The Thirty-Nine Steps

CHAPTER 1

The Man Who Died

I RETURNED FROM THE CITY about three o'clock on that May afternoon pretty well disgusted with life. I had been three months in the Old Country, and was fed up with it. If anyone had told me a year ago that I would have been feeling like that I should have laughed at him; but there was the fact. The weather made me liverish, the talk of the ordinary Englishman made me sick, I couldn't get enough exercise, and the amusements of London seemed as flat as soda-water that has been standing in the sun. "Richard Hannay," I kept telling myself, "you have got into the wrong ditch, my friend, and you had better climb out."

It made me bite my lips to think of the plans I had been building up those last years in Bulawayo. I had got my pile—not one of the big ones, but good enough for me; and I had figured out all kinds of ways of enjoying myself. My father had brought me out from Scotland at the age of six, and I had never been home since; so England was a sort of Arabian Nights to me, and I counted on stopping there for the rest of my days.

But from the first I was disappointed with it. In about a week I was tired of seeing sights, and in less than a month I had had enough of restaurants and theatres and race meetings. I had no real pal to go about with, which probably explains things. Plenty of people invited me to their houses, but they didn't seem much interested in me. They would fling me a question or two about South Africa, and then get onto their own affairs. A lot of Imperialist ladies asked me to tea to meet schoolmasters from New Zealand and editors from Vancouver, and that was the dismallest business of all. Here was I, thirty-seven years old, sound in wind and limb, with enough money to have a good time, yawning my head off all day. I had just about settled to clear out and get back to the veld, for I was the best bored man in the United Kingdom.

That afternoon I had been worrying my brokers about investments to give my mind something to work on, and on my way home I turned into my club—rather a pot-house, which took in Colonial members. I had a long drink, and read the evening papers. They were full of the row in the Near East, and there was an article about Karolides, the Greek Premier. I rather fancied the chap. From all accounts he seemed the one big man in the show; and he played a straight game too, which was more than could be said for most of them. I gathered that they hated him pretty blackly in Berlin and Vienna, but that we were going to stick by him, and one paper said that he was the only barrier between Europe and Armageddon. I remember wondering if I could get a job in those parts. It struck me that Albania was the sort of place that might keep a man from yawning.

About six o'clock I went home, dressed, dined at the Café Royal, and turned into a music-hall. It was a silly show, all capering women and monkey-faced men, and I did not stay long. The night was fine and clear as I walked back to the flat I had hired near Portland Place. The crowd surged past me on the pavements, busy, and chattering, and I envied the people for having something to do. These shopgirls and clerks and dandies and policemen had some interest in life that kept them going. I gave half a crown to a beggar because I saw him yawn; he was a fellow sufferer. At Oxford Circus I looked up into the spring sky and I made a vow. I would give the Old Country another day to fit me into something; if nothing happened, I would take the next boat for the Cape.

My flat was the first floor in a new block behind Langham Place. There was a common staircase, with a porter and a liftman at the entrance, but there was no restaurant or anything of that sort, and each flat was quite shut off from the others. I hate servants on the premises, so I had a fellow to look after me who came in by the day. He arrived before eight o'clock every morning and used to depart at seven, for I never dined at home.

I was just fitting my key into the door when I noticed a man at my elbow. I had not seen him approach, and the sudden appearance made me start. He was a slim man, with a short brown beard and small, gimlety blue eyes. I recognized him as the occupant of a flat on the top floor, with whom I had passed the time of day on the stairs.

"Can I speak to you?" he said. "May I come in for a minute?" He was steadying his voice with an effort, and his hand was pawing my arm.

I got my door open and motioned him in. No sooner was he over the

HE WAS STEADYING HIS VOICE WITH AN EFFORT

threshold than he made a dash for my back room, where I used to smoke and write my letters. Then he bolted back.

"Is the door locked?" he asked feverishly, and he fastened the chain with his own hand.

"I'm very sorry," he said humbly. "It's a mighty liberty, but you looked the kind of man who would understand. I've had you in my mind all this week when things got troublesome. Say, will you do me a good turn?"

"I'll listen to you," I said. "That's all I'll promise." I was getting worried by the antics of this nervous little chap.

There was a tray of drinks on a table beside him, from which he filled himself a stiff whisky and soda. He drank it off in three gulps, and cracked the glass as he set it down.

"Pardon," he said, "I'm a bit rattled tonight. You see, I happen at this moment to be dead."

I sat down in an armchair and lit my pipe.

"What does it feel like?" I asked. I was pretty certain that I had to deal with a madman.

A smile flickered over his drawn face. "I'm not mad—yet. Say, sir, I've been watching you, and I reckon you're a cool customer. I reckon, too, you're an honest man, and not afraid of playing a bold hand. I'm going to confide in you. I need help worse than any man ever needed it, and I want to know if I can count you in."

"Get on with your yarn," I said, "and I'll tell you."

He seemed to brace himself for a great effort, and then started on the queerest rigmarole. I didn't get hold of it at first, and I had to stop and ask him questions. But here is the gist of it:

He was an American, from Kentucky, and after college, being pretty well off, he had started out to see the world. He wrote a bit, and acted as war correspondent for a Chicago paper, and spent a year or two in South-Eastern Europe. I gathered that he was a fine linguist, and had got to know pretty well the society in those parts. He spoke familiarly of many names that I remembered to have seen in the newspapers.

He had played about with politics, he told me, at first for the interest of them, and then because he couldn't help himself. I read him as a sharp, restless fellow, who always wanted to get down to the roots of things. He got a little further down than he wanted.

I am giving you what he told me as well as I could make it out. Away behind all the Governments and the armies there was a big subterranean movement going on, engineered by very dangerous people. He had come on it by accident; it fascinated him; he went further, and then he got caught. I gathered that most of the people in it were the sort of educated anarchists that make revolutions, but that beside them there were financiers who were playing for money. A clever man can make big profits on a falling market, and it suited the book of both classes to set Europe by the ears.

He told me some queer things that explained a lot that had puzzled me—things that happened in the Balkan War, how one state suddenly came out on top, why alliances were made and broken, why certain men disappeared, and where the sinews of war came from. The aim of the whole conspiracy was to get Russia and Germany at loggerheads.

When I asked Why, he said that the anarchist lot thought it would give them their chance. Everything would be in the melting pot, and they looked to see a new world emerge. The capitalists would rake in the shekels, and make fortunes by buying up wreckage. Capital, he said, had no conscience and no fatherland. Besides, the Jew was behind it, and the Jew hated Russia worse than hell.

"Do you wonder?" he cried. "For three hundred years they have been persecuted, and this is the return match for the *pogroms*. The Jew is everywhere, but you have to go far down the backstairs to find him. Take any big Teutonic business concern. If you have dealings with it the first man you meet is Prince *von und zu* Something, an elegant young man who talks Eton-and-Harrow English. But he cuts no ice. If your business is big, you get behind him and find a prognathous Westphalian with a retreating brow and the manners of a hog. He is the German business man that gives your English papers the shakes. But if you're on the biggest kind of job and are bound to get to the real boss, ten to one you are brought up against a little white-faced Jew in a bath-chair with an eye like a rattlesnake. Yes, sir, he is the man who is ruling the world just now, and he has his knife in the Empire of the Tsar, because his aunt was outraged and his father flogged in some one-horse location on the Volga."

I could not help saying that his Jew-anarchists seemed to have got left behind a little.

"Yes and no," he said. "They won up to a point, but they struck a bigger thing than money, a thing that couldn't be bought, the old elemental fighting instincts of man. If you're going to be killed, you invent some kind of flag and country to fight for, and if you survive you get to love the thing. Those foolish devils of soldiers have found something they care for, and that has upset the pretty plan laid in Berlin and Vienna. But my friends haven't played their last card by a long sight. They've gotten the ace up their sleeves, and unless I can keep alive for a month they are going to play it and win."

"But I thought you were dead," I put in.

"*Mors janua vitae,*" he smiled. (I recognized the quotation: it was about all the Latin I knew.) "I'm coming to that, but I've got to put you wise about a lot of things first. If you read your newspaper, I guess you know the name of Constantine Karolides?"

I sat up at that, for I had been reading about him that very afternoon.

"He is the man that has wrecked all their games. He is the one big brain in the whole show, and he happens also to be an honest man. Therefore he has been marked down these twelve months past. I found that out—not that it was difficult, for any fool could guess as much. But I found out the way they were going to get him, and that knowledge was deadly. That's why I have had to decease."

He had another drink, and I mixed it for him myself, for I was getting interested in the beggar.

"They can't get him in his own land, for he has a bodyguard of Epirotes that would skin their grandmothers. But on the 15th day of June he is coming to this city. The British Foreign Office has taken to having International tea parties, and the biggest of them is due on that date. Now Karolides is reckoned the principal guest, and if my friends have their way he will never return to his admiring countrymen."

"That's simple enough, anyhow," I said. "You can warn him and keep him at home."

"And play their game?" he asked sharply. "If he does not come they win, for he's the only man that can straighten out the tangle. And if his Government are warned he won't come, for he does not know how big the stakes will be on June the 15th."

"What about the British Government?" I said. "They're not going to let their guests be murdered. Tip them the wink, and they'll take extra precautions."

"No good. They might stuff your city with plain-clothes detectives and double the police and Constantine would still be a doomed man.

My friends are not playing this game for candy. They want a big occasion for the taking off, with the eyes of all Europe on it. He'll be murdered by an Austrian, and there'll be plenty of evidence to show the connivance of the big folk in Vienna and Berlin. It will all be an infernal lie, of course, but the case will look black enough to the world. I'm not talking hot air, my friend. I happen to know every detail of the hellish contrivance, and I can tell you it will be the most finished piece of blackguardism since the Borgias. But it's not going to come off if there's a certain man who knows the wheels of the business alive right here in London on the 15th day of June. And that man is going to be your servant, Franklin P. Scudder."

I was getting to like the little chap. His jaw had shut like a rat-trap, and there was the fire of battle in his gimlety eyes. If he was spinning me a yarn he could act up to it.

"Where did you find out this story?" I asked.

"I got the first hint in an inn on the Achensee in Tyrol. That set me inquiring, and I collected my other clues in a fur shop in the Galician quarter of Buda, in a Strangers' Club in Vienna, and in a little bookshop off the Racknitzstrasse in Leipsig. I completed my evidence ten days ago in Paris. I can't tell you the details now, for it's something of a history. When I was quite sure in my own mind I judged it my business to disappear, and I reached this city by a mighty queer circuit. I left Parish a dandified young French-American and I sailed from Hamburg a Jew diamond merchant. In Norway I was an English student of Ibsen collecting material for lectures, but when I left Bergen I was a cinema-man with special ski films. And I came here from Leith with a lot of pulpwood propositions in my pocket to put before the London newspapers. Till yesterday I thought I had muddied my trail some, and was feeling pretty happy. Then . . ."

The recollection seemed to upset him, and he gulped down some more whisky.

"Then I saw a man standing in the street outside this block. I used to stay close in my room all day, and only slip out after dark for an hour or two. I watched him for a bit from my window, and I thought I recognized him . . . He came in and spoke to the porter . . . When I came back from my walk last night I found a card in my letterbox. It bore the name of the man I want least to meet on God's earth."

I think that the look in my companion's eyes, the sheer naked scare on his face, completed my conviction of his honesty. My own voice sharpened a bit as I asked him what he did next.

"I realized that I was bottled as sure as a pickled herring, and that there was only one way out. I had to die. If my pursuers knew I was dead they would go to sleep again."

"How did you manage it?"

"I told the man that valets me that I was feeling pretty bad, and I got myself up to look like death. That wasn't difficult, for I'm no slouch at disguises. Then I got a corpse—you can always get a body in London if you know where to go for it. I fetched it back in a trunk on the top of a four-wheeler, and I had to be assisted upstairs to my room. You see I had to pile up some evidence for the inquest. I went to bed and got my man to mix me a sleeping draught, and then told him to clear out. He wanted to fetch a doctor, but I swore some and said I couldn't abide leeches. When I was left alone I started in to fake up that corpse. He was my size, and I judged had perished from too much alcohol, so I put some spirits handy about the place. The jaw was the weak point in the likeness, so I blew it away with a revolver. I dare say there will be somebody tomorrow to swear to having heard a shot, but there are no neighbours on my floor, and I guessed I could risk it. So I left the body in bed dressed up in my pyjamas, with a revolver lying on the bedclothes and a considerable mess around. Then I got into a suit of clothes I had kept waiting for emergencies. I didn't dare to shave for fear of leaving tracks, and besides, it wasn't any kind of use my trying to get into the streets. I had had you in my mind all day, and there seemed nothing to do but to make an appeal to you. I watched from my window till I saw you come home, and then slipped down the stair to meet you . . . There, sir, I guess you know about as much as me of this business."

He sat blinking like an owl, fluttering with nerves and yet desperately determined. By this time I was pretty well convinced that he was going straight with me. It was the wildest sort of narrative, but I had heard in my time many steep tales which had turned out to be true, and I had made a practice of judging the man rather than the story. If he had wanted to get a location in my flat, and then cut my throat, he would have pitched a milder yarn.

"Hand me your key," I said, "and I'll take a look at the corpse. Excuse my caution, but I'm bound to verify a bit if I can."

He shook his head mournfully. "I reckoned you'd ask for that, but I haven't got it. It's on my chain on the dressing-table. I had to leave it behind for I couldn't leave any clues to breed suspicions. The gentry who are after me are pretty bright-eyed citizens. You'll have to take me on trust for the night, and tomorrow you'll get proof of the corpse business right enough."

I thought for an instant or two. "Right. I'll trust you for the night. I'll lock you into this room and keep the key. Just one word, Mr Scudder. I believe you're straight, but if so be you are not I should warn you that I'm a handy man with a gun."

"Sure," he said, jumping up with some briskness. "I haven't the privilege of your name, sir, but let me tell you that you're a white man. I'll thank you to lend me a razor."

I took him into my bedroom and turned him loose. In half an hour's time a figure came out that I scarcely recognized. Only his gimlety, hungry eyes were the same. He was shaved clean, his hair was parted in the middle, and he had cut his eyebrows. Further, he carried himself as if he had been drilled, and was the very model, even to the brown complexion, of some British officer who had had a long spell in India. He had a monocle, too, which he stuck in his eye, and every trace of the American had gone out of his speech.

"My hat! Mr Scudder—" I stammered.

"Not Mr Scudder," he corrected; "Captain Theophilus Digby, of the 40th Gurkhas, presently home on leave. I'll thank you to remember that, sir."

I made him up a bed in my smoking-room and sought my own couch, more cheerful than I had been for the past month. Things did happen occasionally, even in this God-forgotten metropolis.

I WOKE NEXT MORNING to hear my man, Paddock, making the deuce of a row at the smoking-room door. Paddock was a fellow I had done a good turn to out on the Selakwi, and I had inspanned him as my servant as soon as I got to England. He had about as much gift of the gab as a hippopotamus, and was not a great hand at valeting, but I knew I could count on his loyalty.

"Stop that row, Paddock," I said. "There's a friend of mine, Captain—Captain" (I couldn't remember the name) "dossing down in there. Get breakfast for two and then come and speak to me."

I told Paddock a fine story about how my friend was a great swell, with his nerves pretty bad from overwork, who wanted absolute rest and stillness. Nobody had got to know he was here, or he would be besieged by communications from the India Office and the Prime Minister and his cure would be ruined. I am bound to say Scudder played up splendidly when he came to breakfast. He fixed Paddock with his eyeglass, just like a British officer, asked him about the Boer War, and slung out at me a lot of stuff about imaginary pals. Paddock couldn't learn to call me "sir", but he "sirred" Scudder as if his life depended on it.

I left him with the newspaper and a box of cigars, and went down to the City till luncheon. When I got back the liftman had an important face.

"Nawsty business 'ere this morning, sir. Gent in No.15 has been and shot 'isself. They've just took 'im to the mortuary. The police are up there now."

I ascended to No.15, and found a couple of bobbies and an inspector busy making an examination. I asked a few idiotic questions, and they soon kicked me out. Then I found the man that had valeted Scudder, and pumped him, but I could see he suspected nothing. He was a whining fellow with a churchyard face, and half a crown went far to console him.

I attended the inquest next day. A partner of some publishing firm gave evidence that the deceased had brought him woodpulp propositions, and had been, he believed, an agent of an American business. The jury found it a case of suicide while of unsound mind, and the few effects were handed over to the American Consul to deal with. I gave Scudder a full account of the affair, and it interested him greatly. He said he wished he could have attended the inquest, for he reckoned it would be about as spicy as to read one's own obituary notice.

The first two days he stayed with me in that back room he was very peaceful. He read and smoked a bit, and made a heap of jottings in a notebook, and every night we had a game of chess, at which he beat me hollow. I think he was nursing his nerves back to health, for he had had a pretty trying time. But on the third day I could see he was beginning to get restless. He fixed up a list of the days till June 15th, and ticked each off with a red pencil, making remarks in shorthand against them. I would find him sunk in a brown study, with his sharp eyes abstracted, and after those spells of meditation he was apt to be very despondent.

Then I could see that he began to get edgy again. He listened for little noises, and was always asking me if Paddock could be trusted. Once or twice he got very peevish, and apologized for it. I didn't blame him. I made every allowance, for he had taken on a fairly stiff job.

It was not the safety of his own skin that troubled him, but the success of the scheme he had planned. That little man was clean grit all through, without a soft spot in him. One night he was very solemn.

"Say, Hannay," he said, "I judge I should let you a bit deeper into this business. I should hate to go out without leaving somebody else to put up a fight." And he began to tell me in detail what I had only heard from him vaguely.

I did not give him very close attention. The fact is, I was more interested in his own adventures than in his high politics. I reckoned that Karolides and his affairs were not my business, leaving all that to him. So a lot that he said slipped clean out of my memory. I remember that he was very clear that the danger to Karolides would not begin till he had got to London, and would come from the very highest quarters, where there would be no thought of suspicion. He mentioned the name of a woman—Julia Czechenyi—as having something to do with the danger. She would be the decoy, I gathered, to get Karolides out of the care of his guards. He talked, too, about a Black Stone and a man that lisped in his speech, and he described very particularly somebody that he never referred to without a shudder—an old man with a young voice who could hood his eyes like a hawk.

He spoke a good deal about death, too. He was mortally anxious about winning through with his job, but he didn't care a rush for his life.

"I reckon it's like going to sleep when you are pretty well tired out, and waking to find a summer day with the scent of hay coming in at the window. I used to thank God for such mornings way back in the Blue-Grass country, and I guess I'll thank Him when I wake up on the other side of Jordan."

Next day he was much more cheerful, and read the life of Stonewall Jackson much of the time. I went out to dinner with a mining engineer I had got to see on business, and came back about half past ten in time for our game of chess before turning in.

I had a cigar in my mouth, I remember, as I pushed open the smoking-room door. The lights were not lit, which struck me as odd. I wondered if Scudder had turned in already.

I snapped the switch, but there was nobody there. Then I saw something in the far corner which made me drop my cigar and fall into a cold sweat.

My guest was lying sprawled on his back. There was a long knife through his heart which skewered him to the floor.

MY GUEST WAS LYING WITH A KNIFE THROUGH HIS HEART

CHAPTER 2

The Milkman Sets Out on His Travels

I SAT DOWN in an armchair and felt very sick. That lasted for maybe five minutes, and was succeeded by a fit of the horrors. The poor staring white face on the floor was more than I could bear, and I managed to get a tablecloth and cover it. Then I staggered to a cupboard, found the brandy and swallowed several mouthfuls. I had seen men die violently before; indeed I had killed a few myself in the Matabele War; but this cold-blooded indoor business was different. Still I managed to pull myself together. I looked at my watch, and saw that it was half past ten.

An idea seized me, and I went over the flat with a small-tooth comb. There was nobody there, nor any trace of anybody, but I shuttered and bolted all the windows and put the chain on the door.

By this time my wits were coming back to me, and I could think again. It took me about an hour to figure the thing out, and I did not hurry, for, unless the murderer came back, I had till about six o'clock in the morning for my cogitations.

I was in the soup—that was pretty clear. Any shadow of a doubt I might have had about the truth of Scudder's tale was now gone. The proof of it was lying under the tablecloth. The men who knew that he knew what he knew had found him, and had taken the best way to make certain of his silence. Yes; but he had been in my rooms four days, and his enemies must have reckoned that he had confided in me. So I would be the next to go. It might be that very night, or next day, or the day after, but my number was up all right.

Then suddenly I thought of another probability. Supposing I went out now and called in the police, or went to bed and let Paddock find the body and call them in the morning. What kind of a story was I to tell about Scudder? I had lied to Paddock about him, and the whole thing looked desperately fishy. If I made a clean breast of it and told the police everything he had told me, they would simply laugh at me. The odds were a thousand to one that I would be charged with the murder, and the circumstantial evidence was strong enough to hang me. Few people knew me in England; I had no real pal who could come forward and swear to my character. Perhaps that was what those secret enemies were playing for. They were clever enough for anything, and an English prison was as good a way of getting rid of me till after June 15th as a knife in my chest.

Besides, if I told the whole story, and by any miracle was believed, I would be playing their game. Karolides would stay at home, which was what they wanted. Somehow or other the sight of Scudder's dead face had made me a passionate believer in his scheme. He was gone, but he had taken me into his confidence, and I was pretty well bound to carry on his work.

You may think this ridiculous for a man in danger of his life, but that was the way I looked at it. I am an ordinary sort of fellow, not braver than other people, but I hate to see a good man downed, and that long knife would not be the end of Scudder if I could play the game in his place.

It took me an hour or two to think this out, and by that time I had come to a decision. I must vanish somehow, and keep vanished till the end of the second week in June. Then I must somehow find a way to get in touch with the Government people and tell them what Scudder had told me. I wished to Heaven he had told me more, and that I had listened more carefully to the little he had told me. I knew nothing but the barest facts. There was a big risk that, even if I weathered the other dangers, I would not be believed in the end. I must take my chance of that, and hope that something might happen which would confirm my tale in the eyes of the Government.

My first job was to keep going for the next three weeks. It was now the 24th day of May, and that meant twenty days of hiding before I could venture to approach the powers that be. I reckoned that two sets of people would be looking for me—Scudder's enemies to put me out of existence, and the police, who would want me for Scudder's murder. It was going to be a giddy hunt, and it was queer how the prospect comforted me. I had been slack so long that almost any chance of activity was welcome. When I had to sit alone with that corpse and wait on Fortune I was no better than a crushed worm, but if my neck's safety was to hang on my own wits I was prepared to be cheerful about it.

My next thought was whether Scudder had any papers about him to give me a better clue to the business. I drew back the tablecloth and searched his pockets, for I had no longer any shrinking from the body. The face was wonderfully calm for a man who had been struck down in a moment. There was nothing in the breast pocket, and only a few loose coins and a cigar holder in the waistcoat. The trousers held a little penknife and some silver, and the side pocket of his jacket contained an old crocodile-skin cigar case. There was no sign of the little black book in which I had seen him making notes. That had no doubt been taken by his murderer.

But as I looked up from my task I saw that some drawers had been pulled out in the writing-table. Scudder would never have left them in that state, for he was the tidiest of mortals. Someone must have been searching for something—perhaps for the pocketbook.

I went round the flat and found that everything had been ransacked—the inside of books, drawers, cupboards, boxes, even the pockets of the clothes in my wardrobe, and the sideboard in the dining-room. There was no trace of the book. Most likely the enemy had found it, but they had not found it on Scudder's body.

Then I got out an atlas and looked at a big map of the British Isles. My notion was to get off to some wild district, where my veldcraft would be of some use to me, for I would be like a trapped rat in a city. I considered that Scotland would be best, for my people were Scotch and I could pass anywhere as an ordinary Scotsman. I had half an idea at first to be a German tourist, for my father had had German partners, and I had been brought up to speak the tongue pretty fluently, not to mention having put in three years prospecting for copper in German Damaraland. But I calculated that it would be less conspicuous to be a Scot, and less in a line with what the police might know of my past. I fixed on Galloway as the best place to go to. It was the nearest wild part of Scotland, so far as I could figure it out, and from the look of the map was not over thick with population.

A search in Bradshaw informed me that a train left St Pancras at seven-ten, which would land me at any Galloway station in the late afternoon. That was well enough, but a more important matter was how

I was to make my way to St Pancras, for I was pretty certain that Scudder's friends would be watching outside. This puzzled me for a bit; then I had an inspiration, on which I went to bed and slept for two troubled hours.

I got up at four and opened my bedroom shutters. The faint light of a fine summer morning was flooding the skies, and the sparrows had begun to chatter. I had a great revulsion of feeling, and felt a God-forgotten fool. My inclination was to let things slide, and trust to the British police taking a reasonable view of my case. But as I reviewed the situation I could find no arguments to bring against my decision of the previous night, so with a wry mouth I resolved to go on with my plan. I was not feeling in any particular funk; only disinclined to go looking for trouble, if you understand me.

I hunted out a well-used tweed suit, a pair of strong nailed boots, and a flannel shirt with a collar. Into my pockets I stuffed a spare shirt, a cloth cap, some handkerchiefs, and a toothbrush. I had drawn a good sum in gold from the bank two days before, in case Scudder should want money, and I took fifty pounds of it in sovereigns in a belt which I had brought back from Rhodesia. That was about all I wanted. Then I had a bath, and cut my moustache, which was long and drooping, into a short stubby fringe.

Now came the next step. Paddock used to arrive punctually at seven-thirty and let himself in with a latch-key. But about twenty minutes to seven, as I knew from bitter experience, the milkman turned up with a great clatter of cans, and deposited my share outside my door. I had seen that milkman sometimes when I had gone out for an early ride. He was a young man about my own height, with an ill-nourished moustache, and he wore a white overall. On him I staked all my chances.

I went into the darkened smoking-room where the rays of morning light were beginning to creep through the shutters. There I breakfasted off a whisky and soda and some biscuits from the cupboard. By this time it was getting on for six o'clock. I put a pipe in my pocket and filled my pouch from the tobacco jar on the table by the fireplace.

As I poked into the tobacco my fingers touched something hard, and I drew out Scudder's little black pocketbook . . .

That seemed to me a good omen. I lifted the cloth from the body and was amazed at the peace and dignity of the dead face. "Goodbye, old chap," I said; "I am going to do my best for you. Wish me well, wherever you are."

Then I hung about in the hall waiting for the milkman. That was the worst part of the business, for I was fairly choking to get out of doors. Six-thirty passed, then six-forty, but still he did not come. The fool had chosen this day of all days to be late.

At one minute after the quarter to seven I heard the rattle of the cans outside. I opened the front door, and there was my man, singling out my cans from a bunch he carried and whistling through his teeth. He jumped a bit at the sight of me.

"Come in here a moment," I said. "I want a word with you." And I led him into the dining-room.

"I reckon you're a bit of a sportsman," I said, "and I want you to do me a service. Lend me your cap and overall for ten minutes, and here's a sovereign for you."

His eyes opened at the sight of the gold, and he grinned broadly. "Wot's the gyme?" he asked.

"A bet," I said. "I haven't time to explain, but to win it I've got to be a milkman for the next ten minutes. All you've got to do is to stay here till I come back. You'll be a bit late, but nobody will complain, and you'll have that quid for yourself."

"Right-oh!" he said cheerily. "I ain't the man to spoil a bit of sport. 'Ere's the rig, guv'nor."

I stuck on his flat blue hat and his white overall, picked up the cans, banged my door, and went whistling downstairs. The porter at the foot told me to shut my jaw, which sounded as if my make-up was adequate.

At first I thought there was nobody in the street. Then I caught sight of a policeman a hundred yards down, and a loafer shuffling past on the other side. Some impulse made me raise my eyes to the house opposite, and there at a first-floor window was a face. As the loafer passed he looked up, and I fancied a signal was exchanged.

I crossed the street, whistling gaily and imitating the jaunty swing of the milkman. Then I took the first side street, and went up a left-hand turning which led past a bit of vacant ground. There was no one in the little street, so I dropped the milk-cans inside the hoarding and sent the hat and overall after them. I had only just put on my cloth cap when a postman came round the corner. I gave him good morning and he answered me unsuspiciously. At that moment the clock of a neighbour-ing church struck the hour of seven.

There was not a second to spare. As soon as I got to Euston Road I took to my heels and ran. The clock at Euston Station showed five minutes past the hour. At St Pancras I had no time to take a ticket, let alone that I had not settled upon my destination. A porter told me the platform, and as I entered it I saw the train already in motion. Two station officials blocked the way, but I dodged them and clambered into the last carriage.

Three minutes later, as we were roaring through the northern tunnels, an irate guard interviewed me. He wrote out for me a ticket to Newton Stewart, a name which had suddenly come back to my memory, and he conducted me from the first-class compartment where I had ensconced myself to a third-class smoker, occupied by a sailor and a stout woman with a child. He went off grumbling, and as I mopped my brow I observed to my companions in my broadest Scots that it was a sore job catching trains. I had already entered upon my part.

"The impidence o' that gyaird!" said the lady bitterly. "He needit a Scotch tongue to pit him in his place. He was complainin' o' this wean no haein' a ticket and her no fower till August twalmonth, and he was objectin' to this gentleman spittin'."

The sailor morosely agreed, and I started my new life in an atmosphere of protest against authority. I reminded myself that a week ago I had been finding the world dull.

CHAPTER 3

The Adventure of the Literary Innkeeper

I HAD A SOLEMN TIME travelling north that day. It was fine May weather, with the hawthorn flowering on every hedge, and I asked myself why, when I was still a free man, I had stayed on in London and not got the good of this heavenly country. I didn't dare face the restaurant car, but I got a luncheon basket at Leeds and shared it with the fat woman. Also I got the morning's papers, with news about starters for the Derby and the beginning of the cricket season, and some paragraphs about how Balkan affairs were settling down and a British squadron was going to Kiel.

When I had done with them I got out Scudder's little black pocketbook and studied it. It was pretty well filled with jottings, chiefly figures, though now and then a name was printed in. For example, I found the words "Hofgaard", "Luneville", and "Avocado" pretty often, and especially the word "Pavia".

Now I was certain that Scudder never did anything without a reason, and I was pretty sure that there was a cypher in all this. That is a subject which has always interested me, and I did a bit at it myself once as intelligence-officer in Delagoa Bay during the Boer War. I have a head for things like chess and puzzles, and I used to reckon myself pretty good at finding out cyphers. This one looked like the numerical kind where sets of figures correspond to the letters of the alphabet, but any fairly shrewd man can find the clue to that sort after an hour or two's work, and I didn't think Scudder would have been content with anything so easy. So I fastened on the printed words, for you can make a pretty good numerical cypher if you have a key word which gives you the sequence of the letters.

I tried for hours, but none of the words answered. Then I fell asleep and woke at Dumfries just in time to bundle out and get into the slow Galloway train. There was a man on the platform whose looks I didn't like, but he never glanced at me, and when I caught sight of myself in the mirror of an automatic machine I didn't wonder. With my brown face, my old tweeds, and my slouch, I was the very model of one of the hill farmers who were crowding into the third-class carriages.

I travelled with half a dozen in an atmosphere of shag and clay pipes. They had come from the weekly market, and their mouths were full of prices. I heard accounts of how the lambing had gone up the Cairn and the Deuch and a dozen other mysterious waters. Above half the men had lunched heavily and were highly flavoured with whisky, but they took no notice of me. We rumbled slowly into a land of little wooded glens and then to a great wide moorland place, gleaming with lochs, with high hills showing northwards.

About five o'clock the carriage had emptied, and I was left alone as I had hoped. I got out at the next station, a little place whose name I scarcely noted, set right in the heart of a bog. It reminded me of one of those forgotten little stations in the Karroo. An old station-master was digging in his garden, and with his spade over his shoulder sauntered to the train, took charge of a parcel, and went back to his potatoes. A child of ten received my ticket, and I emerged on a white road that straggled over the brown moor.

It was a gorgeous spring evening, with every hill showing as clear as a cut amethyst. The air had the queer, rooty smell of bogs, but it was as fresh as mid-ocean, and it had the strangest effect on my spirits. I actually felt light-hearted. I might have been a boy out for a spring holiday tramp, instead of a man of thirty-seven very much wanted by the police. I felt just as I used to feel when I was starting for a big trek on a frosty morning on the high veld. If you believe me, I swung along that road whistling. There was no plan of campaign in my head, only just to go on and on in this blessed, honest-smelling hill country, for every mile put me in better humour with myself.

In a roadside planting I cut a walking stick of hazel, and presently struck off the highway up a by-path which followed the glen of a brawling stream. I reckoned that I was still far ahead of any pursuit, and for that night might please myself. It was some hours since I had tasted food, and I was getting very hungry when I came to a herd's cottage set in a nook beside a waterfall. A brown-faced woman was standing by the door, and greeted me with the kindly shyness of moorland places. When I asked for a night's lodging she said I was

31

welcome to the "bed in the loft", and very soon she set before me a hearty meal of ham and eggs, scones, and thick sweet milk.

At the darkening her man came in from the hills, a lean giant, who in one step covered as much ground as three paces of ordinary mortals. They asked no questions, for they had the perfect breeding of all dwellers in the wilds, but I could see they set me down as a kind of dealer, and I took some trouble to confirm their view. I spoke a lot about cattle, of which my host knew little, and I picked up from him a good deal about the local Galloway markets, which I tucked away in my memory for future use. At ten I was nodding in my chair, and the "bed in the loft" received a weary man who never opened his eyes till five o'clock set the little homestead a-going once more.

They refused any payment, and by six I had breakfasted and was striding southwards again. My notion was to return to the railway line a station or two farther on than the place where I had alighted yesterday and to double back. I reckoned that that was the safest way, for the police would naturally assume that I was always making farther from London in the direction of some western port. I thought I had still a good bit of a start, for, as I reasoned, it would take some hours to fix the blame on me, and several more to identify the fellow who got on board the train at St Pancras.

It was the same jolly, clear spring weather, and I simply could not contrive to feel careworn. Indeed I was in better spirits than I had been for months. Over a long ridge of moorland I took my road, skirting the side of a high hill which the herd had called Cairnsmore of Fleet. Nesting curlews and plovers were crying everywhere, and the links of green pasture by the streams were dotted with young lambs. All the slackness of the past months was slipping from my bones, and I stepped out like a four-year-old. By and by I came to a swell of moorland which dipped to the vale of a little river, and a mile away in the heather I saw the smoke of a train.

The station, when I reached it, proved to be ideal for my purpose. The moor surged up around it and left room only for the single line, the slender siding, a waiting-room, an office, the station-master's cottage, and a tiny yard of gooseberries and sweet-william. There seemed no road to it from anywhere, and to increase the desolation the waves of a tarn lapped on their grey granite beach half a mile away. I waited in the deep heather till I saw the smoke of an east-going train on the horizon.

Then I approached the tiny booking-office and took a ticket for Dumfries.

The only occupants of the carriage were an old shepherd and his dog—a wall-eyed brute that I mistrusted. The man was asleep, and on the cushions beside him was that morning's *Scotsman*. Eagerly I seized on it, for I fancied it would tell me something.

There were two columns about the Portland Place Murder, as it was called. My man Paddock had given the alarm and had the milkman arrested. Poor devil, it looked as if the latter had earned his sovereign hardly; but for me he had been cheap at the price, for he seemed to have occupied the police the better part of the day. In the latest news I found a further instalment of the story. The milkman had been released, I read, and the true criminal, about whose identity the police were reticent, was believed to have got away from London by one of the northern lines. There was a short note about me as the owner of the flat. I guessed the police had stuck that in, as a clumsy contrivance to persuade me that I was unsuspected.

There was nothing else in the paper, nothing about foreign politics or Karolides, or the things that had interested Scudder. I laid it down, and found that we were approaching the station at which I had got out yesterday. The potato-digging station-master had been gingered up into some activity, for the west-going train was waiting to let us pass, and from it had descended three men who were asking him questions. I supposed that they were the local police, who had been stirred up by Scotland Yard, and had traced me as far as this one-horse siding. Sitting well back in the shadow I watched them carefully. One of them had a book, and took down notes. The old potato-digger seemed to have turned peevish, but the child who had collected my ticket was talking volubly. All the party looked out across the moor where the white road departed. I hoped they were going to take up my tracks there.

As we moved away from the station my companion woke up. He fixed me with a wandering glance, kicked his dog viciously, and inquired where he was. Clearly he was very drunk.

"That's what comes o' bein' a teetotaller," he observed in bitter regret.

I expressed my surprise that in him I should have met a blue-ribbon stalwart.

"Ay, but I'm a strong teetotaller," he said pugnaciously. "I took the pledge last Martinmas, and I havena touched a drop o' whisky sinsyne. No even at Hogmanay, though I was sair temptit."

He swung his heels up on the seat, and burrowed a frowsy head into the cushions.

"And that's a' I get," he moaned. "A heid hetter than hell fire, and twae een lookin' different ways for the Sabbath."

"What did it?" I asked.

"A drink they ca' brandy. Bein' a teetotaller I keepit off the whisky, but I was nip-nippin' a' day at this brandy, and I doubt I'll no be weel for a fortnicht." His voice died away into a stutter, and sleep once more laid its heavy hand on him.

My plan had been to get out at some station down the line, but the train suddenly gave me a better chance, for it came to a standstill at the end of a culvert which spanned a brawling porter-coloured river. I looked out and saw that every carriage window was closed and no human figure appeared in the landscape. So I opened the door, and dropped quickly into the tangle of hazels which edged the line.

It would have been all right but for that infernal dog. Under the impression that I was decamping with its master's belongings, it started to bark, and all but got me by the trousers. This woke up the herd, who stood bawling at the carriage door in the belief that I had committed suicide. I crawled through the thicket, reached the edge of the stream, and in cover of the bushes put a hundred yards or so behind me. Then from my shelter I peered back, and saw the guard and several passengers gathered round the open carriage door and staring in my direction. I could not have made a more public departure if I had left with a bugler and a brass band.

Happily the drunken herd provided a diversion. He and his dog, which was attached by a rope to his waist, suddenly cascaded out of the carriage, landed on their heads on the track, and rolled some way down the bank towards the water. In the rescue which followed the dog bit somebody, for I could hear the sound of hard swearing. Presently they had forgotten me, and when after a quarter of a mile's crawl I ventured to look back, the train had started again and was vanishing in the cutting.

I was in a wide semicircle of moorland, with the brown river as radius, and the high hills forming the northern circumference. There was not a sign or sound of a human being, only the splashing water and the interminable crying of curlews. Yet, oddly enough, for the first time I felt the terror of the hunted on me. It was not the police that I thought of, but the other folk, who knew that I knew Scudder's secret and dared not let me live. I was certain that they would pursue me with a keenness and vigilance unknown to the British law, and that once their grip closed on me I should find no mercy.

I looked back, but there was nothing in the landscape. The sun glinted on the metals of the line and the wet stones in the stream, and you could not have found a more peaceful sight in the world. Nevertheless I started to run. Crouching low in the runnels of the bog, I ran till the sweat blinded my eyes. The mood did not leave me till I had reached the rim of mountain and flung myself panting on a ridge high above the young waters of the brown river.

From my vantage-ground I could scan the whole moor right away to the railway line and to the south of it where green fields took the place of heather. I have eyes like a hawk, but I could see nothing moving in the whole countryside. Then I looked east beyond the ridge and saw a new kind of landscape—shallow green valleys with plentiful fir plantations and the faint lines of dust which spoke of highroads. Last of all I looked into the blue May sky and there I saw that which set my pulses racing. . .

Low down in the south a monoplane was climbing into the heavens. I was as certain as if I had been told that that aeroplane was looking for me, and that it did not belong to the police. For an hour or two I watched it from a pit of heather. It flew low along the hill-tops, and then in narrow circles over the valley up which I had come. Then it seemed to change its mind, rose to a great height, and flew away back to the south.

I did not like this espionage from the air, and I began to think less well of the countryside I had chosen for a refuge. These heather hills were no sort of cover if my enemies were in the sky, and I must find a different kind of sanctuary. I looked with more satisfaction to the green country beyond the ridge, for there I should find woods and stone houses.

About six in the evening I came out of the moorland to a white ribbon of road which wound up the narrow vale of a lowland stream. As I followed it, fields gave place to bent, the glen became a plateau, and presently I had reached a kind of pass where a solitary house smoked in the twilight. The road swung over a bridge, and leaning on the parapet was a young man.

He was smoking a long clay pipe and studying the water with spectacled eyes. In his left hand was a small book with a finger marking the place. Slowly he repeated:

> *"As when a Gryphon through the wilderness*
> *With wingèd step, o'er hill and moory dale*
> *Pursues the Arimaspian."*

He jumped round as my step rung on the keystone, and I saw a pleasant sunburnt boyish face.

"Good evening to you," he said gravely. "It's a fine night for the road."

The smell of peat smoke and of some savoury roast floated to me from the house.

"Is that place an inn?" I asked.

"At your service," he said politely. "I am the landlord, sir, and I hope you will stay the night, for to tell you the truth I have had no company for a week."

I pulled myself up on the parapet of the bridge and filled my pipe. I began to detect an ally.

"You're young to be an innkeeper," I said.

"My father died a year ago and left me the business. I live there with my grandmother. It's a slow job for a young man, and it wasn't my choice of profession."

"Which was?"

He actually blushed. "I want to write books," he said.

"And what better chance could you ask?" I cried. "Man, I've often thought that an innkeeper would make the best story-teller in the world."

"Not now," he said eagerly. "Maybe in the old days when you had pilgrims and ballad-makers and highwaymen and mail coaches on the road. But not now. Nothing comes here but motor-cars full of fat women, who stop for lunch, and a fisherman or two in the spring, and the shooting tenants in August. There is not much material to be got out of that. I want to see life, to travel the world, and write things like Kipling and Conrad. But the most I've done yet is to get some verses printed in *Chambers's Journal*."

I looked at the inn standing golden in the sunset against the brown hills.

"I've knocked a bit about the world, and I wouldn't despise such a hermitage. D'you think that adventure is found only in the tropics or among the gentry in red shirts? Maybe you're rubbing shoulders with it at this moment."

"That's what Kipling says," he said, his eyes brightening, and he quoted some verse about "Romance bringing up the nine-fifteen".

"Here's a true tale for you then," I cried, "and a month from now you can make a novel out of it."

Sitting on the bridge in the soft May gloaming I pitched him a lovely yarn. It was true in essentials, too, though I altered the minor details. I made out that I was a mining magnate from Kimberley, who had had a lot of trouble with I.D.B. and had shown up a gang. They had pursued me across the ocean, and had killed my best friend, and were now on my tracks.

I told the story well, though I say it who shouldn't. I pictured a flight across the Kalahari to German Africa, the crackling, parching days, the wonderful blue-velvet nights. I described an attack on my life on the voyage home, and I made a really horrid affair of the Portland Place murder. "You're looking for adventure," I cried; "well, you've found it here. The devils are after me, and the police are after them. It's a race that I mean to win."

"By God!" he whispered, drawing his breath in sharply. "It is all pure Rider Haggard and Conan Doyle."

"You believe me," I said gratefully.

"Of course I do," and he held out his hand. "I believe everything out of the common. The only thing to distrust is the normal."

He was very young, but he was the man for my money.

"I think they're off my track for the moment, but I must lie close for a couple of days. Can you take me in?"

He caught my elbow in his eagerness and drew me towards the house. "You can lie as snug here as if you were in a moss-hole. I'll see that nobody blabs, either. And you'll give me some more material about your adventures?"

As I entered the inn porch I heard from far off the beat of an engine. There silhouetted against the dusky west was my friend, the monoplane.

HE GAVE ME A ROOM at the back of the house, with a fine outlook over the plateau, and he made me free of his own study, which was stacked with cheap editions of his favourite authors. I never saw the grandmother, so I guess she was bedridden. An old woman called Margit brought me my meals, and the innkeeper was around me at all hours. I wanted some time to myself, so I invented a job for him. He had a motor-bicycle and I sent him off next morning for the daily paper, which usually arrived with the post in the later afternoon. I told him to keep his eyes skinned, and make note of any strange figures he saw, keeping a special sharp look-out for motors and aeroplanes. Then I sat down in real earnest to Scudder's notebook.

He came back at midday with the *Scotsman*. There was nothing in it, except some further evidence of Paddock and the milkman, and a repetition of yesterday's statement that the murderer had gone north. But there was a long article, reprinted from *The Times*, about Karolides and the state of affairs in the Balkans, though there was no mention of any visit to England. I got rid of the innkeeper for the afternoon, for I was getting very warm in my search for the cypher.

As I told you, it was a numerical cypher, and by an elaborate system of experiments I had pretty well discovered what were the nulls and stops. The trouble was the key word, and when I thought of the odd million words he might have used I felt pretty hopeless. But about three o'clock I had a sudden inspiration.

The name Julia Czechenyi flashed across my memory. Scudder had said it was the key to the Karolides business, and it occurred to me to try it on his cypher.

It worked. The five letters of "Julia" gave me the position of the vowels. A was J, the tenth letter of the alphabet, and so represented by X in the cypher. E was U = XXI, and so on. "Czechenyi" gave me the numerals for the principal consonants. I scribbled that scheme on a bit of paper and sat down to read Scudder's pages.

In half an hour I was reading with a whitish face and fingers that drummed on the table.

I glanced out of the window and saw a big touring-car coming up the glen towards the inn. It drew up at the door, and there was the sound of people alighting. There seemed to be two of them, men in Aquascutums and tweed caps.

Ten minutes later the innkeeper slipped into the room, his eyes bright with excitement.

"There's two chaps below looking for you," he whispered. "They're in the dining-room having whiskies and sodas. They asked about you and said they had hoped to meet you here. Oh! and they described you jolly well, down to your boots and shirt. I told them you had been here last night and had gone off on a motor-bicycle this morning, and one of the chaps swore like a navvy."

I made him tell me what they looked like. One was a dark-eyed thin fellow with bushy eyebrows, the other was always smiling and lisped in his talk. Neither was any kind of foreigner; on this my young friend was positive.

I took a bit of paper and wrote these words in German as if they were part of a letter:

Black Stone. Scudder had got on to this, but he could not act for a fortnight. I doubt if I can do any good now, especially as Karolides is uncertain about his plans. But if Mr T. advises I will do the best I . . .

I manufactured it rather neatly, so that it looked like a loose page of a private letter.

"Take this down and say it was found in my bedroom, and ask them to return it to me if they overtake me."

Three minutes later I heard the car begin to move, and peeping from behind the curtain caught sight of the two figures. One was slim, the other was sleek; that was the most I could make of my reconnaissance.

The innkeeper appeared in great excitement. "Your paper woke them up," he said gleefully. "The dark fellow went as white as death and cursed like blazes, and the fat one whistled and looked ugly. They paid for their drinks with half a sovereign and wouldn't wait for change."

"Now I'll tell you what I want you to do," I said. "Get on your bicycle and go off to Newton Stewart to the Chief Constable. Describe the two men, and say you suspect them of having had something to do with the London murder. You can invent reasons. The two will come back, never fear. Not tonight, for they'll follow me forty miles along the road, but first thing tomorrow morning. Tell the police to be here bright and early."

He set off like a docile child, while I worked at Scudder's notes. When he came back we dined together, and in common decency I had to let him pump me. I gave him a lot of stuff about lion hunts and the Matabele War, thinking all the while what tame businesses these were compared to this I was now engaged in. When he went to bed I sat up and finished Scudder. I smoked in a chair till daylight, for I could not sleep.

About eight next morning I witnessed the arrival of two constables and a sergeant. They put their car in a coachhouse under the innkeeper's instructions, and entered the house. Twenty minutes later I saw from my window a second car come across the plateau from the opposite direction. It did not come up to the inn, but stopped two hundred yards off in the shelter of a patch of wood. I noticed that its occupants carefully reversed it before leaving it. A minute or two later I heard their steps on the gravel outside the window.

My plan had been to lie hid in my bedroom, and see what happened. I had a notion that, if I could bring the police and my other more dangerous pursuers together, something might work out of it to my advantage. But now I had a better idea. I scribbled a line of thanks to my host, opened the window, and dropped quietly into a gooseberry bush. Unobserved I crossed the dyke, crawled down the side of a tributary burn, and won the highroad on the far side of the patch of trees. There stood the car, very spick and span in the morning sunlight, but with the dust on her which told of a long journey. I started her, jumped into the chauffeur's seat, and stole gently out on to the plateau.

Almost at once the road dipped so that I lost sight of the inn, but the wind seemed to bring me the sound of angry voices.

CHAPTER 4

The Adventure of the Radical Candidate

YOU MAY PICTURE me driving that 40 hp car for all she was worth over the crisp moor roads on that shining May morning; glancing back at first over my shoulder, and looking anxiously to the next turning; then driving with a vague eye, just wide enough awake to keep on the highway. For I was thinking desperately of what I had found in Scudder's pocket-book.

The little man had told me a pack of lies. All his yarns about the Balkans and the Jew-anarchists and the Foreign Office Conference were eyewash, and so was Karolides. And yet not quite, as you shall hear. I had staked everything on my belief in his story, and had been let down; here was his book telling me a different tale, and instead of being once-bit-twice-shy, I believed it absolutely.

Why, I don't know. It rang desperately true, and the first yarn, if you understand me, had been in a queer way true also in spirit. The fifteenth day of June was going to be a day of destiny, a bigger destiny than the killing of a Dago. It was so big that I didn't blame Scudder for keeping me out of the game and wanting to play a lone hand. That, I was pretty clear, was his intention. He had told me something which sounded big enough, but the real thing was so immortally big that he, the man who had found it out, wanted it all for himself. I didn't blame him. It was risks after all that he was chiefly greedy about.

The whole story was in the notes—with gaps, you understand, which he would have filled up from his memory. He stuck down his authorities, too, and had an odd trick of giving them all a numerical value and then striking a balance, which stood for the reliability of each stage in the yarn. The four names he had printed were authorities, and there was a man, Ducrosne, who got five out of a possible five; and another fellow, Ammersfoort, who got three. The bare bones of the tale

41

were all that was in the book—these, and one queer phrase which occurred half a dozen times inside brackets. ("Thirty-nine steps") was the phrase; and at its last time of use it ran—("Thirty-nine steps, I counted them—high tide 10.17 pm"). I could make nothing of that.

The first thing I learned was that it was no question of preventing a war. That was coming, as sure as Christmas: had been arranged, said Scudder, ever since February 1912. Karolides was going to be the occasion. He was booked all right, and was to hand in his checks on June 14th, two weeks and four days from that May morning. I gathered from Scudder's notes that nothing on earth could prevent that. His talk of Epirote guards that would skin their own grandmothers was all billy-O.

The second thing was that this war was going to come as a mighty surprise to Britain. Karolides' death would set the Balkans by the ears, and then Vienna would chip in with an ultimatum. Russia wouldn't like that, and there would be high words. But Berlin would play the peacemaker, and pour oil on the waters, till suddenly she would find a good cause for a quarrel, pick it up, and in five hours let fly at us. That was the idea, and a pretty good one too. Honey and fair speeches, and then a stroke in the dark. While we were talking about the goodwill and good intentions of Germany our coast would be silently ringed with mines, and submarines would be waiting for every battleship.

But all this depended upon the third thing, which was due to happen on June 15th. I would never have grasped this if I hadn't once happened to meet a French staff officer, coming back from West Africa, who had told me a lot of things. One was that, in spite of all the nonsense talked in Parliament, there was a real working alliance between France and Britain, and that the two General Staffs met every now and then, and made plans for joint action in case of war. Well, in June a very great swell was coming over from Paris, and he was going to get nothing less than a statement of the disposition of the British Home Fleet on mobilization. At least I gathered it was something like that; anyhow, it was something uncommonly important.

But on the 15th day of June there were to be others in London—others, at whom I could only guess. Scudder was content to call them collectively the "Black Stone". They represented not our Allies, but our deadly foes; and the information, destined for France, was to be diverted to their pockets. And it was to be used, remember—used a week or two later, with great guns and swift torpedoes, suddenly in the darkness of a summer night.

This was the story I had been deciphering in a back room of a country inn, overlooking a cabbage garden. This was the story that hummed in my brain as I swung in the big touring-car from glen to glen.

My first impulse had been to write a letter to the Prime Minister, but a little reflection convinced me that that would be useless. Who would believe my tale? I must show a sign, some token in proof, and Heaven knew what that could be. Above all, I must keep going myself, ready to act when things got riper, and that was going to be no light job with the police of the British Isles in full cry after me and the watchers of the Black Stone running silently and swiftly on my trail.

I had no very clear purpose in my journey, but I steered east by the sun, for I remembered from the map that if I went north I would come into a region of coal-pits and industrial towns. Presently I was down from the moorlands and traversing the broad haugh of a river. For miles I ran alongside a park wall, and in a break of the trees I saw a great castle. I swung through little old thatched villages, and over peaceful lowland streams, and past gardens blazing with hawthorn and yellow laburnum. The land was so deep in peace that I could scarcely believe that somewhere behind me were those who sought my life; ay, and that in a month's time, unless I had the almightiest of luck, these round country faces would be pinched and staring, and men would be lying dead in English fields.

About midday I entered a long straggling village, and had a mind to stop and eat. Halfway down was the Post Office, and on the steps of it stood the post-mistress and a policeman hard at work conning a telegram. When they saw me they wakened up, and the policeman advanced with raised hand, and cried on me to stop.

I nearly was fool enough to obey. Then it flashed upon me that the wire had to do with me; that my friends at the inn had come to an understanding, and were united in desiring to see more of me, and that it had been easy enough for them to wire the description of me and the car to thirty villages through which I might pass. I released the brakes just in time. As it was, the policeman made a claw at the hood, and only dropped off when he got my left in his eye.

I saw that main roads were no place for me, and turned into the by-ways. It wasn't an easy job without a map, for there was the risk of getting on to a farm road and ending in a duck-pond or a stable-yard, and I couldn't afford that kind of delay. I began to see what an ass I had been to steal the car. The big green brute would be the safest kind of clue to me over the breadth of Scotland. If I left it and took to my feet, it would be discovered in an hour or two and I would get no start in the race.

The immediate thing to do was to get to the loneliest roads. These I soon found when I struck up a tributary of the big river, and got into a glen with steep hills all about me, and a corkscrew road at the end which climbed over a pass. Here I met nobody, but it was taking me too far north, so I slewed east along a bad track and finally struck a big double-line railway. Away below me I saw another broadish valley, and it occurred to me that if I crossed it I might find some remote inn to pass the night. The evening was now drawing in, and I was furiously hungry, for I had eaten nothing since breakfast except a couple of buns I had bought from a baker's cart.

Just then I heard a noise in the sky, and lo and behold there was that infernal aeroplane, flying low, about a dozen miles to the south and rapidly coming towards me.

I had the sense to remember that on a bare moor I was at the aeroplane's mercy, and that my only chance was to get to the leafy cover of the valley. Down the hill I went like blue lightning, screwing my head round, whenever I dared, to watch that damned flying machine. Soon I was on a road between hedges, and dipping to the deep-cut glen of a stream. Then came a bit of thick wood where I slackened speed.

Suddenly on my left I heard the hoot of another car, and realized to my horror that I was almost upon a couple of gateposts through which a private road debouched on the highway. My horn gave an agonized roar, but it was too late. I clapped on my brakes, but my impetus was too great, and there before me a car was sliding athwart my course. In a second there would have been the deuce of a wreck. I did the only thing possible, and ran slap into the hedge on the right, trusting to find something soft beyond.

But there I was mistaken. My car slithered through the hedge like butter, and then gave a sickening plunge forward. I saw what was coming, leaped on the seat and would have jumped out. But a branch of hawthorn got me in the chest, lifted me up and held me, while a ton or two of expensive metal slipped below me, bucked and pitched, and then dropped with an almighty smash fifty feet to the bed of the stream.

MY CAR SLITHERED THROUGH THE HEDGE

SLOWLY THAT THORN let me go. I subsided first on the hedge, and then very gently on a bower of nettles. As I scrambled to my feet a hand took me by the arm, and a sympathetic and badly scared voice asked me if I were hurt.

I found myself looking at a tall young man in goggles and a leather ulster, who kept on blessing his soul and whinnying apologies. For myself, once I got my wind back, I was rather glad than otherwise. This was one way of getting rid of the car.

"My blame, sir," I answered him. "It's lucky that I did not add homicide to my follies. That's the end of my Scotch motor tour, but it might have been the end of my life."

He plucked out a watch and studied it. "You're the right sort of fellow," he said. "I can spare a quarter of an hour, and my house is two minutes off. I'll see you clothed and fed and snug in bed. Where's your kit, by the way? Is it in the burn along with the car?"

"It's in my pocket," I said, brandishing a toothbrush. "I'm a Colonial and travel light."

"A Colonial," he cried. "By Gad, you're the very man I've been praying for. Are you by any blessed chance a Free Trader?"

"I am," said I, without the foggiest notion of what he meant.

He patted my shoulder and hurried me into his car. Three minutes later we drew up before a comfortable-looking shooting-box set among pine-trees, and he ushered me indoors. He took me first to a bedroom and flung half a dozen of his suits before me, for my own had been pretty well reduced to rags. I selected a loose blue serge, which differed most conspicuously from my former garments, and borrowed a linen collar. Then he haled me to the dining-room, where the remnants of a meal stood on the table, and announced that I had just five minutes to feed. "You can take a snack in your pocket, and we'll have supper when we get back. I've got to be at the Masonic Hall at eight o'clock or my agent will comb my hair."

I had a cup of coffee and some cold ham, while he yarned away on the hearthrug.

"You find me in the deuce of a mess, Mr——; by the by, you haven't told me your name. Twisdon? Any relation of old Tommy Twisdon of the Sixtieth? No? Well, you see I'm Liberal Candidate for this part of the world, and I had a meeting on tonight at Brattleburn—that's my chief town, and an infernal Tory stronghold. I had got the Colonial ex-Premier fellow, Crumpleton, coming to speak for me tonight, and had the thing tremendously billed and the whole place ground-baited. This afternoon I had a wire from the ruffian saying he had got influenza at Blackpool, and here am I left to do the whole thing myself. I had meant to speak for ten minutes and must now go on for forty, and, though I've been racking my brains for three hours to think of something, I simply cannot last the course. Now you've got to be a good chap and help me. You're a Free Trader and can tell our people what a wash-out Protection is in the Colonies. All you fellows have the gift of the gab—I wish to Heaven I had it. I'll be for evermore in your debt."

I had very few notions about Free Trade one way or the other, but I saw no other chance to get what I wanted. My young gentleman was far too absorbed in his own difficulties to think how odd it was to ask a stranger who had just missed death by an ace and had lost a thousand-guinea car to address a meeting for him on the spur of the moment. But my necessities did not allow me to contemplate oddnesses or to pick and choose my supports.

"All right," I said. "I'm not much good as a speaker, but I'll tell them a bit about Australia."

At my words the cares of the ages slipped from his shoulders, and he was rapturous in his thanks. He lent me a big driving coat—and never troubled to ask why I had started on a motor tour without possessing an ulster—and, as we slipped down the dusty roads, poured into my ears the simple facts of his history. He was an orphan, and his uncle had brought him up—I've forgotten the uncle's name, but he was in the Cabinet, and you can read his speeches in the papers. He had gone round the world after leaving Cambridge, and then, being short of a job, his uncle had advised politics. I gathered that he had no preference in parties. "Good chaps in both," he said cheerfully, "and plenty of blighters, too. I'm Liberal, because my family have always been Whigs." But if he was lukewarm politically he had strong views on other things. He found out I knew a bit about horses, and jawed away about the Derby entries; and he was full of plans for improving his shooting. Altogether, a very clean, decent, callow young man.

As we passed through a little town two policemen signalled us to stop, and flashed their lanterns on us.

"Beg pardon, Sir Harry," said one. "We've got instructions to look out for a car, and the description's no unlike yours."

"Right-oh," said my host, while I thanked Providence for the devious ways I had been brought to safety. After that he spoke no more, for his mind began to labour heavily with his coming speech. His lips kept muttering, his eye wandered, and I began to prepare myself for a second catastrophe. I tried to think of something to say myself, but my mind was dry as a stone. The next thing I knew we had drawn up outside a door in a street, and were being welcomed by some noisy gentlemen with rosettes.

The hall had about five hundred in it, women mostly, a lot of bald heads, and a dozen or two young men. The chairman, a weaselly minister with a reddish nose, lamented Crumpleton's absence, soliloquized on his influenza, and gave me a certificate as a "trusted leader of Australian thought". There were two policemen at the door, and I hoped they took note of that testimonial. Then Sir Harry started.

I never heard anything like it. He didn't begin to know how to talk. He had about a bushel of notes from which he read, and when he let go of them he fell into one prolonged stutter. Every now and then he remembered a phrase he had learned by heart, straightened his back, and gave it off like Henry Irving, and the next moment he was bent double and crooning over his papers. It was the most appalling rot, too. He talked about the "German menace", and said it was all a Tory invention to cheat the poor of their rights and keep back the great flood of social reform, but that "organized labour" realized this and laughed the Tories to scorn. He was all for reducing our Navy as a proof of our good faith, and then sending Germany an ultimatum telling her to do the same or we would knock her into a cocked hat. He said that, but for the Tories, Germany and Britain would be fellow workers in peace and reform. I thought of the little black book in my pocket! A giddy lot Scudder's friends cared for peace and reform.

Yet in a queer way I liked the speech. You could see the niceness of the chap shining out behind the muck with which he had been spoon-fed. Also it took a load off my mind. I mightn't be much of an orator, but I was a thousand per cent better than Sir Harry.

I didn't get on so badly when it came to my turn. I simply told them all I could remember about Australia, praying there should be no Australian there—all about its labour party and emigration and universal service. I doubt if I remembered to mention Free Trade, but I said there were no Tories in Australia, only Labour and Liberals. That fetched a cheer, and I woke them up a bit when I started in to tell them the kind of glorious business I thought could be made out of the Empire if we really put our backs into it.

Altogether I fancy I was rather a success. The minister didn't like me, though, and when he proposed a vote of thanks, spoke of Sir Harry's speech as "statesmanlike" and mine as having "the eloquence of an emigration agent".

When we were in the car again my host was in wild spirits at having got his job over. "A ripping speech, Twisdon," he said. "Now, you're coming home with me. I'm all alone, and if you'll stop a day or two I'll show you some very decent fishing."

We had a hot supper—and I wanted it pretty badly—and then drank grog in a big cheery smoking-room with a crackling wood fire. I thought the time had come for me to put my cards on the table. I saw by this man's eye that he was the kind you can trust.

"Listen, Sir Harry," I said. "I've something pretty important to say to you. You're a good fellow, and I'm going to be frank. Where on earth did you get that poisonous rubbish you talked tonight?"

His face fell. "Was it as bad as that?" he asked ruefully. "It did sound rather thin. I got most of it out of the *Progressive Magazine* and pamphlets that agent chap of mine keeps sending me. But you surely don't think Germany would ever go to war with us?"

"Ask that question in six weeks and it won't need an answer," I said. "If you'll give me your attention for half an hour I am going to tell you a story."

I can see yet that bright room with the deers' heads and the old prints on the walls, Sir Harry standing restlessly on the stone curb of the hearth, and myself lying back in an armchair, speaking. I seemed to be another person, standing aside and listening to my own voice, and judging carefully the reliability of my tale. It was the first time I had ever told anyone the exact truth, as far as I understood it, and it did me no end of good, for it straightened out the thing in my own mind. I blinked no detail. He heard all about Scudder, and the milkman, and the notebook, and my doings in Galloway. Presently he got very excited and walked up and down the hearthrug.

"So you see," I concluded, "you have got here in your house the man that is wanted for the Portland Place murder. Your duty is to send your car for the police and give me up. I don't think I'll get very far. There'll be an accident, and I'll have a knife in my ribs an hour or so after arrest. Nevertheless it's your duty, as a law-abiding citizen. Perhaps in a month's time you'll be sorry, but you have no cause to think of that."

He was looking at me with bright steady eyes. "What was your job in Rhodesia, Mr Hannay?" he asked.

"Mining engineer," I said. "I've made my pile cleanly, and I've had a good time in the making of it."

"Not a profession that weakens the nerves, is it?"

I laughed. "Oh, as to that, my nerves are good enough." I took down a hunting-knife from a stand on the wall, and did the old Mashona trick of tossing it and catching it in my lips. That wants a pretty steady heart.

He watched me with a smile. "I don't want proof. I may be an ass on the platform, but I can size up a man. You're no murderer and you're no fool, and I believe you are speaking the truth. I'm going to back you up. Now, what can I do?"

"First, I want you to write a letter to your uncle. I've got to get in touch with the Government people some time before the 15th of June."

He pulled his moustache. "That won't help you. This is Foreign Office business, and my uncle would have nothing to do with it. Besides, you'd never convince him. No, I'll go one better. I'll write to the Permanent Secretary at the Foreign Office. He's my godfather, and one of the best going. What do you want?"

He sat down at a table and wrote to my dictation. The gist of it was that if a man called Twisdon (I thought I had better stick to that name) turned up before June 15th he was to treat him kindly. He said Twisdon would prove his *bona fides* by passing the word "Black Stone" and whistling "Annie Laurie".

"Good," said Sir Harry. "That's the proper style. By the way, you'll find my godfather—his name's Sir Walter Bullivant—down at his country cottage for Whitsuntide. It's close to Artinswell on the Kennet. That's done. Now, what's the next thing?"

"You're about my height. Lend me the oldest tweed suit you've got. Anything will do, so long as the colour is the opposite of the clothes I destroyed this afternoon. Then show me a map of the neighbourhood and explain to me the lie of the land. Lastly, if the police come seeking me, just show them the car in the glen. If the other lot turn up, tell them I caught the south express after your meeting."

He did, or promised to do, all these things. I shaved off the remnants of my moustache, and got inside an ancient suit of what I believe is called heather mixture. The map gave me some notion of my whereabouts, and told me the two things I wanted to know—where the main railway to the south could be joined and what were the wildest districts near at hand.

At two o'clock he wakened me from my slumbers in the smoking-room armchair, and led me blinking into the dark starry night. An old bicycle was found in a tool-shed and handed over to me.

"First turn to the right up by the long fir-wood," he enjoined. "By daybreak you'll be well into the hills. Then I should pitch the machine into a bog and take to the moors on foot. You can put in a week among the shepherds, and be as safe as if you were in New Guinea."

I pedalled diligently up steep roads of hill gravel till the skies grew pale with morning. As the mists cleared before the sun, I found myself in a wide green world with glens falling on every side and a far-away blue horizon. Here, at any rate, I could get early news of my enemies.

CHAPTER 5

The Adventure of the Spectacled Roadman

I SAT DOWN on the very crest of the pass and took stock of my position.

Behind me was the road climbing through a long cleft in the hills, which was the upper glen of some notable river. In front was a flat space of maybe a mile, all pitted with bog-holes and rough with tussocks, and then beyond it the road fell steeply down another glen to a plain whose blue dimness melted into the distance. To left and right were round-shouldered green hills as smooth as pancakes, but to the south—that is, the left hand—there was a glimpse of high heathery mountains, which I remembered from the map as the big knot of hill which I had chosen for my sanctuary. I was on the central boss of a huge upland country, and could see everything moving for miles. In the meadows below the road half a mile back a cottage smoked, but it was the only sign of human life. Otherwise there was only the calling of plovers and the tinkling of little streams.

It was now about seven o'clock, and as I waited I heard once again that ominous beat in the air. Then I realized that my vantage-ground might be in reality a trap. There was no cover for a tomtit in those bald green places.

I sat quite still and hopeless while the beat grew louder. Then I saw an aeroplane coming up from the east. It was flying high, but as I looked it dropped several hundred feet and began to circle round the knot of hill in narrowing circles, just as a hawk wheels before it pounces. Now it was flying very low, and now the observer on board caught sight of me. I could see one of the two occupants examining me through glasses.

Suddenly it began to rise in swift whorls, and the next I knew it was speeding eastward again till it became a speck in the blue morning.

That made me do some savage thinking. My enemies had located me, and the next thing would be a cordon round me. I didn't know what force they could command, but I was certain it would be sufficient. The aeroplane had seen my bicycle, and would conclude that I would try to escape by the road. In that case there might be a chance on the moors to the right or left. I wheeled the machine a hundred yards from the highway, and plunged it into a moss-hole, where it sank among pond-weed and water-buttercups. Then I climbed to a knoll which gave me a view of the two valleys. Nothing was stirring on the long white ribbon that threaded them.

I have said there was not cover in the whole place to hide a rat. As the day advanced it was flooded with soft fresh light till it had the fragrant sunniness of the South African veld. At other times I would have liked the place, but now it seemed to suffocate me. The free moorlands were prison walls, and the keen hill air was the breath of a dungeon.

I tossed a coin—heads right, tails left—and it fell heads, so I turned to the north. In a little I came to the brow of the ridge which was the containing wall of the pass. I saw the highroad for maybe ten miles, and far down it something that was moving, and that I took to be a motor-car. Beyond the ridge I looked on a rolling green moor, which fell away into wooded glens.

Now my life on the veld has given me the eyes of a kite, and I can see things for which most men need a telescope . . . Away down the slope, a couple of miles away, several men were advancing like a row of beaters at a shoot . . .

I dropped out of sight behind the skyline. That way was shut to me, and I must try the bigger hills to the south beyond the highway. The car I had noticed was getting nearer, but it was still a long way off with some very steep gradients before it. I ran hard, crouching low except in the hollows, and as I ran I kept scanning the brow of the hill before me. Was it imagination, or did I see figures—one, two, perhaps more—moving in a glen beyond the stream?

If you are hemmed in on all sides in a patch of land there is only one chance of escape. You must stay in the patch, and let your enemies search it and not find you. That was good sense, but how on earth was I to escape notice in that tablecloth of a place? I would have buried myself to the neck in mud or lain below water or climbed the tallest tree. But there was not a stick of wood, the bog-holes were little puddles, the stream was a slender trickle. There was nothing but short heather, and bare hill bent, and the white highway.

THEN IN A TINY bight of road, beside a heap of stones, I found the roadman.

He had just arrived, and was wearily flinging down his hammer. He looked at me with a fishy eye and yawned.

"Confoond the day I ever left the herdin'!" he said, as if to the world at large. "There I was my ain maister. Now I'm a slave to the Government, tethered to the roadside, wi' sair een, and a back like a suckle."

He took up the hammer, struck a stone, dropped the implement with an oath, and put both hands to his ears. "Mercy on me! My heid's burstin'!" he cried.

He was a wild figure, about my own size but much bent, with a week's beard on his chin, and a pair of big horn spectacles.

"I canna dae't," he cried again. "The Surveyor maun just report me. I'm for my bed."

I asked him what was the trouble, though indeed that was clear enough.

"The trouble is that I'm no sober. Last nicht my dochter Merran was waddit, and they danced till fower in the byre. Me and some ither chiels sat down to the drinkin', and here I am. Peety that I ever lookit on the wine when it was red!"

I agreed with him about bed.

"It's easy speakin'," he moaned. "But I got a post-caird yestreen sayin' that the new Road Surveyor would be round the day. He'll come and he'll no find me, or else he'll find me fou, and either way I'm a done man. I'll awa' back to my bed and say I'm no weel, but I doot that'll no help me, for they ken my kind o' no-weel-ness."

Then I had an inspiration. "Does the new Surveyor know you?" I asked.

"No him. He's just been a week at the job. He rins about in a wee motor-cawr, and wad speir the inside oot o' a whelk."

"Where's your house?" I asked, and was directed by a wavering finger to the cottage by the stream.

"Well, back to your bed," I said, "and sleep in peace. I'll take on your job for a bit and see the Surveyor."

He stared at me blankly; then, as the notion dawned on his fuddled brain, his face broke into the vacant drunkard's smile.

"You're the billy," he cried. "It'll be easy eneuch managed. I've finished that bing o' stanes, so you needna chap ony mair this forenoon. Just take the barry, and wheel eneuch metal frae yon quarry doon the road to make anither bing the morn. My name's Alexander Turnbull, and I've been seeven year at the trade, and twenty afore that herdin', on Leithen Water. My freens ca' me Ecky, and whiles Specky, for I wear glasses, being weak i' the sicht. Just you speak the Surveyor fair, and ca' him Sir, and he'll be fell pleased. I'll be back or midday."

I borrowed his spectacles and filthy old hat; stripped off coat, waistcoat, and collar, and gave him them to carry home; borrowed, too, the foul stump of a clay pipe as an extra property. He indicated my simple tasks, and without more ado set off at an amble bedwards. Bed may have been his chief object, but I think there was also something left in the foot of a bottle. I prayed that he might be safe under cover before my friends arrived on the scene.

Then I set to work to dress for the part. I opened the collar of my shirt—it was a vulgar blue-and-white check such as ploughmen wear—and revealed a neck as brown as any tinker's. I rolled up my sleeves, and there was a forearm which might have been a blacksmith's, sunburnt and rough with old scars. I got my boots and trouser-legs all white from the dust of the road, and hitched up my trousers, tying them with string below the knee. Then I set to work on my face. With a handful of dust I made a watermark round my neck, the place where Mr Turnbull's Sunday ablutions might be expected to stop. I rubbed a good deal of dirt also into the sunburn of my cheeks. A roadman's eyes would no doubt be a little inflamed, so I contrived to get some dust in both of mine, and by dint of vigorous rubbing produced a bleary effect.

The sandwiches Sir Harry had given me had gone off with my coat, but the roadman's lunch, tied up in a red handkerchief, was at my disposal. I ate with great relish several of the thick slabs of scone and cheese and drank a little of the cold tea. In the handkerchief was a local paper tied with string and addressed to Mr Turnbull—obviously meant to solace his midday leisure. I did up the bundle again, and put the paper conspicuously beside it.

My boots did not satisfy me, but by dint of kicking among the stones I reduced them to the granite-like surface which marks a roadman's footgear. Then I bit and scraped my fingernails till the edges were all cracked and uneven. The men I was matched against would miss no detail. I broke one of the bootlaces and retied it in a clumsy knot, and loosed the other so that my thick grey socks bulged over the uppers. Still no sign of anything on the road. The motor I had observed half an hour ago must have gone home.

My toilet complete, I took up the barrow and began my journeys to and from the quarry a hundred yards off.

I remember an old scout in Rhodesia, who had done many queer things in his day, once telling me that the secret of playing a part was to think yourself into it. You could never keep it up, he said, unless you could manage to convince yourself that you were *it*. So I shut off all other thoughts and switched them on to the road-mending. I thought of the little white cottage as my home, I recalled the years I had spent herding on Leithen Water, I made my mind dwell lovingly on sleep in a box-bed and a bottle of cheap whisky. Still nothing appeared on that long white road.

Now and then a sheep wandered off the heather to stare at me. A heron flopped down to a pool in the stream and started to fish, taking no more notice of me than if I had been a milestone. On I went, trundling my loads of stone, with the heavy step of the professional. Soon I grew warm, and the dust on my face changed into solid and abiding grit. I was already counting the hours till evening should put a limit to Mr Turnbull's monotonous toil.

Suddenly a crisp voice from the road, and looking up I saw a little Ford two-seater, and a round-faced young man in a bowler hat.

"Are you Alexander Turnbull?" he asked. "I am the new County Road Surveyor. You live at Blackhopefoot, and have charge of the section from Laidlaw-byres to the Riggs? Good! A fair bit of road, Turnbull, and not badly engineered. A little soft about a mile off, and the edges want cleaning. See you look after that. Good morning. You'll know me the next time you see me."

Clearly my get-up was good enough for the dreaded Surveyor. I went on with my work, and as the morning grew towards noon I was cheered by a little traffic. A baker's van breasted the hill, and sold me a bag of ginger biscuits which I stowed in my trouser pockets against emergencies. Then a herd passed with sheep, and disturbed me somewhat by asking loudly, "What had become o' Specky?"

"In bed wi' the colic," I replied, and the herd passed on . . .

Just about midday a big car stole down the hill, glided past and drew up a hundred yards beyond. Its three occupants descended as if to stretch their legs, and sauntered towards me.

Two of the men I had seen before from the window of the Galloway inn—one lean, sharp, and dark, the other comfortable and smiling. The third had the look of a countryman—a vet, perhaps, or a small farmer. He was dressed in ill-cut knickerbockers, and the eye in his head was as bright and wary as a hen's.

"'Morning," said the last. "That's a fine easy job o' yours."

I had not looked up on their approach, and now, when accosted, I slowly and painfully straightened my back, after the manner of roadmen; spat vigorously, after the manner of the low Scot; and regarded them steadily before replying. I confronted three pairs of eyes that missed nothing.

"There's waur jobs and there's better," I said sententiously. "I wad rather hae yours, sittin' a' day on your hinderlands on thae cushions. It's you and your muckle cawrs that wreck my roads! If we a' had oor richts, ye sud be made to mend what ye break."

The bright-eyed man was looking at the newspaper lying beside Turnbull's bundle.

"I see you get your papers in good time," he said.

I glanced at it casually. "Ay, in gude time. Seein' that that paper cam' out last Setterday I'm just sax days late."

He picked it up, glanced at the superscription, and laid it down again. One of the others had been looking at my boots, and a word in German called the speaker's attention to them.

"You've a fine taste in boots," he said. "These were never made by a country shoemaker."

"They were not," I said readily. "They were made in London. I got them frae the gentleman that was here last year for the shootin'. What was his name now?" And I scratched a forgetful head.

Again the sleek one spoke in German. "Let us get on," he said. "This fellow is all right."

They asked one last question.

"Did you see anyone pass early this morning? He might be on a bicycle or he might be on foot."

I very nearly fell into the trap and told a story of a bicyclist hurrying past in the grey dawn. But I had the sense to see my danger. I pretended to consider very deeply.

"I wasna up very early," I said. "Ye see, my dochter was merrit last nicht, and we keepit it up late. I opened the house door about seeven and there was naebody on the road then. Since I cam' up here there has just been the baker and the Ruchill herd, besides you gentlemen."

One of them gave me a cigar, which I smelt gingerly and stuck in Turnbull's bundle. They got into their car and were out of sight in three minutes.

My heart leaped with an enormous relief, but I went on wheeling my stones. It was as well, for ten minutes later the car returned, one of the occupants waving a hand to me. Those gentry left nothing to chance.

I finished Turnbull's bread and cheese, and pretty soon I had finished the stones. The next step was what puzzled me. I could not keep up this roadmaking business for long. A merciful Providence had kept Mr Turnbull indoors, but if he appeared on the scene there would be trouble. I had a notion that the cordon was still tight round the glen, and that if I walked in any direction I should meet with questioners. But get out I must. No man's nerve could stand more than a day of being spied on.

I stayed at my post till about five o'clock. By that time I had resolved to go down to Turnbull's cottage at nightfall and take my chance of getting over the hills in the darkness. But suddenly a new car came up the road, and slowed down a yard or two from me. A fresh wind had risen, and the occupant wanted to light a cigarette.

It was a touring-car, with the tonneau full of an assortment of baggage. One man sat in it, and by an amazing chance I knew him. His name was Marmaduke Jopley, and he was an offence to creation. He was a sort of blood stockbroker, who did his business by toadying eldest sons and rich young peers and foolish old ladies. 'Marmie' was a familiar figure, I understood, at balls and polo weeks and country houses. He was an adroit scandal-monger, and would crawl a mile on his belly to anything that had a title or a million. I had a business introduction to his firm when I came to London, and he was good

I VERY NEARLY FELL INTO THE TRAP

enough to ask me to dinner at his club. There he showed off at a great rate, and pattered about his duchesses till the snobbery of the creature turned me sick. I asked a man afterwards why nobody kicked him, and was told that Englishmen reverenced the weaker sex.

Anyhow there he was now, nattily dressed, in a fine new car, obviously on his way to visit some of his smart friends. A sudden daftness took me, and in a second I had jumped into the tonneau and had him by the shoulder.

"Hullo, Jopley," I sang out. "Well met, my lad!" He got a horrid fright. His chin dropped as he stared at me. "Who the devil are you?" he gasped.

"My name's Hannay," I said. "From Rhodesia, you remember."

"Good God, the murderer!" he choked.

"Just so. And there'll be a second murder, my dear, if you don't do as I tell you. Give me that coat of yours. That cap, too."

He did as bid, for he was blind with terror. Over my dirty trousers and vulgar shirt I put on his smart driving coat, which buttoned high at the top and thereby hid the deficiencies of my collar. I stuck the cap on my head, and added his gloves to my get-up. The dusty roadman in a minute was transformed into one of the neatest motorists in Scotland. On Mr Jopley's head I clapped Turnbull's unspeakable hat, and told him to keep it there.

Then with some difficulty I turned the car. My plan was to go back the road he had come, for the watchers, having seen it before, would probably let it pass unremarked, and Marmie's figure was in no way like mine.

"Now, my child," I said, "sit quite still and be a good boy. I mean you no harm. I'm only borrowing your car for an hour or two. But if you play me any tricks, and above all if you open your mouth, as sure as there's a God above me I'll wring your neck. *Savez?*"

I enjoyed that evening's ride. We ran eight miles down the valley, through a village or two, and I could not help noticing several strange-looking folk lounging by the roadside. These were the watchers who would have had much to say to me if I had come in other garb or company. As it was, they looked incuriously on. One touched his cap in salute, and I responded graciously.

As the dark fell I turned up a side glen which, as I remembered from the map, led into an unfrequented corner of the hills. Soon the villages were left behind, then the farms, and then even the wayside cottages. Presently we came to a lonely moor where the night was blackening the sunset gleam in the bog pools. Here we stopped, and I obligingly reversed the car and restored to Mr Jopley his belongings.

"A thousand thanks," I said. "There's more use in you than I thought. Now be off and find the police."

As I sat on the hillside, watching the tail-lights dwindle, I reflected on the various kinds of crime I had now sampled. Contrary to general belief, I was not a murderer, but I had become an unholy liar, a shameless impostor, and a highwayman with a marked taste for expensive motor-cars.

CHAPTER 6

The Adventure of the Bald Archaeologist

I SPENT THE NIGHT on a shelf of the hillside, in the lee of a boulder where the heather grew long and soft. It was a cold business, for I had neither coat nor waistcoat. These were in Mr Turnbull's keeping, as was Scudder's little book, my watch and—worst of all—my pipe and tobacco pouch. Only my money accompanied me in my belt, and about half a pound of ginger biscuits in my trousers pocket.

I supped off half those biscuits, and by worming myself deep into the heather got some kind of warmth. My spirits had risen, and I was beginning to enjoy this crazy game of hide-and-seek. So far I had been miraculously lucky. The milkman, the literary innkeeper, Sir Harry, the roadman, and the idiotic Marmie, were all pieces of undeserved good fortune. Somehow the first success gave me a feeling that I was going to pull the thing through.

My chief trouble was that I was desperately hungry. When a Jew shoots himself in the City and there is an inquest, the newspapers usually report that the deceased was 'well-nourished'. I remember thinking that they would not call me well-nourished if I broke my neck in a bog-hole. I lay and tortured myself—for the ginger biscuits merely emphasized the aching void—with the memory of all the good food I had thought so little of in London. There were Paddock's crisp sausages and fragrant shavings of bacon, and shapely poached eggs—how often I had turned up my nose at them! There were the cutlets they did at the club, and a particular ham that stood on the cold table, for which my soul lusted. My thoughts hovered over all varieties of mortal edible, and finally settled on a porter-house steak and a quart of bitter with a welsh rabbit to follow. In longing hopelessly for these dainties I fell asleep.

I woke very cold and stiff about an hour after dawn. It took me a little while to remember where I was, for I had been very weary and had slept heavily. I saw first the pale blue sky through a net of heather, then a big shoulder of hill, and then my own boots placed neatly in a blaeberry bush. I raised myself on my arms and looked down into the valley, and that one look set me lacing up my boots in mad haste.

For there were men below, not more than a quarter of a mile off, spaced out on the hillside like a fan, and beating the heather. Marmie had not been slow in looking for his revenge.

I crawled out of my shelf into the cover of a boulder, and from it gained a shallow trench which slanted up the mountain face. This led me presently into the narrow gully of a burn, by way of which I scrambled to the top of the ridge. From there I looked back, and saw that I was still undiscovered. My pursuers were patiently quartering the hillside and moving upwards.

Keeping behind the skyline I ran for maybe half a mile, till I judged I was above the uppermost end of the glen. Then I showed myself, and was instantly noted by one of the flankers, who passed the word to the others. I heard cries coming up from below, and saw that the line of search had changed its direction. I pretended to retreat over the skyline, but instead went back the way I had come, and in twenty minutes was behind the ridge overlooking my sleeping place. From that viewpoint I had the satisfaction of seeing the pursuit streaming up the hill at the top of the glen on a hopelessly false scent.

I had before me a choice of routes, and I chose a ridge which made an angle with the one I was on, and so would soon put a deep glen between me and my enemies. The exercise had warmed my blood, and I was beginning to enjoy myself amazingly. As I went I breakfasted on the dusty remnants of the ginger biscuits.

I knew very little about the country, and I hadn't a notion what I was going to do. I trusted to the strength of my legs, but I was well aware that those behind me would be familiar with the lie of the land, and that my ignorance would be a heavy handicap. I saw in front of me a sea of hills, rising very high towards the south, but northwards breaking down into broad ridges which separated wide and shallow dales. The ridge I had chosen seemed to sink after a mile or two to a moor which lay like a pocket in the uplands. That seemed as good a direction to take as any other.

My stratagem had given me a fair start—call it twenty minutes—and

I had the width of a glen behind me before I saw the first heads of the pursuers. The police had evidently called in local talent to their aid, and the men I could see had the appearance of herds or gamekeepers. They hallooed at the sight of me, and I waved my hand. Two dived into the glen and began to climb my ridge, while the others kept their own side of the hill. I felt as if I were taking part in a schoolboy game of hare and hounds.

But very soon it began to seem less of a game. Those fellows behind were hefty men on their native heath. Looking back I saw that only three were following direct, and I guessed that the others had fetched a circuit to cut me off. My lack of local knowledge might very well be my undoing, and I resolved to get out of this tangle of glens to the pocket of moor I had seen from the tops. I must so increase my distance as to get clear away from them, and I believed I could do this if I could find the right ground for it. If there had been cover I would have tried a bit of stalking, but on these bare slopes you could see a fly a mile off. My hope must be in the length of my legs and the soundness of my wind, but I needed easier ground for that, for I was not bred a mountaineer. How I longed for a good Afrikander pony!

I put on a great spurt and got off my ridge and down into the moor before any figures appeared on the skyline behind me. I crossed a burn, and came out on a highroad which made a pass between two glens. All in front of me was a big field of heather sloping up to a crest which was crowned with an odd feather of trees. In the dyke by the roadside was a gate, from which a grass-grown track led over the first wave of the moor.

I jumped the dyke and followed it, and after a few hundred yards—as soon as it was out of sight of the highway—the grass stopped and it became a very respectable road, which was evidently kept with some care. Clearly it ran to a house, and I began to think of doing the same. Hitherto my luck had held, and it might be that my best chance would be found in this remote dwelling. Anyhow there were trees there, and that meant cover.

I did not follow the road, but the burnside which flanked it on the right, where the bracken grew deep and the high banks made a tolerable screen. It was well I did so, for no sooner had I gained the hollow than, looking back, I saw the pursuit topping the ridge from which I had descended.

After that I did not look back; I had no time. I ran up the burnside, crawling over the open places, and for a large part wading in the shallow stream. I found a deserted cottage with a row of phantom peat-stacks and an overgrown garden. Then I was among young hay, and very soon had come to the edge of a plantation of wind-blown firs. From there I saw the chimneys of the house smoking a few hundred yards to my left. I forsook the burnside, crossed another dyke, and almost before I knew I was on a rough lawn. A glance back told me that I was well out of sight of the pursuit, which had not yet passed the first lift of the moor.

The lawn was a very rough place, cut with a scythe instead of a mower, and planted with beds of scrubby rhododendrons. A brace of black-game, which are not usually garden birds, rose at my approach. The house before me was the ordinary moorland farm, with a more pretentious whitewashed wing added. Attached to this wing was a glass veranda, and through the glass I saw the face of an elderly gentleman meekly watching me.

I stalked over the border of coarse hill gravel and entered the open veranda door. Within was a pleasant room, glass on one side, and on the other a mass of books. More books showed in an inner room. On the floor, instead of tables, stood cases such as you see in a museum, filled with coins and queer stone implements.

There was a knee-hole desk in the middle, and seated at it, with some papers and open volumes before him, was the benevolent old gentleman. His face was round and shiny, like Mr Pickwick's, big glasses were stuck on the end of his nose, and the top of his head was as bright and bare as a glass bottle. He never moved when I entered, but raised his placid eyebrows and waited on me to speak.

It was not an easy job, with about five minutes to spare, to tell a stranger who I was and what I wanted and to win his aid. I did not attempt it. There was something about the eye of the man before me, something so keen and knowledgeable, that I could not find a word. I simply stared at him and stuttered.

"You seem in a hurry, my friend," he said slowly.

I nodded towards the window. It gave a prospect across the moor through a gap in the plantation, and revealed certain figures half a mile off struggling through the heather.

"Ah, I see," he said, and took up a pair of field-glasses through which he patiently scrutinised the figures.

"A fugitive from justice, eh? Well, we'll go into the matter at our leisure. Meantime I object to my privacy being broken in upon by the clumsy rural policeman. Go into my study, and you will see two doors facing you. Take the one on the left and close it behind you. You will be perfectly safe."

And this extraordinary man took up his pen again.

I did as I was bid, and found myself in a little dark chamber which smelt of chemicals, and was lit only by a tiny window high up in the wall. The door had swung behind me with a click like the door of a safe. Once again I had found an unexpected sanctuary.

All the same I was not comfortable. There was something about the old gentleman which puzzled and rather terrified me. He had been too easy and ready, almost as if he had expected me. And his eyes had been horribly intelligent.

No sound came to me in that dark place. For all I knew the police might be searching the house, and if they did they would want to know what was behind this door. I tried to possess my soul in patience, and to forget how hungry I was.

Then I took a more cheerful view. The old gentleman could scarcely refuse me a meal, and I fell to reconstructing my breakfast. Bacon and eggs would content me, but I wanted the better part of a flitch of bacon and half a hundred eggs. And then, while my mouth was watering in anticipation, there was a click and the door stood open.

I emerged into the sunlight to find the master of the house sitting in a deep armchair in the room he called his study, and regarding me with curious eyes.

"Have they gone?" I asked.

"They have gone. I convinced them that you had crossed the hill. I do not choose that the police should come between me and one whom I am delighted to honour. This is a lucky morning for you, Mr Richard Hannay."

As he spoke his eyelids seemed to tremble and to fall a little over his keen grey eyes. In a flash the phrase of Scudder's came back to me, when he had described the man he most dreaded in the world. He had said that he "could hood his eyes like a hawk." Then I saw that I had walked straight into the enemy's headquarters.

My first impulse was to throttle the old ruffian and make for the open air. He seemed to anticipate my intention, for he smiled gently, and nodded to the door behind me. I turned, and saw two menservants who had me covered with pistols.

He knew my name, but he had never seen me before. And as the reflection darted across my mind I saw a slender chance.

"I don't know what you mean," I said roughly. "And who are you calling Richard Hannay? My name's Ainslie."

"So?" he said, still smiling. "But of course you have others. We won't quarrel about a name."

I was pulling myself together now, and I reflected that my garb, lacking coat and waistcoat and collar, would at any rate not betray me. I put on my surliest face and shrugged my shoulders.

"I suppose you're going to give me up after all, and I call it a damned dirty trick. My God, I wish I had never seen that cursed motor-car! Here's the money and be damned to you," and I flung four sovereigns on the table.

He opened his eyes a little. "Oh no, I shall not give you up. My friends and I will have a little private settlement with you, that is all. You know a little too much, Mr Hannay. You are a clever actor, but not quite clever enough."

He spoke with assurance, but I could see the dawning of a doubt in his mind.

"Oh, for God's sake stop jawing," I cried. "Everything's against me. I haven't had a bit of luck since I came on shore at Leith. What's the harm in a poor devil with an empty stomach picking up some money he finds in a bust-up motor-car? That's all I done, and for that I've been chivvied for two days by those blasted bobbies over those blasted hills. I tell you I'm fair sick of it. You can do what you like, old boy! Ned Ainslie's got no fight left in him."

I could see that the doubt was gaining.

"Will you oblige me with the story of your recent doings?" he asked.

"I can't, guv'nor," I said in a real beggar's whine. "I've not had a bite to eat for two days. Give me a mouthful of food, and then you'll hear God's truth."

I must have showed my hunger in my face, for he signalled to one of the men in the doorway. A bit of cold pie was brought and a glass of beer, and I wolfed them down like a pig—or rather, like Ned Ainslie, for I was keeping up my character. In the middle of my meal he spoke suddenly to me in German, but I turned on him a face as blank as a stone wall.

Then I told him my story—how I had come off an Archangel ship at Leith a week ago, and was making my way overland to my brother at Wigtown. I had run short of cash—I hinted vaguely at a spree—and I was pretty well on my uppers when I had come on a hole in a hedge, and, looking through, had seen a big motor-car lying in the burn. I had poked about to see what had happened, and had found three sovereigns lying on the seat and one on the floor. There was nobody there or any sign of an owner, so I had pocketed the cash. But somehow the law had got after me. When I had tried to change a sovereign in a baker's shop, the woman had cried on the police, and a little later, when I was washing my face in a burn, I had been nearly gripped, and had only got away by leaving my coat and waistcoat behind me.

"They can have the money back," I cried, "for a fat lot of good it's done me. Those perishers are all down on a poor man. Now, if it had been you, guv'nor, that had found the quids, nobody would have troubled you."

"You're a good liar, Hannay," he said.

I flew into a rage. "Stop fooling, damn you! I tell you my name is Ainslie, and I never heard of anyone called Hannay in my born days. I'd sooner have the police than you with your Hannays and your monkey-faced pistol tricks . . . No, guv'nor, I beg pardon, I don't mean that. I'm much obliged to you for the grub, and I'll thank you to let me go now the coast's clear."

It was obvious that he was badly puzzled. You see he had never seen me, and my appearance must have altered considerably from my photographs, if he had got one of them. I was pretty smart and well dressed in London, and now I was a regular tramp.

"I do not propose to let you go. If you are what you say you are, you will soon have a chance of clearing yourself. If you are what I believe you are, I do not think you will see the light much longer."

He rang a bell, and a third servant appeared from the veranda.

"I want the Lanchester in five minutes," he said. "There will be three to luncheon."

Then he looked steadily at me, and that was the hardest ordeal of all. There was something weird and devilish in those eyes, cold, malignant, unearthly, and most hellishly clever. They fascinated me like the bright eyes of a snake. I had a strong impulse to throw myself on his mercy and offer to join his side, and if you consider the way I felt about the whole thing you will see that that impulse must have been purely physical, the weakness of a brain mesmerized and mastered by a stronger spirit. But I managed to stick it out and even to grin.

"You'll know me next time, guv'nor," I said.

"Karl," he spoke in German to one of the men in the doorway, "you will put this fellow in the storeroom till I return, and you will be answerable to me for his keeping."

I was marched out of the room with a pistol at each ear.

THE STOREROOM WAS a damp chamber in what had been the old farmhouse. There was no carpet on the uneven floor, and nothing to sit down on but a school form. It was black as pitch, for the windows were heavily shuttered. I made out by groping that the walls were lined with boxes and barrels and sacks of some heavy stuff. The whole place smelt of mould and disuse. My jailers turned the key in the door, and I could hear them shifting their feet as they stood on guard outside.

I sat down in that chilly darkness in a very miserable frame of mind. The old boy had gone off in a motor to collect the two ruffians who had interviewed me yesterday. Now, they had seen me as the roadman, and they would remember me, for I was in the same rig. What was a roadman doing twenty miles from his beat, pursued by the police? A question or two would put them on the track. Probably they had seen Mr Turnbull, probably Marmie too; most likely they could link me up with Sir Harry, and then the whole thing would be crystal clear. What chance had I in this moorland house with three desperadoes and their armed servants?

I began to think wistfully of the police, now plodding over the hills after my wraith. They at any rate were fellow-countrymen and honest men, and their tender mercies would be kinder than these ghoulish aliens. But they wouldn't have listened to me. That old devil with the eyelids had not taken long to get rid of them. I thought he probably had some kind of graft with the constabulary. Most likely he had letters from Cabinet Ministers saying he was to be given every facility for plotting against Britain. That's the sort of owlish way we run our politics in the Old Country.

The three would be back for lunch, so I hadn't more than a couple of hours to wait. It was simply waiting on destruction, for I could see no way out of this mess. I wished that I had Scudder's courage, for I am free to confess I didn't feel any great fortitude. The only thing that kept me going was that I was pretty furious. It made me boil with rage to think of those three spies getting the pull on me like this. I hoped that at any rate I might be able to twist one of their necks before they downed me.

The more I thought of it the angrier I grew, and I had to get up and move about the room. I tried the shutters, but they were the kind that locked with a key, and I couldn't move them. From the outside came the faint clucking of hens in the warm sun. Then I groped among the sacks and boxes. I couldn't open the latter, and the sacks seemed to be full of things like dog-biscuits that smelt of cinnamon. But, as I circumnavigated the room, I found a handle in the wall which seemed worth investigating.

It was the door of a wall cupboard—what they call a "press" in Scotland—and it was locked. I shook it, and it seemed rather flimsy. For want of something better to do I put out my strength on that door, getting some purchase on the handle by looping my braces round it. Presently the thing gave with a crash which I thought would bring in my warders to inquire. I waited for a bit, and then started to explore the cupboard shelves.

There was a multitude of queer things there. I found an odd vesta or two in my trouser pockets and struck a light. It went out in a second, but it showed me one thing. There was a little stock of electric torches on one shelf. I picked up one, and found it was in working order.

With the torch to help me I investigated further. There were bottles and cases of queer-smelling stuffs, chemicals no doubt for experiments, and there were coils of fine copper wire and hanks and hanks of a thin oiled silk. There was a box of detonators, and a lot of cord for fuses. Then away at the back of a shelf I found a stout brown cardboard box, and inside it a wooden case. I managed to wrench it open, and within lay half a dozen little grey bricks, each a couple of inches square.

I took up one, and found that it crumbled easily in my hand. Then I smelt it and put my tongue to it. After that I sat down to think. I hadn't been a mining engineer for nothing, and I knew lentonite when I saw it.

With one of these bricks I could blow the house to smithereens. I had used the stuff in Rhodesia and knew its power. But the trouble was that my knowledge wasn't exact. I had forgotten the proper charge and the right way of preparing it, and I wasn't sure about the timing. I had only a vague notion, too, as to its power, for though I had used it I had not handled it with my own fingers.

But it was a chance, the only possible chance. It was a mighty risk, but against it was an absolute black certainty. If I used it the odds were, as I reckoned, about five to one in favour of my blowing myself into the tree-tops; but if I didn't I should very likely be occupying a six-foot hole in the garden by the evening. That was the way I had to look at it. The prospect was pretty dark either way, but anyhow there was a chance, both for myself and for my country.

The remembrance of little Scudder decided me. It was about the beastliest moment of my life, for I'm no good at these cold-blooded resolutions. Still I managed to rake up the pluck to set my teeth and choke back the horrid doubts that flooded in on me. I simply shut off my mind and pretended I was doing an experiment as simple as Guy Fawkes' fireworks.

I got a detonator, and fixed it to a couple of feet of fuse. Then I took a quarter of a lentonite brick, and buried it near the door below one of the sacks in a crack of the floor, fixing the detonator in it. For all I knew half those boxes might be dynamite. If the cupboard held such deadly explosives, why not the boxes? In that case there would be a glorious skyward journey for me and the German servants and about an acre of the surrounding country. There was also the risk that the detonation might set off the other bricks in the cupboard, for I had forgotten most that I knew about lentonite. But it didn't do to begin thinking about the possibilities. The odds were horrible, but I had to take them.

I ensconced myself just below the sill of the window, and lit the fuse. Then I waited for a moment or two. There was dead silence—only a shuffle of heavy boots in the passage, and the peaceful cluck of the hens from the warm out-of-doors. I commended my soul to my Maker, and wondered where I would be in five seconds.

A great wave of heat seemed to surge upwards from the floor, and hang for a blistering instant in the air. Then the wall opposite me flashed into a golden yellow and dissolved with a rending thunder that hammered my brain into a pulp. Something dropped on me, catching the point of my left shoulder.

I GOT A DETONATOR AND FIXED A FUSE

And then I think I became unconscious.

My stupor can scarcely have lasted beyond a few seconds. I felt myself being choked by thick yellow fumes, and struggled out of the debris to my feet. Somewhere behind me I felt fresh air. The jambs of the window had fallen, and through the ragged rent the smoke was pouring out to the summer noon. I stepped over the broken lintel, and found myself standing in a yard in a dense and acrid fog. I felt very sick and ill, but I could move my limbs, and I staggered blindly forward away from the house.

A small mill-lade ran in a wooden aqueduct at the other side of the yard, and into this I fell. The cool water revived me, and I had just enough wits left to think of escape. I squirmed up the lade among the slippery green slime till I reached the mill-wheel. Then I wriggled through the axle hole into the old mill and tumbled on to a bed of chaff. A nail caught the seat of my trousers, and I left a wisp of heather-mixture behind me.

The mill had been long out of use. The ladders were rotten with age, and in the loft the rats had gnawed great holes in the floor. Nausea shook me, and a wheel in my head kept turning, while my left shoulder and arm seemed to be stricken with the palsy. I looked out of the window and saw a fog still hanging over the house and smoke escaping from an upper window. Please God I had set the place on fire, for I could hear confused cries coming from the other side.

But I had no time to linger, since this mill was obviously a bad hiding-place. Anybody looking for me would naturally follow the lade, and I made certain the search would begin as soon as they found that my body was not in the storeroom. From another window I saw that on the far side of the mill stood an old stone dovecot. If I could get there without leaving tracks I might find a hiding-place, for I argued that my enemies, if they thought I could move, would conclude I had made for open country, and would go seeking me on the moor.

I crawled down the broken ladder, scattering chaff behind me to cover my footsteps. I did the same on the mill floor, and on the threshold where the door hung on broken hinges. Peeping out, I saw that between me and the dovecot was a piece of bare cobbled ground, where no footmarks would show. Also it was mercifully hid by the mill buildings from any view from the house. I slipped across the space, got to the back of the dovecot and prospected a way of ascent.

That was one of the hardest jobs I ever took on. My shoulder and arm ached like hell, and I was so sick and giddy that I was always on the verge of falling. But I managed it somehow. By the use of out-jutting stones and gaps in the masonry and a tough ivy root I got to the top in the end. There was a little parapet behind which I found space to lie down. Then I proceeded to go off into an old-fashioned swoon.

I woke with a burning head and the sun glaring in my face. For a long time I lay motionless, for those horrible fumes seemed to have loosened my joints and dulled my brain. Sounds came to me from the house— men speaking throatily and the throbbing of a stationary car. There was a little gap in the parapet to which I wriggled, and from which I had some sort of prospect of the yard. I saw figures come out—a servant with his head bound up, and then a younger man in knickerbockers. They were looking for something, and moved towards the mill. Then one of them caught sight of the wisp of cloth on the nail, and cried out to the other. They both went back to the house, and brought two more to look at it. I saw the rotund figure of my late captor, and I thought I made out the man with the lisp. I noticed that all had pistols.

For half an hour they ransacked the mill. I could hear them kicking over the barrels and pulling up the rotten planking. Then they came outside, and stood just below the dovecot, arguing fiercely. The servant with the bandage was being soundly rated. I heard them fiddling with the door of the dovecot, and for one horrid moment I fancied they were coming up. Then they thought better of it, and went back to the house.

All that long blistering afternoon I lay baking on the roof-top. Thirst was my chief torment. My tongue was like a stick, and to make it worse I could hear the cool drip of water from the mill-lade. I watched the course of the little stream as it came in from the moor, and my fancy followed it to the top of the glen, where it must issue from an icy fountain fringed with cool ferns and mosses. I would have given a thousand pounds to plunge my face into that.

I had a fine prospect of the whole ring of moorland. I saw the car speed away with two occupants, and a man on a hill pony riding east. I judged they were looking for me, and I wished them joy of their quest.

But I saw something else more interesting. The house stood almost on the summit of a swell of moorland which crowned a sort of plateau, and there was no higher point nearer than the big hills six miles off. The actual summit, as I have mentioned, was a biggish clump of trees—firs mostly, with a few ashes and beeches. On the dovecot I was almost on a level with the tree-tops, and could see what lay beyond. The wood was not solid, but only a ring, and inside was an oval of green turf, for all the world like a big cricket field.

I didn't take long to guess what it was. It was an aerodrome, and a secret one. The place had been most cunningly chosen. For suppose anyone were watching an aeroplane descending here, he would think it had gone over the hill beyond the trees. As the place was on the top of a rise in the midst of a big amphitheatre, any observer from any direction would conclude it had passed out of view behind the hill. Only a man very close at hand would realize that the aeroplane had not gone over but had descended in the midst of the wood. An observer with a telescope on one of the higher hills might have discovered the truth, but only herds went there, and herds do not carry spy-glasses. When I looked from the dovecot I could see far away a blue line which I knew was the sea, and I grew furious to think that our enemies had this secret conning-tower to rake our waterways.

Then I reflected that if that aeroplane came back the chances were ten to one that I would be discovered. So through the afternoon I lay and prayed for the coming of darkness, and glad I was when the sun went down over the big western hills and the twilight haze crept over the moor. The aeroplane was late. The gloaming was far advanced when I heard the beat of wings and saw it vol-planing downward to its home in the wood. Lights twinkled for a bit and there was much coming and going from the house. Then the dark fell and silence.

Thank God it was black night. The moon was well on its last quarter and would not rise till late. My thirst was too great to allow me to tarry, so about nine o'clock, so far as I could judge, I started to descend. It wasn't easy, and halfway down I heard the back door of the house open, and saw the gleam of a lantern against the mill wall. For some agonizing minutes I hung by the ivy and prayed that whoever it was would not come round by the dovecot. Then the light disappeared, and I dropped as softly as I could on to the hard soil of the yard.

I crawled on my belly in the lee of a stone dyke till I reached the fringe of trees which surrounded the house. If I had known how to do it I would have tried to put that aeroplane out of action, but I realized that any attempt would probably be futile. I was pretty certain that there would be some kind of defence round the house, so I went through the wood on hands and knees, feeling carefully every inch before me. It was as well, for presently I came on a wire about two feet from the ground. If I had tripped over that, it would doubtless have rung some bell in the house and I would have been captured.

A hundred yards farther on I found another wire cunningly placed on the edge of a small stream. Beyond that lay the moor, and in five minutes I was deep in bracken and heather. Soon I was round the shoulder of the rise, in the little glen from which the mill-lade flowed. Ten minutes later my face was in the spring, and I was soaking down pints of the blessed water.

But I did not stop till I had put half a dozen miles between me and that accursed dwelling.

CHAPTER 7

The Dry-Fly Fisherman

I SAT DOWN on a hill-top and took stock of my position. I wasn't feeling very happy, for my natural thankfulness at my escape was clouded by my severe bodily discomfort. Those lentonite fumes had fairly poisoned me, and the baking hours on the dovecot hadn't helped matters. I had a crushing headache, and felt as sick as a cat. Also my shoulder was in a bad way. At first I thought it was only a bruise, but it seemed to be swelling, and I had no use of my left arm.

My plan was to seek Mr Turnbull's cottage, recover my garments, and especially Scudder's notebook, and then make for the main line and get back to the south. It seemed to me that the sooner I got in touch with the Foreign Office man, Sir Walter Bullivant, the better. I didn't see how I could get more proof than I had got already. He must just take or leave my story, and anyway, with him I would be in better hands than those devilish Germans. I had begun to feel quite kindly towards the British police.

It was a wonderful starry night, and I had not much difficulty about the road. Sir Harry's map had given me the lie of the land, and all I had to do was to steer a point or two west of south-west to come to the stream where I had met the roadman. In all these travels I never knew the names of the places, but I believe this stream was no less than the upper waters of the River Tweed. I calculated I must be about eighteen miles distant, and that meant I could not get there before morning. So I must lie up a day somewhere, for I was too outrageous a figure to be seen in the sunlight. I had neither coat, waistcoat, collar, nor hat, my trousers were badly torn, and my face and hands were black with the explosion. I dare say I had other beauties, for my eyes felt as if they were furiously bloodshot. Altogether I was no spectacle for God-fearing citizens to see on a highroad.

Very soon after daybreak I made an attempt to clean myself in a hill burn, and then approached a herd's cottage, for I was feeling the need of food. He was away from home, and his wife was alone, with no neighbour for five miles. She was a decent old body, and a plucky one, for though she got a fright when she saw me, she had an axe handy, and would have used it on any evil-doer. I told her that I had had a fall—I didn't say how—and she saw by my looks that I was pretty sick. Like a true Samaritan she asked no questions, but gave me a bowl of milk with a dash of whisky in it, and let me sit for a little by her kitchen fire. She would have bathed my shoulder, but it ached so badly that I would not let her touch it.

I don't know what she took me for—a repentant burglar, perhaps; for when I wanted to pay her for the milk and tendered a sovereign, which was the smallest coin I had, she shook her head and said something about "giving it to them that had a right to it". At this I protested so strongly that I think she believed me honest, for she took the money and gave me a warm new plaid for it, and an old hat of her man's. She showed me how to wrap the plaid round my shoulders, and when I left that cottage I was the living image of the kind of Scotsman you see in the illustrations to Burns's poems. But at any rate I was more or less clad.

It was as well, for the weather changed before midday to a thick drizzle of rain. I found shelter below an overhanging rock in the crook of a burn, where a drift of dead brackens made a tolerable bed. There I managed to sleep till nightfall, waking very cramped and wretched, with my shoulder gnawing like a toothache. I ate the oatcake and cheese the old wife had given me and set out again just before the darkening.

I pass over the miseries of that night among the wet hills. There were no stars to steer by, and I had to do the best I could from my memory of the map. Twice I lost my way, and I had some nasty falls into peat-bogs. I had only about ten miles to go as the crow flies, but my mistakes made it nearer twenty. The last bit was completed with set teeth and a very light and dizzy head. But I managed it, and in the early dawn I was knocking at Mr Turnbull's door. The mist lay close and thick, and from the cottage I could not see the highroad.

Mr Turnbull himself opened to me—sober and something more than sober. He was primly dressed in an ancient but well-tended suit of black; he had been shaved not later than the night before; he wore a linen collar; and in his left hand he carried a pocket Bible. At first he did not recognize me.

"Whae are ye that comes stravaigin' here on the Sabbath mornin'?" he asked.

I had lost all count of the days. So the Sabbath was the reason for this strange decorum.

My head was swimming so wildly that I could not frame a coherent answer. But he recognized me, and he saw that I was ill.

"Hae ye got my specs?" he asked.

I fetched them out of my trouser pocket and gave him them.

"Ye'll hae come for your jacket and westcoat," he said. "Come in-bye. Losh, man, ye're terrible dune i' the legs. Haud up till I get ye to a chair."

I perceived I was in for a bout of malaria. I had a good deal of fever in my bones, and the wet night had brought it out, while my shoulder and the effects of the fumes combined to make me feel pretty bad. Before I knew, Mr Turnbull was helping me off with my clothes, and putting me to bed in one of the two cupboards that lined the kitchen walls.

He was a true friend in need, that old roadman. His wife was dead years ago, and since his daughter's marriage he lived alone.

For the better part of ten days he did all the rough nursing I needed. I simply wanted to be left in peace while the fever took its course, and when my skin was cool again I found that the bout had more or less cured my shoulder. But it was a baddish go, and though I was out of bed in five days, it took me some time to get my legs again.

He went out each morning, leaving me milk for the day, and locking the door behind him; and came in in the evening to sit silent in the chimney corner. Not a soul came near the place. When I was getting better, he never bothered me with a question. Several times he fetched me a two days' old *Scotsman*, and I noticed that the interest in the Portland Place murder seemed to have died down. There was no mention of it, and I could find very little about anything except a thing called the General Assembly—some ecclesiastical spree, I gathered.

One day he produced my belt from a lockfast drawer. "There's a terrible heap o' siller in't," he said. "Ye'd better coont it to see it's a' there."

He never even sought my name. I asked him if anybody had been around making inquiries subsequent to my spell at the roadmaking.

"Ay, there was a man in a motor-cawr. He speired whae had ta'en my place that day, and I let on I thocht him daft. But he keepit on at me, and syne I said he maun be thinkin' o' my gude-brither frae the Cleuch that whiles lent me a haun'. He was a wersh-lookin' sowl, and I couldna understand the half o' his English tongue."

I was getting restless those last days, and as soon as I felt myself fit I decided to be off. That was not till the twelfth day of June, and as luck would have it a drover went past that morning taking some cattle to Moffat. He was a man named Hislop, a friend of Turnbull's, and he came in to his breakfast with us and offered to take me with him.

I made Turnbull accept five pounds for my lodging, and a hard job I had of it. There never was a more independent being. He grew positively rude when I pressed him, and shy and red, and took the money at last without a thank-you. When I told him how much I owed him, he grunted something about "ae guid turn deservin' anither". You would have thought from our leave-taking that we had parted in disgust.

Hislop was a cheery soul, who chattered all the way over the pass and down the sunny vale of Annan. I talked of Galloway markets and sheep prices, and he made up his mind I was a "pack-shepherd" from those parts—whatever that may be. My plaid and my old hat, as I have said, gave me a fine theatrical Scots look. But driving cattle is a mortally slow job, and we took the better part of the day to cover a dozen miles.

If I had not had such an anxious heart I would have enjoyed that time. It was shining blue weather, with a constantly changing prospect of brown hills and far green meadows, and a continual sound of larks and curlews and falling streams. But I had no mind for the summer, and little for Hislop's conversation, for as the fateful fifteenth of June drew near I was overweighted with the hopeless difficulties of my enterprise.

I got some dinner in a humble Moffat public-house, and walked the two miles to the junction on the main line. The night express for the south was not due till near midnight, and to fill up the time I went up on the hillside and fell asleep, for the walk had tired me. I all but slept too long, and had to run to the station and catch the train with two minutes to spare. The feel of the hard third-class cushions and the smell of stale tobacco cheered me up wonderfully. At any rate, I felt now that I was getting to grips with my job.

I WAS DECANTED at Crewe in the small hours and had to wait till six to get a train for Birmingham. In the afternoon I got to Reading, and changed into a local train which journeyed into the deeps of Berkshire.

Presently I was in a land of lush water-meadows and slow reedy streams. About eight o'clock in the evening, a weary and travel-stained being—a cross between a farm-labourer and a vet—with a checked black-and-white plaid over his arm (for I did not dare to wear it south of the Border), descended at the little station of Artinswell. There were several people on the platform, and I thought I had better wait to ask my way till I was clear of the place.

The road led through a wood of great beeches and then into a shallow valley, with the green backs of downs peeping over the distant trees. After Scotland the air smelt heavy and flat, but infinitely sweet, for the limes and chestnuts and lilac bushes were domes of blossom. Presently I came to a bridge, below which a clear slow stream flowed between snowy beds of water-buttercups. A little above it was a mill; and the lasher made a pleasant cool sound in the scented dusk. Somehow the place soothed me and put me at my ease. I fell to whistling as I looked into the green depths, and the tune which came to my lips was "Annie Laurie".

A fisherman came up from the waterside, and as he neared me he too began to whistle. The tune was infectious, for he followed my suit. He was a huge man in untidy old flannels and a wide-brimmed hat, with a canvas bag slung on his shoulder. He nodded to me, and I thought I had never seen a shrewder or better-tempered face. He leaned his delicate ten-foot split-cane rod against the bridge, and looked with me at the water.

"Clear, isn't it?" he said pleasantly. "I back our Kennet any day against the Test. Look at that big fellow. Four pounds if he's an ounce. But the evening rise is over and you can't tempt 'em."

"I don't see him," said I.

"Look! There! A yard from the reeds just above that stickle."

"I've got him now. You might swear he was a black stone."

"So," he said, and whistled another bar of "Annie Laurie".

"Twisdon's the name, isn't it?" he said over his shoulder, his eyes still fixed on the stream.

"No," I said. "I mean to say, Yes." I had forgotten all about my *alias*.

"It's a wise conspirator that knows his own name," he observed, grinning broadly at a moor-hen that emerged from the bridge's shadow.

I stood up and looked at him, at the square, cleft jaw and broad, lined brow and the firm folds of cheek, and began to think that here at last was an ally worth having. His whimsical blue eyes seemed to go very deep.

Suddenly he frowned. "I call it disgraceful," he said, raising his voice. "Disgraceful that an able-bodied man like you should dare to beg. You can get a meal from my kitchen, but you'll get no money from me."

A dog-cart was passing, driven by a young man who raised his whip to salute the fisherman. When he had gone, he picked up his rod.

"That's my house," he said, pointing to a white gate a hundred yards on. "Wait five minutes and then go round to the back door." And with that he left me.

I did as I was bidden. I found a pretty cottage with a lawn running down to the stream, and a perfect jungle of guelder-rose and lilac flanking the path. The back door stood open, and a grave butler was awaiting me.

"Come this way, sir," he said, and he led me along a passage and up a back staircase to a pleasant bedroom looking towards the river. There I found a complete outfit laid out for me—dress clothes with all the fixings, a brown flannel suit, shirts, collars, ties, shaving things and hair-brushes, even a pair of patent shoes. "Sir Walter thought as how Mr Reggie's things would fit you, sir," said the butler. "He keeps some clothes 'ere, for he comes regular on the weekends. There's a bathroom next door, and I've prepared a 'ot bath. Dinner in 'alf an hour, sir. You'll 'ear the gong."

The grave being withdrew, and I sat down in a chintz-covered easy chair and gaped. It was like a pantomime, to come suddenly out of beggardom into this orderly comfort. Obviously Sir Walter believed in me, though why he did I could not guess. I looked at myself in the mirror and saw a wild, haggard brown fellow, with a fortnight's ragged beard, and dust in ears and eyes, collarless, vulgarly shirted, with shapeless old tweed clothes and boots that had not been cleaned for the better part of a month. I made a fine tramp and a fair drover; and here I was ushered by a prim butler into this temple of gracious ease. And the best of it was that they did not even know my name.

I resolved not to puzzle my head but to take the gifts the gods had provided. I shaved and bathed luxuriously and got into the dress clothes, and clean crackling shirt, which fitted me not so badly. When I had finished the looking-glass showed a not unpersonable young man.

Sir Walter awaited me in a dusky dining-room where a little round table was lit with silver candles. The sight of him—so respectable and established and secure, the embodiment of law and government and all the conventions—took me aback and made me feel an interloper. He couldn't know the truth about me, or he wouldn't treat me like this. I simply could not accept his hospitality on false pretences.

"I'm more obliged to you than I can say, but I'm bound to make things clear," I said. "I'm an innocent man, but I'm wanted by the police. I've got to tell you this, and I won't be surprised if you kick me out."

He smiled. "That's all right. Don't let that interfere with your appetite. We can talk about these things after dinner."

I never ate a meal with greater relish, for I had had nothing all day but railway sandwiches. Sir Walter did me proud, for we drank a good champagne and had some uncommon fine port afterwards. It made me almost hysterical to be sitting there, waited on by a footman and a sleek butler, and remember that I had been living for three weeks like a brigand, with every man's hand against me. I told Sir Walter about tiger-fish in the Zambesi that bite off your fingers if you give them a chance, and we discussed sport up and down the globe, for he had hunted a bit in his day.

We went to his study for coffee, a jolly room full of books and trophies and untidiness and comfort. I made up my mind that if ever I got rid of this business and had a house of my own, I would create just such a room. Then when the coffee-cups were cleared away, and we had got our cigars alight, my host swung his long legs over the side of his chair and bade me get started with my yarn.

"I've obeyed Harry's instructions," he said, "and the bribe he offered me was that you would tell me something to wake me up. I'm ready, Mr Hannay."

I noticed with a start that he called me by my proper name.

I began at the very beginning. I told of my boredom in London, and the night I had come back to find Scudder gibbering on my doorstep. I told him all Scudder had told me about Karolides and the Foreign Office conference, and that made him purse his lips and grin.

Then I got to the murder, and he grew solemn again. He heard all about the milkman and my time in Galloway, and my deciphering Scudder's notes at the inn.

"You've got them here?" he asked sharply, and drew a long breath when I whipped the little book from my pocket.

I said nothing of the contents. Then I described my meeting with Sir Harry, and the speeches at the hall. At that he laughed uproariously.

"Harry talked dashed nonsense, did he? I quite believe it. He's as good a chap as ever breathed, but his idiot of an uncle has stuffed his head with maggots. Go on, Mr Hannay."

My day as roadman excited him a bit. He made me describe the two fellows in the car very closely and seemed to be raking back in his memory. He grew merry again when he heard of the fate of that ass Jopley.

But the old man in the moorland house solemnized him. Again I had to describe every detail of his appearance.

"Bland and bald-headed and hooded his eyes like a bird . . . He sounds a sinister wild-fowl! And you dynamited his hermitage, after he had saved you from the police. Spirited piece of work, that!"

Presently I reached the end of my wanderings. He got up slowly, and looked down at me from the hearthrug.

"You may dismiss the police from your mind," he said. "You're in no danger from the law of this land."

"Great Scot!" I cried. "Have they got the murderer?"

"No. But for the last fortnight they have dropped you from the list of possibles."

"Why?" I asked in amazement.

"Principally because I received a letter from Scudder. I knew something of the man, and he did several jobs for me. He was half crank, half genius, but he was wholly honest. The trouble about him was his partiality for playing a lone hand. That made him pretty well useless in any Secret Service—a pity, for he had uncommon gifts. I think he was the bravest man in the world, for he was always shivering with fright, and yet nothing would choke him off. I had a letter from him on the 31st of May."

"But he had been dead a week by then."

"The letter was written and posted on the 23rd. He evidently did not anticipate an immediate decease. His communications usually took a week to reach me, for they were sent under cover to Spain and then to Newcastle. He had a mania, you know, for concealing his tracks."

"What did he say?" I stammered.

"Nothing. Merely that he was in danger, but had found shelter with a good friend, and that I would hear from him before the 15th of June. He gave me no address, but said he was living near Portland Place. I think his object was to clear you if anything happened. When I got it I went to Scotland Yard, went over the details of the inquest, and concluded that you were the friend. We made inquiries about you, Mr Hannay, and found you were respectable. I thought I knew the motives for your disappearance—not only the police, the other one too—and when I got Harry's scrawl I guessed at the rest. I have been expecting you any time this past week."

You can imagine what a load this took off my mind. I felt a free man once more, for I was now up against my country's enemies only, and not my country's law.

"Now let us have the little notebook," said Sir Walter.

It took us a good hour to work through it. I explained the cypher, and he was jolly quick at picking it up. He emended my reading of it on several points, but I had been fairly correct, on the whole. His face was very grave before he had finished, and he sat silent for a while.

"I don't know what to make of it," he said at last. "He is right about one thing—what is going to happen the day after tomorrow. How the devil can it have got known? That is ugly enough in itself. But all this about war and the Black Stone—it reads like some wild melodrama. If only I had more confidence in Scudder's judgment. The trouble about him was that he was too romantic. He had the artistic temperament, and wanted a story to be better than God meant it to be. He had a lot of odd biases, too. Jews, for example, made him see red. Jews and the high finance.

"The Black Stone," he repeated. *"Der Schwarzestein.* It's like a penny novelette. And all this stuff about Karolides. That is the weak part of the tale, for I happen to know that the virtuous Karolides is likely to outlast us both. There is no state in Europe that wants him gone. Besides, he has just been playing up to Berlin and Vienna and giving my Chief some uneasy moments. No! Scudder has gone off the track there. Frankly, Hannay, I don't believe that part of his story. There's some nasty business afoot, and he found out too much and lost his life over it. But I am ready to take my oath that it is ordinary spy work. A certain great European Power makes a hobby of her spy system, and her methods are not too particular. Since she pays by piecework her blackguards are not likely to stick at a murder or two. They want our naval dispositions for their collection at the Marinamt; but they will be pigeonholed—nothing more."

Just then the butler entered the room.

"There's a trunk call from London, Sir Walter. It's Mr 'Eath, and he wants to speak to you personally."

My host went off to the telephone.

He returned in five minutes with a whitish face. "I apologize to the shade of Scudder," he said. "Karolides was shot dead this evening at a few minutes after seven."

CHAPTER 8

The Coming of the Black Stone

I CAME DOWN to breakfast next morning, after eight hours of blessed dreamless sleep, to find Sir Walter decoding a telegram in the midst of muffins and marmalade. His fresh rosiness of yesterday seemed a thought tarnished.

"I had a busy hour on the telephone after you went to bed," he said. "I got my Chief to speak to the First Lord and the Secretary for War, and they are bringing Royer over a day sooner. This wire clinches it. He will be in London at five. Odd that the code word for a *Sous-chef d'Etat Major-General* should be 'Porker'."

He directed me to the hot dishes and went on.

"Not that I think it will do much good. If your friends were clever enough to find out the first arrangement they are clever enough to discover the change. I would give my head to know where the leak is. We believed there were only five men in England who knew about Royer's visit, and you may be certain there were fewer in France, for they manage these things better there."

While I ate he continued to talk, making me to my surprise a present of his full confidence.

"Can the dispositions not be changed?" I asked.

"They could," he said. "But we want to avoid that if possible. They are the result of immense thought, and no alteration would be as good. Besides, on one or two points change is simply impossible. Still, something could be done, I suppose, if it were absolutely necessary. But you see the difficulty, Hannay. Our enemies are not going to be such fools as to pick Royer's pocket or any childish game like that. They know that would mean a row and put us on our guard. Their aim is to get the details without any one of us knowing, so that Royer will go back to Paris in the belief that the whole business is still deadly secret.

If they can't do that they fail, for, once we suspect, they know that the whole thing must be altered."

"Then we must stick by the Frenchman's side till he is home again," I said. "If they thought they could get the information in Paris they would try there. It means that they have some deep scheme on foot in London which they reckon is going to win out."

"Royer dines with my Chief, and then comes to my house where four people will see him—Whittaker from the Admiralty, myself, Sir Arthur Drew, and General Winstanley. The First Lord is ill, and has gone to Sheringham. At my house he will get a certain document from Whittaker, and after that he will be motored to Portsmouth where a destroyer will take him to Havre. His journey is too important for the ordinary boat-train. He will never be left unattended for a moment till he is safe on French soil. The same with Whittaker till he meets Royer. That is the best we can do, and it's hard to see how there can be any miscarriage. But I don't mind admitting that I'm horribly nervous. This murder of Karolides will play the deuce in the chancelleries of Europe."

After breakfast he asked me if I could drive a car.

"Well, you'll be my chauffeur today and wear Hudson's rig. You're about his size. You have a hand in this business and we are taking no risks. There are desperate men against us, who will not respect the country retreat of an overworked official."

When I first came to London I had bought a car and amused myself with running about the south of England, so I knew something of the geography. I took Sir Walter to town by the Bath Road and made good going. It was a soft breathless June morning, with a promise of sultriness later, but it was delicious enough swinging through the little towns with their freshly watered streets, and past the summer gardens of the Thames valley. I landed Sir Walter at his house in Queen Anne's Gate punctually by half past eleven. The butler was coming up by train with the luggage.

The first thing he did was to take me round to Scotland Yard. There we saw a prim gentleman, with a clean-shaven, lawyer's face.

"I've brought you the Portland Place murderer," was Sir Walter's introduction.

The reply was a wry smile. "It would have been a welcome present,

Bullivant. This, I presume, is Mr Richard Hannay, who for some days greatly interested my department."

"Mr Hannay will interest it again. He has much to tell you, but not today. For certain grave reasons his tale must wait for twenty-four hours. Then, I can promise you, you will be entertained and possibly edified. I want you to assure Mr Hannay that he will suffer no further inconvenience."

This assurance was promptly given. "You can take up your life where you left off," I was told. "Your flat, which probably you no longer wish to occupy, is waiting for you, and your man is still there. As you were never publicly accused, we considered that there was no need of a public exculpation. But on that, of course, you must please yourself."

"We may want your assistance later on, MacGillivray," Sir Walter said as we left.

Then he turned me loose.

"Come and see me tomorrow, Hannay. I needn't tell you to keep deadly quiet. If I were you I would go to bed, for you must have considerable arrears of sleep to overtake. You had better lie low, for if one of your Black Stone friends saw you there might be trouble."

I FELT CURIOUSLY at a loose end. At first it was very pleasant to be a free man, able to go where I wanted without fearing anything. I had only been a month under the ban of the law, and it was quite enough for me. I went to the Savoy and ordered very carefully a very good luncheon, and then smoked the best cigar the house could provide. But I was still feeling nervous. When I saw anybody look at me in the lounge, I grew shy, and wondered if they were thinking about the murder.

After that I took a taxi and drove miles away up into North London. I walked back through fields and lines of villas and terraces and then slums and mean streets, and it took me pretty nearly two hours. All the while my restlessness was growing worse. I felt that great things, tremendous things, were happening or about to happen, and I, who was the cog-wheel of the whole business, was out of it. Royer would be landing at Dover, Sir Walter would be making plans with the few people in England who were in the secret, and somewhere in the darkness the Black Stone would be working. I felt the sense of danger and impending calamity, and I had the curious feeling, too, that I alone could avert it, alone could grapple with it. But I was out of the game now. How could it be otherwise? It was not likely that Cabinet Ministers and Admiralty Lords and Generals would admit me to their councils.

I actually began to wish that I could run up against one of my three enemies. That would lead to developments. I felt that I wanted enormously to have a vulgar scrap with those gentry, where I could hit out and flatten something. I was rapidly getting into a very bad temper.

I didn't feel like going back to my flat. That had to be faced some time, but as I still had sufficient money I thought I would put it off till next morning, and go to an hotel for the night.

My irritation lasted through dinner, which I had at a restaurant in Jermyn Street. I was no longer hungry, and let several courses pass untasted. I drank the best part of a bottle of Burgundy, but it did nothing to cheer me. An abominable restlessness had taken possession of me. Here was I, a very ordinary fellow, with no particular brains, and yet I was convinced that somehow I was needed to help this business through—that without me it would all go to blazes. I told myself it was sheer silly conceit, that four or five of the cleverest people living, with all the might of the British Empire at their back, had the job in hand. Yet I couldn't be convinced. It seemed as if a voice kept speaking in my ear, telling me to be up and doing, or I would never sleep again.

The upshot was that about half past nine I made up my mind to go to Queen Anne's Gate. Very likely I would not be admitted, but it would ease my conscience to try.

I walked down Jermyn Street, and at the corner of Duke Street passed a group of young men. They were in evening dress, had been dining somewhere, and were going on to a music-hall. One of them was Mr Marmaduke Jopley.

He saw me and stopped short.

"By God, the murderer!" he cried. "Here, you fellows, hold him! That's Hannay, the man who did the Portland Place murder!" He gripped me by the arm, and the others crowded round.

I wasn't looking for any trouble, but my ill-temper made me play the fool. A policeman came up, and I should have told him the truth, and, if he didn't believe it, demanded to be taken to Scotland Yard, or for that matter to the nearest police station. But a delay at that moment seemed to me unendurable, and the sight of Marmie's imbecile face was more than I could bear. I let out with my left, and had the satisfaction of seeing him measure his length in the gutter.

Then began an unholy row. They were all on me at once, and the policeman took me in the rear. I got in one or two good blows, for I think, with fair play, I could have licked the lot of them, but the policeman pinned me behind, and one of them got his fingers on my throat.

Through a black cloud of rage I heard the officer of the law asking what was the matter, and Marmie, between his broken teeth, declaring that I was Hannay the murderer.

"Oh, damn it all," I cried, "make the fellow shut up. I advise you to leave me alone, constable. Scotland Yard knows all about me, and you'll get a proper wigging if you interfere with me."

"You've got to come along of me, young man," said the policeman. "I saw you strike that gentleman crool 'ard. You began it too, for he wasn't doing nothing. I seen you. Best go quietly or I'll have to fix you up."

Exasperation and an overwhelming sense that at no cost must I delay gave me the strength of a bull elephant. I fairly wrenched the constable off his feet, floored the man who was gripping my collar, and set off at my best pace down Duke Street. I heard a whistle being blown, and the rush of men behind me.

I have a very fair turn of speed, and that night I had wings. In a jiffy I was in Pall Mall and had turned down towards St James's Park. I dodged the policeman at the Palace gates, dived through a press of carriages at the entrance to the Mall, and was making for the bridge before my pursuers had crossed the roadway. In the open ways of the Park I put on a spurt. Happily there were few people about and no one tried to stop me. I was staking all on getting to Queen Anne's Gate.

When I entered that quiet thoroughfare it seemed deserted. Sir Walter's house was in the narrow part, and outside it three or four motor-cars were drawn up. I slackened speed some yards off and walked briskly up to the door. If the butler refused me admission, or if he even delayed to open the door, I was done.

He didn't delay. I had scarcely rung before the door opened.

"I must see Sir Walter," I panted. "My business is desperately important."

That butler was a great man. Without moving a muscle he held the door open, and then shut it behind me. "Sir Walter is engaged, sir, and I have orders to admit no one. Perhaps you will wait."

The house was of the old-fashioned kind, with a wide hall and rooms on both sides of it. At the far end was an alcove with a telephone and a couple of chairs, and there the butler offered me a seat.

"See here," I whispered. "There's trouble about and I'm in it. But Sir Walter knows, and I'm working for him. If anyone comes and asks if I am here, tell him a lie."

He nodded, and presently there was a noise of voices in the street, and a furious ringing at the bell. I never admired a man more than that butler. He opened the door, and with a face like a graven image waited to be questioned. Then he gave them it. He told them whose house it was, and what his orders were, and simply froze them off the doorstep. I could see it all from my alcove, and it was better than any play.

I HADN'T WAITED LONG till there came another ring at the bell. The butler made no bones about admitting this new visitor.

While he was taking off his coat I saw who it was. You couldn't open a newspaper or a magazine without seeing that face—the grey beard cut like a spade, the firm fighting mouth, the blunt square nose, and the keen blue eyes. I recognized the First Sea Lord, the man, they say, that made the new British Navy.

He passed my alcove and was ushered into a room at the back of the hall. As the door opened I could hear the sound of low voices. It shut, and I was left alone again. For twenty minutes I sat there, wondering what I was to do next. I was still perfectly convinced that I was wanted, but when or how I had no notion. I kept looking at my watch, and as the time crept on to half past ten I began to think that the conference must soon end. In a quarter of an hour Royer should be speeding along the road to Portsmouth . . .

Then I heard a bell ring, and the butler appeared. The door of the back room opened, and the First Sea Lord came out. He walked past me, and in passing he glanced in my direction, and for a second we looked each other in the face.

Only for a second, but it was enough to make my heart jump. I had never seen the great man before, and he had never seen me. But in that fraction of time something sprang into his eyes, and that something was recognition. You can't mistake it. It is a flicker, a spark of light, a minute shade of difference which means one thing and one thing only. It came involuntarily, for in a moment it died, and he passed on. In a maze of wild fancies I heard the street door close behind him.

I picked up the telephone book and looked up the number of his house. We were connected at once, and I heard a servant's voice.

"Is his Lordship at home?" I asked.

"His Lordship returned half an hour ago," said the voice, "and has gone to bed. He is not very well tonight. Will you leave a message, sir?"

I rang off and almost tumbled into a chair. My part in this business was not yet ended. It had been a close shave, but I had been in time.

Not a moment could be lost, so I marched boldly to the door of that back room and entered without knocking.

Five surprised faces looked up from a round table. There was Sir Walter, and Drew the War Minister, whom I knew from his photographs. There was a slim elderly man, who was probably Whittaker, the Admiralty official, and there was General Winstanley, conspicuous from the long scar on his forehead. Lastly there was a short stout man with an iron-grey moustache and bushy eyebrows, who had been arrested in the middle of a sentence.

Sir Walter's face showed surprise and annoyance.

"This is Mr Hannay, of whom I have spoken to you," he said apologetically to the company. "I'm afraid, Hannay, this visit is ill-timed."

I was getting back my coolness. "That remains to be seen, sir," I said; "but I think it may be in the nick of time. For God's sake, gentlemen, tell me who went out a minute ago?"

"Lord Alloa," Sir Walter said, reddening with anger.

"It was not," I cried; "it was his living image, but it was not Lord Alloa. It was someone who recognized me, someone I have seen in the last month. He had scarcely left the doorstep when I rang up Lord Alloa's house and was told he had come in half an hour before and had gone to bed."

"Who—who—" someone stammered.

"The Black Stone," I cried, and I sat down in the chair so recently vacated and looked round at five badly scared gentlemen.

CHAPTER 9

The Thirty-Nine Steps

ONSENSE!" said the official from the Admiralty.

Sir Walter got up and left the room while we looked blankly at the table. He came back in ten minutes with a long face. "I have spoken to Alloa," he said. "Had him out of bed—very grumpy. He went straight home after Mulross's dinner."

"But it's madness," broke in General Winstanley. "Do you mean to tell me that that man came here and sat beside me for the best part of half an hour and that I didn't detect the imposture? Alloa must be out of his mind."

"Don't you see the cleverness of it?" I said. "You were too interested in other things to have any eyes. You took Lord Alloa for granted. If it had been anybody else you might have looked more closely, but it was natural for him to be here, and that put you all to sleep."

Then the Frenchman spoke, very slowly, and in good English.

"The young man is right! His psychology is good. Our enemies have not been foolish!"

He bent his wise brows on the assembly.

"I will tell you a tale," he said. "It happened many years ago in Senegal. I was quartered in a remote station, and to pass the time used to go fishing for big barbel in the river. A little Arab mare used to carry my luncheon basket—one of the salted dun breed you got at Timbuctoo in the old days. Well, one morning I had good sport, and the mare was unaccountably restless. I could hear her whinnying and squealing and stamping her feet, and I kept soothing her with my voice while my mind was intent on fish. I could see her all the time, as I thought, out of a corner of my eye, tethered to a tree twenty yards away. After a couple of hours I began to think of food. I collected my fish in a tarpaulin bag, and moved down the stream towards the mare, trolling my line. When I got up to her I flung the tarpaulin on her back . . ."

He paused and looked round.

"It was the smell that gave me warning. I turned my head and found

94

myself looking at a lion three feet off . . . An old man-eater, that was the terror of the village . . . What was left of the mare, a mass of blood and bones and hide, was behind him."

"What happened?" I asked. I was enough of a hunter to know a true yarn when I heard it.

"I stuffed my fishing-rod into his jaws, and I had a pistol. Also my servants came presently with rifles. But he left his mark on me." He held up a hand which lacked three fingers.

"Consider," he said. "The mare had been dead more than an hour, and the brute had been patiently watching me ever since. I never saw the kill, for I was accustomed to the mare's fretting, and I never marked her absence, for my consciousness of her was only of something tawny, and the lion filled that part. If I could blunder thus, gentlemen, in a land where men's senses are keen, why should we busy preoccupied urban folk not err also?"

Sir Walter nodded. No one was ready to gainsay him.

"But I don't see," went on Winstanley. "Their object was to get these dispositions without our knowing it. Now it only required one of us to mention to Alloa our meeting tonight for the whole fraud to be exposed."

Sir Walter laughed dryly. "The selection of Alloa shows their acumen. Which of us was likely to speak to him about tonight? Or was he likely to open the subject?"

I remembered the First Sea Lord's reputation for taciturnity and shortness of temper.

"The one thing that puzzles me," said the General, "is what good his visit here would do that spy fellow? He could not carry away several pages of figures and strange names in his head."

"That is not difficult," the Frenchman replied. "A good spy is trained to have a photographic memory. Like your own Macaulay. You noticed he said nothing, but went through these papers again and again. I think we may assume that he has every detail stamped on his mind. When I was younger I could do the same trick."

"Well, I suppose there is nothing for it but to change the plans," said Sir Walter ruefully.

Whittaker was looking very glum. "Did you tell Lord Alloa what has happened?" he asked. "No? Well, I can't speak with absolute assurance, but I'm nearly certain we can't make any serious change unless we alter the geography of England."

"Another thing must be said." It was Royer who spoke. "I talked freely when that man was here. I told something of the military plans of my Government. I was permitted to say so much. But that information would be worth many millions to our enemies. No, my friends, I see no other way. The man who came here and his confederates must be taken, and taken at once."

"Good God," I cried, "and we have not a rag of a clue."

"Besides," said Whittaker, "there is the post. By this time the news will be on its way."

"No," said the Frenchman. "You do not understand the habits of the spy. He receives personally his reward, and he delivers personally his intelligence. We in France know something of the breed. There is still a chance, *mes amis*. These men must cross the sea, and there are ships to be searched and ports to be watched. Believe me, the need is desperate for both France and Britain."

Royer's grave good sense seemed to pull us together. He was the man of action among fumblers. But I saw no hope in any face, and I felt none. Where among the fifty millions of these islands and within a dozen hours were we to lay hands on the three cleverest rogues in Europe?

THEN SUDDENLY I had an inspiration.

"Where is Scudder's book?" I cried to Sir Walter. "Quick, man, I remember something in it."

He unlocked the door of a bureau and gave it to me.

I found the place. "*Thirty-nine steps,*" I read, and again, "*Thirty-nine steps—I counted them—High tide, 10.17 pm.*"

The Admiralty man was looking at me as if he thought I had gone mad.

"Don't you see it's a clue," I shouted. "Scudder knew where these fellows laired—he knew where they were going to leave the country, though he kept the name to himself. Tomorrow was the day, and it was some place where high tide was at ten-seventeen."

"They may have gone tonight," someone said.

"Not they. They have their own snug secret way, and they won't be hurried. I know Germans, and they are mad about working to a plan. Where the devil can I get a book of Tide Tables?"

Whittaker brightened up. "It's a chance," he said. "Let's go over to the Admiralty."

We got into two of the waiting motor-cars—all but Sir Walter, who went off to Scotland Yard—to "mobilize MacGillivray", so he said.

We marched through empty corridors and big bare chambers where the charwomen were busy, till we reached a little room lined with books and maps. A resident clerk was unearthed, who presently fetched from the library the Admiralty Tide Tables. I sat at the desk and the others stood round, for somehow or other I had got charge of this expedition.

It was no good. There were hundreds of entries, and so far as I could see ten-seventeen might cover fifty places. We had to find some way of narrowing the possibilities.

I took my head in my hands and thought. There must be some way of reading this riddle. What did Scudder mean by steps? I thought of dock steps, but if he had meant that I didn't think he would have mentioned the number. It must be some place where there were several staircases, and one marked out from the others by having thirty-nine steps.

Then I had a sudden thought, and hunted up all the steamer sailings. There was no boat which left for the Continent at 10.17 pm.

Why was high tide important? If it was a harbour it must be some little place where the tide mattered, or else it was a heavy-draught boat. But there was no regular steamer sailing at that hour, and somehow I didn't think they would travel by a big boat from a regular harbour. So it must be some little harbour where the tide was important, or perhaps no harbour at all.

But if it was a little port I couldn't see what the steps signified. There were no sets of staircases on any harbour that I had ever seen. It must be some place which a particular staircase identified, and where the tide was full at ten-seventeen. On the whole it seemed to me that the place must be a bit of open coast. But the staircases kept puzzling me.

Then I went back to wider considerations. Whereabouts would a man be likely to leave for Germany, a man in a hurry, who wanted a speedy and a secret passage? Not from any of the big harbours. And not from the Channel or the West Coast or Scotland, for, remember, he was starting from London. I measured the distance on the map, and tried to put myself in the enemy's shoes. I should try for Ostend or Antwerp or Rotterdam, and I should sail from somewhere on the East Coast between Cromer and Dover.

All this was very loose guessing, and I don't pretend it was ingenious or scientific. I wasn't any kind of Sherlock Holmes. But I have always fancied I had a kind of instinct about questions like this. I don't know if I can explain myself, but I used to use my brains as far as they went, and after they came to a blank wall I guessed, and I usually found my guesses pretty right.

So I set out all my conclusions on a bit of Admiralty paper. They ran like this:

FAIRLY CERTAIN

(1) Place where there are several sets of stairs; one that matters distinguished by having thirty-nine steps.
(2) Full tide at 10.17 pm. Leaving shore only possible at full tide.
(3) Steps not dock steps, and so place probably not harbour.
(4) No regular night steamer at 10.17. Means of transport must be tramp (unlikely), yacht, or fishing-boat.

There my reasoning stopped. I made another list, which I headed "Guessed", but I was just as sure of the one as the other.

GUESSED

(1) Place not harbour but open coast.
(2) Boat small—trawler, yacht, or launch.
(3) Place somewhere on East Coast between Cromer and Dover.

It struck me as odd that I should be sitting at that desk with a Cabinet Minister, a Field-Marshal, two high Government officials, and a French General watching me, while from the scribble of a dead man I was trying to drag a secret which meant life or death for us.

Sir Walter had joined us, and presently MacGillivray arrived. He had sent out instructions to watch the ports and railway stations for the three men whom I had described to Sir Walter. Not that he or anybody else thought that that would do much good.

"Here's the most I can make of it," I said. "We have got to find a place where there are several staircases down to the beach, one of which has thirty-nine steps. I think it's a piece of open coast with biggish cliffs, somewhere between the Wash and the Channel. Also it's a place where full tide is at ten-seventeen tomorrow night."

Then an idea struck me. "Is there no Inspector of Coastguards or some fellow like that who knows the East Coast?"

Whittaker said there was, and that he lived in Clapham. He went off in a car to fetch him, and the rest of us sat about the little room and talked of anything that came into our heads. I lit a pipe and went over the whole thing again till my brain grew weary.

About one in the morning the coastguard man arrived. He was a fine old fellow, with the look of a naval officer, and was desperately respectful to the company. I left the War Minister to cross-examine him, for I felt he would think it cheek in me to talk.

"We want you to tell us the places you know on the East Coast where there are cliffs, and where several sets of steps run down to the beach."

He thought for a bit. "What kind of steps do you mean, sir? There are plenty of places with roads cut down through the cliffs, and most roads have a step or two in them. Or do you mean regular staircases— all steps, so to speak?"

Sir Arthur looked towards me. "We mean regular staircases," I said.

He reflected a minute or two. "I don't know that I can think of any. Wait a second. There's a place in Norfolk—Brattlesham—beside a golf course, where there are a couple of staircases to let the gentlemen get a lost ball."

"That's not it," I said.

"Then there are plenty of Marine Parades, if that's what you mean. Every seaside resort has them."

I shook my head.

"It's got to be more retired than that," I said.

"Well, gentlemen, I can't think of anywhere else. Of course, there's the Ruff—"

"What's that?" I asked.

"The big chalk headland in Kent, close to Bradgate. It's got a lot of villas on the top, and some of the houses have staircases down to a private beach. It's a very high-toned sort of place, and the residents there like to keep by themselves."

I tore open the Tide Tables and found Bradgate. High tide there was at 10.27 pm on the 15th of June.

"We're on the scent at last," I cried excitedly. "How can I find out what is the tide at the Ruff?"

"I can tell you that, sir," said the coastguard man. "I once was lent a house there in this very month, and I used to go out at night to the deep-sea fishing. The tide's ten minutes before Bradgate."

I closed the book and looked round at the company.

"If one of those staircases has thirty-nine steps we have solved the mystery, gentlemen," I said. "I want the loan of your car, Sir Walter, and a map of the roads. If Mr MacGillivray will spare me ten minutes, I think we can prepare something for tomorrow."

It was ridiculous of me to take charge of the business like this, but they didn't seem to mind, and after all I had been in the show from the start. Besides, I was used to rough jobs, and these eminent gentlemen were too clever not to see it. It was General Royer who gave me my commission. "I for one," he said, "am content to leave the matter in Mr Hannay's hands."

By half past three I was tearing past the moonlit hedgerows of Kent, with MacGillivray's best man on the seat beside me.

CHAPTER 10

Various Parties Converging on the Sea

A PINK AND BLUE June morning found me at Bradgate looking from the Griffin Hotel over a smooth sea to the lightship on the Cock sands which seemed the size of a bell-buoy. A couple of miles farther south and much nearer the shore a small destroyer was anchored. Scaife, MacGillivray's man, who had been in the Navy, knew the boat, and told me her name and her commander's, so I sent off a wire to Sir Walter.

After breakfast Scaife got from a house-agent a key for the gates of the staircases on the Ruff. I walked with him along the sands, and sat down in a nook of the cliffs while he investigated the half dozen of them. I didn't want to be seen, but the place at this hour was quite deserted, and all the time I was on that beach I saw nothing but the seagulls.

It took him more than an hour to do the job, and when I saw him coming towards me, conning a bit of paper, I can tell you my heart was in my mouth. Everything depended, you see, on my guess proving right.

He read aloud the number of steps in the different stairs. "Thirty-four, thirty-five, thirty-nine, forty-two, forty-seven," and "twenty-one" where the cliffs grew lower. I almost got up and shouted.

We hurried back to the town and sent a wire to MacGillivray. I wanted half a dozen men, and I directed them to divide themselves among different specified hotels. Then Scaife set out to prospect the house at the head of the thirty-nine steps.

He came back with news that both puzzled and reassured me. The house was called Trafalgar Lodge, and belonged to an old gentleman called Appleton—a retired stockbroker, the house-agent said. Mr Appleton was there a good deal in the summertime, and was in residence now—had been for the better part of a week. Scaife could pick up very little information about him, except that he was a decent old fellow, who paid his bills regularly, and was always good for a fiver for a local charity. Then Scaife seems to have penetrated to the back door of the house, pretending he was an agent for sewing-machines. Only three servants were kept, a cook, a parlourmaid, and a housemaid, and they were just the sort that you would find in a respectable middle-class household. The cook was not the gossiping kind, and had pretty soon shut the door in his face, but Scaife said he was positive she knew nothing. Next door there was a new house building which would give good cover for observation, and the villa on the other side was to let, and its garden was rough and shrubby.

I borrowed Scaife's telescope, and before lunch went for a walk along the Ruff. I kept well behind the rows of villas, and found a good observation point on the edge of the golf course. There I had a view of the line of turf along the cliff-top, with seats placed at intervals, and the little square plots, railed in and planted with bushes, whence the staircases descended to the beach. I saw Trafalgar Lodge very plainly, a red-brick villa with a veranda, a tennis lawn behind, and in front the ordinary seaside flower-garden full of marguerites and scraggy geraniums. There was a flagstaff from which an enormous Union Jack hung limply in the still air.

Presently I observed someone leave the house and saunter along the cliff. When I got my glasses on him I saw it was an old man, wearing white flannel trousers, a blue serge jacket, and a straw hat. He carried field-glasses and a newspaper, and sat down on one of the iron seats and began to read. Sometimes he would lay down the paper and turn his glasses on the sea. He looked for a long time at the destroyer. I watched him for half an hour, till he got up and went back to the house for his luncheon, when I returned to the hotel for mine.

I wasn't feeling very confident. This decent commonplace dwelling was not what I had expected. The man might be the bald archaeologist of the horrible moorland farm, or he might not. He was exactly the kind of satisfied old bird you will find in every suburb and every holiday place. If you wanted a type of the perfectly harmless person you would probably pitch on that.

But after lunch, as I sat in the hotel porch, I perked up, for I saw the thing I hoped for and had dreaded to miss. A yacht came up from the south and dropped anchor pretty well opposite the Ruff. She seemed about a hundred and fifty tons, and I saw she belonged to the Squadron from the white ensign. So Scaife and I went down to the harbour and hired a boatman for an afternoon's fishing.

I spent a warm and peaceful afternoon. We caught between us about twenty pounds of cod and lythe, and out in that dancing blue sea I took a cheerier view of things. Above the white cliffs of the Ruff I saw the green and red of the villas, and especially the great flagstaff of Trafalgar Lodge. About four o'clock, when we had fished enough, I made the boatman row us round the yacht, which lay like a delicate white bird, ready at a moment to flee. Scaife said she must be a fast boat from her build, and that she was pretty heavily engined.

Her name was the *Ariadne*, as I discovered from the cap of one of the men who was polishing brasswork. I spoke to him, and got an answer in the soft dialect of Essex. Another hand that came along passed me the time of day in an unmistakable English tongue. Our boatman had an argument with one of them about the weather, and for a few minutes we lay on our oars close to the starboard bow.

Then the men suddenly disregarded us and bent their heads to their work as an officer came along the deck. He was a pleasant, clean-looking young fellow, and he put a question to us about our fishing in very good English. But there could be no doubt about him. His close-cropped head and the cut of his collar and tie never came out of England.

That did something to reassure me, but as we rowed back to Bradgate my obstinate doubts would not be dismissed. The thing that worried me was the reflection that my enemies knew that I had got my knowledge from Scudder, and it was Scudder who had given me the clue to this place. If they knew that Scudder had this clue, would they not be certain to change their plans? Too much depended on their success for them to take any risks. The whole question was how much they understood about Scudder's knowledge. I had talked confidently last night about Germans always sticking to a scheme, but if they had any suspicions that I was on their track they would be fools not to cover it. I wondered if the man last night had seen that I recognized him. Somehow I did not think he had, and to that I clung. But the whole business had never seemed so difficult as that afternoon when by all calculations I should have been rejoicing in assured success.

In the hotel I met the commander of the destroyer, to whom Scaife introduced me, and with whom I had a few words. Then I thought I would put in an hour or two watching Trafalgar Lodge.

I found a place farther up the hill, in the garden of an empty house. From that I had a full view of the court, on which two figures were having a game of tennis. One was the old man, whom I had already seen; the other was a younger fellow, wearing some club colours in the scarf round his middle. They played with tremendous zest, like two city gents who wanted hard exercise to open their pores. You couldn't conceive a more innocent spectacle. They shouted and laughed and stopped for drinks, when a maid brought out two tankards on a salver. I rubbed my eyes and asked myself if I was not the most immortal fool on earth. Mystery and darkness had hung about the men who hunted me over the Scotch moor in aeroplane and motor-car, and notably about that infernal antiquarian. It was easy enough to connect those folk with the knife that pinned Scudder to the floor, and with fell designs on the world's peace. But here were two guileless citizens taking their innocuous exercise, and soon about to go indoors to a humdrum dinner, where they would talk of market prices and the last cricket scores and the gossip of their native Surbiton. I had been making a net to catch vultures and falcons, and lo and behold! two plump thrushes had blundered into it.

Presently a third figure arrived, a young man on a bicycle, with a bag of golf clubs slung on his back. He strolled round to the tennis lawn and was welcomed riotously by the players. Evidently they were chaffing him, and their chaff sounded horribly English. Then the plump man, mopping his brow with a silk handkerchief, announced that he must have a tub. I heard his very words—"I've got into a proper lather," he said. "This will bring down my weight and my handicap, Bob. I'll take you on tomorrow and give you a stroke a hole." You couldn't find anything much more English than that.

They all went into the house, and left me feeling a precious idiot. I had been barking up the wrong tree this time. These men might be acting; but if they were, where was their audience? They didn't know I was sitting thirty yards off in a rhododendron. It was simply impossible to believe that these three hearty fellows were anything but what they seemed—three ordinary, game-playing, suburban Englishmen, wearisome, if you like, but sordidly innocent.

AND YET THERE WERE three of them; and one was old, and one was plump, and one was lean and dark; and their house chimed in with Scudder's notes; and half a mile off was lying a steam yacht with at least one German officer. I thought of Karolides lying dead, and all Europe trembling on the edge of earthquake, and the men I had left behind me in London who were waiting anxiously for the events of the next hours. There was no doubt that hell was afoot somewhere. The Black Stone had won, and if it survived this June night would bank its winnings.

There seemed only one thing to do—go forward as if I had no doubts, and if I was going to make a fool of myself to do it handsomely. Never in my life have I faced a job with greater disinclination. I would rather in my then mind have walked into a den of anarchists, each with his Browning handy, or faced a charging lion with a popgun, than enter that happy home of three cheerful Englishmen and tell them that their game was up. How they would laugh at me!

But suddenly I remembered a thing I once heard in Rhodesia from old Peter Pienaar. I have quoted Peter already in this narrative. He was the best scout I ever knew, and before he had turned respectable he had been pretty often on the windy side of the law, when he had been wanted badly by the authorities. Peter once discussed with me the question of disguises, and he had a theory which struck me at the time. He said, barring absolute certainties like fingerprints, mere physical traits were very little use for identification if the fugitive really knew his business. He laughed at things like dyed hair and false beards and such childish follies. The only thing that mattered was what Peter called "atmosphere".

If a man could get into perfectly different surroundings from those in which he had been first observed, and—this is the important part—really play up to these surroundings and behave as if he had never been out of them, he would puzzle the cleverest detectives on earth. And he used to tell a story of how he once borrowed a black coat and went to church and shared the same hymn-book with the man that was looking for him. If that man had seen him in decent company before he would have recognized him; but he had only seen him snuffing the lights in a public-house with a revolver.

The recollection of Peter's talk gave me the first real comfort I had

had that day. Peter had been a wise old bird, and these fellows I was after were about the pick of the aviary. What if they were playing Peter's game? A fool tries to look different: a clever man looks the same and *is* different.

Again, there was that other maxim of Peter's which had helped me when I had been a roadman. "If you are playing a part, you will never keep it up unless you convince yourself that you are *it*." That would explain the game of tennis. Those chaps didn't need to act, they just turned a handle and passed into another life, which came as naturally to them as the first. It sounds a platitude, but Peter used to say that it was the big secret of all the famous criminals.

It was now getting on for eight o'clock, and I went back and saw Scaife to give him his instructions. I arranged with him how to place his men, and then I went for a walk, for I didn't feel up to any dinner. I went round the deserted golf course, and then to a point on the cliffs farther north beyond the line of the villas.

On the little trim newly made roads I met people in flannels coming back from tennis and the beach, and a coastguard from the wireless station, and donkeys and pierrots padding homewards. Out at sea in the blue dusk I saw lights appear on the *Ariadne* and on the destroyer away to the south, and beyond the Cock sands the bigger lights of steamers making for the Thames. The whole scene was so peaceful and ordinary that I got more dashed in spirits every second. It took all my resolution to stroll towards Trafalgar Lodge about half past nine.

On the way I got a piece of solid comfort from the sight of a greyhound that was swinging along at a nursemaid's heels. He reminded me of a dog I used to have in Rhodesia, and of the time when I took him hunting with me in the Pali hills. We were after rhebok, the dun kind, and I recollected how we had followed one beast, and both he and I had clean lost it. A greyhound works by sight, and my eyes are good enough, but that buck simply leaked out of the landscape. Afterwards I found out how it managed it. Against the grey rock of the kopje it showed no more than a crow against a thunder-cloud. It didn't need to run away; all it had to do was to stand still and melt into the background.

Suddenly as these memories chased across my brain I thought of my present case and applied the moral. The Black Stone didn't need to bolt. They were quietly absorbed into the landscape. I was on the right track, and I jammed that down in my mind and vowed never to forget it. The last word was with Peter Pienaar.

Scaife's men would be posted now, but there was no sign of a soul. The house stood as open as a market-place for anybody to observe. A three-foot railing separated it from the cliff road; the windows on the ground floor were all open, and shaded lights and the low sound of voices revealed where the occupants were finishing dinner. Everything was as public and above-board as a charity bazaar. Feeling the greatest fool on earth, I opened the gate and rang the bell.

A MAN OF MY SORT, who has travelled about the world in rough places, gets on perfectly well with two classes, what you may call the upper and the lower. He understands them and they understand him. I was at home with herds and tramps and roadmen, and I was sufficiently at my ease with people like Sir Walter and the men I had met the night before. I can't explain why, but it is a fact. But what fellows like me don't understand is the great comfortable, satisfied middle-class world, the folk that live in villas and suburbs. He doesn't know how they look at things, he doesn't understand their conventions, and he is as shy of them as of a black mamba. When a trim parlourmaid opened the door, I could hardly find my voice.

I asked for Mr Appleton, and was ushered in. My plan had been to walk straight into the dining-room, and by a sudden appearance wake in the men that start of recognition which would confirm my theory. But when I found myself in that neat hall the place mastered me. There were the golf clubs and tennis rackets, the straw hats and caps, the rows of gloves, the sheaf of walking sticks, which you will find in ten thousand British homes. A stack of neatly folded coats and waterproofs covered the top of an old oak chest; there was a grandfather clock ticking; and some polished brass warming-pans on the walls, and a barometer, and a print of Chiltern winning the St Leger. The place was as orthodox as an Anglican church. When the maid asked me for my name I gave it automatically, and was shown into the smoking-room, on the right side of the hall.

That room was even worse. I hadn't time to examine it, but I could see some framed group photographs above the mantelpiece, and I could have sworn they were English public school or college. I had only one glance, for I managed to pull myself together and go after the maid. But

I was too late. She had already entered the dining-room and given my name to her master, and I had missed the chance of seeing how the three took it.

When I walked into the room the old man at the head of the table had risen and turned round to meet me. He was in evening dress—a short coat and black tie—as was the other, whom I called in my own mind the plump one. The third, the dark fellow, wore a blue serge suit and a soft white collar, and the colours of some club or school.

The old man's manner was perfect. "Mr Hannay?" he said hesitatingly. "Did you wish to see me? One moment, you fellows, and I'll rejoin you. We had better go to the smoking-room."

Though I hadn't an ounce of confidence in me, I forced myself to play the game. I pulled up a chair and sat down on it.

"I think we have met before," I said, "and I guess you know my business."

The light in the room was dim, but so far as I could see their faces, they played the part of mystification very well.

"Maybe, maybe," said the old man. "I haven't a very good memory, but I'm afraid you must tell me your errand, sir, for I really don't know it."

"Well, then," I said, and all the time I seemed to myself to be talking pure foolishness—"I have come to tell you that the game's up. I have here a warrant for the arrest of you three gentlemen."

"Arrest," said the old man, and he looked really shocked. "Arrest! Good God, what for?"

"For the murder of Franklin Scudder in London on the 23rd day of last month."

"I never heard the name before," said the old man in a dazed voice.

One of the others spoke up. "That was the Portland Place murder. I read about it. Good Heavens, you must be mad, sir! Where do you come from?"

"Scotland Yard," I said.

After that for a minute there was utter silence. The old man was staring at his plate and fumbling with a nut, the very model of innocent bewilderment.

Then the plump one spoke up. He stammered a little, like a man picking his words.

"Don't get flustered, uncle," he said. "It is all a ridiculous mistake;

but these things happen sometimes, and we can easily set it right. It won't be hard to prove our innocence. I can show that I was out of the country on the 23rd of May, and Bob was in a nursing home. You were in London, but you can explain what you were doing."

"Right, Percy! Of course that's easy enough. The 23rd! That was the day after Agatha's wedding. Let me see. What was I doing? I came up in the morning from Woking, and lunched at the club with Charlie Symons. Then—oh yes, I dined with the Fishmongers. I remember, for the punch didn't agree with me, and I was seedy next morning. Hang it all, there's the cigar-box I brought back from the dinner." He pointed to an object on the table, and laughed nervously.

"I think, sir," said the young man, addressing me respectfully, "you will see you are mistaken. We want to assist the law like all Englishmen, and we don't want Scotland Yard to be making fools of themselves. That's so, uncle?"

"Certainly, Bob." The old fellow seemed to be recovering his voice. "Certainly, we'll do anything in our power to assist the authorities. But—but this is a bit too much. I can't get over it."

"How Nellie will chuckle," said the plump man. "She always said that you would die of boredom because nothing ever happened to you. And now you've got it thick and strong," and he began to laugh very pleasantly.

"By Jove, yes. Just think of it! What a story to tell at the club. Really, Mr Hannay, I suppose I should be angry, to show my innocence, but it's too funny! I almost forgive you the fright you gave me! You looked so glum, I thought I might have been walking in my sleep and killing people."

It couldn't be acting, it was too confoundedly genuine. My heart went into my boots, and my first impulse was to apologize and clear out. But I told myself I must see it through, even though I was to be the laughing-stock of Britain. The light from the dinner-table candlesticks was not very good, and to cover my confusion I got up, walked to the door and switched on the electric light. The sudden glare made them blink, and I stood scanning the three faces.

Well, I made nothing of it. One was old and bald, one was stout, one was dark and thin. There was nothing in their appearance to prevent them being the three who had hunted me in Scotland, but there was nothing to identify them. I simply can't explain why I who, as a roadman, had looked into two pairs of eyes, and as Ned Ainslie into another pair, why I, who have a good memory and reasonable powers of observation, could find no satisfaction. They seemed exactly what they professed to be, and I could not have sworn to one of them.

There in that pleasant dining-room, with etchings on the walls, and a picture of an old lady in a bib above the mantelpiece, I could see nothing to connect them with the moorland desperadoes. There was a silver cigarette-box beside me, and I saw that it had been won by Percival Appleton, Esq., of the St Bede's Club, in a golf tournament. I had to keep firm hold of Peter Pienaar to prevent myself bolting out of that house.

"Well," said the old man politely, "are you reassured by your scrutiny, sir?"

I couldn't find a word.

"I hope you'll find it consistent with your duty to drop this ridiculous business. I make no complaint, but you'll see how annoying it must be to respectable people."

I shook my head.

"O Lord," said the young man. "This is a bit too thick!"

"Do you propose to march us off to the police station?" asked the plump one. "That might be the best way out of it, but I suppose you won't be content with the local branch. I have the right to ask to see your warrant, but I don't wish to cast any aspersions upon you. You are only doing your duty. But you'll admit it's horribly awkward. What do you propose to do?"

There was nothing to do except to call in my men and have them arrested, or to confess my blunder and clear out. I felt mesmerized by the whole place, by the air of obvious innocence—not innocence merely, but frank honest bewilderment and concern in the three faces.

"Oh, Peter Pienaar," I groaned inwardly, and for a moment I was very near damning myself for a fool and asking their pardon.

"Meantime I vote we have a game of bridge," said the plump one. "It will give Mr Hannay time to think over things, and you know we have been wanting a fourth player. Do you play, sir?"

I accepted as if it had been an ordinary invitation at the club. The whole business had mesmerized me. We went into the smoking-room where a card-table was set out, and I was offered things to smoke and drink. I took my place at the table in a kind of dream. The window was open and the moon was flooding the cliffs and sea with a great tide of yellow light. There was moonshine, too, in my head. The three had recovered their composure, and were talking easily—just the kind of slangy talk you will hear in any golf club-house. I must have cut a rum figure, sitting there knitting my brows with my eyes wandering.

My partner was the young dark one. I play a fair hand at bridge, but I must have been rank bad that night. They saw that they had got me puzzled, and that put them more than ever at their ease. I kept looking at their faces, but they conveyed nothing to me. It was not that they looked different; they *were* different. I clung desperately to the words of Peter Pienaar.

THEN SOMETHING AWOKE ME.

The old man laid down his hand to light a cigar. He didn't pick it up at once, but sat back for a moment in his chair, with his fingers tapping on his knees.

It was the movement I remembered when I had stood before him in the moorland farm, with the pistols of his servants behind me.

A little thing, lasting only a second, and the odds were a thousand to one that I might have had my eyes on my cards at the time and missed it. But I didn't, and, in a flash, the air seemed to clear. Some shadow lifted from my brain, and I was looking at the three men with full and absolute recognition.

The clock on the mantelpiece struck ten o'clock.

The three faces seemed to change before my eyes and reveal their secrets. The young one was the murderer. Now I saw cruelty and ruthlessness, where before I had only seen good humour. His knife, I made certain, had skewered Scudder to the floor. His kind had put the bullet in Karolides.

The plump man's features seemed to dislimn, and form again, as I looked at them. He hadn't a face, only a hundred masks that he could assume when he pleased. That chap must have been a superb actor. Perhaps he had been Lord Alloa of the night before; perhaps not, it didn't matter. I wondered if he was the fellow who had first tracked Scudder, and left his card on him. Scudder had said he lisped, and I could imagine how the adoption of a lisp might add terror.

But the old man was the pick of the lot. He was sheer brain, icy, cool, calculating, as ruthless as a steam hammer. Now that my eyes were opened I wondered where I had seen the benevolence. His jaw was like chilled steel, and his eyes had the inhuman luminosity of a bird's. I went on playing, and every second a greater hate welled up in my heart. It almost choked me, and I couldn't answer when my partner spoke. Only a little longer could I endure their company.

"Whew! Bob! Look at the time," said the old man. "You'd better think about catching your train. Bob's got to go to town tonight," he added, turning to me. The voice rang now as false as hell.

I looked at the clock, and it was nearly half past ten.

"I am afraid he must put off his journey," I said.

"Oh, damn," said the young man, "I thought you had dropped that rot. I've simply got to go. You can have my address, and I'll give any security you like."

"No," I said, "you must stay."

At that I think they must have realized that the game was desperate. Their only chance had been to convince me that I was playing the fool, and that had failed. But the old man spoke again.

"I'll go bail for my nephew. That ought to content you, Mr Hannay." Was it fancy, or did I detect some halt in the smoothness of that voice?

There must have been, for as I glanced at him, his eyelids fell in that hawk-like hood which fear had stamped on my memory.

I blew my whistle.

In an instant the lights were out. A pair of strong arms gripped me round the waist, covering the pockets in which a man might be expected to carry a pistol.

"*Schnell, Franz,*" cried a voice, "*das Boot, das Boot!*" As it spoke, I saw two of my fellows emerge on the moonlit lawn.

The young dark man leaped for the window, was through it, and over the low fence before a hand could touch him. I grappled the old chap, and the room seemed to fill with figures. I saw the plump one collared, but my eyes were all for the out-of-doors, where Franz sped on over the road towards the railed entrance to the beach stairs. One man followed him, but he had no chance. The gates of the stairs locked behind the fugitive, and I stood staring, with my hands on the old boy's throat, for such a time as a man might take to descend those steps to the sea.

Suddenly my prisoner broke from me and flung himself on the wall. There was a click as if a lever had been pulled. Then came a low

I BLEW MY WHISTLE

rumbling, far far below the ground, and through the window I saw a cloud of chalky dust pouring out of the shaft of the stairway.

Someone switched on the light.

The old man was looking at me with blazing eyes.

"He is safe," he cried. "You cannot follow in time . . . He is gone. He has triumphed . . . *Der Schwarzestein ist in der Siegeskrone.*"

There was more in those eyes than any common triumph. They had been hooded like a bird of prey, and now they flamed with a hawk's pride. A white fanatic heat burned in them, and I realized for the first time the terrible thing I had been up against. This man was more than a spy; in his foul way he had been a patriot.

As the handcuffs clinked on his wrists I said my last word to him.

"I hope Franz will bear his triumph well. I ought to tell you that the *Ariadne* for the last hour has been in our hands."

SEVEN WEEKS LATER, as all the world knows, we went to war. I joined the New Army the first week, and owing to my Matabele experience got a captain's commission straight off. But I had done my best service, I think, before I put on khaki.

GREENMANTLE

With illustrations by L.B. Black

GREENMANTLE

CHAPTER 1

A Mission is Proposed

I HAD JUST FINISHED breakfast and was filling my pipe when I got Bullivant's telegram. It was at Furling, the big country house in Hampshire where I had come to convalesce after Loos, and Sandy, who was in the same case, was hunting for the marmalade. I flung him the flimsy with the blue strip pasted down on it, and he whistled.

"Hullo, Dick, you've got the battalion. Or maybe it's a staff billet. You'll be a blighted brass-hat, coming it heavy over the hard-working regimental officer. And to think of the language you've wasted on brass-hats in your time!"

I sat and thought for a bit, for that name "Bullivant" carried me back eighteen months to the hot summer before the war. I had not seen the man since, though I had read about him in the papers. For more than a year I had been a busy battalion officer, with no other thought than to hammer a lot of raw stuff into good soldiers. I had succeeded pretty well, and there was no prouder man on earth than Richard Hannay when he took his Lennox Highlanders over the parapets on that glorious and bloody 25th day of September. Loos was no picnic, and we had had some ugly bits of scrapping before that, but the worst bit of the campaign I had seen was a tea-party to the show I had been in with Bullivant before the war started.

The sight of his name on a telegram form seemed to change all my outlook on life. I had been hoping for the command of the battalion, and looking forward to being in at the finish with Brother Boche. But this message jerked my thoughts on to a new road. There might be other things in the war than straightforward fighting. Why on earth should the Foreign Office want to see an obscure major of the New Army, and want to see him in double-quick time?

"I'm going up to town by the ten train," I announced; "I'll be back in time for dinner."

"Try my tailor," said Sandy. "He's got a very nice taste in red tabs. You can use my name."

An idea struck me. "You're pretty well all right now. If I wire for you, will you pack your own kit and mine and join me?"

"Right-o! I'll accept a job on your staff if they give you a corps. If so be as you come down to-night, be a good chap and bring a barrel of oysters from Sweeting's."

I travelled up to London in a regular November drizzle, which cleared up about Wimbledon to watery sunshine. I never could stand London during the war. It seemed to have lost its bearings and broken out into all manner of badges and uniforms which did not fit in with my notion of it. One felt the war more in its streets than in the field, or rather one felt the confusion of war without feeling the purpose. I dare say it was all right; but since August 1914 I never spent a day in town without coming home depressed to my boots.

I took a taxi and drove straight to the Foreign Office. Sir Walter did not keep me waiting long. But when his secretary took me to his room I would not have recognized the man I had known eighteen months before.

His big frame seemed to have dropped flesh and there was a stoop in the square shoulders. His face had lost its rosiness and was red in patches, like that of a man who gets too little fresh air. His hair was much greyer and very thin about the temples, and there were lines of overwork below the eyes. But the eyes were the same as before, keen and kindly and shrewd, and there was no change in the firm set of the jaw.

"We must on no account be disturbed for the next hour," he told his secretary. When the young man had gone he went across to both doors and turned the keys in them.

"Well, Major Hannay," he said, flinging himself into a chair beside the fire. "How do you like soldiering?"

"Right enough," I said, "though this isn't just the kind of war I would have picked myself. It's a comfortless, bloody business. But we've got the measure of the old Boche now, and it's dogged as does it. I count on getting back to the front in a week or two."

"Will you get the battalion?" he asked. He seemed to have followed my doings pretty closely.

"I believe I've a good chance. I'm not in this show for honour and glory, though. I want to do the best I can, but I wish to Heaven it was

122

over. All I think of is coming out of it with a whole skin."

He laughed. "You do yourself an injustice. What about the forward observation post at the Lone Tree? You forgot about the whole skin then."

I felt myself getting red. "That was all rot," I said, "and I can't think who told you about it. I hated the job, but I had to do it to prevent my subalterns going to glory. They were a lot of fire-eating young lunatics. If I had sent one of them he'd have gone on his knees to Providence and asked for trouble."

Sir Walter was still grinning.

"I'm not questioning your caution. You have the rudiments of it, or our friends of the Black Stone would have gathered you in at our last merry meeting. I would question it as little as your courage. What exercises my mind is whether it is best employed in the trenches."

"Is the War Office dissatisfied with me?" I asked sharply.

"They are profoundly satisfied. They propose to give you command of your battalion. Presently, if you escape a stray bullet, you will no doubt be a Brigadier. It is a wonderful war for youth and brains. But, I take it you are in this business to serve your country, Hannay?"

"I reckon I am," I said. "I am certainly not in it for my health."

He looked at my leg, where the doctors had dug out the shrapnel fragments, and smiled quizzically.

"Pretty fit again?" he asked.

"Tough as a sjambok. I thrive on the racket and eat and sleep like a schoolboy."

He got up and stood with his back to the fire, his eyes staring abstractedly out of the window at the wintry park.

"It is a great game, and you are the man for it, no doubt. But there are others who can play it, for soldiering to-day asks for the average rather than the exception in human nature. It is like a big machine where the parts are standardized. You are fighting, not because you are short of a job, but because you want to help England. How if you could help her better than by commanding a battalion—or brigade—or, if it comes to that, a division? How if there is a thing which you alone can do? Not some *embusqué* business in an office, but a thing compared to which your fight at Loos was a Sunday-school picnic. You are not afraid of danger? Well, in this job you would not be fighting with an army around you, but alone. You are fond of tackling difficulties? Well, I can give you a task which will try all your powers. Have you anything to say?"

My heart was beginning to thump uncomfortably. Sir Walter was not the man to pitch a case too high.

"I am a soldier," I said, "and under orders."

"True; but what I am about to propose does not come by any conceivable stretch within the scope of a soldier's duties. I shall perfectly understand if you decline. You will be acting as I should act myself—as any sane man would. I would not press you for worlds. If you wish it, I will not even make the proposal, but let you go here and now, and wish you good luck with your battalion. I do not wish to perplex a good soldier with impossible decisions."

This piqued me and put me on my mettle.

"I am not going to run away before the guns fire. Let me hear what you propose."

Sir Walter crossed to a cabinet, unlocked it with a key from his chain, and took a piece of paper from a drawer. It looked like an ordinary half-sheet of note-paper.

"I take it," he said, "that your travels have not extended to the East."

"No," I said, "barring a shooting trip in East Africa."

"Have you by any chance been following the present campaign there?"

"I've read the newspapers pretty regularly since I went to hospital. I've got some pals in the Mesopotamia show, and of course I'm keen to know what is going to happen at Gallipoli and Salonika. I gather that Egypt is pretty safe."

"If you will give me your attention for ten minutes I will supplement your newspaper reading."

Sir Walter lay back in an arm-chair and spoke to the ceiling. It was the best story, the clearest and the fullest, I had ever got of any bit of the war. He told me just how and why and when Turkey had left the rails. I heard about her grievances over our seizure of her ironclads, of the mischief the coming of the *Goeben* had wrought, of Enver and his precious Committee and the way they had got a cinch on the old Turk. When he had spoken for a bit, he began to question me.

"You are an intelligent fellow, and you will ask how a Polish adventurer, meaning Enver, and a collection of Jews and gipsies should have got control of a proud race. The ordinary man will tell you that it was German organization backed up with German money and German arms. You will inquire again how, since Turkey is primarily a religious power, Islam has played so small a part in it all. The Sheikh-ul-Islam is neglected, and though the Kaiser proclaims a Holy War and calls himself Hadji Mohammed Guilliamo, and says the Hohenzollerns are descended from the Prophet, that seems to have fallen pretty flat. The ordinary man again will answer that Islam in Turkey is becoming a back number, and that Krupp guns are the new gods. Yet—I don't know. I do not quite believe in Islam becoming a back number.

"Look at it in another way," he went on. "If it were Enver and Germany alone dragging Turkey into a European war for purposes that no Turk cared a rush about, we might expect to find the regular army obedient, and Constantinople. But in the provinces, where Islam is strong, there would be trouble. Many of us counted on that. But we have been disappointed. The Syrian army is as fanatical as the hordes of the Mahdi. The Senussi have taken a hand in the game. The Persian Moslems are threatening trouble. There is a dry wind blowing through the East, and the parched grasses wait the spark. And the wind is blowing towards the Indian border. Whence comes that wind, think you?"

Sir Walter had lowered his voice and was speaking very slow and distinct. I could hear the rain dripping from the eaves of the window, and far off the hoot of taxis in Whitehall.

"Have you an explanation, Hannay?" he asked again.

"It looks as if Islam had a bigger hand in the thing than we thought," I said. "I fancy religion is the only thing to knit up such a scattered empire."

"You are right," he said. "You must be right. We have laughed at the Holy War, the Jehad that old Von der Goltz prophesied. But I believe that stupid old man with the big spectacles was right. There is a Jehad preparing. The question is, How?"

"I'm hanged if I know," I said; "but I'll bet it won't be done by a pack of stout German officers in *Pickelhaubes*. I fancy you can't manufacture Holy Wars out of Krupp guns alone and a few staff officers and a battle cruiser with her boilers burst."

"Agreed. They are not fools, however much we try to persuade ourselves of the contrary. But supposing they had got some tremendous sacred sanction—some holy thing, some book or gospel or some new prophet from the desert, something which would cast over the whole ugly mechanism of German war the glamour of the old torrential raids which crumpled the Byzantine Empire and shook the walls of Vienna? Islam is a fighting creed, and the mullah still stands in the pulpit with the Koran in one hand and a drawn sword in the other. Supposing there is some Ark of the Covenant which will madden the remotest Moslem peasant with dreams of Paradise? What then, my friend?"

"Then there will be hell let loose in those parts pretty soon."

"Hell which may spread. Beyond Persia, remember, lies India."

"You keep to suppositions. How much do you know?" I asked.

"Very little, except the fact. But the fact is beyond dispute. I have reports from agents everywhere—pedlars in South Russia, Afghan horse-dealers, Turcoman merchants, pilgrims on the road to Mecca, sheikhs in North Africa, sailors on the Black Sea coasters, sheep-skinned Mongols, Hindu fakirs, Greek traders in the Gulf, as well as respectable Consuls who use cyphers. They tell the same story. The East is waiting for a revelation. It has been promised one. Some star—man, prophecy, or trinket—is coming out of the West. The Germans know, and that is the card with which they are going to astonish the world."

"And the mission you spoke of for me is to go and find out?"

He nodded gravely. "That is the crazy and impossible mission."

"Tell me one thing, Sir Walter," I said. "I know it is the fashion in this country if a man has a special knowledge to set him to some job exactly the opposite. I know all about Damaraland, but instead of being put on Botha's staff, as I applied to be, I was kept in Hampshire mud till the campaign in German South West Africa was over. I know a man who could pass as an Arab, but do you think they would send him to the East? They left him in my battalion—a lucky thing for me, for he saved my live at Loos. I know the fashion, but isn't this just carrying it a bit too far? There must be thousands of men who have spent years in the East and talk any language. They're the fellows for this job. I never saw a Turk in my life except a chap who did wrestling turns in a show at

Kimberley. You've picked about the most useless man on earth."

"You've been a mining engineer, Hannay," Sir Walter said. "If you wanted a man to prospect for gold in Barotseland you would of course like to get one who knew the country and the people and the language. But the first thing you would require in him would be that he had a nose for finding gold and knew his business. That is the position now. I believe that you have a nose for finding out what our enemies try to hide. I know that you are brave and cool and resourceful. That is why I tell you the story. Besides . . ."

He unrolled a big map of Europe on the wall.

"I can't tell you where you'll get on the track of the secret, but I can put a limit to the quest. You won't find it east of the Bosporus—not yet. It is still in Europe. It may be in Constantinople, or in Thrace. It may be farther west. But it is moving eastwards. If you are in time you may cut into its march to Constantinople. That much I can tell you. The secret is known in Germany, too, to those whom it concerns. It is in Europe that the seeker must search—at present."

"Tell me more," I said. "You can give me no details and no instructions. Obviously you can give me no help if I come to grief."

He nodded. "You would be beyond the pale."

"You give me a free hand."

"Absolutely. You can have what money you like, and you can get what help you like. You can follow any plan you fancy, and go anywhere you think fruitful. We can give no directions."

"One last question. You say it is important. Tell me just how important."

"It is life and death," he said solemnly. "I can put it no higher and no lower. Once we know what is the menace we can meet it. As long as we are in the dark it works unchecked and we may be too late. The war must be won or lost in Europe. Yes; but if the East blazes up, our effort will be distracted from Europe and the great *coup* may fail. The stakes are no less than victory and defeat, Hannay."

I got out of my chair and walked to the window. It was a difficult moment in my life. I was happy in my soldiering; above all, happy in the company of my brother officers. I was asked to go off into the enemy's lands on a quest for which I believed I was manifestly unfitted—a business of lonely days and nights, of nerve-racking strain, of deadly peril shrouding me like a garment. Looking out on the bleak weather I shivered. It was too grim a business, too inhuman for flesh and blood. But Sir Walter had called it a matter of life and death, and I had told him that I was out to serve my country. He could not give me orders, but was I not under orders—higher orders than my Brigadier's? I thought myself incompetent, but cleverer men than me thought me competent, or at least competent enough for a sporting chance. I knew in my soul that if I declined I should never be quite at peace in the world again. And yet Sir Walter had called the scheme madness, and said that he himself would never have accepted.

How does one make a great decision? I swear that when I turned round to speak I meant to refuse. But my answer was Yes, and I had crossed the Rubicon. My voice sounded cracked and far away.

Sir Walter shook hands with me and his eyes blinked a little.

"I may be sending you to your death, Hannay—Good God, what a damned task-mistress duty is!—If so, I shall be haunted with regrets, but *you* will never repent. Have no fear of that. You have chosen the roughest road, but it goes straight to the hill-tops."

He handed me the half-sheet of note-paper. On it were written three words—"*Kasredin*", "*cancer*", and "*v. I*".

"That is the only clue we possess," he said. "I cannot construe it, but I can tell you the story. We have had our agents working in Persia and Mesopotamia for years—mostly young officers of the Indian Army. They carry their lives in their hands, and now and then one disappears, and the sewers of Bagdad might tell a tale. But they find out many things, and they count the game worth the candle. They have told us of the star rising in the West, but they could give us no details. All but one—the best of them. He had been working between Mosul and the Persian frontier as a muleteer, and had been south into the Bakhtiari hills. He found out something, but his enemies knew that he knew and he was pursued. Three months ago, just before Kut, he staggered into Delamain's camp with ten bullet holes in him and a knife slash on his forehead. He mumbled his name, but beyond that and the fact that there was a Something coming from the West he told them nothing. He died in ten minutes. They found this paper on him, and since he cried out the word 'Kasredin' in his last moments, it must have had something to do with his quest. It is for you to find out if it has any meaning."

I folded it up and placed it in my pocket-book.

"What a great fellow! What was his name?" I asked.

Sir Walter did not answer at once. He was looking out of the window. "His name," he said at last, "was Harry Bullivant. He was my son. God rest his brave soul!"

CHAPTER 2

The Gathering
of the Missionaries

I WROTE OUT a wire to Sandy, asking him to come up by the two-fifteen train and meet me at my flat.

"I have chosen my colleague," I said.

"Billy Arbuthnot's boy? His father was at Harrow with me. I know the fellow—Harry used to bring him down to fish—tallish, with a lean, high-boned face and a pair of brown eyes like a pretty girl's. I know his record, too. There's a good deal about him in this office. He rode through Yemen, which no white man ever did before. The Arabs let him pass, for they thought him stark mad and argued that the hand of Allah was heavy enough on him without their efforts. He's blood-brother to every kind of Albanian bandit. Also he used to take a hand in Turkish politics, and got a huge reputation. Some Englishman was once complaining to old Mahmoud Shevkat about the scarcity of statesmen in Western Europe, and Mahmoud broke in with, 'Have you not the Honourable Arbuthnot?' You say he's in your battalion. I was wondering what had become of him, for we tried to get hold of him here, but he had left no address. Ludovick Arbuthnot—yes, that's the man. Buried deep in the commissioned ranks of the New Army? Well, we'll get him out pretty quick!"

"I knew he had knocked about the East, but I didn't know he was that kind of swell. Sandy's not the chap to buck about himself."

"He wouldn't," said Sir Walter. "He had always a more than Oriental reticence. I've got another colleague for you, if you like him."

He looked at his watch. "You can get to the Savoy Grill Room in five minutes by taxi-cab. Go in from the Strand, turn to your left, and you will see in the alcove on the right-hand side a table with one large American gentleman sitting at it. They know him there, so he will have the table to himself. I want you to go and sit down beside him. Say you come from me. His name is Mr John Scantlebury Blenkiron, now a citizen of Boston, Mass., but born and raised in Indiana. Put this envelope in your pocket, but don't read its contents till you have talked to him. I want you to form your own opinion about Mr Blenkiron."

I went out of the Foreign Office in as muddled a frame of mind as any diplomatist who ever left its portals. I was most desperately depressed. To begin with, I was in a complete funk. I had always thought I was about as brave as the average man, but there's courage and courage, and mine was certainly not the impassive kind. Stick me down in a trench and I could stand being shot at as well as most people, and my blood could get hot if it were given the chance. But I think I had too much imagination. I couldn't shake off the beastly forecasts that kept crowding my mind.

In about a fortnight, I calculated, I would be dead. Shot as a spy—a rotten sort of ending! At the moment I was quite safe, looking for a taxi in the middle of Whitehall, but the sweat broke on my forehead. I felt as I had felt in my adventure before the war. But this was far worse, for it was more cold-blooded and premeditated, and I didn't seem to have even a sporting chance. I watched the figures in khaki passing on the pavement, and thought what a nice safe prospect they had compared to mine. Yes, even if next week they were in the Hohenzollern, or the Hairpin trench at the Quarries, or that ugly angle at Hooge. I wondered why I had not been happier that morning before I got that infernal wire. Suddenly all the trivialities of English life seemed to me inexpressibly dear and terribly far away. I was very angry with Bullivant, till I remembered how fair he had been. My fate was my own choosing.

When I was hunting the Black Stone the interest of the problem had helped to keep me going. But now I could see no problem. My mind had nothing to work on but three words of gibberish on a sheet of paper and a mystery of which Sir Walter had been convinced, but to which he couldn't give a name. It was like the story I had read of St Teresa setting off at the age of ten with her small brother to convert the Moors. I sat huddled in the taxi with my chin on my breast, wishing that I had lost a leg at Loos and been comfortably tucked away for the rest of the war.

Sure enough I found my man in the Grill Room. There he was, feeding solemnly, with a napkin tucked under his chin. He was a big fellow with a fat, sallow, clean-shaven face. I disregarded the hovering waiter and pulled up a chair beside the American at the little table. He turned on me a pair of full sleepy eyes, like a ruminating ox.

"Mr Blenkiron?" I asked.

"You have my name, sir," he said. "Mr John Scantlebury Blenkiron. I would wish you a good morning if I saw anything good in this darned British weather."

"I come from Sir Walter Bullivant," I said, speaking low.

"So?" said he. "Sir Walter is a very good friend of mine. Pleased to meet you, Mr—or I guess it's Colonel—"

"Hannay," I said; "Major Hannay." I was wondering what this sleepy Yankee could do to help me.

"Allow me to offer you luncheon, Major. Here, waiter, bring the *carte*. I regret that I cannot join you in sampling the efforts of the management of this ho-tel. I suffer, sir, from dyspepsia—duo-denal dyspepsia. It gets me two hours after a meal and gives me hell just below the breast-bone. So I am obliged to adopt a diet. My nourishment is fish, sir, and boiled milk and a little dry toast. It's a melancholy descent from the days when I could do justice to a lunch at Sherry's and sup off oyster-crabs and devilled bones." He sighed from the depths of his capacious frame.

I ordered an omelette and a chop, and took another look at him. The large eyes seemed to be gazing steadily at me without seeing me. They were as vacant as an abstracted child's; but I had an uncomfortable feeling that they saw more than mine.

"You have been fighting, Major? The Battle of Loos? Well, I guess that must have been some battle. We in America respect the fighting of the British soldier, but we don't quite catch on to the de-vices of the British Generals. We opine that there is more bellicosity than science among your highbrows. That is so? My father fought at Chattanooga, but these eyes have seen nothing gorier than a Presidential election. Say, is there any way I could be let into a scene of real bloodshed?"

His serious tone made me laugh. "There are plenty of your countrymen in the present show," I said. "The French Foreign Legion is full of young Americans, and so is our Army Service Corps. Half the chauffeurs you strike in France seem to come from the States."

He sighed. "I did think of some belligerent stunt a year back. But I reflected that the good God had not given John S. Blenkiron the kind of martial figure that would do credit to the tented field. Also I recollected that we Americans were nootrals—benevolent nootrals—and that it did not become me to be butting into the struggles of the effete monarchies of Europe. So I stopped at home. It was a big renunciation, Major, for I was lying sick during the Philippines business, and I have never seen the lawless passions of men let loose on a battlefield. And, as a stoodent of humanity, I hankered for the experience."

"What have you been doing?" I asked. The calm gentleman had begun to interest me.

"Waal," he said, "I just waited. The Lord has blessed me with money to burn, so I didn't need to go scrambling like a wild cat for war contracts. But I reckoned I would get let into the game somehow, and I was. Being a nootral, I was in an advantageous position to take a hand. I had a pretty hectic time for a while, and then I reckoned I would leave God's country and see what was doing in Europe. I have counted myself out of the bloodshed business, but, as your poet sings, peace has its victories not less renowned than war, and I reckon that means that a nootral can have a share in a scrap as well as a belligerent."

"That's the best kind of neutrality I've ever heard of," I said.

"It's the right kind," he replied solemnly. "Say, Major, what are your lot fighting for? For your own skins and your Empire and the peace of Europe. Waal, those ideals don't concern us one cent. We're not Europeans, and there aren't any German trenches on Long Island yet. You've made the ring in Europe, and if we came butting in it wouldn't be the rules of the game. You wouldn't welcome us, and I guess you'd be right. We're that delicate-minded we can't interfere and that was what my friend, President Wilson, meant when he opined that America was too proud to fight. So we're nootrals. But likewise we're benevolent nootrals. As I follow events, there's a skunk been let loose in the world, and the odour of it is going to make life none too sweet till it is cleared away. It wasn't us that stirred up that skunk, but we've got to take a hand in disinfecting the planet. See? We can't fight, but, by God! some of us are going to sweat blood to sweep the mess up. Officially we do nothing except give off Notes like a leaky boiler gives off steam. But as individooal citizens we're in it up to the neck. So, in the spirit of Jefferson Davis and Woodrow Wilson, I'm going to be the nootralist kind of nootral till Kaiser will be sorry he didn't declare war on America at the beginning."

I was completely recovering my temper. This fellow was a perfect jewel, and his spirit put purpose into me.

"I guess you British were the same kind of nootral when your Admiral warned off the German fleet from interfering with Dewey in Manila Bay in '98." Mr Blenkiron drank up the last drop of his boiled milk, and lit a thin black cigar.

I leaned forward. "Have you talked to Sir Walter?" I asked.

"I have talked to him, and he has given me to understand that there's a deal ahead which you're going to boss. There are no flies on that big man, and if he says it's good business then you can count me in."

"You know that it's uncommonly dangerous?"

"I judged so. But it don't do to begin counting risks. I believe in an all-wise beneficent Providence, but you have got to trust Him and give Him a chance. What's life anyhow? For me, it's living on a strict diet and having frequent pains in my stomach. It isn't such an almighty lot to give up, provided you get a good price in the deal. Besides, how big is the risk? About one o'clock in the morning, when you can't sleep, it will be the size of Mount Everest, but if you run out to meet it, it will be a hillock you can jump over. The grizzly looks very fierce when you're taking your ticket for the Rockies and wondering if you'll come back, but he's just an ordinary bear when you've got the sight of your rifle on him. I won't think about risks till I'm up to my neck in them and don't see the road out."

I scribbled my address on a piece of paper and handed it to the stout philosopher. "Come to dinner to-night at eight," I said.

"I thank you, Major. A little fish, please, plain-boiled, and some hot milk. You will forgive me if I borrow your couch after the meal and spend the evening on my back. That is the advice of my noo doctor."

I got a taxi and drove to my club. On the way I opened the envelope Sir Walter had given me. It contained a number of jottings, the dossier of Mr Blenkiron. He had done wonders for the Allies in the States. He had nosed out the Dumba plot, and had been instrumental in getting the portfolio of Dr Albert. Von Papen's spies had tried to murder him, after he had defeated an attempt to blow up one of the big gun factories. Sir Walter had written at the end: "The best man we ever had. Better than Scudder. He would go through hell with a box of bismuth tablets and a pack of Patience cards."

I went into the little back smoking-room, borrowed an atlas from the library, poked up the fire, and sat down to think. Mr Blenkiron had given me the fillip I needed. My mind was beginning to work now, and was running wide over the whole business. Not that I hoped to find anything by my cogitations. It wasn't thinking in an arm-chair that would solve the mystery. But I was getting a sort of grip on a plan of operations. And to my relief I had stopped thinking about the risks. Blenkiron had shamed me out of that. If a sedentary dyspeptic could show that kind of nerve, I wasn't going to be behind him.

I went back to my flat about five o'clock. My man Paddock had gone to the wars long ago, so I had shifted to one of the new blocks in Park Lane where they provide food and service. I kept the place on to have a home to go to when I got leave. It's a miserable business holidaying in an hotel.

Sandy was devouring tea-cakes with the serious resolution of a convalescent.

"Well, Dick, what's the news? Is it a brass-hat or the boot?"

"Neither," I said. "But you and I are going to disappear from His Majesty's forces. Seconded for special service."

"O my sainted aunt!" said Sandy. "What is it? For Heaven's sake put me out of pain. Have we to tout deputations of suspicious neutrals over munition works or take the shivering journalist in a motor-car where he can imagine he sees a Boche?"

"The news will keep. But I can tell you this much. It's about as safe and easy as to go through the German lines with a walking-stick."

"Come, that's not so dusty," said Sandy, and began cheerfully on the muffins.

I must spare a moment to introduce Sandy to the reader, for he cannot be allowed to slip into this tale by a side-door. If you will consult the Peerage you will find that to Edward Cospatrick, fifteenth Baron Clanroyden, there was born in the year 1882, as his second son, Ludovick Gustavus Arbuthnot, commonly called the Honourable, etc. The said son was educated at Eton and New College, Oxford, was a captain in the Tweeddale Yeomanry, and served for some years as honorary attaché at various embassies. The Peerage will stop short at this point, but that is by no means the end of the story. For the rest you must consult very different authorities. Lean brown men from the ends of the earth may be seen on the London pavements now and then in creased clothes, walking with the light outland step, slinking into clubs as if they could not remember whether or not they belonged to them. From them you may get news of Sandy. Better still, you will hear of him at little forgotten fishing ports where the Albanian mountains dip to the Adriatic. If you struck a Mecca pilgrimage the odds are you would meet a dozen of Sandy's friends in it. In shepherds' huts in the Caucasus you will find bits of his cast-off clothing, for he has a knack of shedding garments as he goes. In the caravanserais of Bokhara and Samarkand he is known, and there are shikaris in the Pamirs who still speak of him around their fires. If you were going to visit Petrograd or Rome or Cairo it would be no use asking him for introductions; if he gave them, they would lead you into strange haunts. But if Fate compelled you to go to Llasa or Yarkand or Seistan he could map out your road for you and pass the word to potent friends. We call ourselves insular, but the truth is that we are the only race on earth that can produce men capable of getting inside the skin of remote peoples. Perhaps the Scots are better than the English, but we're all a thousand per cent better than anybody else. Sandy was the wandering Scot carried to the pitch of genius. In old days he would have led a crusade or discovered a new road to the Indies. To-day he merely roamed as the spirit moved him, till the war swept him up and dumped him down in my battalion.

I got out Sir Walter's half-sheet of note-paper. It was not the original—naturally he wanted to keep that—but it was a careful tracing. I took it that Harry Bullivant had not written down the words as a memo for his own use. People who follow his career have good memories. He must have written them in order that, if he perished and his body was found, his friends might get a clue. Wherefore, I argued, the words must be intelligible to somebody or other of our persuasion, and likewise they must be pretty well gibberish to any Turk or German that found them.

The first, *"Kasredin"*, I could make nothing of.

I asked Sandy.

"You mean Nasr-ed-din," he said, still munching crumpets.

"What's that?" I asked sharply.

"He's the General believed to be commanding against us in Mesopotamia. I remember him years ago in Aleppo. He talked bad French and drank the sweetest of sweet champagne."

I looked closely at the paper. The "K" was unmistakable.

"Kasredin is nothing. It means in Arabic the House of Faith, and might cover anything from Hagia Sofia to a suburban villa. What's your next puzzle, Dick? Have you entered for a prize competition in a weekly paper?"

"*Cancer*," I read out.

"It is the Latin for a crab. Likewise it is the name of a painful disease. It is also a sign of the Zodiac."

"*v. I*," I read.

"There you have me. It sounds like the number of a motor-car. The police would find out for you. I call this a rather difficult competition. What's the prize?"

I passed him the paper. "Who wrote it? It looks as if he had been in a hurry."

"Harry Bullivant," I said. Sandy's face grew solemn. "Old Harry. He was at my tutor's. The best fellow God ever made. I saw his name in the casualty list before Kut . . . Harry didn't do things without a purpose. What's the story of this paper?"

"Wait till after dinner," I said. "I'm going to change and have a bath. There's an American coming to dine, and he's part of the business."

Mr Blenkiron arrived punctual to the minute in a fur coat like a Russian prince's. Now that I saw him on his feet I could judge him better. He had a fat face, but was not too plump in figure, and very muscular wrists showed below his shirt-cuffs. I fancied that, if the occasion called, he might be a good man with his hands.

Sandy and I ate a hearty meal, but the American picked at his boiled fish and sipped his milk a drop at a time. When the servant had cleared away, he was as good as his word and laid himself out on my sofa. I offered him a good cigar, but he preferred one of his own lean black abominations. Sandy stretched his length in an easy-chair and lit his pipe. "Now for your story, Dick," he said.

I began, as Sir Walter had begun with me, by telling them about the puzzle in the Near East. I pitched a pretty good yarn, for I had been thinking a lot about it, and the mystery of the business had caught my fancy. Sandy got very keen.

"It is possible enough. Indeed, I've been expecting it, though I'm hanged if I can imagine what card the Germans have got up their sleeve. It might be any one of twenty things. Thirty years ago there was a bogus prophecy that played the devil in Yemen. Or it might be a flag such as Ali Wad Helu had, or a jewel like Solomon's necklace in Abyssinia. You never know what will start off a Jehad! But I rather think it's a man."

"Where could he get his purchase?" I asked.

"It's hard to say. If it were merely wild tribesmen like the Bedouin he might have got a reputation as a saint and miracle-worker. Or he might be a fellow that preached a pure religion, like the chap that founded the Senussi. But I'm inclined to think he must be something extra special if he can put a spell on the whole Moslem world. The Turk and the Persian wouldn't follow the ordinary new theology game. He must be of the Blood. Your Mahdis and Mullahs and Imams were nobodies, but they had only a local prestige. To capture all Islam—and I gather that is what we fear—the man must be of the Koreish, the tribe of the Prophet himself."

"But how could any impostor prove that? for I suppose he's an impostor."

"He would have to combine a lot of claims. His descent must be pretty good to begin with, and there are families, remember, that claim the Koreish blood. Then he'd have to be rather a wonder on his own account—saintly, eloquent, and that sort of thing. And I expect he'd have to show a sign, though what that could be I haven't a notion."

"You know the East about as well as any living man. Do you think that kind of thing is possible?" I asked.

"Perfectly," said Sandy, with a grave face.

"Well, there's the ground cleared to begin with. Then there's the evidence of pretty well every secret agent we possess. That all seems to prove the fact. But we have no details and no clues except that bit of paper." I told them the story of it.

Sandy studied it with wrinkled brows. "It beats me. But it may be the key for all that. A clue may be dumb in London and shout aloud at Bagdad."

"That's just the point I was coming to. Sir Walter says this thing is about as important for our cause as big guns. He can't give me orders, but he offers the job of going out to find what the mischief is. Once he knows that, he says he can checkmate it. But it's got to be found out soon, for the mine may be sprung at any moment. I've taken on the job. Will you help?"

Sandy was studying the ceiling.

"I should add that it's about as safe as playing chuck-farthing at the Loos Cross-roads, the day you and I went in. And if we fail nobody can help us."

"Oh, of course, of course," said Sandy in an abstracted voice.

Mr Blenkiron, having finished his after-dinner recumbency, had sat up and pulled a small table towards him. From his pocket he had taken a pack of Patience cards and had begun to play the game called the Double Napoleon. He seemed to be oblivious of the conversation.

Suddenly I had the feeling that the whole affair was stark lunacy. Here were we three simpletons sitting in a London flat and projecting a mission into the enemy's citadel without an idea what we were to do or how we were to do it. And one of the three was looking at the ceiling, and whistling softly through his teeth, and another was playing Patience. The farce of the thing struck me so keenly that I laughed.

Sandy looked at me sharply. "You feel like that? Same with me. It's idiocy, but all war is idiotic, and the most whole-hearted idiot is apt to win. We're to go on this mad trail wherever we think we can hit it. Well, I'm with you. But I don't mind admitting that I'm in a blue funk. I had got myself adjusted to this trench business and was quite happy. And now you have hoicked me out, and my feet are cold."

"I don't believe you know what fear is," I said.

"There you're wrong, Dick," he said earnestly. "Every man who isn't a maniac knows fear. I have done some daft things, but I never started on them without wishing they were over. Once I'm in the show I get easier, and by the time I'm coming out I'm sorry to leave it. But at the start my feet are icy."

"Then I take it you're coming?"

"Rather," he said. "You didn't imagine I would go back on you?"

"And you, sir?" I addressed Blenkiron.

His game of Patience seemed to be coming out. He was completing eight little heaps of cards with a contented grunt. As I spoke, he raised his sleepy eyes and nodded.

"Why, yes," he said. "You gentlemen mustn't think that I haven't been following your most engrossing conversation. I guess I haven't missed a syllable. I find that a game of Patience stimulates the digestion after meals and conduces to quiet reflection. John S. Blenkiron is with you all the time."

AS I SPOKE, HE RAISED HIS SLEEPY EYES AND NODDED

He shuffled the cards and dealt for a new game.

I don't think I ever expected a refusal, but this ready assent cheered me wonderfully. I couldn't have faced the thing alone.

"Well, that's settled. Now for ways and means. We three have got to put ourselves in the way of finding out Germany's secret, and we have to go where it is known. Somehow or other we have to reach Constantinople, and to beat the biggest area of country we must go by different roads. Sandy, my lad, you've got to get into Turkey. You're the only one of us that knows that engaging people. You can't get in by Europe very easily, so you must try Asia. What about the coast of Asia Minor?"

"It could be done," he said. "You'd better leave that entirely to me. I'll find out the best way. I suppose the Foreign Office will help me to get to the jumping-off place?"

"Remember," I said, "it's no good getting too far east. The secret, so far as concerns us, is still west of Constantinople."

"I see that. I'll blow in on the Bosporus by a short tack."

"For you, Mr Blenkiron, I would suggest a straight journey. You're an American, and can travel through Germany direct. But I wonder how far your activities in New York will allow you to pass as a neutral?"

"I have considered that, sir," he said. "I have given some thought to the pecooliar psychology of the great German nation. As I read them they're as cunning as cats, and if you play the feline game they will outwit you every time. Yes, sir, they are no slouches at sleuth-work. If I were to buy a pair of false whiskers and dye my hair and dress like a Baptist parson and go into Germany on the peace racket, I guess they'd be on my trail like a knife, and I should be shot as a spy inside of a week or doing solitary in the Moabit prison. But they lack the larger vision. They can be bluffed, sir. With your approval I shall visit the Fatherland as John S. Blenkiron, once a thorn in the side of their brightest boys on the other side. But it will be a different John S. I reckon he will have experienced a change of heart. He will have come to appreciate the great, pure, noble soul of Germany, and he will be sorrowing for his past like a converted gun-man at a camp meeting. He will be a victim of the meanness and perfidy of the British Government. I am going to have a first-class row with your Foreign Office about my passport, and I am going to speak harsh words about them up and down this metropolis. I am going to be shadowed by your sleuths at my port of embarkation, and I guess I shall run up hard against the British Le-gations in Scandinavia. By that time our Teutonic friends will have begun to wonder what has happened to John S., and to think that maybe they have been mistaken in that child. So, when I get to Germany they will be waiting for me with an open mind. Then I judge my conduct will surprise and encourage them. I will confide to them valuable secret information about British preparations, and I will show up the British lion as the meanest kind of cur. You may trust me to make a good impression. After that I'll move eastwards, to see the de-molition of the British Empire in those parts. By the way, where is the rendezvous?"

"This is the 17th day of November. If we can't find out what we want in two months we may chuck the job. On the 17th of January we should forgather in Constantinople. You fix the meeting-place."

"I've already thought of that," he said, and going to the writing-table he drew a little plan on a sheet of paper. "That lane runs down from the Kurdish Bazaar in Galata to the ferry of Ratchik. Halfway down on the left-hand side is a café kept by a Greek called Kuprasso. Behind the café is a garden, surrounded by high walls which were parts of the old Byzantine Theatre. At the end of the garden is a shanty called the Garden-House of Suliman the Red. It has been in its time a dancing-hall and a gambling hell and God knows what else. It's not a place for respectable people, but the ends of the earth converge there and no questions are asked. That's the best spot I can think of for a meeting-place."

The kettle was simmering by the fire, the night was raw, and it seemed the hour for whisky-punch. I made a brew for Sandy and myself and boiled some milk for Blenkiron.

"What about language?" I asked. "You're all right, Sandy?"

"I know German fairly well; and I can pass anywhere as a Turk. The first will do for eavesdropping and the second for ordinary business."

"And you?" I asked Blenkiron.

"I was left out at Pentecost," he said. "I regret to confess I have no gift of tongues. But the part I have chosen for myself don't require the polyglot. Never forget I'm plain John S. Blenkiron, a citizen of the great American Republic."

"You haven't told us your own line, Dick," Sandy said.

"I am going to the Bosporus through Germany, and, not being a neutral, it won't be a very cushioned journey."

Sandy looked grave.

"That sounds pretty desperate. Is your German good enough?"

"Pretty fair; quite good enough to pass as a native. But officially I shall not understand one word. I shall be a Boer from Western Cape Colony: one of Maritz's old lot who after a bit of trouble has got through Angola and reached Europe. I shall talk Dutch and nothing else. And, my hat! I shall be pretty bitter about the British. There's a powerful lot of good swear-words in the *taal*. I shall know all about Africa, and be panting to get another whack at the *verdommt rooinek*. With luck they may send me to the Uganda show or to Egypt, and I shall take care to go by Constantinople. If I'm to deal with the Mohammedan natives they're bound to show me what hand they hold. At least, that's the way I look at it."

We filled our glasses—two of punch and one of milk—and drank to our next merry meeting. Then Sandy began to laugh, and I joined in. The sense of hopeless folly again descended on me. The best plans we could make were like a few buckets of water to ease the drought of the Sahara or the old lady who would have stopped the Atlantic with a broom. I thought with sympathy of little St Teresa.

CHAPTER 3

Peter Pienaar

OUR VARIOUS DEPARTURES were unassuming, all but the American's. Sandy spent a busy fortnight in his subterranean fashion, now in the British Museum, now running about the country to see old exploring companions, now at the War Office, now at the Foreign Office, but mostly in my flat, sunk in an arm-chair and meditating. He left finally on December 1 as a King's Messenger for Cairo. Once there I knew the King's Messenger would disappear, and some queer Oriental ruffian take his place. It would have been impertinence in me to inquire into his plans. He was the real professional, and I was only a dabbler.

Blenkiron was a different matter. Sir Walter told me to look out for squalls, and the twinkle in his eye gave me a notion of what was coming. The first thing the sportsman did was to write a letter to the papers signed with his name. There had been a debate in the House of Commons on foreign policy, and the speech of some idiot there gave him his cue. He declared that he had been heart and soul with the British at the start, but that he was reluctantly compelled to change his views. He said our blockade of Germany had broken all the laws of God and humanity, and he reckoned that Britain was now the worst exponent of Prussianism going. That letter made a fine racket, and the paper that printed it had a row with the Censor.

But that was only the beginning of Mr Blenkiron's campaign. He got mixed up with some mountebanks called the League of Democrats against Aggression, gentlemen who thought that Germany was all right if we could only keep from hurting her feelings. He addressed a meeting under their auspices, which was broken up by the crowd, but not before John S. had got off his chest a lot of amazing stuff. I wasn't there, but a man who was told me that he never heard such clotted nonsense. He said that Germany was right in wanting the freedom of the seas, and that America would back her up, and that the British Navy was a bigger menace to the peace of the world than the Kaiser's army. He admitted that he had once thought differently, but he was an honest man and not afraid to face facts. The oration closed suddenly, when he got a brussels-sprout in the eye, at which my friend said he swore in a very unpacifist style.

After that he wrote other letters to the Press, saying that there was no more liberty of speech in England, and a lot of scallywags backed him up. Some Americans wanted to tar and feather him, and he got kicked out of the Savoy. There was an agitation to get him deported, and questions were asked in Parliament, and the Under-Secretary for Foreign Affairs said his department had the matter in hand. I was beginning to think that Blenkiron was carrying his tomfoolery too far, so I went to see Sir Walter, but he told me to keep my mind easy.

"Our friend's motto is 'Thorough'," he said, "and he knows very well what he is about. We have officially requested him to leave, and he sails from Newcastle on Monday. He will be shadowed wherever he goes, and we hope to provoke more outbreaks. He is a very capable fellow."

The last I saw of him was on the Saturday afternoon when I met him in St James's Street and offered to shake hands. He told me that my uniform was a pollution, and made a speech to a small crowd about it. They hissed him and he had to get into a taxi. As he departed there was just the suspicion of a wink in his left eye. On Monday I read that he had gone off, and the papers observed that our shores were well quit of him.

I sailed on December 3 from Liverpool in a boat bound for the Argentine that was due to put in at Lisbon. I had of course to get a Foreign Office passport to leave England, but after that my connexion with the Government ceased. All the details of my journey were carefully thought out. Lisbon would be a good jumping-off place, for it was the rendezvous of scallywags from most parts of Africa. My kit was an old Gladstone bag, and my clothes were the relics of my South African wardrobe. I let my beard grow for some days before I sailed, and, since it grows fast, I went on board with the kind of hairy chin you will see on the young Boer. My name was now Brandt, Cornelis Brandt—at least so my passport said, and passports never lie.

There were just two other passengers on that beastly boat, and they never appeared till we were out of the Bay. I was pretty bad myself, but managed to move about all the time, for the frowst in my cabin would have sickened a hippo. The old tub took two days and a night to waddle from Ushant to Finisterre. Then the weather changed and we came out of snow-squalls into something very like summer. The hills of Portugal were all blue and yellow like the Kalahari, and before we made the Tagus I was beginning to forget I had ever left Rhodesia. There was a Dutchman among the sailors with whom I used to patter the *taal*, and but for "Good morning" and "Good evening" in broken English to the captain, that was about all the talking I did on the cruise.

We dropped anchor off the quays of Lisbon on a shiny blue morning, pretty near warm enough to wear flannels. I had now got to be very wary. I did not leave the ship with the shore-going boat, but made a leisurely breakfast. Then I strolled on deck, and there, just casting anchor in the middle of the stream, was another ship with the blue and white funnel I knew so well. I calculated that a month before she had been smelling the mangrove swamps of Angola. Nothing could better answer my purpose. I proposed to board her, pretending I was looking for a friend, and come on shore from her, so that anyone in Lisbon who chose to be curious would think I had landed straight from Portuguese Africa.

I hailed one of the adjacent ruffians, and got into his row-boat, with my kit. We reached the vessel—they called her the *Henry the Navigator*—just as the first shore-boat was leaving. The crowd in it were all Portuguese, which suited my book.

But when I went up the ladder the first man I met was old Peter Pienaar.

Here was a piece of sheer monumental luck. Peter had opened his eyes and his mouth, and had got as far as *"Allemachtig"*, when I shut him up.

"Brandt," I said, "Cornelis Brandt. That's my name now, and don't you forget it. Who is the captain here? Is it still old Sloggett?"

"*Ja*," said Peter, pulling himself together. "He was speaking about you yesterday."

This was better and better. I sent Peter below to get hold of Sloggett, and presently I had a few words with that gentleman in his cabin with the door shut.

"You've got to enter my name in the ship's books. I came aboard at Mossamedes. And my name's Cornelis Brandt."

At first Sloggett was for objecting. He said it was a felony. I told him that I dared say it was, but he had got to do it, for reasons which I couldn't give, but which were highly creditable to all parties. In the end he agreed, and I saw it done. I had a pull on old Sloggett, for I had known him ever since he owned a dissolute tug-boat at Delagoa Bay.

Then Peter and I went ashore and swaggered into Lisbon as if we owned De Beers. We put up at the big hotel opposite the railway station, and looked and behaved like a pair of low-bred South Africans home for a spree. It was a fine bright day, so I hired a motor-car and said I would drive it myself. We asked the name of some beauty-spot to visit, and were told Cintra and shown the road to it. I wanted a quiet place to talk, for I had a good deal to say to Peter Pienaar.

I christened that car the Lusitanian Terror, and it was a marvel that we did not smash ourselves up. There was something immortally wrong with its steering gear. Half a dozen times we slewed across the road, inviting destruction. But we got there in the end, and had luncheon in an hotel opposite the Moorish palace. There we left the car and wandered up the slopes of a hill, where, sitting among scrub very like the veld, I told Peter the situation of affairs.

But first a word must be said about Peter. He was the man that taught me all I ever knew of veldcraft, and a good deal about human nature besides. He was out of the Old Colony—Burgersdorp, I think—but he had come to the Transvaal when the Lydenburg goldfields started. He was prospector, transport-rider, and hunter in turns, but principally hunter. In those early days he was none too good a citizen. He was in Swaziland with Bob Macnab, and you know what that means. Then he took to working off bogus gold propositions on Kimberley and Johannesburg magnates, and what he didn't know about salting a mine wasn't knowledge. After that he was in the Kalahari, where he and Scotty Smith were familiar names. An era of comparative respectability dawned for him with the Matabele War, when he did uncommon good scouting and transport work. Cecil Rhodes wanted to establish him on a stock farm down Salisbury way, but Peter was an independent devil and would call no man master. He took to big-game hunting, which was what God intended him for, for he could track a tsessebe in thick bush, and was far the finest shot I have seen in my life. He took parties to the Pungwe flats, and Barotseland, and up to Tanganyika. Then he made a speciality of the Ngami region, where I once hunted with him, and he was with me when I went prospecting in Damaraland.

When the Boer War started, Peter, like many of the very great hunters, took the British side and did most of our intelligence work in the North Transvaal. Beyers would have hanged him if he could have caught him, and there was no love lost between Peter and his own people for many a day. When it was all over and things had calmed down a bit, he settled in Bulawayo and used to go with me when I went on trek. At the time when I left Africa two years before, I had lost sight of him for months, and heard that he was somewhere on the Congo poaching elephants. He had always a great idea of making things hum so loud in Angola that the Union Government would have to step in and annex it. After Rhodes Peter had the biggest notions south of the Line.

He was a man of about five foot ten, very thin and active, and as strong as a buffalo. He had pale blue eyes, a face as gentle as a girl's, and a soft sleepy voice. From his present appearance it looked as if he had been living hard lately. His clothes were of the cut you might expect to get at Lobito Bay, he was as lean as a rake, deeply browned with the sun, and there was a lot of grey in his beard. He was fifty-six years old, and used to be taken for forty. Now he looked about his age.

I first asked him what he had been up to since the war began. He spat, in the Kaffir way he had, and said he had been having hell's time.

"I got hung up on the Kafue," he said. "When I heard from old Letsitela that the white men were fighting I had a bright idea that I might get into German South West from the north. You see I knew that Botha couldn't long keep out of the war. Well, I got into German territory all right, and then a *skellum* of an officer came along, and commandeered all my mules, and wanted to commandeer me with them for his fool army. He was a very ugly man with a yellow face." Peter filled a deep pipe from a kudu-skin pouch.

"Were you commandeered?" I asked.

"No. I shot him—not so as to kill, but to wound badly. It was all right, for he fired first on me. Got me too in the left shoulder. But that was the beginning of bad trouble. I trekked east pretty fast, and got over the border among the Ovamba. I have made many journeys, but that was the worst. Four days I went without water, and six without food. Then by bad luck I fell in with 'Nkitla—you remember, the half-caste chief. He said I owed him money for cattle which I bought when I came there with Carowab. It was a lie, but he held to it, and would give me no transport. So I crossed the Kalahari on my feet. Ugh, it was as slow as a vrouw coming from *nachtmaal*. It took weeks and weeks, and when I came to Lechwe's kraal, I heard that the fighting was over and that Botha had conquered the Germans. That, too, was a lie, but it deceived me, and I went north into Rhodesia, where I learned the truth. But by then I judged the war had gone too far for me to make any profit out of it, so I went into Angola to look for German refugees. By that time I was hating Germans worse than hell."

"But what did you propose to do with them?" I asked.

"I had a notion they would make trouble with the Government in those parts. I don't specially love the Portugoose, but I'm for him against the Germans every day. Well, there was trouble, and I had a merry time for a month or two. But by and by it petered out, and I thought I had better clear for Europe, for South Africa was settling down just as the big show was getting really interesting. So here I am, Cornelis, my old friend. If I shave my beard will they let me join the Flying Corps?"

I looked at Peter sitting there smoking, as imperturbable as if he had been growing mealies in Natal all his life and had run home for a month's holiday with his people in Peckham.

"You're coming with me, my lad," I said. "We're going into Germany."

Peter showed no surprise. "Keep in mind that I don't like the Germans," was all he said. "I'm a quiet Christian man, but I've the devil of a temper."

Then I told him the story of our mission.

"You and I have got to be Maritz's men. We went into Angola, and now we're trekking for the Fatherland to get a bit of our own back from the infernal English. Neither of us knows any German—publicly. We'd better plan out the fighting we were in—Kakamas will do for one, and Schuit Drift. You were a Ngamiland hunter before the war. They won't have your dossier, so you can tell any lie you like. I'd better be an educated Afrikander, one of Beyer's bright lads, and a pal of old Hertzog. We can let our imagination loose about that part, but we must stick to the same yarn about the fighting."

"*Ja*, Cornelis," said Peter. (He had called me Cornelis ever since I had told him my new name. He was a wonderful chap for catching on to any game.) "But after we get into Germany, what then? There can't be much difficulty about the beginning. But once we're among the beer-swillers I don't quite see our line. We're to find out about something that's going on in Turkey? When I was a boy the predikant used to preach about Turkey. I wish I was better educated and remembered whereabouts in the map it was."

"You leave that to me," I said; "I'll explain it all to you before we get there. We haven't got much of a spoor, but we'll cast about, and with luck will pick it up. I've seen you do it often enough when we hunted kudu on the Kafue."

Peter nodded. "Do we sit still in a German town?" he asked anxiously. "I shouldn't like that, Cornelis."

"We move gently eastward to Constantinople," I said.

Peter grinned. "We should cover a lot of new country. You can reckon on me, friend Cornelis. I've always had a hankering to see Europe."

He rose to his feet and stretched his long arms.

"We'd better begin at once. God, I wonder what's happened to old Solly Maritz, with his bottle face? Yon was a fine battle at the drift when I was sitting up to my neck in the Orange praying that Brits' lads would take my head for a stone."

Peter was as thorough a mountebank, when he got started, as Blenkiron himself. All the way back to Lisbon he yarned about Maritz and his adventures in German South West till I half believed they were true. He made a very good story of our doings, and by his constant harping on it I pretty soon got it into my memory. That was always Peter's way. He said if you were going to play a part, you must think yourself into it, convince yourself that you were *it*, till you really were it and didn't act but behaved naturally. The two men who had started that morning from the hotel door had been bogus enough, but the two men that returned were genuine desperadoes itching to get a shot at England.

We spent the evening piling up evidence in our favour. Some kind of republic had been started in Portugal, and ordinarily the cafés would have been full of politicians, but the war had quieted all these local squabbles, and the talk was of nothing but what was doing in France and Russia. The place we went to was a big, well-lighted show on a main street, and there were a lot of sharp-eyed fellows wandering about that I guessed were spies and police agents. I knew that Britain was the one country that doesn't bother about this kind of game, and that it would be safe enough to let ourselves go.

I talked Portuguese fairly well, and Peter spoke it like a Lourenço Marques bar-keeper, with a lot of Shangaan words to fill up. He started on curaçao, which I reckoned was a new drink to him, and presently his tongue ran freely. Several neighbours pricked up their ears, and soon we had a small crowd round our table.

We talked to each other of Maritz and our doings. It didn't seem to be a popular subject in that café. One big blue-black fellow said that Maritz was a dirty swine who would soon be hanged. Peter quickly caught his knife-wrist with one hand and his throat with the other, and demanded an apology. He got it. The Lisbon *boulevardiers* have not lost any lions.

After that there was a bit of a squash in our corner. Those near to us were very quiet and polite, but the outer fringe made remarks. When Peter said that if Portugal, which he admitted he loved, was going to stick to England she was backing the wrong horse, there was a murmur of disapproval. One decent-looking fellow, who had the air of a ship's captain, flushed all over his honest face, and stood up looking straight at Peter. I saw that we had struck an Englishman, and mentioned it to Peter in Dutch.

Peter played his part perfectly. He suddenly shut up, and, with furtive looks around him, began to jabber to me in a low voice. He was the very picture of the old stage conspirator.

The old fellow stood staring at us. "I don't very well understand this damned lingo," he said; "but if so be you dirty Dutchmen are sayin' anything against England, I'll ask you to repeat it. And if so be as you repeats it I'll take either of you on and knock the face off him."

He was a chap after my own heart, but I had to keep the game up. I said in Dutch to Peter that we mustn't get brawling in a public-house. "Remember the big thing," I said darkly. Peter nodded, and the old fellow, after staring at us for a bit, spat scornfully, and walked out.

"The time is coming when the Englander will sing small," I observed to the crowd. We stood drinks to one or two, and then swaggered into the street. At the door a hand touched my arm, and, looking down, I saw a little scrap of a man in a fur coat.

"Will the gentleman walk a step with me and drink a glass of beer?" he said in very stiff Dutch.

"Who the devil are you?" I asked.

"*Gott strafe England!*" was his answer, and, turning back the lapel of his coat, he showed some kind of ribbon in his buttonhole.

"Amen," said Peter. "Lead on, friend. We don't mind if we do."

He led us to a back street and then up two pairs of stairs to a very snug little flat. The place was filled with fine red lacquer, and I guessed that art-dealing was his nominal business. Portugal, since the republic broke up the convents and sold up the big royalist grandees, was full of bargains in the lacquer and curio line.

He filled us two long tankards of very good Munich beer.

"*Prosit,*" he said, raising his glass. "You are from South Africa. What make you in Europe?"

We both looked sullen and secretive.

"That's our own business," I answered. "You don't expect to buy our confidence with a glass of beer."

"So?" he said. "Then I will put it differently. From your speech in the café I judge you do not love the English."

Peter said something about stamping on their grandmothers, a Kaffir phrase which sounded gruesome in Dutch.

The man laughed. "That is all I want to know. You are on the German side?"

"That remains to be seen," I said. "If they treat me fair I'll fight for them, or for anybody else that makes war on England. England has stolen my country and corrupted my people and made me an exile. We Afrikanders do not forget. We may be slow but we win in the end. We two are men worth a great price. Germany fights England in East Africa. We know the natives as no Englishmen can ever know them. They are too soft and easy and the Kaffirs laugh at them. But we can handle the blacks so that they will fight like devils for fear of us. What is the reward, little man, for our services? I will tell you. There will be no reward. We ask none. We fight for hate of England."

Peter grunted a deep approval.

"That is good talk," said our entertainer, and his close-set eyes flashed. "There is room in Germany for such men as you. Where are you going now, I beg to know?"

"To Holland," I said. "Then maybe we will go to Germany. We are tired with travel and may rest a bit. This war will last long and our chance will come."

"But you may miss your market," he said significantly. "A ship sails to-morrow for Rotterdam. If you take my advice, you will go with her."

This was what I wanted, for if we stayed in Lisbon some real soldier of Maritz might drop in any day and blow the gaff.

"I recommend you to sail in the *Machado*," he repeated. "There is work for you in Germany—oh yes, much work; but if you delay the chance may pass. I will arrange your journey. It is my business to help the allies of my fatherland."

He wrote down our names and an epitome of our doings contributed by Peter, who required two mugs of beer to help him through. He was a Bavarian, it seemed, and we drank to the health of Prince Rupprecht, the same blighter I was trying to do in at Loos. That was an irony which Peter unfortunately could not appreciate. If he could he would have enjoyed it.

The little chap saw us back to our hotel, and was with us the next morning after breakfast, bringing the steamer tickets. We got on board about two in the afternoon, but on my advice he did not see us off. I told him that, being British subjects and rebels at that, we did not want to run any risks on board, assuming a British cruiser caught us up and searched us. But Peter took twenty pounds off him for travelling expenses, it being his rule never to miss an opportunity of spoiling the Egyptians.

As we were dropping down the Tagus we passed the old *Henry the Navigator*.

"I met Sloggett in the street this morning," said Peter, "and he told me a little German man had been off in a boat at daybreak looking up the passenger list. Yon was a right notion of yours, Cornelis. I am glad we are going among Germans. They are careful people whom it is a pleasure to meet."

CHAPTER 4

Adventures of Two Dutchmen on the Loose

T HE GERMANS, as Peter said, are a careful people. A man met us on the quay at Rotterdam. I was a bit afraid that something might have turned up in Lisbon to discredit us, and that our little friend might have warned his pals by telegram. But apparently all was serene.

Peter and I had made our plans pretty carefully on the voyage. We had talked nothing but Dutch, and had kept up between ourselves the rôle of Maritz's men, which Peter said was the only way to play a part well. Upon my soul, before we got to Holland I was not very clear in my own mind what my past had been. Indeed the danger was that the other side of my mind, which should be busy with the great problem, would get atrophied, and that I should soon be mentally on a par with the ordinary backveld desperado. We had agreed that it would be best to get into Germany at once, and when the agent on the quay told us of a train at midday we decided to take it.

I had another fit of cold feet before we got over the frontier. At the station there was a King's Messenger whom I had seen in France, and a war correspondent who had been trotting round our part of the front before Loos. I heard a woman speaking pretty clean-cut English, which amid the hoarse Dutch jabber sounded like a lark among crows. There were copies of the English papers for sale, and English cheap editions. I felt pretty bad about the whole business, and wondered if I should ever see these homely sights again.

But the mood passed when the train started. It was a clear blowing day, and as we crawled through the flat pastures of Holland my time was taken up answering Peter's questions. He had never been in Europe before, and formed a high opinion of the farming. He said he reckoned that such land would carry four sheep a morgen. We were thick in talk when we reached the frontier station and jolted over a canal bridge into Germany.

I had expected a big barricade with barbed wire and entrenchments. But there was nothing to see on the German side but half a dozen sentries in the field-grey I had hunted at Loos. An under-officer, with the black-and-gold button of the Landsturm, hoicked us out of the train, and we were all shepherded in a big bare waiting-room where a large stove burned. They took us two at a time into an inner room for examination. I had explained to Peter all about this formality, but I was glad we went in together, for they made us strip to the skin, and I had to curse him pretty seriously to make him keep quiet. The men who did the job were fairly civil, but they were mighty thorough. They took down a list of all we had in our pockets and bags, and all the details from the passports the Rotterdam agent had given us.

We were dressing when a man in a lieutenant's uniform came in with a paper in his hand. He was a fresh-faced lad of about twenty, with short-sighted spectacled eyes.

"Herr Brandt," he called out.

I nodded.

"And this is Herr Pienaar?" he asked in Dutch.

He saluted. "Gentlemen, I apologize. I am late because of the slowness of the Herr Commandant's motor-car. Had I been in time you would not have been required to go through this ceremony. We have been advised of your coming, and I am instructed to attend you on your journey. The train for Berlin leaves in half an hour. Pray do me the honour to join me in a bock."

With a feeling of distinction we stalked out of the ordinary ruck of passengers and followed the lieutenant to the station restaurant. He plunged at once into conversation, talking the Dutch of Holland, which Peter, who had forgotten his schooldays, found a bit hard to follow. He was unfit for active service, because of his eyes and a weak heart, but he was a desperate fire-eater in that stuffy restaurant. By his way of it Germany could gobble up the French and the Russians whenever she cared, but she was aiming at getting all the Middle East in her hands first, so that she could come out conqueror with the practical control of half the world.

"Your friends the English," he said grinning, "will come last. When we have starved them and destroyed their commerce with our under-sea boats we will show them what our navy can do. For a year they have been wasting their time in brag and politics, and we have been building great ships—oh, so many! My cousin at Kiel—" and he looked over his shoulder.

But we never heard about that cousin at Kiel. A short sunburnt man came in and our friend sprang up and saluted, clicking his heels like a pair of tongs.

"These are the South African Dutch, Herr Captain," he said.

The new-comer looked us over with bright intelligent eyes, and started questioning Peter in the *taal*. It was well that we had taken some pains with our story, for this man had been years in German South West, and knew every mile of the borders. Zorn was his name, and both Peter and I thought we remembered hearing him spoken of.

I am thankful to say that we both showed up pretty well. Peter told his story to perfection, not pitching it too high, and asking me now and then for a name or to verify some detail. Captain Zorn looked satisfied.

"You seem the right kind of fellows," he said. "But remember" —and he bent his brows on us—"we do not understand slimness in this land. If you are honest you will be rewarded, but if you dare to play a double game you will be shot like dogs. Your race has produced over many traitors for my taste."

"I ask no reward," I said gruffly. "We are not Germans or Germany's slaves. But so long as she fights against England we will fight for her."

"Bold words," he said; "but you must bow your stiff necks to discipline first. Discipline has been the weak point of you Boers, and you have suffered for it. You are no more a nation. In Germany we put discipline first and last, and therefore we will conquer the world. Off with you now. Your train starts in three minutes. We will see what von Stumm will make of you."

That fellow gave me the best "feel" of any German I had yet met. He was a white man and I could have worked with him. I liked his stiff chin and steady blue eyes.

My chief recollection of our journey to Berlin was its commonplaceness. The spectacled lieutenant fell asleep, and for the most part we had the carriage to ourselves. Now and again a soldier on leave would drop in, most of them tired men with heavy eyes. No wonder, poor devils, for they were coming back from the Yser or the Ypres salient. I would have liked to talk to them, but officially of course I knew no German, and the conversation I overheard did not signify much. It was mostly about regimental details, though one chap, who was in better spirits than the rest, observed that this was the last Christmas of misery, and that next year he would be holidaying at home with full pockets. The others assented, but without much conviction.

The winter day was short, and most of the journey was made in the dark. I could see from the window the lights of little villages, and now and then the blaze of ironworks and forges. We stopped at a town for dinner, where the platform was crowded with drafts waiting to go westward. We saw no signs of any scarcity of food, such as the English newspapers wrote about. We had an excellent dinner at the station restaurant, which, with a bottle of white wine, cost just three shillings apiece. The bread, to be sure, was poor, but I can put up with the absence of bread if I get a juicy fillet of beef and as good vegetables as you will see in the Savoy.

I was a little afraid of our giving ourselves away in our sleep, but I need have had no fear, for our escort slumbered like a hog with his mouth wide open. As we roared through the darkness I kept pinching myself to make myself feel that I was in the enemy's land on a wild mission. The rain came on, and we passed through dripping towns, with the lights shining from the wet streets. As we went eastward the lighting seemed to grow more generous. After the murk of London it was queer to slip through garish stations with a hundred arc lights glowing, and to see long lines of lamps running to the horizon. Peter dropped off early, but I kept awake till midnight, trying to focus thoughts that persistently strayed. Then I, too, dozed, and did not awake till about five in the morning, when we ran into a great busy terminus as bright as midday. It was the easiest and most unsuspicious journey I ever made.

The lieutenant stretched himself and smoothed his rumpled uniform. We carried our scanty luggage to a *droschke*, for there seemed to be no porters. Our escort gave the address of some hotel and we rumbled out into brightly lit empty streets.

"A mighty dorp," said Peter. "Of a truth the Germans are a great people."

The lieutenant nodded good-humouredly.

"The greatest people on earth," he said, "as their enemies will soon bear witness."

I would have given a lot for a bath, but I felt that it would be outside my part, and Peter was not of the washing persuasion. But we had a very good breakfast of coffee and eggs, and then the lieutenant started on the telephone. He began by being dictatorial, then he seemed to be switched on to higher authorities, for he grew more polite, and at the end he fairly crawled. He made some arrangements, for he informed us that in the afternoon we would see some fellow whose title he could not translate into Dutch. I judged he was a great swell, for his voice became reverential at the mention of him.

He took us for a walk that morning after Peter and I had attended to our toilets. We were an odd pair of scallywags to look at, but as South African as a wait-a-bit bush. Both of us had ready-made tweed suits, grey flannel shirts with flannel collars, and felt hats with broader brims than they like in Europe. I had strong nailed brown boots, Peter a pair of those mustard-coloured abominations which the Portuguese affect and which made him hobble like a Chinese lady. He had a scarlet satin tie which you could hear a mile off. My beard had grown to quite a respectable length, and I trimmed it like General Smuts'. Peter's was the kind of loose flapping thing the *taakhaar* loves, which has scarcely ever been shaved, and is combed once in a blue moon. I must say we made a pretty solid pair. Any South African would have set us down as a Boer from the backveld who had bought a suit of clothes in the nearest store, and his cousin from some one-horse dorp who had been to school and thought himself the devil of a fellow. We fairly reeked of the sub-continent, as the papers call it.

It was a fine morning after the rain, and we wandered about in the streets for a couple of hours. They were busy enough, and the shops looked rich and bright with their Christmas goods, and one big store where I went to buy a pocket-knife was packed with customers. One didn't see very many young men, and most of the women wore mourning. Uniforms were everywhere, but their wearers generally looked like dug-outs or office fellows. We had a glimpse of the squat building which housed the General Staff and took off our hats to it. Then we stared at the Marinamt, and I wondered what plots were hatching there behind old Tirpitz's whiskers. The capital gave one an impression of ugly cleanness and a sort of dreary effectiveness. And yet

I found it depressing—more depressing than London. I don't know how to put it, but the whole big concern seemed to have no soul in it, to be like a big factory instead of a city. You won't make a factory look like a house, though you decorate its front and plant rose-bushes all round it. The place depressed and yet cheered me. It somehow made the German people seem smaller.

At three o'clock the lieutenant took us to a plain white building in a side street with sentries at the door. A young staff officer met us and made us wait for five minutes in an ante-room. Then we were ushered into a big room with a polished floor on which Peter nearly sat down. There was a log fire burning, and seated at a table was a little man in spectacles with his hair brushed back from his brow like a popular violinist. He was the boss, for the lieutenant saluted him and announced our names. Then he disappeared, and the man at the table motioned us to sit down in two chairs before him.

"Herr Brandt and Herr Pienaar?" he asked, looking over his glasses.

But it was the other man that caught my eye. He stood with his back to the fire leaning his elbows on the mantelpiece. He was a perfect mountain of a fellow, six and a half feet if he was an inch, with shoulders on him like a shorthorn bull. He was in uniform, and the black-and-white ribbon of the Iron Cross showed at a buttonhole. His tunic was all wrinkled and strained as if it could scarcely contain his huge chest, and mighty hands were clasped over his stomach. That man must have had the length of reach of a gorilla. He had a great, lazy, smiling face, with a square cleft chin which stuck out beyond the rest. His brow retreated and the stubby back of his head ran forward to meet it, while his neck below bulged out over his collar. His head was exactly the shape of a pear with the sharp end topmost.

He stared at me with his small bright eyes and I stared back. I had struck something I had been looking for for a long time, and till that moment I wasn't sure that it existed. Here was the German of caricature, the real German, the fellow we were up against. He was as hideous as a hippopotamus, but effective. Every bristle on his odd head was effective.

The man at the table was speaking. I took him to be a civilian official of sorts, pretty high up from his surroundings, perhaps an Under-Secretary. His Dutch was slow and careful, but good—too good for Peter. He had a paper before him and was asking us questions from it.

BUT IT WAS THE OTHER MAN THAT CAUGHT MY EYE

They did not amount to much, being pretty well a repetition of those
Zorn had asked us at the frontier. I answered fluently, for I had all our
lies by heart.

Then the man on the hearthrug broke in. "I'll talk to them,
Excellency," he said in German. "You are too academic for these
outland swine."

He began in the *taal*, with the thick guttural accent that you get in
German South West. "You have heard of me," he said. "I am the
Colonel von Stumm who fought the Hereros."

Peter pricked up his ears. "*Ja*, Baas, you cut off the chief Baviaan's
head and sent it in pickle about the country. I have seen it."

The big man laughed. "You see I am not forgotten," he said to his
friend, and then to us: "So I treat my enemies, and so will Germany
treat hers. You, too, if you fail me by a fraction of an inch." And he
laughed loud again.

There was something horrible in that boisterousness. Peter was
watching him from below his eyelids, as I have seen him watch a lion
about to charge.

He flung himself on a chair, put his elbows on the table, and thrust
his face forward.

"You have come from a damned muddled show. If I had Maritz in
my power I would have him flogged at a wagon's end. Fools and
pig-dogs, they had the game in their hands and they flung it away. We
could have raised a fire that would have burned the English into the sea,
and for lack of fuel they let it die down. Then they try to fan it when the
ashes are cold."

He rolled a paper pellet and flicked it into the air. "That is what I
think of your idiot general," he said, "and of all you Dutch. As slow as
a fat vrouw and as greedy as an aasvogel."

We looked very glum and sullen.

"A pair of dumb dogs," he cried. "A thousand Brandenburgers
would have won in a fortnight. Seitz hadn't much to boast of, mostly
clerks and farmers and half-castes, and no soldier worth the name to
lead them, but it took Botha and Smuts and a dozen generals to hunt
him down. But Maritz!" His scorn came like a gust of wind.

"Maritz did all the fighting there was," said Peter sulkily. "At any
rate he wasn't afraid of the sight of khaki like you lot."

"Maybe he wasn't," said the giant in a cooing voice; "maybe he had his reasons for that. You Dutchmen have always a feather-bed to fall on. You can always turn traitor. Maritz now calls himself Robinson, and has a pension from his friend Botha."

"That," said Peter, "is a very damned lie."

"I asked for information," said Stumm with a sudden politeness. "But that is all past and done with. Maritz matters no more than your old Cronjes and Krugers. The show is over, and you are looking for safety. For a new master perhaps? But, man, what can you bring? What can you offer? You and your Dutch are lying in the dust with the yoke on your necks. The Pretoria lawyers have talked you round. You see that map," and he pointed to a big one on the wall. "South Africa is coloured green. Not red for the English, or yellow for the Germans. Some day it will be yellow, but for a little it will be green—the colour of neutrals, of nothings, of boys and young ladies and chicken-hearts."

I kept wondering what he was playing at.

Then he fixed his eyes on Peter. "What do you come here for? The game's up in your own country. What can you offer us Germans? If we gave you ten million marks and sent you back you could do nothing. Stir up a village row, perhaps, and shoot a policeman. South Africa is counted out in this war. Botha is a cleverish man and has beaten you calves'-heads of rebels. Can you deny it?"

Peter couldn't. He was terribly honest in some things, and these were for certain his opinions.

"No," he said, "that is true, Baas."

"Then what in God's name can you do?" shouted Stumm.

Peter mumbled some foolishness about nobbling Angola for Germany and starting a revolution among the natives. Stumm flung up his arms and cursed, and the Under-Secretary laughed.

It was high time for me to chip in. I was beginning to see the kind of fellow this Stumm was, and as he talked I thought of my mission, which had got overlaid by my Boer past. It looked as if he might be useful.

"Let me speak," I said. "My friend is a great hunter, but he fights better than he talks. He is no politician. You speak truth. South Africa is a closed door for the present, and the key to it is elsewhere. Here in Europe, and in the East, and in other parts of Africa. We have come to help you to find the key."

Stumm was listening. "Go on, my little Boer. It will be a new thing to hear a *taakhaar* on world-politics."

"You are fighting," I said, "in East Africa; and soon you may fight in Egypt. All the east coast north of the Zambesi will be your battle-ground. The English run about the world with little expeditions. I do not know where the places are, though I read of them in the papers. But I know my Africa. You want to beat them here in Europe and on the seas. Therefore, like wise generals, you try to divide them and have them scattered throughout the globe while you stick at home. That is your plan?"

"A second Falkenhayn," said Stumm, laughing.

"Well, England will not let East Africa go. She fears for Egypt and she fears, too, for India. If you press her there she will send armies and more armies till she is so weak in Europe that a child can crush her. That is England's way. She cares more for her Empire than for what may happen to her allies. So I say press and still press there, destroy the railway to the Lakes, burn her capital, pen up every Englishman in Mombasa island. At this moment it is worth for you a thousand Damaralands."

The man was really interested and the Under-Secretary, too, pricked up his ears.

"We can keep our territory," said the former; "but as for pressing, how the devil are we to press? The accursed English hold the sea. We cannot ship men or guns there. South are the Portuguese and west the Belgians. You cannot move a mass without a lever."

"The lever is there, ready for you," I said.

"Then for God's sake show it me," he cried.

I looked at the door to see that it was shut, as if what I had to say was very secret.

"You need men, and the men are waiting. They are black, but they are the stuff of warriors. All round your borders you have the remains of great fighting tribes, the Angoni, the Masai, the Manyumwezi, and above all the Somalis of the north, and the dwellers on the Upper Nile. The British recruit their black regiments there, and so do you. But to get recruits is not enough. You must set whole nations moving, as the Zulu under Tchaka flowed over South Africa."

"It cannot be done," said the Under-Secretary.

"It can be done," I said quietly. "We two are here to do it."

This kind of talk was jolly difficult for me, chiefly because of Stumm's asides in German to the official. I had, above all things, to get the credit of knowing no German, and, if you understand a language well, it is not very easy when you are interrupted not to show that you know it, either by a direct answer, or by referring to the interruption in what you say next. I had to be always on my guard, and yet it was up to me to be very persuasive and convince these fellows that I would be useful. Somehow or other I had to get into their confidence.

"I have been for years up and down in Africa—Uganda and the Congo and the Upper Nile. I know the ways of the Kaffir as no Englishman does. We Afrikanders see into the black man's heart, and though he may hate us he does our will. You Germans are like the English; you are too big folk to understand plain men. 'Civilize,' you cry. 'Educate,' say the English. The black man obeys and puts away his gods, but he worships them all the time in his soul. We must get his gods on our side, and then he will move mountains. We must do as John Laputa did with Sheba's necklace."

"That's all in the air," said Stumm, but he did not laugh.

"It is sober common sense," I said. "But you must begin at the right end. First find the race that fears its priests. It is waiting for you—the Mussulmans of Somaliland and the Abyssinian border and the Blue and White Nile. They would be like dried grasses to catch fire if you used the flint and steel of their religion. Look what the English suffered from a crazy mullah who ruled only a dozen villages. Once get the flames going and they will lick up the pagans of the west and south. That is the way of Africa. How many thousands, think you, were in the Mahdi's army who never heard of the Prophet till they saw the black flags of the Emirs going into battle?"

Stumm was smiling. He turned his face to the official and spoke with his hand over his mouth, but I caught his words. They were: "This is the man for Hilda." The other pursed his lips and looked a little scared.

Stumm rang a bell and the lieutenant came in and clicked his heels. He nodded towards Peter. "Take this man away with you. We have done with him. The other fellow will follow presently."

Peter went out with a puzzled face and Stumm turned to me.

"You are a dreamer, Brandt," he said. "But I do not reject you on that account. Dreams sometimes come true, when an army follows the visionary. But who is going to kindle the flame?"

"You," I said.

"What the devil do you mean?" he asked.

"That is your part. You are the cleverest people in the world. You have already half the Mussulman lands in your power. It is for you to show us how to kindle a Holy War, for clearly you have the secret of it. Never fear but we will carry out your order."

"We have no secret," he said shortly, and glanced at the official, who stared out of the window.

I dropped my jaw and looked the picture of disappointment. "I do not believe you," I said slowly. "You play a game with me. I have not come six thousand miles to be made a fool of."

"Discipline, by God," Stumm cried. "This is none of your ragged commandos." In two strides he was above me and had lifted me out of my seat. His great hands clutched my shoulders, and his thumbs gouged my armpits. I felt as if I were in the grip of a big ape. Then very slowly he shook me so that my teeth seemed loosened and my head swam. He let me go and I dropped limply back in the chair.

"Now, go! *Futsack!* And remember that I am your master. I, Ulric von Stumm, who owns you as a Kaffir owns his mongrel. Germany may have some use for you, my friend, when you fear me as you never feared your God."

As I walked dizzily away the big man was smiling in his horrible way, and that little official was blinking and smiling too. I had struck a dashed queer country, so queer that I had had no time to remember that for the first time in my life I had been bullied without hitting back. When I realized it I nearly choked with anger. But I thanked Heaven I had shown no temper, for I remembered my mission. Luck seemed to have brought me into useful company.

CHAPTER 5

Further Adventures of the Same

NEXT MORNING there was a touch of frost and a nip in the air which stirred my blood and put me in buoyant spirits. I forgot my precarious position and the long road I had still to travel. I came down to breakfast in great form, to find Peter's even temper badly ruffled. He had remembered Stumm in the night and disliked the memory; this he muttered to me as we rubbed shoulders at the dining-room door. Peter and I got no opportunity for private talk. The lieutenant was with us all the time, and at night we were locked in our rooms. Peter discovered this through trying to get out to find matches, for he had the bad habit of smoking in bed.

Our guide started on the telephone, and announced that we were to be taken to see a prisoners' camp. In the afternoon I was to go somewhere with Stumm, but the morning was for sightseeing. "You will see," he told us, "how merciful is a great people. You will also see some of the hated English in our power. That will delight you. They are the forerunners of all their nation."

We drove in a taxi through the suburbs and then over a stretch of flat market-garden-like country to a low rise of wooded hills. After an hour's ride we entered the gate of what looked like a big reformatory or hospital. I believe it had been a home for destitute children. There were sentries at the gate and massive concentric circles of barbed wire through which we passed under an arch that was let down like a portcullis at nightfall. The lieutenant showed his permit, and we ran the car into a brick-paved yard and marched through a lot more sentries to the office of the commandant.

He was away from home, and we were welcomed by his deputy, a pale young man with a head nearly bald. There were introductions in German which our guide translated into Dutch, and a lot of elegant

166

speeches about how Germany was foremost in humanity as well as martial valour. Then they stood us sandwiches and beer, and we formed a procession for a tour of inspection. There were two doctors, both mild-looking men in spectacles, and a couple of warders—under-officers of the good old burly, bullying sort I knew well. That was the cement which kept the German army together. Her men were nothing to boast of on the average; no more were the officers, even in crack corps like the Guards and the Brandenburgers; but they seemed to have an inexhaustible supply of hard, competent N.C.O.s.

We marched round the wash-houses, the recreation-ground, the kitchens, the hospital—with nobody in it save one chap with the 'flu. It didn't seem to be badly done. This place was entirely for officers, and I expect it was a show place where American visitors were taken. If half the stories one heard were true there were some pretty ghastly prisons away in South and East Germany.

I didn't half like the business. To be a prisoner has always seemed to me about the worst thing that could happen to a man. The sight of German prisoners used to give me a bad feeling inside, whereas I looked at dead Boches with nothing but satisfaction. Besides, there was the off-chance that I might be recognized. So I kept very much in the shadow whenever we passed anybody in the corridors. The few we met passed us incuriously. They saluted the deputy-commandant, but scarcely wasted a glance on us. No doubt they thought we were inquisitive Germans come to gloat over them. They looked fairly fit, but a little puffy about the eyes, like men who get too little exercise. They seemed thin, too. I expect the food, for all the commandant's talk, was nothing to boast of. In one room people were writing letters. It was a big place with only a tiny stove to warm it, and the windows were shut so that the atmosphere was a cold frowst. In another room a fellow was lecturing on something to a dozen hearers and drawing figures on a blackboard. Some were in ordinary khaki, others in any old thing they could pick up, and most wore greatcoats. Your blood gets thin when you have nothing to do but hope against hope and think of your pals and the old days.

I was moving along, listening with half an ear to the lieutenant's prattle and the loud explanations of the deputy-commandant, when I pitchforked into what might have been the end of my business. We were going through a sort of convalescent room, where people were sitting who had been in hospital. It was a big place, a little warmer than the rest of the building, but still abominably fuggy. There were about half a dozen men in the room, reading and playing games. They looked at us with lack-lustre eyes for a moment, and then returned to their occupations. Being convalescents I suppose they were not expected to get up and salute.

All but one, who was playing Patience at a little table by which we passed. I was feeling very bad about the thing, for I hated to see these good fellows locked away in this infernal German hole when they might have been giving the Boche his deserts at the front. The commandant went first with Peter, who had developed a great interest in prisons. Then came our lieutenant with one of the doctors; then a couple of warders; and then the second doctor and myself. I was absent-minded at the moment and was last in the queue.

The Patience-player suddenly looked up and I saw his face. I'm hanged if it wasn't Dolly Riddell, who was our brigade machine-gun officer at Loos. I had heard that the Germans had got him when they blew up a mine at the Quarries.

I had to act pretty quick, for his mouth was agape, and I saw he was going to speak. The doctor was a yard ahead of me.

I stumbled and spilt his cards on the floor. Then I kneeled to pick them up and gripped his knee. His head bent to help me and I spoke low in his ear.

"I'm Hannay all right. For God's sake don't wink an eye. I'm here on a secret job."

The doctor had turned to see what was the matter. I got a few more words in. "Cheer up, old man. We're winning hands down."

Then I began to talk excited Dutch and finished the collection of the cards. Dolly was playing his part well, smiling as if he was amused by the antics of a monkey. The others were coming back, the deputy-commandant with an angry light in his dull eye. "Speaking to the prisoners is forbidden," he shouted.

I looked blankly at him till the lieutenant translated.

"What kind of fellow is he?" said Dolly in English to the doctor. "He spoils my game and then jabbers High-Dutch at me."

Officially I knew English, and that speech of Dolly's gave me my cue. I pretended to be very angry with the very damned Englishman, and went out of the room close by the deputy-commandant, grumbling like a sick jackal. After that I had to act a bit. The last place we visited was the close-confinement part where prisoners were kept as a punishment for some breach of the rules. They looked cheerless enough, but I pretended to gloat over the sight, and said so to the lieutenant, who passed it on to the others. I have rarely in my life felt such a cad.

On the way home the lieutenant discoursed a lot about prisoners and detention-camps, for at one time he had been on duty at Ruhleben. Peter, who had been in quod more than once in his life, was deeply interested and kept on questioning him. Among other things he told us was that they often put bogus prisoners among the rest, who acted as spies. If any plot to escape was hatched these fellows got into it and encouraged it. They never interfered till the attempt was actually made and then they had them on toast. There was nothing the Boche liked so much as an excuse for sending a poor devil to "solitary".

THAT AFTERNOON Peter and I separated. He was left behind with the lieutenant and I was sent off to the station with my bag in the company of a Landsturm sergeant. Peter was very cross, and I didn't care for the look of things; but I brightened up when I heard I was going somewhere with Stumm. If he wanted to see me again he must think me of some use, and if he was going to use me he was bound to let me into his game. I liked Stumm about as much as a dog likes a scorpion, but I hankered for his society.

At the station platform, where the ornament of the Landsturm saved me all the trouble about tickets, I could not see my companion. I stood waiting, while a great crowd, mostly of soldiers, swayed past me and filled all the front carriages. An officer spoke to me gruffly and told me to stand aside behind a wooden rail. I obeyed, and suddenly found Stumm's eyes looking down at me.

"You know German?" he asked sharply.

"A dozen words," I said carelessly. "I've been to Windhuk and learned enough to ask for my dinner. Peter—my friend—speaks it a bit."

"So," said Stumm. "Well, get into the carriage. Not that one! There, thickhead!"

I did as I was bid, he followed, and the door was locked behind us. The precaution was needless, for the sight of Stumm's profile at the platform end would have kept out the most brazen. I wondered if I had woken up his suspicions. I must be on my guard to show no signs of intelligence if he suddenly tried me in German, and that wouldn't be easy, for I knew it as well as I knew Dutch.

We moved into the country, but the windows were blurred with frost, and I saw nothing of the landscape. Stumm was busy with papers and let me alone. I read on a notice that one was forbidden to smoke, so to show my ignorance of German I pulled out my pipe. Stumm raised his head, saw what I was doing, and gruffly bade me put it away, as if he were an old lady that disliked the smell of tobacco.

In half an hour I got very bored, for I had nothing to read and my pipe was *verboten*. People passed now and then in the corridors, but no one offered to enter. No doubt they saw the big figure in uniform and thought he was the deuce of a staff swell who wanted solitude. I thought of stretching my legs in the corridor, and was just getting up to do it when somebody slid the door back and a big figure blocked the light.

He was wearing a heavy ulster and a green felt hat. He saluted Stumm, who looked up angrily, and smiled pleasantly on us both.

"Say, gentlemen," he said, "have you room in here for a little one? I guess I'm about smoked out of my car by your brave soldiers. I've gotten a delicate stomach . . ."

Stumm had risen with a brow of wrath, and looked as if he were going to pitch the intruder off the train. Then he seemed to halt and collect himself, and the other's face broke into a friendly grin.

"Why, it's Colonel Stumm," he cried. (He pronounced it like the first syllable in "stomach".) "Very pleased to meet you again, Colonel. I had the honour of making your acquaintance at our Embassy. I reckon Ambassador Gerard didn't cotton to our conversation that night." And the new-comer plumped himself down in the corner opposite me.

I had been pretty certain I would run across Blenkiron somewhere in Germany, but I didn't think it would be so soon. There he sat staring at me with his full, unseeing eyes, rolling out platitudes to Stumm, who was nearly bursting in his effort to keep civil. I looked moody and suspicious, which I took to be the right line.

"Things are getting a bit dead at Salonika," said Mr Blenkiron, by way of a conversational opening.

Stumm pointed to a notice which warned officers to refrain from discussing military operations with mixed company in a railway carriage.

"Sorry," said Blenkiron, "I can't read that tombstone language of yours. But I reckon that that notice to trespassers, whatever it signifies, don't apply to you and me. I take it this gentleman is in your party."

I sat and scowled, fixing the American with suspicious eyes.

"He is a Dutchman," said Stumm; "South African Dutch, and he is not happy, for he doesn't like to hear English spoken."

"We'll shake on that," said Blenkiron cordially. "But who said I spoke English? It's good American. Cheer up, friend, for it isn't the call that makes the big wapiti, as they say out west in my country. I hate John Bull worse than a poison rattle. The Colonel can tell you that."

I dare say he could, but at that moment we slowed down at a station and Stumm got up to leave. "Good day to you, Herr Blenkiron," he cried over his shoulder. "If you consider your comfort, don't talk English to strange travellers. They don't distinguish between the different brands."

I followed him in a hurry, but was recalled by Blenkiron's voice.

"Say, friend," he shouted, "you've left your grip," and he handed me my bag from the luggage rack. But he showed no sign of recognition, and the last I saw of him was sitting sunk in a corner with his head on his chest as if he were going to sleep. He was a man who kept up his parts well.

THERE WAS A MOTOR-CAR waiting—one of the grey military kind— and we started at a terrific pace over bad forest roads. Stumm had put away his papers in a portfolio, and flung me a few sentences on the journey.

"I haven't made up my mind about you, Brandt," he announced. "You may be a fool or a knave or a good man. If you are a knave, we will shoot you."

"And if I am a fool?" I asked.

"Send you to the Yser or the Dvina. You will be respectable cannon-fodder."

"You cannot do that unless I consent," I said.

"Can't we?" he said, smiling wickedly. "Remember you are a citizen of nowhere. Technically, you are a rebel, and the British, if you go to them, will hang you, supposing they have any sense. You are in our power, my friend, to do precisely what we like with you." He was silent for a second, and then he said, meditatively:

"But I don't think you are a fool. You may be a scoundrel. Some kinds of scoundrel are useful enough. Other kinds are strung up with a rope. Of that we shall know more soon."

"And if I am a good man?"

"You will be given a chance to serve Germany, the proudest privilege a mortal man can have." The strange man said this with a ringing sincerity in his voice that impressed me.

The car swung out from the trees into a park lined with saplings, and in the twilight I saw before me a biggish house like an overgrown Swiss chalet. There was a kind of archway with a sham portcullis, and a terrace with battlements which looked as if they were made of stucco. We drew up at a Gothic front door, where a thin middle-aged man in a shooting jacket was waiting.

As we moved into the lighted hall I got a good look at our host. He was very lean and brown, with the stoop in the shoulder that one gets from being constantly on horseback. He had untidy grizzled hair and a ragged beard, and a pair of pleasant, short-sighted brown eyes.

"Welcome, my Colonel," he said. "Is this the friend you spoke of?"

"This is the Dutchman," said Stumm. "His name is Brandt. Brandt, you see before you Herr Gaudian."

I knew the name, of course; there weren't many in my profession that didn't. He was one of the biggest railway engineers in the world, the man who had built the Bagdad and Syrian railways, and the new lines in German East. I suppose he was about the greatest living authority on tropical construction. He knew the East and he knew Africa; clearly I had been brought down for him to put me through my paces.

A blonde maidservant took me to my room, which had a bare polished floor, a stove, and windows that, unlike most of the German kind I had sampled, seemed made to open. When I had washed I descended to the hall, which was hung round with trophies of travel, like Dervish jibbahs and Masai shields and one or two good buffalo heads. Presently a bell was rung. Stumm appeared with his host, and we went in to supper.

I was jolly hungry and would have made a good meal if I hadn't constantly had to keep jogging my wits. The other two talked in

German, and when a question was put to me Stumm translated. The first thing I had to do was to pretend I didn't know German and look listlessly round the room while they were talking. The second was to miss not a word, for there lay my chance. The third was to be ready to answer questions at any moment, and to show in the answering that I had not followed the previous conversation. Likewise, I must not prove myself a fool in these answers, for I had to convince them that I was useful. It took some doing, and I felt like a witness in a box under a stiff cross-examination, or a man trying to play three games of chess at once.

I heard Stumm telling Gaudian the gist of my plan. The engineer shook his head.

"Too late," he said. "It should have been done at the beginning. We neglected Africa. You know the reason why."

Stumm laughed. "The von Einem! Perhaps, but her charm works well enough."

Gaudian glanced towards me while I was busy with an orange salad. "I have much to tell you of that. But it can wait. Your friend is right in one thing. Uganda is a vital spot for the English, and a blow there will make their whole fabric shiver. But how can we strike? They have still the coast, and our supplies grow daily smaller."

"We can send no reinforcements, but have we used all the local resources? That is what I cannot satisfy myself about. Zimmerman says we have, but Tressler thinks differently, and now we have this fellow coming out of the void with a story which confirms my doubt. He seems to know his job. You try him."

Thereupon Gaudian set about questioning me, and his questions were very thorough. I knew just enough and no more to get through, but I think I came out with credit. You see I have a capacious memory, and in my time I had met scores of hunters and pioneers and listened to their yarns, so I could pretend to knowledge of a place even when I hadn't been there. Besides, I had once been on the point of undertaking a job up Tanganyika way, and I had got up that countryside pretty accurately.

"You say that with our help you can make trouble for the British on the three borders?" Gaudian asked at length.

"I can spread the fire if someone else will kindle it," I said.

"But there are thousands of tribes with no affinities."

"They are all African. You can bear me out. All African peoples are alike in one thing—they can go mad, and the madness of one infects the others. The English know this well enough."

"Where would you start the fire?" he asked.

"Where the fuel is dryest. Up in the North among the Mussulman peoples. But there you must help me. I know nothing about Islam, and I gather that you do."

"Why?" he asked.

"Because of what you have done already," I answered.

Stumm had translated all this time, and had given the sense of my words very fairly. But with my last answer he took liberties. What he gave was: "Because the Dutchman thinks that we have some big card in dealing with the Moslem world." Then, lowering his voice and raising his eyebrows, he said some word like "Uhnmantl".

The other looked with a quick glance of apprehension at me. "We had better continue our talk in private, Herr Colonel," he said. "If Herr Brandt will forgive us, we will leave him for a little to entertain himself." He pushed the cigar-box towards me and the two got up and left the room.

I pulled my chair up to the stove, and would have liked to drop off to sleep. The tension of the talk at supper had made me very tired. I was accepted by these men for exactly what I professed to be. Stumm might suspect me of being a rascal, but it was a Dutch rascal. But all the same I was skating on thin ice. I could not sink myself utterly in the part, for if I did I would get no good out of being there. I had to keep my wits going all the time, and join the appearance and manners of a backveld Boer with the mentality of a British intelligence-officer. Any moment the two parts might clash and I would be faced with the most alert and deadly suspicion.

There would be no mercy from Stumm. That large man was beginning to fascinate me, even though I hated him. Gaudian was clearly a good fellow, a white man and a gentleman. I could have worked with him for he belonged to my own totem. But the other was an incarnation of all that makes Germany detested, and yet he wasn't altogether the ordinary German, and I couldn't help admiring him. I noticed he neither smoked nor drank. His grossness was apparently not in the way of fleshly appetites. Cruelty, from all I had heard of him in German South West, was his hobby; but there were other things in him, some of them good, and he had that kind of crazy patriotism which becomes a religion. I wondered why he had not some high command in the field, for he had had the name of a good soldier. But probably he was a big man in his own line, whatever it was, for the Under-Secretary fellow had talked small in his presence, and so great a man as Gaudian clearly respected him. There must be no lack of brains inside that funny pyramidal head.

As I sat beside the stove I was casting back to think if I had got the slightest clue to my real job. There seemed to be nothing so far. Stumm had talked of a von Einem woman who was interested in his department, perhaps the same woman as the Hilda he had mentioned the day before to the Under-Secretary. There was not much in that. She was probably some minister's or ambassador's wife who had a finger in high politics. If I could have caught the word Stumm had whispered to Gaudian which made him start and look askance at me! But I had only heard a gurgle of something like "Uhnmantl", which wasn't any German word that I knew.

The heat put me into a half-doze and I began dreamily to wonder what other people were doing. Where had Blenkiron been posting to in that train, and what was he up to at this moment? He had been hobnobbing with ambassadors and swells—I wondered if he had found out anything. What was Peter doing? I fervently hoped he was behaving himself, for I doubted if Peter had really tumbled to the delicacy of our job. Where was Sandy, too? As like as not bucketing in the hold of some Greek coaster in the Aegean. Then I thought of my battalion somewhere on the line between Hulluch and La Bassée, hammering at the Boche, while I was five hundred miles or so inside the Boche frontier.

It was a comic reflection, so comic that it woke me up. After trying in vain to find a way of stoking that stove, for it was a cold night, I got up and walked about the room. There were portraits of two decent old fellows, probably Gaudian's parents. There were enlarged photographs, too, of engineering works, and a good picture of Bismarck. And close to the stove there was a case of maps mounted on rollers.

I pulled out one at random. It was a geological map of Germany, and with some trouble I found out where I was. I was an enormous distance from my goal, and moreover I was clean off the road to the East. To go there I must first go to Bavaria and then into Austria. I noticed the

Danube flowing eastwards and remembered that that was one way to Constantinople.

Then I tried another map. This one covered a big area, all Europe from the Rhine and as far east as Persia. I guessed that it was meant to show the Bagdad railway and the through routes from Germany to Mesopotamia. There were markings on it; and, as I looked closer, I saw that there were dates scribbled in blue pencil, as if to denote the stages of a journey. The dates began in Europe, and continued right on into Asia Minor and then south to Syria.

For a moment my heart jumped, for I thought I had fallen by accident on the clue I wanted. But I never got that map examined. I heard footsteps in the corridor, and very gently I let the map roll up and turned away. When the door opened I was bending over the stove trying to get a light for my pipe.

It was Gaudian, to bid me join him and Stumm in his study.

On our way there he put a kindly hand on my shoulder. I think he thought I was bullied by Stumm and wanted to tell me that he was my friend, and he had no other language than a pat on the back.

The soldier was in his old position with his elbows on the mantelpiece and his formidable great jaw stuck out.

"Listen to me," he said. "Herr Gaudian and I are inclined to make use of you. You may be a charlatan, in which case you will be in the devil of a mess and have yourself to thank for it. If you are a rogue you will have little scope for roguery. We will see to that. If you are a fool, you will yourself suffer for it. But if you are a good man, you will have a fair chance, and if you succeed we will not forget it. To-morrow I go home and you will come with me and get your orders."

I made shift to stand at attention and salute.

Gaudian spoke in a pleasant voice, as if he wanted to atone for Stumm's imperiousness. "We are men who love our Fatherland, Herr Brandt," he said. "You are not of that Fatherland, but at least you hate its enemies. Therefore we are allies, and trust each other like allies. Our victory is ordained by God, and we are none of us more than His instruments."

Stumm translated in a sentence, and his voice was quite solemn. He held up his right hand and so did Gaudian, like a man taking an oath or a parson blessing his congregation. Then I realized something of the might of Germany. She produced good and bad, cads and gentlemen, but she could put a bit of the fanatic into them all.

CHAPTER 6

The Indiscretions of the Same

I WAS STANDING STARK NAKED next morning in that icy bedroom, trying to bathe in about a quart of water, when Stumm entered. He strode up to me and stared me in the face. I was half a head shorter than him to begin with, and a man does not feel his stoutest when he has no clothes, so he had the pull on me every way.

"I have reason to believe that you are a liar," he growled.

I pulled the bed-cover round me, for I was shivering with cold, and the German idea of a towel is a pocket-handkerchief. I own I was in a pretty blue funk.

"A liar!" he repeated. "You and that swine Pienaar."

With my best effort at surliness I asked what we had done.

"You lied, because you said you knew no German. Apparently your friend knows enough to talk treason and blasphemy."

This gave me back some heart.

"I told you I knew a dozen words. But I told you Peter could talk it a bit. I told you that yesterday at the station." Fervently I blessed my luck for that casual remark.

He evidently remembered, for his tone became a trifle more civil.

"You are a precious pair. If one of you is a scoundrel, why not the other?"

"I take no responsibility for Peter," I said. I felt I was a cad in saying it, but that was the bargain we had made at the start. "I have known him for years as a great hunter and a brave man. I know he fought well against the English. But more I cannot tell you. You have to judge him for yourself. What has he done?"

I was told, for Stumm had got it that morning on the telephone. While telling it he was kind enough to allow me to put on my trousers.

It was just the sort of thing I might have foreseen. Peter, left alone, had become first bored and then reckless. He had persuaded the lieutenant to take him out to supper at a big Berlin restaurant. There, inspired by the lights and music—novel things for a backveld hunter—and no doubt bored stiff by his company, he had proceeded to get

177

drunk. That had happened in my experience with Peter about once in every three years, and it always happened for the same reason. Peter, bored and solitary in a town, went on the spree. He had a head like a rock, but he got to the required condition by wild mixing. He was quite a gentleman in his cups, and not in the least violent, but he was apt to be very free with his tongue. And that was what occurred at the Franciscana.

He had begun by insulting the Emperor, it seemed. He drank his health, but said he reminded him of a wart-hog, and thereby scarified the lieutenant's soul. Then an officer—some tremendous swell—at an adjoining table had objected to his talking so loud, and Peter had replied insolently in respectable German. After that things became mixed. There was some kind of a fight, during which Peter calumniated the German army and all its female ancestry. How he wasn't shot or run through I can't imagine, except that the lieutenant loudly proclaimed that he was a crazy Boer. Anyhow the upshot was that Peter was marched off to gaol, and I was left in a pretty pickle.

"I don't believe a word of it," I said firmly. I had most of my clothes on now and felt more courageous. "It is all a plot to get him into disgrace and draft him off to the front."

Stumm did not storm as I expected, but smiled.

"That was always his destiny," he said, "ever since I saw him. He was no use to us except as a man with a rifle. Cannon-fodder, nothing else. Do you imagine, you fool, that this great Empire in the thick of a world-war is going to trouble its head to lay snares for an ignorant *taakhaar*?"

"I wash my hands of him," I said. "If what you say of his folly is true I have no part in it. But he was my companion and I wish him well. What do you propose to do with him?"

"We will keep him under our eye," he said, with a wicked twist of the mouth. "I have a notion that there is more at the back of this than appears. We will investigate the antecedents of Herr Pienaar. And you, too, my friend. On you also we have our eye."

I did the best thing I could have done, for what with anxiety and disgust I lost my temper.

"Look here, sir," I cried, "I've had about enough of this. I came to Germany abominating the English and burning to strike a blow for you.

But you haven't given me much cause to love you. For the last two days I've had nothing from you but suspicion and insult. The only decent man I've met is Herr Gaudian. It's because I believe that there are many in Germany like him that I'm prepared to go on with this business and do the best I can. But, by God, I wouldn't raise my little finger for your sake."

He looked at me very steadily for a minute. "That sounds like honesty," he said at last in a civil voice. "You had better come down and get your coffee."

I was safe for the moment but in very low spirits. What on earth would happen to poor old Peter? I could do nothing even if I wanted, and, besides, my first duty was to my mission. I had made this very clear to him at Lisbon and he had agreed, but all the same it was a beastly reflection. Here was the ancient worthy left to the tender mercies of the people he most detested on earth. My only comfort was that they couldn't do very much with him. If they sent him to the front, which was the worst they could do, he would escape, for I would have backed him to get through any mortal lines. It wasn't much fun for me either. Only when I was to be deprived of it did I realize how much his company had meant to me. I was absolutely alone now, and I didn't like it. I seemed to have about as much chance of joining Blenkiron and Sandy as of flying to the moon.

After breakfast I was told to get ready. When I asked where I was going Stumm advised me to mind my own business, but I remembered that last night he had talked of taking me home with him and giving me my orders. I wondered where his home was.

Gaudian patted me on the back when we started and wrung my hand. He was a capital good fellow, and it made me feel sick to think that I was humbugging him. We got into the same big grey car, with Stumm's servant sitting beside the chauffeur. It was a morning of hard frost, the bare fields were white with rime, and the fir-trees powdered like a wedding-cake. We took a different road from the night before, and after a run of half a dozen miles came to a little town with a big railway station. It was a junction on some main line, and after five minutes' waiting we found our train.

Once again we were alone in the carriage. Stumm must have had some colossal graft, for the train was crowded.

I had another three hours of complete boredom. I dared not smoke, and could do nothing but stare out of the window. We soon got into hilly country, where a good deal of snow was lying. It was the 23rd day of December, and even in war time one had a sort of feel of Christmas. You could see girls carrying evergreens, and when we stopped at a station the soldiers on leave had all the air of holiday making. The middle of Germany was a cheerier place than Berlin or the western parts. I liked the look of the old peasants, and the women in their neat Sunday best, but I noticed, too, how pinched they were. Here in the country, where no neutral tourists came, there was not the same stage-management as in the capital.

Stumm made no attempt to talk to me on the journey. I could see his aim. Before this he had cross-examined me, but now he wanted to draw me into ordinary conversation. He had no notion how to do it. He was either peremptory and provocative, like a drill-sergeant, or so obviously diplomatic that any fool would have been put on his guard. That is the weakness of the German. He has no gift for laying himself alongside different types of men. He is such a hard-shell being that he cannot put out feelers to his kind. He may have plenty of brains, as Stumm had, but he has the poorest notion of psychology of any of God's creatures. In Germany only the Jew can get outside himself, and that is why, if you look into the matter, you will find that the Jew is at the back of most German enterprises.

After midday we stopped at a station for luncheon. We had a very good meal in the restaurant, and when we were finishing two officers entered. Stumm got up and saluted and went aside to talk to them. Then he came back and made me follow him to a waiting-room, where he told me to stay till he fetched me. I noticed that he called a porter and had the door locked when he went out.

It was a chilly place with no fire, and I kicked my heels there for twenty minutes. I was living by the hour now, and did not trouble to worry about this strange behaviour. There was a volume of time-tables on a shelf, and I turned the pages idly till I struck a big railway map. Then it occurred to me to find out where we were going. I had heard Stumm take my ticket for a place called Schwandorf, and after a lot of searching I found it. It was away south in Bavaria, and so far as I could make out less than fifty miles from the Danube. That cheered me enormously. If Stumm lived there he would most likely start me off on my travels by the railway which I saw running to Vienna and then on to the East. It looked as if I might get to Constantinople after all. But I feared it would be a useless achievement, for what could I do when I got there? I was being hustled out of Germany without picking up the slenderest clue.

The door opened and Stumm entered. He seemed to have got bigger in the interval and to carry his head higher. There was a proud light, too, in his eye.

"Brandt," he said, "you are about to receive the greatest privilege that ever fell to one of your race. His Imperial Majesty is passing through here, and has halted for a few minutes. He has done me the honour to receive me, and when he heard my story he expressed a wish to see you. You will follow me to his presence. Do not be afraid. The All-Highest is merciful and gracious. Answer his questions like a man."

I followed him with a quickened pulse. Here was a bit of luck I had never dreamed of. At the far side of the station a train had drawn up, a train consisting of three big coaches, chocolate-coloured and picked out with gold. On the platform beside it stood a small group of officers, tall men in long grey-blue cloaks. They seemed to be mostly elderly, and one or two of the faces I thought I remembered from photographs in the picture papers.

As we approached they drew apart, and left us face to face with one man. He was a little below middle height, and all muffled in a thick coat with a fur collar. He wore a silver helmet with an eagle atop of it, and kept his left hand resting on his sword. Below the helmet was a face the colour of grey paper, from which shone curious sombre restless eyes with dark pouches beneath them. There was no fear of my mistaking him. These were the features which, since Napoleon, have been best known to the world.

I stood as stiff as a ramrod and saluted. I was perfectly cool and most desperately interested. For such a moment I would have gone through fire and water.

"Majesty, this is the Dutchman I spoke of," I heard Stumm say.

"What language does he speak?" the Emperor asked.

"Dutch," was the reply; "but being a South African he also speaks good English."

A spasm of pain seemed to flit over the face before me. Then he addressed me in English.

"You have come from a land which will yet be our ally to offer your sword to our service? I accept the gift and hail it as a good omen. I would have given your race its freedom, but there were fools and traitors among you who misjudged me. But that freedom I shall yet give you in spite of yourselves. Are there many like you in your country?"

"There are thousands, sire," I said, lying cheerfully. "I am one of many who think that my race's life lies in your victory. And I think that that victory must be won not in Europe alone. In South Africa for the moment there is no chance, so we look to other parts of the continent. You will win in Europe. You have won in the East, and it now remains to strike the English where they cannot fend the blow. If we take Uganda, Egypt will fall. By your permission I go there to make trouble for your enemies."

A flicker of a smile passed over the worn face. It was the face of one who slept little and whose thoughts rode him like a nightmare.

"That is well," he said. "Some Englishman once said that he would call in the New World to redress the balance of the Old. We Germans will summon the whole earth to suppress the infamies of England. Serve us well, and you will not be forgotten."

Then he suddenly asked: "Did you fight in the last South African War?"

"Yes, sire," I said. "I was in the commando of that Smuts who has now been bought by England."

"What were your countrymen's losses?" he asked eagerly.

I did not know, but I hazarded a guess. "In the field some twenty thousand. But many more by sickness and in the accursed prison-camps of the English."

Again a spasm of pain crossed his face.

"Twenty thousand," he repeated huskily. "A mere handful. To-day we lose as many in a skirmish in the Polish marshes."

Then he broke out fiercely.

"I did not seek the war . . . It was forced on me . . . I laboured for peace . . . The blood of millions is on the heads of England and Russia, but England most of all. God will yet avenge it. He that takes the sword will perish by the sword. Mine was forced from the scabbard in self-defence, and I am guiltless. Do they know that among your people?"

"All the world knows it, sire," I said.

He gave his hand to Stumm and turned away. The last I saw of him was a figure moving like a sleep-walker, with no spring in his step, amid his tall suite. I felt that I was looking on at a far bigger tragedy than any I had seen in action. Here was one that had loosed Hell, and the furies of Hell had got hold of him. He was no common man, for in his presence I felt an attraction which was not merely the mastery of one used to command. That would not have impressed me, for I had never owned a master. But here was a human being who, unlike Stumm and his kind, had the power of laying himself alongside other men. That was the irony of it. Stumm would not have cared a tinker's curse for all the massacres in history. But this man, the chief of a nation of Stumms, paid the price in war for the gifts that had made him successful in peace. He had imagination and nerves, and the one was white hot and the others were quivering. I would not have been in his shoes for the throne of the Universe . . .

ALL AFTERNOON WE SPED SOUTHWARD, mostly in a country of hills and wooded valleys. Stumm, for him, was very pleasant. His Imperial master must have been gracious to him, and he passed a bit of it on to me. But he was anxious to see that I had got the right impression.

"The All-Highest is merciful, as I told you," he said.

I agreed with him.

"Mercy is the prerogative of kings," he said sententiously, "but for us lesser folks it is a trimming we can well do without."

I nodded my approval.

"I am not merciful," he went on, as if I needed telling that. "If any man stands in my way I trample the life out of him. That is the German fashion. That is what has made us great. We do not make war with lavender gloves and fine phrases, but with hard steel and hard brains. We Germans will cure the green-sickness of the world. The nations rise against us. Pouf! They are soft flesh, and flesh cannot resist iron. The shining ploughshare will cut its way through acres of mud."

I hastened to add that these were also my opinions.

"What the hell do your opinions matter? You are a thickheaded boor of the veld . . . Not but what," he added, "there is metal in you slow Dutchmen once we Germans have had the forging of it!"

The winter evening closed in, and I saw that we had come out of the hills and were in flat country. Sometimes a big sweep of river showed, and, looking out at one station, I saw a funny church with a thing like an onion on top of its spire. It might almost have been a mosque, judging from the pictures I remembered of mosques. I wished to Heaven I had given geography more attention in my time.

Presently we stopped, and Stumm led the way out. The train must have been specially halted for him, for it was a one-horse little place whose name I could not make out. The station-master was waiting, bowing and saluting, and outside was a motor-car with big headlights. Next minute we were sliding through dark woods where the snow lay far deeper than in the north. There was a mild frost in the air, and the tyres slipped and skidded at the corners.

We hadn't far to go. We climbed a little hill and on the top of it stopped at the door of a big black castle. It looked enormous in the winter night, with not a light showing anywhere on its front. The door was opened by an old fellow who took a long time about it and got well cursed for his slowness. Inside the place was very noble and ancient. Stumm switched on the electric light, and there was a great hall with black tarnished portraits of men and women in old-fashioned clothes, and mighty horns of deer on the walls.

There seemed to be no superfluity of servants. The old fellow said that food was ready, and without more ado we went into the dining-room—another vast chamber with rough stone walls above the panelling—and found some cold meats on a table beside a big fire. The servant presently brought in a ham omelette, and on that and the cold stuff we dined. I remember there was nothing to drink but water. It puzzled me how Stumm kept his great body going on the very moderate amount of food he ate. He was the type you expect to swill beer by the bucket and put away a pie at a sitting.

When we had finished, he rang for the old man and told him that we should be in the study for the rest of the evening. "You can lock up and go to bed when you like," he said, "but see you have coffee ready at seven sharp in the morning."

Ever since I entered that house I had the uncomfortable feeling of being in a prison. Here was I alone in this great place with a fellow who could, and would, wring my neck if he wanted. Berlin and all the rest of it had seemed comparatively open country; I had felt that I could move freely and at the worst make a bolt for it. But here I was trapped, and I had to tell myself every minute that I was there as a friend and colleague. The fact is, I was afraid of Stumm, and I don't mind admitting it. He was a new thing in my experience and I didn't like it. If only he had drunk and guzzled a bit I should have been happier.

We went up a staircase to a room at the end of a long corridor. Stumm locked the door behind him and laid the key on the table. That room took my breath away, it was so unexpected. In place of the grim bareness of downstairs here was a place all luxury and colour and light. It was very large, but low in the ceiling, and the walls were full of little recesses with statues in them. A thick grey carpet of velvet pile covered the floor, and the chairs were low and soft and upholstered like a lady's boudoir. A pleasant fire burned on the hearth and there was a flavour of scent in the air, something like incense or burnt sandalwood. A French clock on the mantelpiece told me that it was ten minutes past eight. Everywhere on little tables and in cabinets was a profusion of knick-knacks, and there was some beautiful embroidery framed on screens. At first sight you would have said it was a woman's drawing-room.

But it wasn't. I soon saw the difference. There had never been a woman's hand in that place. It was the room of a man who had a passion for frippery, who had a perverted taste for soft delicate things. It was the complement to his bluff brutality. I began to see the queer other side of my host, that evil side which gossip had spoken of as not unknown in the German army. The room seemed a horribly unwholesome place, and I was more than ever afraid of Stumm.

The hearthrug was a wonderful old Persian thing, all faint greens and pinks. As he stood on it he looked uncommonly like a bull in a china-shop. He seemed to bask in the comfort of it, and sniffed like a satisfied animal. Then he sat down at an escritoire, unlocked a drawer and took out some papers.

"We will now settle your business, friend Brandt," he said. "You will go to Egypt and there take your orders from one whose name and address are in this envelope. This card," and he lifted a square piece of grey pasteboard with a big stamp at the corner and some code words stencilled on it, "will be your passport. You will show it to the man you seek. Keep it jealously, and never use it save under orders or in the last necessity. It is your badge as an accredited agent of the German Crown."

I took the card and the envelope and put them in my pocket-book.

"Where do I go after Egypt?" I asked.

"That remains to be seen. Probably you will go up the Blue Nile. Riza, the man you will meet, will direct you. Egypt is a nest of our agents who work peacefully under the nose of the English Secret Service."

"I am willing," I said. "But how do I reach Egypt?"

"You will travel by Holland and London. Here is your route," and he took a paper from his pocket. "Your passports are ready and will be given you at the frontier."

This was a pretty kettle of fish. I was to be packed off to Cairo by sea, which would take weeks, and God knows how I would get from Egypt to Constantinople. I saw all my plans falling to pieces about my ears, and just when I thought they were shaping nicely.

Stumm must have interpreted the look on my face as fear.

"You have no cause to be afraid," he said. "We have passed the word to the English police to look out for a suspicious South African named Brandt, one of Maritz's rebels. It is not difficult to have that kind of a hint conveyed to the proper quarter. But the description will not be yours. Your name will be Van der Linden, a respectable Java merchant going home to his plantations after a visit to his native shores. You had better get your dossier by heart, but I guarantee you will be asked no questions. We manage these things well in Germany."

I kept my eyes on the fire, while I did some savage thinking. I knew they would not let me out of their sight till they saw me in Holland, and, once there, there would be no possibility of getting back. When I left this house I would have no chance of giving them the slip. And yet I was well on my way to the East, the Danube could not be fifty miles off, and that way ran the road to Constantinople. It was a fairly desperate position. If I tried to get away Stumm would prevent me, and the odds were that I would go to join Peter in some infernal prison-camp.

Those moments were some of the worst I ever spent. I was absolutely and utterly baffled, like a rat in a trap. There seemed nothing for it but to go back to London and tell Sir Walter the game was up. And that was about as bitter as death.

He saw my face and laughed.

"Does your heart fail you, my little Dutchman? You funk the English? I will tell you one thing for your comfort. There is nothing in the world to be feared except me. Fail, and you have cause to shiver. Play me false and you had far better never have been born."

His ugly sneering face was close above mine. Then he put out his hands and gripped my shoulders as he had done the first afternoon.

I forget if I mentioned that part of the damage I got at Loos was a shrapnel bullet low down at the back of my neck. The wound had healed well enough, but I had pains there on a cold day. His fingers found the place and it hurt like hell.

There is a very narrow line between despair and black rage. I had about given up the game, but the sudden ache of my shoulders gave me purpose again. He must have seen the rage in my eyes for his own became cruel.

"The weasel would like to bite," he cried. "But the poor weasel has found its master. Stand still, vermin. Smile, look pleasant, or I will make pulp of you. Do you dare to frown at me?"

I shut my teeth and said never a word. I was choking in my throat and could not have uttered a syllable if I had tried.

Then he let me go, grinning like an ape.

I stepped back a pace and gave him my left between the eyes.

For a second he did not realize what had happened, for I don't suppose anyone had dared to lift a hand to him since he was a child. He blinked at me mildly. Then his face grew as red as fire.

"God in Heaven," he said quietly. "I am going to kill you," and he flung himself on me like a mountain.

I was expecting him and dodged the attack. I was quite calm now, but pretty helpless. The man had a gorilla's reach and could give me at least a couple of stone. He wasn't soft either, but looked as hard as granite. I was only just from hospital and absurdly out of training. He would certainly kill me if he could, and I saw nothing to prevent him.

My only chance was to keep him from getting to grips, for he could have squeezed in my ribs in two seconds. I fancied I was lighter on my legs than him, and I had a good eye. Black Monty at Kimberley had taught me to fight a bit, but there is no art on earth which can prevent a big man in a narrow space from sooner or later cornering a lesser one. That was the danger.

Backwards and forwards we padded on the soft carpet. He had no notion of guarding himself, and I got in a good few blows. Then I saw a queer thing. Every time I hit him he blinked and seemed to pause. I guessed the reason for that. He had gone through life keeping the crown of the causeway, and nobody had ever stood up to him. He wasn't a coward by a long chalk, but he was a bully, and had never been struck in his life. He was getting struck now in real earnest, and he didn't like it. He had lost his bearings and was growing as mad as a hatter.

I kept half an eye on the clock. I was hopeful now, and was looking for the right kind of chance. The risk was that I might tire sooner than him and be at his mercy.

Then I learned a truth I have never forgotten. If you are fighting a man who means to kill you, he will be apt to down you unless you mean to kill him too. Stumm did not know any rules to this game, and I forgot to allow for that. Suddenly, when I was watching his eyes, he launched a mighty kick at my stomach. If he had got me, this yarn would have had an abrupt ending. But by the mercy of God I was moving sideways when he let out, and his heavy boot just grazed my left thigh.

It was the place where most of the shrapnel had lodged, and for a second I was sick with pain and stumbled. Then I was on my feet again but with a new feeling in my blood. I had to smash Stumm or never sleep in my bed again.

I got a wonderful power from this new cold rage of mine. I felt I couldn't tire, and I danced round and dotted his face till it was streaming with blood. His bulky padded chest was no good to me, so I couldn't try for the mark.

He began to snort now and his breath came heavily. "You infernal cad," I said in good round English, "I'm going to knock the stuffing out of you," but he didn't know what I was saying.

Then at last he gave me my chance. He half tripped over a little table and his face stuck forward. I got him on the point of the chin, and put every ounce of weight I possessed behind the blow. He crumpled up in a heap and rolled over, upsetting a lamp and knocking a big china jar in two. His head, I remember, lay under the escritoire from which he had taken my passport.

I picked up the key and unlocked the door. In one of the gilded mirrors I smoothed my hair and tidied up my clothes. My anger had completely gone and I had no particular ill-will left against Stumm. He was a man of remarkable qualities, which would have brought him to the highest distinction in the Stone Age. But for all that he and his kind were back numbers.

I stepped out of the room, locked the door behind me, and started out on the second stage of my travels.

CHAPTER 7

Christmastide

EVERYTHING DEPENDED on whether the servant was in the hall. I had put Stumm to sleep for a bit, but I couldn't flatter myself he would long be quiet, and when he came to he would kick the locked door to matchwood. I must get out of the house without a minute's delay, and if the door was shut and the old man gone to bed I was done.

I met him at the foot of the stairs, carrying a candle.

"Your master wants me to send off an important telegram. Where is the nearest office? There's one in the village, isn't there?" I spoke in my best German, the first time I had used the tongue since I crossed the frontier.

"The village is five minutes off at the foot of the avenue," he said. "Will you be long, sir?"

"I'll be back in a quarter of an hour," I said. "Don't lock up till I get in."

I put on my ulster and walked out into a clear starry night. My bag I left lying on a settle in the hall. There was nothing in it to compromise me, but I wished I could have got a toothbrush and some tobacco out of it. So began one of the craziest escapades you can well imagine. I couldn't stop to think of the future yet, but must take one step at a time. I ran down the avenue, my feet crackling on the hard snow, planning hard my programme for the next hour.

I found the village—half a dozen houses with one biggish place that looked like an inn. The moon was rising, and as I approached I saw that it was some kind of store. A funny little two-seated car was purring before the door, and I guessed this was also the telegraph office.

I marched in and told my story to a stout woman with spectacles on her nose who was talking to a young man.

"It is too late," she shook her head. "The Herr Burgrave knows that well. There is no connexion from here after eight o'clock. If the matter is urgent you must go to Schwandorf."

"How far is that?" I asked, looking for some excuse to get decently out of the shop.

"Seven miles," she said, "but here is Franz and the post-wagon. Franz, you will be glad to give the gentleman a seat beside you."

The sheepish-looking youth muttered something which I took to be assent, and finished off a glass of beer. From his eyes and manner he looked as if he were half drunk.

I thanked the woman, and went out to the car, for I was in a fever to take advantage of this unexpected bit of luck. I could hear the post-mistress enjoining Franz not to keep the gentleman waiting, and presently he came out and flopped into the driver's seat. We started in a series of voluptuous curves, till his eyes got accustomed to the darkness.

At first we made good going along the straight, broad highway lined with woods on one side and on the other snowy fields melting into haze. Then he began to talk, and, as he talked, he slowed down. This by no means suited my book, and I seriously wondered whether I should pitch him out and take charge of the thing. He was obviously a weakling, left behind in the conscription, and I could have done it with one hand. But by a fortunate chance I left him alone.

"That is a fine hat of yours, mein Herr," he said. He took off his own blue peaked cap, the uniform, I suppose, of the driver of the post-wagon, and laid it on his knee. The night air ruffled a shock of tow-coloured hair.

Then he calmly took my hat and clapped it on his head.

"With this thing I should be a gentleman," he said.

I said nothing, but put on his cap and waited.

"That is a noble overcoat, mein Herr," he went on. "It goes well with the hat. It is the kind of garment I have always desired to own. In two days it will be the holy Christmas, when gifts are given. Would that the good God sent me such a coat as yours!"

"You can try it on to see how it looks," I said good-humouredly.

He stopped the car with a jerk, and pulled off his blue coat. The exchange was soon effected. He was about my height, and my ulster fitted not so badly. I put on his overcoat, which had a big collar that buttoned round the neck.

The idiot preened himself like a girl. Drink and vanity had primed him for any folly. He drove so carelessly for a bit that he nearly put us into a ditch. We passed several cottages and at the last he slowed down.

"A friend of mine lives here," he announced. "Gertrud would like to see me in the fine clothes which the most amiable Herr has given me. Wait for me, I will not be long." And he scrambled out of the car and lurched into the little garden.

I took his place and moved very slowly forward. I heard the door open and the sound of laughing and loud voices. Then it shut, and looking back I saw that my idiot had been absorbed into the dwelling of his Gertrud. I waited no longer, but sent the car forward at its best speed.

Five minutes later the infernal thing began to give trouble—a nut loose in the antiquated steering-gear. I unhooked a lamp, examined it, and put the mischief right, but I was a quarter of an hour doing it. The highway ran now in a thick forest and I noticed branches going off now and then to the right. I was just thinking of turning up one of them, for I had no anxiety to visit Schwandorf, when I heard behind me the sound of a great car driven furiously.

I drew in to the right side—thank goodness I remembered the rule of the road—and proceeded decorously, wondering what was going to happen. I could hear the brakes being clamped on and the car slowing down. Suddenly a big grey bonnet slipped past me and as I turned my head I heard a familiar voice.

It was Stumm, looking like something that has been run over. He had his jaw in a sling, so that I wondered if I had broken it, and his eyes were beautifully bunged up. It was that that saved me, that and his raging temper. The collar of the postman's coat was round my chin, hiding my beard, and I had his cap pulled well down on my brow. I remembered what Blenkiron had said—that the only way to deal with the Germans was naked bluff. Mine was naked enough, for it was all that was left to me.

"Where is the man you brought from Andersbach?" he roared, as well as his jaw would allow him.

I pretended to be mortally scared, and spoke in the best imitation I could manage of the postman's high cracked voice.

"He got out a mile back, Herr Burgrave," I quavered. "He was a rude fellow who wanted to go to Schwandorf, and then changed his mind."

"Where, you fool? Say exactly where he got down or I will wring your neck."

"In the wood this side of Gertrud's cottage . . . on the left hand . . . I left him running among the trees." I put all the terror I knew into my pipe, and it wasn't all acting.

"He means the Henrichs' cottage, Herr Colonel," said the chauffeur. "This man is courting the daughter."

Stumm gave an order and the great car backed, and, as I looked round, I saw it turning. Then as it gathered speed it shot forward, and presently was lost in the shadows. I had got over the first hurdle.

But there was no time to be lost. Stumm would meet the postman and would be tearing after me any minute. I took the first turning, and bucketed along a narrow woodland road. The hard ground would show very few tracks, I thought, and I hoped the pursuit would think I had gone on to Schwandorf. But it wouldn't do to risk it, and I was determined very soon to get the car off the road, leave it, and take to the forest. I took out my watch and calculated I could give myself ten minutes.

I was very nearly caught. Presently I came on a bit of rough heath, with a slope away from the road and here and there a patch of black which I took to be a sandpit. Opposite one of these I slewed the car to the edge, got out, started it again and saw it pitch head-foremost into the darkness. There was a splash of water and then silence. Craning over I could see nothing but murk, and the marks at the lip where the wheels had passed. They would find my tracks in the daylight but scarcely at this time of night.

Then I ran across the road to the forest. I was only just in time, for the echoes of the splash had hardly died away when I heard the sound of another car. I lay flat in a hollow below a tangle of snow-laden brambles and looked between the pine-trees at the moonlit road. It was Stumm's car again and to my consternation it stopped just a little short of the sandpit.

I saw an electric torch flashed, and Stumm himself got out and examined the tracks on the highway. Thank God, they would be still there for him to find, but had he tried half a dozen yards on he would have seen them turn towards the sandpit. If that had happened he would have beaten the adjacent woods and most certainly found me. There was a third man in the car, with my hat and coat on him. That poor devil of a postman had paid dear for his vanity.

They took a long time before they started again, and I was jolly well relieved when they went scouring down the road. I ran deeper into the woods till I found a track which—as I judged from the sky which I saw in a clearing—took me nearly due west. That wasn't the direction I wanted, so I bore off at right angles, and presently struck another road which I crossed in a hurry. After that I got entangled in some confounded kind of enclosure and had to climb paling after paling of rough stakes plaited with osiers. Then came a rise in the ground and I was on a low hill of pines which seemed to last for miles. All the time I was going at a good pace, and before I stopped to rest I calculated I had put six miles between me and the sandpit.

My mind was getting a little more active now; for the first part of the journey I had simply staggered from impulse to impulse. These impulses had been uncommon lucky, but I couldn't go on like that for ever. *Ek sal 'n plan maak*, says the old Boer when he gets into trouble, and it was up to me now to make a plan.

As soon as I began to think I saw the desperate business I was in for. Here was I, with nothing except what I stood up in—including a coat and cap that weren't mine—alone in mid-winter in the heart of South Germany. There was a man behind me looking for my blood, and soon there would be a hue-and-cry for me up and down the land. I had heard that the German police were pretty efficient, and I couldn't see that I stood the slimmest chance. If they caught me they would shoot me beyond doubt. I asked myself on what charge, and answered, "For knocking about a German officer." They couldn't have me up for espionage, for as far as I knew they had no evidence. I was simply a Dutchman that had got riled and had run amok. But if they cut down a cobbler for laughing at a second lieutenant—which is what happened at Zabern—I calculated that hanging would be too good for a man that had broken a colonel's jaw.

To make things worse my job was not to escape—though that would have been hard enough—but to get to Constantinople, more than a thousand miles off, and I reckoned I couldn't get there as a tramp. I had to be sent there, and now I had flung away my chance. If I had been a Catholic I would have said a prayer to St Teresa, for she would have understood my troubles.

My mother used to say that when you felt down on your luck it was a good cure to count your mercies. So I set about counting mine. The first was that I was well started on my journey, for I couldn't be above two score miles from the Danube. The second was that I had Stumm's

I LAY FLAT IN A HOLLOW AND LOOKED OUT

pass. I didn't see how I could use it, but there it was. Lastly I had plenty of money—fifty-three English sovereigns and the equivalent of three pounds in German paper which I had changed at the hotel. Also I had squared accounts with old Stumm. That was the biggest mercy of all.

I thought I'd better get some sleep, so I found a dryish hole below an oak root and squeezed myself into it. The snow lay deep in these woods and I was sopping wet up to my knees. All the same I managed to sleep for some hours, and got up and shook myself just as the winter's dawn was breaking through the tree-tops. Breakfast was the next thing, and I must find some sort of dwelling.

Almost at once I struck a road, a big highway running north and south. I trotted along in the bitter morning to get my circulation started, and presently I began to feel a little better. In a little I saw a church-spire, which meant a village. Stumm wouldn't be likely to have got on my tracks yet, I calculated, but there was always the chance that he had warned all the villages round by telephone and that they might be on the look-out for me. But that risk had to be taken, for I must have food.

It was the day before Christmas, I remembered, and people would be holidaying. The village was quite a big place, but at this hour—just after eight o'clock—there was nobody in the street except a wandering dog. I chose the most unassuming shop I could find, where a little boy was taking down the shutters—one of those general stores where they sell everything. The boy fetched a very old woman, who hobbled in from the back, fitting on her spectacles.

"*Grüss Gott*," she said in a friendly voice, and I took off my cap. I saw from my reflection in a saucepan that I looked moderately respectable in spite of my night in the woods.

I told her a story of how I was walking from Schwandorf to see my mother at an imaginary place called Judenfeld, banking on the ignorance of villagers about any place five miles from their homes. I said my luggage had gone astray, and I hadn't time to wait for it, since my leave was short. The old lady was sympathetic and unsuspecting. She sold me a pound of chocolate, a box of biscuits, the better part of a ham, two tins of sardines and a rucksack to carry them. I also bought some soap, a comb and a cheap razor, and a small Tourists' Guide, published by a Leipzig firm. As I was leaving I saw what seemed like garments hanging up in the back shop, and turned to have a look at them. They were the kind of thing that Germans wear on their summer walking tours—long shooting capes made of a green stuff they call *loden*. I bought one, and a green felt hat and an alpenstock to keep it company. Then wishing the old woman and her belongings a merry Christmas, I departed and took the shortest cut out of the village. There were one or two people about now, but they did not seem to notice me.

I went into the woods again and walked for two miles till I halted for breakfast. I was not feeling quite so fit now, and I did not make much of my provisions, beyond eating a biscuit and some chocolate. I felt very thirsty and longed for hot tea. In an icy pool I washed and with infinite agony shaved my beard. That razor was the worst of its species, and my eyes were running all the time with the pain of the operation. Then I took off the postman's coat and cap, and buried them below some bushes. I was now a clean-shaven German pedestrian with a green cape and hat, and an absurd walking-stick with an iron-shod end—the sort of person who roams in thousands over the Fatherland in summer, but is a rarish bird in mid-winter.

The Tourists' Guide was a fortunate purchase, for it contained a big map of Bavaria which gave me my bearings. I was certainly not forty miles from the Danube—more like thirty. The road through the village I had left would have taken me to it. I had only to walk due south and I would reach it before night. So far as I could make out there were long tongues of forest running down to the river, and I resolved to keep to the woodlands. At the worst I would meet a forester or two, and I had a good enough story for them. On the highroad there might be awkward questions.

When I started out again I felt very stiff and the cold seemed to be growing intense. This puzzled me, for I had not minded it much up to now, and, being warm-blooded by nature, it never used to worry me. A sharp winter night on the high-veld was a long sight chillier than anything I had struck so far in Europe. But now my teeth were chattering and the marrow seemed to be freezing in my bones.

The day had started bright and clear, but a wrack of grey clouds soon covered the sky, and a wind from the east began to whistle. As I stumbled along through the snowy undergrowth I kept longing for bright warm places. I thought of those long days on the veld when the earth was like a great yellow bowl, with white roads running to the horizon and a tiny white farm basking in the heart of it, with its blue dam and patches of bright green lucerne. I thought of those baking days on the east coast, when the sea was like mother-of-pearl and the sky one burning turquoise. But most of all I thought of warm scented noons on trek, when one dozed in the shadow of the wagon and sniffed the wood smoke from the fire where the boys were cooking dinner.

From these pleasant pictures I returned to the beastly present—the thick snowy woods, the lowering sky, wet clothes, a hunted present, and a dismal future. I felt miserably depressed, and I couldn't think of any mercies to count. It struck me that I might be falling sick.

About midday I awoke with a start to the belief that I was being pursued. I cannot explain how or why the feeling came, except that it is a kind of instinct that men get who have lived much in wild countries. My senses, which had been numbed, suddenly grew keen, and my brain began to work double quick.

I asked myself what I would do if I were Stumm, with hatred in my heart, a broken jaw to avenge, and pretty well limitless powers. He must have found the car in the sandpit and seen my tracks in the wood opposite. I didn't know how good he and his men might be at following a spoor, but I knew that any ordinary Kaffir could have nosed it out easily. But he didn't need to do that. This was a civilized country full of roads and railways. I must some time and somewhere come out of the woods. He could have all the roads watched, and the telephone would set everyone on my track within a radius of fifty miles. Besides, he would soon pick up my trail in the village I had visited that morning. From the map I learned that it was called Greif, and it was likely to live up to that name with me.

Presently I came to a rocky knoll which rose out of the forest. Keeping well in shelter I climbed to the top and cautiously looked around me. Away to the east I saw the vale of a river with broad fields and church-spires. West and south the forest rolled unbroken in a wilderness of snowy tree-tops. There was no sign of life anywhere, not even a bird, but I knew very well that behind me in the woods were men moving swiftly on my track, and that it was pretty well impossible for me to get away.

There was nothing for it but to go on till I dropped or was taken. I shaped my course south with a shade of west in it, for the map showed me that in that direction I would soonest strike the Danube. What I was going to do when I got there I didn't trouble to think. I had fixed the river as my immediate goal and the future must take care of itself.

I was now certain that I had fever on me. It was still in my bones, as a legacy from Africa, and had come out once or twice when I was with the battalion in Hampshire. The bouts had been short for I had known of their coming and dosed myself. But now I had no quinine, and it looked as if I were in for a heavy go. It made me feel desperately wretched and stupid, and I all but blundered into capture.

For suddenly I came on a road and was going to cross it blindly, when a man rode slowly past on a bicycle. Luckily I was in the shade of a clump of hollies and he was not looking my way, though he was not three yards off. I crawled forward to reconnoitre. I saw about half a mile of road running straight through the forest and every two hundred yards was a bicyclist. They wore uniform and appeared to be acting as sentries.

This could only have one meaning. Stumm had picketed all the roads and cut me off in an angle of the woods. There was no chance of getting across unobserved. As I lay there with my heart sinking, I had the horrible feeling that the pursuit might be following me from behind, and that at any moment I would be enclosed between two fires.

For more than an hour I stayed there with my chin in the snow. I didn't see any way out, and I was feeling so ill that I didn't seem to care. Then my chance came suddenly out of the skies.

The wind rose, and a great gust of snow blew from the east. In five minutes it was so thick that I couldn't see across the road. At first I thought it a new addition to my troubles, and then very slowly I saw the opportunity. I slipped down the bank and made ready to cross.

I almost blundered into one of the bicyclists. He cried out and fell off his machine, but I didn't wait to investigate. A sudden access of strength came to me and I darted into the woods on the farther side. I knew I would be soon swallowed from sight in the drift, and I knew that the falling snow would hide my tracks. So I put my best foot forward.

I must have run miles before the hot fit passed, and I stopped from sheer bodily weakness. There was no sound except the crush of falling snow, the wind seemed to have gone, and the place was very solemn and quiet. But Heavens! how the snow fell! It was partly screened by the branches, but all the same it was piling itself up deep everywhere. My legs seemed made of lead, my head burned, and there were fiery pains over all my body. I stumbled on blindly, without a notion of any direction, determined only to keep going to the last. For I knew that if I once lay down I would never rise again.

When I was a boy I was fond of fairy tales, and most of the stories I remembered had been about great German forests and snow and charcoal burners and woodmen's huts. Once I had longed to see these things, and now I was fairly in the thick of them. There had been wolves, too, and I wondered idly if I should fall in with a pack. I felt myself getting light-headed. I fell repeatedly and laughed sillily every time. Once I dropped into a hole and lay for some time at the bottom giggling. If anyone had found me then he would have taken me for a madman.

The twilight of the forest grew dimmer, but I scarcely noticed it. Evening was falling, and soon it would be night, a night without morning for me.

My body was going on without the direction of my brain, for my mind was filled with craziness. I was like a drunk man who keeps running, for he knows that if he stops he will fall, and I had a sort of bet with myself not to lie down—not at any rate just yet. If I lay down I should feel the pain in my head worse. Once I had ridden for five days down country with fever on me and the flat bush trees had seemed to melt into one big mirage and dance quadrilles before my eyes. But then I had more or less kept my wits. Now I was fairly daft, and every minute growing dafter.

Then the trees seemed to stop and I was walking on flat ground. It was a clearing, and before me twinkled a little light. The change restored me to consciousness, and suddenly I felt with horrid intensity the fire in my head and bones and the weakness of my limbs. I longed to sleep, and I had a notion that a place to sleep was before me. I moved towards the light and presently saw through a screen of snow the outline of a cottage.

I had no fear, only an intolerable longing to lie down. Very slowly I made my way to the door and knocked. My weakness was so great that I could hardly lift my hand.

There were voices within, and a corner of the curtain was lifted from the window. Then the door opened and a woman stood before me, a woman with a thin, kindly face.

"*Grüss Gott,*" she said, while children peeped from behind her skirts.

"*Grüss Gott,*" I replied. I leaned against the door-post, and speech forsook me.

She saw my condition. "Come in, sir," she said. "You are sick and it is no weather for a sick man."

I stumbled after her and stood dripping in the centre of the little kitchen, while three wondering children stared at me. It was a poor place, scantily furnished, but a good log-fire burned on the hearth. The shock of warmth gave me one of those minutes of self-possession which come sometimes in the middle of a fever.

"I am sick, mother, and I have walked far in the storm and lost my way. I am from Africa, where the climate is hot, and your cold brings me fever. It will pass in a day or two if you can give me a bed."

"You are welcome," she said; "but first I will make you coffee."

I took off my dripping cloak, and crouched close to the hearth. She gave me coffee—poor washy stuff, but blessedly hot. Poverty was spelled large in everything I saw. I felt the tides of fever beginning to overflow my brain again, and I made a great attempt to set my affairs straight before I was overtaken. With difficulty I took out Stumm's pass from my pocket-book.

"That is my warrant," I said. "I am a member of the Imperial Secret Service and for the sake of my work I must move in the dark. If you will permit it, mother, I will sleep till I am better, but no one must know that I am here. If anyone comes, you must deny my presence."

She looked at the big seal as if it were a talisman.

"Yes, yes," she said, "you will have the bed in the garret and be left in peace till you are well. We have no neighbours near, and the storm will shut the roads. I will be silent, I and the little ones."

My head was beginning to swim, but I made one more effort.

"There is food in my rucksack—biscuits and ham and chocolate. Pray take it for your use. And here is some money to buy Christmas fare for the little ones." And I gave her some of the German notes.

After that my recollection becomes dim. She helped me up a ladder to the garret, undressed me, and gave me a thick coarse nightgown. I seem to remember that she kissed my hand, and that she was crying. "The good Lord has sent you," she said. "Now the little ones have their prayers answered and the Christkind will not pass by our door."

CHAPTER 8

The Essen Barges

I LAY FOR FOUR DAYS like a log in that garret bed. The storm died down, the thaw set in, and the snow melted. The children played about the doors and told stories at night round the fire. Stumm's myrmidons no doubt beset every road and troubled the lives of innocent wayfarers. But no one came near the cottage, and the fever worked itself out while I lay in peace.

It was a bad bout, but on the fifth day it left me, and I lay, as weak as a kitten, staring at the rafters and the little skylight. It was a leaky, draughty old place, but the woman of the cottage had heaped deerskins and blankets on my bed and kept me warm. She came in now and then, and once she brought me a brew of some bitter herbs which greatly refreshed me. A little thin porridge was all the food I could eat, and some chocolate made from the slabs in my rucksack.

I lay and dozed through the day, hearing the faint chatter of children below, and getting stronger hourly. Malaria passes as quickly as it comes and leaves a man little the worse, though this was one of the sharpest turns I ever had. As I lay I thought, and my thoughts followed curious lines. One queer thing was that Stumm and his doings seemed to have been shot back into a lumber-room of my brain and the door locked. He didn't seem to be a creature of the living present, but a distant memory on which I could look calmly. I thought a good deal about my battalion and the comedy of my present position. You see I was getting better, for I called it comedy now, not tragedy.

But chiefly I thought of my mission. All that wild day in the snow it had seemed the merest farce. The three words Harry Bullivant had scribbled had danced through my head in a crazy fandango. They were present to me now, but coolly and sanely in all their meagreness.

I remember that I took each one separately and chewed on it for hours. *Kasredin*—there was nothing to be got out of that. *Cancer*—there were too many meanings, all blind. *v. I*—that was the worst gibberish of all.

Before this I had always taken the *I* as the letter of the alphabet. I had thought the *v.* must stand for *von*, and I had considered the German names beginning with I—Ingolstadt, Ingeburg, Ingenohl, and all the rest of them. I had made a list of about seventy at the British Museum before I left London.

Now I suddenly found myself taking the *I* as the numeral One. Idly, not thinking what I was doing, I put it into German.

Then I nearly fell out of the bed. *Von Einem*—the name I had heard at Gaudian's house, the name Stumm had spoken behind his hand, the name to which Hilda was probably the prefix. It was a tremendous discovery—the first real bit of light I had found. Harry Bullivant knew that some man or woman called von Einem was at the heart of the mystery. Stumm had spoken of the same personage with respect and in connexion with the work I proposed to do in raising the Moslem Africans. If I found von Einem I would be getting very warm. What was the word that Stumm had whispered to Gaudian and scared that worthy? It had sounded like Uhnmantl. If I could only get that clear, I would solve the riddle.

I think that discovery completed my cure. At any rate on the evening of the fifth day—it was Wednesday, the 29th of December—I was well enough to get up. When the dark had fallen and it was too late to fear a visitor, I came downstairs and, wrapped in my green cape, took a seat by the fire.

As we sat there in the firelight, with the three white-headed children staring at me with saucer eyes, and smiling when I looked their way, the woman talked. Her man had gone to the wars on the Eastern front, and the last she had heard from him he was in a Polish bog and longing for his dry native woodlands. The struggle meant little to her. It was an act of God, a thunderbolt out of the sky, which had taken a husband from her, and might soon make her a widow and her children fatherless. She knew nothing of its causes and purposes, and thought of the Russians as a gigantic nation of savages, heathens who had never been converted, and who would eat up German homes if the good Lord and the brave German soldiers did not stop them. I tried hard to find out if she had any notion of affairs in the West, but she hadn't beyond the fact that there was trouble with the French. I doubt if she knew of England's share in it. She was a decent soul, with no bitterness against anybody, not even the Russians if they would spare her man.

That night I realized the crazy folly of war. When I saw the splintered

shell of Ypres and heard hideous tales of German doings, I used to want
to see the whole land of the Boche given up to fire and sword. I thought
we could never end the war properly without giving the Huns some of
their own medicine. But that woodcutter's cottage cured me of such
nightmares. I was for punishing the guilty but letting the innocent go
free. It was our business to thank God and keep our hands clean from
the ugly blunders to which Germany's madness had driven her. What
good would it do Christian folk to burn poor little huts like this and
leave children's bodies by the wayside? To be able to laugh and to be
merciful are the only things that make man better than the beasts.

The place, as I have said, was desperately poor. The woman's face
had the skin stretched tight over the bones and that transparency which
means under-feeding; I fancied she did not have the liberal allowance
that soldiers' wives get in England. The children looked better
nourished, but it was by their mother's sacrifice. I did my best to cheer
them up. I told them long yarns about Africa and lions and tigers, and I
got some pieces of wood and whittled them into toys. I am fairly good
with a knife, and I carved very presentable likenesses of a monkey, a
springbok, and a rhinoceros. The children went to bed hugging the first
toys, I expect, they ever possessed.

It was clear to me that I must leave as soon as possible. I had to get on
with my business, and besides, it was not fair to the woman. Any
moment I might be found here, and she would get into trouble for
harbouring me. I asked her if she knew where the Danube was, and her
answer surprised me. "You will reach it in an hour's walk," she said.
"The track through the wood runs straight to the ferry."

Next morning after breakfast I took my departure. It was drizzling
weather, and I was feeling very lean. Before going I presented my
hostess and the children with two sovereigns apiece. "It is English
gold," I said, "for I have to travel among our enemies and use our
enemies' money. But the gold is good, and if you go to any town they
will change it for you. But I advise you to put it in your stocking-foot
and use it only if all else fails. You must keep your home going, for
some day there will be peace and your man will come back from the
wars."

I kissed the children, shook the woman's hand, and went off down
the clearing. They had cried *"Auf Wiedersehen,"* but it wasn't likely I
would ever see them again.

The snow had all gone, except in patches in the deep hollows. The ground was like a full sponge, and a cold rain drifted in my eyes. After half an hour's steady trudge the trees thinned, and presently I came out on a knuckle of open ground cloaked in dwarf junipers. And there before me lay the plain, and a mile off a broad brimming river.

I sat down and looked dismally at the prospect. The exhilaration of my discovery the day before had gone. I had stumbled on a worthless piece of knowledge, for I could not use it. Hilda von Einem, if such a person existed and possessed the great secret, was probably living in some big house in Berlin, and I was about as likely to get anything out of her as to be asked to dine with the Kaiser. Blenkiron might do something, but where on earth was Blenkiron? I dared say Sir Walter would value the information, but I could not get to Sir Walter. I was to go on to Constantinople, running away from the people who really pulled the ropes. But if I stayed I could do nothing, and I could not stay. I must go on and I didn't see how I could go on. Every course seemed shut to me, and I was in as pretty a tangle as any man ever stumbled into.

For I was morally certain that Stumm would not let the thing drop. I knew too much, and besides I had outraged his pride. He would beat the countryside till he got me, and he undoubtedly would get me if I waited much longer. But how was I to get over the border? My passport would be no good, for the number of that pass would long ere this have been wired to every police station in Germany, and to produce it would be to ask for trouble. Without it I could not cross the borders by any railway. My studies of the Tourists' Guide had suggested that once I was in Austria I might find things slacker and move about easier. I thought of having a try at the Tyrol and I also thought of Bohemia. But these places were a long way off, and there were several thousand chances each day that I would be caught on the road.

This was Thursday, the 30th of December, the second last day of the year. I was due in Constantinople on the 17th of January. Constantinople! I had thought myself a long way from it in Berlin, but now it seemed as distant as the moon.

But that big sullen river in front of me led to it. And as I looked my attention was caught by a curious sight. On the far eastern horizon, where the water slipped round a corner of hill, there was a long trail of smoke. The streamers thinned out, and seemed to come from some boat well round the corner, but I could see at least two boats in view. Therefore there must be a long train of barges, with a tug in tow.

I looked to the west and saw another such procession coming into sight. First went a big river steamer—it can't have been much less than 1,000 tons—and after came a string of barges. I counted no less than six besides the tug. They were heavily loaded and their draught must have been considerable, but there was plenty of depth in the flooded river.

A moment's reflection told me what I was looking at. Once Sandy, in one of the discussions you have in hospital, had told us just how the Germans munitioned their Balkan campaign. They were pretty certain of dishing Serbia at the first go, and it was up to them to get through guns and shells to the old Turk, who was running pretty short in his first supply. Sandy said that they wanted the railway, but they wanted still more the river, and they could make certain of that in a week. He told us how endless strings of barges, loaded up at the big factories of Westphalia, were moving through the canals from the Rhine or the Elbe to the Danube. Once the first reached Turkey, there would be regular delivery, you see—as quick as the Turks could handle the stuff. And they didn't return empty, Sandy said, but came back full of Turkish cotton and Bulgarian beef and Rumanian corn. I don't know where Sandy got the knowledge, but there was the proof of it before my eyes.

It was a wonderful sight, and I could have gnashed my teeth to see those loads of munitions going snugly off to the enemy. I calculated they would give our poor chaps hell in Gallipoli. And then, as I looked, an idea came into my head and with it an eighth part of a hope.

There was only one way for me to get out of Germany, and that was to leave in such good company that I would be asked no questions. That was plain enough. If I travelled to Turkey, for instance, in the Kaiser's suite, I would be as safe as the mail; but if I went on my own I was done. I had, so to speak, to get my passport *inside* Germany, to join some caravan which had free marching powers. And there was the kind of caravan before me—the Essen barges.

It sounded lunacy, for I guessed that munitions of war would be as jealously guarded as old Hindenburg's health. All the safer, I replied to myself, once I get there. If you are looking for a deserter you don't seek him at the favourite regimental public-house. If you're after a thief, among the places you'd be apt to leave unsearched would be Scotland Yard.

It was sound reasoning, but how was I to get on board? Probably the beastly things did not stop once in a hundred miles, and Stumm would get me long before I struck a halting-place. And even if I did get a chance like that, how was I to get permission to travel?

One step was clearly indicated—to get down to the river bank at once. So I set off at a sharp walk across squelchy fields, till I struck a road where the ditches had overflowed so as almost to meet in the middle. The place was so bad that I hoped travellers might be few. And as I trudged, my thoughts were busy with my prospects as a stowaway. If I bought food, I might get a chance to lie snug on one of the barges. They would not break bulk till they got to their journey's end.

Suddenly I noticed that the steamer, which was now abreast me, began to move towards the shore, and as I came over a low rise, I saw on my left a straggling village with a church, and a small landing-stage. The houses stood about a quarter of a mile from the stream, and between them was a straight, poplar-fringed road.

Soon there could be no doubt about it. The procession was coming to a standstill. The big tug nosed her way in and lay up alongside the pier, where in that season of flood there was enough depth of water. She signalled to the barges and they also started to drop anchors, which showed that there must be at least two men aboard each. Some of them dragged a bit and it was rather a cock-eyed train that lay in mid-stream. The tug got out a gangway, and from where I lay I saw half a dozen men leave it, carrying something on their shoulders.

It could be only one thing—a dead body. Someone of the crew must have died, and this halt was to bury him. I watched the procession move towards the village and I reckoned they would take some time there, though they might have wired ahead for a grave to be dug. Anyhow, they would be long enough to give me a chance.

For I had decided upon the brazen course. Blenkiron had said you couldn't cheat the Boche, but you could bluff him. I was going to put up the most monstrous bluff. If the whole countryside was hunting for Richard Hannay, Richard Hannay would walk through as a pal of the hunters. For I remembered the pass Stumm had given me. If that was worth a tinker's curse it should be good enough to impress a ship's captain.

Of course there were a thousand risks. They might have heard of me in the village and told the ship's party the story. For that reason I resolved not to go there but to meet the sailors when they were returning to the boat. Or the captain might have been warned and got the number of my pass, in which case Stumm would have his hands on me pretty soon. Or the captain might be an ignorant fellow who had never seen a Secret Service pass and did not know what it meant, and would refuse me transport by the letter of his instructions. In that case I might wait on another convoy.

I had shaved and made myself a fairly respectable figure before I left the cottage. It was my cue to wait for the men when they left the church, wait on that quarter-mile of straight highway. I judged the captain must be in the party. The village, I was glad to observe, seemed very empty. I have my own notions about the Bavarians as fighting men, but I am bound to say that, judging by my observations, very few of them stayed at home.

That funeral took hours. They must have had to dig the grave, for I waited near the road in a clump of cherry-trees, with my feet in two inches of mud and water, till I felt chilled to the bone. I prayed to God it would not bring back my fever, for I was only one day out of bed. I had very little tobacco left in my pouch, but I stood myself one pipe, and I ate one of the three cakes of chocolate I still carried.

At last, well after midday, I could see the ship's party returning. They marched two by two and I was thankful to see that they had no villagers with them. I walked to the road, turned up it, and met the vanguard, carrying my head as high as I knew how.

"Where's your captain?" I asked, and a man jerked his thumb over his shoulder. The others wore thick jerseys and knitted caps, but there was one man at the rear in uniform. He was a short, broad man with a weather-beaten face and an anxious eye.

"May I have a word with you, Herr Captain?" I said, with what I hoped was a judicious blend of authority and conciliation.

He nodded to his companion, who walked on.

"Yes?" he asked rather impatiently.

I proffered him my pass. Thank Heaven he had seen the kind of thing before, for his face at once took on that curious look which one person in authority always wears when he is confronted with another. He studied it closely and then raised his eyes.

"Well, sir?" he said. "I observe your credentials. What can I do for you?"

"I take it you are bound for Constantinople?" I asked.

"The boats go as far as Rustchuk," he replied. "There the stuff is transferred to the railway."

"And you reach Rustchuk when?"

"In ten days, bar accidents. Let us say twelve to be safe."

"I want to accompany you," I said. "In my profession, Herr Captain, it is necessary sometimes to make journeys by other than the common route. That is now my desire. I have the right to call upon some other branch of our country's service to help me. Hence my request."

Very plainly he did not like it.

"I must telegraph about it. My instructions are to let no one aboard, not even a man like you. I am sorry, sir, but I must get authority first before I can fall in with your desire. Besides, my boat is ill-found. You had better wait for the next batch and ask Dreyser to take you. I lost Walter to-day. He was ill when he came aboard—a disease of the heart—but he would not be persuaded. And last night he died."

"Was that him you have been burying?" I asked.

"Even so. He was a good man and my wife's cousin, and now I have no engineer. Only a fool of a boy from Hamburg. I have just come from wiring to my owners for a fresh man, but even if he comes by the quickest train he will scarcely overtake us before Vienna or even Buda."

I saw light at last.

"We will go together," I said, "and cancel that wire. For behold, Herr Captain, I am an engineer, and will gladly keep an eye on your boilers till we get to Rustchuk."

He looked at me doubtfully.

"I am speaking truth," I said. "Before the war I was an engineer in Damaraland. Mining was my branch, but I had a good general training, and I know enough to run a river-boat. Have no fear. I promise you I will earn my passage."

His face cleared, and he looked what he was, an honest, good-humoured North German seaman.

"Come then in God's name," he cried, "and we will make a bargain. I will let the telegraph sleep. I require authority from the Government to take a passenger, but I need none to engage a new engineer."

He sent one of the hands back to the village to cancel his wire. In ten minutes I found myself on board, and ten minutes later we were out in mid-stream and our tows were lumbering into line. Coffee was being made ready in the cabin, and while I waited for it I picked up the captain's binoculars and scanned the place I had left.

I saw some curious things. On the first road I had struck on leaving the cottage there were men on bicycles moving rapidly. They seemed to wear uniform. On the next parallel road, the one that ran through the village, I could see others. I noticed, too, that several figures appeared to be beating the intervening fields.

Stumm's cordon had got busy at last, and I thanked my stars that not one of the villagers had seen me. I had not got away much too soon, for in another half-hour he would have had me.

CHAPTER 9

The Return of the Straggler

BEFORE I TURNED in that evening I had done some good hours' work in the engine-room. The boat was oil-fired, and in very fair order, so my duties did not look as if they would be heavy. There was nobody who could be properly called an engineer; only, besides the furnace-men, a couple of lads from Hamburg who had been a year ago apprentices in a ship-building yard. They were civil fellows, both of them consumptive, who did what I told them and said little. By bed-time, if you had seen me in my blue jumper, a pair of carpet slippers, and a flat cap—all the property of the deceased Walter—you would have sworn I had been bred to the firing of river-boats, whereas I had acquired most of my knowledge on one run down the Zambesi, when the proper engineer got drunk and fell overboard among the crocodiles.

The captain—they called him Schenk—was out of his bearings in the job. He was a Frisian and a first-class deep-water seaman, but, since he knew the Rhine delta, and because the German mercantile marine was laid on the ice till the end of war, they had turned him on to this show. He was bored by the business, and didn't understand it very well. The river charts puzzled him, and though it was pretty plain going for hundreds of miles, yet he was in a perpetual fidget about the pilotage. You could see that he would have been far more in his element smelling his way through the shoals of the Ems mouth, or beating against a north-easter in the shallow Baltic. He had six barges in tow, but the heavy flood of the Danube made it an easy job except when it came to going slow. There were two men on each barge, who came aboard every morning to draw rations. That was a funny business, for we never lay to if we could help it. There was a dinghy belonging to each barge, and the men used to row to the next and get a lift in that barge's dinghy, and so forth. Six men would appear in the dinghy of the barge nearest us and carry off supplies for the rest. The men were mostly Frisians, slow-spoken, sandy-haired lads, very like the breed you strike on the Essex coast.

It was the fact that Schenk was really a deep-water sailor, and so a novice to the job, that made me get on with him. He was a good fellow and quite willing to take a hint, so before I had been twenty-four hours on board he was telling me all his difficulties, and I was doing my best to cheer him. And difficulties came thick, because the next night was New Year's Eve.

I knew that that night was a season of gaiety in Scotland, but Scotland wasn't in it with the Fatherland. Even Schenk, though he was in charge of valuable stores and was voyaging against time, was quite clear that the men must have permission for some kind of beano. Just before darkness we came abreast a fair-sized town, whose name I never discovered, and decided to lie to for the night. The arrangement was that one man should be left on guard in each barge, and the other get four hours' leave ashore. Then he would return and relieve his friend, who should proceed to do the same thing. I foresaw that there would be some fun when the first batch returned, but I did not dare to protest. I was desperately anxious to get past the Austrian frontier, for I had a half-notion we might be searched there, but Schenk took this *Sylvesterabend* business so seriously that I would have risked a row if I had tried to argue.

The upshot was what I expected. We got the first batch aboard about midnight, blind to the world, and the others straggled in at all hours next morning. I stuck to the boat for obvious reasons, but next day it became too serious, and I had to go ashore with the captain to try and round up the stragglers. We got them all in but two, and I am inclined to think these two had never meant to come back. If I had a soft job like a river-boat I shouldn't be inclined to run away in the middle of Germany with the certainty that my best fate would be to be scooped up for the trenches, but your Frisian has no more imagination than a haddock. The absentees were both watchmen from the barges, and I fancy the monotony of the life had got on their nerves.

The captain was in a raging temper, for he was short-handed to begin with. He would have started a press-gang, but there was no superfluity of men in that township: nothing but boys and grandfathers. As I was helping to run the trip I was pretty annoyed also, and I sluiced down the drunkards with icy Danube water, using all the worst language I knew in Dutch and German. It was a raw morning, and as we raged through the riverside streets I remember I heard the dry crackle of wild geese going overhead, and wished I could get a shot at them. I told one fellow—he was the most troublesome—that he was a disgrace to a great Empire, and was only fit to fight with the filthy English.

"God in Heaven!" said the captain, "we can delay no longer. We must make shift the best we can. I can spare one man from the deck hands, and you must give up one from the engine-room."

That was arranged, and we were tearing back rather short in the wind when I espied a figure sitting on a bench beside the booking-office on the pier. It was a slim figure, in an old suit of khaki: some cast-off duds which had long lost the semblance of a uniform. It had a gentle face, and was smoking peacefully, looking out upon the river and the boats and us noisy fellows with meek philosophical eyes. If I had seen General French sitting there and looking like nothing on earth I couldn't have been more surprised.

The man stared at me without recognition. He was waiting for his cue.

I spoke rapidly in Sesutu, for I was afraid the captain might know Dutch.

"Where have you come from?" I asked.

"They shut me up in *tronk*," said Peter, "and I ran away. I am tired, Cornelis, and want to continue the journey by boat."

"Remember you have worked for me in Africa," I said. "You are just home from Damaraland. You are a German who has lived thirty years away from home. You can tend a furnace and have worked in mines."

Then I spoke to the captain.

"Here is a fellow who used to be in my employ, Captain Schenk. It's almighty luck we've struck him. He's old, and not very strong in the head, but I'll go bail he's a good worker. He says he'll come with us and I can use him in the engine-room."

"Stand up," said the captain.

Peter stood up, light and slim and wiry as a leopard. A sailor does not judge men by girth and weight.

"He'll do," said Schenk, and the next minute he was readjusting his crews and giving the strayed revellers the rough side of his tongue. As it chanced, I couldn't keep Peter with me, but had to send him to one of the barges, and I had time for no more than five words with him, when I told him to hold his tongue and live up to his reputation as a half-wit. That accursed *Sylvesterabend* had played havoc with the whole outfit, and the captain and I were weary men before we got things straight.

In one way it turned out well. That afternoon we passed the frontier and I never knew it till I saw a man in a strange uniform come aboard, who copied some figures on a schedule, and brought us a mail. With my dirty face and general air of absorption in duty, I must have been an unsuspicious figure. He took down the names of the men in the barges, and Peter's name was given as it appeared on the ship's roll—Anton Blum.

"You must feel it strange, Herr Brandt," said the captain, "to be scrutinized by a policeman, you who give orders, I doubt not, to many policemen."

I shrugged my shoulders. "It is my profession. It is my business to go unrecognized often by my own servants." I could see that I was becoming rather a figure in the captain's eyes. He liked the way I kept the men up to their work, for I hadn't been a nigger-driver for nothing.

Late on that Sunday night we passed through a great city which the captain told me was Vienna. It seemed to last for miles and miles, and to be as brightly lit as a circus. After that, we were in big plains and the air grew perishing cold. Peter had come aboard once for his rations, but usually he left it to his partner, for he was lying very low. But one morning—I think it was the 5th of January, when we had passed Buda and were moving through great sodden flats just sprinkled with snow—the captain took it into his head to get me to overhaul the barge loads. Armed with a mighty typewritten list, I made a tour of the barges, beginning with the hindmost. There was a fine old stock of deadly weapons—mostly machine-guns and some field-pieces, and enough shells to blow up the Gallipoli peninsula. All kinds of shell were there, from the big 14-inch crumps to rifle grenades and trench-mortars. It made me fairly sick to see all these good things preparing for our own fellows, and I wondered whether I would not be doing my best service if I engineered a big explosion. Happily I had the common sense to remember my job and my duty and to stick to it.

Peter was in the middle of the convoy, and I found him pretty unhappy, principally through not being allowed to smoke. His companion was an ox-eyed lad, whom I ordered to look-out while Peter and I went over the lists.

"Cornelis, my old friend," he said, "there are some pretty toys here. With a spanner and a couple of clear hours I could make these maxims about as deadly as bicycles. What do you say to a try?"

"I've considered that," I said, "but it won't do. We're on a bigger business than wrecking munition convoys. I want to know how you got here."

He smiled with that extraordinary Sunday-school docility of his.

"It was very simple, Cornelis. I was foolish in the café—but they have told you of that. You see I was angry and did not reflect. They had separated us, and I could see would treat me as dirt. Therefore, my bad temper came out, for, as I have told you, I do not like Germans."

Peter gazed lovingly at the little bleak farms which dotted the Hungarian plain.

"All night I lay in *tronk* with no food. In the morning they fed me, and took me hundreds of miles in a train to a place which I think is called Neuburg. It was a great prison, full of English officers . . . I asked myself many times on the journey what was the reason of this treatment, for I could see no sense in it. If they wanted to punish me for insulting them they had the chance to send me off to the trenches. No one could have objected. If they thought me useless they could have turned me back to Holland. I could not have stopped them. But they treated me as if I were a dangerous man, whereas all their conduct hitherto had shown that they thought me a fool. I could not understand it.

"But I had not been one night in that Neuburg place before I thought of the reason. They wanted to keep me under observation as a check upon you, Cornelis. I figured it out this way. They had given you some very important work which required them to let you into some big secret. So far, good. They evidently thought much of you, even yon Stumm man, though he was as rude as a buffalo. But they did not know you fully, and they wanted a check on you. That check they found in Peter Pienaar. Peter was a fool, and if there was anything to blab, sooner or later Peter would blab it. Then they would stretch out a long arm and nip you short, wherever you were. Therefore they must keep old Peter under their eye."

"That sounds likely enough," I said.

"It was God's truth," said Peter. "And when it was all clear to me I settled that I must escape. Partly because I am a free man and do not like to be in prison, but mostly because I was not sure of myself. Some day my temper would go again, and I might say foolish things for which Cornelis would suffer. So it was very certain that I must escape.

"Now, Cornelis, I noticed pretty soon that there were two kinds among the prisoners. There were the real prisoners, mostly English and French, and there were humbugs. The humbugs were treated, apparently, like the others, but not really, as I soon perceived. There was one man who passed as an English officer, another as a French Canadian, and the others called themselves Russians. None of the honest men suspected them, but they were there as spies to hatch plots for escape and get the poor devils caught in the act, and to worm out confidences which might be of value. That is the German notion of good business. I am not a British soldier to think all men are gentlemen. I know that amongst men there are desperate *skellums*, so I soon picked up this game. It made me very angry, but it was a good thing for my plan. I made my resolution to escape the day I arrived at Neuburg, and on Christmas Day I had a plan made."

"Peter, you're an old marvel. Do you mean to say you were quite certain of getting away whenever you wanted?"

"Quite certain, Cornelis. You see, I have been wicked in my time and know something about the inside of prisons. You may build them like great castles, or they may be like a backveld *tronk*, only mud and corrugated iron, but there is always a key and a man who keeps it, and that man can be bested. I knew I could get away, but I did not think it would be so easy. That was due to the bogus prisoners, my friends, the spies.

"I made great pals with them. On Christmas night we were very jolly together. I think I spotted every one of them the first day. I bragged about my past and all I had done, and I told them I was going to escape. They backed me up and promised to help. Next morning I had a plan. In the afternoon, just after dinner, I had to go to the commandant's room. They treated me a little differently from the others, for I was not a prisoner of war, and I went there to be asked questions and to be cursed as a stupid Dutchman. There was no strict guard kept there, for the place was on the second floor, and distant by many yards from any staircase. In the corridor outside the commandant's room there was a window which had no bars, and four feet from the window the limb of a great tree. A man might reach that limb, and if he were active as a monkey might descend to the ground. Beyond that I knew nothing, but I am a good climber, Cornelis.

"I told the others of my plan. They said it was good, but no one offered to come with me. They were very noble; they declared that the scheme was mine and I should have the fruit of it, for if more than one tried, detection was certain. I agreed and thanked them—thanked them with tears in my eyes. Then one of them very secretly produced a map. We planned out my road, for I was going straight to Holland. It was a long road, and I had no money, for they had taken all my sovereigns when I was arrested, but they promised to get a subscription up among themselves to start me. Again I wept tears of gratitude. This was on Sunday, the day after Christmas. I settled to make the attempt on the Wednesday afternoon.

"Now, Cornelis, when the lieutenant took us to see the British prisoners, you remember, he told us many things about the ways of prisons. He told us how they loved to catch a man in the act of escape, so that they could use him harshly with a clear conscience. I thought of that, and calculated that now my friends would have told everything to the commandant, and that they would be waiting to bottle me on the Wednesday. Till then I reckoned I would be slackly guarded, for they would look on me as safe in the net . . .

"So I went out of the window the next day. It was the Monday afternoon . . ."

"That was a bold stroke," I said admiringly.

"The plan was bold, but it was not skilful," said Peter modestly. "I had no money beyond seven marks, and I had but one stick of chocolate. I had no overcoat, and it was snowing hard. Further, I could not get down the tree, which had a trunk as smooth and branchless as a blue gum. For a little I thought I should be compelled to give in, and I was not happy.

"But I had leisure, for I did not think I would be missed before nightfall, and given time a man can do most things. By and by I found a branch which led beyond the outer wall of the yard and hung above the river. This I followed, and then dropped from it into the stream. It was a drop of some yards, and the water was very swift, so that I nearly drowned. I would rather swim the Limpopo, Cornelis, among all the crocodiles than that icy river. Yet I managed to reach the shore and get my breath lying in the bushes . . .

"After that it was plain going, though I was very cold. I knew that I would be sought on the northern roads, as I had told my friends, for no one would dream of an ignorant Dutchman going south away from his kinsfolk. But I had learned enough from the map to know that our road lay south-east, and I had marked this big river."

"Did you hope to pick me up?" I asked.

"No, Cornelis. I thought you would be travelling in first-class carriages while I should be plodding on foot. But I was set on getting to the place you spoke of (how do you call it? Constant Nople?), where our big business lay. I thought I might be in time for that."

"You're an old Trojan, Peter," I said; "but go on. How did you get to that landing-stage where I found you?"

"It was a hard journey," he said meditatively. "It was not easy to get beyond the barbed-wire entanglements which surrounded Neuburg— yes, even across the river. But in time I reached the woods and was safe, for I did not think any German could equal me in wild country. The best of them, even their foresters, are but babes in veldcraft compared with such as me . . . My troubles came only from hunger and cold. Then I met a Peruvian smouse,* and sold him my clothes and bought from him these. I did not want to part with my own, which were better, but he gave me ten marks on the deal. After that I went into a village and ate heavily."

"Were you pursued?" I asked.

"I do not think so. They had gone north, as I expected, and were looking for me at the railway stations which my friends had marked for me. I walked happily and put a bold face on it. If I saw a man or woman look at me suspiciously I went up to them at once and talked. I told a sad tale, and all believed it. I was a poor Dutchman travelling home on foot to see a dying mother, and I had been told that by the Danube I should find the main railway to take me to Holland. There were kind people who gave me food, and one woman gave me half a mark, and

---

* Peter meant a Polish-Jew pedlar.

wished me God speed . . . Then on the last day of the year I came to the river and found many drunkards."

"Was that when you resolved to get on one of the river-boats?"

"*Ja*, Cornelis. As soon as I heard of the boats I saw where my chance lay. But you might have knocked me over with a straw when I saw you come on shore. That was good fortune, my friend . . . I have been thinking much about the Germans, and I will tell you the truth. It is only boldness that can baffle them. They are a most diligent people. They will think of all likely difficulties, but not of all possible ones. They have not much imagination. They are like steam engines which must keep to prepared tracks. There they will hunt any man down, but let him trek for open country and they will be at a loss. Therefore boldness, my friend; for ever boldness. Remember as a nation they wear spectacles, which means that they are always peering."

Peter broke off to gloat over the wedges of geese and the strings of wild swans that were always winging across those plains. His tale had bucked me up wonderfully. Our luck had held beyond all belief, and I had a kind of hope in the business now which had been wanting before. That afternoon, too, I got another fillip.

I came on deck for a breath of air and found it pretty cold after the heat of the engine-room. So I called to one of the deck hands to fetch me up my cloak from the cabin—the same I had bought that first morning in the Greif village.

"*Der grüne mantel?*" the man shouted up, and I cried, "Yes." But the words seemed to echo in my ears, and long after he had given me the garment I stood staring abstractedly over the bulwarks.

His tone had awakened a chord of memory, or, to be accurate, they had given emphasis to what before had been only blurred and vague. For he had spoken the words which Stumm had uttered behind his hand to Gaudian. I had heard something like "*Uhnmantl*," and could make nothing of it. Now I was as certain of those words as of my own existence. They had been "*Grüne mantel*". *Grüne mantel*, whatever it might be, was the name which Stumm had not meant me to hear, which was some talisman for the task I had proposed, and which was connected in some way with the mysterious von Einem.

This discovery put me in high fettle. I told myself that, considering the difficulties, I had managed to find out a wonderful amount in a very few days. It only shows what a man can do with the slenderest evidence if he keeps chewing and chewing on it . . .

Two mornings later we lay alongside the quays at Belgrade, and I took the opportunity of stretching my legs. Peter had come ashore for a smoke, and we wandered among the battered riverside streets, and looked at the broken arches of the great railway bridge which the Germans were working at like beavers. There was a big temporary pontoon affair to take the railway across, but I calculated that the main bridge would be ready inside a month. It was a clear, cold, blue day, and as one looked south one saw ridge after ridge of snowy hills. The upper streets of the city were still fairly whole, and there were shops open where food could be got. I remember hearing English spoken, and seeing some Red Cross nurses in the custody of Austrian soldiers coming from the railway station.

It would have done me a lot of good to have had a word with them. I thought of the gallant people whose capital this had been, how three times they had flung the Austrians back over the Danube, and then had only been beaten by the black treachery of their so-called allies. Somehow that morning in Belgrade gave both Peter and me a new purpose in our task. It was our business to put a spoke in the wheel of this monstrous bloody Juggernaut that was crushing the life out of the little heroic nations.

We were just getting ready to cast off when a distinguished party arrived at the quay. There were all kinds of uniforms—German, Austrian, and Bulgarian, and amid them one stout gentleman in a fur coat and a black felt hat. They watched the barges up-anchor, and before we began to jerk into line I could hear the conversation. The fur coat was talking English.

"I reckon that's pretty good noos, General," it said; "if the English have run away from Gally-poly we can use these noo consignments for the bigger game. I guess it won't be long before we see the British lion moving out of Egypt with sore paws."

They all laughed. "The privilege of that spectacle may soon be ours," was the reply.

I did not pay much attention to the talk; indeed I did not realize till weeks later that that was the first tidings of the great evacuation of Cape Helles. What rejoiced me was the sight of Blenkiron, as bland as a barber among those swells. Here were two of the missionaries within reasonable distance of their goal.

CHAPTER 10

The Garden-House of Suliman the Red

W E REACHED RUSTCHUK on January 10, but by no means
landed on that day. Something had gone wrong with the
unloading arrangements, or more likely with the railway
behind them, and we were kept swinging all day well out in
the turbid river. On the top of this Captain Schenk got an
ague, and by that evening was a blue and shivering wreck. He had done
me well, and I reckoned I would stand by him. So I got his ship's
papers, and the manifests of cargo, and undertook to see to the
transhipment. It wasn't the first time I had tackled that kind of
business, and I hadn't much to learn about steam cranes. I told him I
was going on to Constantinople and would take Peter with me, and he
was agreeable. He would have to wait at Rustchuk to get his return
cargo, and could easily inspan a fresh engineer.

I worked about the hardest twenty-four hours of my life getting the
stuff ashore. The landing officer was a Bulgarian, quite a competent
man if he could have made the railways give him the trucks he needed.
There was a collection of hungry German transport officers always
putting in their oars, and being infernally insolent to everybody. I took
the high and mighty line with them; and, as I had the Bulgarian
commandant on my side, after about two hours' blasphemy got them
quieted.

But the big trouble came the next morning when I had got nearly all
the stuff aboard the trucks.

A young officer in what I took to be a Turkish uniform rode up with
an aide-de-camp. I noticed the German guards saluting him, so I judged
he was rather a swell. He came up to me and asked me very civilly in
German for the way-bills. I gave him them and he looked carefully
through them, marking certain items with a blue pencil. Then he coolly

handed them to his aide-de-camp and spoke to him in Turkish.

"Look here, I want these back," I said. "I can't do without them, and we've no time to waste."

"Presently," he said, smiling, and went off.

I said nothing, reflecting that the stuff was for the Turks and they naturally had to have some say in its handling. The loading was practically finished when my gentleman returned. He handed me a neatly typed new set of way-bills. One glance at them showed that some of the big items had been left out.

"Here, this won't do," I cried. "Give me back the right set. This thing's no good to me."

For answer he winked gently, smiled like a dusky seraph, and held out his hand. In it I saw a roll of money.

"For yourself," he said. "It is the usual custom."

It was the first time anyone had ever tried to bribe me, and it made me boil up like a geyser. I saw his game clearly enough. Turkey would pay for the lot to Germany: probably had already paid the bill: but she would pay double for the things not on the way-bills, and pay to this fellow and his friends. This struck me as rather steep even for Oriental methods of doing business.

"Now look here, sir," I said, "I don't stir from this place till I get the correct way-bills. If you won't give me them, I will have every item out of the trucks and make a new list. But a correct list I have, or the stuff stays here till Doomsday."

He was a slim, foppish fellow, and he looked more puzzled than angry.

"I offer you enough," he said, again stretching out his hand.

At that I fairly roared. "If you try to bribe me, you infernal little haberdasher, I'll have you off that horse and chuck you in the river."

He no longer misunderstood me. He began to curse and threaten, but I cut him short.

"Come along to the commandant, my boy," I said, and I marched away, tearing up his typewritten sheets as I went and strewing them behind me like a paper chase.

We had a fine old racket in the commandant's office. I said it was my business, as representing the German Government, to see the stuff delivered to the consignee at Constantinople ship-shape and Bristol-fashion. I told him it wasn't my habit to proceed with cooked

HE NO LONGER MISUNDERSTOOD ME

documents. He couldn't but agree with me, but there was that wrathful Oriental with his face as fixed as a Buddha.

"I am sorry, Rasta Bey," he said; "but this man is in the right."

"I have authority from the Committee to receive the stores," he said sullenly.

"Those are not my instructions," was the answer. "They are consigned to the Artillery commandant at Chataldja, General von Oesterzee."

The man shrugged his shoulders. "Very well. I will have a word to say to General von Oesterzee, and many to this fellow who flouts the Committee." And he strode away like an impudent boy.

The harassed commandant grinned. "You've offended his lordship, and he is a bad enemy. All those damned Comitadjis are. You would be well advised not to go on to Constantinople."

"And have that blighter in the red hat loot the trucks on the road. No, thank you. I am going to see them safe at Chataldja, or whatever they call the artillery depot."

I said a good deal more, but that is an abbreviated translation of my remarks. My word for "blighter" was *Trottel*, but I used some other expressions which would have ravished my Young Turk friend to hear. Looking back, it seems pretty ridiculous to have made all this fuss about guns which were going to be used against my own people. But I didn't see that at the time. My professional pride was up in arms, and I couldn't bear to have a hand in a crooked deal.

"Well, I advise you to go armed," said the commandant. "You will have a guard for the trucks, of course, and I will pick you good men. They may hold you up all the same. I can't help you once you are past the frontier, but I'll send a wire to Oesterzee and he'll make trouble if anything goes wrong. I still think you would have been wiser to humour Rasta Bey."

As I was leaving he gave me a telegram. "Here's a wire for your Captain Schenk." I slipped the envelope in my pocket and went out.

Schenk was pretty sick, so I left a note for him. At one o'clock I got the train started, with a couple of German Landwehr in each truck and Peter and I in a horse-box. Presently I remembered Schenk's telegram, which still reposed in my pocket. I took it out and opened it, meaning to wire it from the first station we stopped at. But I changed my mind when I read it. It was from some official at Regensburg, asking him to put under arrest and send back by the first boat a man called Brandt, who was believed to have come aboard at Absthafen on the 30th of December.

I whistled and showed it to Peter. The sooner we were at Constantinople the better, and I prayed we would get there before the fellow who sent this wire repeated it and got the commandant to send on the message and have us held up at Chataldja. For my back had fairly got stiffened about these munitions, and I was going to take any risk to see them safely delivered to their proper owner. Peter couldn't understand me at all. He still hankered after a grand destruction of the lot somewhere down the railway. But then, this wasn't the line of Peter's profession, and his pride was not at stake.

We had a mortally slow journey. It was bad enough in Bulgaria, but when we crossed the frontier at a place called Mustafa Pasha we struck the real supineness of the East. Happily I found a German officer there who had some notion of hustling, and, after all, it was his interest to get the stuff moved. It was the morning of the 16th, after Peter and I had been living like pigs on black bread and condemned tin stuff, that we came in sight of a blue sea on our right hand and knew we couldn't be very far from the end.

It was jolly near the end in another sense. We stopped at a station and were stretching our legs on the platform when I saw a familiar figure approaching. It was Rasta, with half a dozen Turkish gendarmes.

I called Peter, and we clambered into the truck next our horse-box. I had been half expecting some move like this and had made a plan.

The Turk swaggered up and addressed us. "You can get back to Rustchuk," he said. "I take over from you here. Hand me the papers."

"Is this Chataldja?" I asked innocently.

"It is the end of your affair," he said haughtily. "Quick, or it will be the worse for you."

"Now, look here, my son," I said; "you're a kid and know nothing. I hand over to General von Oesterzee and to no one else."

"You are in Turkey," he cried, "and will obey the Turkish Government."

"I'll obey the Government right enough," I said; "but if you're the Government I could make a better one with a bib and a rattle."

He said something to his men, who unslung their rifles.

"Please don't begin shooting," I said. "There are twelve armed

227

guards in this train who will take their orders from me. Besides, I and my friend can shoot a bit."

"Fool!" he cried, getting very angry. "I can order up a regiment in five minutes."

"Maybe you can," I said; "but observe the situation. I am sitting on enough toluol to blow up this countryside. If you dare to come aboard I will shoot you. If you call in your regiment I will tell you what I'll do. I'll fire this stuff, and I reckon they'll be picking up the bits of you and your regiment off the Gallipoli peninsula."

He had put up a bluff—a poor one—and I had called it. He saw I meant what I said, and became silken.

"Good-bye, sir," he said. "You have had a fair chance and rejected it. We shall meet again soon, and you will be sorry for your insolence."

He strutted away and it was all I could do to keep from running after him. I wanted to lay him over my knee and spank him.

WE GOT SAFELY to Chataldja, and were received by von Oesterzee like long-lost brothers. He was the regular gunner-officer, not thinking about anything except his guns and shells. I had to wait about three hours while he was checking the stuff with the invoices, and then he gave me a receipt which I still possess. I told him about Rasta, and he agreed that I had done right. It didn't make him as mad as I expected, because, you see, he got his stuff safe in any case. It was only that the wretched Turks had to pay twice for the lot of it.

He gave Peter and me luncheon, and was altogether very civil and inclined to talk about the war. I would have liked to hear what he had to say, for it would have been something to get the inside view of Germany's Eastern campaign, but I did not dare to wait. Any moment there might arrive an incriminating wire from Rustchuk. Finally he lent us a car to take us the few miles to the city.

So it came about that at five past three on the 16th day of January, with only the clothes we stood up in, Peter and I entered Constantinople.

I was in considerable spirits, for I had got the final lap successfully over, and I was looking forward madly to meeting my friends; but, all the same, the first sight was a mighty disappointment. I don't quite know what I had expected—a sort of fairyland Eastern city, all white marble and blue water, and stately Turks in surplices, and veiled houris, and roses and nightingales, and some sort of string band discoursing sweet music. I had forgotten that winter is pretty much the same everywhere. It was a drizzling day, with a south-east wind blowing, and the streets were long troughs of mud. The first part I struck looked like a dingy colonial suburb—wooden houses and corrugated iron roofs, and endless dirty, sallow children. There was a cemetery, I remember, with Turks' caps stuck at the head of each grave. Then we got into narrow steep streets which descended to a kind of big canal. I saw what I took to be mosques and minarets, and they were about as impressive as factory chimneys. By and by we crossed a bridge, and paid a penny for the privilege. If I had known it was the famous Golden Horn I would have looked at it with more interest, but I saw nothing save a lot of moth-eaten barges and some queer little boats like gondolas. Then we came into busier streets, where ramshackle cabs drawn by lean horses spluttered through the mud. I saw one old fellow who looked like my notion of a Turk, but most of the population had the appearance of London old-clothes men. All but the soldiers, Turk and German, who seemed well-set-up fellows.

Peter had paddled along at my side like a faithful dog, not saying a word, but clearly not approving of this wet and dirty metropolis.

"Do you know that we are being followed, Cornelis?" he said suddenly, "ever since we came into this evil-smelling dorp."

Peter was infallible in a thing like that. The news scared me badly, for I feared that the telegram had come to Chataldja. Then I thought it couldn't be that, for if von Oesterzee had wanted me he wouldn't have taken the trouble to stalk me. It was more likely my friend Rasta.

I found the ferry of Ratchik by asking a soldier and a German sailor there told me where the Kurdish Bazaar was. He pointed up a steep street which ran past a high block of warehouses with every window broken. Sandy had said the left-hand side coming down, so it must be the right-hand side going up. We plunged into it, and it was the filthiest place of all. The wind whistled up it and stirred the garbage. It seemed densely inhabited, for at all the doors there were groups of people squatting, with their heads covered, though scarcely a window showed in the blank walls.

The street corkscrewed endlessly. Sometimes it seemed to stop; then it found a hole in the opposing masonry and edged its way in. Often it was almost pitch dark; then would come a greyish twilight where it opened out to the width of a decent lane. To find a house in that murk was no easy job, and by the time we had gone a quarter of a mile I began to fear we had missed it. It was no good asking any of the crowd we met. They didn't look as if they understood any civilized tongue.

At last we stumbled on it—a tumble-down coffee-house, with A. Kuprasso above the door in queer amateur lettering. There was a lamp burning inside, and two or three men smoking at small wooden tables.

We ordered coffee, thick black stuff like treacle, which Peter anathematized. A negro brought it, and I told him in German I wanted to speak to Mr Kuprasso. He paid no attention, so I shouted louder at him, and the noise brought a man out of the back parts.

He was a fat, oldish fellow with a long nose, very like the Greek traders you see on the Zanzibar coast. I beckoned to him and he waddled forward, smiling oilily. Then I asked him what he would take, and he replied, in very halting German, that he would have a sirop.

"You are Mr Kuprasso," I said. "I wanted to show this place to my friend. He has heard of your garden-house and the fun there."

"The Signor is mistaken. I have no garden-house."

"Rot," I said; "I've been here before, my boy. I recall your shanty at the back and many merry nights there. What was it you called it? Oh, I remember—the Garden-House of Suliman the Red."

He put his finger to his lip and looked incredibly sly. "The Signor remembers that. But that was in the old happy days before war came. The place is long since shut. The people here are too poor to dance and sing."

"All the same I would like to have another look at it," I said, and I slipped an English sovereign into his hand.

He glanced at it in surprise and his manner changed. "The Signor is a Prince, and I will do his will." He clapped his hands and the negro appeared, and at his nod took his place behind a little side-counter.

"Follow me," he said, and led us through a long, noisome passage, which was pitch dark and very unevenly paved. Then he unlocked a door and with a swirl the wind caught it and blew it back on us.

We were looking into a mean little yard, with on one side a high curving wall, evidently of great age, with bushes growing in the cracks of it. Some scraggy myrtles stood in broken pots, and nettles flourished in a corner. At one end was a wooden building like a dissenting chapel, but painted a dingy scarlet. Its windows and skylights were black with dirt, and its door, tied with rope, flapped in the wind.

"Behold the Pavilion," Kuprasso said proudly.

"That is the old place," I observed with feeling. "What times I've seen there! Tell me, Mr Kuprasso, do you ever open it?"

He put his thick lips to my ear.

"If the Signor will be silent I will tell him. It is sometimes open—not often. Men must amuse themselves even in war. Some of the German officers come here for their pleasure, and but last week we had the ballet of Mademoiselle Cici. The police approve—but not often, for this is no time for too much gaiety. I will tell you a secret. To-morrow afternoon there will be dancing—wonderful dancing! Only a few of my patrons know. Who, think you, will be there?"

He bent his head closer and said in a whisper—

"The Compagnie des Heures Roses."

"Oh, indeed," I said with a proper tone of respect, though I hadn't a notion what he meant.

"Will the Signor wish to come?"

"Sure," I said. "Both of us. We're all for the rose hours."

"Then the fourth hour after midday. Walk straight through the café and one will be there to unlock the door. You are new-comers here? Take the advice of Angelo Kuprasso and avoid the streets after nightfall. Stamboul is no safe place nowadays for quiet men."

I asked him to name an hotel, and he rattled off a list from which I chose one that sounded modest and in keeping with our get-up. It was not far off, only a hundred yards to the right at the top of the hill.

When we left his door the night had begun to drop. We hadn't gone twenty yards before Peter drew very near to me and kept turning his head like a hunted stag.

"We are being followed close, Cornelis," he said calmly.

Another ten yards and we were at a cross-road, where a little *place* faced a biggish mosque. I could see in the waning light a crowd of people who seemed to be moving towards us. I heard a high-pitched voice cry out a jabber of excited words, and it seemed to me that I had heard the voice before.

CHAPTER 11

The Companions of the Rosy Hours

WE BATTLED TO A CORNER, where a jut of building stood out into the street. It was our only chance to protect our backs, to stand up with the rib of stone between us. It was only the work of seconds. One instant we were groping our solitary way in the darkness, the next we were pinned against a wall with a throaty mob surging round us.

It took me a moment or two to realize that we were attacked. Every man has one special funk in the back of his head, and mine was to be the quarry of an angry crowd. I hated the thought of it—the mess, the blind struggle, the sense of unleashed passions different from those of any single blackguard. It was a dark world to me, and I don't like darkness. But in my nightmares I had never imagined anything just like this. The narrow, fetid street, with the icy winds fanning the filth, the unknown tongue, the hoarse savage murmur, and my utter ignorance as to what it might all be about, made me cold in the pit of my stomach.

"We've got it in the neck this time, old man," I said to Peter, who had out the pistol the commandant at Rustchuk had given him. These pistols were our only weapons. The crowd saw them and hung back, but if they chose to rush us it wasn't much of a barrier two pistols would make.

Rasta's voice had stopped. He had done his work, and had retired to the background. There were shouts from the crowd—"*Alleman*" and a word "*Khafiyeh*" constantly repeated. I didn't know what it meant at the time, but now I know that they were after us because we were Boches and spies. There was no love lost between the Constantinople scum and their new masters. It seemed an ironical end for Peter and me to be done in because we were Boches. And done in we should be. I had heard of the East as a good place for people to disappear in; there were no inquisitive newspapers or incorruptible police.

I wished to Heaven I had a word of Turkish. But I made my voice heard for a second in a pause of the din, and shouted that we were German sailors who had brought down big guns for Turkey, and were going home next day. I asked them what the devil they thought we had done? I don't know if any fellow there understood German; anyhow, it only brought a pandemonium of cries in which that ominous word *Khafiyeh* was predominant.

Then Peter fired over their heads. He had to, for a chap was pawing at his throat. The answer was a clatter of bullets on the wall above us. It looked as if they meant to take us alive, and that I was very clear should not happen. Better a bloody end in a street scrap than the tender mercies of that bandbox bravo.

I don't quite know what happened next. A press drove down at me and I fired. Someone squealed, and I looked the next moment to be strangled. And then, suddenly, the scrimmage ceased, and there was a wavering splash of light in that pit of darkness.

I never went through many worse minutes than these. When I had been hunted in the past weeks there had been mystery enough, but no immediate peril to face. When I had been up against a real, urgent, physical risk, like Loos, the danger at any rate had been clear. One knew what one was in for. But here was a threat I couldn't put a name to, and it wasn't in the future, but pressing hard at our throats.

And yet I couldn't feel it was quite real. The patter of the pistol bullets against the wall, like so many crackers, the faces felt rather than seen in the dark, the clamour which to me was pure gibberish, had all the madness of a nightmare. Only Peter, cursing steadily in Dutch by my side, was real. And then the light came, and made the scene more eerie!

It came from one or two torches carried by wild fellows with long staves who drove their way into the heart of the mob. The flickering glare ran up the steep walls and made monstrous shadows. The wind swung the flame into long streamers, dying away in a fan of sparks.

And now a new word was heard in the crowd. It was *Chinganeh*, shouted not in anger but in fear.

At first I could not see the new-comers. They were hidden in the deep darkness under their canopy of light, for they were holding their torches high at the full stretch of their arms. They were shouting, too, wild shrill cries ending sometimes in a gush of rapid speech. Their words did not seem to be directed against us, but against the crowd. A sudden hope came to me that for some unknown reason they were on our side.

The press was no longer heavy against us. It was thinning rapidly and I could hear the scuffle as men made off down the side streets. My first notion was that these were the Turkish police. But I changed my mind when the leader came out into the patch of light. He carried no torch, but a long stave with which he belaboured the heads of those who were too tightly packed to flee.

It was the most eldritch apparition you can conceive. A tall man dressed in skins, with bare legs and sandal-shod feet. A wisp of scarlet cloth clung to his shoulders, and, drawn over his head down close to his eyes, was a skull-cap of some kind of pelt with the tail waving behind it. He capered like a wild animal, keeping up a strange high monotone that fairly gave me the creeps.

I was suddenly aware that the crowd had gone. Before us was only this figure and his half-dozen companions, some carrying torches and all wearing clothes of skin. But only the one who seemed to be their leader wore the skull-cap; the rest had bare heads and long tangled hair.

The fellow was shouting gibberish at me. His eyes were glassy, like a man who smokes hemp, and his legs were never still for a second. You would think such a figure no better than a mountebank, and yet there was nothing comic in it. Fearful and sinister and uncanny it was; and I wanted to do anything but laugh.

As he shouted he kept pointing with his stave up the street which climbed the hillside.

"He means us to move," said Peter. "For God's sake let us get away from this witch-doctor."

I couldn't make sense of it, but one thing was clear. These maniacs had delivered us for the moment from Rasta and his friends.

Then I did a dashed silly thing. I pulled out a sovereign and offered it to the leader. I had some kind notion of showing gratitude, and as I had no words I had to show it by deed.

He brought his stick down on my wrist and sent the coin spinning in the gutter. His eyes blazed, and he made his weapon sing round my head. He cursed me—oh, I could tell cursing well enough, though I didn't follow a word; and he cried to his followers and they cursed me too. I had offered him a mortal insult and stirred up a worse hornet's nest than Rasta's push.

Peter and I, with a common impulse, took to our heels. We were not looking for any trouble with demoniacs. Up the steep narrow lane we ran with that bedlamite crowd at our heels. The torches seemed to have gone out, for the place was black as pitch, and we tumbled over heaps of offal and splashed through running drains. The men were close behind us, and more than once I felt a stick on my shoulder. But fear lent us wings, and suddenly before us was a blaze of light and we saw the debouchment of our street in a main thoroughfare. The others saw it, too, for they slackened off. Just before we reached the light we stopped and looked round. There was no sound or sight behind us in the dark lane which dipped to the harbour.

"This is a queer country, Cornelis," said Peter, feeling his limbs for bruises. "Too many things happen in too short a time. I am breathless."

The big street we had struck seemed to run along the crest of the hill. There were lamps in it, and crawling cabs, and quite civilized-looking shops. We soon found the hotel to which Kuprasso had directed us, a big place in a courtyard with a very tumble-down-looking portico, and green sun shutters which rattled drearily in the winter's wind. It proved, as I had feared, to be packed to the door, mostly with German officers. With some trouble I got an interview with the proprietor, the usual Greek, and told him that we had been sent there by Mr Kuprasso. That didn't affect him in the least, and we would have been shot into the street if I hadn't remembered about Stumm's pass.

So I explained that we had come from Germany with munitions and only wanted rooms for one night. I showed him the pass and blustered a good deal, till he became civil and said he would do the best he could for us.

That best was pretty poor. Peter and I were doubled up in a small room which contained two camp-beds and little else, and had broken windows through which the wind whistled. We had a wretched dinner of stringy mutton, boiled with vegetables, and a white cheese strong enough to raise the dead. But I got a bottle of whisky, for which I paid a sovereign, and we managed to light the stove in our room, fasten the shutters, and warm our hearts with a brew of toddy. After that we went to bed and slept like logs for twelve hours. On the road from Rustchuk we had had uneasy slumbers.

I woke next morning and, looking out from the broken window, saw that it was snowing. With a lot of trouble I got hold of a servant and made him bring us some of the treacly Turkish coffee. We were both in pretty low spirits. "Europe is a poor cold place," said Peter, "not worth fighting for. There is only one white man's land, and that is South Africa." At the time I heartily agreed with him.

I remember that, sitting on the edge of my bed, I took stock of our position. It was not very cheering. We seemed to have been amassing enemies at a furious pace. First of all, there was Rasta, whom I had insulted and who wouldn't forget it in a hurry. He had his crowd of Turkish riff-raff and was bound to get us sooner or later. Then there was the maniac in the skin hat. He didn't like Rasta, and I made a guess that he and his weird friends were of some party hostile to the Young Turks. But, on the other hand, he didn't like us, and there would be bad trouble the next time we met him. Finally, there was Stumm and the German Government. It could only be a matter of hours at the best before he got the Rustchuk authorities on our trail. It would be easy to trace us from Chataldja, and once they had us we were absolutely done. There was a big black dossier against us, which by no conceivable piece of luck could be upset.

It was very clear to me that, unless we could find sanctuary and shed all our various pursuers during this day, we should be done in for good and all. But where on earth were we to find sanctuary? We had neither of us a word of the language, and there was no way I could see of taking on new characters. For that we wanted friends and help, and I could think of none anywhere. Somewhere, to be sure, there was Blenkiron, but how could we get in touch with him? As for Sandy, I had pretty well given him up. I always thought his enterprise the craziest of the lot and bound to fail. He was probably somewhere in Asia Minor, and a month or two later would get to Constantinople and hear in some pot-house the yarn of the two wretched Dutchmen who had dis-appeared so soon from men's sight.

That rendezvous at Kuprasso's was no good. It would have been all right if we had got here unsuspected, and could have gone on quietly frequenting the place till Blenkiron picked us up. But to do that we wanted leisure and secrecy, and here we were with a pack of hounds at our heels. The place was horribly dangerous already. If we showed ourselves there we should be gathered in by Rasta, or by the German military police, or by the madman in the skin cap. It was a stark impossibility to hang about on the off-chance of meeting Blenkiron.

I reflected with some bitterness that this was the 17th day of January, the day of our assignation. I had had high hopes all the way down the Danube of meeting with Blenkiron—for I knew *he* would be in time—of giving him the information I had had the good fortune to collect, of piecing it together with what he had found out, and of getting the whole story which Sir Walter hungered for. After that, I thought it wouldn't be hard to get away by Rumania, and to get home through Russia. I had hoped to be back with my battalion in February, having done as good a bit of work as anybody in the war. As it was, it looked as if my information would die with me, unless I could find Blenkiron before the evening.

I talked the thing over with Peter, and he agreed that we were fairly up against it. We decided to go to Kuprasso's that afternoon, and to trust to luck for the rest. It wouldn't do to wander about the streets, so we sat tight in our room all morning, and swopped old hunting yarns to keep our minds from the beastly present. We got some food at midday—cold mutton and the same cheese, and finished our whisky. Then I paid the bill, for I didn't dare to stay there another night. About half past three we went into the street, without the foggiest notion where we would find our next quarters.

It was snowing heavily, which was a piece of luck for us. Poor old Peter had no greatcoat, so we went into a Jew's shop and bought a ready-made abomination, which looked as if it might have been meant for a dissenting parson. It was no good saving my money when the future was so black. The snow made the streets deserted, and we turned down the long lane which led to Ratchik ferry, and found it perfectly quiet. I do not think we met a soul till we got to Kuprasso's shop.

We walked straight through the café, which was empty, and down the dark passage, till we were stopped by the garden door. I knocked and it swung open. There was the bleak yard, now puddled with snow, and a blaze of light from the pavilion at the other end. There was a scraping of fiddles, too, and the sound of human talk. We paid the negro at the door, and passed from the bitter afternoon into a garish saloon.

There were forty or fifty people there, drinking coffee and sirops and filling the air with the fumes of latakia. Most of them were Turks in European clothes and the fez, but there were some German officers and what looked like German civilians—Army Service Corps clerks, probably, and mechanics from the Arsenal. A woman in cheap finery was tinkling at the piano, and there were several shrill females with the officers. Peter and I sat down modestly in the nearest corner, where old Kuprasso saw us and sent us coffee. A girl who looked like a Jewess came over to us and talked French, but I shook my head and she went off again.

Presently a girl came on the stage and danced, a silly affair, all a clashing of tambourines and wriggling. I have seen native women do the same thing better in a Mozambique kraal. Another sang a German song, a simple, sentimental thing about golden hair and rainbows, and the Germans present applauded. The place was so tinselly and common that, coming to it from weeks of rough travelling, it made me impatient. I forgot that, while for the others it might be a vulgar little dancing-hall, for us it was as perilous as a brigands' den.

Peter did not share my mood. He was quite interested in it, as he was interested in everything new. He had a genius for living in the moment.

I remember there was a drop-scene on which was daubed a blue lake with very green hills in the distance. As the tobacco smoke grew thicker and the fiddles went on squealing, this tawdry picture began to mesmerize me. I seemed to be looking out of a window at a lovely summer landscape where there were no wars or danger. I seemed to feel the warm sun and to smell the fragrance of blossom from the islands. And then I became aware that a queer scent had stolen into the atmosphere.

There were braziers burning at both ends to warm the room, and the thin smoke from these smelt like incense. Somebody had been putting a powder in the flames, for suddenly the place became very quiet. The fiddles still sounded, but far away like an echo. The lights went down, all but a circle on the stage, and into that circle stepped my enemy of the skin cap.

He had three others with him. I heard a whisper behind me, and the words were those which Kuprasso had used the day before. These bedlamites were called the Companions of the Rosy Hours, and Kuprasso had promised great dancing.

I hoped to goodness they would not see us, for they had fairly given me the horrors. Peter felt the same, and we both made ourselves very small in that dark corner. But the new-comers had no eyes for us.

In a twinkling the pavilion changed from a common saloon, which might have been in Chicago or Paris, to a place of mystery—yes, and of beauty. It became the Garden-House of Suliman the Red, whoever that sportsman may have been. Sandy had said that the ends of the earth converged there, and he had been right. I lost all consciousness of my neighbours—stout German, frock-coated Turk, frowsy Jewess—and saw only strange figures leaping in a circle of light, figures that came out of the deepest darkness to make a big magic.

The leader flung some stuff into the brazier, and a great fan of blue light flared up. He was weaving circles, and he was singing something shrill and high, whilst his companions made a chorus with their deep monotone. I can't tell you what the dance was. I had seen the Russian ballet just before the war, and one of the men in it reminded me of this man. But the dancing was the least part of it. It was neither sound nor movement nor scent that wrought the spell, but something far more potent. In an instant I found myself reft away from the present with its dull dangers, and looking at a world all young and fresh and beautiful. The gaudy drop-scene had vanished. It was a window I was looking from, and I was gazing at the finest landscape on earth, lit by the pure clean light of morning.

It seemed to be part of the veld, but like no veld I had ever seen. It was wider and wilder and more gracious. Indeed, I was looking at my first youth. I was feeling the kind of immortal light-heartedness which only a boy knows in the dawning of his days. I had no longer any fear of these magic-makers. They were kindly wizards, who had brought me into fairyland.

Then slowly from the silence there distilled drops of music. They came like water falling a long way into a cup, each the essential quality of pure sound. We, with our elaborate harmonies, have forgotten the charm of single notes. The African natives know it, and I remember a learned man once telling me that the Greeks had the same art. Those silver bells broke out of infinite space, so exquisite and perfect that no mortal words could have been fitted to them. That was the music, I expect, that the morning stars made when they sang together.

Slowly, very slowly, it changed. The glow passed from blue to purple, and then to an angry red. Bit by bit the notes spun together till they had made a harmony—a fierce, restless harmony. And I was conscious again of the skin-clad dancers beckoning out of their circle.

There was no mistake about the meaning now. All the daintiness and youth had fled, and passion was beating the air—terrible, savage passion, which belonged neither to day nor night, life nor death, but to the half-world between them. I suddenly felt the dancers as monstrous, inhuman, devilish. The thick scents that floated from the brazier seemed to have a tang of new-shed blood. Cries broke from the hearers—cries of anger and lust and terror. I heard a woman sob, and Peter, who is as tough as any mortal, took tight hold of my arm.

I now realized that these Companions of the Rosy Hours were the only thing in the world to fear. Rasta and Stumm seemed feeble simpletons by contrast. The window I had been looking out of was changed to a prison wall—I could see the mortar between the massive blocks. In a second these devils would be smelling out their enemies like some foul witch-doctors. I felt the burning eyes of their leader looking for me in the gloom. Peter was praying audibly beside me, and I could have choked him. His infernal chatter would reveal us, for it seemed to me that there was no one in the place except us and the magic-workers.

THEN SUDDENLY THE SPELL was broken. The door was flung open and a great gust of icy wind swirled through the hall, driving clouds of ashes from the braziers. I heard loud voices without, and a hubbub began inside. For a moment it was quite dark, and then someone lit one of the flare lamps by the stage. It revealed nothing but the common squalor of a low saloon—white faces, sleepy eyes, and frowsy heads. The drop-piece was there in all its tawdriness.

The Companions of the Rosy Hours had gone. But at the door stood men in uniform. I heard a German a long way off murmur, "Enver's bodyguards," and I heard him distinctly; for, though I could not see clearly, my hearing was desperately acute. That is often the way when you suddenly come out of a swoon.

The place emptied like magic. Turk and German tumbled over each other, while Kuprasso wailed and wept. No one seemed to stop them, and then I saw the reason. Those guards had come for us. This must be Stumm at last. The authorities had tracked us down, and it was all up with Peter and me.

A sudden revulsion leaves a man with a low vitality. I didn't seem to care greatly. We were done, and there was an end of it. It was Kismet, the act of God, and there was nothing for it but to submit. I hadn't a flicker of a thought of escape or resistance. The game was utterly and absolutely over.

A man who seemed to be a sergeant pointed to us and said something to Kuprasso, who nodded. We got heavily to our feet and stumbled towards them. With one on each side of us we crossed the yard, walked through the dark passage and the empty shop, and out into the snowy street. There was a closed carriage waiting which they motioned to us to get into. It looked exactly like the Black Maria.

Both of us sat still, like truant schoolboys, with our hands on our knees. I didn't know where I was going and I didn't care. We seemed to be rumbling up the hill, and then I caught the glare of lighted streets.

"This is the end of it, Peter," I said.

"*Ja*, Cornelis," he replied, and that was all our talk.

By and by—hours later it seemed—we stopped. Someone opened the door and we got out, to find ourselves in a courtyard with a huge dark building around. The prison, I guessed, and I wondered if they would give us blankets, for it was perishing cold.

We entered a door, and found ourselves in a big stone hall. It was quite warm, which made me more hopeful about our cells. A man in some kind of uniform pointed to the staircase, up which we plodded wearily. My mind was too blank to take clear impressions, or in any way to forecast the future. Another warder met us and took us down a passage till we halted at a door. He stood aside and motioned us to enter.

I guessed that this was the governor's room, and we should be put through our first examination. My head was too stupid to think, and I made up my mind to keep perfectly mum. Yes, even if they tried thumbscrews. I had no kind of story, but I resolved not to give anything away. As I turned the handle I wondered idly what kind of sallow Turk or bulging-necked German we should find inside.

It was a pleasant room, with a polished wood floor and a big fire burning on the hearth. Beside the fire a man lay on a couch, with a little table drawn up beside him. On that table was a small glass of milk and a number of Patience cards spread in rows.

I stared blankly at the spectacle, till I saw a second figure. It was the man in the skin cap, the leader of the dancing maniacs. Both Peter and I backed sharply at the sight and then stood stock still.

For the dancer crossed the room in two strides and gripped both of my hands.

"Dick, old man," he cried, "I'm most awfully glad to see you again!"

CHAPTER 12

Four Missionaries See Light in Their Mission

SPASM OF INCREDULITY, a vast relief, and that sharp joy which comes of reaction chased each other across my mind. I had come suddenly out of very black waters into an unbelievable calm. I dropped into the nearest chair and tried to grapple with something far beyond words.

"Sandy," I said, as soon as I got my breath, "you're an incarnate devil. You've given Peter and me the fright of our lives."

"It was the only way, Dick. If I hadn't come mewing like a tom-cat at your heels yesterday, Rasta would have had you long before you got to your hotel. You two have given me a pretty anxious time, and it took some doing to get you safe here. However, that is all over now. Make yourselves at home, my children."

"Over!" I cried incredulously, for my wits were still wool-gathering. "What place is this?"

"You may call it my humble home"—it was Blenkiron's sleek voice that spoke. "We've been preparing for you, Major, but it was only yesterday I heard of your friend."

I introduced Peter.

"Mr Pienaar," said Blenkiron, "pleased to meet you. Well, as I was observing, you're safe enough here, but you've cut it mighty fine. Officially, a Dutchman called Brandt was to be arrested this afternoon and handed over to the German authorities. When Germany begins to trouble about that Dutchman she will find difficulty in getting the body; but such are the languid ways of an Oriental despotism. Meantime the Dutchman will be no more. He will have ceased upon the midnight without pain, as your poet sings."

"But I don't understand," I stammered. "Who arrested us?"

"My men," said Sandy. "We have a bit of a graft here, and it wasn't difficult to manage it. Old Moellendorff will be nosing after the business to-morrow, but he will find the mystery too deep for him. That is the advantage of a Government run by a pack of adventurers. But, by Jove, Dick, we hadn't any time to spare. If Rasta had got you, or the Germans had had the job of lifting you, your goose would have been jolly well cooked. I had some unquiet hours this morning."

The thing was too deep for me. I looked at Blenkiron, shuffling his Patience cards with his old sleepy smile, and Sandy, dressed like some bandit in melodrama, his lean face as brown as a nut, his bare arms all tattooed with crimson rings, and the fox pelt drawn tight over brow and ears. It was still a nightmare world, but the dream was getting pleasanter. Peter said not a word, but I could see his eyes heavy with his own thoughts.

Blenkiron hove himself from the sofa and waddled to a cupboard.

"You boys must be hungry," he said. "My duo-denum has been giving me hell as usual, and I don't eat no more than a squirrel. But I laid in some stores, for I guessed you would want to stoke up some after your travels."

He brought out a couple of Strassburg pies, a cheese, a cold chicken, a loaf, and three bottles of champagne.

"Fizz," said Sandy rapturously. "And a dry Heidsieck too! We're in luck, Dick, old man."

I never ate a more welcome meal, for we had starved in that dirty hotel. But I had still the old feeling of the hunted, and before I began I asked about the door.

"That's all right," said Sandy. "My fellows are on the stair and at the gate. If the *Metreb* are in possession, you may bet that other people will keep off. Your past is blotted out, clean vanished away, and you begin to-morrow morning with a new sheet. Blenkiron's the man you've got to thank for that. He was pretty certain you'd get here, but he was also certain that you'd arrive in a hurry with a good many inquiries behind you. So he arranged that you should leak away and start fresh."

"Your name is Richard Hanau," Blenkiron said, "born in Cleveland, Ohio, of German parentage on both sides. One of our brightest mining engineers, and the apple of Guggenheim's eye. You arrived this afternoon from Constanza, and I met you at the packet. The clothes for the part are in your bedroom next door. But I guess all that can wait, for I'm anxious to get to business. We're not here on a joy-ride, Major, so I reckon we'll leave out the dime-novel adventures. I'm just dying to hear them, but they'll keep. I want to know how our mutual inquiries have prospered."

He gave Peter and me cigars, and we sat ourselves in arm-chairs in front of the blaze. Sandy squatted cross-legged on the hearthrug and lit a foul old briar pipe, which he extricated from some pouch among his skins. And so began that conversation which had never been out of my thoughts for four hectic weeks.

"If I presume to begin," said Blenkiron, "it's because I reckon my story is the shortest. I have to confess to you, gentlemen, that I have failed."

He drew down the corners of his mouth till he looked a cross between a music-hall comedian and a sick child.

"If you were looking for something in the root of the hedge, you wouldn't want to scour the road in a high-speed automobile. And still less would you want to get a bird's-eye view in an aeroplane. That parable about fits my case. I have been in the clouds and I've been scorching on the pikes, but what I was wanting was in the ditch all the time, and I naturally missed it . . . I had the wrong stunt, Major. I was too high up and refined. I've been processing through Europe like Barnum's Circus, and living with generals and transparencies. Not that I haven't picked up a lot of noos, and got some very interesting sidelights on high politics. But the thing I was after wasn't to be found on my beat, for those that knew it weren't going to tell. In that kind of society they don't get drunk and blab after their tenth cocktail. So I guess I've no contribution to make to quieting Sir Walter Bullivant's mind, except that he's dead right. Yes, sir, he has hit the spot and rung the bell. There is a mighty miracle-working proposition being floated in these parts, but the promoters are keeping it to themselves. They aren't taking in more than they can help on the ground floor."

Blenkiron stopped to light a fresh cigar. He was leaner than when he left London and there were pouches below his eyes. I fancy his journey had not been as fur-lined as he made out.

"I've found out one thing, and that is, that the last dream Germany will part with is the control of the Near East. That is what your statesmen don't figure enough on. She'll give up Belgium and Alsace-Lorraine and Poland, but by God! she'll never give up the road to Mesopotamia till you have her by the throat and make her drop it. Sir Walter is a pretty bright-eyed citizen, and he sees it right enough. If the worst happens, Kaiser will fling overboard a lot of ballast in Europe, and it will look like a big victory for the Allies, but he won't be beaten if he has the road to the East safe. Germany's like a scorpion: her sting's in her tail, and that tail stretches way down into Asia.

"I got that clear, and I also made out that it wasn't going to be dead easy for her to keep that tail healthy. Turkey's a bit of an anxiety, as you'll soon discover. But Germany thinks she can manage it, and I won't say she can't. It depends on the hand she holds, and she reckons it a good one. I tried to find out, but they gave me nothing but eyewash. I had to pretend to be satisfied, for the position of John S. wasn't so strong as to allow him to take liberties. If I asked one of the highbrows he looked wise and spoke of the might of German arms and German organization and German staff-work. I used to nod my head and get enthusiastic about these stunts, but it was all soft soap. She has a trick in hand—that much I know, but I'm darned if I can put a name to it. I pray to God you boys have been cleverer."

His tone was quite melancholy, and I was mean enough to feel rather glad. He had been the professional with the best chance. It would be a good joke if the amateur succeeded where the expert failed.

I looked at Sandy. He filled his pipe again, and pushed back his skin cap from his brows. What with his long dishevelled hair, his high-boned face, and stained eyebrows he had the appearance of some mad mullah.

"I went straight to Smyrna," he said. "It wasn't difficult, for you see I had laid down a good many lines in former travels. I reached the town as a Greek money-lender from the Fayum, but I had friends there I could count on, and the same evening I was a Turkish gipsy, a member of the most famous fraternity in Western Asia. I had long been a member, and I'm blood-brother of the chief boss, so I stepped into the part ready made. But I found out that the Company of the Rosy Hours was not what I had known it in 1910. Then it had been all for the Young Turks and reform; now it hankered after the old régime and was the last hope of the Orthodox. It had no use for Enver and his friends, and it did not regard with pleasure the *beaux yeux* of the Teuton. It stood for Islam and the old ways, and might be described as a Conservative–Nationalist caucus. But it was uncommon powerful in the provinces, and Enver and Talaat daren't meddle with it. The dangerous thing about it was that it said nothing and apparently did nothing. It just bided its time and took notes.

"You can imagine that this was the very kind of crowd for my purpose. I knew of old its little ways, for with all its orthodoxy it dabbled a good deal in magic, and owed half its power to its atmosphere of the uncanny. The Companions could dance the heart out of the ordinary Turk. You saw a bit of one of our dances this afternoon, Dick—pretty good, wasn't it? They could go anywhere, and no questions asked. They knew what the ordinary man was thinking, for they were the best intelligence department in the Ottoman Empire—far better than Enver's *Khafiyeh*. And they were popular, too, for they had never bowed the knee to the *Nemesh*—the Germans who are squeezing out the life-blood of the Osmanli for their own ends. It would have been as much as the life of the Committee or its German masters was worth to lay a hand on us, for we clung together like leeches and we were not in the habit of sticking at trifles.

"Well, you may imagine it wasn't difficult for me to move where I wanted. My dress and the pass-word franked me anywhere. I travelled from Smyrna by the new railway to Panderma on the Marmora, and got there just before Christmas. That was after Anzac and Suvla had been evacuated, but I could hear the guns going hard at Cape Helles. From Panderma I started to cross to Thrace in a coasting steamer. And there an uncommon funny thing happened—I got torpedoed.

"It must have been about the last effort of a British submarine in those waters. But she got us all right. She gave us ten minutes to take to the boats, and then sent the blighted old packet and a fine cargo of 6-inch shells to the bottom. There weren't many passengers, so it was easy enough to get ashore in the ship's boats. The submarine sat on the surface watching us, as we wailed and howled in the true Oriental way, and I saw the captain quite close in the conning-tower. Who do you think it was? Tommy Elliot, who lives on the other side of the hill from me at home.

"I gave Tommy the surprise of his life. As we bumped past him, I started the 'Flowers of the Forest'—the old version—on the antique stringed instrument I carried, and I sang the words very plain. Tommy's eyes bulged out of his head, and he shouted at me in English to know who the devil I was. I replied in the broadest Scots, which no man in the submarine or in our boat could have understood a word of. 'Maister Tammy,' I cried, 'what for wad ye skail a dacent tinkler lad intil a cauld sea? I'll gie ye your kail through the reek for this ploy the next time I forgaither wi' ye on the tap o' Caerdon.'

"Tommy spotted me in a second. He laughed till he cried, and as we moved off shouted to me in the same language to 'pit a stoot hert tae a stey brae'. I hope to Heaven he had the sense not to tell my father, or the old man will have had a fit. He never much approved of my wanderings, and thought I was safely anchored in the battalion.

"Well, to make a long story short, I got to Constantinople, and pretty soon found touch with Blenkiron. The rest you know . . . And now for business. I have been fairly lucky—but no more, for I haven't got to the bottom of the thing nor anything like it. But I've solved the first of Harry Bullivant's riddles. I know the meaning of *Kasredin*.

"Sir Walter was right, as Blenkiron has told us. There's a great stirring in Islam, something moving on the face of the waters. They make no secret of it. Those religious revivals come in cycles, and one was due about now. And they are quite clear about the details. A seer has arisen of the blood of the Prophet, who will restore the Khalifate to its old glories and Islam to its old purity. His sayings are everywhere in the Moslem world. All the orthodox believers have them by heart. That is why they are enduring grinding poverty and preposterous taxation, and that is why their young men are rolling up to the armies and dying without complaint in Gallipoli and Transcaucasia. They believe they are on the eve of a great deliverance.

"Now the first thing I found out was that the Young Turks had nothing to do with this. They are unpopular and unorthodox, and no true Turks. But Germany has. How, I don't know, but I could see quite plainly that in some subtle way Germany was regarded as a collaborator in the movement. It is that belief that is keeping the present régime going. The ordinary Turk loathes the Committee, but he has some queer perverted expectation from Germany. It is not a case of Enver and the rest carrying on their shoulders the unpopular Teuton; it is a case of the Teuton carrying the unpopular Committee. And Germany's graft is just this and nothing more—that she has some hand in the coming of the new deliverer.

"They talk about the thing quite openly. It is called the *Kaába-i-*

hurriyeh, the Palladium of Liberty. The prophet himself is known as Zimrud—'the Emerald'—and his four Ministers are called also after jewels—Sapphire, Ruby, Pearl, and Topaz. You will hear their names as often in the talk of the towns and villages as you will hear the names of generals in England. But no one knew where Zimrud was or when he would reveal himself, though every week came his messages to the faithful. All that I could learn was that he and his followers were coming from the West.

"You will say, what about *Kasredin*? That puzzled me dreadfully, for no one used the phrase. The Home of the Spirit! It is an obvious cliché, just as in England some new sect might call itself the Church of Christ. Only no one seemed to use it.

"But by and by I discovered that there was an inner and an outer circle in this mystery. Every creed has an esoteric side which is kept from the common herd. I struck this side in Constantinople. Now there is a very famous Turkish *shaka* called *Kasredin*, one of those old half-comic miracle plays with an allegorical meaning which they call *orta oyun*, and which take a week to read. That tale tells of the coming of a prophet, and I found that the select of the faith spoke of the new revelation in terms of it. The curious thing is that in that tale the prophet is aided by one of the few women who play much part in the hagiology of Islam. That is the point of the tale, and it is partly a jest, but mainly a religious mystery. The prophet, too, is not called Emerald."

"I know," I said; "he is called Greenmantle."

Sandy scrambled to his feet, letting his pipe drop in the fireplace.

"Now how on earth did you find out that?" he cried.

Then I told them of Stumm and Gaudian and the whispered words I had not been meant to hear. Blenkiron was giving me the benefit of a steady stare, unusual from one who seemed always to have his eyes abstracted, and Sandy had taken to ranging up and down the room.

"Germany's in the heart of the plan. That is what I always thought. If we're to find the Kaábi-i-hurriyeh it is no good fossicking among the Committee or in the Turkish provinces. The secret's in Germany. Dick, you should not have crossed the Danube."

"That's what I half feared," I said. "But on the other hand it is obvious that the thing must come east, and sooner rather than later. I take it they can't afford to delay too long before they deliver the goods.

249

If we can stick it out here we must hit the trail . . . I've got another bit of evidence. I have solved Harry Bullivant's third puzzle."

Sandy's eyes were very bright and I had an audience on wires.

"Did you say that in the tale of *Kasredin* a woman is the ally of the prophet?"

"Yes," said Sandy; "what of that?"

"Only that the same thing is true of Greenmantle. I can give you her name."

I fetched a piece of paper and a pencil from Blenkiron's desk and handed it to Sandy.

"Write down Harry Bullivant's third word."

He promptly wrote down "*v. I.*"

Then I told them of the other name Stumm and Gaudian had spoken. I told of my discovery as I lay in the woodman's cottage.

"The '*I*' is not the letter of the alphabet, but the numeral. The name is von Einem—Hilda von Einem."

"Good old Harry," said Sandy softly. "He was a dashed clever chap. Hilda von Einem? Who and where is she? for if we find her we have done the trick."

Then Blenkiron spoke. "I reckon I can put you wise on that, gentlemen," he said. "I saw her no later than yesterday. She is a lovely lady. She happens also to be the owner of this house."

Both Sandy and I began to laugh. It was too comic to have stumbled across Europe and lighted on the very headquarters of the puzzle we had set out to unriddle.

But Blenkiron did not laugh. At the mention of Hilda von Einem he had suddenly become very solemn, and the sight of his face pulled me up short.

"I don't like it, gentlemen," he said. "I would rather you had mentioned any other name on God's earth. I haven't been long in this city, but I have been long enough to size up the various political bosses. They haven't much to them. I reckon they wouldn't stand up against what we could show them in the U-nited States. But I have met the Frau von Einem, and that lady's a very different proposition. The man that will understand her has got to take a biggish size in hats."

"Who is she?" I asked.

"Why, that is just what I can't tell you. She was a great excavator of Babylonish and Hittite ruins, and she married a diplomat who went to glory three years back. It isn't what she has been, but what she is, and that's a mighty clever woman."

Blenkiron's respect did not depress me. I felt as if at last we had got our job narrowed to a decent compass, for I had hated casting about in the dark. I asked where she lived.

"That I don't know," said Blenkiron. "You won't find people unduly anxious to gratify your natural curiosity about Frau von Einem."

"I can find that out," said Sandy. "That's the advantage of having a push like mine. Meantime, I've got to clear, for my day's work isn't finished. Dick, you and Peter must go to bed at once."

"Why?" I asked in amazement. Sandy spoke like a medical adviser.

"Because I want your clothes—the things you've got on now. I'll take them off with me and you'll never see them again."

"You've a queer taste in souvenirs," I said.

"Say rather the Turkish police. The current in the Bosporus is pretty strong, and these sad relics of two misguided Dutchmen will be washed up to-morrow about Seraglio Point. In this game you must drop the curtain neat and pat at the end of each scene, if you don't want trouble later with the missing heir and the family lawyer."

CHAPTER 13

I Move in Good Society

I WALKED OUT of that house next morning with Blenkiron's arm in mine, a different being from the friendless creature who had looked vainly the day before for sanctuary. To begin with, I was splendidly dressed. I had a navy-blue suit with square padded shoulders, a neat black bow-tie, shoes with a hump at the toe, and a brown bowler. Over that I wore a greatcoat lined with wolf fur. I had a smart malacca cane, and one of Blenkiron's cigars in my mouth. Peter had been made to trim his beard, and, dressed in unassuming pepper-and-salt, looked with his docile eyes and quiet voice a very respectable servant. Old Blenkiron had done the job in style, for, if you'll believe it, he had brought the clothes all the way from London. I realized now why he and Sandy had been fossicking in my wardrobe. Peter's suit had been of Sandy's procuring, and it was not the fit of mine. I had no difficulty about the accent. Any man brought up in the colonies can get his tongue round American, and I flattered myself I made a very fair shape at the lingo of the Middle West.

The wind had gone to the south and the snow was melting fast. There was a blue sky above Asia, and away to the north masses of white cloud drifting over the Black Sea. What had seemed the day before the dingiest of cities now took on a strange beauty, the beauty of unexpected horizons and tongues of grey water winding below cypress-studded shores. A man's temper has a lot to do with his appreciation of scenery. I felt a free man once more, and could use my eyes.

That street was a jumble of every nationality on earth. There were Turkish regulars in their queer conical khaki helmets, and wild-looking levies who had no kin with Europe. There were squads of Germans in flat forage-caps, staring vacantly at novel sights, and quick to salute any officer on the side-walk. Turks in closed carriages passed, and Turks on good Arab horses, and Turks who looked as if they had come out of the Ark. But it was the rabble that caught the eye—very wild, pinched, miserable rabble. I never in my life saw such swarms of beggars, and you walked down that street to the accompaniment of entreaties for alms in all the tongues of the Tower of Babel. Blenkiron and I behaved as if we were interested tourists. We would stop and laugh at one fellow and give a penny to a second, passing comments in high-pitched Western voices.

We went into a café and had a cup of coffee. A beggar came in and asked alms. Hitherto Blenkiron's purse had been closed, but now he took out some small nickels and planked five down on the table. The man cried down blessings and picked up three. Blenkiron very swiftly swept the other two into his pocket.

That seemed to me queer, and I remarked that I had never before seen a beggar who gave change. Blenkiron said nothing, and presently we moved on and came to the harbour-side.

There were a number of small tugs moored alongside, and one or two bigger craft—fruit boats, I judged, which used to ply in the Aegean. They looked pretty well moth-eaten from disuse. We stopped at one of them and watched a fellow in a blue nightcap splicing ropes. He raised his eyes once and looked at us, and then kept on with his business.

Blenkiron asked him where he came from, but he shook his head, not understanding the tongue. A Turkish policeman came up and stared at us suspiciously, till Blenkiron opened his coat, as if by accident, and displayed a tiny square of ribbon, at which he saluted. Failing to make conversation with the sailor, Blenkiron flung him three of his black cigars. "I guess you can smoke, friend, if you can't talk," he said.

The man grinned and caught the three neatly in the air. Then to my amazement he tossed one of them back.

The donor regarded it quizzically as it lay on the pavement. "That boy's a connoisseur of tobacco," he said. As we moved away I saw the Turkish policeman pick it up and put it inside his cap.

We returned by the long street on the crest of the hill. There was a man selling oranges on a tray, and Blenkiron stopped to look at them. I noticed that the man shuffled fifteen into a cluster. Blenkiron felt the oranges, as if to see that they were sound, and pushed two aside. The man instantly restored them to the group, never raising his eyes.

"This ain't the time of year to buy fruit," said Blenkiron as we passed on. "Those oranges are rotten as medlars."

We were almost on our own doorstep before I guessed the meaning of the business.

"Is your morning's work finished?" I said.

"Our morning's walk?" he asked innocently.

"I said 'work'."

He smiled blandly. "I reckoned you'd tumble to it. Why, yes, except that I've some figuring still to do. Give me half an hour and I'll be at your service, Major."

That afternoon, after Peter had cooked a wonderfully good luncheon, I had a heart-to-heart talk with Blenkiron.

"My business is to get noos," he said; "and before I start on a stunt I make considerable preparations. All the time in London when I was yelping at the British Government, I was busy with Sir Walter arranging things ahead. We used to meet in queer places and at all hours of the night. I fixed up a lot of connexions in this city before I arrived, and especially a noos service with your Foreign Office by way of Rumania and Russia. In a day or two I guess our friends will know all about our discoveries."

At that I opened my eyes very wide.

"Why, yes. You Britishers haven't any notion how wide-awake your Intelligence Service is. I reckon it's easy the best of all the belligerents. You never talked about it in peace time, and you shunned the theatrical ways of the Teuton. But you had the wires laid good and sure. I calculate there isn't much that happens in any corner of the earth that you don't know within twenty-four hours. I don't say your highbrows use the noos well. I don't take much stock in your political push. They're a lot of silver-tongues, no doubt, but it ain't oratory that is wanted in this racket. The William Jennings Bryan stunt languishes in war time. Politics is like a chicken-coop, and those inside get to behave as if their little run were all the world. But if the politicians make mistakes it isn't from lack of good instruction to guide their steps. If I had a big proposition to handle and could have my pick of helpers I'd plump for the Intelligence Department of the British Admiralty. Yes, sir, I take off my hat to your Government sleuths."

"Did they provide you with ready-made spies here?" I asked in astonishment.

"Why, no," he said. "But they gave me the key, and I could make my own arrangements. In Germany I buried myself deep in the local atmosphere and never peeped out. That was my game, for I was looking for something in Germany itself, and didn't want any foreign cross-bearings. As you know, I failed where you succeeded. But so soon as I crossed the Danube I set about opening up my lines of communication, and I hadn't been two days in this metropolis before I had got my telephone exchange buzzing. Some time I'll explain the thing to you, for it's a pretty little business. I've got the cutest cypher . . . No, it ain't my invention. It's your Government's. Anyone, babe, imbecile, or dotard, can carry my messages—you saw some of them to-day—but it takes some mind to set the piece, and it takes a lot of figuring at my end to work out the results. Some day you shall hear it all, for I guess it would please you."

"How do you use it?" I asked.

"Well, I get early noos of what is going on in this cabbage-patch. Likewise I get authentic noos of the rest of Europe, and I can send a message to Mr X. in Petrograd and Mr Y. in London, or, if I wish, to Mr Z. in Noo York. What's the matter with that for a post-office? I'm the best-informed man in Constantinople, for old General Liman only hears one side, and mostly lies at that, and Enver prefers not to listen at all. Also, I could give them points on what is happening at their very door, for our friend Sandy is a big boss in the best-run crowd of mountebanks that ever fiddled secrets out of men's hearts. Without their help I wouldn't have cut much ice in this city."

"I want you to tell me one thing, Blenkiron," I said. "I've been playing a part for the past month, and it wears my nerves to tatters. Is this job very tiring, for if it is, I doubt I may buckle up?"

He looked thoughtful. "I can't call our business an absolute rest-cure any time. You've got to keep your eyes skinned, and there's always the risk of the little packet of dynamite going off unexpected. But as these things go, I rate this stunt as easy. We've only got to be natural. We wear our natural clothes, and talk English, and sport a Teddy Roosevelt smile, and there isn't any call for theatrical talent. Where I've found the job tight was when I have got to be natural, and my naturalness was the same brand as that of everybody round about, and all the time I had to do unnatural things. It isn't easy to be going down town to business and taking cocktails with Mr Carl Rosenheim, and next hour being engaged trying to blow Mr Rosenheim's friends sky high. And it isn't easy to keep up a part which is clean outside your ordinary life. I've never tried that. My line has always been to keep my normal personality. But you have, Major, and I guess you found it wearing."

"Wearing's a mild word," I said. "But I want to know another thing.

It seems to me that the line you've picked is as good as could be. But it's a cast-iron line. It commits us pretty deep and it won't be a simple job to drop it."

"Why, that's just the point I was coming to," he said. "I was going to put you wise about that very thing. When I started out I figured on some situation like this. I argued that unless I had a very clear part with a big bluff in it I wouldn't get the confidences which I needed. We've got to be at the heart of the show, taking a real hand and not just looking on. So I settled I would be a big engineer—there was a time when there weren't many bigger in the United States than John S. Blenkiron. I talked large about what might be done in Mesopotamia in the way of washing the British down the river. Well, that talk caught on. They knew of my reputation as an hydraulic expert, and they were tickled to death to rope me in. I told them I wanted a helper, and I told them about my friend Richard Hanau, as good a German as ever supped sauerkraut, who was coming through Russia and Rumania as a benevolent neutral; but when he got to Constantinople would drop his neutrality and double his benevolence. They got reports on you by wire from the States—I arranged that before I left London. So you're going to be welcomed and taken to their bosoms just like John S. was. We've both got jobs we can hold down, and now you're in these pretty clothes you're the dead ringer of the brightest kind of American engineer . . . But we can't go back on our tracks. If we wanted to leave for Constanza next week they'd be very polite, but they'd never let us. We've got to go on with this adventure and nose our way down into Mesopotamia, hoping that our luck will hold . . . God knows how we will get out of it; but it's no good going out to meet trouble. As I observed before, I believe in an all-wise and beneficent Providence, but you've got to give Him a chance."

I am bound to confess the prospect staggered me. We might be let in for fighting—and worse than fighting—against our own side. I wondered if it wouldn't be better to make a bolt for it, and said so.

He shook his head. "I reckon not. In the first place we haven't finished our inquiries. We've got Greenmantle located right enough, thanks to you, but we still know mighty little about that holy man. In the second place it won't be as bad as you think. This show lacks cohesion, sir. It is not going to last for ever. I calculate that before you and I strike the site of the garden that Adam and Eve frequented there will be a queer turn of affairs. Anyhow, it's good enough to gamble on."

Then he got some sheets of paper and drew me a plan of the disposition of the Turkish forces. I had no notion he was such a close student of war, for his exposition was as good as a staff lecture. He made out that the situation was none too bright anywhere. The troops released from Gallipoli wanted a lot of refitment, and would be slow in reaching the Transcaucasian frontier, where the Russians were threatening. The army of Syria was pretty nearly a rabble under the lunatic Djemal. There wasn't the foggiest chance of a serious invasion of Egypt being undertaken. Only in Mesopotamia did things look fairly cheerful, owing to the blunders of British strategy. "And you may take it from me," he said, "that if the old Turk mobilized a total of a million men, he has lost 40 per cent of them already. And if I'm anything of a prophet he's going pretty soon to lose more."

He tore up the papers and enlarged on politics. "I reckon I've got the measure of the Young Turks and their precious Committee. Those boys aren't any good. Enver's bright enough, and for sure he's got sand. He'll stick out a fight like a Vermont game-chicken, but he lacks the larger vision, sir. He doesn't understand the intricacies of the job no more than a sucking-child, so the Germans play with him, till his temper goes and he bucks like a mule. Talaat is a sulky dog who wants to batter mankind with a club. Both these boys would have made good cow-punchers in the old days, and they might have got a living out West as the gun-men of a Labour Union. They're about the class of Jesse James or Bill the Kid, excepting that they're college-reared and can patter languages. But they haven't the organizing power to manage the Irish vote in a ward election. Their one notion is to get busy with their firearms, and people are getting tired of the Black Hand stunt. Their hold on the country is just the hold that a man with a Browning has over a crowd with walking-sticks. The cooler heads in the Committee are growing shy of them, and an old fox like Djavid is lying low till his time comes. Now it doesn't want arguing that a gang of that kind has got to hang close together or they may hang separately. They've got no grip on the ordinary Turk, barring the fact that they are active and he is sleepy, and that they've got their guns loaded."

"What about the Germans here?" I asked.

Blenkiron laughed. "It is no sort of a happy family. But the Young

Turks know that without the German boost they'll be strung up like Haman, and the Germans can't afford to neglect an ally. Consider what would happen if Turkey got sick of the game and made a separate peace. The road would be open for Russia to the Aegean. Ferdy of Bulgaria would take his depreciated goods to the other market, and not waste a day thinking about it. You'd have Rumania coming in on the Allies' side. Things would look pretty black for that control of the Near East on which Germany has banked her winnings. Kaiser says that's got to be prevented at all costs, but how is it going to be done?"

Blenkiron's face had become very solemn again. "It won't be done unless Germany's got a trump card to play. Her game's mighty near bust, but it's still got a chance. And that chance is a woman and an old man. I reckon our landlady has a bigger brain than Enver and Liman. She's the real boss of the show. When I came here, I reported to her, and presently you've got to do the same. I am curious as to how she'll strike you, for I'm free to admit that she impressed me considerable."

"It looks as if our job were a long way from the end," I said.

"It's scarcely begun," said Blenkiron.

THAT TALK DID A LOT to cheer my spirits, for I realized that it was the biggest of big game we were hunting this time. I'm an economical soul, and if I'm going to be hanged I want a good stake for my neck.

Then began some varied experiences. I used to wake up in the morning, wondering where I should be at night, and yet quite pleased at the uncertainty. Greenmantle became a sort of myth with me. Somehow I couldn't fix any idea in my head of what he was like. The nearest I got was a picture of an old man in a turban coming out of a bottle in a cloud of smoke, which I remembered from a child's edition of the *Arabian Nights*. But if he was dim, the lady was dimmer. Sometimes I thought of her as a fat old German crone, sometimes as a harsh-featured woman like a schoolmistress with thin lips and eye-glasses. But I had to fit the East into the picture, so I made her young and gave her a touch of the languid houri in a veil. I was always wanting to pump Blenkiron on the subject, but he shut up like a rat-trap. He was looking for bad trouble in that direction, and was disinclined to speak about it beforehand.

We led a peaceful existence. Our servants were two of Sandy's lot, for

Blenkiron had very rightly cleared out the Turkish caretakers, and they worked like beavers under Peter's eye, till I reflected I had never been so well looked after in my life. I walked about the city with Blenkiron, keeping my eyes open, and speaking very civil. The third night we were bidden to dinner at Moellendorff's, so we put on our best clothes and set out in an ancient cab. Blenkiron had fetched a dress suit of mine, from which my own tailor's label had been cut and a New York one substituted.

General Liman and Metternich the Ambassador had gone up the line to Nish to meet the Kaiser, who was touring in those parts, so Moellendorff was the biggest German in the city. He was a thin, foxy-faced fellow, cleverish but monstrously vain, and he was not very popular either with the Germans or the Turks. He was polite to both of us, but I am bound to say that I got a bad fright when I entered the room, for the first man I saw was Gaudian.

I doubt if he would have recognized me even in the clothes I had worn in Stumm's company, for his eyesight was wretched. As it was, I ran no risk in dress clothes, with my hair brushed back and a fine American accent. I paid him high compliments as a fellow engineer, and translated part of a very technical conversation between him and Blenkiron. Gaudian was in uniform, and I liked the look of his honest face better than ever.

But the great event was the sight of Enver. He was a slim fellow of Rasta's build, very foppish and precise in his dress, with a smooth oval face like a girl's and rather fine straight black eyebrows. He spoke perfect German, and had the best kind of manners, neither pert nor overbearing. He had a pleasant trick, too, of appealing all round the table for confirmation, and so bringing everybody into the talk. Not that he spoke a great deal, but all he said was good sense, and he had a smiling way of saying it. Once or twice he ran counter to Moellendorff, and I could see there was no love lost between these two. I didn't think I wanted him as a friend—he was too cold-blooded and artificial; and I was pretty certain that I didn't want those steady black eyes as an enemy. But it was no good denying his quality. The little fellow was all cold courage, like the fine polished blue steel of a sword.

I fancy I was rather a success at that dinner. For one thing I could speak German, and so had a pull on Blenkiron. For another I was in a good temper, and really enjoyed putting my back into my part. They talked very high-flown stuff about what they had done and were going to do, and Enver was great on Gallipoli. I remember he said that he could have destroyed the whole British Army if it hadn't been for somebody's cold feet—at which Moellendorff looked daggers. They were so bitter about Britain and all her works that I gathered they were getting pretty panicky, and that made me as jolly as a sandboy. I'm afraid I was not free from bitterness myself on that subject. I said things about my own country that I sometimes wake in the night and sweat to think of.

Gaudian got on to the use of water power in war, and that gave me a chance.

"In my country," I said, "when we want to get rid of a mountain we wash it away. There's nothing on earth that will stand against water. Now, speaking with all respect, gentlemen, and as an absolute novice in the military art, I sometimes ask why this God-given weapon isn't more used in the present war. I haven't been to any of the fronts, but I've studied them some from maps and the newspapers. Take your German position in Flanders, where you've got the high ground. If I were a British general I reckon I would very soon make it no sort of position."

Moellendorff asked, "How?"

"Why, I'd wash it away. Wash away the fourteen feet of soil down to the stone. There's a heap of coalpits behind the British front where they could generate power, and I judge there's ample water supply from the rivers and canals. I'd guarantee to wash you away in twenty-four hours—yes, in spite of all your big guns. It beats me why the British haven't got on to this notion. They used to have some bright engineers."

Enver was on the point like a knife, far quicker than Gaudian. He cross-examined me in a way that showed he knew how to approach a technical subject, though he mightn't have much technical knowledge. He was just giving me a sketch of the flooding in Mesopotamia when an aide-de-camp brought in a chit which fetched him to his feet.

"I have gossiped long enough," he said. "My kind host, I must leave you. Gentlemen all, my apologies and farewells."

Before he left he asked my name and wrote it down. "This is an unhealthy city for strangers, Mr Hanau," he said in very good English. "I have some small power of protecting a friend, and what I have is at your disposal." This with the condescension of a king promising his favour to a subject.

The little fellow amused me tremendously, and rather impressed me too. I said so to Gaudian after he had left, but that decent soul didn't agree.

"I do not love him," he said. "We are allies—yes; but friends—no. He is no true son of Islam, which is a noble faith and despises liars and boasters and betrayers of their salt."

That was the verdict of one honest man on this ruler in Israel. The next night I got another from Blenkiron on a greater than Enver.

He had been out alone and had come back pretty late, with his face grey and drawn with pain. The food we ate—not at all bad of its kind—and the cold east wind played havoc with his dyspepsia. I can see him yet, boiling milk on a spirit-lamp, while Peter worked at a Primus stove to get him a hot-water bottle. He was using horrid language about his inside.

"My God, Major, if I were you with a sound stomach I'd fairly conquer the world. As it is, I've got to do my work with half my mind, while the other half is dwelling in my intestines. I'm like the child in the Bible that had a fox gnawing at its vitals."

He got his milk boiling and began to sip it.

"I've been to see our pretty landlady," he said. "She sent for me and I hobbled off with a grip full of plans, for she's mighty set on Mesopotamy."

"Anything about Greenmantle?" I asked eagerly.

"Why, no, but I have reached one conclusion. I opine that the hapless prophet has no sort of time with that lady. I opine that he will soon wish himself in Paradise. For if Almighty God ever created a female devil it's Madam von Einem."

He sipped a little more milk with a grave face.

"That isn't my duo-denal dyspepsia, Major. It's the verdict of a ripe experience, for I have a cool and penetrating judgement, even if I've a deranged stomach. And I give it as my con-sidered conclusion that that woman's mad and bad—but principally bad."

CHAPTER 14

The Lady of the Mantilla

SINCE THAT FIRST NIGHT I had never clapped eyes on Sandy. He had gone clean out of the world, and Blenkiron and I waited anxiously for a word of news. Our own business was in good trim, for we were presently going east towards Mesopotamia, but unless we learned more about Greenmantle our journey would be a grotesque failure. And learn about Greenmantle we could not, for nobody by word or deed suggested his existence, and it was impossible of course for us to ask questions. Our only hope was Sandy, for what we wanted to know was the prophet's whereabouts and his plans. I suggested to Blenkiron that we might do more to cultivate Frau von Einem, but he shut his jaw like a rat-trap. "There's nothing doing for us in that quarter," he said. "That's the most dangerous woman on earth; and if she got any kind of notion that we were wise about her pet schemes I reckon you and I would very soon be in the Bosporus."

This was all very well; but what was going to happen if the two of us were bundled off to Bagdad with instructions to wash away the British? Our time was getting pretty short, and I doubted if we could spin out more than three days more in Constantinople. I felt just as I had felt with Stumm that last night when I was about to be packed off to Cairo and saw no way of avoiding it. Even Blenkiron was getting anxious. He played Patience incessantly, and was disinclined to talk. I tried to find out something from the servants, but they either knew nothing or wouldn't speak—the former, I think. I kept my eyes lifting, too, as I walked about the streets, but there was no sign anywhere of the skin coats or the weird stringed instruments. The whole Company of the Rosy Hours seemed to have melted into the air, and I began to wonder if they had ever existed.

Anxiety made me restless, and restlessness made me want exercise. It was no good walking about the city. The weather had become foul again, and I was sick of the smells and the squalor and the flea-bitten crowds. So Blenkiron and I got horses, Turkish cavalry mounts with heads like trees, and went out through the suburbs into the open country.

It was a grey drizzling afternoon, with the beginnings of a sea fog which hid the Asiatic shores of the straits. It wasn't easy to find open ground for a gallop, for there were endless small patches of cultivation and the gardens of country houses. We kept on the high land above the sea, and when we reached a bit of downland came on squads of Turkish soldiers digging trenches. Whenever we let the horses go we had to pull up sharp for a digging party or a stretch of barbed wire. Coils of the beastly thing were lying loose everywhere, and Blenkiron nearly took a nasty toss over one. Then we were always being stopped by sentries and having to show our passes. Still the ride did us good and shook up our livers, and by the time we turned for home I was feeling more like a white man.

We jogged back in the short winter twilight, past the wooded grounds of white villas, held up every few minutes by transport-wagons and companies of soldiers. The rain had come on in real earnest, and it was two very bedraggled horsemen that crawled along the muddy lanes. As we passed one villa, shut in by a high white wall, a pleasant smell of wood smoke was wafted towards us, which made me sick for the burning veld. My ear, too, caught the twanging of a zither, which somehow reminded me of the afternoon in Kuprasso's garden-house.

I pulled up and proposed to investigate, but Blenkiron very testily declined.

"Zithers are as common here as fleas," he said. "You don't want to be fossicking around somebody's stables and find a horse-boy entertaining his friends. They don't like visitors in this country; and you'll be asking for trouble if you go inside those walls. I guess it's some old Buzzard's harem." Buzzard was his own private peculiar name for the Turk, for he said he had had as a boy a natural history book with a picture of a bird called the turkey-buzzard, and couldn't get out of the habit of applying it to the Ottoman people.

I wasn't convinced, so I tried to mark down the place. It seemed to be about three miles out from the city, at the end of a steep lane on the inland side of the hill coming from the Bosporus. I fancied somebody of distinction lived there, for a little farther on we met a big empty motor-car snorting its way up, and I had a notion that the car belonged to the walled villa.

Next day Blenkiron was in grievous trouble with his dyspepsia. About midday he was compelled to lie down, and having nothing better to do I had out the horses again and took Peter with me. It was funny to see Peter in a Turkish army-saddle, riding with the long Boer stirrup and the slouch of the backveld.

That afternoon was unfortunate from the start. It was not the mist and drizzle of the day before, but a stiff northern gale which blew sheets of rain in our faces and numbed our bridle hands. We took the same road, but pushed west of the trench-digging parties and got to a shallow valley with a white village among the cypresses. Beyond that there was a very respectable road which brought us to the top of a crest that in clear weather must have given a fine prospect. Then we turned our horses, and I shaped our course so as to strike the top of the long lane that abutted on the down. I wanted to investigate the white villa.

But we hadn't gone far on our road back before we got into trouble. It arose out of a sheep-dog, a yellow mongrel brute that came at us like a thunderbolt. It took a special fancy to Peter, and bit savagely at his horse's heels and sent it capering off the road. I should have warned him, but I did not realize what was happening, till too late. For Peter, being accustomed to mongrels in Kaffir kraals, took a summary way with the pest. Since it despised his whip, he out with his pistol and put a bullet through its head.

The echoes of the shot had scarcely died away when the row began. A big fellow appeared running towards us, shouting wildly. I guessed he was the dog's owner, and proposed to pay no attention. But his cries summoned two other fellows—soldiers by the look of them—who closed in on us, unslinging their rifles as they ran. My first idea was to show them our heels, but I had no desire to be shot in the back, and they looked like men who wouldn't stop short of shooting. So we slowed down and faced them.

They made as savage-looking a trio as you would want to avoid. The shepherd looked as if he had been dug up, a dirty ruffian with matted hair and a beard like a bird's nest. The two soldiers stood staring with sullen faces, fingering their guns, while the other chap raved and stormed and kept pointing at Peter, whose mild eyes stared unwinkingly at his assailant.

The mischief was that neither of us had a word of Turkish. I tried German, but it had no effect. We sat looking at them and they stood storming at us, and it was fast getting dark. Once I turned my horse round as if to proceed, and the two soldiers jumped in front of me.

They jabbered among themselves, and then one said very slowly: "He . . . want . . . pounds," and he held up five fingers. They evidently saw by the cut of our jib that we weren't Germans.

"I'll be hanged if he gets a penny," I said angrily, and the conversation languished.

The situation was getting serious, so I spoke a word to Peter. The soldiers had their rifles loose in their hands, and before they could lift them we had the pair covered with our pistols.

"If you move," I said, "you are dead." They understood that all right and stood stock still, while the shepherd stopped his raving and took to muttering like a gramophone when the record is finished.

"Drop your guns," I said sharply. "Quick, or we shoot."

The tone, if not the words, conveyed my meaning. Still staring at us, they let the rifles slide to the ground. The next second we had forced our horses on the top of them, and the three were off like rabbits. I sent a shot over their heads to encourage them. Peter dismounted and tossed the guns into a bit of scrub where they would take some finding.

This hold-up had wasted time. By now it was getting very dark, and we hadn't ridden a mile before it was black night. It was an annoying predicament, for I had completely lost my bearings and at the best I had only a foggy notion of the lie of the land. The best plan seemed to be to try and get to the top of a rise in the hope of seeing the lights of the city, but all the countryside was so pockety that it was hard to strike the right kind of rise.

We had to trust to Peter's instinct. I asked him where our line lay, and he sat very still for a minute sniffing the air. Then he pointed the direction. It wasn't what I would have taken myself, but on a point like that he was pretty near infallible.

Presently we came to a long slope which cheered me. But at the top there was no light visible anywhere—only a black void like the inside of a shell. As I stared into the gloom it seemed to me that there were patches of deeper darkness that might be woods.

"There is a house half-left in front of us," said Peter.

I peered till my eyes ached and saw nothing.

"Well, for Heaven's sake, guide me to it," I said, and with Peter in front we set off down the hill.

It was a wild journey, for darkness clung as close to us as a vest. Twice we stepped into patches of bog, and once my horse saved himself by a hair from going head forward into a gravel pit. We got tangled up in strands of wire, and often found ourselves rubbing our noses against tree-trunks. Several times I had to get down and make a gap in barricades of loose stones. But after a ridiculous amount of slipping and stumbling we finally struck what seemed the level of a road, and a piece of special darkness in front which turned out to be a high wall.

I argued that all mortal walls had doors, so we set to groping along it, and presently found a gap. There was an old iron gate on broken hinges, which we easily pushed open, and found ourselves on a back path to some house. It was clearly disused, for masses of rotting leaves covered it, and by the feel of it underfoot it was grass-grown.

We dismounted now, leading our horses, and after about fifty yards the path ceased and came out on a well-made carriage drive. So, at least, we guessed, for the place was as black as pitch. Evidently the house couldn't be far off, but in which direction I hadn't a notion.

Now, I didn't want to be paying calls on any Turk at that time of day. Our job was to find where the road opened into the lane, for after that our way to Constantinople was clear. One side the lane lay, and the other the house, and it didn't seem wise to take the risk of tramping up with horses to the front door. So I told Peter to wait for me at the end of the back-road, while I would prospect a bit. I turned to the right, my intention being if I saw the light of a house to return, and with Peter take the other direction.

I walked like a blind man in that nether-pit of darkness. The road seemed well kept, and the soft wet gravel muffled the sounds of my feet. Great trees overhung it, and several times I wandered into dripping bushes. And then I stopped short in my tracks, for I heard the sound of whistling.

It was quite close, about ten yards away. And the strange thing was that it was a tune I knew, about the last tune you would expect to hear in this part of the world. It was the Scots air: "Ca' the yowes to the knowes" which was a favourite of my father's.

The whistler must have felt my presence, for the air suddenly stopped in the middle of a bar. An unbounded curiosity seized me to know who the fellow could be. So I started in and finished it myself.

There was silence for a second, and then the unknown began again and stopped. Once more I chipped in and finished it.

Then it seemed to me that he was coming nearer. The air in that dank tunnel was very still, and I thought I heard a light foot. I think I took a step backward. Suddenly there was a flash of an electric torch from a yard off, so quick that I could see nothing of the man who held it.

Then a low voice spoke out of the darkness—a voice I knew well—and, following it, a hand was laid on my arm. "What the devil are you doing here, Dick?" it said, and there was something like consternation in the tone.

I told him in a hectic sentence, for I was beginning to feel badly rattled myself.

"You've never been in greater danger in your life," said the voice. "Great God, man, what brought you wandering here to-day of all days?"

You can imagine that I was pretty scared, for Sandy was the last man to put a case too high. And the next second I felt worse, for he clutched my arm and dragged me in a bound to the side of the road. I could see nothing, but I felt that his head was screwed round, and mine followed suit. And there, a dozen yards off, were the acetylene lights of a big motor-car.

It came along very slowly, purring like a great cat, while we pressed into the bushes. The headlights seemed to spread a fan far to either side, showing the full width of the drive and its borders, and about half the height of the over-arching trees. There was a figure in uniform sitting beside the chauffeur, whom I saw dimly in the reflex glow, but the body of the car was dark.

It crept towards us, passed, and my mind was just getting easy again when it stopped. A switch was snapped within, and the limousine was brightly lit up. Inside I saw a woman's figure.

The servant had got out and opened the door and a voice came from within—a clear soft voice speaking in some tongue I didn't understand. Sandy had started forward at the sound of it, and I followed him. It would never do for me to be caught skulking in the bushes.

I was so dazzled by the suddenness of the glare that at first I blinked and saw nothing. Then my eyes cleared and I found myself looking at the inside of a car upholstered in some soft dove-coloured fabric, and beautifully finished off in ivory and silver. The woman who sat in it had a mantilla of black lace over her head and shoulders, and with one slender jewelled hand she kept its fold over the greater part of her face. I saw only a pair of pale grey-blue eyes—these and the slim fingers.

I remember that Sandy was standing very upright with his hands on his hips, by no means like a servant in the presence of his mistress. He was a fine figure of a man at all times, but in those wild clothes, with his head thrown back and his dark brows drawn below his skull-cap, he looked like some savage king out of an older world. He was speaking Turkish, and glancing at me now and then as if angry and perplexed. I took the hint that he was not supposed to know any other tongue, and that he was asking who the devil I might be.

Then they both looked at me, Sandy with the slow unwinking stare of the gipsy, the lady with those curious, beautiful pale eyes. They ran over my clothes, my brand-new riding-breeches, my splashed boots, my wide-brimmed hat. I took off the last and made my best bow.

"Madam," I said, "I have to ask pardon for trespassing in your garden. The fact is, I and my servant—he's down the road with the horses and I guess you noticed him—the two of us went for a ride this afternoon, and got good and well lost. We came in by your back gate, and I was prospecting for your front door to find someone to direct us, when I bumped into this brigand-chief who didn't understand my talk. I'm American, and I'm here on a big Government proposition. I hate to trouble you, but if you'd send a man to show us how to strike the city I'd be very much in your debt."

Her eyes never left my face. "Will you come into the car?" she said in English. "At the house I will give you a servant to direct you."

She drew in the skirts of her fur cloak to make room for me, and in my muddy boots and sopping clothes I took the seat she pointed out. She said a word in Turkish to Sandy, switched off the light, and the car moved on.

Women had never come much my way, and I knew about as much of their ways as I knew about the Chinese language. All my life I had lived with men only, and rather a rough crowd at that. When I made my pile and came home I looked to see a little society, but I had first the business of the Black Stone on my hands, and then the war, so my education languished. I had never been in a motor-car with a lady before, and I felt like a fish on a dry sandbank. The soft cushions and the subtle scents filled me with acute uneasiness. I wasn't thinking now about Sandy's grave words, or about Blenkiron's warning, or about my job and the part this woman must play in it. I was thinking only that I felt mortally shy. The darkness made it worse. I was sure that my companion was looking at me all the time and laughing at me for a clown.

The car stopped and a tall servant opened the door. The lady was over the threshold before I was at the step. I followed her heavily, the wet squelching from my field-boots. At that moment I noticed that she was very tall.

She led me through a long corridor to a room where two pillars held lamps in the shape of torches. The place was dark but for their glow, and it was as warm as a hothouse from invisible stoves. I felt soft carpets underfoot, and on the walls hung some tapestry or rug of an amazingly intricate geometrical pattern, but with every strand as rich as jewels. There, between the pillars, she turned and faced me. Her furs were thrown back, and the black mantilla had slipped down to her shoulders.

"I have heard of you," she said. "You are called Richard Hanau, the American. Why have you come to this land?"

"To have a share in the campaign," I said. "I'm an engineer, and I thought I could help out with some business like Mesopotamia."

"You are on Germany's side?" she asked.

"Why, yes," I replied. "We Americans are supposed to be nootrals. That means we're free to choose any side we fancy. I'm for the Kaiser."

Her cool eyes searched me, but not in suspicion. I could see she wasn't troubled with the question whether I was speaking the truth. She was sizing me up as a man. I cannot describe that calm appraising look. There was no sex in it, nothing even of that implicit sympathy with which one human being explores the existence of another. I was a chattel, a thing infinitely removed from intimacy. Even so I have myself looked at a horse which I thought of buying, scanning his shoulders and hocks and paces. Even so must the old lords of Constantinople have looked at the slaves which the chances of war brought to their markets, assessing their usefulness for some task or other with no thought of a humanity common to purchased and purchaser. And yet—not quite. This woman's eyes were weighing me, not for any special duty, but for my essential qualities. I felt that I was under the scrutiny of one who was a connoisseur in human nature.

I see I have written that I knew nothing about women. But every man has in his bones a consciousness of sex. I was shy and perturbed, but horribly fascinated. This slim woman, poised exquisitely like some statue between the pillared lights, with her fair cloud of hair, her long delicate face, and her pale bright eyes, had the glamour of a wild dream. I hated her instinctively, hated her intensely, but I longed to arouse her interest. To be valued coldly by those eyes was an offence to my manhood, and I felt antagonism rising within me. I am a strong fellow, well set up, and rather above the average height, and my irritation stiffened me from heel to crown. I flung my head back and gave her cool glance for cool glance, pride against pride.

Once, I remember, a doctor on board ship who dabbled in hypnotism told me that I was the most unsympathetic person he had ever struck. He said I was about as good a mesmeric subject as Table Mountain. Suddenly I began to realize that this woman was trying to cast some spell over me. The eyes grew large and luminous, and I was conscious for just an instant of some will battling to subject mine. I was aware, too, in the same moment of a strange scent which recalled that wild hour in Kuprasso's garden-house. It passed quickly, and for a second her eyes drooped. I seemed to read in them failure, and yet a kind of satisfaction, too, as if they had found more in me than they expected.

"What life have you led?" the soft voice was saying.

I was able to answer quite naturally, rather to my surprise. "I have been a mining engineer up and down the world."

"You have faced danger many times?"

"I have faced danger."

"You have fought with men in battles?"

"I have fought in battles."

Her bosom rose and fell in a kind of sigh. A smile—a very beautiful thing—flitted over her face. She gave me her hand.

"The horses are at the door now," she said, "and your servant is with them. One of my people will guide you to the city."

She turned away and passed out of the circle of light into the darkness beyond . . .

Peter and I jogged home in the rain with one of Sandy's skin-clad Companions loping at our side. We did not speak a word, for my thoughts were running like hounds on the track of the past hours. I had seen the mysterious Hilda von Einem, I had spoken to her, I had held

"I HAVE HEARD OF YOU," SHE SAID

her hand. She had insulted me with the subtlest of insults and yet I was not angry. Suddenly the game I was playing became invested with a tremendous solemnity. My old antagonists, Stumm and Rasta and the whole German Empire, seemed to shrink into the background, leaving only the slim woman with her inscrutable smile and devouring eyes. "Mad and bad," Blenkiron had called her, "but principally bad." I did not think they were the proper terms, for they belonged to the narrow world of our common experience. This was something beyond and above it, as a cyclone or an earthquake is outside the decent routine of nature. Mad and bad she might be, but she was also great.

Before we arrived our guide had plucked my knee and spoken some words which he had obviously got by heart. "The Master says," ran the message, "expect him at midnight."

CHAPTER 15

An Embarrassed Toilet

I WAS SOAKED to the bone, and while Peter set off to look for dinner I went to my room to change. I had a rub down and then got into pyjamas for some dumb-bell exercises with two chairs, for that long wet ride had stiffened my arm and shoulder muscles. They were a vulgar suit of primitive blue, which Blenkiron had looted from my London wardrobe. As Cornelis Brandt I had sported a flannel nightgown.

My bedroom opened off the sitting-room, and while I was busy with my gymnastics I heard the door open. I thought at first it was Blenkiron, but the briskness of the tread was unlike his measured gait. I had left the light burning there, and the visitor, whoever he was, had made himself at home. I slipped on a green dressing-gown Blenkiron had lent me, and sallied forth to investigate.

My friend Rasta was standing by the table, on which he had laid an envelope. He looked round at my entrance and saluted.

"I come from the Minister of War, sir," he said, "and bring you your passports for to-morrow. You will travel by . . ." And then his voice tailed away and his black eyes narrowed to slits. He had seen something which switched him off the metals.

At that moment I saw it too. There was a mirror on the wall behind him, and as I faced him I could not help seeing my reflection. It was the exact image of the engineer on the Danube boat—blue jeans, *loden* cloak, and all. The accursed mischance of my costume had given him the clue to an identity which was otherwise buried deep in the Bosporus.

I am bound to say for Rasta that he was a man of quick action. In a trice he had whipped round to the other side of the table between me and the door, where he stood regarding me wickedly.

By this time I was at the table and stretched out a hand for the envelope. My one hope was nonchalance.

"Sit down, sir," I said, "and have a drink. It's a filthy night to move about in."

273

"Thank you, no, Herr Brandt," he said. "You may burn these passports for they will not be used."

"Whatever's the matter with you?" I cried. "You've mistaken the house, my lad. I'm called Hanau—Richard Hanau—and my partner's Mr John S. Blenkiron. He'll be here presently. Never knew anyone of the name of Brandt, barring a tobacconist in Denver City."

"You have never been to Rustchuk?" he said with a sneer.

"Not that I know of. But, pardon me, sir, if I ask your name and your business here. I'm darned if I'm accustomed to be called by Dutch names or have my word doubted. In my country we consider that impolite as between gentlemen."

I could see that my bluff was having its effect. His stare began to waver, and when he next spoke it was in a more civil tone.

"I will ask pardon if I'm mistaken, sir, but you're the image of a man who a week ago was at Rustchuk, a man much wanted by the Imperial Government."

"A week ago I was tossing in a dirty little hooker coming from Constanza. Unless Rustchuk's in the middle of the Black Sea I've never visited the township. I guess you're barking up the wrong tree. Come to think of it, I was expecting passports. Say, do you come from Enver Damad?"

"I have that honour," he said.

"Well, Enver is a very good friend of mine. He's the brightest citizen I've struck this side of the Atlantic."

The man was calming down, and in another minute his suspicions would have gone. But at that moment, by the crookedest kind of luck, Peter entered with a tray of dishes. He did not notice Rasta, and walked straight to the table and plumped down his burden on it. The Turk had stepped aside at his entrance, and I saw by the look in his eyes that his suspicions had become a certainty. For Peter, stripped to shirt and breeches, was the identical shabby little companion of the Rustchuk meeting.

I had never doubted Rasta's pluck. He jumped for the door and had a pistol out in a trice pointing at my head.

"*Bonne fortune*," he cried. "Both the birds at one shot." His hand was on the latch, and his mouth was open to cry. I guessed there was an orderly waiting on the stairs.

He had what you call the strategic advantage, for he was at the door while I was at the other end of the table and Peter at the side of it at least two yards from him. The road was clear before him, and neither of us was armed. I made a despairing step forward, not knowing what I meant to do, for I saw no light. But Peter was before me.

He had never let go of the tray, and now, as a boy skims a stone on a pond, he skimmed it with its contents at Rasta's head. The man was opening the door with one hand while he kept me covered with the other, and he got the contrivance fairly in the face. A pistol shot cracked out, and the bullet went through the tray, but the noise was drowned in the crash of glasses and crockery. The next second Peter had wrenched the pistol from Rasta's hand and had gripped his throat.

A dandified Young Turk, brought up in Paris and finished in Berlin, may be as brave as a lion, but he cannot stand in a rough-and-tumble against a backveld hunter, though more than double his age. There was no need for me to help him. Peter had his own way, learned in a wild school, of knocking the sense out of a foe. He gagged him scientifically, and trussed him up with his own belt and two straps from a trunk in my bedroom.

"This man is too dangerous to let go," he said, as if his procedure were the most ordinary thing in the world. "He will be quiet now till we have time to make a plan."

At that moment there came a knocking at the door. That is the sort of thing that happens in melodrama, just when the villain has finished off his job neatly. The correct thing to do is to pale to the teeth, and with a rolling, conscience-stricken eye glare round the horizon. But that was not Peter's way.

"We'd better tidy up if we're to have visitors," he said calmly.

Now there was one of those big oak German cupboards against the wall which must have been brought in in sections, for complete it would never have got through the door. It was empty now, but for Blenkiron's hatbox. In it he deposited the unconscious Rasta, and turned the key. "There's enough ventilation through the top," he observed, "to keep the air good." Then he opened the door.

A magnificent *kavass* in blue and silver stood outside. He saluted and proffered a card on which was written in pencil, "Hilda von Einem".

I would have begged for time to change my clothes, but the lady was behind him. I saw the black mantilla and the rich sable furs. Peter vanished through my bedroom and I was left to receive my guest in a room littered with broken glass and a senseless man in the cupboard.

There are some situations so crazily extravagant that they key up the spirit to meet them. I was almost laughing when that stately lady stepped over my threshold.

"Madam," I said, with a bow that shamed my old dressing-gown and strident pyjamas. "You find me at a disadvantage. I came home soaking from my ride, and was in the act of changing. My servant has just upset a tray of crockery, and I fear this room's no fit place for a lady. Allow me three minutes to make myself presentable."

She inclined her head gravely and took a seat by the fire. I went into my bedroom, and as I expected found Peter lurking by the other door. In a hectic sentence I bade him get Rasta's orderly out of the place on any pretext, and tell him his master would return later. Then I hurried into decent garments, and came out to find my visitor in a brown study.

At the sound of my entrance she started from her dream and stood up on the hearthrug, slipping the long robe of fur from her slim body.

"We are alone?" she said. "We will not be disturbed?"

Then an inspiration came to me. I remembered that Frau von Einem, according to Blenkiron, did not see eye to eye with the Young Turks; and I had a queer instinct that Rasta could not be to her liking. So I spoke the truth.

"I must tell you that there's another guest here to-night. I reckon he's feeling pretty uncomfortable. At present he's trussed up on a shelf in that cupboard."

She did not trouble to look round.

"Is he dead?" she asked calmly.

"By no means," I said, "but he's fixed so he can't speak, and I guess he can't hear much."

"He was the man who brought you this?" she asked, pointing to the envelope on the table which bore the big blue stamp of the Ministry of War.

"The same," I said. "I'm not perfectly sure of his name, but I think they call him Rasta."

Not a flicker of a smile crossed her face, but I had a feeling that the news pleased her.

"Did he thwart you?" she asked.

"Why, yes. He thwarted me some. His head is a bit swelled, and an hour or two on the shelf will do him good."

"He is a powerful man," she said, "a jackal of Enver's. You have made a dangerous enemy."

"I don't value him at two cents," said I, though I thought grimly that as far as I could see the value of him was likely to be about the price of my neck.

"Perhaps you are right," she said with serious eyes. "In these days no enemy is dangerous to a bold man. I have come to-night, Mr Hanau, to talk business with you, as they say in your country. I have heard well of you, and to-day I have seen you. I may have need of you, and you assuredly will have need of me . . ."

She broke off, and again her strange potent eyes fell on my face. They were like a burning searchlight which showed up every cranny and crack of the soul. I felt it was going to be horribly difficult to act a part under that compelling gaze. She could not mesmerize me, but she could strip me of my fancy dress and set me naked in the masquerade.

"What came you forth to seek?" she asked. "You are not like the stout American Blenkiron, a lover of shoddy power and a devotee of a feeble science. There is something more than that in your face. You are on our side, but you are not of the Germans with their hankerings for a rococo Empire. You come from America, the land of pious follies, where men worship gold and words. I ask, what came you forth to seek?"

As she spoke I seemed to get a vision of a figure, like one of the old gods looking down on human nature from a great height, a figure disdainful and passionless, but with its own magnificence. It kindled my imagination, and I answered with the stuff I had often cogitated when I had tried to explain to myself just how a case could be made out against the Allied cause.

"I will tell you, Madam," I said. "I am a man who has followed a science, but I have followed it in wild places, and I have gone through it and come out at the other side. The world, as I see it, had become too easy and cushioned. Men had forgotten their manhood in soft speech, and imagined that the rules of their smug civilization were the laws of the universe. But that is not the teaching of science, and it is not the teaching of life. We have forgotten the greater virtues, and we were becoming emasculated humbugs whose gods were our own weaknesses. Then came war, and the air was cleared. Germany, in spite of her blunders and her grossness, stood forth as the scourge of cant. She had the courage to cut through the bonds of humbug and to laugh at the fetishes of the herd. Therefore I am on Germany's side. But I came here for another reason. I know nothing of the East, but as I read history it is from the desert that the purification comes. When mankind is smothered with shams and phrases and painted idols a wind blows out of the wild to cleanse and simplify life. The world needs space and fresh air. The civilization we have boasted of is a toy-shop and a blind alley, and I hanker for the open country."

This confounded nonsense was well received. Her pale eyes had the cold light of the fanatic. With her bright hair and the long exquisite oval of her face she looked like some destroying fury of a Norse legend. At that moment I think I first really feared her; before I had half hated and half admired. Thank Heaven, in her absorption she did not notice that I had forgotten the speech of Cleveland, Ohio.

"You are of the Household of Faith," she said. "You will presently learn many things, for the Faith marches to victory. Meantime I have one word for you. You and your companion travel eastward."

"We go to Mesopotamia," I said. "I reckon these are our passports," and I pointed to the envelope.

She picked it up, opened it, and then tore it in pieces and tossed it in the fire.

"The orders are countermanded," she said. "I have need of you and you go with me. Not to the flats of the Tigris, but to the great hills. To-morrow you will receive new passports."

She gave me her hand and turned to go. At the threshold she paused, and looked towards the oak cupboard. "To-morrow I will relieve you of your prisoner. He will be safer in my hands."

SHE LEFT ME in a condition of pretty blank bewilderment. We were to be tied to the chariot-wheels of this fury, and started on an enterprise compared to which fighting against our friends at Kut seemed tame and reasonable. On the other hand, I had been spotted by Rasta, and had got the envoy of the most powerful man in Constantinople locked in a cupboard. At all costs we had to keep Rasta safe, but I was very determined that he should not be handed over to the lady. I was going to be no party to cold-blooded murder, which I judged to be her expedient. It was a pretty kettle of fish, but in the meantime I must have food, for I had eaten nothing for nine hours. So I went in search of Peter.

I had scarcely begun my long-deferred meal when Sandy entered. He was before his time, and he looked as solemn as a sick owl. I seized on him as a drowning man clutches a spar.

He heard my story of Rasta with a lengthening face.

"That's bad," he said. "You say he spotted you, and your subsequent doings of course would not disillusion him. It's an infernal nuisance, but there's only one way out of it. I must put him in charge of my own people. They will keep him safe and sound till he's wanted. Only he mustn't see me." And he went out in a hurry.

I fetched Rasta from his prison. He had come to his senses by this time, and lay regarding me with stony, malevolent eyes.

"I'm very sorry, sir," I said, "for what has happened. But you left me no alternative. I've got a big job on hand and I can't have it interfered with by you or anyone. You're paying the price of a suspicious nature. When you know a little more you'll want to apologize to me. I'm going to see that you are kept quiet and comfortable for a day or two. You've no cause to worry, for you'll suffer no harm. I give you my word of honour as an American citizen."

Two of Sandy's miscreants came in and bore him off, and presently Sandy himself returned. When I asked him where he was being taken, Sandy said he didn't know. "They've got their orders, and they'll carry them out to the letter. There's a big unknown area in Constantinople to hide a man, into which the *Khafiyeh* never enter."

Then he flung himself in a chair and lit his old pipe.

"Dick," he said, "this job is getting very difficult and very dark. But my knowledge has grown in the last few days. I've found out the meaning of the second word that Harry Bullivant scribbled."

"*Cancer?*" I asked.

"Yes. It means just what it reads and no more. Greenmantle is dying—has been dying for months. This afternoon they brought a German doctor to see him, and the man gave him a few hours of life. By now he may be dead."

The news was a staggerer. For a moment I thought it cleared up things. "Then that busts the show," I said. "You can't have a crusade without a prophet."

"I wish I thought it did. It's the end of one stage, but the start of a new and blacker one. Do you think that woman will be beaten by such a small thing as the death of her prophet? She'll find a substitute—one of the four Ministers, or someone else. She's a devil incarnate, but she has the soul of a Napoleon. The big danger is only beginning."

Then he told me the story of his recent doings. He had found out the house of Frau von Einem without much trouble, and had performed with his ragamuffins in the servants' quarters. The prophet had a large retinue, and the fame of his minstrels—for the Companions were known far and wide in the land of Islam—came speedily to the ears of the Holy Ones. Sandy, a leader in this most orthodox coterie, was taken into favour and brought to the notice of the four Ministers. He and his half-dozen retainers became inmates of the villa, and Sandy, from his knowledge of Islamic lore and his ostentatious piety, was admitted to the confidence of the household. Frau von Einem welcomed him as an ally, for the Companions had been the most devoted propagandists of the new revelation.

As he described it, it was a strange business. Greenmantle was dying and often in great pain, but he struggled to meet the demands of his protectress. The four Ministers, as Sandy saw them, were unworldly ascetics; the prophet himself was a saint, though a practical saint with some notions of policy; but the controlling brain and will were those of the lady. Sandy seemed to have won his favour, even his affection. He spoke of him with a kind of desperate pity.

"I never saw such a man. He is the greatest gentleman you can picture, with a dignity like a high mountain. He is a dreamer and a poet, too—a genius if I can judge these things. I think I can assess him rightly, for I know something of the soul of the East, but it would be too long a story to tell now. The West knows nothing of the true Oriental. It pictures him as lapped in colour and idleness and luxury and gorgeous dreams. But it is all wrong. The *Kâf* he yearns for is an austere thing. It is the austerity of the East that is its beauty and its terror . . . It always wants the same things at the back of its head. The Turk and the Arab came out of big spaces, and they have the desire of them in their bones. They settle down and stagnate, and by the by they degenerate into that appalling subtlety which is their ruling passion gone crooked. And then comes a new revelation and a great simplifying. They want to live face to face with God without a screen of ritual and images and priestcraft. They want to prune life of its foolish fringes and get back to the noble bareness of the desert. Remember, it is always the empty desert and the empty sky that cast their spell over them — these, and the hot, strong, antiseptic sunlight which burns up all rot and decay . . . It isn't inhuman. It's the humanity of one part of the human race. It isn't ours, it isn't as good as ours, but it's jolly good all the same. There are times when it grips me so hard that I'm inclined to forswear the gods of my fathers!

"Well, Greenmantle is the prophet of this great simplicity. He speaks straight to the heart of Islam, and it's an honourable message. But for our sins it's been twisted into part of that damned German propaganda. His unworldliness has been used for a cunning political move, and his creed of space and simplicity for the furtherance of the last word in human degeneracy. My God, Dick, it's like seeing St Francis run by Messalina."

"The woman has been here to-night," I said. "She asked me what I stood for, and I invented some infernal nonsense which she approved of. But I can see one thing. She and her prophet may run for different stakes, but it's the same course."

Sandy started. "She has been here!" he cried. "Tell me, Dick, what do you think of her?"

"I thought she was about two parts mad, but the third part was uncommon like inspiration."

"That's about right," he said. "I was wrong in comparing her to Messalina. She's something a dashed sight more complicated. She runs the prophet just because she shares his belief. Only what in him is sane and fine, in her is mad and horrible. You see, Germany also wants to simplify life."

"I know," I said. "I told her that an hour ago, when I talked more rot to the second than any mortal man ever achieved. It will come between me and my sleep for the rest of my days."

"Germany's simplicity is that of the neurotic, not the primitive. It is megalomania and egotism and the pride of the man in the Bible that waxed fat and kicked. But the results are the same. She wants to destroy and simplify; but it isn't the simplicity of the ascetic, which is of the spirit, but the simplicity of the madman that grinds down all the contrivances of civilization to a featureless monotony. The prophet wants to save the souls of his people; Germany wants to rule the inanimate corpse of the world. But you can get the same language to cover both. And so you have the partnership of St Francis and Messalina. Dick, did you ever hear of a thing called the Superman?"

"There was a time when the papers were full of nothing else," I answered. "I gather it was invented by a sportsman called Nietzsche."

"Maybe," said Sandy. "Old Nietzsche has been blamed for a great deal of rubbish he would have died rather than acknowledge. But it's a craze of the new, fatted Germany. It's a fancy type which could never really exist, any more than the Economic Man of the politicians. Mankind has a sense of humour which stops short of the final absurdity. There never has been, and there never could be a real Superman . . . But there might be a Superwoman."

"You'll get into trouble, my lad, if you talk like that," I said.

"It's true all the same. Women have got a perilous logic which we never have, and some of the best of them don't see the joke of life like the ordinary man. They can be far greater than men, for they can go straight to the heart of things. There never was a man so near the divine as Joan of Arc. But I think, too, they can be more entirely damnable than anything that ever was breeched, for they don't stop still now and then and laugh at themselves . . . There is no Superman. The poor old donkeys that fancy themselves in the part are either crack-brained professors who couldn't rule a Sunday-school class, or bristling soldiers with pint-pot heads who imagine that the shooting of a Duc d'Enghien made a Napoleon. But there is a Superwoman, and her name's Hilda von Einem."

"I thought our job was nearly over," I groaned, "and now it looks as if it hadn't well started. Bullivant said that all we had to do was to find out the truth."

"Bullivant didn't know. No man knows except you and me. I tell you, the woman has immense power. The Germans have trusted her with their trump card, and she's going to play it for all she is worth. There's no crime that will stand in her way. She has set the ball rolling, and if need be she'll cut all her prophets' throats and run the show herself . . . I don't know about your job, for honestly I can't quite see what you and Blenkiron are going to do. But I'm very clear about my own duty. She's let me into the business, and I'm going to stick to it in the hope that I'll find a chance of wrecking it . . . We're moving eastward to-morrow—with a new prophet if the old one is dead."

"Where are you going?" I asked.

"I don't know. But I gather it's a long journey, judging by the preparations. And it must be to a cold country, judging by the clothes provided."

"Well, wherever it is, we're going with you. You haven't heard the end of our yarn. Blenkiron and I have been moving in the best circles as skilled American engineers who are going to play Old Harry with the British on the Tigris. I'm a pal of Enver's now, and he has offered me his protection. The lamented Rasta brought our passports for the journey to Mesopotamia to-morrow, but an hour ago your lady tore them up and put them in the fire. We are going with her, and she vouchsafed the information that it was towards the great hills."

Sandy whistled long and low. "I wonder what the deuce she wants with you? This thing is getting dashed complicated, Dick . . . Where, more by token, is Blenkiron? He's the fellow to know about high politics."

The missing Blenkiron, as Sandy spoke, entered the room with his slow, quiet step. I could see by his carriage that for once he had no dyspepsia, and by his eyes that he was excited.

"Say, boys," he said, "I've got something pretty considerable in the way of noos. There's been big fighting on the Eastern border, and the Buzzards have taken a bad knock."

His hands were full of papers, from which he selected a map and spread it on the table.

"They keep mum about this thing in the capital, but I've been piecing the story together these last days and I think I've got it straight. A fortnight ago old man Nicholas descended from his mountains and scuppered his enemies there—at Kuprikeui, where the main road eastwards crosses the Araxes. That was only the beginning of the stunt, for he pressed on on a broad front, and the gentleman called Kiamil, who commands in those parts, was not up to the job of holding him. The Buzzards were shepherded in from north and east and south, and now the Muscovite is sitting down outside the forts of Erzerum. I can tell you they're pretty miserable about the situation in the highest quarters . . . Enver is sweating blood to get fresh divisions to Erzerum from Gally-poly, but it's a long road and it looks as if they would be too late for the fair . . . You and I, Major, start for Mesopotamy to-morrow, and that's about the meanest bit of bad luck that ever happened to John S. We're missing the chance of seeing the goriest fight of this campaign."

I picked up the map and pocketed it. Maps were my business, and I had been looking for one.

"We're not going to Mesopotamia," I said. "Our orders have been cancelled."

"But I've just seen Enver, and he said he had sent round our passports."

"They're in the fire," I said. "The right ones will come along to-morrow morning."

Sandy broke in, his eyes bright with excitement.

"The great hills! . . . We're going to Erzerum . . . Don't you see that the Germans are playing their big card? They're sending Greenmantle to the point of danger in the hope that his coming will rally the Turkish defence. Things are beginning to move, Dick, old man. No more kicking the heels for us. We're going to be in it up to the neck, and Heaven help the best man . . . I must be off now, for I've a lot to do. *Au revoir.* We meet some time soon in the hills."

Blenkiron still looked puzzled, till I told him the story of that night's doings. As he listened, all the satisfaction went out of his face, and that funny, childish air of bewilderment crept in.

"It's not for me to complain, for it's in the straight line of our dooty, but I reckon there's going to be big trouble ahead of this caravan. It's Kismet, and we've got to bow. But I won't pretend that I'm not considerable scared at the prospect."

"Oh, so am I," I said. "The woman frightens me into fits. We're up against it this time all right. All the same I'm glad we're to be let into the real star metropolitan performance. I didn't relish the idea of touring the provinces."

"I guess that's correct. But I could wish that the good God would see fit to take that lovely lady to Himself. She's too much for a quiet man at my time of life. When she invites us to go in on the ground floor I feel like taking the elevator to the roof-garden."

CHAPTER 16

The Battered Caravanserai

TWO DAYS LATER, in the evening, we came to Angora, the first stage in our journey.

The passports had arrived next morning, as Frau von Einem had promised, and with them a plan of our journey. More, one of the Companions, who spoke a little English, was detailed to accompany us—a wise precaution, for no one of us had a word of Turkish. These were the sum of our instructions. I heard nothing more of Sandy or Greenmantle or the lady. We were meant to travel in our own party.

We had the railway to Angora, a very comfortable German *Schlafwagen*, tacked to the end of a troop-train. There wasn't much to be seen of the country, for after we left the Bosporus we ran into scuds of snow, and except that we seemed to be climbing on to a big plateau I had no notion of the landscape. It was a marvel that we made such good time, for that line was congested beyond anything I have ever seen. The place was crawling with the Gallipoli troops, and every siding was packed with supply trucks. When we stopped—which we did on an average about once an hour—you could see vast camps on both sides of the line, and often we struck regiments on the march along the railway track. They looked a fine, hardy lot of ruffians, but many were deplorably ragged, and I didn't think much of their boots. I wondered how they would do the five hundred miles of road to Erzerum.

Blenkiron played Patience, and Peter and I took a hand at picquet, but mostly we smoked and yarned. Getting away from that infernal city had cheered us up wonderfully. Now we were out on the open road, moving to the sound of the guns. At the worst, we should not perish like rats in a sewer. We would be all together, too, and that was a comfort. I think we felt the relief which a man who has been on a lonely out-post feels when he is brought back to his battalion. Besides, the thing had gone clean beyond our power to direct. It was no good planning and scheming, for none of us had a notion what the next step might be. We were fatalists now, believing in Kismet, and that is a comfortable faith.

All but Blenkiron. The coming of Hilda von Einem into the business had put a very ugly complexion on it for him. It was curious to see how she affected the different members of our gang. Peter did not care a rush; man, woman, and hippogriff were the same to him; he met it all as calmly as if he were making plans to round up an old lion in a patch of bush, taking the facts as they came and working at them as if they were a sum in arithmetic. Sandy and I were impressed—it's no good denying it: horribly impressed—but we were too interested to be scared, and we weren't a bit fascinated. We hated her too much for that. But she fairly struck Blenkiron dumb. He said himself it was just like a rattlesnake and a bird.

I made him talk about her, for if he sat and brooded he would get worse. It was a strange thing that this man, the most imperturbable and, I think, about the most courageous I have ever met, should be paralysed by a slim woman. There was no doubt about it. The thought of her made the future to him as black as a thunder-cloud. It took the power out of his joints, and if she was going to be much around, it looked as if Blenkiron might be counted out.

I suggested that he was in love with her, but this he vehemently denied.

"No; sir; I haven't got no sort of affection for the lady. My trouble is that she puts me out of countenance, and I can't fit her in as an antagonist. I guess we Americans haven't got the right poise for dealing with that kind of female. We've exalted our womenfolk into little tin gods, and at the same time left them out of the real business of life. Consequently, when we strike one playing the biggest kind of man's game we can't place her. We aren't used to regarding them as anything except angels and children. I wish I had had you boys' upbringing."

Angora was like my notion of some place such as Amiens in the retreat from Mons. It was one mass of troops and transport—the neck of the bottle, for more arrived every hour, and the only outlet was the single eastern road. The town was pandemonium into which distracted German officers were trying to introduce some order. They didn't worry much about us, for the heart of Anatolia wasn't a likely hunting-ground for suspicious characters. We took our passports to the commandant, who viséd them readily, and told us he'd do his best to get us transport. We spent the night in a sort of hotel, where all four crowded into one little bedroom, and next morning I had my work cut out getting a motor-car. It took four hours, and the use of every great name in the Turkish Empire, to raise a dingy sort of Studebaker, and another two to get the petrol and spare tyres. As for a chauffeur, love or money couldn't find him, and I was compelled to drive the thing myself.

We left just after midday and swung out into bare bleak downs patched with scrubby woodlands. There was no snow here, but a wind was blowing from the east which searched the marrow. Presently we climbed up into hills, and the road, though not badly engineered to begin with, grew as rough as the channel of a stream. No wonder, for the traffic was like what one saw on that awful stretch between Cassel and Ypres, and there were no gangs of Belgian roadmakers to mend it up. We found troops by the thousands striding along with their impassive Turkish faces, ox convoys, mule convoys, wagons drawn by sturdy little Anatolian horses, and, coming in the contrary direction, many shabby Red Crescent cars and wagons of the wounded. We had to crawl for hours on end, till we got past a block. Just before the darkening we seemed to outstrip the first press, and had a clear run for about ten miles over a low pass in the hills. I began to get anxious about the car, for it was a poor one at the best, and the road was guaranteed sooner or later to knock even a Rolls-Royce into scrap iron.

All the same it was glorious to be out in the open again. Peter's face wore a new look, and he sniffed the bitter air like a stag. There floated up from little wayside camps the odour of wood smoke and dung-fires. That, and the curious acrid winter smell of great wind-blown spaces, will always come to my memory as I think of that day. Every hour brought me peace of mind and resolution. I felt as I had felt when the battalion first marched from Aire towards the firing-line, a kind of keying-up and wild expectation. I'm not used to cities, and lounging about Constantinople had slackened my fibre. Now, as the sharp wind buffeted us, I felt braced to any kind of risk. We were on the great road to the East and the border hills, and soon we should stand upon the farthest battle-front of the war. This was no commonplace intelligence job. That was all over, and we were going into the firing-line, going to take part in what might be the downfall of our enemies. I didn't reflect that we were among those enemies, and would probably share their downfall if we were not shot earlier. The truth is, I had got out of the way of regarding the thing as a struggle between armies and nations. I hardly bothered to think where my sympathies lay. First and foremost it was a contest between the four of us and a crazy woman, and this personal antagonism made the strife of armies only a dimly felt background.

We slept that night like logs on the floor of a dirty khan, and started next morning in a powder of snow. We were getting very high up now, and it was perishing cold. The Companion—his name sounded like Hussin—had travelled the road before and told me what the places were, but they conveyed nothing to me. All morning we wriggled through a big lot of troops, a brigade at least, who swung along at a great pace with a fine free stride that I don't think I have ever seen bettered. I must say I took a fancy to the Turkish fighting man: I remembered the testimonial our fellows gave him as a clean fighter, and I felt very bitter that Germany should have lugged him into this dirty business. They halted for a meal, and we stopped, too, and lunched off some brown bread and dried figs and a flask of very sour wine. I had a few words with one of the officers who spoke a little German. He told me they were marching straight for Russia, since there had been a great Turkish victory in the Caucasus. "We have beaten the French and the British, and now it is Russia's turn," he said stolidly, as if repeating a lesson. But he added that he was mortally sick of war.

In the afternoon we cleared the column and had an open road for some hours. The land now had a tilt eastward, as if we were moving towards the valley of a great river. Soon we began to meet little parties of men coming from the East with a new look in their faces. The first lots of wounded had been the ordinary thing you see on every front, and there had been some pretence at organization. But these new lots were very weary and broken; they were often barefoot, and they seemed to have lost their transport and to be starving. You would find a group stretched by the roadside in the last stages of exhaustion. Then would come a party limping along, so tired that they never turned their heads to look at us. Almost all were wounded, some badly, and most were horribly thin. I wondered how my Turkish friend behind would explain the sight to his men, if he believed in a great victory. They had not the air of the backwash of a conquering army.

Even Blenkiron, who was no soldier, noticed it.

"These boys look mighty bad," he observed. "We've got to hustle, Major, if we're going to get seats for the last act."

That was my own feeling. The sight made me mad to get on faster, for I saw that big things were happening in the East. I had reckoned that four days would take us from Angora to Erzerum, but here was the second nearly over and we were not yet a third of the way. I pressed on recklessly, and that hurry was our undoing.

I have said that the Studebaker was a rotten old car. Its steering-gear was pretty dicky, and the bad surface and continual hairpin bends of the road didn't improve it. Soon we came into snow lying fairly deep, frozen hard and rutted by the big transport-wagons. We bumped and bounced horribly, and were shaken about like peas in a bladder. I began to be acutely anxious about the old boneshaker, the more as we seemed a long way short of the village I had proposed to spend the night in. Twilight was falling and we were still in an unfeatured waste, crossing the shallow glen of a stream. There was a bridge at the bottom of a slope—a bridge of logs and earth which had apparently been freshly strengthened for heavy traffic. As we approached it at a good pace the car ceased to answer to the wheel.

I struggled desperately to keep it straight, but it swerved to the left and we plunged over a bank into a marshy hollow. There was a sickening bump as we struck the lower ground, and the whole party were shot out into the frozen slush. I don't yet know how I escaped, for the car turned over and by rights I should have had my back broken. But no one was hurt. Peter was laughing, and Blenkiron, after shaking the snow out of his hair, joined him. For myself I was feverishly examining the machine. It was about as ugly as it could be, for the front axle was broken.

Here was a piece of hopeless bad luck. We were stuck in the middle of Asia Minor with no means of conveyance, for to get a new axle there was as likely as to find snowballs on the Congo. It was all but dark and there was no time to lose. I got out the petrol tins and spare tyres and cached them among some rocks on the hillside. Then we collected our scanty baggage from the derelict Studebaker. Our only hope was Hussin. He had got to find us some lodging for the night, and next day we would have a try for horses or a lift in some passing wagon. I had no hope of another car. Every automobile in Anatolia would now be at a premium.

It was so disgusting a mishap that we all took it quietly. It was too bad to be helped by hard swearing. Hussin and Peter set off on different sides of the road to prospect for a house, and Blenkiron and I sheltered under the nearest rock and smoked savagely.

Hussin was the first to strike oil. He came back in twenty minutes with news of some kind of dwelling a couple of miles up the stream. He went off to collect Peter, and, humping our baggage, Blenkiron and I plodded up the waterside. Darkness had fallen thick by this time, and we took some bad tosses among the bogs. When Hussin and Peter overtook us they found a better road, and presently we saw a light twinkle in the hollow ahead.

It proved to be a wretched tumble-down farm in a grove of poplars—a foul-smelling, muddy yard, a two-roomed hovel of a house, and a barn which was tolerably dry and which we selected for our sleeping-place. The owner was a broken old fellow whose sons were all at the war, and he received us with the profound calm of one who expects nothing but unpleasantness from life.

By this time we had recovered our tempers, and I was trying hard to put my new Kismet philosophy into practice. I reckoned that if risks were foreordained, so were difficulties, and both must be taken as part of the day's work. With the remains of our provisions and some curdled milk we satisfied our hunger and curled ourselves up among the pease straw of the barn. Blenkiron announced with a happy sigh that he had now been for two days quit of his dyspepsia.

That night, I remember, I had a queer dream. I seemed to be in a wild place among mountains, and I was being hunted, though who was after me I couldn't tell. I remember sweating with fright, for I seemed to be quite alone and the terror that was pursuing me was more than human. The place was horribly quiet and still, and there was deep snow lying everywhere, so that each step I took was heavy as lead. A very ordinary sort of nightmare, you will say. Yes, but there was one strange feature in this one. The night was pitch dark, but ahead of me in the throat of the pass there was one patch of light, and it showed a rum little hill with a rocky top: what we call in South Africa a *castrol* or saucepan. I had a notion that if I could get to that *castrol* I should be safe, and I panted through the drifts towards it with the avenger of blood at my heels. I woke, gasping, to find the winter morning struggling through the cracked rafters, and to hear Blenkiron say cheerily that his duodenum had behaved all night like a gentleman. I lay still for a bit trying to fix the dream, but it all dissolved into haze except the picture of the little hill, which was quite clear in every detail. I told myself it was a reminiscence of the veld, some spot down in the Wakkerstroom country, though for the life of me I couldn't place it.

I pass over the next three days, for they were one uninterrupted series of heart-breaks. Hussin and Peter scoured the country for horses, Blenkiron sat in the barn and played Patience, while I haunted the roadside near the bridge in the hope of picking up some kind of conveyance. My task was perfectly futile. The columns passed, casting wondering eyes on the wrecked car among the frozen rushes, but they could offer no help. My friend the Turkish officer promised to wire to Angora from some place or other for a fresh car, but, remembering the state of affairs at Angora, I had no hope from that quarter. Cars passed, plenty of them, packed with staff-officers, Turkish and German, but they were in far too big a hurry even to stop and speak. The only conclusion I reached from my roadside vigil was that things were getting very warm in the neighbourhood of Erzerum. Everybody on that road seemed to be in mad haste either to get there or to get away.

Hussin was the best chance, for, as I have said, the Companions had a very special and peculiar graft throughout the Turkish Empire. But the first day he came back empty-handed. All the horses had been commandeered for the war, he said; and though he was certain that some had been kept back and hidden away, he could not get on their track. The second day he returned with two—miserable screws and deplorably short in the wind from a diet of beans. There was no decent corn or hay left in that countryside. The third day he picked up a nice little Arab stallion: in poor condition, it is true, but perfectly sound. For these beasts we paid good money, for Blenkiron was well supplied and we had no time to spare for the interminable Oriental bargaining.

Hussin said he had cleaned up the countryside, and I believed him. I dared not delay another day, even though it meant leaving him behind. But he had no notion of doing anything of the kind. He was a good runner, he said, and could keep up with such horses as ours for ever. If this was the manner of our progress, I reckoned we would be weeks in getting to Erzerum.

We started at dawn on the morning of the fourth day, after the old farmer had blessed us and sold us some stale rye-bread. Blenkiron bestrode the Arab, being the heaviest, and Peter and I had the screws. My worst forebodings were soon realized, and Hussin, loping along at my side, had an easy job to keep up with us. We were about as slow as an ox-wagon. The brutes were unshod, and with the rough roads I saw that their feet would very soon go to pieces. We jogged along like a tinker's caravan, about five miles to the hour, as feckless a party as ever disgraced a highroad.

The weather was now a cold drizzle, which increased my depression. Cars passed us and disappeared in the mist, going at thirty miles an hour to mock our slowness. None of us spoke, for the futility of the business clogged our spirits. I bit hard on my lip to curb my restlessness, and I think I would have sold my soul there and then for anything that could move fast. I don't know any sorer trial than to be mad for speed and have to crawl at a snail's pace. I was getting ripe for any kind of desperate venture.

About midday we descended on a wide plain full of the marks of rich cultivation. Villages became frequent, and the land was studded with olive groves and scarred with water furrows. From what I remembered of the map I judged that we were coming to that champagne country near Siwas, which is the granary of Turkey, and the home of the true Osmanli stock.

Then at the turning of the road we came to the caravanserai.

It was a dingy, battered place, with the pink plaster falling in patches from its walls. There was a courtyard abutting on the road, and a flat-topped house with a big hole in its side. It was a long way from any battle-ground, and I guessed that some explosion had wrought the damage. Behind it, a few hundred yards off, a detachment of cavalry were encamped beside a stream, with their horses tied up in long lines of pickets.

And by the roadside, quite alone and deserted, stood a large new motor-car.

In all the road before and behind there was no man to be seen except the troops by the stream. The owners, whoever they were, must be inside the caravanserai.

I have said I was in the mood for some desperate deed, and lo and behold Providence had given me the chance! I coveted that car as I have never coveted anything on earth. At the moment all my plans had narrowed down to a feverish passion to get to the battlefield. We had to find Greenmantle at Erzerum, and once there we should have Hilda von Einem's protection. It was a time of war, and a front of brass was the surest safety. But, indeed, I could not figure out any plan worth speaking of. I saw only one thing—a fast car which might be ours.

I said a word to the others, and we dismounted and tethered our horses at the near end of the courtyard. I heard the low hum of voices from the cavalrymen by the stream, but they were three hundred yards off and could not see us. Peter was sent forward to scout in the courtyard. In the building itself there was but one window looking on the road, and that was in the upper floor. Meantime I crawled along beside the wall to where the car stood, and had a look at it. It was a splendid six-cylinder affair, brand new, with the tyres little worn. There were seven tins of petrol stacked behind as well as spare tyres, and, looking in, I saw map-cases and field-glasses strewn on the seats as if the owners had only got out for a minute to stretch their legs.

Peter came back and reported that the courtyard was empty. "There are men in the upper room," he said; "more than one, for I heard their voices. They are moving about restlessly, and may soon be coming out."

I reckoned that there was no time to be lost, so I told the others to slip down the road fifty yards beyond the caravanserai and be ready to climb in as I passed. I had to start the infernal thing, and there might be shooting.

I waited by the car till I saw them reach the right distance. I could hear voices from the second floor of the house and footsteps moving up and down. I was in a fever of anxiety, for any moment a man might come to the window. Then I flung myself on the starting handle and worked like a demon.

The cold made the job difficult, and my heart was in my mouth, for the noise in that quiet place must have woke the dead. Then, by the mercy of Heaven, the engine started, and I sprang to the driving seat, released the clutch, and opened the throttle. The great car shot forward, and I seemed to hear behind me shrill voices. A pistol bullet bored through my hat, and another buried itself in a cushion beside me.

In a second I was clear of the place and the rest of the party were embarking. Blenkiron got on the step and rolled himself like a sack of coals into the tonneau. Peter nipped up beside me, and Hussin scrambled in from the back over the folds of the hood. We had our baggage in our pockets and had nothing to carry.

Bullets dropped round us, but did no harm. Then I heard a report at my ear, and out of a corner of my eye saw Peter lower his pistol. Presently we were out of range, and, looking back, I saw three men gesticulating in the middle of the road.

"May the devil fly away with this pistol," said Peter ruefully. "I never could make good shooting with a little gun. Had I had my rifle . . ."

"What did you shoot for?" I asked in amazement. "We've got the fellows' car, and we don't want to do them any harm."

"It would have saved trouble had I had my rifle," said Peter, quietly. "The little man you call Rasta was there, and he knew you. I heard him cry your name. He is an angry little man, and I observe that on this road there is a telegraph."

CHAPTER 17

Trouble by the Waters of Babylon

ROM THAT MOMENT I date the beginning of my madness. Suddenly I forgot all cares and difficulties of the present and future and became foolishly light-hearted. We were rushing towards the great battle where men were busy at my proper trade. I realized how much I had loathed the lonely days in Germany, and still more the dawdling week in Constantinople. Now I was clear of it all, and bound for the clash of armies. It didn't trouble me that we were on the wrong side of the battle-line. I had a sort of instinct that the darker and wilder things grew the better chance for us.

"Seems to me," said Blenkiron, bending over me, "that this joy-ride is going to come to an untimely end pretty soon. Peter's right. That young man will set the telegraph going, and we'll be held up at the next township."

"He's got to get to a telegraph office first," I answered. "That's where we have the pull on him. He's welcome to the screws we left behind, and if he finds an operator before the evening I'm the worst kind of a Dutchman. I'm going to break all the rules and bucket this car for what's she's worth. Don't you see that the nearer we get to Erzerum the safer we are?"

'I don't follow," he said slowly. "At Erzerum I reckon they'll be waiting for us with the handcuffs. Why in thunder couldn't those hairy ragamuffins keep the little cuss safe? Your record's a bit too precipitous, Major, for the most innocent-minded military boss."

"Do you remember what you said about the Germans being open to bluff? Well, I'm going to put up the steepest sort of bluff. Of course they'll stop us. Rasta will do his damnedest. But remember that he and his friends are not very popular with the Germans, and Madame von Einem is. We're her protégés, and the bigger the German swell I get before the safer I'll feel. We've got our passports and our orders, and he'll be a bold man that will stop us once we get into the German zone. Therefore I'm going to hurry as fast as God will let me."

It was a ride that deserved to have an epic written about it. The car was good, and I handled her well, though I say it who shouldn't. The road in that big central plain was fair, and often I knocked fifty miles an hour out of her. We passed troops by a circuit over the veld, where we took some awful risks, and once we skidded by some transport with our off wheels almost over the lip of a ravine. We went through the narrow streets of Siwas like a fire-engine, while I shouted out in German that we carried despatches for headquarters. We shot out of drizzling rain into brief spells of winter sunshine, and then into a snow blizzard which all but whipped the skin from our faces. And always before us the long road unrolled, with somewhere at the end of it two armies clinched in a death-grapple.

That night we looked for no lodging. We ate a sort of meal in the car with the hood up, and felt our way on in the darkness, for the headlights were in perfect order. Then we turned off the road for four hours' sleep, and I had a go at the map. Before dawn we started again, and came over a pass into the vale of a big river. The winter dawn showed its gleaming stretches, ice-bound among the sprinkled meadows. I called to Blenkiron:

"I believe that river is the Euphrates," I said.

"So," he said, acutely interested. "Then that's the waters of Babylon. Great snakes, that I should have lived to see the fields where King Nebuchadnezzar grazed! Do you know the name of that big hill, Major?"

"Ararat, as like as not," I cried, and he believed me.

We were among the hills now, great, rocky black slopes, and, seen through side-glens, a hinterland of snowy peaks. I remember I kept looking for the *castrol* I had seen in my dream. The thing had never left off haunting me, and I was pretty clear now that it did not belong to my South African memories. I am not a superstitious man, but the way that little *kranz* clung to my mind made me think it was a warning sent by Providence. I was pretty certain that when I clapped eyes on it I would be in for bad trouble.

All morning we travelled up that broad vale, and just before noon it spread out wider, the road dipped to the water's edge, and I saw before me the white roofs of a town. The snow was deep now, and lay down to the riverside, but the sky had cleared, and against a space of blue heaven some peaks to the south rose glittering like jewels. The arches of a bridge, spanning two forks of the stream, showed in front, and as I slowed down at the bend a sentry's challenge rang out from a block-house. We had reached the fortress of Erzingjan, the headquarters of a Turkish corps and the gate of Armenia.

I showed the man our passports, but he did not salute and let us move on. He called another fellow from the guard-house, who motioned us to keep pace with him as he stumped down a side lane. At the other end was a big barracks with sentries outside. The man spoke to us in Turkish, which Hussin interpreted. There was somebody in that barracks who wanted badly to see us.

"By the waters of Babylon we sat down and wept," quoted Blenkiron softly. "I fear, Major, we'll soon be remembering Zion."

I tried to persuade myself that this was merely the red tape of a frontier fortress, but I had an instinct that difficulties were in store for us. If Rasta had started wiring I was prepared to put up the brazenest bluff, for we were still eighty miles from Erzerum, and at all costs we were going to be landed there before night.

A fussy staff-officer met us at the door. At the sight of us he cried to a friend to come and look.

"Here are the birds safe. A fat man and two lean ones and a savage who looks like a Kurd. Call the guard and march them off. There's no doubt about their identity."

"Pardon me, sir," I said, "but we have no time to spare and we'd like to be in Erzerum before the dark. I would beg you to get through any formalities as soon as possible. This man," and I pointed to the sentry, "has our passports."

"Compose yourself," he said impudently; "you're not going on just yet, and when you do it won't be in a stolen car." He took the passports and fingered them casually. Then something he saw there made him cock his eyebrows.

"Where did you steal these?" he asked, but with less assurance in his tone.

I spoke very gently. "You seem to be the victim of a mistake, sir. These are our papers. We are under orders to report ourselves at Erzerum without an hour's delay. Whoever hinders us will have to answer to General von Liman. We will be obliged if you will conduct us at once to the Governor."

"You can't see General Posselt," he said; "this is my business. I have a wire from Siwas that four men stole a car belonging to one of Enver Damad's staff. It describes you all, and says that two of you are notorious spies wanted by the Imperial Government. What have you to say to that?"

"Only that it is rubbish. My good sir, you have seen our passes. Our errand is not to be cried on the housetops, but five minutes with General Posselt will make things clear. You will be exceedingly sorry for it if you delay another minute."

He was impressed in spite of himself, and after pulling his moustache turned on his heel and left us. Presently he came back and said very gruffly that the Governor would see us. We followed him along a corridor into a big room looking out on the river, where an oldish fellow sat in an arm-chair by a stove, writing letters with a fountain pen.

This was Posselt, who had been Governor of Erzerum till he fell sick and Ahmed Fevzi took his place. He had a peevish mouth and big blue pouches below his eyes. He was supposed to be a good engineer and to have made Erzerum impregnable, but the look on his face gave me the impression that his reputation at the moment was a bit unstable.

The staff-officer spoke to him in an undertone.

"Yes, yes, I know," he said testily. "Are these the men? They look a pretty lot of scoundrels. What's that you say? They deny it. But they've got the car. They can't deny that. Here, you," and he fixed on Blenkiron, "who the devil are you?" Blenkiron smiled sleepily at him, not understanding one word, and I took up the parable.

"Our passports, sir, give our credentials," I said. He glanced through them, and his face lengthened.

"They're right enough. But what about this story of stealing a car?"

"It is quite true," I said, "but I would prefer to use a pleasanter word. You will see from our papers that every authority on the road is directed to give us the best transport. Our own car broke down, and after a long delay we got some wretched horses. It is vitally important that we should be in Erzerum without delay, so I took the liberty of appropriating an empty car we found outside an inn. I am sorry for the discomfort of the owners, but our business was too grave to wait."

"But the telegram says you are notorious spies!"

I smiled. "Who sent the telegram?"

"I see no reason why I shouldn't give you his name. It was Rasta Bey. You've picked an awkward fellow to make an enemy of."

I did not smile but laughed. "Rasta!" I cried. "He's one of Enver's satellites. That explains many things. I should like a word with you alone, sir."

He nodded to the staff-officer, and when he had gone I put on my most Bible face and looked as important as a provincial mayor at a royal visit.

"I can speak freely," I said, "for I am speaking to a soldier of Germany. There is no love lost between Enver and those I serve. I need not tell you that. This Rasta thought he had found a chance of delaying us, so he invents this trash about spies. Those Comitadjis have spies on the brain . . . Especially he hates Frau von Einem."

He jumped at the name.

"You have orders from her?" he asked, in a respectful tone.

"Why, yes," I answered, "and those orders will not wait."

He got up and walked to a table, whence he turned a puzzled face on me. "I'm torn in two between the Turks and my own countrymen. If I please one I offend the other, and the result is a damnable confusion. You can go on to Erzerum, but I shall send a man with you to see that you report to headquarters there. I'm sorry, gentlemen, but I'm obliged to take no chances in this business. Rasta's got a grievance against you, but you can easily hide behind the lady's skirts. She passed through this town two days ago."

Ten minutes later we were coasting through the slush of the narrow streets with a stolid German lieutenant sitting beside me.

The afternoon was one of those rare days when in the pauses of snow you have a spell of weather as mild as May. I remembered several like it during our winter's training in Hampshire. The road was a fine one, well engineered, and well kept too, considering the amount of traffic. We were little delayed, for it was sufficiently broad to let us pass troops and transport without slackening pace. The fellow at my side was good-humoured enough, but his presence naturally put the lid on our conversation. I didn't want to talk, however. I was trying to piece together a plan, and making very little of it, for I had nothing to go upon. We must find Hilda von Einem and Sandy, and between us we must wreck the Greenmantle business. That done, it didn't matter so much what happened to us. As I reasoned it out, the Turks must be in a bad way, and, unless they got a fillip from Greenmantle, would crumple up before the Russians. In the rout I hoped we might get a chance to change our sides. But it was no good looking so far forward; the first thing was to get to Sandy.

Now I was still in the mood of reckless bravado which I had got from bagging the car. I did not realize how thin our story was, and how easily Rasta might have a big graft at headquarters. If I had, I would have shot out the German lieutenant long before we got to Erzerum, and found some way of getting mixed up in the ruck of the population. Hussin could have helped me to that. I was getting so confident since our interview with Posselt that I thought I could bluff the whole outfit.

But my main business that afternoon was pure nonsense. I was trying to find my little hill. At every turn of the road I expected to see the *castrol* before us. You must know that ever since I could stand I have been crazy about high mountains. My father took me to Basutoland when I was a boy, and I reckon I have scrambled over almost every bit of upland south of the Zambesi, from the Hottentots Holland to the Zoutpansberg, and from the ugly yellow kopjes of Damaraland to the noble cliffs of Mont aux Sources. One of the things I had looked forward to in coming home was the chance of climbing the Alps. But now I was among peaks that I fancied were bigger than the Alps, and I could hardly keep my eyes on the road. I was pretty certain that my *castrol* was among them, for that dream had taken an almighty hold on my mind. Funnily enough, I was ceasing to think it a place of evil omen, for one soon forgets the atmosphere of nightmare. But I was convinced that it was a thing I was destined to see, and to see pretty soon.

Darkness fell when we were some miles short of the city, and the last part was difficult driving. On both sides of the road transport and engineers' stores were parked, and some of it strayed into the highway. I noticed lots of small details—machine-gun detachments, signalling parties, squads of stretcher-bearers—which mean the fringe of an army, and as soon as the night began the white fingers of searchlights began to grope in the skies.

And then, above the hum of the roadside, rose the voice of the great guns. The shells were bursting four or five miles away, and the guns must have been as many more distant. But in that upland pocket of plain in the frosty night they sounded most intimately near. They kept up their solemn litany, with a minute's interval between each—no *rafale* which rumbles like a drum, but the steady persistence of artillery exactly ranged on a target. I judged they must be bombarding the outer forts, and once there came a loud explosion and a red glare as if a magazine had suffered.

It was a sound I had not heard for five months, and it fairly crazed me. I remembered how I had first heard it on the ridge before Laventie. Then I had been half afraid, half solemnized, but every nerve had been quickened. Then it had been the new thing in my life that held me breathless with anticipation; now it was the old thing, the thing I had shared with so many good fellows, my proper work, and the only task for a man. At the sound of the guns I felt that I was moving in natural air once more. I felt that I was coming home.

We were stopped at a long line of ramparts, and a German sergeant stared at us till he saw the lieutenant beside me, when he saluted and we passed on. Almost at once we dipped into narrow twisting streets, choked with soldiers, where it was hard business to steer. There were few lights—only now and then the flare of a torch which showed the grey stone houses, with every window latticed and shuttered. I had put out my headlights and had only side lamps, so we had to pick our way gingerly through the labyrinth. I hoped we would strike Sandy's quarters soon, for we were all pretty empty, and a frost had set in which made our thick coats seem as thin as paper.

The lieutenant did the guiding. We had to present our passports, and I anticipated no more difficulty than in landing from the boat at Boulogne. But I wanted to get it over, for my hunger pinched me and it was fearsome cold. Still the guns went on, like hounds baying before a quarry. The city was out of range, but there were strange lights on the ridge to the east.

At last we reached our goal and marched through a fine old carved archway into a courtyard, and thence into a draughty hall.

"You must see the *Sektionschef*," said our guide. I looked round to see if we were all there, and noticed that Hussin had disappeared. It did not matter, for he was not on the passports.

We followed as we were directed through an open door. There was a man standing with his back towards us looking at a wall map, a very big man with a neck that bulged over his collar.

I would have known that neck among a million. At the sight of it I made a half-turn to bolt back. It was too late, for the door had closed behind us and there were two armed sentries beside it.

The man slewed round and looked into my eyes. I had a despairing hope that I might bluff it out, for I was in different clothes and had shaved my beard. But you cannot spend ten minutes in a death-grapple without your adversary getting to know you.

He went very pale, then recollected himself and twisted his features into the old grin.

"So," he said, "the little Dutchmen! We meet after many days."

It was no good lying or saying anything. I shut my teeth and waited.

"And you, Herr Blenkiron? I never liked the look of you. You babbled too much, like all your damned Americans."

"I guess your personal dislikes haven't got anything to do with the matter," said Blenkiron, calmly. "If you're the boss here, I'll thank you to cast your eye over these passports, for we can't stand waiting for ever."

This fairly angered him. "I'll teach you manners," he cried, and took a step forward to reach for Blenkiron's shoulder—the game he had twice played with me.

Blenkiron never took his hands from his coat pockets. "Keep your distance," he drawled in a new voice. "I've got you covered, and I'll make a hole in your bullet head if you lay a hand on me."

With an effort Stumm recovered himself. He rang a bell and fell to smiling. An orderly appeared to whom he spoke in Turkish, and presently a file of soldiers entered the room.

"I'm going to have you disarmed, gentlemen," he said. "We can conduct our conversation more pleasantly without pistols."

It was idle to resist. We surrendered our arms, Peter almost in tears with vexation. Stumm swung his legs over a chair, rested his chin on the back and looked at me.

"Your game is up, you know," he said. "These fools of Turkish police said the Dutchmen were dead, but I had the happier inspiration. I believed the good God had spared them for me. When I got Rasta's telegram I was certain, for your doings reminded me of a little trick you once played me on the Schwandorf road. But I didn't think to find this plump old partridge," and he smiled at Blenkiron. "Two eminent American engineers and their servant bound for Mesopotamia on business of high Government importance! It was a good lie; but if I had been in Constantinople it would have had a short life. Rasta and his friends are no concern of mine. You can trick them as you please. But you have attempted to win the confidence of a certain lady, and her interests are mine. Likewise you have offended me, and I do not forgive. By God," he cried, his voice growing shrill with passion, "by the time I have done with you your mothers in their graves will weep that they ever bore you!"

It was Blenkiron who spoke. His voice was as level as the chairman's of a bogus company, and it fell on that turbid atmosphere like acid on grease.

"I don't take no stock in high-falutin'. If you're trying to scare me by that dime-novel talk I guess you've hit the wrong man. You're like the sweep that stuck in the chimney, a bit too big for your job. I reckon you've a talent for ro-mance that's just wasted in soldiering. But if you're going to play any ugly games on me I'd like you to know that I'm an American citizen, and pretty well considered in my own country and in yours, and you'll sweat blood for it later. That's a fair warning, Colonel Stumm."

I don't know what Stumm's plans were, but that speech of Blenkiron's put into his mind just the needed amount of uncertainty. You see, he had Peter and me right enough, but he hadn't properly connected Blenkiron with us, and was afraid either to hit out at all three, or to let Blenkiron go. It was lucky for us that the American had cut such a dash in the Fatherland.

"There is no hurry," he said blandly. "We shall have long happy hours together. I'm going to take you all home with me, for I am a hospitable soul. You will be safer with me than in the town gaol, for it's a trifle draughty. It lets things in, and it might let things out."

Again he gave an order, and we were marched out, each with a soldier at his elbow. The three of us were bundled into the back seat of the car, while two men sat before us with their rifles between their knees, one got up behind on the baggage rack, and one sat beside Stumm's chauffeur. Packed like sardines we moved into the bleak streets, above which the stars twinkled in ribbons of sky.

Hussin had disappeared from the face of the earth, and quite right too. He was a good fellow, but he had no call to mix himself up in our troubles.

CHAPTER 18

Sparrows on the Housetops

I'VE OFTEN REGRETTED," said Blenkiron, "that miracles have left off happening."

He got no answer, for I was feeling the walls for something in the nature of a window.

"For I reckon," he went on, "that it wants a good old-fashioned copper-bottomed miracle to get us out of this fix. It's plumb against all my principles. I've spent my life using the talents God gave me to keep things from getting to the point of rude violence, and so far I've succeeded. But now you come along, Major, and you hustle a respectable middle-aged citizen into an aboriginal mix-up. It's mighty indelicate. I reckon the next move is up to you, for I'm no good at the housebreaking stunt."

"No more am I," I answered; "but I'm hanged if I'll chuck up the sponge. Sandy's somewhere outside, and he's got a hefty crowd at his heels."

I simply could not feel the despair which by every law of common sense was due to the case. The guns had intoxicated me. I could still hear their deep voices, though yards of wood and stone separated us from the upper air.

What vexed us most was our hunger. Barring a few mouthfuls on the road we had eaten nothing since the morning, and as our diet for the past days had not been generous we had some leeway to make up. Stumm had never looked near since we were shoved into the car. We had been brought to some kind of house and bundled into a place like a wine-cellar. It was pitch dark, and after feeling round the walls, first on my feet and then on Peter's back, I decided that there were no windows. It must have been lit and ventilated by some lattice in the ceiling. There was not a stick of furniture in the place: nothing but a damp earth floor and bare stone sides. The door was a relic of the Iron Age, and I could hear the paces of a sentry outside it.

When things get to the pass that nothing you can do can better them, the only thing is to live for the moment. All three of us sought in sleep a refuge from our empty stomachs. The floor was the poorest kind of bed, but we rolled up our coats for pillows and made the best of it. Soon I knew by Peter's regular breathing that he was asleep, and I presently followed him . . .

I was awakened by a pressure below my left ear. I thought it was Peter, for it is the old hunter's trick of waking a man so that he makes no noise. But another voice spoke. It told me that there was no time to lose and to rise and follow, and the voice was the voice of Hussin.

Peter was awake, and we stirred Blenkiron out of heavy slumber. We were bidden take off our boots and hang them by their laces round our necks as country boys do when they want to go barefoot. Then we tiptoed to the door, which was ajar.

Outside was a passage with a flight of steps at one end which led to the open air. On these steps lay a faint shine of starlight, and by its help I saw a man huddled up at the foot of them. It was our sentry, neatly and scientifically gagged and tied up.

The steps brought us to a little courtyard about which the walls of the houses rose like cliffs. We halted while Hussin listened intently. Apparently the coast was clear and our guide led us to one side, which was clothed by a stout wooden trellis. Once it may have supported fig-trees, but now the plants were dead and only withered tendrils and rotten stumps remained.

It was child's play for Peter and me to go up that trellis, but it was the deuce and all for Blenkiron. He was in poor condition and puffed like a grampus, and he seemed to have no sort of head for heights. But he was as game as a buffalo, and started in gallantly till his arms gave out and he fairly stuck. So Peter and I went up on each side of him, taking an arm apiece, as I had once seen done to a man with vertigo in the Kloof Chimney on Table Mountain. I was mighty thankful when I got him panting on the top and Hussin had shinned up beside us.

We crawled along a broadish wall, with an inch or two of powdery snow on it, and then up a sloping buttress on to the flat roof of the house. It was a miserable business for Blenkiron, who would certainly have fallen if he could have seen what was below him, and Peter and I had to stand to attention all the time. Then began a more difficult job. Hussin pointed out a ledge which took us past a stack of chimneys to another building slightly lower, this being the route he fancied. At that I sat down resolutely and put on my boots, and the others followed.

Frost-bitten feet would be a poor asset in this kind of travelling.

It was a bad step for Blenkiron, and we only got him past it by Peter and I spread-eagling ourselves against the wall and passing him in front of us with his face towards us. We had no grip, and if he had stumbled we should all three have been in the courtyard. But we got it over, and dropped as softly as possible on to the roof of the next house. Hussin had his finger to his lips, and I soon saw why. For there was a lighted window in the wall we had descended.

Some imp prompted me to wait behind and explore. The others followed Hussin and were soon at the far end of the roof, where a kind of wooden pavilion broke the line, while I tried to get a look inside. The window was curtained, and had two folding sashes which clasped in the middle. Through a gap in the curtain I saw a little lamp-lit room and a big man sitting at a table littered with papers.

I watched him, fascinated, as he turned to consult some document and made a marking on the map before him. Then he suddenly rose, stretched himself, cast a glance at the window, and went out of the room, making a great clatter in descending the wooden staircase. He left the door ajar and the lamp burning.

I guessed he had gone to have a look at his prisoners, in which case the show was up. But what filled my mind was an insane desire to get a sight of his map. It was one of those mad impulses which utterly cloud right reason, a thing independent of any plan, a crazy leap in the dark. But it was so strong that I would have pulled that window out by its frame, if need be, to get to that table.

There was no need, for the flimsy clasp gave at the first pull, and the sashes swung open. I scrambled in, after listening for steps on the stairs. I crumpled up the map and stuck it in my pocket, as well as the paper from which I had seen him copying. Very carefully I removed all marks of my entry, brushed away the snow from the boards, pulled back the curtain, got out and refastened the window. Still there was no sound of his return. Then I started off to catch up the others.

I found them shivering in the roof pavilion. "We've got to move pretty fast," I said, "for I've just been burgling old Stumm's private cabinet. Hussin, my lad, d'you hear that? They may be after us any moment, so I pray Heaven we soon strike better going."

Hussin understood. He led us at a smart pace from one roof to another, for here they were all the same height, and only low parapets and screens divided them. We never saw a soul, for a winter's night is not the time you choose to saunter on your housetop. I kept my ears open for trouble behind us, and in about five minutes I heard it. A riot of voices broke out, with one louder than the rest, and, looking back, I saw lanterns waving. Stumm had realized his loss and found the tracks of the thief.

Hussin gave one glance behind and then hurried us on at break-neck pace, with old Blenkiron gasping and stumbling. The shouts behind us grew louder, as if some eye quicker than the rest had caught our movement in the starlit darkness. It was very evident that if they kept up the chase we should be caught, for Blenkiron was about as useful on a roof as a hippo.

Presently we came to a big drop, with a kind of ladder down it, and at the foot a shallow ledge running to the left into a pit of darkness. Hussin gripped my arm and pointed down it. "Follow it," he whispered, "and you will reach a roof which spans a street. Cross it, and on the other side is a mosque. Turn to the right there and you will find easy going for fifty metres, well screened from the higher roofs. For Allah's sake keep in the shelter of the screen. Somewhere there I will join you."

He hurried us along the ledge for a bit and then went back, and with snow from the corners covered up our tracks. After that he went straight on himself, taking strange short steps like a bird. I saw his game. He wanted to lead our pursuers after him, and he had to multiply the tracks and trust to Stumm's fellows not spotting that they all were made by one man.

But I had quite enough to think of in getting Blenkiron along that ledge. He was pretty nearly foundered, he was in a sweat of terror, and as a matter of fact he was taking one of the biggest risks of his life, for we had no rope and his neck depended on himself. I could hear him invoking some unknown deity called Holy Mike. But he ventured gallantly, and we got to the roof which ran across the street. That was easier, though ticklish enough, but it was no joke skirting the cupola of that infernal mosque. At last we found the parapet and breathed more freely, for we were now under shelter from the direction of danger. I spared a moment to look round, and thirty yards off, across the street, I saw a weird spectacle.

The hunt was proceeding along the roofs parallel to the one we were lodged on. I saw the flicker of the lanterns, waved up and down as the bearers slipped in the snow, and I heard their cries like hounds on a trail. Stumm was not among them: he had not the shape for that sort of business. They passed us and continued to our left, now hid by a jutting chimney, now clear to view against the skyline. The roofs they were on were perhaps six feet higher than ours, so even from our shelter we could mark their course. If Hussin were going to be hunted across Erzerum it was a bad look-out for us, for I hadn't the foggiest notion where we were or where we were going to.

But as we watched we saw something more. The wavering lanterns were now three or four hundred yards away, but on the roofs just opposite us across the street there appeared a man's figure. I thought it was one of the hunters, and we all crouched lower, and then I recognized the lean agility of Hussin. He must have doubled back, keeping in the dusk to the left of the pursuit, and taking big risks in the open places. But there he was now, exactly in front of us, and separated only by the width of the narrow street.

He took a step backward, gathered himself for a spring, and leaped clean over the gap. Like a cat he lighted on the parapet above us, and stumbled forward with the impetus right on our heads.

"We are safe for the moment," he whispered, "but when they miss me they will return. We must make good haste."

The next half-hour was a maze of twists and turns, slipping down icy roofs and climbing icier chimney-stacks. The stir of the city had gone, and from the black streets below came scarcely a sound. But always the great tattoo of guns beat in the east. Gradually we descended to a lower level, till we emerged on the top of a shed in a courtyard. Hussin gave an odd sort of cry, like a demented owl, and something began to stir below us.

It was a big covered wagon, full of bundles of forage, and drawn by four mules. As we descended from the shed into the frozen litter of the yard, a man came out of the shade and spoke low to Hussin. Peter and I lifted Blenkiron into the cart, and scrambled in beside him, and I never felt anything more blessed than the warmth and softness of that place after the frosty roofs. I had forgotten all about my hunger, and only yearned for sleep. Presently the wagon moved out of the courtyard into the dark streets.

Then Blenkiron began to laugh, a deep internal rumble which shook him violently and brought down a heap of forage on his head. I thought it was hysterics, the relief from the tension of the past hour. But it wasn't. His body might be out of training, but there was never anything the matter with his nerves. He was consumed with honest merriment.

"Say, Major," he gasped, "I don't usually cherish dislikes for my fellow men, but somehow I didn't cotton to Colonel Stumm. But now I almost love him. You hit his jaw very bad in Germany, and now you've annexed his private file, and I guess it's important or he wouldn't have been so mighty set on steeple-chasing over those roofs. I haven't done such a thing since I broke into neighbour Brown's woodshed to steal his tame 'possum, and that's forty years back. It's the first piece of genooine amusement I've struck in this game, and I haven't laughed so much since old Jim Hooker told the tale of 'Cousin Sally Dillard' when we were hunting ducks in Michigan and his wife's brother had an apoplexy in the night and died of it."

To the accompaniment of Blenkiron's chuckles I did what Peter had done in the first minute, and fell asleep.

When I woke it was still dark. The wagon had stopped in a courtyard which seemed to be shaded by great trees. The snow lay deeper here, and by the feel of the air we had left the city and climbed to higher ground. There were big buildings on one side, and on the other what looked like the lift of a hill. No lights were shown, the place was in profound gloom, but I felt the presence near me of others besides Hussin and the driver.

We were hurried, Blenkiron only half awake, into an out-building, and then down some steps to a roomy cellar. There Hussin lit a lantern, which showed what had once been a storehouse for fruit. Old husks still strewed the floor and the place smelt of apples. Straw had been piled in corners for beds, and there was a rude table and a divan of boards covered with sheepskins.

"Where are we?" I asked Hussin.

"In the house of the Master," he said. "You will be safe here, but you must keep still till the Master comes."

"Is the Frankish lady here?" I asked.

Hussin nodded, and from a wallet brought out some food—raisins and cold meat and a loaf of bread. We fell on it like vultures, and as we ate Hussin disappeared. I noticed that he locked the door behind him.

As soon as the meal was ended the others returned to their

interrupted sleep. But I was wakeful now and my mind was sharp-set on many things. I got Blenkiron's electric torch and lay down on the divan to study Stumm's map.

The first glance showed me that I had lit on a treasure. It was the staff map of the Erzerum defences, showing the forts and the field-trenches, with little notes scribbled in Stumm's neat small handwriting. I got out the big map which I had taken from Blenkiron, and made out the general lie of the land. I saw the horseshoe of Deve Boyun to the east which the Russian guns were battering. Stumm's was just like the kind of squared artillery map we used in France, 1 in 10,000, with spidery red lines showing the trenches, but with the difference that it was the Turkish trenches that were shown in detail and the Russian only roughly indicated. The thing was really a confidential plan of the whole Erzerum *enceinte*, and would be worth untold gold to the enemy. No wonder Stumm had been in a wax at its loss.

The Deve Boyun lines seemed to me monstrously strong, and I remembered the merits of the Turk as a fighter behind strong defences. It looked as if Russia were up against a second Plevna or a new Gallipoli.

Then I took to studying the flanks. South lay the Palantuken range of mountains, with forts defending the passes, where ran the roads to Mush and Lake Van. That side, too, looked pretty strong. North in the valley of the Euphrates I made out two big forts, Tafta and Kara Gubek, defending the road from Olti. On this part of the map Stumm's notes were plentiful, and I gave them all my attention. I remembered Blenkiron's news about the Russians advancing on a broad front, for it was clear that Stumm was taking pains about the flank of the fortress.

Kara Gubek was the point of interest. It stood on a rib of land between two peaks, which from the contour lines rose very steep. So long as it was held it was clear that no invader could move down the Euphrates glen. Stumm had appended a note to the peaks—*"not fortified"*; and about two miles to the north-east there was a red cross and the name *"Prjevalsky"*. I assumed that to be the farthest point yet reached by the right wing of the Russian attack.

Then I turned to the paper from which Stumm had copied the jottings on to his map. It was typewritten, and consisted of notes on different points. One was headed *Kara Gubek* and read: *No time to fortify adjacent peaks. Difficult for enemy to get batteries there, but not impossible. This the real point of danger, for if Prjevalsky wins the peaks Kara Gubek and Tafta must fall, and enemy will be on left rear of Deve Boyun main position.*

I was soldier enough to see the tremendous importance of this note. On Kara Gubek depended the defence of Erzerum, and it was a broken reed if one knew where the weakness lay. Yet, searching the map again, I could not believe that any mortal commander would see any chance in the adjacent peaks, even if he thought them unfortified. That was information confined to the Turkish and German staff. But if it could be conveyed to the Grand Duke he would have Erzerum in his power in a day. Otherwise he would go on battering at the Deve Boyun ridge for weeks, and long ere he won it the Gallipoli divisions would arrive, he would be out-numbered by two to one, and his chance would have vanished.

My discovery set me pacing up and down that cellar in a perfect fever of excitement. I longed for wireless, a carrier pigeon, an aeroplane—anything to bridge over that space of half a dozen miles between me and the Russian lines. It was maddening to have stumbled on vital news and to be wholly unable to use it. How could three fugitives in a cellar, with the whole hornet's nest of Turkey and Germany stirred up against them, hope to send this message of life and death?

I went back to the map and examined the nearest Russian positions. They were carefully marked. Prjevalsky in the north, the main force beyond Deve Boyun, and the southern columns up to the passes of the Palantuken but not yet across them. I could not know which was nearest to us till I discovered where we were. And as I thought of this I began to see the rudiments of a desperate plan. It depended on Peter, now slumbering like a tired dog on a couch of straw.

Hussin had locked the door and I must wait for information till he came back. But suddenly I noticed a trap in the roof, which had evidently been used for raising and lowering the cellar's stores. It looked ill-fitting and might be unbarred, so I pulled the table below it, and found that with a little effort I could raise the flap. I knew I was taking immense risks, but I was so keen on my plan that I disregarded them. After some trouble I got the thing prised open, and catching the edges of the hole with my fingers raised my body and got my knees on the edge.

It was the out-building of which our refuge was the cellar, and it was half filled with light. Not a soul was there, and I hunted about till I found what I wanted. This was a ladder leading to a sort of loft, which in turn gave access to the roof. Here I had to be very careful, for I might be overlooked from the high buildings. But by good luck there was a trellis for grape vines across the place, which gave a kind of shelter. Lying flat on my face I stared over a great expanse of country.

Looking north I saw the city in a haze of morning smoke, and, beyond, the plain of the Euphrates and the opening of the glen where the river left the hills. Up there, among the snowy heights, were Tafta and Kara Gubek. To the east was the ridge of Deve Boyun, where the mist was breaking before the winter's sun. On the roads up to it I saw transport moving, I saw the circle of the inner forts, but for a moment the guns were silent. South rose a great wall of white mountain, which I took to be the Palantuken. I could see the roads running to the passes, and the smoke of camps and horse-lines right under the cliffs.

I had learned what I needed. We were in the out-buildings of a big country house two or three miles south of the city. The nearest point of the Russian front was somewhere in the foothills of the Palantuken.

As I descended I heard, thin and faint and beautiful, like the cry of a wild bird, the muezzin from the minarets of Erzerum.

When I dropped through the trap the others were awake. Hussin was setting food on the table, and viewing my descent with anxious disapproval.

"It's all right," I said; "I won't do it again, for I've found out all I wanted. Peter, old man, the biggest job of your life is before you!"

CHAPTER 19

Greenmantle

P ETER SCARCELY LOOKED up from his breakfast.

"I'm willing, Dick," he said. "But you mustn't ask me to be friends with Stumm. He makes my stomach cold, that one."

For the first time he had stopped calling me "Cornelis". The day of make-believe was over for all of us.

"Not to be friends with him," I said, "but to bust him and all his kind."

"Then I'm ready," said Peter cheerfully. "What is it?"

I spread out the maps on the divan. There was no light in the place but Blenkiron's electric torch, for Hussin had put out the lantern. Peter got his nose into the things at once, for his intelligence work in the Boer War had made him handy with maps. It didn't want much telling from me to explain to him the importance of the one I had looted.

"That news is worth many a million pounds," said he, wrinkling his brows, and scratching delicately the tip of his left ear. It was a way he had when he was startled.

"How can we get it to our friends?"

Peter cogitated. "There is but one way. A man must take it. Once, I remember, when we fought the Matabele it was necessary to find out whether the chief Makapan was living. Some said he had died, others that he'd gone over the Portuguese border, but I believed he lived. No native could tell us, and since his kraal was well defended no runner could get through. So it was necessary to send a man."

Peter lifted up his head and laughed. "The man found the chief Makapan. He was very much alive, and made good shooting with a shot-gun. But the man brought the chief Makapan out of his kraal and handed him over to the Mounted Police. You remember Captain Arcoll, Dick—Jim Arcoll? Well, Jim laughed so much that he broke open a wound in his head, and had to have a doctor."

"You were that man, Peter," I said.

"*Ja*. I was the man. There are more ways of getting into kraals than there are ways of keeping people out."

313

"Will you take this chance?"

"For certain, Dick. I am getting stiff with doing nothing, and if I sit in houses much longer I shall grow old. A man bet me five pounds on the ship that I could not get through a trench-line, and if there had been a trench-line handy I would have taken him on. I will be very happy, Dick, but I do not say I will succeed. It is new country to me, and I will be hurried, and hurry makes bad stalking."

I showed him what I thought the likeliest place—in the spurs of the Palantuken mountains. Peter's way of doing things was all his own. He scraped earth and plaster out of a corner and sat down to make a little model of the landscape on the table, following the contours of the map. He did it extraordinarily neatly, for, like all great hunters, he was as deft as a weaver bird. He puzzled over it for a long time, and conned the map till he must have got it by heart. Then he took his field-glasses—a very good single Zeiss which was part of the spoils from Rasta's motor-car—and announced that he was going to follow my example and get on to the housetop. Presently his legs disappeared through the trap, and Blenkiron and I were left to our reflections.

Peter must have found something uncommon interesting, for he stayed on the roof the better part of the day. It was a dull job for us, since there was no light, and Blenkiron had not even the consolation of a game of Patience. But for all that he was in good spirits, for he had had no dyspepsia since we left Constantinople, and announced that he believed he was at last getting even with his darned duodenum. As for me I was pretty restless, for I could not imagine what was detaining Sandy. It was clear that our presence must have been kept secret from Hilda von Einem, for she was a pal of Stumm's, and he must by now have blown the gaff on Peter and me. How long could this secrecy last, I asked myself. We had now no sort of protection in the whole outfit. Rasta and the Turks wanted our blood: so did Stumm and the Germans; and once the lady found we were deceiving her she would want it most of all. Our only hope was Sandy, and he gave no sign of his existence. I began to fear that with him, too, things had miscarried.

And yet I wasn't really depressed, only impatient. I could never again get back to the beastly stagnation of that Constantinople week. The guns kept me cheerful. There was the devil of a bombardment all day, and the thought that our Allies were thundering there half a dozen miles off gave me a perfectly groundless hope. If they burst through the defence Hilda von Einem and her prophet and all our enemies would be overwhelmed in the deluge. And that blessed chance depended very much on old Peter, now brooding like a pigeon on the housetops.

It was not till the late afternoon that Hussin appeared again. He took no notice of Peter's absence, but lit a lantern and set it on the table. Then he went to the door and waited. Presently a light step fell on the stairs, and Hussin drew back to let someone enter. He promptly departed and I heard the key turn in the lock behind him.

Sandy stood there, but a new Sandy who made Blenkiron and me jump to our feet. The pelts and skin cap had gone, and he wore instead a long linen tunic clasped at the waist by a broad girdle. A strange green turban adorned his head, and as he pushed it back I saw that his hair had been shaved. He looked like some acolyte—a weary acolyte, for there was no spring in his walk or nerve in his carriage. He dropped numbly on the divan and laid his head in his hands. The lantern showed his haggard eyes with dark lines beneath them.

"Good God, old man, have you been sick?" I cried.

"Not sick," he said hoarsely. "My body is right enough, but the last few days I have been living in hell."

Blenkiron nodded sympathetically. That was how he himself would have described the company of the lady.

I marched across to him and gripped both his wrists.

"Look at me," I said, "straight in the eyes."

His eyes were like a sleep-walker's, unwinking, unseeing. "Great Heavens, man, you've been drugged!" I said.

"Drugged," he cried, with a weary laugh. "Yes, I have been drugged, but not by any physic. No one has been doctoring my food. But you can't go through hell without getting your eyes red-hot."

I kept my grip on his wrists. "Take your time, old chap, and tell us about it. Blenkiron and I are here, and old Peter's on the roof not far off. We'll look after you."

"It does me good to hear your voice, Dick," he said. "It reminds me of clean, honest things."

"They'll come back, never fear. We're at the last lap now. One more spurt and it's over. You've got to tell me what the new snag is. Is it that woman?"

He shivered like a frightened colt. "Woman!" he cried. "Does a woman drag a man through the nether-pit? She's a she-devil. Oh, it

315

isn't madness that's wrong with her. She's as sane as you and as cool as Blenkiron. Her life is an infernal game of chess, and she plays with souls for pawns. She is evil—evil—evil . . ." And once more he buried his head in his hands.

It was Blenkiron who brought sense into this hectic atmosphere. His slow, beloved drawl was an antiseptic against nerves.

"Say, boy," he said, "I feel just like you about the lady. But our job is not to investigate her character. Her Maker will do that good and sure some day. We've got to figure how to circumvent her, and for that you've got to tell us what exactly's been occurring since we parted company."

Sandy pulled himself together with a great effort.

"Greenmantle died that night I saw you. We buried him secretly by her order in the garden of the villa. Then came the trouble about his successor . . . The four Ministers would be no party to a swindle. They were honest men, and vowed that their task now was to make a tomb for their master and pray for the rest of their days at his shrine. They were as immovable as a granite hill and she knew it . . . Then they, too, died."

"Murdered?" I gasped.

"Murdered . . . all four in one morning. I do not know how, but I helped to bury them. Oh, she had Germans and Kurds to do her foul work, but their hands were clean compared to hers. Pity me, Dick, for I have seen honesty and virtue put to the shambles and have abetted the deed when it was done. It will haunt me to my dying day."

I did not stop to console him, for my mind was on fire with his news.

"Then the prophet is gone, and the humbug is over," I cried.

"The prophet still lives. She has found a successor."

He stood up in his linen tunic.

"Why do I wear these clothes? Because I am Greenmantle. I am the Kaába-i-hurriyeh for all Islam. In three days' time I will reveal myself to my people and wear on my breast the green ephod of the prophet."

He broke off with an hysterical laugh.

"Only you see, I won't. I will cut my throat first."

"Cheer up!" said Blenkiron soothingly. "We'll find some prettier way than that."

"There is no way," he said, "no way but death. We're done for, all of us. Hussin got you out of Stumm's clutches, but you're in danger every moment. At the best you have three days, and then you, too, will be dead."

I had no words to reply. This change in the bold and unshakable Sandy took my breath away.

"She made me her accomplice," he went on. "I should have killed her on the graves of those innocent men. But instead I did all she asked and joined in her game . . . She was very candid, you know . . . She cares no more than Enver for the faith of Islam. She can laugh at it. But she has her own dreams, and they consume her as a saint is consumed by his devotion. She has told me them, and if the day in the garden was hell, the days since have been the innermost fires of Tophet. I think—it is horrible to say it—that she has got some kind of crazy liking for me. When we have reclaimed the East I am to be by her side when she rides on her milk-white horse into Jerusalem . . . And there have been moments—only moments, I swear to God—when I have been fired myself by her madness . . ."

Sandy's figure seemed to shrink and his voice grew shrill and wild. It was too much for Blenkiron. He indulged in a torrent of blasphemy such as I believe had never before passed his lips.

"I'm blessed if I'll listen to this God-darned stuff. It isn't delicate. You get busy, Major, and pump some sense into your afflicted friend."

I was beginning to see what had happened. Sandy was a man of genius—as much as anybody I ever struck—but he had the defects of such high-strung, fanciful souls. He would take more than mortal risks, and you couldn't scare him by any ordinary terror. But let his old conscience get cross-eyed, let him find himself in some situation which in his eyes involved his honour, and he might go stark crazy. The woman, who roused in me and Blenkiron only hatred, could catch his imagination and stir in him—for the moment only—an unwilling response. And then came bitter and morbid repentance, and the last desperation.

It was no time to mince matters. "Sandy, you old fool," I cried, "be thankful you have friends to keep you from playing the fool. You saved my life at Loos, and I'm jolly well going to get you through this show. I'm bossing the outfit now, and for all your confounded prophetic manners, you've got to take your orders from me. You aren't going to reveal yourself to your people, and still less are you going to cut your throat. Greenmantle will avenge the murder of his Ministers, and make that bedlamite woman sorry she was born. We're going to get clear away, and inside of a week we'll be having tea with the Grand Duke Nicholas."

I wasn't bluffing. Puzzled as I was about ways and means I had still the blind belief that we should win out. And as I spoke two legs dangled through the trap and a dusty and blinking Peter descended in our midst.

I took the maps from him and spread them on the table.

"First, you must know that we've had an almighty piece of luck. Last night Hussin took us for a walk over the roofs of Erzerum, and by the blessing of Providence I got into Stumm's room, and bagged his staff map . . . Look here . . . d'you see his notes? That's the danger-point of the whole defence. Once the Russians get that fort, Kara Gubek, they've turned the main position. And it can be got; Stumm knows it can; for these two adjacent hills are not held . . . It looks a mad enterprise on paper, but Stumm knows that it is possible enough. The question is: Will the Russians guess that? I say no, not unless someone tells them. Therefore, by hook or by crook, we've got to get that information through to them."

Sandy's interest in ordinary things was beginning to flicker up again. He studied the map and began to measure distances.

"Peter's going to have a try for it. He thinks there's a sporting chance of his getting through the lines. If he does—if he gets this map to the Grand Duke's staff—then Stumm's goose is cooked. In three days the Cossacks will be in the streets of Erzerum."

"What are the chances?" Sandy asked.

I glanced at Peter. "We're hard-bitten fellows and can face the truth. I think the chances against success are about five to one."

"Two to one," said Peter modestly. "Not worse than that. I don't think you're fair to me, Dick, my old friend."

I looked at that lean, tight figure and the gentle, resolute face, and I changed my mind. "I'm hanged if I think there are any odds," I said. "With anybody else it would want a miracle, but with Peter I believe the chances are level."

"Two to one," Peter persisted. "If it was evens I wouldn't be interested."

"Let me go," Sandy cried. "I talk the lingo, and can pass as a Turk, and I'm a million times likelier to get through. For God's sake, Dick, let me go."

"Not you. You're wanted here. If you disappear the whole show's busted too soon, and the three of us left behind will be strung up before morning . . . No, my son. You're going to escape, but it will be in company with Blenkiron and me. We've got to blow the whole Greenmantle business so high that the bits of it will never come to earth again . . . First, tell me how many of your fellows will stick by you? I mean the Companions."

"The whole half-dozen. They are very worried already about what has happened. She made me sound them in her presence, and they were quite ready to accept me as Greenmantle's successor. But they have their suspicions about what happened at the villa, and they've no love for the woman . . . They'd follow me through hell if I bade them, but they would rather it was my own show."

"That's all right," I cried. "It is the one thing I've been doubtful about. Now observe this map. Erzerum isn't invested by a long chalk. The Russians are round it in a broad half-moon. That means that all the west, south-west, and north-west is open and undefended by trench-lines. There are flanks far away to the north and south in the hills which can be turned, and once we get round a flank there's nothing between us and our friends . . . I've figured out our road," and I traced it on the map. "If we can make that big circuit to the west and get over that pass unobserved we're bound to strike a Russian column the next day. It'll be a rough road, but I fancy we've all ridden as bad in our time. But one thing we must have, and that's horses. Can we and your six ruffians slip off in the darkness on the best beasts in this township? If you can manage that, we'll do the trick."

Sandy sat down and pondered. Thank Heaven, he was thinking now of action and not of his own conscience.

"It must be done," he said at last, "but it won't be easy. Hussin's a great fellow, but as you know well, Dick, horses right up at the battle-front are not easy to come by. Tomorrow I've got some kind of infernal fast to observe, and the next day that woman will be coaching me for my part. We'll have to give Hussin time . . . I wish to Heaven it could be to-night."

He was silent again for a bit, and then he said: "I believe the best time would be the third night, the eve of the revelation. She's bound to leave me alone that night."

"Right-o," I said. "It won't be much fun sitting waiting in this cold sepulchre; but we must keep our heads and risk nothing by being in a hurry. Besides, if Peter wins through, the Turk will be a busy man by the day after to-morrow."

The key turned in the door and Hussin stole in like a shade. It was the signal for Sandy to leave.

"You fellows have given me a new lease of life," he said. "I've got a plan now, and I can set my teeth and stick it out."

He went up to Peter and gripped his hand. "Good luck. You're the bravest man I've ever met, and I've seen a few." Then he turned abruptly and went out, followed by an exhortation from Blenkiron to "Get busy about the quadrupeds."

THEN WE SET ABOUT equipping Peter for his crusade. It was a simple job, for we were not rich in properties. His get-up, with his thick fur-collared greatcoat, was not unlike the ordinary Turkish officer seen in a dim light. But Peter had no intention of passing for a Turk, or indeed of giving anybody the chance of seeing him, and he was more concerned to fit in with the landscape. So he stripped off the greatcoat and pulled a grey sweater of mine over his jacket, and put on his head a woollen helmet of the same colour. He had no need of the map for he had long since got his route by heart, and what was once fixed in that mind stuck like wax; but I made him take Stumm's plan and paper, hidden below his shirt. The big difficulty, I saw, would be getting to the Russians without getting shot, assuming he passed the Turkish trenches. He could only hope that he would strike someone with a smattering of English or German. Twice he ascended to the roof and came back cheerful, for there was promise of wild weather.

Hussin brought in our supper, and Peter made up a parcel of food. Blenkiron and I had both small flasks of brandy and I gave him mine.

Then he held out his hand quite simply, like a good child who is going off to bed. It was too much for Blenkiron. With large tears rolling down his face he announced that, if we all came through, he was going to fit him into the softest berth that money could buy. I don't think he was understood, for old Peter's eyes had now the faraway absorption of the hunter who has found game. He was thinking only of his job.

Two legs and a pair of very shabby boots vanished through the trap, and suddenly I felt utterly lonely and desperately sad. The guns were beginning to roar again in the east, and in the intervals came the whistle of the rising storm.

CHAPTER 20

Peter Pienaar Goes to the Wars

THIS CHAPTER is the tale that Peter told me—long after, sitting beside a stove in the hotel at Bergen, where we were waiting for our boat.

HE CLIMBED ON THE ROOF and shinned down the broken bricks of the outer wall. The out-building we were lodged in abutted on a road, and was outside the proper *enceinte* of the house. At ordinary times I have no doubt there were sentries, but Sandy and Hussin had probably managed to clear them off this end for a little. Anyhow he saw nobody as he crossed the road and dived into the snowy fields.

He knew very well that he must do the job in the twelve hours of darkness ahead of him. The immediate front of a battle is a bit too public for anyone to lie hidden in by day, especially when two or three feet of snow make everything kenspeckle. Now hurry in a job of this kind was abhorrent to Peter's soul, for, like all Boers, his tastes were for slowness and sureness, though he could hustle fast enough when haste was needed. As he pushed through the winter fields he reckoned up the things in his favour, and found the only one the dirty weather. There was a high, gusty wind, blowing scuds of snow but never coming to any great fall. The frost had gone, and the lying snow was as soft as butter. That was all to the good, he thought, for a clear, hard night would have been the devil.

The first bit was through farmlands, which were seamed with little snow-filled water furrows. Now and then would come a house and a patch of fruit-trees, but there was nobody abroad. The roads were crowded enough, but Peter had no use for roads. I can picture him swinging along with his bent back, stopping every now and then to sniff and listen, alert for the foreknowledge of danger. When he chose he could cover country like an antelope.

Soon he struck a big road full of transport. It was the road from Erzerum to the Palantuken pass, and he waited his chance and crossed it. After that the ground grew rough with boulders and patches of thorn-trees, splendid cover where he could move fast without worrying. Then he was pulled up suddenly on the bank of a river. The map had warned him of it, but not that it would be so big.

It was a torrent swollen with melting snow and rains in the hills, and it was running fifty yards wide. Peter thought he could have swum it, but he was very averse to a drenching. "A wet man makes too much noise," he said, and besides, there was the off-chance that the current would be too much for him. So he moved up stream to look for a bridge.

In ten minutes he found one, a new-made thing of trestles, broad enough to take transport-wagons. It was guarded, for he heard the tramp of a sentry, and as he pulled himself up the bank he observed a couple of long wooden huts, obviously some kind of billets. These were on the near side of the stream, about a dozen yards from the bridge. A door stood open and a light showed in it, and from within came the sound of voices . . . Peter had a sense of hearing like a wild animal, and he could detect even from the confused gabble that the voices were German.

As he lay and listened someone came over the bridge. It was an officer, for the sentry saluted. The man disappeared in one of the huts. Peter had struck the billets and repairing shop of a squad of German sappers.

He was just going ruefully to retrace his steps and try to find a good place to swim the stream when it struck him that the officer who had passed him wore clothes very like his own. He, too, had had a grey sweater and a Balaclava helmet, for even a German officer ceases to be dressy on a mid-winter's night in Anatolia. The idea came to Peter to walk boldly across the bridge and trust to the sentry not seeing the difference.

He slipped round a corner of the hut and marched down the road. The sentry was now at the far end, which was lucky, for if the worst came to the worst he could throttle him. Peter, mimicking the stiff German walk, swung past him, his head down as if to protect him from the wind.

The man saluted. He did more, for he offered conversation. The officer must have been a genial soul. "It's a rough night, Captain," he said in German. "The wagons are late. Pray God, Michael hasn't got a shell in his lot. They've begun putting over some big ones."

Peter grunted good night in German and strode on. He was just leaving the road when he heard a great halloo behind him.

The real officer must have appeared on his heels, and the sentry's doubts had been stirred. A whistle was blown, and, looking back, Peter saw lanterns waving in the gale. They were coming out to look for the duplicate.

He stood still for a second, and noticed the lights spreading out south of the road. He was just about to dive off it on the north side when he was aware of a difficulty. On that side a steep bank fell to a ditch, and the bank beyond bounded a big flood. He could see the dull ruffle of the water under the wind.

On the road itself he would soon be caught; south of it the search was beginning; and the ditch itself was no place to hide, for he saw a lantern moving up it. Peter dropped into it all the same and made a plan. The side below the road was a little undercut and very steep. He resolved to plaster himself against it, for he would be hidden from the road, and a searcher in the ditch would not be likely to explore the unbroken sides. It was always a maxim of Peter's that the best hiding-place was the worst, the least obvious to the minds of those who were looking for you.

He waited until the lights both in the road and the ditch came nearer, and then he gripped the edge with his left hand, where some stones gave him purchase, dug the toes of his boots into the wet soil and stuck like a limpet. It needed some strength to keep the position for long, but the muscles of his arms and legs were like whipcord.

The searcher in the ditch soon got tired, for the place was very wet, and joined his comrades on the road. They came along, running, flashing the lanterns into the trench, and exploring all the immediate countryside.

Then rose a noise of wheels and horses from the opposite direction. Michael and the delayed wagons were approaching. They dashed up at a great pace, driven wildly, and for one horrid second Peter thought they were going to spill into the ditch at the very spot where he was concealed. The wheels passed so close to the edge that they almost grazed his fingers. Somebody shouted an order and they pulled up a yard or two nearer the bridge. The others came up and there was a consultation.

Michael swore he had passed no one on the road.

"That fool Hannus has seen a ghost," said the officer testily. "It's too cold for this child's play."

Hannus, almost in tears, repeated his tale. "The man spoke to me in good German," he cried.

"Ghost or no ghost he is safe enough up the road," said the officer. "Kind God, that was a big one!" He stopped and stared at a shell-burst, for the bombardment from the east was growing fiercer.

They stood discussing the fire for a minute and presently moved off. Peter gave them two minutes' law and then clambered back to the highway and set off along it at a run. The noise of the shelling and the wind, together with the thick darkness, made it safe to hurry.

He left the road at the first chance and took to the broken country. The ground was now rising towards a spur of the Palantuken, on the far slope of which were the Turkish trenches. The night had begun by being pretty nearly as black as pitch; even the smoke from the shell explosions, which is often visible in darkness, could not be seen. But as the wind blew the snow-clouds athwart the sky patches of stars came out. Peter had a compass, but he didn't need to use it, for he had a kind of "feel" for landscape, a special sense which is born in savages and can only be acquired after long experience by the white man. I believe he could smell where the north lay. He had settled roughly which part of the line he would try, merely because of its nearness to the enemy. But he might see reason to vary this, and as he moved he began to think that the safest place was where the shelling was hottest. He didn't like the notion, but it sounded sense.

Suddenly he began to puzzle over queer things in the ground, and, as he had never seen big guns before, it took him a moment to fix them. Presently one went off at his elbow with a roar like the Last Day. These were Austrian howitzers—nothing over eight-inch, I fancy, but to Peter they looked like leviathans. Here, too, he saw for the first time a big and quite recent shell-hole, for the Russian guns were searching out the position. He was so interested in it all that he poked his nose where he shouldn't have been, and dropped plump into the pit behind a gun-emplacement.

Gunners all the world over are the same—shy people, who hide themselves in holes and hibernate and mortally dislike being detected.

A gruff voice cried "*Wer da?*" and a heavy hand seized his neck.

Peter was ready with his story. He belonged to Michael's wagon-team and had been left behind. He wanted to be told the way to the sappers' camp. He was very apologetic, not to say obsequious.

"It is one of those Prussian swine from the Marta bridge," said a gunner. "Land him a kick to teach him sense. Bear to your right, mannikin, and you will find a road. And have a care when you get there, for the Russkoes are registering on it."

Peter thanked them and bore off to the right. After that he kept a wary eye on the howitzers, and was thankful when he got out of their area on to the slopes up the hill. Here was the type of country that was familiar to him, and he defied any Turk or Boche to spot him among the scrub and boulders. He was getting on very well, when once more, close to his ear, came a sound like the crack of doom.

It was the field-guns now, and the sound of a field-gun close at hand is bad for the nerves if you aren't expecting it. Peter thought he had been hit, and lay flat for a little to consider. Then he found the right explanation, and crawled forward very warily.

Presently he saw his first Russian shell. It dropped half a dozen yards to his right, making a great hole in the snow and sending up a mass of mixed earth, snow, and broken stones. Peter spat out the dirt and felt very solemn. You must remember that never in his life had he seen big shelling, and was now being landed in the thick of a first-class show without any preparation. He said he felt cold in his stomach, and very wishful to run away, if there had been anywhere to run to. But he kept on to the crest of the ridge, over which a big glow was broadening like sunrise. He tripped once over a wire, which he took for some kind of snare, and after that went very warily. By and by he got his face between two boulders and looked over into the true battlefield.

He told me it was exactly what the predikant used to say that Hell would be like. About fifty yards down the slope lay the Turkish trenches—they were dark against the snow, and now and then a black figure like a devil showed for an instant and disappeared. The Turks clearly expected an infantry attack, for they were sending up calcium rockets and Very flares. The Russians were battering their line and spraying all the hinterland, not with shrapnel, but with good, solid high-explosives. The place would be as bright as day for a moment, all smothered in a scurry of smoke and snow and debris, and then a black pall would fall on it, when only the thunder of the guns told of the battle.

Peter felt very sick. He had not believed there could be so much noise in the world, and the drums of his ears were splitting. Now, for a man to whom courage is habitual, the taste of fear—naked, utter fear—is a horrible thing. It seems to wash away all his manhood. Peter lay on the crest, watching the shells burst, and confident that any moment he might be a shattered remnant. He lay and reasoned with himself, calling himself every name he could think of, but conscious that nothing would get rid of that lump of ice below his heart.

Then he could stand it no longer. He got up and ran for his life.

But he ran forward.

It was the craziest performance. He went hell-for-leather over a piece of ground which was being watered with H.E., but by the mercy of Heaven nothing hit him. He took some fearsome tosses in shell-holes, but partly erect and partly on all fours he did the fifty yards and tumbled into a Turkish trench right on top of a dead man.

The contact with that body brought him to his senses. That men could die at all seemed a comforting, homely thing after that unnatural pandemonium. The next moment a crump took the parapet of the trench some yards to his left, and he was half buried in an avalanche.

He crawled out of that, pretty badly cut about the head. He was quite cool now and thinking hard about his next step. There were men all around him, sullen dark faces as he saw them when the flares went up. They were manning the parapets and waiting tensely for something else than the shelling. They paid no attention to him, for I fancy in that trench units were pretty well mixed up, and under a bad bombardment no one bothers about his neighbour. He found himself free to move as he pleased. The ground of the trench was littered with empty cartridge-cases, and there were many dead bodies.

The last shell, as I have said, had played havoc with the parapet. In the next spell of darkness Peter crawled through the gap and twisted among some snowy hillocks. He was no longer afraid of shells, any more than he was afraid of a veld thunderstorm. But he was wondering very hard how he should ever get to the Russians. The Turks were behind him now, but there was the biggest danger in front.

Then the artillery ceased. It was so sudden that he thought he had gone deaf, and could hardly realize the blessed relief of it. The wind, too, seemed to have fallen, or perhaps he was sheltered by the lee of the hill. There were a lot of dead here also, and that he couldn't understand, for they were new dead. Had the Turks attacked and been driven back? When he had gone about thirty yards he stopped to take his bearings. On the right were the ruins of a large building set on fire by the guns. There was a blur of woods and the debris of walls round it. Away to the left another hill ran out farther to the east, and the place he was in seemed to be a kind of cup between the spurs. Just before him was a little ruined building, with the sky seen through its rafters, for the smouldering ruin on the right gave a certain light. He wondered if the Russian firing-line lay there.

Just then he heard voices—smothered voices—not a yard away and apparently below the ground. He instantly jumped to what this must mean. It was a Turkish trench—a communication trench. Peter didn't know much about modern warfare, but he had read in the papers, or heard from me, enough to make him draw the right moral. The fresh dead pointed to the same conclusion. What he had got through were the Turkish support trenches, not their firing-line. That was still before him.

He didn't despair, for the rebound from panic had made him extra courageous. He crawled forward, an inch at a time, taking no sort of risk, and presently found himself looking at the parados of a trench. Then he lay quiet to think out the next step.

The shelling had stopped, and there was that queer kind of peace which falls sometimes on two armies not a quarter of a mile distant. Peter said he could hear nothing but the far-off sighing of the wind. There seemed to be no movement of any kind in the trench before him, which ran through the ruined building. The light of the burning was dying, and he could just make out the mound of earth a yard in front. He began to feel hungry, and got out his packet of food and had a swig at the brandy flask. That comforted him, and he felt a master of his fate again. But the next step was not so easy. He must find out what lay behind that mound of earth.

Suddenly a curious sound fell on his ears. It was so faint that at first he doubted the evidence of his senses. Then as the wind fell it came louder. It was exactly like some hollow piece of metal being struck by a stick, musical and oddly resonant.

He concluded it was the wind blowing a branch of a tree against an old boiler in the ruin before him. The trouble was that there was scarcely enough wind now for that in this sheltered cup.

But as he listened he caught the note again. It was a bell, a fallen bell, and the place before him must have been a chapel. He remembered that an Armenian monastery had been marked on the big map, and he guessed it was the burned building on his right.

The thought of a chapel and a bell gave him the notion of some human agency. And then suddenly the notion was confirmed. The sound was regular and concerted—dot, dash, dot—dash, dot, dot. The branch of a tree and the wind may play strange pranks, but they do not produce the longs and shorts of the Morse Code.

This was where Peter's intelligence work in the Boer War helped him. He knew the Morse, he could read it, but he could make nothing of the signalling. It was either in some special code or in a strange language.

He lay still and did some calm thinking. There was a man in front of him, a Turkish soldier, who was in the enemy's pay. Therefore he could fraternize with him, for they were on the same side. But how was he to approach him without getting shot in the process? Again, how could a man send signals to the enemy from a firing-line without being detected? Peter found an answer in the strange configuration of the ground. He had not heard a sound until he was a few yards from the place, and they would be inaudible to men in the reserve trenches and even in the communication trenches. If somebody moving up the latter caught the noise, it would be easy to explain it naturally. But the wind blowing down the cup would carry it far in the enemy's direction.

There remained the risk of being heard by those parallel with the bell in the firing trenches. Peter concluded that that trench must be very thinly held, probably only by a few observers, and the nearest might be a dozen yards off. He had read about that being the French fashion under a big bombardment.

The next thing was to find out how to make himself known to this ally. He decided that the only way was to surprise him. He might get shot, but he trusted to his strength and agility against a man who was almost certainly wearied. When he had got him safe, explanations might follow.

Peter was now enjoying himself hugely. If only those infernal guns kept silent he would play out the game in the sober, decorous way he loved. So very delicately he began to wriggle forward to where the sound was.

The night was now as black as ink around him, and very quiet, too, except for soughings of the dying gale. The snow had drifted a little in the lee of the ruined walls, and Peter's progress was naturally very slow. He could not afford to dislodge one ounce of snow. Still the tinkling went on, now in greater volume. Peter was in terror lest it should cease before he got his man.

Presently his hand clutched at empty space. He was on the lip of the front trench. The sound was now a yard to his right, and with infinite care he shifted his position. Now the bell was just below him, and he felt the big rafter of the woodwork from which it had fallen. He felt something else—a stretch of wire fixed in the ground with the far end hanging in the void. That would be the spy's explanation if anyone heard the sound and came seeking the cause.

Somewhere in the darkness before him and below was the man, not a yard off. Peter remained very still, studying the situation. He could not see, but he could feel the presence, and he was trying to decide the relative position of the man and bell and their exact distance from him. The thing was not so easy as it looked, for if he jumped for where he believed the figure was, he might miss it and get a bullet in the stomach. A man who played so risky a game was probably handy with his firearms. Besides, if he should hit the bell, he would make a hideous row and alarm the whole front.

Fate suddenly gave him the right chance. The unseen figure stood up and moved a step, till his back was against the parados. He actually brushed against Peter's elbow, who held his breath.

There is a catch that the Kaffirs have which would need several diagrams to explain. It is partly a neck hold, and partly a paralysing backward twist of the right arm, but if it is practised on a man from behind, it locks him as sure as if he were handcuffed. Peter slowly got his body raised and his knees drawn under him, and reached for his prey.

He got him. A head was pulled backward over the edge of the trench, and he felt in the air the motion of the left arm pawing feebly but unable to reach behind.

"Be still," whispered Peter in German; "I mean you no harm. We are friends of the same purpose. Do you speak German?"

"*Nein*," said a muffled voice.

"English?"

"Yes," said the voice.

"Thank God," said Peter. "Then we can understand each other. I've watched your notion of signalling, and a very good one it is. I've got to get through to the Russian lines somehow before morning, and I want you to help me. I'm English—a kind of English, so we're on the same side. If I let go your neck will you be good and talk reasonably?"

The voice assented. Peter let go, and in the same instant slipped to the side. The man wheeled round and flung out an arm but gripped vacancy.

"Steady, friend," said Peter; "you mustn't play tricks with me or I'll be angry."

"Who are you? Who sent you?" asked the puzzled voice.

Peter had a happy thought. "The Companions of the Rosy Hours?" he said.

"Then are we friends indeed," said the voice. "Come out of the darkness, friend, and I will do you no harm. I am a good Turk, and I fought beside the English in Kordofan and learned their tongue. I live only to see the ruin of Enver, who has beggared my family and slain my twin brother. Therefore I serve the *Muscov ghiaours*."

"I don't know what the Musky Jaws are, but if you mean the Russians I'm with you. I've got news for them which will make Enver green. The question is, how I'm to get to them, and that is where you shall help me, my friend."

"How?"

"By playing that little tune of yours again. Tell them to expect within the next half-hour a deserter with an important message. Tell them, for God's sake, not to fire at anybody till they've made certain it isn't me."

The man took the blunt end of his bayonet and squatted beside the bell. The first stroke brought out a clear, searching note which floated down the valley. He struck three notes at slow intervals. For all the world, Peter said, he was like a telegraph operator calling up a station.

"Send the message in English," said Peter.

"They may not understand it," said the man.

"Then send it any way you like. I trust you, for we are brothers."

After ten minutes the man ceased and listened. From far away came the sound of a trench-gong, the kind of thing they used on the Western Front to give the gas-alarm.

"They say they will be ready," he said. "I cannot take down messages in the darkness, but they have given me the signal which means 'Consent'."

"Come, that is pretty good," said Peter. "And now I must be moving. You take a hint from me. When you hear big firing up to the north get ready to beat a quick retreat, for it will be all up with that city of yours. And tell your folk, too, that they're making a bad mistake letting those fool Germans rule their land. Let them hang Enver and his little friends, and we'll be happy once more."

"May Satan receive his soul!" said the Turk. "There is wire before us, but I will show you a way through. The guns this evening made many rents in it. But haste, for a working party may be here presently to repair it. Remember there is much wire before the other lines."

Peter, with certain directions, found it pretty easy to make his way through the entanglement. There was one bit which scraped a hole in his back, but very soon he had come to the last posts and found himself in open country. The place, he said, was a graveyard of the unburied dead that smelt horribly as he crawled among them. He had no inducements to delay, for he thought he could hear behind him the movement of the Turkish working party, and was in terror that a flare might reveal him and a volley accompany his retreat.

From one shell-hole to another he wormed his way, till he struck an old ruinous communication trench which led in the right direction. The Turks must have been forced back in the past week, and the Russians were now in the evacuated trenches. The thing was half full of water, but it gave Peter a feeling of safety, for it enabled him to get his head below the level of the ground. Then it came to an end and he found before him a forest of wire.

The Turk in his signal had mentioned half an hour, but Peter thought it was nearer two hours before he got through that noxious entanglement. Shelling had made little difference to it. The uprights were all there, and the barbed strands seemed to touch the ground.

Remember, he had no wire-cutter; nothing but his bare hands. Once again fear got hold of him. He felt caught in a net, with monstrous vultures waiting to pounce on him from above. At any moment a flare might go up and a dozen rifles find their mark. He had altogether forgotten about the message which had been sent, for no message could dissuade the ever-present death he felt around him. It was, he said, like following an old lion into bush when there was but one narrow way in, and no road out.

The guns began again—the Turkish guns from behind the ridge—and a shell tore up the wire a short way before him. Under cover of the burst he made good a few yards, leaving large portions of his clothing in the strands. Then, quite suddenly, when hope had almost died in his heart, he felt the ground rise steeply. He lay very still, a star-rocket from the Turkish side lit up the place, and there in front was a rampart with the points of bayonets showing beyond it. It was the Russian hour for stand-to.

He raised his cramped limbs from the ground and shouted "Friend! English!"

A face looked down at him, and then the darkness again descended.

"Friend," he said hoarsely. "English."

He heard speech behind the parapet. An electric torch was flashed on him for a second. A voice spoke, a friendly voice, and the sound of it seemed to be telling him to come over.

He was now standing up, and as he got his hands on the parapet he seemed to feel bayonets very near him. But the voice that spoke was kindly, so with a heave he scrambled over and flopped into the trench. Once more the electric torch was flashed, and revealed to the eyes of the onlookers an indescribably dirty, lean, middle-aged man with a bloody head, and scarcely a rag of shirt on his back. The said man, seeing friendly faces around him, grinned cheerfully.

"That was a rough trek, friends," he said; "I want to see your general pretty quick, for I've got a present for him."

He was taken to an officer in a dug-out, who addressed him in French, which he did not understand. But the sight of Stumm's plan worked wonders. After that he was fairly bundled down communication trenches and then over swampy fields to a farm among trees. There he found staff officers, who looked at him and looked at his map, and then put him on a horse and hurried him eastwards. At last he came to a big ruined house, and was taken into a room which seemed to be full of maps and generals.

The conclusion must be told in Peter's words.

"There was a big man sitting at a table drinking coffee, and when I saw him my heart jumped out of my skin. For it was the man I hunted with on the Pungwe in '98—him whom the Kaffirs called 'Buck's Horn', because of his long curled moustaches. He was a prince even then, and now he is a very great general. When I saw him, I ran forward and gripped his hand and cried, '*Hoe gat het, Mynheer?*' and he knew me and shouted in Dutch, 'Damn, if it isn't old Peter Pienaar!' Then he gave me coffee and ham and good bread, and he looked at my map.

" 'What is this?' he cried, growing red in the face.

" 'It is the staff map of one Stumm, a German *skellum* who commands in yon city,' I said.

"He looked at it close and read the markings, and then he read the other paper which you gave me, Dick. And then he flung up his arms and laughed. He took a loaf and tossed it into the air so that it fell on the head of another general. He spoke to them in their own tongue, and they, too, laughed, and one or two ran out as if on some errand. I have never seen such merrymaking. They were clever men, and knew the worth of what you gave me.

"Then he got to his feet and hugged me, all dirty as I was, and kissed me on both cheeks.

" 'Before God, Peter,' he said, 'you're the mightiest hunter since Nimrod. You've often found me game, but never game so big as this!' "

CHAPTER 21

The Little Hill

I T WAS A WISE MAN who said that the biggest kind of courage was to be able to sit still. I used to feel that when we were getting shelled in the reserve trenches outside Vermelles. I felt it before we went over the parapets at Loos, but I never felt it so much as on the last two days in that cellar. I had simply to set my teeth and take a pull on myself. Peter had gone on a crazy errand which I scarcely believed could come off. There were no signs of Sandy; somewhere within a hundred yards he was fighting his own battles, and I was tormented by the thought that he might get jumpy again and wreck everything. A strange Companion brought us food, a man who spoke only Turkish and could tell us nothing; Hussin, I judged, was busy about the horses. If I could only have done something to help on matters I could have scotched my anxiety, but there was nothing to be done, nothing but wait and brood. I tell you I began to sympathize with the general behind the lines in a battle, the fellow who makes the plan which others execute. Leading a charge can be nothing like so nerve-shaking a business as sitting in an easy-chair and waiting on the news of it.

It was bitter cold, and we spent most of the day wrapped in our greatcoats and buried deep in the straw. Blenkiron was a marvel. There was no light for him to play Patience by, but he never complained. He slept a lot of the time, and when he was awake talked as cheerily as if he were starting out on a holiday. He had one great comfort, his dyspepsia was gone. He sang hymns constantly to the benign Providence that had squared his duo-denum.

My only occupation was to listen for the guns. The first day after Peter left they were very quiet on the front nearest us, but in the late evening they started a terrific racket. The next day they never stopped from dawn to dusk, so that it reminded me of that tremendous forty-eight hours before Loos. I tried to read into this some proof that Peter had got through, but it would not work. It looked more like the opposite, for this desperate hammering must mean that the frontal assault was still the Russian game.

Two or three times I climbed on the housetop for fresh air. The day was foggy and damp, and I could see very little of the countryside. Transport was still bumping southward along the road to the Palantuken, and the slow wagon-loads of wounded returning. One thing I noticed, however. There was a perpetual coming and going between the house and the city. Motors and mounted messengers were constantly arriving and departing, and I concluded that Hilda von Einem was getting ready for her part in the defence of Erzerum.

These ascents were all on the first day after Peter's going. The second day, when I tried the trap, I found it closed and heavily weighted. This must have been done by our friends, and very right, too. If the house were becoming a place of public resort, it would never do for me to be journeying roofward.

Late on the second night Hussin reappeared. It was after supper, when Blenkiron had gone peacefully to sleep and I was beginning to count the hours till the morning. I could not close an eye during these days and not much at night.

Hussin did not light a lantern. I heard his key in the lock, and then his light step close to where we lay

"Are you asleep?" he said, and when I answered he sat down beside me.

"The horses are found," he said, "and the Master bids me tell you that we start in the morning three hours before dawn."

It was welcome news. "Tell me what is happening," I begged; "we have been lying in this tomb for three days and heard nothing."

"The guns are busy," he said. "The Allemans come to this place every hour, I know not for what. Also there has been a great search for you. The searchers have been here, but they were sent away empty . . . Sleep, my lord, for there is wild work before us."

I did not sleep much, for I was strung too high with expectation, and I envied Blenkiron his now eupeptic slumbers. But for an hour or so I dropped off, and my old nightmare came back. Once again I was in the throat of a pass, hotly pursued, straining for some sanctuary which I knew I must reach. But I was no longer alone. Others were with me: how many I could not tell, for when I tried to see their faces they dissolved in mist. Deep snow was underfoot, a grey sky was over us, black peaks were on all sides, but ahead in the mist of the pass was that curious *castrol* which I had first seen in my dream on the Erzerum road.

I saw it distinct in every detail. It rose to the left of the road through the pass, above a hollow where great boulders stood out in the snow. Its sides were steep, so that the snow had slipped off in patches, leaving stretches of glistening black shale. The *kranz* at the top did not rise sheer, but sloped at an angle of forty-five, and on the very summit there seemed a hollow, as if the earth within the rock-rim had been beaten by weather into a cup.

That is often the way with a South African *castrol*, and I knew it was so with this. We were straining for it, but the snow clogged us, and our enemies were very close behind.

Then I was awakened by a figure at my side. "Get ready, my lord," it said; "it is the hour to ride."

LIKE SLEEP-WALKERS we moved into the sharp air. Hussin led us out of an old postern and then through a place like an orchard to the shelter of some tall evergreen trees. There horses stood, champing quietly from their nosebags. "Good," I thought; "a feed of oats before a big effort."

There were nine beasts for nine riders. We mounted without a word and filed through a grove of trees to where a broken paling marked the beginning of cultivated land. There for the matter of twenty minutes Hussin chose to guide us through deep, clogging snow. He wanted to avoid any sound till we were well beyond earshot of the house. Then we struck a by-path which presently merged in a hard highway, running, as I judged, south-west by west. There we delayed no longer, but galloped furiously into the dark.

I had got back all my exhilaration. Indeed I was intoxicated with the movement, and could have laughed out loud and sung. Under the black canopy of the night perils are either forgotten or terribly alive. Mine were forgotten. The darkness I galloped into led me to freedom and friends. Yes, and success, which I had not dared to hope and scarcely even to dream of.

Hussin rode first, with me at his side. I turned my head and saw Blenkiron behind me, evidently mortally unhappy about the pace we set and the mount he sat. He used to say that horse-exercise was good for his liver, but it was a gentle amble and a short gallop that he liked, and not this mad helter-skelter. His thighs were too round to fit a saddle leather. We passed a fire in a hollow, the bivouac of some

337

Turkish unit, and all the horses shied violently. I knew by Blenkiron's oaths that he had lost his stirrups and was sitting on his horse's neck.

Beside him rode a tall figure swathed to the eyes in wrappings, and wearing round his neck some kind of shawl whose ends floated behind him. Sandy, of course, had no European ulster, for it was months since he had worn proper clothes. I wanted to speak to him, but somehow I did not dare. His stillness forbade me. He was a wonderful fine horseman, with his firm English hunting seat, and it was as well, for he paid no attention to his beast. His head was still full of unquiet thoughts.

Then the air around me began to smell acrid and raw, and I saw that a fog was winding up from the hollows.

"Here's the devil's own luck," I cried to Hussin. "Can you guide us in a mist?"

"I do not know." He shook his head. "I had counted on seeing the shape of the hills."

"We've a map and compass, anyhow. But these make slow travelling. Pray God it lifts!"

Presently the black vapour changed to grey, and the day broke. It was little comfort. The fog rolled in waves to the horses' ears, and riding at the head of the party I could but dimly see the next rank.

"It is time to leave the road," said Hussin, "or we may meet inquisitive folk."

We struck to the left, over ground which was for all the world like a Scotch moor. There were pools of rain on it, and masses of tangled snow-laden junipers, and long reefs of wet slaty stone. It was bad going, and the fog made it hopeless to steer a good course. I had out the map and the compass, and tried to fix our route so as to round the flank of a spur of the mountains which separated us from the valley we were aiming at.

"There's a stream ahead of us," I said to Hussin. "Is it fordable?"

"It is only a trickle," he said, coughing. "This accursed mist is from Eblis." But I knew long before we reached it that it was no trickle. It was a hill stream coming down in spate, and, as I soon guessed, in a deep ravine. Presently we were at its edge, one long whirl of yeasty falls and brown rapids. We could as soon get horses over it as to the topmost cliffs of the Palantuken.

Hussin stared at it in consternation. "May Allah forgive my folly, for

I should have known. We must return to the highway and find a bridge. My sorrow, that I should have led my lords so ill."

Back over that moor we went with my spirits badly damped. We had none too long a start, and Hilda von Einem would rouse heaven and earth to catch us up. Hussin was forcing the pace, for his anxiety was as great as mine.

Before we reached the road the mist blew back and revealed a wedge of country right across to the hills beyond the river. It was a clear view, every object standing out wet and sharp in the light of morning. It showed the bridge with horsemen drawn up across it, and it showed, too, cavalry pickets moving along the road.

They saw us at the same instant. A word was passed down the road, a shrill whistle blew, and the pickets put their horses at the bank and started across the moor.

"Did I not say this mist was from Eblis?" growled Hussin, as we swung round and galloped back on our tracks. "These cursed Zaptiehs have seen us, and our road is cut."

I was for trying the stream at all costs, but Hussin pointed out that it would do us no good. The cavalry beyond the bridge was moving up the other bank. "There is a path through the hills that I know, but it must be travelled on foot. If we can increase our lead and the mist cloaks us, there is yet a chance."

It was a weary business plodding up to the skirts of the hills. We had the pursuit behind us now, and that put an edge on every difficulty. There were long banks of broken screes, I remember, where the snow slipped in wreaths from under our feet. Great boulders had to be circumvented, and patches of bog, where the streams from the snows first made contact with the plains, mired us to our girths. Happily the mist was down again, but this, though it hindered the chase, lessened the chances of Hussin finding the path.

He found it nevertheless. There was the gully and the rough mule-track leading upwards. But there also had been a land-slip, quite recent from the marks. A large scar of raw earth had broken across the hillside, which with the snow above it looked like a slice cut out of an iced chocolate-cake.

We stared blankly for a second, till we recognized its hopelessness.

"I'm trying for the crags," I said. "Where there once was a way another can be found."

"And be picked off at their leisure by these marksmen," said Hussin grimly. "Look!"

The mist had opened again, and a glance behind showed me the pursuit closing up on us. They were now less than three hundred yards off. We turned our horses and made off eastward along the skirts of the cliffs.

Then Sandy spoke for the first time. "I don't know how you fellows feel, but I'm not going to be taken. There's nothing much to do except to find a good place and put up a fight. We can sell our lives dearly."

"That's about all," said Blenkiron cheerfully. He had suffered such tortures on that gallop that he welcomed any kind of stationary fight.

"Serve out the arms," said Sandy.

The Companions all carried rifles slung across their shoulders. Hussin, from a deep saddle-bag, brought out rifles and bandoliers for the rest of us. As I laid mine across my saddle-bow I saw it was a German Mauser of the latest pattern.

"It's hell-for-leather till we find a place for a stand," said Sandy. "The game's against us this time."

Once more we entered the mist, and presently found better going on a long stretch of even slope. Then came a rise, and on the crest of it I saw the sun. Presently we dipped into bright daylight and looked down on a broad glen, with a road winding up it to a pass in the range. I had expected this. It was one way to the Palantuken pass, some miles south of the house where we had been lodged.

And then, as I looked southward, I saw what I had been watching for for days. A little hill split the valley, and on its top was a *kranz* of rocks. It was the *castrol* of my persistent dream.

On that I promptly took charge. "There's our fort," I cried. "If we once get there we can hold it for a week. Sit down and ride for it."

We bucketed down that hillside like men possessed, even Blenkiron sticking on manfully among the twists and turns and slithers. Presently we were on the road and were racing past marching infantry and gun teams and empty wagons. I noted that most seemed to be moving downward and few going up. Hussin screamed some words in Turkish that secured us a passage, but indeed our crazy speed left them staring. Out of a corner of my eye I saw that Sandy had flung off most of his wrappings and seemed to be all a dazzle of rich colour. But I had thought for nothing except the little hill, now almost fronting us across the shallow glen.

No horses could breast that steep. We urged them into the hollow, and then hastily dismounted, humped the packs, and began to struggle up the side of the *castrol*. It was strewn with great boulders, which gave a kind of cover that very soon was needed. For, snatching a glance back, I saw that our pursuers were on the road above us and were getting ready to shoot.

At normal times we would have been easy marks, but, fortunately, wisps and streamers of mist now clung about that hollow. The rest could fend for themselves, so I stuck to Blenkiron and dragged him, wholly breathless, by the least exposed route. Bullets spattered now and then against the rocks, and one sang unpleasantly near my head. In this way we covered three-fourths of the distance, and had only the bare dozen yards where the gradient eased off up to the edge of the *kranz*.

Blenkiron got hit in the leg, our only casualty. There was nothing for it but to carry him, so I swung him on my shoulders, and with a bursting heart did that last lap. It was hottish work, and the bullets were pretty thick about us, but we all got safely to the *kranz* and a short scramble took us over the edge. I laid Blenkiron inside the *castrol* and started to prepare our defence.

We had little time to do it. Out of the thin fog figures were coming, crouching in cover. The place we were in was a natural redoubt, except that there were no loopholes or sandbags. We had to show our heads over the rim to shoot, but the danger was lessened by the superb field of fire given by those last dozen yards of glacis. I posted the men and waited, and Blenkiron, with a white face, insisted on taking his share, announcing that he used to be handy with a gun.

I gave the order that no man was to shoot till the enemy had come out of the rocks on to the glacis. The thing ran right round the top, and we had to watch all sides to prevent them getting us in flank or rear. Hussin's rifle cracked out presently from the back, so my precautions had not been needless.

We were all three fair shots, though none of us up to Peter's miraculous standard, and the Companions, too, made good practice. The Mauser was the weapon I knew best, and I didn't miss much. The attackers never had a chance, for their only hope was to rush us by numbers, and, the whole party being not above two dozen, they were far too few. I think we killed three, for their bodies were left lying, and wounded at least six, while the rest fell back towards the road. In a quarter of an hour it was all over.

"They are dogs of Kurds," I heard Hussin say fiercely. "Only a Kurdish *ghiaour* would fire on the livery of the Kaába."

Then I had a good look at Sandy. He had discarded shawls and wrappings, and stood up in the strangest costume man ever wore in battle. Somehow he had procured field-boots and an old pair of riding-breeches. Above these, reaching well below his middle, he had a wonderful silken jibbah or ephod of a bright emerald. I call it silk, but it was like no silk I have ever known, so exquisite in the mesh, with such a sheen and depth in it. Some strange pattern was woven on the breast, which in the dim light I could not trace. I'll warrant no rarer or costlier garment was ever exposed to lead on a bleak winter hill.

Sandy seemed unconscious of his garb. His eye, listless no more, scanned the hollow. "That's only the overture," he cried. "The opera will soon begin. We must put a breastwork up in these gaps or they'll pick us off from a thousand yards."

I had meantime roughly dressed Blenkiron's wound with a linen rag which Hussin provided. It was from a ricochet bullet which had chipped into his left shin. Then I took a hand with the others in getting up earthworks to complete the circuit of the defence. It was no easy job, for we wrought only with our knives and had to dig deep down below the snowy gravel. As we worked I took stock of our refuge.

The *castrol* was a rough circle about ten yards in diameter, its interior filled with boulders and loose stones, and its parapet about four feet high. The mist had cleared for a considerable space, and I could see the immediate surroundings. West, beyond the hollow, was the road we had come, where now the remnants of the pursuit were clustered. North, the hill fell steeply to the valley bottom, but to the south, after a dip there was a ridge which shut the view. East lay another fork of the stream, the chief fork I guessed, and it was evidently followed by the main road to the pass, for I saw it crowded with transport. The two roads seemed to converge somewhere farther south of my sight.

I guessed we could not be very far from the front, for the noise of guns sounded very near, both the sharp crack of the field-pieces, and the deeper boom of the howitzers. More, I could hear the chatter of the

. . . THE STRANGEST COSTUME MAN EVER WORE IN BATTLE

machine-guns, a magpie note among the baying of hounds. I even saw the bursting of Russian shells, evidently trying to reach the main road. One big fellow—an eight-inch—landed not ten yards from a convoy to the east of us, and another in the hollow through which we had come. These were clearly ranging shots, and I wondered if the Russians had observation-posts on the heights to mark them. If so, they might soon try a curtain, and we should be very near its edge. It would be an odd irony if we were the target of friendly shells.

"By the Lord Harry," I heard Sandy say, "if we had a brace of machine-guns we could hold this place against a division."

"What price shells?" I asked. "If they get a gun up they can blow us to atoms in ten minutes."

"Please God the Russians keep them too busy for that," was his answer.

With anxious eyes I watched our enemies on the road. They seemed to have grown in numbers. They were signalling, too, for a white flag fluttered. Then the mist rolled down on us again, and our prospect was limited to ten yards of vapour.

"Steady," I cried; "they may try to rush us at any moment. Every man keep his eye on the edge of the fog, and shoot at the first sign."

For nearly half an hour by my watch we waited in that queer white world, our eyes smarting with the strain of peering. The sound of the guns seemed to be hushed, and everything grown deathly quiet. Blenkiron's squeal, as he knocked his wounded leg against a rock, made every man start.

THEN OUT OF THE MIST there came a voice.

It was a woman's voice, high, penetrating, and sweet, but it spoke in no tongue I knew. Only Sandy understood. He made a sudden movement as if to defend himself against a blow.

The speaker came into clear sight on the glacis a yard or two away. Mine was the first face she saw.

"I come to offer terms," she said in English. "Will you permit me to enter?"

I could do nothing except take off my cap and say, "Yes, ma'am." Blenkiron, snuggled up against the parapet, was cursing furiously below his breath.

She climbed up the *kranz* and stepped over the edge as lightly as a deer. Her clothes were strange—spurred boots and breeches over which fell a short green kirtle. A little cap skewered with a jewelled pin was on her head, and a cape of some coarse country cloth hung from her shoulders. She had rough gauntlets on her hands, and she carried for weapon a riding-whip. The fog-crystals clung to her hair, I remember, and a silvery film of fog lay on her garments.

I had never before thought of her as beautiful. Strange, uncanny, wonderful, if you like, but the word beauty had too kindly and human a sound for such a face. But as she stood with heightened colour, her eyes like stars, her poise like a wild bird's, I had to confess that she had her own loveliness. She might be a devil, but she was also a queen. I considered that there might be merits in the prospect of riding by her side into Jerusalem.

Sandy stood rigid, his face very grave and set. She held out both hands to him, speaking softly in Turkish. I noticed that the six Companions had disappeared from the *castrol* and were somewhere out of sight on the farther side.

I do not know what she said, but from her tone, and above all from her eyes, I judged that she was pleading—pleading for his return, for his partnership in her great adventure; pleading, for all I knew, for his love.

His expression was like a death-mask, his brows drawn tight in a little frown and his jaw rigid.

"Madam," he said, "I ask you to tell your business quick and to tell it in English. My friends must hear it as well as me."

"Your friends!" she cried. "What has a prince to do with these hirelings? Your slaves, perhaps, but not your friends."

"My friends," Sandy repeated grimly. "You must know, Madam, that I am a British officer."

That was beyond doubt a clean staggering stroke. What she had thought of his origin God knows, but she had never dreamed of this. Her eyes grew larger and more lustrous, her lips parted as if to speak, but her voice failed her. Then by an effort she recovered herself, and out of that strange face went all the glow of youth and ardour. It was again the unholy mask I had first known.

"And these others?" she asked in a level voice.

"One is a brother officer of my regiment. The other is an American friend. But all three of us are on the same errand. We came east to destroy Greenmantle and your devilish ambitions. You have yourself destroyed your prophets, and now it is your turn to fail and disappear. Make no mistake, Madam; that folly is over. I will tear this sacred garment into a thousand pieces and scatter them on the wind. The people wait to-day for the revelation, but none will come. You may kill us if you can, but we have at least crushed a lie and done service to our country."

I would not have taken my eyes from her face for a king's ransom. I have written that she was a queen, and of that there is no manner of doubt. She had the soul of a conqueror, for not a flicker of weakness or disappointment marred her air. Only pride and the stateliest resolution looked out of her eyes.

"I said I came to offer terms. I will still offer them, though they are other than I thought. For the fat American, I will send him home safely to his own country. I do not make war on such as he. He is Germany's foe, not mine. You," she said, turning fiercely on me, "I will hang before dusk."

Never in my life had I been so pleased. I had got my revenge at last. This woman had singled me out above the others as the object of her wrath, and I almost loved her for it.

She turned to Sandy, and the fierceness went out of her face.

"You seek the truth," she said. "So also do I, and if we use a lie it is only to break down a greater. You are of my household in spirit, and you alone of all men I have seen are fit to ride with me on my mission. Germany may fail, but I shall not fail. I offer you the greatest career that mortal has known. I offer you a task which will need every atom of brain and sinew and courage. Will you refuse this destiny?"

I do not know what effect this vapouring might have had in hot scented rooms, or in the languor of some rich garden; but up on that cold hill-top it was as unsubstantial as the mist around us. It sounded not even impressive, only crazy.

"I stay with my friends," said Sandy.

"Then I will offer more. I will save your friends. They, too, shall share in my triumph."

This was too much for Blenkiron. He scrambled to his feet to speak the protest that had been wrung from his soul, forgot his game leg, and rolled back on the ground with a groan.

Then she seemed to make a last appeal. She spoke in Turkish now, and I do not know what she said, but I judged it was the plea of a woman to her lover. Once more she was the proud beauty, but there was a tremor in her pride—I had almost written tenderness. To listen to her was like horrid treachery, like eavesdropping on something pitiful. I know my cheeks grew scarlet and Blenkiron turned away his head.

Sandy's face did not move. He spoke in English.

"You can offer me nothing that I desire," he said. "I am the servant of my country, and her enemies are mine. I can have neither part nor lot with you. That is my answer, Madam von Einem."

Then her steely restraint broke. It was like a dam giving before a pent-up mass of icy water. She tore off one of her gauntlets and hurled it in his face. Implacable hate looked out of her eyes.

"I have done with you," she cried. "You have scorned me, but you have dug your own grave."

She leaped on the parapet and the next second was on the glacis. Once more the mist had fled, and across the hollow I saw a field-gun in place and men around it who were not Turkish. She waved her hand to them, and hastened down the hillside.

But at that moment I heard the whistle of a long-range Russian shell. Among the boulders there was the dull shock of an explosion and a mushroom of red earth. It all passed in an instant of time: I saw the gunners on the road point their hands and I heard them cry; I heard, too, a kind of sob from Blenkiron—all this before I realized myself what had happened. The next thing I saw was Sandy, already beyond the glacis, leaping with great bounds down the hill. They were shooting at him, but he heeded them not. For the space of a minute he was out of sight, and his whereabouts was shown only by the patter of bullets.

Then he came back—walking quite slowly up the last slope, and he was carrying something in his arms. The enemy fired no more; they realized what had happened.

He laid his burden down gently in a corner of the *castrol*. The cap had fallen off, and the hair was breaking loose. The face was very white but there was no wound or bruise on it.

"She was killed at once," I heard him saying. "Her back was broken by a shell-fragment. Dick, we must bury her here . . . You see, she . . . she liked me. I can make her no return but this."

We set the Companions to guard, and with infinite slowness, using our hands and our knives, we made a shallow grave below the eastern parapet. When it was done we covered her face with the linen cloak which Sandy had worn that morning. He lifted the body and laid it reverently in its place.

"I did not know that anything could be so light," he said.

IT WASN'T FOR ME to look on at that kind of scene. I went to the parapet with Blenkiron's field-glasses and had a stare at our friends on the road. There was no Turk there, and I guessed why, for it would not be easy to use the men of Islam against the wearer of the green ephod. The enemy were German or Austrian, and they had a field-gun. They seemed to have got it laid on our fort; but they were waiting. As I looked I saw behind them a massive figure I seemed to recognize. Stumm had come to see the destruction of his enemies.

To the east I saw another gun in the fields just below the main road. They had got us on both sides, and there was no way of escape. Hilda von Einem was to have a noble pyre and goodly company for the dark journey.

Dusk was falling now, a clear bright dusk where the stars pricked through a sheen of amethyst. The artillery were busy all around the horizon, and towards the pass on the other road, where Fort Palantuken stood, there was the dust and smoke of a furious bombardment. It seemed to me, too, that the guns on the other fronts had come nearer. Deve Boyun was hidden by a spur of hill, but up in the north, white clouds, like the streamers of evening, were hanging over the Euphrates glen. The whole firmament hummed and twanged like a taut string that has been struck . . .

As I looked, the gun to the west fired—the gun where Stumm was. The shell dropped ten yards to our right. A second later another fell behind us.

Blenkiron had dragged himself to the parapet. I don't suppose he had ever been shelled before, but his face showed curiosity rather than fear.

"Pretty poor shooting, I reckon," he said.

"On the contrary," I said, "they know their business. They're bracketing . . ."

The words were not out of my mouth when one fell right among us. It struck the far rim of the *castrol*, shattering the rock, but bursting mainly outside. We all ducked, and barring some small scratches no one was a penny the worse. I remember that much of the debris fell on Hilda von Einem's grave.

I pulled Blenkiron over the far parapet, and called on the rest to follow, meaning to take cover on the rough side of the hill. But as we showed ourselves shots rang out from our front, shots fired from a range of a few hundred yards. It was easy to see what had happened. Riflemen had been sent to hold us in rear. They would not assault so long as we remained in the *castrol*, but they would block any attempt to find safety outside it. Stumm and his gun had us at their mercy.

We crouched below the parapet again. "We may as well toss for it," I said. "There's only two ways—to stay here and be shelled or try to break through those fellows behind. Either's pretty unhealthy."

But I knew there was no choice. With Blenkiron crippled we were pinned to the *castrol*. Our numbers were up all right.

CHAPTER 22

The Guns of the North

BUT NO MORE shells fell.

The night grew dark and showed a field of glittering stars, for the air was sharpening again towards frost. We waited for an hour, crouching just behind the far parapets, but never came that ominous familiar whistle.

Then Sandy rose and stretched himself. "I'm hungry," he said. "Let's have out the food, Hussin. We've eaten nothing since before daybreak. I wonder what is the meaning of this respite?"

I fancied I knew.

"It's Stumm's way," I said. "He wants to torture us. He'll keep us hours on tenterhooks, while he sits over yonder exulting in what he thinks we're enduring. He has just enough imagination for that . . . He would rush us if he had the men. As it is, he's going to blow us to pieces, but do it slowly and smack his lips over it."

Sandy yawned. "We'll disappoint him, for we won't be worried, old man. We three are beyond that kind of fear."

"Meanwhile we're going to do the best we can," I said. "He's got the exact range for his whizz-bangs. We've got to find a hole somewhere just outside the *castrol*, and some sort of head-cover. We're bound to get damaged whatever happens, but we'll stick it out to the end. When they think they have finished with us and rush the place, there may be one of us alive to put a bullet through old Stumm. What do you say?"

They agreed, and after our meal Sandy and I crawled out to prospect, leaving the others on guard in case there should be an attack. We found a hollow in the glacis a little south of the *castrol*, and, working very quietly, managed to enlarge it and cut a kind of shallow cave in the hill. It would be no use against a direct hit, but it would give some cover from flying fragments. As I read the situation, Stumm could land as many shells as he pleased in the *castrol* and wouldn't bother to attend to the flanks. When the bad shelling began there would be shelter for one or two in the cave.

Our enemies were watchful. The riflemen on the east burnt Very

350

flares at intervals, and Stumm's lot sent up a great star-rocket. I remember that just before midnight hell broke loose round Fort Palantuken. No more Russian shells came into our hollow, but all the road to the east was under fire, and at the Fort itself there was a shattering explosion and a queer scarlet glow which looked as if a magazine had been hit. For about two hours the firing was intense, and then it died down. But it was towards the north that I kept turning my head. There seemed to be something different in the sound there, something sharper in the report of the guns, as if shells were dropping in a narrow valley whose rock walls doubled the echo. Had the Russians by any blessed chance worked round that flank?

I got Sandy to listen, but he shook his head. "Those guns are a dozen miles off," he said. "They're no nearer than three days ago. But it looks as if the sportsmen on the south might have a chance. When they break through and stream down the valley, they'll be puzzled to account for what remains of us . . . We're no longer three adventurers in the enemy's country. We're the advance guard of the Allies. Our pals don't know about us, and we're going to be cut off, which has happened to advance guards before now. But all the same, we're in our own battle-line again. Doesn't that cheer you, Dick?"

It cheered me wonderfully, for I knew now what had been the weight on my heart ever since I accepted Sir Walter's mission. It was the loneliness of it. I was fighting far away from my friends, far away from the true fronts of battle. It was a side-show which, whatever its importance, had none of the exhilaration of the main effort. But now we had come back to familiar ground. We were like the Highlanders cut off at Cité St Auguste on the first day of Loos, or those Scots Guards at Festubert of whom I had heard. Only, the others did not know of it, would never hear of it. If Peter succeeded he might tell the tale, but most likely he was lying dead somewhere in the no-man's-land between the lines. We should never be heard of again any more, but our work remained. Sir Walter would know that, and he would tell our few belongings that we had gone out in our country's service.

We were in the *castrol* again, sitting under the parapets. The same thoughts must have been in Sandy's mind, for he suddenly laughed.

"It's a queer ending, Dick. We simply vanish into the infinite. If the Russians get through they will never recognize what is left of us among so much of the wreckage of battle. The snow will soon cover us, and when the spring comes there will only be a few bleached bones. Upon my soul it is the kind of death I always wanted." And he quoted softly to himself a verse of an old Scots ballad:

> *"Mony's the ane for him maks mane,*
> *But nane sall ken whar he is gane.*
> *Ower his white banes, when they are bare,*
> *The wind sall blaw for evermair."*

"But our work lives," I cried, with a sudden great gasp of happiness. "It's the job that matters, not the men that do it. And our job's done. We have won, old chap—won hands down—and there is no going back on that. We have won anyway; and if Peter has had a slice of luck, we've scooped the pool . . . After all, we never expected to come out of this thing with our lives."

Blenkiron, with his leg stuck out stiffly before him, was humming quietly to himself, as he often did when he felt cheerful. He had only one song, "John Brown's Body"; usually only a line at a time, but now he got as far as the whole verse:

> *"He captured Harper's Ferry, with his nineteen men so true,*
> *And he frightened old Virginny till she trembled through and through.*
> *They hung him for a traitor, themselves the traitor crew,*
> *But his soul goes marching along."*

"Feeling good?" I asked.

"Fine. I'm about the luckiest man on God's earth, Major. I've always wanted to get into a big show, but I didn't see how it would come the way of a homely citizen like me, living in a steam-warmed house and going down town to my office every morning. I used to envy my old dad that fought at Chattanooga, and never forgot to tell you about it. But I guess Chattanooga was like a scrap in a Bowery bar compared to this. When I meet the old man in Glory he'll have to listen some to me . . ."

IT WAS JUST AFTER Blenkiron spoke that we got a reminder of Stumm's presence. The gun was well laid, for a shell plumped on the near edge of the *castrol*. It made an end of one of the Companions who was on guard there, badly wounded another, and a fragment gashed my thigh. We took refuge in the shallow cave, but some wild shooting from the east side brought us back to the parapets, for we feared an attack. None came, nor any more shells, and once again the night was quiet.

I asked Blenkiron if he had any near relatives.

"Why, no, except a sister's son, a college-boy who has no need of his uncle. It's fortunate that we three have no wives. I haven't any regrets, neither, for I've had a mighty deal out of life. I was thinking this morning that it was a pity I was going out when I had just got my duo-denum to listen to reason. But I reckon that's another of my mercies. The good God took away the pain in my stomach so that I might go to Him with a clear head and a thankful heart."

"We're lucky fellows," said Sandy; "we've all had our whack. When I remember the good times I've had I could sing a hymn of praise. We've lived long enough to know ourselves, and to shape ourselves into some kind of decency. But think of those boys who have given their lives freely when they scarcely knew what life meant. They were just at the beginning of the road, and they didn't know what dreary bits lay before them. It was all sunshiny and bright-coloured, and yet they gave it up without a moment's doubt. And think of the men with wives and children and homes that were the biggest things in life to them. For fellows like us to shirk would be black cowardice. It's small credit for us to stick it out. But when those others shut their teeth and went forward, they were blessed heroes . . ."

After that we fell silent. A man's thoughts at a time like that seem to be double-powered, and the memory becomes very sharp and clear. I don't know what was in the others' minds, but I know what filled my own . . .

I fancy it isn't the men who get most out of the world and are always buoyant and cheerful that most fear to die. Rather it is the weak-engined souls who go about with dull eyes, that cling most fiercely to life. They have not the joy of being alive which is a kind of earnest of immortality . . . I know that my thoughts were chiefly about the jolly things that I had seen and done; not regret, but gratitude. The panorama of blue moons on the veld unrolled itself before me, and hunter's nights in the bush, the taste of food and sleep, the bitter stimulus of dawn, the joy of wild adventure, the voices of old staunch friends. Hitherto the war had seemed to make a break with all that had gone before, but now the war was only part of the picture. I thought of my battalion, and the good fellows there, many of whom had fallen on the Loos parapets. I had never looked to come out of that myself. But I had been spared, and given the chance of a greater business, and I had succeeded. That was the tremendous fact, and my mood was humble gratitude to God and exultant pride. Death was a small price to pay for it. As Blenkiron would have said, I had got good value in the deal.

The night was getting bitter cold, as happens before dawn. It was frost again, and the sharpness of it woke our hunger. I got out the remnants of the food and wine and we had a last meal. I remember we pledged each other as we drank.

"We have eaten our Passover Feast," said Sandy. "When do you look for the end?"

"After dawn," I said. "Stumm wants daylight to get the full savour of his revenge."

SLOWLY THE SKY PASSED from ebony to grey, and black shapes of hill outlined themselves against it. A wind blew down the valley, bringing the acrid smell of burning, but something too of the freshness of morn. It stirred strange thoughts in me, and woke the old morning vigour of the blood which was never to be mine again. For the first time in that long vigil I was torn with a sudden regret.

"We must get into the cave before it is full light," I said. "We had better draw lots for the two to go."

The choice fell on one of the Companions and Blenkiron.

"You can count me out," said the latter. "If it's your wish to find a man to be alive when our friends come up to count their spoil, I guess I'm the worst of the lot. I'd prefer, if you don't mind, to stay here. I've made my peace with my Maker, and I'd like to wait quietly on His call. I'll play a game of Patience to pass the time."

He would take no denial, so we drew again, and the lot fell to Sandy.

"If I'm the last to go," he said, "I promise I don't miss. Stumm won't be long in following me."

He shook hands with his cheery smile, and he and the Companion slipped over the parapet in the final shadows before dawn.

BLENKIRON SPREAD his Patience cards on a flat rock, and dealt out the Double Napoleon. He was perfectly calm, and hummed to himself his only tune. For myself I was drinking in my last draught of the hill air. My contentment was going. I suddenly felt bitterly loath to die.

Something of the same kind must have passed through Blenkiron's head. He suddenly looked up and asked, "Sister Anne, Sister Anne, do you see anybody coming?"

I stood close to the parapet, watching every detail of the landscape as shown by the revealing daybreak. Up on the shoulders of the Palantuken snowdrifts lipped over the edges of the cliffs. I wondered when they would come down as avalanches. There was a kind of croft on one hillside, and from a hut the smoke of breakfast was beginning to curl. Stumm's gunners were awake and apparently holding council. Far down on the main road a convoy was moving—I heard the creak of the wheels two miles away, for the air was deathly still.

Then, as if a spring had been loosed, the world suddenly leaped to a hideous life. With a growl the guns opened round all the horizon. They were especially fierce to the south, where a *rafale* beat as I had never heard it before. The one glance I cast behind me showed the gap in the hills choked with fumes and dust.

But my eyes were on the north. From Erzerum city tall tongues of flame leaped from a dozen quarters. Beyond, towards the opening of the Euphrates glen, there was the sharp crack of field-guns. I strained eyes and ears, mad with impatience, and I read the riddle.

"Sandy," I yelled, "Peter has got through. The Russians are round the flank. The town is burning. Glory to God, we've won, we've won!"

And as I spoke the earth seemed to split beside me, and I was flung forward on the gravel which covered Hilda von Einem's grave.

As I PICKED MYSELF UP, and to my amazement found myself uninjured, I saw Blenkiron rubbing the dust out of his eyes and arranging a disordered card. He was singing aloud:

> *"He captured Harper's Ferry, with his nineteen men so true,*
> *And he frightened old Virginny . . ."*

"Say, Major," he cried, "I believe this game of mine is coming out."

I was now pretty well mad. The thought that old Peter had won, that *we* had won beyond our wildest dreams, that if we died there were those coming who would exact the uttermost vengeance, rode my brain like a fever. I sprang on the parapet and waved my hand to Stumm, shouting defiance. Rifle shots cracked out from behind, and I leaped back just in time for the next shell.

The charge must have been short, for it was a bad miss, landing somewhere on the glacis. The next was better and crashed on the near parapet, carving a great hole in the rocky *kranz*. This time my arm hung limp, broken by a fragment of stone, but I felt no pain. Blenkiron seemed to bear a charmed life, for he was smothered in dust, but unhurt. He blew the dust away from his cards very gingerly and went on playing.

"Sister Anne," he asked, "do you see anybody coming?"

Then came a dud which dropped neatly inside on the soft ground. I was determined to break for the open and chance the rifle fire, for if Stumm went on shooting the *castrol* was certain death. I caught Blenkiron round the middle, scattering his cards to the winds, and jumped over the parapet.

"Don't apologize, Sister Anne," said he. "The game was as good as won. But for God's sake drop me, for if you wave me like the banner of freedom I'll get plugged sure and good."

My one thought was to get cover for the next minutes, for I had an instinct that our vigil was near its end. The defences of Erzerum were crumbling like sand-castles, and it was a proof of the tenseness of my nerves that I seemed to be deaf to the sound. Stumm had seen us cross the parapet, and he started to sprinkle all the surroundings of the *castrol*. Blenkiron and I lay like a working party between the lines caught by machine-guns, taking a pull on ourselves as best we could. Sandy had some kind of cover, but we were on the bare farther slope, and the riflemen on that side might have had us at their mercy.

But no shots came from them. As I looked east, the hillside, which a little before had been held by our enemies, was as empty as the desert. And then I saw on the main road a sight which for a second time made me yell like a maniac. Down that glen came a throng of men and galloping limbers—a crazy, jostling crowd, spreading away beyond the road to the steep slopes, and leaving behind it many black dots to darken the snows. The gates of the South had yielded, and our friends were through them.

At that sight I forgot all about our danger. I didn't give a cent for Stumm's shells. I didn't believe he could hit me. The fate which had mercifully preserved us for the first taste of victory would see us through to the end.

I remember bundling Blenkiron along the hill to find Sandy. But our news was anticipated. For down our own side-glen came the same broken tumult of men. More; for at their backs, far up at the throat of the pass, I saw horsemen—the horsemen of the pursuit. Old Nicholas had flung his cavalry in.

Sandy was on his feet, with his lips set and his eye abstracted. If his face hadn't been burned black by weather it would have been pale as a dish-clout. A man like him doesn't make up his mind for death and then be given his life again without being wrenched out of his bearings. I thought he didn't understand what had happened, so I beat him on the shoulders.

"Man, d'you see?" I cried. "The Cossacks! The Cossacks! God! how they're taking that slope! They're into them now. By Heaven, we'll ride with them! We'll get the gun horses!"

A little knoll prevented Stumm and his men from seeing what was happening farther up the glen, till the first wave of the rout was on them. He had gone on bombarding the *castrol* and its environs while the world was cracking over his head. The gun team was in the hollow below the road, and down the hill among the boulders we crawled, Blenkiron as lame as a duck, and me with a limp left arm.

The poor beasts were straining at their pickets and sniffing the morning wind, which brought down the thick fumes of the great bombardment and the indescribable babbling cries of a beaten army. Before we reached them that maddened horde had swept down on them, men panting and gasping in their flight, many of them bloody from wounds, many tottering in the first stages of collapse and death. I saw the horses seized by a dozen hands, and a desperate fight for their possession. But as we halted there our eyes were fixed on the battery on the road above us, for round it was now sweeping the van of the retreat.

I had never seen a rout before, when strong men come to the end of their tether and only their broken shadows stumble towards the refuge they never find. No more had Stumm, poor devil. I had no ill-will left for him, though coming down that hill I was rather hoping that the two of us might have a final scrap. He was a brute and a bully, but, by God! he was a man. I heard his great roar when he saw the tumult, and the next I saw was his monstrous figure working at the gun. He swung it south and turned it on the fugitives.

But he never fired it. The press was on him, and the gun was swept sideways. He stood up, a foot higher than any of them, and he seemed to be trying to check the rush with his pistol. There is power in numbers, even though every unit is broken and fleeing. For a second to that wild crowd Stumm was the enemy, and they had strength enough to crush him. The wave flowed round and then across him. I saw the butt-ends of rifles crash on his head and shoulders, and the next second the stream had passed over his body.

That was God's judgement on the man who had set himself above his kind.

Sandy gripped my shoulder and was shouting in my ear:

"They're coming, Dick. Look at the grey devils! . . . Oh, God be thanked, it's our friends!"

The next minute we were tumbling down the hillside, Blenkiron hopping on one leg between us. I heard dimly Sandy crying, "Oh, well done our side!" and Blenkiron declaiming about Harper's Ferry, but I had no voice at all and no wish to shout. I know the tears were in my eyes, and that if I had been left alone I would have sat down and cried with pure thankfulness. For sweeping down the glen came a cloud of grey cavalry on little wiry horses, a cloud which stayed not for the rear of the fugitives, but swept on like a flight of rainbows, with the steel of their lance-heads glittering in the winter sun. They were riding for Erzerum.

Remember that for three months we had been with the enemy and had never seen the face of an Ally in arms. We had been cut off from the fellowship of a great cause, like a fort surrounded by an army. And now we were delivered, and there fell around us the warm joy of comradeship as well as the exultation of victory.

We flung caution to the winds, and went stark mad. Sandy, still in his emerald coat and turban, was scrambling up the farther slope of the hollow, yelling greetings in every language known to man. The leader saw him, with a word checked his men for a moment—it was marvellous to see the horses reined in in such a break-neck ride—and from the squadron half a dozen troopers swung loose and wheeled towards us. Then a man in a grey overcoat and a sheepskin cap was on the ground beside us wringing our hands.

"You are safe, my old friends"—it was Peter's voice that spoke—"I will take you back to our army, and get you breakfast."

"No, by the Lord, you won't," cried Sandy. "We've had the rough end of the job and now we'll have the fun. Look after Blenkiron and these fellows of mine. I'm going to ride knee by knee with your sportsmen for the city."

Peter spoke a word, and two of the Cossacks dismounted. The next I knew I was mixed up in the cloud of greycoats, galloping down the road up which the morning before we had strained to the *castrol*.

That was the great hour of my life, and to live through it was worth a dozen years of slavery. With a broken left arm I had little hold on my beast, so I trusted my neck to him and let him have his will. Black with dirt and smoke, hatless, with no kind of uniform, I was a wilder figure than any Cossack. I soon was separated from Sandy, who had two hands and a better horse, and seemed resolute to press forward to the very van. That would have been suicide for me, and I had all I could do to keep my place in the bunch I rode with.

But, Great God! what an hour it was! There was loose shooting on our flank, but nothing to trouble us, though the gun team of some Austrian howitzer, struggling madly at a bridge, gave us a bit of a tussle. Everything flitted past me like smoke, or like the mad *finale* of a dream just before waking. I knew the living movement under me, and the companionship of men, but all dimly, for at heart I was alone, grappling with the realization of a new world. I felt the shadows of the Palantuken glen fading, and the great burst of light as we emerged on the wider valley. Somewhere before us was a pall of smoke seamed with red flames, and beyond the darkness of still higher hills. All that time I was dreaming, crooning daft catches of song to myself, so happy, so deliriously happy that I dared not try to think. I kept muttering a kind of prayer made up of Bible words to Him who had shown me His goodness in the land of the living.

But as we drew out from the skirts of the hills and began the long slope to the city, I woke to clear consciousness. I felt the smell of sheepskin and lathered horses, and above all the bitter smell of fire. Down in the trough lay Erzerum, now burning in many places, and from the east, past the silent forts, horsemen were closing in on it. I yelled to my comrades that we were nearest, that we would be first in the city, and they nodded happily and shouted their strange war-cries. As we topped the last ridge I saw below me the van of our charge—a dark mass on the snow—while the broken enemy on both sides were flinging away their arms and scattering in the fields.

In the very front, now nearing the city ramparts, was one man. He was like the point of the steel spear soon to be driven home. In the clear morning air I could see that he did not wear the uniform of the invaders. He was turbaned and rode like one possessed, and against the snow I caught the dark sheen of emerald. As he rode it seemed that the fleeing Turks were stricken still, and sank by the roadside with eyes strained after his unheeding figure . . .

Then I knew that the prophecy had been true, and that their prophet had not failed them. The long-looked-for revelation had come. Greenmantle had appeared at last to an awaiting people.

AFTERWORD

By Brian Stableford, BA, D.Phil

Afterword

I T IS EXTREMELY USEFUL both to have *The Thirty-Nine Steps* and *Greenmantle* within a single cover. The former stands perfectly well on its own, but is perhaps best regarded as a prologue to its much more substantial sequel. *Greenmantle*, likewise, can be read without prior knowledge of Richard Hannay's exploits in *The Thirty-Nine Steps*, but it will be enjoyed far more by readers already familiar with the character of Buchan's hero, as it is described and developed in the first adventure.

Buchan wrote *The Thirty-Nine Steps* in 1914, in a relatively short space of time, when ill-health forced him to rest. He did not view the writing of the novel as a serious literary project, but rather as a way of alleviating the frustration he felt at having to delay his participation in the First World War. Perhaps because of this very relaxed approach, Buchan succeeded in endowing his story with a marvellous spontaneity and frankness of feeling. When it was finished, he sent it to *Blackwood's Magazine*, which had earlier serialized his weightier thriller, *The Power-House*. But this time he was published under the pseudonym "H.de V". He did not attach his own name to *The Thirty-Nine Steps* until it was issued in book form in 1915, by which time it had received considerable praise from the magazine's readers and reviewers.

John Buchan dedicated the book to Thomas Nelson, the friend and publisher for whom he worked for many years. In his dedication he referred to his story as a "shocker", thus associating it with the kind of novels which at that time were produced in a cheap format (retailing at a shilling rather than the 7s 6d that was standard for longer and more luxuriously bound volumes) and which usually dealt in lurid fashion with matters of crime and espionage—or, in Buchan's words: "romance where the incidents defy the probabilities, and march just inside the borders of the possible". Buchan may have modestly judged *The Thirty-Nine Steps* to be an "elementary type of tale", but he filled it with his customary grace, his usual loving and atmospheric descriptions of the Scottish countryside, and put into its hero's mind the hopeful and determinedly pacifist ideals which preoccupied his own mind as the world entered the long-anticipated "war to end war".

The Thirty-Nine Steps is probably best known these days as a film. The version made by Alfred Hitchcock in 1935, with Robert Donat as Hannay, is one of the director's classics, a cardinal example of the kind of thriller he loved to make, in which an ordinary man becomes accidentally caught up in matters of international espionage and is forced to flee from the villains and the forces of law and order alike, while keeping uneasy custody of the key to the mystery. Much of the film is, however, pure invention on Hitchcock's part. Donat's Hannay spends a great deal of his time handcuffed to Madeleine Carroll—a situation made even more theatrical by her belief that he is a murderer—and this device is repeated in the 1959 version starring Kenneth More and the 1978 version starring Robert Powell. The addition of a female role was considered necessary, not merely because every popular film had to have one, but because a film, unlike a book, cannot give the viewer access to a hero's thoughts unless he has an interlocutor.

In the memoir which she wrote after her husband's death, *John Buchan by his Wife and Friends* (1947), Baroness Tweedsmuir says that, in her opinion, the 1935 film would have been better had it stuck to the original story, but notes that Buchan himself had no objection to the alteration and enjoyed the film. There is no doubt, however, that Hitchcock altered the mood and manner of Buchan's story, and in the process lost some of the aspects which make it unique and precious. The strengths of *The Thirty-Nine Steps* lie in its descriptions of the Scottish landscape and, most particularly, in the steadfast character of Richard Hannay.

Hannay introduces himself as an ordinary man, but not an ordinary Englishman (the talk of the ordinary Englishman, he tells us in the very first paragraph, makes him sick). His personality has been invigorated, as Buchan thought his own had been, by time spent in Africa. He has brought back from that experience not merely the Imperialist convictions that Buchan held dear, but also an awesomely competent pragmatism, born of his exploits as a mining engineer, which makes him want to do things and do them properly, fearless of getting his hands dirty. Boredom impels him into his adventure, but a hardheaded sense of duty and necessity pulls him through it. He is a rank amateur in the business of international espionage, but takes to it like a duck to water.

One can see why Alfred Hitchcock despaired of the climax of the novel, when Hannay and his enemies, having come face to face at a critical moment, sit down to play bridge, but it is a fittingly quiet conclusion to the process of personal development which Hannay has been through. Buchan always intended his hero to triumph through gentleness, courtesy and intelligence rather than melodramatic derring-do. Indeed, he stated as much in an address to the English Association in 1931 when he set out a manifesto for all thrillers, stressing that the odds must be heavily weighed against the hero, so that the magnitude of his achievement might properly be appreciated, and that his must be a victory in which "weakness [wins] against might, gentleness and courtesy against brutality, brains . . . against mere animal strength".

Greenmantle, published in 1916, just two years after *The Thirty-Nine Steps*, was one of the first, and certainly one of the best, novels of wartime secret service ever written. Hannay has now become a professional secret agent. His varied experience makes him useful for such work, but he requires assistance from others of equally varied experience: the American agent John Blenkiron, the matter-of-fact Boer Peter Pienaar (whose good example is cited more than once in *The Thirty-Nine Steps*); and the remarkable Sandy Arbuthnot, who has the gift of being able to fit himself perfectly to the role of an Islamic Holy Man. Some critics have assumed Arbuthnot was based on T.E. Lawrence, later a close friend of Buchan's, but the character was actually based on Aubrey Herbert, the younger brother of one of Buchan's Oxford friends who served in Turkey during the war.

It is largely because Hannay's associates have lived long among men of other nations and other races that they are able to blend themselves, chameleon-fashion, into almost any social situation on either side of enemy lines. This ability is crucial to the plot, but it also gives Buchan's characters a useful insight into the motives and ambitions of their adversaries. Unlike other thriller writers, Buchan never demonizes the enemy or reduces him to a single ugly stereotype. Given the tenor of First World War propaganda, it was a brave and generous move on Buchan's part to portray the Kaiser so sympathetically in the novel.

The plot of *Greenmantle* draws upon Buchan's eventual experience as a correspondent at the front, and upon the information which he routinely gathered for *The Times*, and for the partwork history of the war which he produced for Nelson's throughout the conflict. The story not only has a conviction and an immediacy which no other contemporary work matched, but it also encapsulates Buchan's evolving consciousness of the war and the lessons he learned from it. Much later he was to write: "Slowly I began to see the war as a gigantic cosmic drama, embracing every quarter of the globe and the whole orbit of man's life . . . it had an apocalyptic splendour of design . . . It was a war won not by the genius of the few, but by the faithfulness of the many. There was no leader, civil or military, to whom I felt I could give unreasoned trust, but I could confide implicitly in the mass of my own people." One can see in the pages of *Greenmantle* the first emergence of Buchan's notion of the war as something more than a political struggle, as a vital phase in the evolution of great idea-systems like Islam and the Empire and also as an arena in which human nature itself was being subjected to searching examination. It is nowadays unfashionable to see the First World War in those terms—or, if we do, to find anything in its record of mass slaughter to compliment or admire—but the heartening effect that *Greenmantle* had on those who were fighting the war, while its end was still far off, must have been profound. The novel offers modern readers a way to see the war as its proudest and most ardent combatants saw it, and is as valuable in its own fashion as the agonized poetry penned in the trenches of Flanders.

Like its predecessor, *Greenmantle* is gripping not simply because of its brisk pace, but because the text communicates a strong sense of the importance of what is going on. The reader is aware that an awesomely large matter is at stake—the possible complication of the Great War by an all-out Islamic jihad—but is never allowed to lose sight of the ideals of duty, heroism and civilized behaviour whose preservation is as vital as the successful completion of the mission. For Buchan, the end never justifies the means; Richard Hannay is not the kind of hero who is inclined to casual homicide. Indeed, he does not play a particularly active role in the story he narrates, and the only real episode of impulsive derring-do is entrusted to Peter Pienaar. Hannay's own heroics consist of showing resourcefulness and grace, even in retreat and under fire. He is perpetually escaping disaster by a hair's-breadth, but this never instils in him any bitter lust for revenge, and the respect which he has for his enemies, even the thoroughly nasty Stumm, is always evident.

The fact that Buchan chose a bizarrely charismatic woman as his villain may seem to some to give the book a misogynistic subtext, but such figures were by no means uncommon in the kind of "boys' books" which were read at the time as avidly by adults as juveniles—Rider Haggard's *She* is the most obvious example. The other device which might seem out of place to some contemporary readers, the premonitory dream which leads Hannay and his companions to the scene of their climactic last stand, is a kind of incident which Buchan took seriously, and believed in. Many of his short stories revolve around such momentary revelations of a supernatural framework within which the observable world is contained, and his autobiography, *Memory Hold-the-Door*, refers to incidents in his own life which gave rise to similarly uncanny feelings.

The central characters of *Greenmantle* subsequently reappeared in *Mr Standfast* (1919), *The Three Hostages* (1924), *The Courts of the Morning* (1929) and *The Island of Sheep* (1936). All of these are eminently readable adventure stories, but the series suffered a certain loss of vitality and sense of direction as the characters and their devoted readers found themselves further distanced from the stable and war-free world which the Great War had been intended to bring into being. None of these subsequent books has the immediacy of *Greenmantle* because all of them are backward-looking, and the later ones are defiantly nostalgic, as if the author were haunted by an awareness of their own dubious relevance. *The Thirty-Nine Steps* and *Greenmantle* labour under no such handicap. They are both forward-looking and forward-moving, and in no way diminished by the shadow of doubt that history has cast over the ideals which they encapsulate. Both novels retain all their candour, verve and stoutness of heart, and are fully capable of rewarding the modern reader.

ISBN 978-0-656-66362-0
PIBN 10480173

Protokoll

über die

Verhandlungen des Parteitages

der

Sozialdemokratischen Partei Deutschlands.

Abgehalten zu Halle a. S.

vom 12. bis 18. Oktober 1890.

Berlin 1890.

Verlag der Expedition des „Berliner Volksblatt".

(Th. Glocke.)

Das Programm der Partei.

I. Die Arbeit ist die Quelle alles Reichthums und aller Kultur, und da allgemein nutzbringende Arbeit nur durch die Gesellschaft möglich ist, so gehört der Gesellschaft, das heißt allen ihren Gliedern, das gesammte Arbeitsprodukt, bei allgemeiner Arbeitspflicht, nach gleichem Recht, Jedem nach seinen vernunftgemäßen Bedürfnissen.

In der heutigen Gesellschaft sind die Arbeitsmittel Monopol der Kapitalistenklasse; die hierdurch bedingte Abhängigkeit der Arbeiterklasse ist die Ursache des Elends und der Knechtschaft in allen Formen.

Die Befreiung der Arbeit erfordert die Verwandlung der Arbeitsmittel in Gemeingut der Gesellschaft und die genossenschaftliche Regelung der Gesammtarbeit mit gemeinnütziger Verwendung und gerechter Vertheilung des Arbeitsertrages.

Die Befreiung der Arbeit muß das Werk der Arbeiterklasse sein, der gegenüber alle anderen Klassen nur eine reaktionäre Masse sind.

II. Von diesen Grundsätzen ausgehend, erstrebt die sozialistische Arbeiterpartei Deutschlands mit allen Mitteln den freien Staat und die sozialistische Gesellschaft, die Zerbrechung des ehernen Lohngesetzes durch Abschaffung des Systems der Lohnarbeit, die Aufhebung der Ausbeutung in jeder Gestalt, die Beseitigung aller sozialen und politischen Ungleichheit.

Die sozialistische Arbeiterpartei Deutschlands, obgleich zunächst im nationalen Rahmen wirkend, ist sich des internationalen Charakters der Arbeiterbewegung bewußt und entschlossen, alle Pflichten, welche derselbe den Arbeitern auferlegt, zu erfüllen, um die Verbrüderung aller Menschen zur Wahrheit zu machen.

Die sozialistische Arbeiterpartei Deutschlands fordert, um die Lösung der sozialen Frage anzubahnen, die Errichtung von sozialistischen Produktivgenossenschaften mit Staatshülfe unter der demokratischen Kontrolle des arbeitenden Volkes. Die Produktivgenossenschaften sind für Industrie und Ackerbau in solchem Umfange in's Leben zu rufen, daß aus ihnen die sozialistische Organisation der Gesammtarbeit entsteht.

1*

Die sozialistische Arbeiterpartei fordert als Grundlagen des Staates:

1. Allgemeines, gleiches, direktes Wahl- und Stimmrecht, mit geheimer und obligatorischer Stimmabgabe aller Staatsangehörigen vom zwanzigsten Lebensjahre an für alle Wahlen und Abstimmungen in Staat und Gemeinde. Der Wahl- oder Abstimmungstag muß ein Feiertag sein.

2. Direkte Gesetzgebung durch das Volk. Entscheidung über Krieg und Frieden durch das Volk.

3. Allgemeine Wehrhaftigkeit. Volkswehr an Stelle der stehenden Heere.

4. Abschaffung aller Ausnahmegesetze, namentlich der Preß-, Vereins- und Versammlungsgesetze, überhaupt aller Gesetze, welche die freie Meinungsäußerung, das freie Denken und Forschen beschränken.

5. Rechtsprechung durch das Volk. Unentgeltliche Rechtspflege.

6. Allgemeine und gleiche Volkserziehung durch den Staat. Allgemeine Schulpflicht. Unentgeltlicher Unterricht in allen Bildungsanstalten. Erklärung der Religion zur Privatsache.

Die sozialistische Arbeiterpartei Deutschlands fordert innerhalb der heutigen Gesellschaft:

1. Möglichste Ausdehnung der politischen Rechte und Freiheiten im Sinne der obigen Forderungen.

2. Eine einzige progressive Einkommensteuer für Staat und Gemeinde, anstatt aller bestehenden, insbesondere der das Volk belastenden indirekten Steuern.

3. Unbeschränktes Koalitionsrecht.

4. Ein den Gesellschaftsbedürfnissen entsprechender Normalarbeitstag. Verbot der Sonntagsarbeit.

5. Verbot der Kinderarbeit und aller die Gesundheit und Sittlichkeit schädigenden Frauenarbeit.

6. Schutzgesetze für Leben und Gesundheit der Arbeiter. Sanitätliche Kontrolle der Arbeiterwohnungen. Ueberwachung der Bergwerke, der Fabrik-, Werkstatt-, und Haus-Industrie durch von den Arbeitern gewählte Beamte. Ein wirksames Haftpflichtgesetz.

7. Regelung der Gefängnisarbeit.

8. Volle Selbstverwaltung für alle Arbeiterhülfs- und Unterstützungskassen.

Die Organisation der Partei.

§ 1.

Zur Partei gehörig wird jede Person betrachtet, die sich zu den Grundsätzen des Parteiprogramms bekennt und die Partei nach Kräften unterstützt.

§ 2.

Zur Partei kann nicht gehören, wer sich eines groben Verstoßes gegen die Grundsätze des Parteiprogramms oder wer sich ehrloser Handlungen schuldig gemacht hat.

Ueber die Zugehörigkeit zur Partei entscheiden die Parteigenossen der einzelnen Orte oder Reichstagswahlkreise.

Gegen diese Entscheidungen steht den Betroffenen die Berufung an die Parteileitung und den Parteitag zu. .

Vertrauensmänner.

§ 3.

Die Parteigenossen in den einzelnen Reichstags = Wahlkreisen wählen in öffentlichen Versammlungen zur Wahrnehmung der Parteiinteressen einen oder mehrere Vertrauensmänner. Die Art der Wahl dieser Vertrauensmänner ist Sache der in den einzelnen Kreisen wohnenden Genossen.

§ 4.

Die Wahl der Vertrauensmänner erfolgt alljährlich und zwar im Anschlusse an den voraufgegangenen Parteitag.

Die Vertrauensmänner haben ihre Wahl mit Angabe ihrer genauen Adresse sofort der Parteileitung mitzutheilen.

§ 5.

Tritt ein Vertrauensmann zurück oder tritt sonstwie eine Vakanz ein, so haben die Parteigenossen umgehend eine Neuwahl vorzunehmen und davon entsprechend § 4 Abs. 2 der Parteileitung Mittheilung zu machen.

§ 6.

Da wo aus gesetzlichen Gründen die in den vorstehenden Paragraphen gegebenen Vorschriften unausführbar sind, haben die Parteigenossen den örtlichen Verhältnissen entsprechende Einrichtungen zu treffen.

Parteitag.

§ 7.

Alljährlich findet ein Parteitag statt, der von der Parteileitung einzuberufen ist.

Hat der vorhergehende Parteitag über den Ort, an welchem der nächste Parteitag stattfinden soll, keine Bestimmung getroffen, so hat die Parteileitung mit der Reichstags-Vertretung hierüber sich zu verständigen.

§ 8.

Die Einberufung des Parteitages muß spätestens 4 Wochen vor dem Termin der Abhaltung desselben durch das offizielle Parteiorgan mit Angabe der provisorischen Tagesordnung erfolgen. Die Einladung zur Beschickung des Parteitages ist mindestens dreimal in angemessenen Zwischenräumen zu wiederholen.

Anträge der Parteigenossen für die Tagesordnung des Parteitages sind bei der Parteileitung einzureichen, die dieselben spätestens 10 Tage vor der des Parteitages durch das offizielle Parteiorgan bekannt zu geben hat.

§ 9.

Der Parteitag bildet die oberste Vertretung der Partei.

Zur Theilnahme an demselben sind berechtigt:

1. die Delegirten der Partei aus den einzelnen Wahlkreisen, mit der Einschränkung, daß in der Regel kein Wahlkreis durch mehr als 3 Personen vertreten sein darf.

    Insoweit nicht unter den gewählten Vertretern des Wahlkreises Frauen sich befinden, können weibliche Vertreter in besonderen Frauenversammlungen gewählt werden.

2. die Mitglieder der Reichstags-Fraktion,

3. die Mitglieder der Parteileitung.

Die Mitglieder der Reichstags-Fraktion und der Parteileitung haben in allen die parlamentarische und die geschäftliche Leitung der Partei betreffenden Fragen nur berathende Stimme.

Der Parteitag prüft die Legitimation seiner Theilnehmer, wählt seine Leitung und bestimmt seine Geschäftsordnung selbst.

§ 10.

Zu den Aufgaben des Parteitages gehören:

1. Entgegennahme des Berichts über die Geschäftsthätigkeit der Parteileitung und über die parlamentarische Thätigkeit der Abgeordneten.

2. Die Bestimmung des Orts, an welchem die Parteileitung ihren Sitz zu nehmen hat.

8. Die Wahl der Parteileitung.

4. Die Beschlußfassung über die Parteiorganisation und alle das Parteileben berührenden Fragen.

5. Die Beschlußfassung über die eingegangenen Anträge.

§ 11.

Ein außerordentlicher Parteitag kann einberufen werden:

1. durch die Parteileitung;

2. auf Antrag der Reichstags-Fraktion;

3. auf Antrag von mindestens 15 Wahlkreisen.

Falls die Parteileitung sich weigert, einem Antrag auf Einberufung eines außerordentlichen Parteitages stattzugeben, so ist derselbe durch die Reichstags-Fraktion einzuberufen. Als Versammlungsort eines außerordentlichen Parteitages ist ein geographisch möglichst günstig gelegener Ort zu bestimmen.

§ 12.

Die Einberufung des außerordentlichen Parteitages muß spätestens 14 Tage vor dem Termin der Abhaltung desselben durch das offizielle Parteiorgan in wenigstens drei aufeinanderfolgenden Nummern mit Angabe der Tagesordnung erfolgen.

Anträge der Parteigenossen sind spätestens 7 Tage vor der Abhaltung des Parteitages im offiziellen Parteiorgan zu veröffentlichen.

Im Uebrigen gelten für die außerordentlichen Parteitage dieselben Bestimmungen wie für die ordentlichen Parteitage (§§ 8—10).

Parteileitung.

§ 13.

Die Parteileitung besteht aus 12 Personen, und zwar aus 2 Vorsitzenden, 2 Schriftführern, 1 Kassirer und 7 Kontrolleuren.

Die Wahl der Parteileitung erfolgt durch den Parteitag mittelst Stimmzettel.

Nach erfolgter Wahl hat die Parteileitung ihre Konstituirung vorzunehmen und dieselbe im offiziellen Parteiorgan bekannt zu machen.

Die Parteileitung verfügt nach eigenem Ermessen über die vorhandenen Gelder.

§ 14.

Die Mitglieder der Parteileitung können für ihre Thätigkeit eine Besoldung beziehen. Die Höhe derselben wird durch den Parteitag festgesetzt.

§ 15.

Die Parteileitung besorgt die Parteigeschäfte, kontrollirt die prinzipielle Haltung der Parteiorgane, beruft die Parteitage und erstattet auf denselben über ihre Thätigkeit Bericht.

§ 16.

Scheidet einer der Vorsitzenden, Schriftführer oder der Kassirer aus, so ist die Vakanz durch eine von den Kontrolleuren vorzunehmende Neuwahl zu ergänzen.

Parteiorgan.

§ 17.

Zum offiziellen Parteiorgan wird das „Berliner Volksblatt" bestimmt. Dasselbe erhält vom 1. Januar 1891 ab den Titel:

„Vorwärts"

Berliner Volksblatt.

Central-Organ der sozialdemokratischen Partei Deutschlands.

Alle offiziellen Bekanntmachungen sind an hervorragender Stelle des redaktionellen Theils zu veröffentlichen.

Abänderung der Organisation.

§ 18.

Aenderungen an der Organisation der Partei können nur durch einen Parteitag vorgenommen werden, doch muß die absolute Mehrheit der anwesenden Vertreter sich dafür erklären.

Anträge auf Abänderung der Organisation können nur berathen werden, wenn sie innerhalb der Fristen, welche die §§ 8 und 12 vorschreiben, zur öffentlichen Kenntniß der Parteigenossen gelangten.

Eine Abweichung von der letzteren Bestimmung ist nur dann zulässig, wenn mindestens 3/4 der anwesenden Vertreter auf einem Parteitag sich für die Abweichung entscheiden.

Tagesordnung des Parteitages.

Sonntag den 12. Oktober, Abends 7 Uhr:

Vorversammlung. Konstituirung des Parteitages und Wahl einer Kommission für die Prüfung der Vollmachten.

Montag den 13. Oktober und die folgenden Tage:

1. Bericht der Parteileitung. Berichterstatter: Bebel.
2. Bericht der Revisoren.
3. Bericht über die parlamentarische Thätigkeit der Reichstags-Fraktion. Berichterstatter: Singer.
4. Die Organisation der Partei. Berichterstatter: Auer.
5. Vornahme der Wahlen auf Grund der angenommenen Organisation.
6. Das Programm der Partei. Berichterstatter: Liebknecht.
7. Die Parteipresse. Berichterstatter: Auer und Bebel.
8. Die Stellung der Partei zu Streiks und Boykotts. Berichterstatter: Grillenberger und Kloß-Stuttgart.
9. Anträge aus der Mitte des Parteitages.

Bureau des Parteitages.

Vorsitzende:

Singer, Berlin. — Dietz, Stuttgart.

Schriftführer:

Agster, Stuttgart.	Ernst, Berlin.	Oertel, Nürnberg.
Blos, Stuttgart.	Frohme, Hannover.	Schippel, Friedrichsh.
Bruhns, Bremen.	Müller, Schkeuditz.	Schwartz, Lübeck.

Mandats=Prüfungs=Kommission:

Ewald, Brandenburg.	Hirsch, Weißensee.	Pfannkuch, Kassel.
Grothe, Halle.	Hosang, Dessau.	Schwarz, Hamburg.
Hahn, Gera.	Kloß, Stuttgart.	Wernau, Berlin.

Neuner=Kommission.

Ewald, Brandenburg.	Kaden, Dresden.	Müller, Darmstadt.
Geck, Offenbach.	Kloß, Stuttgart.	Pfannkuch, Kassel.
Grimpe, Elberfeld.	Meist, Köln a'. Rh.	Reißhaus, Erfurt.

Fünfundzwanziger=Kommission.

Auer, Berlin.	Frau Ihrer, Velten.	Scherm, Nürnberg.
Bebel, Berlin.	Kandt, Rostock.	Schönfeld, Dresden.
Behrend, Frankf. a. O.	Keßler, Berlin.	Schulz, Berlin.
Bertram, Hannover.	Kühn, Langenbielau.	Segitz, Fürth.
Daßbach, Hanau.	Lorenz, Königsberg.	Slomke, Bielefeld.
Eumel, Frankf. a. M.	Lütjens, Hamburg.	Stern, Stuttgart.
Hänsler, Mannheim.	Malke, Flensburg.	Theiß, Hamburg.
Herbert, Stettin.	Riemann, Chemnitz.	Vollmar, München.
	Wernau, Berlin.	

Auswärtige Gäste.

Dr. Adler, Wien.	Domela = Nieuwen-	Ladour, Paris.
Anseele, Gent.	huis, Haag.	Frau Marx-Aveling,
Beck, Zürich.	Duc-Quercy, Paris.	London.
Branting, Stockholm.	Férroul, Paris.	Mundberg, Kopenhg.
Frl. Cohen, Amster-	Guesde, Paris.	Pokorny, Wien.
dam.	Hanser, Wien.	Scherrer, St. Gallen.
	Wobsty, Warschau.	Wullschleger, Basel.

Protokoll.

Eröffnungs-Sitzung: Sonntag, 12. Oktober, Abends 7 Uhr, im großen Saale des Lokals „Zum Hofjäger".

Der Saal ist festlich geschmückt. Von den Wänden grüßen die umkränzten Bilder unserer Todten herab: Geib, Bracke, Hasenclever, Kräcker, York und Kayser. Marx' und Lassalle's Bildnisse sind über der Tribüne vereint unter der Gestalt einer Freiheitsgöttin; unten im Bilde geht die Sonne der Gerechtigkeit auf, während das Schiff der Sozialdemokratie die Wellen kühn durchschneidet und der Zukunft entgegeneilt. Quer über der Tribüne steht auf breitem Bande der alte Schlachtruf: Proletarier aller Länder vereinigt Euch! Zwei rothe Fahnen wallen zu beiden Seiten der Tribüne herab. Auf der einen liest man: Sozialdemokratischer Parteitag zu Halle; auf der anderen: Gleichheit, Freiheit und Brüderlichkeit.

Zahlreiche Schilder hängen an den Wänden, welche die bedeutendsten Tage der Geschichte der deutschen Sozialdemokratie nennen.

Ungefähr 400 Delegirte, fast alle Mitglieder der Reichstags-Fraktion, zahlreiche Hallenser, sowie eine Anzahl ausländischer Genossen sind anwesend.

Im Namen der Reichstags-Fraktion, der Einberuferin des Parteitages, eröffnet Genosse Liebknecht die Verhandlungen: Als dem ältesten der Einberufer dieses Kongresses ist mir die ehrenvolle Aufgabe geworden, die hier versammelten Delegirten der deutschen Arbeiter, sowie die fremden Gäste, welche unseren Kongreß mit ihrer Anwesenheit beehrt haben, zu begrüßen. Ich thue dies hiermit und eröffne zugleich den Kongreß der deutschen Sozialdemokratie. Die Zahl der Theilnehmer war von uns von Anfang an hoch geschätzt worden; aber unsere höchsten Schätzungen hat die Wirklichkeit weit übertroffen. Die zahlreiche Anwesenheit von Delegirten verkündet bereits das gewaltige Wachsthum der deutschen Sozialdemokratie. Der Kongreß, welcher heute beginnt, ist der erste welcher nach dreizehn Jahren wieder auf deutschem Boden tagt' In diesen dreizehn Jahren liegen zwölf Jahre der Herrschaft des Sozialistengesetzes — zwölf Jahre des Kampfes, heißen, ununterbrochenen, alle Kräfte anspannenden Kampfes. Die Gegner schonten

uns nicht; und wir, zu stolz und zu stark, um uns feig zu fügen,
gaben Schlag auf Schlag zurück, und so haben wir das Gesetz
überwunden. Der Kampf aber hat auch schwere Opfer gekostet
und wie viele der tapferften Kämpfer find auf dem Feld der Ehre
geblieben! Da an den Wänden fchauen manche derfelben auf uns
herab, ein Geib, ein Bracke, ein Hafenclever, ein Kayfer und wie
fie fonft alle heißen. Und wie groß ift die Zahl der Ungenannten
und zum Theil Unbekannten, die in diefem Kampfe ihr Leben
gelaffen, und auch Derer, die ihre Gefundheit, ihr Vermögen eingebüßt haben. So fchwer aber auch die Opfer waren, fie find nicht
umfonft gebracht worden. Und fie haben unfere Kräfte nicht ge-
fchwächt, fondern geftärkt. An die Stelle der Niedergeworfenen
traten Andere, und wenn auch unfere vormarfchirende Armee eine
lange Linie Gefallener oder müde Zurückgebliebener aufzuweifen
hat, unfer Vormarfch ift nicht aufgehalten, unfere Reihen find nicht
gelichtet worden; im Gegentheil: je zahlreicher die Opfer, defto zahlreicher der Zuzug, defto größer die Begeifterung. Und je höher
und ftolzer wir unfere Fahne trugen, defto mehr erkannten weite
Kreife des Volkes außerhalb der Partei, daß durch die Sozialdemokratie allein die Erlöfung für das arbeitende Volk, für die
gefammte darbende Menfchheit zu finden fei.

Wir find nicht hierhergekommen, um Reden zu halten, wir
haben ernfte Gefchäfte zu erledigen, ernft nach beftem Können zu
beforgen die Gefchäfte der Partei, der eine neue, den neuen Ver-
hältniffen entfprechende Organifation gefchaffen werden muß.

Wir tagen hier im vollften Lichte der Oeffentlichkeit. Es ift
Ihnen bekannt, daß in den letzten Tagen durch die gegnerifche
Preffe verbreitet worden ift, die Sozialdemokraten hätten zwar im
erften Moment in großmüthiger Aufwallung erklärt, der Eintritt
zum Kongreß folle frei, feine Verhandlungen öffentlich fein, aber
fie hätten fich fchließlich vor ihrem eigenen Befchluffe gefürchtet; —
der Befchluß fei zurückgenommen worden, weil wir viel Heimliches
zu verhandeln, viel fchmutzige Wäfche zu wafchen hätten. Wohlan,
nun tagen wir hier im Lichte der vollften Oeffentlichkeit; die Vertreter der Preffe aller Parteien dürfen anwefend fein. Wir ftellen
uns der Kritik. Unfere Partei hat nichts zu vertufchen,
nichts zu verbergen, ihre Ziele liegen klar da. Es giebt freilich Leute, welche behaupten, die Ziele, die wir in unferem Programm aufftellen, feien bloß zum Schein aufgeftellt und hinter
ihnen lägen andere — die wahren Ziele. Es find Thoren, die fo
reden, fie verrathen dadurch, daß fie von dem Wefen unferer Partei
keinen Begriff haben und ftellen ihrem Verftand ein fehr fchlechtes
Zeugniß aus. Wäre das wahr, fo trieben wir eine felbftmörderifche
Politik, wir würden gerade im entfcheidenden Moment, wenn das
wahre Programm zu enthüllen wäre, von den Maffen verlaffen

werden! Genug, hier stehen wir. Wir fordern die Kritik heraus, wir haben nichts zu scheuen.

Ihnen hier, meine Genossen, brauche ich nicht Worte der Mahnung zu sagen, Ihnen brauche ich keine Rathschläge zu geben: Sie sind fast ohne Ausnahme im Kampfe erprobt, — die Ehre und das Interesse der Partei wird Ihr Leitstern sein, der Gedanke an das Wohl der Partei wird Ihr Rathen und Handeln beherrschen und uns mit Sicherheit dem Ziele immer näher führen. Man pflegt den Soldaten, wenn sie in den Kampf gehen, zu sagen: „Das Vaterland blickt auf Euch und erwartet, daß Ihr Eure Schuldigkeit thut!" — Wir gehen jetzt nicht in den Kampf, aber ein welt=geschichtlicher Moment ist es, in dem die deutsche Sozial=demokratie sich auf diesem Parteitag konstituirt, und dessen müssen wir eingedenk sein. — Nicht bloß das Vaterland blickt auf uns — die gesammte deutsche Arbeiterschaft voll Vertrauen, unsere Feinde voller Haß und Angst —, die ganze gebildete Welt blickt auf diesen Kongreß. Seit Jahren — das zeigt ein Blick in die Presse des Auslandes — hat kein Ereigniß in den weitesten Kreisen ein solches Aufsehen erregt, wie der Sieg der Sozialdemokratie am 20. Februar dieses Jahres, der Fall des Sozialistengesetzes und das Zusammen=treten dieses Kongresses. In England, Frankreich, Amerika, überall beschäftigt sich die Presse mit diesem unserm Kongreß als mit dem wichtigsten Ereigniß der Gegenwart, damit bezeugend, daß das Proletariat eine Macht geworden ist, daß mit der Sozial=demokratie gerechnet werden muß und daß sie eine Summe von Kraft repräsentirt, welche ausschlaggebend in die Wagschale der Zeit fällt. Haben wir doch durch die Zahl unserer Stimmen am 20. Februar bewiesen, daß wir die zahlreichste, die stärkste, ja in gewisser Beziehung die leitende Partei Deutschlands sind. Oder dreht sich nicht gegenwärtig die Gesetzgebung, das ganze politische Leben wesentlich um unsere Partei, um die von uns formulirten Forderungen des arbeitenden Volks? Der Sieg vom 20. Februar, das wunderbare Wachsthum der deutschen Sozialdemokratie, welche aus einer Sekte zu einer kleinen Partei, aus einer kleinen Partei zu einer großen, aus einer großen zur größten Partei in Deutsch=land geworden ist, legt uns auch erhöhte Pflichten, schwierigere Aufgaben auf; Sie alle sind sich dessen bewußt, sind sich bewußt der Bedeutung des Moments und der Verantwortlichkeit, die auf Ihnen, auf uns allen ruht, — Sie werden die Hoffnungen des arbeitenden Volks aller Länder nicht täuschen; auf der andern Seite aber werden Sie auch die Hoffnungen Derjenigen zu Schanden machen, welche da wähnen, die Sozialdemokratie, die von ihren Feinden nicht besiegt werden konnte, werde sich selbst durch inneren Zwiespalt besiegen.

Wohlan, ich schließe mit einem Hoch auf die internationale

Sozialdemokratie, sie lebe hoch! hoch! hoch! (Die Versammelten
stimmen begeistert in den dreimaligen Hochruf ein.) — Und nun
erwächst mir die Pflicht, den Parteitag zu konstituiren. Ich erwarte
Ihre Vorschläge.

Ewald-Brandenburg schlägt vor, die Delegirten Singer und
Dietz zu Vorsitzenden zu wählen und zwar mit gleichen Rechten.

Weitere Vorschläge erfolgen nicht, der Vorschlag Ewald's
wird durch Akklamation einstimmig angenommen.

Singer: Im Auftrage unseres Genossen Dietz und für mich
sage ich der Versammlung herzlichen Dank für die hohe Ehre,
die Sie uns durch die eben vollzogene Wahl erwiesen haben.
Wir wissen das in uns gesetzte Vertrauen zu schätzen; wir werden
mit allen Kräften bemüht sein, es zu rechtfertigen und, soweit an
uns liegt, dafür sorgen, daß der Parteitag, der seit 13 Jahren
zum ersten Male wieder auf deutschem Boden abgehalten werden
kann, würdig der Partei, würdig der Sozialdemokratie verlaufe.
Wir können dieses Vorhaben aber nur ausführen, wenn wir der
Unterstützung jedes einzelnen Genossen sicher sind, und ich bin
überzeugt, daß, da für jeden Einzelnen von uns die Ehre der
Partei die eigene Ehre ist, jeder Genosse die hiermit namens des
Bureaus ausgesprochene Bitte erfüllen und uns in der Geschäftsführung nach Möglichkeit unterstützen wird. Wir nehmen die Wahl
mit herzlichem Dank an. (Lebhafter, andauernder Beifall.)

Auf Vorschlag des Vorsitzenden Singer werden acht Schriftführer gewählt, von denen in jeder Sitzung abwechselnd drei an
den Bureaugeschäften theilnehmen sollen, zwei für das Protokoll,
einer für die Rednerliste. Die Versammlung stimmt dem zu und
erfolgt die Wahl der Schriftführer ebenfalls per Akklamation.

Die drei Erstgenannten treten sofort ihr Amt an.

Vorsitzender Singer: Es würde nun zunächst das Einverständniß
des Parteitages darüber herbeizuführen sein, daß die provisorisch
Ihnen vorgelegte Tagesordnung als für unsere Verhandlungen maßgebend angesehen wird. Ich bitte Diejenigen, welche anderer Meinung
sind, das Wort zu nehmen.

Werner-Teltow: Ich möchte den Parteigenossen vorschlagen,
daß bei der Verhandlung über die verschiedenen Punkte der Tagesordnung jedesmal ein Referent von Seiten der Abgeordneten und
dann ein Korreferent aus der Mitte der Delegirten gehört wird,
welche Korreferenten sich freiwillig zu melden hätten. Nach der
provisorischen Geschäftsordnung soll den einzelnen Rednern nur
eine Redezeit von 10 Minuten zustehen, während die Referenten
über eine Stunde verfügen. Ich besorge, daß dann eine etwaige
gegentheilige Meinung nicht richtig und nicht ausreichend zum Aus-
trag kommen würde. Außerdem meine ich, daß bei den beiden
Punkten der Tagesordnung, wo zwei Abgeordnete als Referenten

genannt sind, einer zu Gunsten eines Korreferenten aus der Mitte der Delegirten zurücktreten sollte. Das würde bei den Referaten über die Presse und über Strikes und Boykotts zu geschehen haben.

Förster-Hamburg widerspricht diesem Vorschlage, dessen Nothwendigkeit er nicht einsehen könne, wie er auch die von Werner ausgesprochene Besorgniß seinerseits nicht theile. Die provisorische Tagesordnung sei vollständig sachgemäß festgesetzt.

Leutert-Apolda kann der Ansicht Werner's ebenfalls nicht beitreten. In der Diskussion genüge eine Redezeit von 10 Minuten, um eine bestimmte Ansicht zur Geltung zu bringen. Das Verfahren nach dem Vorschlage Werner's würde eine kolossale Vergeudung der Zeit herbeiführen, das könne er nicht unterstützen.

Schultze-Magdeburg empfiehlt dagegen, den Antrag anzunehmen. Trage man jeder hier auf dem Parteitage auftretenden Meinung Rechnung, so werde das am besten zur Förderung unserer Parteiinteressen dienen. Es köune nicht zur Klärung beitragen, wenn eine Majorität die Minorität unterdrücke.

Prinz-Frankfurt a. M.: Wir werden einen Fehler begehen, wenn wir die Tagesordnung nicht erledigen, wie sie uns vorgeschlagen ist. Wir sollen heute den Parteitag konstituiren und eine Kommission zur Prüfung der Vollmachten wählen. Geht die Debatte so weiter, so kommen möglicherweise zahlreiche Personen zum Worte, die gar nicht Delegirte sind.

Metzner-Berlin I: Wir haben uns gegenwärtig doch über die Tagesordnung schlüssig zu machen. Ich begreife nicht, warum man damit schon jetzt eine Anregung zur Geschäftsordnung vermengt.

Bebel: Ich glaube, die Absicht, die Genosse Werner mit seinem Antrage verfolgt, wird durch den Vorschlag selbst total verfehlt. Wenn ich recht verstehe, beabsichtigt er nämlich dafür Sorge zu tragen, daß nach jedem Referenten auch ein Redner zum Worte kommt, der vielleicht gegentheiliger Meinung ist. Es wird sich aber doch einmal fragen, ob solche sich melden, und dann, ob der Parteitag Neigung hat, sie zu hören. Es wird eventuell nothwendig sein, darüber eine Abstimmung herbeizuführen. Das sind Komplikationen, die uns unnütz eine Menge Zeit kosten würden. Weiter aber ist der Antrag auch deshalb nicht acceptabel, weil zu dem Bericht der Parteileitung aus der Mitte der Versammlung ein Korreferent doch gar nicht ernannt werden kann. Bei der Diskussion über die parlamentarische Thätigkeit der Fraktion werden diejenigen, die mit derselben nicht einverstanden sind, ebenso das Wort haben wie die andern; mehr können Sie doch nicht verlangen. Es hat also Niemand ein Recht, sich beschwert zu fühlen. Dem Wunsche, daß da, wo zwei Referenten in der provisorischen Tagesordnung bestellt sind, einer zurücktreten möge, erkläre ich persönlich schon jetzt, beim Punkte „Parteipresse" mit Vergnügen nachkommen zu wollen. Bei dem anderen Punkte „Streiks und Boykotts" geht das nicht an, weil da gar keine zwei Abgeordnete zu Referenten ernannt sind. Wir haben hiernach keine Veranlassung, von der früheren bewährten Praxis abzugehen.

Meist-Köln beantragt den Schluß der Diskussion über den Antrag Werner.

Vorsitzender Singer: Da wir noch keine Geschäftsordnung haben, behandeln wir diesen Antrag Meist in der üblichen Weise, indem wir einem Redner für, einem gegen den Schluß das Wort geben. (Zustimmung der Versammlung.)

Meist-Köln befürwortet den Schluß, da schon je zwei Redner für und gegen den Antrag Werner sich geäußert haben.

Das Wort gegen den Schluß wird nicht verlangt.

Mit großer Mehrheit wird darauf der Schlußantrag angenommen und der Antrag Werner abgelehnt.

Der Vorsitzende Singer konstatirt das Einverständniß des Parteitages, die provisorische Tagesordnung für seine Verhandlungen als maßgebend anzusehen.

Weiter macht der Vorsitzende dem Parteitage den Vorschlag, sich eine Geschäftsordnung zu geben. Es liegt unter den gedruckten Vorlagen folgender Entwurf einer solchen vor:

Geschäftsordnungs-Entwurf
für die
Verhandlungen des Parteitages.

1.

Die Meldungen zum Wort sind schriftlich einzureichen und erhalten die Redner nach der Reihenfolge der Anmeldung das Wort.

2.

Alle Anträge, außer denen zur Geschäftsordnung, sind schriftlich einzureichen und müssen dieselben, falls sie zur Verhandlung gelangen sollen, von mindestens 30 Delegirten unterstützt sein. Die Unterstützung kann durch Unterschrift oder Zuruf erfolgen.

3.

Sobald ein Antrag die nöthige Unterstützung gefunden, erhält bei der Verhandlung darüber zunächst der Antragsteller das Wort.

4.

Bei Geschäftsordnungs-Anträgen genügt eine Unterstützung von 15 Delegirten. Bei Anträgen auf Schluß der Debatte oder auf Vertagung erhält nur ein Redner für und einer gegen das Wort. Das Wort zur Geschäftsordnung wird außer der Reihenfolge der vorgemerkten Redner ertheilt. Persönliche Bemerkungen sind erst am Schlusse der Debatte zu machen.

5.

Die Redezeit der Referenten wird auf eine Stunde festgesetzt. Die Einbringer selbstständiger Anträge haben zur Begründung derselben eine Redezeit von 20 Minuten. In der Diskussion erhält jeder Redner 10 Minuten das Wort. Kein Redner — mit Ausnahme der Referenten und Einbringer selbstständiger Anträge — darf mehr als 2mal in einer Sache das Wort nehmen.

6.

Die Beschlüsse werden mit absoluter Mehrheit der Abstimmenden gefaßt. Stimmengleichheit gilt als Ablehnung des Antrages.

7.

Auf Antrag von mindestens 30 Mitgliedern des Parteitages muß die namentliche Abstimmung über einen Antrag stattfinden.

Nach eingehender Diskussion wird vorstehende Geschäftsordnung, mit dem Zusatzantrag, daß vor Schluß des Parteitages abreisende Delegirte dies dem Bureau anzuzeigen haben und ihre Namen im Protokoll vermerkt werden sollen, angenommen.

Der Vorsitzende schlägt vor, eine Mandats-Prüfungskommission von 9 Mitgliedern zu wählen, welche dem Parteitage Bericht zu erstatten hat. Der Vorschlag wird nach kurzer Diskussion angenommen und findet die Wahl per Akklamation statt.

Zu Mitgliedern der Mandats-Prüfungskommission werden gewählt die Genossen: Wernau-Berlin, Hosang-Dessau, Hahn-Gera, Ewald-Brandenburg, Hirsch-Niederbarnim, Pfannkuch-Kassel, Schwarz-Hamburg, Metzger-Hamburg, Heinzel-Kiel.

Nach Schluß der Wahl bemerkt Slomke-Bielefeld, daß Genosse Metzger-Hamburg kein Mandat zum Parteitag habe und deshalb auch nicht die Mandate prüfen dürfe.

Der Vorsitzende bedauert, daß dieses Bedenken nicht schon vor der Wahl des Genossen Metzger ausgesprochen worden ist. Derselbe sei gewählt; indessen der Parteitag sei souverän.

Arnold-Constanz hätte gewünscht, daß auch ein Genosse aus Süddeutschland in die Kommission gewählt worden wäre.

Die Genossen Metzger-Hamburg und Heinzel-Kiel verzichten zu Gunsten süddeutscher Genossen, worauf die Kommission durch die Wahl von Kloß-Stuttgart und Grothe-Halle (Vorsitzender des Lokalkomitees) komplettirt wird.

Der Vorsitzende macht nunmehr Vorschläge über Zeit und Dauer der Sitzungen des Parteitages. Es empfehle sich für den Parteitag die Einführung des achtstündigen Normalarbeitstages (Heiterkeit). Es sei am besten, wenn der Parteitag von 9—1 und von 3—7 Uhr tage.

Brühne-Frankfurt a. M. schlägt vor: 8—12 und 2—6, Bremer dagegen 8—12 und 5—9 mit Rücksicht auf die beschäftigten Arbeiter.

Grothe-Halle bittet, am Montag wenigstens von 9—1 und 4—8 Uhr zu tagen, weil er die Versammlung in dieser Weise polizeilich angemeldet habe.

Lücke-Cöln und Pfannkuch-Cassel glauben, daß eine Rücksprache mit der Polizeibehörde wohl zu einer Aenderung der Anmeldung im Sinne des Vorschlages des Vorsitzenden führen könne.

Grothe erklärt sich bereit, sich zu diesem Zwecke mit der Polizeibehörde ins Einvernehmen zu setzen.

Es verbleibt bei dem Vorschlage des Vorsitzenden.

Meist-Cöln beantragt, eine Kommission von 12 Mitgliedern zu wählen, welcher alle Anträge auf Aenderung des Parteiprogramms einzureichen sind und die durch einen Referenten zu Punkt 6 der Tagesordnung Bericht zu erstatten hat.

Bebel: Ich bitte, den Antrag Meist abzulehnen (Zustimmung). Nach meiner Ueberzeugung ist in Bezug auf das Parteiprogramm diesmal doch nicht an ein endgiltiges Resultat zu denken (Sehr richtig!). Ich denke mir die Sache so, daß, nachdem wir den Referenten gehört haben, in der Diskussion die verschiedensten Wünsche und Ansichten laut werden und daß schließlich alle hier gestellten Anträge einer Kommission überwiesen werden, die alsdann das Programm definitiv festzustellen und mindestens 3 Monate vor dem nächsten Parteitag zu veröffentlichen hätte, so daß dieser zu einem allen Wünschen entsprechenden Parteiprogramm kommen könnte.

Meist zieht seinen Antrag zurück.

Der Vorsitzende verspricht auf eine Anregung mehrerer Genossen, daß das Bureau in Verbindung mit dem Lokalkomitee dafür Sorge tragen wird, daß die Delegirten möglichst im Hauptsaale Platz finden und jede Störung der Verhandlungen vermieden wird. Den ausländischen Genossen soll ein besonderer Tisch reservirt und Rauchen sowie das Biertrinken im Sitzungssaale vermieden werden.

Nachdem der Vorsitzende noch mitgetheilt, daß die Protokolle der Sitzungen auf dem Bureau zur Einsicht offen liegen und über die gesammten Verhandlungen ein ausführliches Protokoll auf Grund stenographischer Aufzeichnungen erscheinen wird, schließt er die Sitzung um 9 Uhr.

Erster Verhandlungstag.

Montag, den 13. Oktober, Vormittags 9 Uhr.

Singer eröffnet die Sitzung mit folgender Ansprache:

Parteigenossen! Wir haben die Freude, die ausländischen Genossen Mundberg-Kopenhagen, Labour-Paris, Anseele-Gent, Wobsky-Warschau, Pokorny-Wien, Hanser-Wien, Dr. Adler-Wien, Domela-Nieuwenhuis-Haag, Branting-Stockholm und Duc-Quercy-

Paris, unter uns zu sehen. Ich glaube, ich kann die Verhandlungen des Parteitages der deutschen Sozialdemokratie nicht besser einleiten, als indem ich die ausländischen Genossen namens des Parteitages brüderlich und herzlich willkommen heiße. (Allseitige Zustimmung.) In ihrer Theilnahme an unseren Arbeiten manifestirt sich die von den Gegnern so oft angezweifelte und bestrittene Solidarität der Arbeiterklasse der ganzen Welt in der glänzendsten Weise; wir danken den ausländischen Genossen, daß sie zu uns gekommen; wenn wir auf unserem Parteitag auch nur die Geschäfte der Sozialdemokratie Deutschlands erledigen werden, so mögen unsere Gäste doch die Ueberzeugung mit in ihre Länder nehmen, daß die deutsche Sozialdemokratie sich ihrer internationalen Aufgaben ebenso bewußt ist, wie der Pflichten, welche sie gegen die deutsche Arbeiterklasse zu erfüllen hat. Die Anwesenheit der ausländischen Genossen, deren Zahl sich, wie zu erwarten steht, im Laufe des Parteitages noch vermehren wird, beweist uns, daß das Wort unseres großen Führers Carl Marx zur Wahrheit geworden ist, daß die Proletarier aller Länder seinem Mahnwort gemäß sich vereinigt haben, und daß sie gewillt und bereit sind, je nach den Verhältnissen ihrer Länder, in gemeinsamer Arbeit die geschichtliche Mission der Arbeiterklasse zu erfüllen, daß sie erkämpfen wollen die Befreiung der Menschheit aus den Banden der Unwissenheit, aus dem Joche der Armuth, aus der Sklaverei des Lohnsystems. (Lebhafter Beifall.) Ich begrüße die ausländischen Genossen in unseren Reihen und bitte sie, den Verhandlungen des Parteitages mit demselben Interesse zu folgen, welches sie in so hohem Maaße durch ihr Erscheinen bereits bekundet haben. (Allseitiger lebhafter Beifall.) Nun, Parteigenossen, drängt es mich, bei Beginn unseres Parteitages, der seit 13 Jahren zum ersten Male wieder auf deutschem Boden stattfindet, jener Treuen und Tapferen zu gedenken, welche im Laufe der Jahre seit dem Parteitage von St. Gallen durch den Tod aus unseren Reihen geschieden sind. Ich bin überzeugt, im Sinne der Gesammtpartei zu handeln, wenn ich die Delegirten bitte, sich zum ehrenden Angedenken an die Genossen, welche bis zum letzten Athemzuge in nie versagender Treue, Schulter an Schulter mit uns gekämpft haben, von ihren Sitzen zu erheben. (Geschieht.) Eine sehr große Anzahl von Begrüßungs- und Zustimmungstelegrammen ist beim Bureau des Parteitages eingelaufen; dieselben wünschen sämmtlich den Vertretern der deutschen Sozialdemokratie erfolgreiches Arbeiten, und enthalten die Versicherung, daß überall die Verhandlungen des Parteitages mit den lebhaftesten Sympathien begleitet werden. Von der Vorlesung des Wortlauts wird Abstand genommen und nur die Liste der Orte verkündet, woher die Telegramme und Zuschriften stammen. — Außerdem sind bereits durch die Presse diejenigen Zuschriften an die deutsche Sozialdemokratie

2*

veröffentlicht worden, die vor der Constituirung des Parteitages eingegangen sind.

Eine Liste der Adressen, Telegramme und Zuschriften wird dem Protokoll einverleibt werden. (Siehe Anhang.)

Namens des Parteitages spricht der Vorsitzende unter lebhaftem Beifall der Versammlung den Veranlassern dieser Zusendungen für die darin ausgedrückte Theilnahme den Dank aus.

Auf Antrag von Körner-Anhalt II, dem die Versammlung zustimmt, wird der Wortlaut der Gesammtadresse der italienischen Genossen, deren Verlesung letztere ausdrücklich gewünscht haben, in der vom Verfasser Professor Labrieola hergestellten deutschen Uebersetzung vom Antragsteller verlesen.

Unterzeichnet ist die Adresse von einer großen Anzahl von Vereinen; außerdem hat dieselbe eine lange Reihe persönlicher Unterschriften von Zeitungsvertretern und Vereinsvorständen, darunter eine ganze Anzahl von Universitätsprofessoren.

Es folgt nun eine Reihe von Ansprachen der ausländischen Genossen an die Delegirten zum Parteitage.

Domela Nieuwenhuis-Haag: Kampfesgenossen! Ich danke dem Vorsitzenden des Kongresses für die freundliche Aufnahme, welche wir hier gefunden haben, die wir gekommen sind, um dem Parteitag der deutschen Sozialdemokratie beizuwohnen. Es ist immer schwer, in einer fremden Sprache zu reden, aber unter Ihnen nicht; denn ich fühle mich nicht fremd unter Ihnen (Beifall), ich fühle mich als ein Freund unter Freunden; denn wir haben eine Sprache des Herzens, eine Sprache des Gefühls, und darum sollten wir Sozialdemokraten der Welt einander verstehen, auch wenn ich nicht zu Ihnen sprechen, wenn ich Ihnen nur die Hand drücken könnte. Ich bringe Ihnen einen Gruß der Freundschaft und des Wohlwollens aus Holland, dem kleinen Lande, das einmal der Keim der Freiheit und der Revolution war, wo man gelitten und gestritten hat gegen die Unterdrücker, und wo der Geist der Revolution nie ausgelöscht worden ist. Wir sind stammverwandt; aber nicht nur stammverwandt, auch geistesverwandt (Lebhafter Beifall). Ihr Leiden war unser Leiden, und nun ist Ihre Freude auch unsere Freude. Keine Grenze, willkürlich gezogen durch die Diplomatie, keine Nationalität, keine Religion kann uns trennen; wir sind eins von Herzen und eins von Sinn, denn wir haben denselben Feind zu bekämpfen: den internationalen Kapitalismus. Darum müssen wir auch international sein. Ja, die Sozialdemokratie sei international oder sie sei nicht! In diesem Augenblick klopft Ihr Herz stolz; denn Sie haben nach 12 Jahren des Kampfes und Leidens einen Sieg errungen; Sie haben ihn errungen nicht blos für Deutschland, nein für die ganze Menschheit. Aber noch sind wir nicht am Ende; es ist nur eine andere Form des Streites, welche eintritt, wir bleiben noch immer im Kampf. Wir gedenken Aller, welche als Märtyrer gestorben sind und gelitten haben, wir gedenken auch Derer, welche noch im Kerker sind.

Als 1789 die Bastille genommen war, das Volk im ersten Augenblicke siegestrunken frohlockte, da war es der edle, viel verkannte Marat, der in einem seiner glänzenden Artikel seinem Volke zurief: „Wachet auf und schlafet nicht ein!" So auch wir. Ja, wir müssen wachen, denn der Feind lauert stets auf uns. Einen Augenblick freundlich, wird er uns zerschmettern wenn er kann, und wenn wir uns nicht fügen nach seinem Willen. Die Freundschaft der Feinde ist öfter viel gefährlicher als ihre Wuth. Darum laßt Euch nicht verlocken. Wir begreifen, wie erfreut Ihr seid, Ihr habt Ursache zur Freude; denn hatte der Altmeister Jacoby Recht, wenn er sagte, daß die Stiftung des kleinsten Arbeitervereins für die Kulturarbeit wichtiger sei als Sadowa, wie wichtig muß dann dieser Tag wohl sein! Gewiß viel wichtiger, als alle Kriege in diesem Jahrhundert zusammen. Mit goldenen Lettern soll dieser Tag geschrieben stehen in den Jahrbüchern der Geschichte, und Sie, meine Freunde, sind sich vollkommen bewußt, hier zusammen zu sein als Träger der Kultur, als Vorarbeiter einer neuen Zukunft, einer neuen Epoche in der Weltgeschichte, wo nicht die brutale Gewalt, sondern Recht und Gleichheit regiert. Noch ist Ruhe nicht unser Theil, sondern Kampf, unermüdlicher Kampf. Nein, wir werden nicht ruhen, so lange noch ein Mensch auf der Welt gefunden wird, welcher darbt und elend ist, so lange noch ein Mensch Unrecht leidet und ausgebeutet wird, so lange noch ein Mensch in Unkenntniß herumläuft; und in diesem Streite streiten wir nicht nur nebeneinander, nein, miteinander. Wir Holländer sind ein kleines Volk, aber die revolutionäre Tradition ist nicht untergegangen, und wir versprechen Ihnen, daß wir unsere Pflicht thun werden. Und sollten wir untergehen, unsere Fahne wird rein bleiben; wir werden fallen mit Ehre; denn wir haben nur ein Vaterland: die Menschheit, nur eine Sittenlehre: Liebe und Gerechtigkeit, nur einen Sinn: die Erlösung der darbenden Menschheit! Und alle, welche dafür mit uns arbeiten, sie sind unsere Brüder, unsere Kampfesgenossen. Darum hoch die deutsche Sozialdemokratie! Dreifach hoch die internationale Sozialdemokratie! (Die Versammlung stimmt mit erhobener Rechten begeistert dreimal in den Hochruf ein.)

Dr. Adler-Wien: Werthe Genossen und Freunde! Im Namen der österreichischen Sozialdemokratie sind wir hier, um Sie zu begrüßen. Die österreichische Sozialdemokratie weiß, was es bedeutet, daß Sie heute wieder öffentlich Ihre Ziele verfolgen können. Die österreichische Sozialdemokratie ist noch enger mit der deutschen verknüpft, als alle anderen Arbeiterparteien; wir sind ihr jüngerer Bruder, verknüpft mit ihr durch eine Reihe von Beziehungen, welche

auch die politischen Beziehungen dieser beiden Staaten zum Ausdruck
bringen. Wir haben aber auch noch etwas anderes mit Ihnen
gemeinsam. Wir wissen, was Sie gelitten haben während des
Ausnahmegesetzes, wir in Oesterreich vielleicht am meisten von allen
hier Anwesenden. Ich bin nicht hier erschienen, um zu klagen über
das, was in Oesterreich vorgeht, wir bringen unsere Klagen und
Beschwerden im eigenen Lande vor; erinnern aber darf ich hier
daran, daß in Oesterreich ein Zustand herrscht, welcher Ihr Ausnahmegesetz noch bei weitem übertrifft, daran erinnern, daß wir
noch nicht den 1. Oktober gefeiert haben. Aber, wie der Freund
aus Holland soeben gesagt hat, die deutsche Sozialdemokratie hat
nicht nur für sich gekämpft, sie hat für die Arbeiter aller Nationen
gekämpft, sie hat nicht nur für sich, sie hat für uns alle gesiegt.
Wenn auch noch weiter in einzelnen Ländern die Politik des Zwanges
in ihrer brutalsten Form ausgeübt wird, moralisch ist diese Politik
am 1. Oktober gerichtet worden. (Sehr gut!) Daß dies geschehen
ist, haben wir Oesterreicher den allermeisten Grund, den deutschen
Sozialdemokraten zu danken. Ebenso wie Sie heute unbestritten
unter allen Völkern die rothe Fahne vorantragen, werden wir, das
darf ich hier versichern, soweit unsere politischen und ökonomischen
Verhältnisse es erlauben, Ihnen in gutem Schritt und Tritt folgen.
Wir wissen, daß Sie das Recht erworben haben, uns den Weg zu
weisen; wir wissen, daß Sie der außerordentlichen Verantwortung
nicht nur für Sie hier im Lande, sondern für die gesammte internationale kämpfende proletarische Partei sich bewußt sind, und in
diesem Sinne begrüßen wir Sie. Sie hier in Deutschland sind viel
mehr der klare, bewußte, vollständige Ausdruck der Bewegung des
arbeitenden Volkes überhaupt, als in irgend einem anderen Lande.
Die proletarische Bewegung ist in den anderen Ländern und auch
in Oesterreich noch nicht sich selbst so sehr zum Bewußtsein gekommen,
wie es in Deutschland der Fall ist. Wenn Sie österreichische Verhältnisse beurtheilen, müssen Sie sich erinnern, daß die Bewegung
des arbeitenden Volkes in Oesterreich weit über das hinausgeht,
was durch den Begriff der österreichischen Sozialdemokratie gedeckt
wird. Die Bewegung wird aber auch jeden Moment eine tiefere,
und ich glaube, der Augenblick ist nicht mehr fern, wo auch die
österreichische Sozialdemokratie wird sagen können, sie sei der Ausdruck aller jener Kräfte, die im Proletariat sich zu seiner Befreiung
regen, wo überall aus dem unbewußten ein bewußter Kampf geworden sein wird. Nun, Genossen, wir haben hier auch die Aufgabe, zu lernen; wir haben von den deutschen Sozialdemokraten
viel gelernt, wir werden hoffentlich noch viel von ihnen zu lernen
haben. Unsere Bewegung ist in einer so raschen, so überraschenden
Art des Fortschreitens begriffen, daß sie sich einfach nicht mehr verfolgen läßt; aber eins wissen die Oesterreicher und die meisten

andern, die Sie hier begrüßen und begrüßt haben, daß theoretisch
und praktisch jener Weg, den die deutsche Sozialdemokratie ein-
geschlagen hat, derjenige ist, welchen die einzelnen Völker, nach ihren
Verhältnissen angemessen abgeändert, werden gehen müssen. In
diesem Sinne bringe ich Ihnen den Gruß der Oesterreicher und
schließe mit einem Hoch auf die deutsche Sozialdemokratie, mit einem
dreifachen Hoch auf die internationale proletarische Bewegung!
(Stürmischer dreifacher Hochruf.)

Von Werner-Teltow ist mittlerweile folgender Antrag eingelaufen:

Der Parteitag möge Entscheidung treffen, ob diejenigen Reichstagsabgeordneten, welche kein Mandat als Delegirte besitzen,
beschließende Stimme haben.

Der Antrag wird als Geschäftsordnungsantrag behandelt, für
welchen die Unterstützung von 15 Stimmen genügt. Er findet die
nöthige Unterstützung und kommt sofort vor Eintritt in die Tagesordnung zur Verhandlung.

Werner-Teltow verweist zur Begründung des Antrages auf
das gestrige Vorgehen der Hamburger Delegirten gegen Metzger-
Hamburg; er hält es deshalb für zweckdienlich, daß die Versammlung eine Entscheidung treffe, damit für die Zukunft alle Streitigkeiten in dieser Frage aus der Welt geschafft würden.

Auer ersucht, feststellen zu lassen, wieviel Abgeordnete ohne Delegation vorhanden sind; er gehöre selbst zu denen, die sich um ein Mandat
nicht umgesehen hätten; zu haben wären sie zu Dutzenden gewesen.

Die Zahl der Reichstagsmitglieder ohne Delegirtenmandat wird
ermittelt; sie beläuft sich auf 11.

Prinz-Frankfurt a. M. ersucht den Parteitag, sich gegen die
Stimmberechtigung zu erklären; berathende Stimme hätten die Abgeordneten ohnehin, und die übrigen Mitglieder des Parteitages
würden ja doch allein wissen, was sie zu thun haben.

Bebel: Die Frage wird thatsächlich durch die später zu berathende Parteiorganisation erledigt werden; es heißt in § 8 des
Ihnen vorgelegten Entwurfs ausdrücklich:

„Der Parteitag bildet die oberste Vertretung der Partei.

Zur Theilnahme an demselben sind berechtigt:

1. die Delegirten der Partei aus den einzelnen Wahlkreisen, mit
der Einschränkung, daß kein Wahlkreis durch mehr als 3 Personen vertreten sein darf;
2. die Mitglieder der Reichstagsfraktion;
3. die Mitglieder des Parteivorstandes.

Die Mitglieder der Reichstagsfraktion und des Parteivorstandes haben in allen die parlamentarische und die geschäftliche
Leitung der Partei betreffenden Fragen nur berathende Stimme.“

Dieser Entwurf steht allerdings zunächst auf dem Papier und

der Parteitag hat das Recht, ihn abzuändern; in diesem Sinne ist
aber der Antrag Werner präjudizirlich. Er regt zwar nur die
Frage an; aber da er das Beispiel Hamburgs herbeigezogen hat, so
scheint er doch denjenigen Abgeordneten, welche kein Mandat zum
Parteitage haben, in den allgemeinen Parteifragen nur berathende,
unter keinen Umständen aber beschließende Stimme zugestehen zu
wollen. Es hätten aber alle mit Leichtigkeit ein Mandat haben können,
wenn sie sich darum hätten bewerben wollen; sie haben sich das er-
spart, da sie wünschten, daß möglichst viel Nichtabgeordnete delegirt
würden. Soll nun ausgesprochen werden, daß die Fraktionsgenossen,
die so verfahren sind, vom Stimmrecht ausgeschlossen werden sollen,
während sie andererseits notorisch ein Mandat sehr leicht hätten
erlangen können, und als Abgeordnete ein Parteimandat im höchsten
Sinne bereits inne haben, dann werden diese Fraktionsgenossen zu
Parteigenossen zweiter Klasse degradirt (sehr richtig!), und wenn es
dahin kommen sollte, wie es bereits mehrfach geschehen ist, daß man
in der That solchen Unterschied macht und die Abgeordneten in
gewissen Rechten und Beziehungen einzuschränken sucht, dann würde
ich allerdings künftig vorziehen, kein Fraktionsgenosse zu sein, um
vollwichtiger Parteigenosse sein zu können. Ich beantrage, daß Sie
sich jetzt schon so entscheiden mögen, wie es § 8 des Entwurfs vorsieht;
der dort angegebene Ausweg ist korrekt und für Alle annehmbar.

Kühn-Langenbielau: Ich bin ja auch mit dem „Makel" behaftet,
der Fraktion angehört zu haben. Bebel hat mit vollem Recht
betont, daß die Annahme des Antrags Werner eine Degradation
der Abgeordneten-Genossen bedeutet. Die letzte Konsequenz des
Antrags wäre, daß die befähigten Genossen sich nicht mehr in den
Reichstag würden wählen lassen und dann jede parlamentarische
Thätigkeit unsererseits aufhören würde. Bei der Zusammensetzung
dieser Versammlung glaube ich mich nicht weiter darauf einlassen
zu sollen, welche Wichtigkeit immerhin die Theilnahme an den
Reichstagsarbeiten für uns hat. Wir wissen das, wie wir auch
wissen, daß wir damit die Welt nicht aus den Angeln heben werden.
Wir würden uns das denkbar größte Armuthszeugniß mit der Erklärung ausstellen, daß unsere Abgeordneten z. B. nicht das Recht
haben sollen, die Mandate der Kongreßtheilnehmer mit prüfen zu
können.

Schmidt-Zwickau: Man hat wohl durchgehends in Deutschland die Meinung gehabt, daß die Abgeordneten der Partei sitz- und
stimmberechtigt hier sind; aus diesem Grunde hat eben eine Anzahl
Abgeordneter kein Mandat erhalten. Ich stimme im Sinne des
Organisationsentwurfs für die Stimmberechtigung der Abgeordneten
in allen Angelegenheiten mit Ausschluß der parlamentarischen (Beifall).

Guttenstein-Karlsruhe: Der Vorschlag Werner's zeugt sehr
wenig von Sozialismus. Wer hier ist, soll auch gleichberechtigt sein.

Wenn wir in dieser Art und Weise in rein formellen Erörterungen unsere kostbare Zeit vergeuden wollen, dann kommen wir überhaupt zu nichts. Wir sind hier eine Versammlung unter Gleichen. Ein Armuthszeugniß in der That würden wir uns ausstellen, wollten wir denen, die im Reichstage, in der Oeffentlichkeit für uns gekämpft haben, jetzt versagen, in unseren Angelegenheiten mit zu entscheiden.

Von drei verschiedenen Seiten wird der Schluß der Diskussion beantragt, von Förster-Hamburg befürwortet, von Wilschke-Berlin bekämpft und darauf mit sehr großer Mehrheit angenommen.

Vorsitzender Singer: Nach unserer Geschäftsordnung würde dem Antragsteller zu diesem Geschäftsordnungsantrage das Schlußwort nicht zu ertheilen sein. Ich bin aber der Meinung, der Parteitag hat alle Ursache, sich auch nur von der Möglichkeit des Vorwurfs frei zu halten, irgend jemand das Wort abschneiden zu wollen; ich bitte demnach, mich zu ermächtigen, ausnahmsweise von der Geschäftsordnung abweichen zu dürfen. (Zustimmung und Widerspruch.) Da Widerspruch laut wird, werden wir darüber abstimmen.

Die große Mehrheit der Versammlung stimmt dem Vorschlag des Vorsitzenden zu, welcher darauf dem Antragsteller das Schlußwort ertheilt.

Werner-Teltow: Parteigenossen! Ich weiß nicht, wie man zu einer solchen Praxis greifen kann, um Gedanken, die gar nicht in dem Antrage enthalten sind, herauszusuchen. Es heißt, ich hätte wohl dieses oder jenes gemeint, und man fragt, ob der Antrag mit dem Sozialismus etwas gemein hätte. Der Antrag hat gar nichts mit dem Sozialismus gemein. Mit Worten wie Armuthszeugniß und dergleichen sollte man dem Antrag doch nicht entgegentreten. Ich will nichts weiter, als Streitigkeiten für die Zukunft vermeiden; ich protestire hier dagegen, daß mir unlautere Motive untergeschoben werden, und ich verbitte mir für die Zukunft derartige Unterstellungen.

Vorsitzender Singer: Ich habe dem nur hinzuzufügen, daß ich mir ebenfalls vorgenommen hatte, darauf hinzuweisen, daß der Antrag ausdrücklich dem Parteitage nur eine Frage zur Entscheidung gestellt hat.

Der Antrag Bebels, für die bevorstehenden Abstimmungen vorbehaltlich der definitiven Entscheidung über das Organisationsstatut den § 8 des bezüglichen Entwurfs maßgebend sein zu lassen, wird mit großer Mehrheit angenommen. Damit ist der Antrag Werner erledigt.

In der Reihe der ausländischen Vertreter erhält nunmehr das Wort Mundberg-Kopenhagen: Deutsche Parteigenossen! Ich habe von der dänischen sozialdemokratischen Partei einen Dank zu bringen nicht nur für den großartigen Eindruck Ihres jetzigen Kongresses, sondern vor allem für die großartige Art und Weise, wie die deutsche Sozialdemokratie den Ausnahmezustand überwunden hat. Mit Freuden gedenkt unsere Partei dabei des Umstandes, daß auch wir seiner Zeit Gelegenheit hatten, Freundschaft gegen die deutsche Sozialdemokratie zu zeigen, indem wir Ihnen anbieten konnten, einen Ihrer Kongresse bei uns abzuhalten in einer Zeit, als die Verfolgungen hier in Deutschland gegen Sie tobten. Es freut uns im Auslande, wenn wir sehen, daß die Sozialdemokratie in Deutschland so stark dasteht, und es wird ebenso sehr die deutsche Sozialdemokratie freuen, wenn sie hören kann, daß es mit der Sozialdemokratie in den anderen Ländern gut steht. Ich konstatire deshalb an dieser Stelle, daß die dänische Sozialdemokratie jetzt eine sehr starke Stellung einnimmt, daß sie einen sehr bedeutenden Einfluß im Lande hat. Ich kann auch sagen, daß die prinzipielle sozialistische Politik in Dänemark schon sehr starke Wurzeln geschlagen hat, nicht allein in den Städten, sondern auch auf dem Lande. Bei unserem letzten Kongresse waren die Landarbeiter sehr stark vertreten, sie waren an Delegirten ebenso zahlreich, wie die städtischen. In dem Hauptvorstand der Partei sitzen viele Landarbeiter. Ueberhaupt haben wir in Dänemark in hohem Grade unsere Aufmerksamkeit auf die Landfrage gerichtet, indem wir erkannten, daß, um die Zustände in den Städten zu bessern, der Zuzug vom Lande verringert werden müsse, und das kann nur dadurch geschehen, daß man die Aufmerksamkeit ganz besonders der Landfrage zuwendet. Sie werden selbstverständlich einen größeren Einfluß auf die Entwicklung üben, als wir in den kleineren Ländern; letztere können in dieser Richtung mit Deutschland nicht konkurriren. Aber ich darf hier sagen: wenn es sich darum handelt, die sozialistische Fahne hoch und rein zu halten, unsere Politik energisch und umsichtig fortzuführen, dann wird man auch in den kleineren Ländern, auch in Dänemark, die Konkurrenz mit jedem anderen Lande aufnehmen (Bravo!) Ich schließe mit der Wiederholung unseres Dankes: Wir danken der deutschen Sozialdemokratie für das, was sie bisher gethan hat, wie für das, was sie, wie wir wissen, in der Zukunft thun will! (Stürmischer Beifall und Händeklatschen.)

Beck-Zürich: Werthe Genossen! Gestatten Sie mir, die Grüße der deutschen Genossen in der Schweiz hier abzustatten und unserer Freude Ausdruck zu geben, daß es uns wieder möglich ist, auf heimathlichem, vaterländischem Boden zu tagen. Ich betone das „vaterländisch", weil man uns immer vorwirft, wir hätten dafür keine Sympathie, wir wären Reichsfeinde. Ich kenne keine Gesellschaftsklasse im Auslande, die so an den Angelegenheiten des Vaterlandes Antheil nimmt, als die dort weilenden Angehörigen der Arbeiterklasse. (Bravo!) — Es ist sehr fraglich, ob es noch

einmal möglich gewesen wäre, in der Schweiz einen Parteitag abzuhalten — die schlechten Beispiele fangen bald an, die guten Sitten
zu verderben (Heiterkeit). Wie dem nun auch sei, wir sind überall,
wo wir waren, im Auslande oder im Inlande, mit großer Liebe
an der Partei gehangen. Es ist da ein Unterschied: man kann
z. B. eine Mutter recht lieb haben, weniger häufig die Schwieger-
mutter, und etwas schwiegermütterlich wurden wir ja behandelt
(Heiterkeit). Von diesem Standpunkt aus müssen Sie unterscheiden,
was ich davon halte, wenn ich von Vaterlandsliebe spreche. — Wir
sind jenem Volke in der Alpenrepublik zu großem Dank verpflichtet.
Was auch geschehen ist, wenn man auch zu Ausweisungen gegriffen
hat, machen Sie nicht das Volk, machen Sie die Regierung dafür
verantwortlich. Mancher biedere Republikaner hat damals den
Kopf geschüttelt, mancher tolerante Arbeitgeber hat zweifelnd gefragt, wie es möglich sei, daß man bloß der Ansichten wegen gemaßregelt, als Parteigenosse ausgewiesen werden könne. Ich kann
den Gefühlen, die mich bewegen, nicht Ausdruck geben; ich beziehe
mich auf Liebknecht, der mit Recht sagte: „Das Proletariat der
ganzen Welt sieht jetzt hierher. Die Genossen im Auslande erwarten, daß die deutsche Sozialdemokratie sich ihrer kulturhistorischen
Mission bewußt ist und auch ferner an der Spitze des weltbefreienden
Proletariats marschirt!" (Lebhafter Beifall.)

Branting-Stockholm: Deutsche Genossen! Auch die schwedische
Sozialdemokratie wünscht durch mich ihren Gruß Ihrem Parteitage
auszurichten. Wenn wir auch jetzt noch eine junge Partei sind, die
noch nicht auf Siege zurückblicken kann, auch nur annähernd so groß
wie die Ihrigen, so sind wir doch von dem wahren Geist der internationalen, revolutionären Sozialdemokratie durchdrungen und werden
niemals ermüdet unsere Fahne sinken lassen, sondern immerdar vorwärts schauen und streben, und da stärkt uns das Bewußtsein, in
der großen proletarischen Bewegung Deutschlands unser leuchtendes
Beispiel vor uns zu haben. Wir wollen alles mögliche thun, um
auch Schweden bald in die Reihen der Sozialdemokratie mehr
vordringen zu lassen. Das Unmögliche aber können auch wir nicht
thun; es ist Sache der Entwicklung und der wirthschaftlichen Verhältnisse, wie schnell unsere Bewegung vorwärts kommt. Vorläufig
ist die theoretische Entwicklung bei uns der ökonomischen noch voraus. Ich wünsche im Namen der schwedischen Parteigenossen den
deutschen Brüdern allen auf's herzlichste Glück. Ein Hoch der
internationalen, revolutionären Sozialdemokratie! (Dreifache jubelnde
Hochrufe.)

Anseele-Gent: Werthe Genossen! Ich kann nicht gut deutsch
sprechen, darum werde ich sehr kurz sein. Im Namen der belgischen
Parteigenossen bringe ich auch unsern Glückwunsch an die deutsche
Sozialdemokratie. Wir sind vielleicht die Vertreter des kleinsten

hier vertretenen Landes, aber ich glaube versichern zu können, daß
wir unser Bestes thun wollen, um die muthigsten Soldaten in der
Armee zu sein. (Bravo!) Wir haben in Belgien kein Sozialistengesetz gehabt und haben es heute nicht; aber ohne Gesetz thun
unsere Meister alles, was ihnen beliebt, ohne Gesetz verbieten sie
unsere Versammlungen, verbieten sie den Verkauf und selbst die
Ausstellung unserer Blätter. Und alles das unter dem Grundgesetz,
welches alle Freiheiten giebt! Ein Zustand also, noch schlechter, als
es der in Deutschland war. Sie wissen ja auch, daß wir in Belgien
das Unglück haben, im Eden des Kapitalismus zu sein. Wir wollen
alles thun, um mit Ihrer Hilfe und derjenigen der Parteigenossen
der ganzen Welt das Eden der Arbeiter daraus zu machen (Bravo!).
Wir belgischen Sozialisten haben uns verpflichtet, vorzuschlagen, daß
der nächste internationale Kongreß in Brüssel, in Belgien stattfinden
möchte. Wir hoffen, daß Sie sich im Sinne der belgischen Arbeiter
entscheiden werden. Ich habe einige Worte in schlechtem Deutsch,
aber aus gutem Herzen gesprochen (Beifall). Ich bringe ein Hoch
auf die Sozialdemokratie, die internationale Sozialdemokratie!
Wenn Sie so wie bisher fortschreiten, ist der Sieg unser trotz
alledem! (Lebhafter, andauernder Beifall.)

Hierauf wird in die Tagesordnung eingetreten.

Klein-Berlin ersucht (zur Geschäftsordnung) den Parteitag,
die Voreingenommenheit gegen die Berliner fallen zu lassen . . . .
(Glocke des Vorsitzenden.)

Vorsitzender Singer: Das ist keine Bemerkung zur Geschäfts-
ordnung (Unruhe). Ich halte mich dem soeben ausgedrückten
Wunsche gegenüber verpflichtet, zu konstatiren, daß ich namens des
Parteitages die Insinuation zurückweise (sehr gut!), als ob der
Parteitag gegen irgend eine Parteigruppe des Reiches voreingenom-
men wäre. Das Recht der Berliner Genossen wird in gleichem
Maaße geachtet werden, wie das jedes anderen Genossen. (Lebhafte
Zustimmung.)

Punkt 1 der Tagesordnung:
Bericht der Parteileitung.

Berichterstatter Bebel: Parteigenossen! Die Freunde aus dem
Auslande, die soeben nacheinander das Wort ergriffen, haben uns
mit Lob und Anerkennung überschüttet; von allen Seiten tönt es
uns entgegen, daß sie uns als eine Art Musterpartei ansehen. Ich
soll jetzt über die Thätigkeit der Partei Bericht erstatten, und da
wünsche ich nur, daß es mir vergönnt sein möge, an der Hand der
vorzuführenden Thatsachen darzuthun, daß das reichlich gespendete
Lob einigermaßen verdient ist. Ich hoffe dann aber auch, daß die
Errungenschaften, die wir zu verzeichnen haben, uns ein fernerer
Ansporn sein werden, künftig unter der sogenannten „neuen Aera"

nur noch in höherem Maße unsere Kräfte und Anstrengungen im Interesse unserer Sache zu bethätigen.

Es sind genau drei Jahre, daß ich zum letzten Mal die Ehre hatte, vor den Vertretern der Partei Bericht zu erstatten; Sie wissen alle, unter welchen Umständen wir jene Berichte zu geben gezwungen waren. Während der 12 Jahre des Ausnahmegesetzes waren wir nicht in der Lage, innerhalb Deutschlands einen Parteitag abzuhalten; aus diesem zwingenden Grunde mußte der Turnus bei der Abhaltung der Parteitage ein sehr unregelmäßiger sein, wir konnten nur in weit auseinanderliegenden Zeiträumen uns sprechen und verständigen. Diesen Zuständen, die wir nicht verschuldet, mußten wir uns aber nach Möglichkeit akkomodiren. Dafür sind aber auch gerade die unter dem Ausnahmegesetz im Auslande, und zwar 1880 in Wyden in der Schweiz, 1883 in Kopenhagen und 1887 in St. Gallen abgehaltenen Parteitage als die eigentlichen Merksteine in der Entwicklung der Partei zu betrachten. Es waren Freuden- und Ehrentage für die Partei, die, weil sie im Auslande unter großen Kosten, Opfern und Gefahren abgehalten werden mußten, das schönste und erhebendste Beispiel des Muthes und der Opferwilligkeit geboten haben. Heute endlich, nach mehr als 13 Jahren, sind wir zum ersten Male wieder in Deutschland unter der Herrschaft des allgemeinen Rechts versammelt, und zwar so zahlreich, wie nie zuvor. Da dürfte es wohl am Platze sein, einen flüchtigen Blick auf die Hauptereignisse und die Entwicklung der Partei unter dem Ausnahmegesetz zu werfen. Als das Gesetz verkündet und dann sofort mit aller Schärfe gegen uns angewandt wurde, da haben wohl viele kaum die Hoffnung gehegt, daß wir eines Tages wieder so wie heute uns versammelt sehen würden. Leider ist die Zahl derer sehr, sehr groß, die diesen großen Tag des Sieges nicht mehr erlebten. Es sind eine große Anzahl Genossen aus den verschiedensten Lebensstellungen, die von den Handhabern des Gesetzes gehetzt, verfolgt, zu Grunde gerichtet und dadurch in ihrem Lebensfaden verkürzt in's frühe Grab sanken. Viele Hunderte andere wurden in den ersten Jahren der Herrschaft des Gesetzes durch die Vernichtung ihrer materiellen Existenz gezwungen, im Auslande Zuflucht und Unterkunft zu suchen. Von denjenigen, die in der vorsozialistengesetzlichen Zeit als Agitator und in öffentlichen Stellungen, als Redakteure, Abgeordnete u. s. w. in der Partei thätig waren, haben in den ersten Jahren über 80 Personen, darunter unsere tüchtigsten, besten und intelligentesten Genossen den deutschen Boden verlassen müssen, und nur sehr wenige von ihnen können oder werden in die Heimath zurückkehren. Es war ein Aderlaß an Kräften, wie nach einer verlorenen Schlacht, aber um so größer steht die Partei da, indem sie diesen Aderlaß nicht blos ertragen, sondern das ihr abgezapfte

Blut auch so reichlich wiedererseßt hat. Sie wissen Alle, welcher
Art die Schläge waren, die fielen, als am 19. Oktober 1878 das
Ausnahmegeseß mit 221 gegen 149 Stimmen angenommen worden
war und am 21. Oktober 1878 in Kraft trat. Wer, wie ich und
mancher andere, damals den Reichstagsverhandlungen über das
Ausnahmegeseß beiwohnte, und daran Theil nehmen mußte, wird
vor allem die Thatsache haben beobachten können, daß in demselben
Maaße, wie jenesmal die Verhandlungen sich in die Länge zogen,
in dem Maaße wie unsere Parteivertreter immer entschiedener gegen
dieses Schandgeseß Protest erhoben, der Eifer für das Gesetz und
die feindselige Stimmung gegen uns im Reichstage zunahm. Es
ist das eine Thatsache, auf die meines Wissens bisher noch nicht
aufmerksam gemacht wurde. Entsprechend dieser erbitterten, feind-
seligen Stimmung fielen denn auch die Schläge gegen die Partei.
Alle unsere Preßorgane, und zwar 42 politische und 14 gewerkschaftliche Organe, eine ungeheure Zahl von Vereinen, verschiedene
Kassen und Gewerkschaften fielen innerhalb weniger Monate der
Polizeimacht zum Opfer. Binnen wenigen Wochen war die ganze
Organisation der Partei vernichtet, hunderte und aber hunderte von
Genossen lagen existenzlos auf dem Pflaster. Daß damals Viele
eine gewisse Muthlosigkeit befiel, ganze Schaaren, wie nach einer
verlorenen Schlacht, von uns abgesprengt wurden, wer will sich
darüber verwundern und wer will das übel nehmen? Keine andere
Partei in Deutschland würde solche Schläge ausgehalten und überwunden haben. (Sehr richtig.)

Im Laufe dieser Jahre sind unter der Herrschaft des Ausnahmegesetzes 155 periodische Druckschriften verboten worden, und unter
diesen an 80 Einzelnummern von periodischen Druckschriften. Weiter
wurden 1200 nichtperiodische Druckschriften, darunter unsere ganze, sehr
ansehnliche Broschüren-Literatur verboten, im Ganzen ca. 1400 Druckschriften. Ausweisungen auf Grund der Herrschaft des sog. kleinen
Belagerungszustandes in Berlin, Potsdam und Berlin, Hamburg-
Altona-Harburg und Umgegend, Leipzig und Umgegend, Frankfurt a. M.-Offenbach, Hanau, Stettin und Spremberg, sind nahe
an 900 erfolgt. Prozesse, die namentlich nach Ablauf der ersten
2 Jahre der Herrschaft des Gesetzes begannen, als die Partei von
den ersten furchtbaren Schlägen sich wieder erholt hatte, und dann
die Genossen dem Drange nach Vereinigung vielfach folgend, sich in
den verschiedensten Orten in sogenannten geheimen Verbindungen
zusammen fanden, diese Prozesse wurden allmählich zahlreich und
führten zur Verurtheilung von über 300 Personen. Daneben ver-
fielen den Maschen des Sozialistengesetzes nahezu an 1200 Personen,
so daß allein auf Grund und als Folge der Ausnahmegesetzgebung
volle 1500 Personen in die Gefängnisse wandern mußten. Dazu
kommen die Verurtheilungen, die genauer festzustellen mir nicht

möglich, war, wegen Majestätsbeleidigung, wegen Verstoßes gegen §§ 130 und 131 des Strafgesetzbuchs, wegen Aufruhr, Landfriedensbruch u. s. w. Die Zahl dieser Verurtheilten mag im Verhältniß zu der anderen klein sein; aber sie erhöht nicht nur die Zahl der Opfer, sondern sie fällt auch in's Gewicht durch die Schwere der Verurtheilungen. Das Gesammtmaaß der Freiheitsstrafen beläuft sich auf nahe an 1000 Jahre Gefängniß, darunter eine Anzahl Jahre Zuchthaus.

Diese keineswegs vollständige Liste der Verfolgungen giebt ein klares Bild sowohl von den Schlägen, die wir zu ertragen, auch von den Opfern, die wir bringen mußten, um diese Schläge nach Möglichkeit zu pariren. Und wir haben sie parirt, gründlich parirt, dafür legt nicht nur Zeugniß die Vergangenheit ab, sondern auch das deutlichste Zeugniß dieser Parteitag. Aber eins halte ich mich für verpflichtet auch auszusprechen: Wenn der Muth und die Opferwilligkeit der Genossen in Deutschland in erster Linie dazu beigetragen hat, daß es so gekommen ist, dann wollen wir auch derer dankbar gedenken, die vom Auslande immerfort ermuthigend und anfeuernd auf unsere Reihen gewirkt haben, an die Gründer und Leiter des „Sozialdemokrat“, die während zehn Jahren unter oft schwierigen Verhältnissen fortgesetzt ihn für Deutschland herstellten, an alle die, die ungekannt und ungenannt es für ihre heiligste Pflicht ansahen, dieses Organ und die im Ausland erscheinenden Brochüren ins Volk zu tragen und vielfach dafür schwer büßen mußten. Ihnen allen sind wir zu ganz besonderem Dank verpflichtet. Diesen Hunderten und Tausenden, die im Auslande und im Inlande öffentlich und geheim für unsere Sache unermüdlich gewirkt und vielfach gelitten haben, wollen wir heute dadurch unseren Dank abstatten, daß der Parteitag ihnen zu Ehren von den Plätzen sich erhebt. (Die Versammlung leistet unter Beifallsrufen der Aufforderung einmüthig Folge.)

Man hat, und ich halte es für nöthig, gerade hier darauf zu sprechen zu kommen, in den verschiedensten Geheimbundprozessen seitens der Staatsanwälte und theilweise auch der Gerichte den Versuch gemacht, nachzuweisen, daß eine große allgemeine, geheime Verbindung über ganz Deutschland bestehe, in der alle Einzelverbindungen, soweit solche bestanden, unter gemeinsamer Leitung ständen, weil man sich anders nicht unsere Existenz und unsere Erfolge erklären konnte. Ich muß auch hier ausdrücklich konstatiren, daß nie und zu keiner Zeit eine solche allgemeine Verbindung in Deutschland bestand, nie die Rede davon war und nicht davon sein konnte, schon wegen der Sicherheit ihrer Entdeckung in allerkürzester Frist. Die Fraktion, als Leiterin der Partei, konnte schon durch die Oeffentlichkeit ihrer Stellung auf eine solche Verbindung unmöglich eingehen. Was geschehen ist, ist ohne eine solche allgemeine geheime Verbindung geschehen, einzig durch den Geist und das Band der Zusammengehörigkeit, und was auch unsere Gegner immer sagen und aufrecht erhalten mögen, ich konstatire, sie hat zu keiner Zeit bestanden, es ist nicht einmal der Versuch gemacht worden, sie in's Leben zu rufen.

Wir haben dann im Laufe dieser 12 Jahre die Wahrnehmung gemacht, daß in dem Maaße, wie auf der einen Seite die herrschende Gewalt mit Gewalt- und Zwangsmitteln aller Art zu unserer Unterdrückung vorging, sie andererseits gezwungen war, der Bewegung gegenüber allerlei Konzessionen zu machen. In demselben Augenblick, in dem man von höchster Stelle die Nothwendigkeit des Ausnahmegesetzes betonte und es verlangte, sah man sich auch genöthigt, anzuerkennen, daß man einem gewissen berechtigten Kern der Bewegung Rechnung tragen müsse. Sogar Fürst Bismarck erklärte etwas später, die herrschenden Klassen müßten sich daran gewöhnen, daß es ohne ein bischen Sozialismus künftig nicht mehr gehe. Nun, wie er und die herrschenden Klassen dieses bischen Sozialismus verstanden haben, wissen wir Alle (Heiterkeit). Wäre es nach ihm gegangen, die Partei wäre nicht, was sie ist, und nach ihm würde noch heute der Ausnahmezustand mit allen seinen Un- gerechtigkeiten auf uns lasten. Nun kam ja im Laufe der Jahre allerdings die sogenannte „milde Praxis", aber sie griff Platz, weil sich zeigte, daß die Partei sich nicht unterdrücken ließ. Die mittler- weile vorgekommenen Reichstagswahlen hatten nicht nur ihre Fort- existenz, sondern, allen Verfolgungen zum Trotz, auch ihr Wachsthum ergeben. Die Masse unserer Anhänger war allmählich wieder zur Besinnung gekommen. Das Beispiel des Muthes der Anderen wirkte ansteckend. Dazu kam die selbst- und zielbewußte Agitation, die auch der sogenannten öffentlichen Meinung mehr und mehr den Beweis lieferte, daß die Art und Weise, wie wir verfolgt wurden, unerhört sei, daß die Anklagen, die man gegen uns erhob, nicht gerechtfertigt waren, und daß eine Behandlung, wie wir sie erfuhren, mit den allgemeinen Rechtsgrundsätzen, die nun einmal dem modernen Staat zu Grunde liegen und, will er existiren, zu Grunde liegen müssen, unvereinbar sei. Diese Erkenntniß ist allmählich in immer weitere Kreise gedrungen, und ganz besonders durch die planmäßige und zielbewußte Thätigkeit der Partei so mächtig gefördert worden, daß man endlich einsah, in der alten Weise geht's nicht mehr, die Zügel müssen lockerer gehandhabt werden!

Ein Rückblick auf die Entwickelung der Partei in den letzten 20 Jahren an der Hand der durch die Ausübung der Wahl- berechtigung vorgenommenen Kraftproben ergiebt folgendes für uns sehr lehrreiche Resultat. Es wurden abgegeben bei den allgemeinen Wahlen im Jahre 1871: 102 000 Stimmen, 1874: 352 000 Stimmen, 1877, zwei Jahre nach dem Vereinigungskongreß der bis 1875 gespaltenen Partei: 493 000 Stimmen. Das war der höchste Stand der Stimmen vor dem Ausnahmegesetz. Ein Jahr darauf bereits wurde in Folge der beiden Attentate der Reichstag aufgelöst, eine ungeheure Hetze gegen unsere Partei, der man infamer Weise die Urheberschaft der Attentate zuschrieb, wurde in Szene gesetzt, und unter dem Hochdruck jener Hatz ging im Sommer 1878 die Zahl der Wahlstimmen von 493 000 auf 437 000 zurück, wir erhielten 56 000 Stimmen weniger als anderthalb Jahre zuvor. Dann kam das Gesetz mit seinen Schlägen, aber trotz alledem erhielten wir 1881 bei den allgemeinen Wahlen, die unter ganz beispiellosen Verhältnissen sich vollzogen, 312 000 Stimmen. Das war um so höher anzuschlagen, als unter den Ausnahmezuständen und dem Drucke jener Zeit ein großer Theil der Wahlkreise nicht einmal Flugblätter, nicht einmal Stimmzettel erhalten konnte, weil keine gegnerische Druckerei sie uns drucken wollte und die eigenen Druckereien fast sämmtlich vernichtet waren, und auch Flugblätter, wo man sie hatte, nur mit den größten Schwierigkeiten und Fährlichkeiten verbreitet werden konnten. Dann kamen die Wahlen von 1884. Diese Wahlen zeigten schon ein ganz anderes Bild. Die Partei hatte sich mittlerweile mächtig erholt, die Parteitage von Wyden und Kopenhagen waren vorüber und hatten das Selbstgefühl der Partei bedeutend gehoben. Hier und da waren auch mit Erfolg Versuche gemacht, neue Blätter ins Leben zu rufen, Druckereien zu erhalten u. s. w. und so gelang es diesmal 550 000 Stimmen, 238 000 mehr als 1881, aufzubringen. Aber 1887 wuchsen wir auf 763 000 und bei den letzten allgemeinen Wahlen dieses Jahres, die noch in Aller Erinnerung sind, auf 1 427 000 Stimmen. Die Partei war damit zugleich die stärkste Partei in Deutschland geworden.

Wir werden im Laufe unserer Verhandlungen noch hinlänglich Gelegenheit haben, über den Werth der Wahlen und der parlamentarischen Thätigkeit überhaupt zu sprechen. Ich erkläre indeß schon jetzt, daß die Agitation bei den allgemeinen Wahlen und die Thätigkeit der gewählten Abgeordneten im Reichstage nach meiner Ueberzeugung das allerwesentlichste und wirksamste Agitationsmittel für die großartige Entwickelung der Partei unter dem Sozialistengesetz gewesen sind. (Sehr richtig!) Wäre uns unter dem Gesetz auch die Reichstagstribüne verschlossen und die Ausübung des Stimmrechtes unmöglich gemacht gewesen, wir hätten kein Mittel besessen, auch nur annähernd festzustellen, in welcher Art und Gestalt die Partei sich entwickelt hatte und fortgeschritten war, wir hätten nicht entfernt unsere Agitation so ausgiebig, wie geschehen, entfalten können. Wie weit die parlamentarische Taktik der Fraktion den Wünschen der Parteigenossen entspricht, das zu erörtern wird Sache späterer Diskussion sein. Nach meiner Ueberzeugung hat die Partei alle Ursache, die bisherige Taktik auch fernerhin beizubehalten. Dafür

3

giebt es gar kein besseres Zeugniß, als die Worte, die heute von allen Seiten unsere Freunde und Genossen aus dem Auslande an uns gerichtet haben, und worin sie uns versicherten, in gleicher Weise, wie wir, thätig sein und arbeiten zu wollen, und daß auch sie die Möglichkeit zu besitzen wünschen, sich auf dem von uns betretenen Wege bethätigen zu können, was ja leider in verschiedenen von ihnen vertretenen Ländern wegen des Fehlens des allgemeinen Wahlrechts noch nicht möglich war.

Wir haben aber auch weiter gesehen, daß im Laufe der Jahre, und zwar durch die steigende Macht unserer Partei, das Interesse an der sozialen Bewegung die weitesten Kreise unserer Gegner ergriff. Sie wurden gezwungen, der Bewegung ihre Aufmerksamkeit zu schenken und sie zu studiren. Ich erinnere an den bekannten Erlaß vom 4. Februar, der unzweifelhaft ein großer moralischer Erfolg der Bestrebungen ist, welche im Juli vorigen Jahres auf dem internationalen Arbeiterkongreß in Paris zum Ausdruck gekommen waren. Selbst der Ultramontanismus sah sich in den letzten Monaten genöthigt, einen internationalen Kongreß zusammenzuberufen, um zu berathen, wie er am besten im Stande sei, dem stetigen Vordringen des Sozialismus einen Damm entgegenzusetzen. Ferner hat vor wenigen Tagen in Frankfurt a. M. ein Kongreß aus Vertretern mehr gelehrter Kreise stattgefunden, welcher ebenfalls die Nothwendigkeit internationaler Arbeitergesetzgebung anerkannte. Alles das sind die großen moralischen Erfolge nicht allein der deutschen, sondern der Sozialdemokratie aller Länder. Eine ganz besondere Aufmerksamkeit und erfreuliche Beachtung verdient aber unsererseits die Thatsache, daß seit den Tagen von Paris das Solidaritätsbewußtsein der Arbeiter der verschiedensten Länder sich in großartigster Weise entwickelt hat, wie ja schon der Pariser Kongreß selbst durch eine bisher nie dagewesene zahlreiche Vertretung der Arbeiter aller Länder für das Vorhandensein dieses internationalen Solidaritätsbewußtseins Zeugniß abgelegt und die Gegner gezwungen hat, mehr und mehr ihre Aufmerksamkeit der internationalen Bewegung zuzuwenden, um wo möglich der Bewegung Herr zu bleiben. Daß das letztere nicht geschehen wird, daß sie vielmehr unsern Gegnern ebenso wie die nationalen Bewegungen in den einzelnen Ländern über die Köpfe wachsen wird, davon sind wir Alle vollkommen überzeugt (Beifall).

Ich komme nun auf unsere jetzt vorhandene Presse, um auch an diesem Punkte darzuthun, wie die agitatorische Wirksamkeit der Partei innerhalb der letzten drei Jahre sich entfaltet hat. 1887 und früher konnten wir keine genaue Uebersicht der Preßorgane geben, welche unter der Herrschaft des Gesetzes ins Leben getreten waren; es war auch vielleicht nicht zweckmäßig, darüber öffentlich zu reden. Heute dagegen erscheint es mir sehr am Platze, zu untersuchen, wie unsere Preßverhältnisse innerhalb der Jahre von 1878 bis 1890 sich gestaltet haben.

Bei Erlaß des Sozialistengesetzes bestanden in Deutschland 42 politische Parteiblätter und 14 Gewerkschaftsorgane. Der gesammte Abonnentenbestand derselben ist nie genau festgestellt worden, er dürfte aber nach sachverständiger Schätzung 160—170 000 nicht überschritten haben. Von den 42 politischen Zeitungen erschienen 18 wöchentlich 6 Mal, 18 wöchentlich 3 Mal, 8 wöchentlich 2 Mal und 13 wöchentlich 1 Mal.

Gegenwärtig können wir eine genauere Uebersicht geben, aber vollständig zutreffende Mittheilungen vermag ich auch jetzt nicht zu geben, da mehrere Blattverwaltungen der Aufforderung, den Abonnentenbestand ihrer Blätter mitzutheilen, nicht Folge geleistet haben und demgemäß in der nachstehenden Aufstellung nicht berücksichtigt werden konnten. Die Uebersicht datirt von Ende September, die Umgestaltungen und Vermehrungen, die am 1. Oktober in verschiedenen Gegenden in erfreulichstem Maße stattgefunden haben, konnten hier also nicht berücksichtigt werden. — Es erschienen:

wöchentlich 6 Mal 19 Blätter, welche zwischen 80 000 u. 1100, im Ganzen 120 400 Abonnenten hatten,

wöchentlich 3 Mal 25 Blätter, welche zwischen 9 000 u. 250, im Ganzen 58 000 Abonnenten hatten,

wöchentlich 2 Mal 6 Blätter, welche zwischen 6 000 u. 450, im Ganzen 14 850 Abonnenten hatten,

wöchentlich 1 Mal 10 Blätter, welche zwischen 14 500 u. 1000, im Ganzen 60 850 Abonnenten hatten.

Insgesammt also 60 politische Blätter mit 254 100 Abonnenten.

Der Stand der Gewerkschaftspresse war folgender.

Es erschienen:

wöchentlich 1 Mal 17 Blätter, von welchen eins, dasjenige der Bergarbeiter, 27 000, das Zweite 16 000, das Dritte 15 000, das Vierte 12 500, das Fünfte 11 000, das Letzte 800 Abonnenten hatte. Im Ganzen hatten diese Blätter 155 350 Abonnenten,

monatlich 2 Mal bezw. 3 Mal 2 Blätter mit zusammen 4 400 Abonnenten,

alle 14 Tage bezw. monatlich 2 Mal 20 Blätter, welche zwischen 6 000 und 400, im Ganzen 39 750 Abonnenten hatten,

monatlich 1 Mal 2 Blätter mit zusammen 1500 Abonnenten.

Insgesammt 41 Blätter mit 201 000 Abonnenten.

Zu den angeführten Blättern kamen weiter: 1 wissenschaftliche Zeitschrift, die „Neue Zeit", die monatlich erschien und 2500 Abonnenten hatte, 1 Unterhaltungsblatt in Hamburg, der „Gesellschafter" wöchentlich erscheinend, mit 19 000 Abonnenten, und 2 Witzblätter mit über 107 000 Abonnenten.

Für Sie, die Sie fast ohne Ausnahme auch thätige Mitglieder der Gewerkschaftsbewegung sind, ist es kein Geheimniß, daß diese

3*

Bewegung sich mächtig entwickelt hat und ein wichtiges Bindeglied in der ganzen Arbeiterbewegung repräsentirt. Die Gesammtzahl aller Organe ist 104, die der Abonnenten ca. 600 000.

Daneben hat auch die sonstige Parteiliteratur einen ganz bedeutenden Aufschwung genommen, nicht nur die in Deutschland erschienene, sondern auch die nach Deutschland hereinspedirte. Zu keiner Periode der vorsozialistengesetzlichen Zeit sind auch nur annähernd solche Auflagen von Parteischriften hergestellt worden, als in der Periode der Herrschaft des Gesetzes, und dieser Aufschwung wird noch viel größer werden, wenn wir nächstens die Neuauflegung und weitere Ausgestaltung unserer Parteiliteratur vornehmen. Es ist selbstverständlich, daß kein Privatverleger ohne Zustimmung des Autors und der Partei eine Schrift erscheinen lassen darf. Ich nehme an, wir werden künftig keine Schrift unter einer Auflage von 20 bis 30 Tausend herzustellen haben, und für viele wird sie bedeutend höher werden, so groß ist die Nachfrage von allen Seiten. Vor dem Gesetz hatten wir in der Regel Auflagen von höchstens 5 Tausend.

Entsprechend dieser Entwicklung unserer agitatorischen Thätigkeit bei den Wahlen, in Parlament und Presse haben sich auch die materiellen Verhältnisse der Partei entwickelt, soweit die Parteileitung darüber Kenntniß hat und die Mittel bei ihr zusammengeflossen sind. Auch hier sind gegen früher Resultate zu verzeichnen, die wir wohl glänzend nennen dürfen.

Die im August 1880 auf dem Wydener Kongreß verrechneten Einnahmen betrugen für die Zeit vom November 1878 bis 1. August 1880 rund 37 100 Mark; auf dem Kopenhagener Kongreß, Anfang April 1883, wurden als Einnahme rund 95 000 Mark verrechnet, auf dem Parteitag in St. Gallen, Anfang Oktober 1887, rund 188 600 Mark. Unter dieser letzteren Einnahme waren auch die Posten verbucht, welche die deutschen Genossen in der Schweiz und die Inhaber des „Sozialdemokrat" vereinnahmt und an gemaßregelte deutsche Genossen verausgabt hatten.

Seit der Abrechnung auf dem Parteitag zu St. Gallen, die bis Ende August 1887 reichte, sind eingegangen:

	Einnahme:	Ausgabe:
für den Wahl- und Diätenfond . .	197 125,30 M.	95 388,50 M.
für den Unterstützungsfond	104 241,72 „	70 825,17 „
für den Elberfelder Prozeß	19 080,65 „	13 421,45 „
Vermischtes	3 884,40 „	12 449,95 „
Zinsen	6 071,65 „	— „
Kapital und Darlehnskonto	41 305,— „	191 240,25 „
Kassenbestand am 1. September 1887 bezw. 1. Oktober 1890	18 800,80 „	7 184,20 „
	390 509,52 M.	390 509,52 M.

Hierzu habe ich folgende Bemerkungen zu machen: Beim Wahl- und Diätenfond betrugen die Ausgaben für Wahlen 78 088,50 Mark, für Diäten und Reichstagskosten 17 300 Mark; beim Unterstützungs- fond für Unterstützungen 60,662,10, für Gerichts- und Prozeßkosten 10 163,07 Mark. Der besondere Fond für den Elberfelder Prozeß brauchte nur theilweise in Anspruch genommen zu werden, da die hierin nicht enthaltenen, von den Parteigenossen von Barmen- Elberfeld und Umgegend aufgebrachten Beträge sehr bedeutend waren, so daß bei diesem Prozeß für die Parteikasse ein ganz anständiges Plus abgefallen ist (Heiterkeit und Beifall). Die vermischten Ein- nahmen setzen sich zusammen aus Geschenken, aus Kursgewinnen — wir sind, wie Sie gehört haben, im Augenblicke Kapitalisten und haben auch manchmal Börsengeschäfte vorzunehmen (große Heiter- keit), und damit auch selbstverständlich mit Gewinn und Verlust zu rechnen. Unter den vermischten Ausgaben sind inbegriffen Porto- und Bureau-Ausgaben, Kosten der Konferenzen der Fraktion, Kosten für den Parteitag in St. Gallen und theilweise für Halle, Kosten für den Pariser Kongreß, die vergleichsweise hoch waren, weil wir außer den offiziellen Vertretern noch den französischen Freunden sehr namhafte Beiträge zur Deckung der Kongreßkosten übergaben; weiter finanzielle Unterstützung des auf Grund der vorjährigen Pariser Beschlüsse herausgegebenen Journals „Der Achtstundentag"; Zuschuß zu den Kosten der Errichtung eines Denksteins an dem Orte, wo Lassalle 1864 erschossen wurde; Kosten für Herstellung der Kongreß- protokolle, denen andererseits entsprechende Einnahmen aus dem Absatz gegenüberstehen. Am 1. Oktober 1890 war ein Kassenbestand von 7184,20 Mark vorhanden.

Die Einnahmen und die Ausgaben, ohne diejenigen für das Kapital- und das Darlehnskonto, die nur als durchlaufende Posten zu betrachten sind, und ohne die Zinsen und den Kassenbestand vom 1. Oktober 1890, stellen sich folgendermaßen:

	Einnahme:	Ausgabe:
Wahl- und Diätenfond . . .	197 125,30 M.	95 388,30 M.
Elberfelder Prozeß	19 080,65 „	13 421,45 „
Unterstützungsfond	104 241,72 „	70 825,17 „
Vermischtes	3 884,40 „	12 449,95 „
	324 332,07 M.	192 085,07 M.

Diese 324 322,07 Mark sind die wirklichen Einnahmen, die durch die Partei aufgebracht wurden. Mit den Zinsen (6071,65) und dem Kassenbestand (18 800,80) belief sich die gesammte Kassen- einnahme auf 349 204,52 Mark, die gesammten Ausgaben auf 192 085,07 Mark, so daß also das vorhandene Vermögen sich auf 157 119,45 Mark beliefe; in Wirklichkeit beläuft es sich auf

171 829,20 Mark, mit dem von früher vorhandenen Vermögensbestand. (Lebhafter Beifall.)

Das ist eine Summe, wie sie bisher die Partei nie aufzuweisen gehabt hat, ein recht schönes Handgeld, welches die neue Parteileitung in ihre Verwaltung bekommt. (Heiterkeit und wiederholter Beifall.)

Außer den hier angeführten Einnahmen sind durch die Partei aufgebracht worden:

für den Hasencleverfond . . . . 15 388,31 M.
für den Kayser-Kräckerfond . . . . . . 4 099,40 „
für die gemaßregelten Bergleute . . . 5 909,25 „

Diese zusammen mit den übrigen von der Partei aufgebrachten Beiträgen von 324 332,07 Mark ergeben 349 729,03 Mark, welchen für alle aufgeführten Fonds eine Ausgabe von 217 399,18 Mark gegenübersteht.

Unter diesen Summen sind selbstverständlich diejenigen Einnahmen und Ausgaben gar nicht enthalten, welche die Parteigenossen der einzelnen Orte und für die verschiedensten politischen Zwecke, so namentlich für die Reichstagswahlen, aufgebracht haben. Die Genossen der großen Städte, insbesondere Berlins und Hamburgs, haben es für ihre Pflicht gehalten, eine große Zahl von Nachbarkreisen materiell zu unterstützen. So haben die Hamburger Genossen einen großen Theil der Wahlkreise in Schleswig-Holstein und Mecklenburg und einen kleineren Theil der Wahlkreise in der Provinz Hannover aus ihren reicheren Mitteln unterstützt, und die Berliner Genossen haben einem großen Theil der Wahlkreise in den Provinzen Brandenburg und Pommern materiell kräftig beigestanden. Wie hoch alle die hier für ganz Deutschland in Betracht kommenden Summen sind, vermag ich natürlich nicht anzugeben; sie sind aber sehr bedeutend und um das mehrfache wohl höher, als die von mir angeführten Summen. Bemerken will ich weiter, daß sich unter den von mir aufgeführten Beiträgen auch diejenigen befinden, die als Ueberschüsse von den Eigenthümern verschiedener Parteiblätter zur Verfügung gestellt wurden. Ferner bin ich verpflichtet, hervorzuheben, daß unsere ausländischen Genossen einen sehr greifbaren Beweis ihres internationalen Solidaritätsgefühls bei der diesmaligen Wahlagitation unserer Partei dadurch gaben, daß sie es nicht nur bei Worten bewenden ließen, sondern ihre Gefühle auch durch klingende Münze zum Ausdruck brachten, indem sie Geldbeiträge uns sandten; das geschah durch unsere Genossen in Amerika, Holland, Belgien, der Schweiz, Oesterreich, Rumänien und sogar in Rußland. Ich glaube in Ihrer aller Sinne zu sprechen, wenn ich Sie bitte, sich zum Zeichen unseres Dankes von den Plätzen zu erheben. (Geschieht.) Ich will dann noch als besonders interessant anführen, und dieser Vorfall dürfte im Parteileben einzig dastehen, daß unsere Partei am 1. April, also nach Abschluß ihrer Wahlrechnungen, reicher war als am 15. Januar, wo wir offiziell in die Wahlagitation eintraten. (Heiterkeit und Beifall.)

Nun entsteht die Frage, in welch' nutzbringender Weise soll die künftige Parteileitung mit den ihr bereits zur Verfügung stehenden Fonds und den weiter zu erwartenden Mitteln wirthschaften. Dies gehört zwar nicht zu den Aufgaben meines Berichts, aber ich glaube es ist nützlich diese Frage zu streifen; zunächst wird es sich darum handeln, daß in den ländlichen und kleinstädtischen Bezirken weit lebhafter und umfänglicher wird agitirt werden müssen, als das bisher der Fall war und sein konnte, ich betrachte das als selbstverständlich. Ob wir dabei, wie vor dem Sozialistengesetz besoldete Agitatoren zu diesem Zweck bestellen sollen oder einen anderen, zweckmäßigeren Weg beschreiten müssen, lasse ich hier unerörtert. Dann aber wollen wir auch jetzt, wo wir wieder gleiches Recht für uns haben, obwohl ich glaube, daß auch dieses gleiche Recht unter Umständen für uns ein Ausnahmerecht werden wird. (Sehr richtig.) Denjenigen, die mit besonderem Stolz und Hochmuth darauf gepocht haben, daß die Sozialdemokratie ihnen nichts anhaben könnte, beweisen, wie sehr sie sich geirrt haben, ich meine die ultramontane Partei. (Lebhafte Zustimmung.) Dem Thurm des Centrums, der so zweifellos fest stehen soll, daß keine Macht der Erde ihn wankend machen oder gar stürzen soll können, hat, glaube ich, die Sozialdemokratie bereits bei den letzten Wahlen einige ganz gehörige Stöße versetzt. (Sehr richtig.) Und ich meine, wir sollten in der jetzt kommenden Periode erst recht zeigen, daß wir diesem Thurm nicht nur Stöße geben können, sondern daß wir auch das Untergrabungsgeschäft, dessen man uns so gern bezichtigt, (Heiterkeit), und das wir in den letzten 12 Jahren weiter so vortrefflich gelernt haben (große Heiterkeit), gründlich in Anwendung zu bringen verstehen.

Auch nach einer anderen Richtung wollen wir unsere agitatorischen Fühlhörner ausstrecken, ich meine in Bezug auf die ländliche Bevölkerung. (Sehr gut.) Es wird uns und der neuen Parteileitung allerdings nicht leicht fallen, und es wird uns auf den ersten Schlag nicht möglich sein, ein Organ für die ländlichen Arbeiter zu gründen, aber sie wird dieses als eine Hauptaufgabe im Auge behalten müssen. (Sehr wahr.) Ich muß mich zwar für meine Person dagegen erklären, daß aus allgemeinen Parteifonds die lokale Presse unterstützt wird — wir werden ja später noch darüber sprechen — ich halte es aber für nothwendig, daß dieser Fonds überall da zur Gründung von Preßorganen in erster Linie Verwendung findet, wo durch die Natur der Verhältnisse die betreffenden

Arbeiterschichten aus eigner Kraft absolut nichts zu schaffen vermögen, und hier kommen die ländlichen Arbeiter zunächst in Frage.
Wir werden ferner unsere agitatorische Thätigkeit erweitern müssen
durch Gründung eines polnischen Arbeiterorgans. (Bravo.) Die
polnische Arbeiter- und Industriebevölkerung ist weit stärker als
wir gemeiniglich glauben. Es ist ein Gegenstand der lebhaftesten
Klage unter den Bergarbeitern in Rheinland und Westfalen, daß
ihnen die polnisch sprechenden Bergarbeiter bei ihren Lohnbestrebungen
die größten Hindernisse bereiten, und daß insbesondere das Centrum
mit ganz besonderer Macht und Erfolg dieser polnisch sprechenden
Arbeiter sich bemächtigt hat. Es sind sogar eigene polnisch sprechende
Geistliche nach Rheinland und Westfalen geschickt worden, welche
dort predigen und agitatorisch thätig sein müssen, um durch polnische
Flugblätter die Arbeiter an sich zu fesseln. Dem gegenüber ist die
Gründung eines polnischen Arbeiterorgans und die Verbreitung
polnischer Flugblätter eine Nothwendigkeit.

Ebenso werden wir aus allgemeinen Mitteln für die Herausgabe
eines Parteiorgans für Elsaß-Lothringen Sorge tragen müssen.
(Sehr gut.) Unsere Genossen in Elsaß-Lothringen sind dazu nicht
im Stande, weil die dortige französische Preßgesetzgebung, die aber
nach preußisch-deutscher Manier gehandhabt wird (Heiterkeit), dies
außerordentlich erschwert. Weiter halte ich es im agitatorischen,
parlamentarischen und sozialgesetzlichen Interesse für dringend nothwendig, daß dem Beispiel einer Reihe jüngerer Gelehrten entsprechend, überall in besonders durch schlechte Lage sich auszeichnenden
Gewerbezweigen sozialstatistische Untersuchungen über die Lage der
Arbeiter angestellt werden. Sie wissen, wie von unseren Gegnern
allgemein bestritten wird, daß die Lage der Arbeiter so sei, wie
wir sie darstellen. Ich bin überzeugt, daß eine solche statistische
Untersuchung zu dem für unsere Gegner überraschenden Resultat
führen wird, daß die Verhältnisse der meisten Arbeiter in der That
viel schlechter sind, als allgemein angenommen wird. (Sehr richtig!)
Das muß aber durch gewissenhafte Untersuchungen festgestellt
werden, und dazu brauchen wir einen Generalstab tüchtiger und
fähiger Leute, die für ihre Reisen und ihre Arbeiten unterstützt
werden. Die Kosten werden zum Theil wieder aus dem Erlös der
durch den Buchhandel zum Verkauf gelangenden Schriften, die auf
Grund jener sozialstatistischen Untersuchungen erscheinen, eingebracht
werden können. Sollten diese Arbeiten aber auch 10 und 20000 Mark
und selbst mehr Zuschuß benöthigen, so wäre dies kein Schaden;
ich würde diese Anlage der Gelder für die nutzbringendste ansehen,
die von der Partei gemacht werden kann. (Sehr wahr!)

So stehen also nach allen Richtungen der neu zu organisirenden
Partei große Aufgaben bevor. Zeigen wir durch die Berathungen
auch dieses Parteitages, daß wir uns vollkommen der weltgeschicht-

lichen Miſſion bewußt ſind, die das Proletariat, und als Führerin des Proletariats, die Sozialdemokratie zugewieſen bekommen hat. Wir wollen den Gegnern, wie auch den zweifelnden Freunden in unſeren eigenen Reihen, zeigen, daß unſer Ruf iſt: Vorwärts, vorwärts und immer vorwärts! (Stürmiſches Bravo und Händeklatſchen.)

Vorſitzender Singer: Auf dem Parteitag in St. Gallen iſt bezüglich einer Reviſionskommiſſion für die Prüfung der Kaſſenverhältniſſe kein Beſchluß gefaßt worden. Da zur Zeit, als die Einberufer die Abhaltung dieſes Parteitages beſchloſſen haben, keine Körperſchaft in Deutſchland vorhanden war, der die Wahl der Reviſionskommiſſion übertragen werden konnte, hat die Fraktion es für richtig gehalten, ihrerſeits drei Genoſſen in Deutſchland mit dieſer Aufgabe zu betrauen, es ſind die Genoſſen Geck-Offenburg, Segitz-Fürth und Kloß-Stuttgart. Die Fraktion konnte dieſe Anordnung um ſo leichter treffen, als ſie mit der Führung der finanziellen Geſchäfte niemals etwas zu thun gehabt hat, vielmehr dieſe Angelegenheit einzig und allein dem Fraktionsvorſtande, der gleichzeitig als Parteivorſtand funktionirt, überlaſſen war. Die Fraktion war alſo, abgeſehen von den den Parteivorſtand bildenden Mitgliedern, in dieſer Frage vollkommen unintereſſirt.

Es wird alſo nach dieſer Richtung ein Zweifel nicht erhoben werden können.

Namens der Reviſionskommiſſion nimmt nunmehr das Wort Genoſſe Geck: Dem Auftrage der Fraktion entſprechend, begaben wir uns vor 8 Tagen in die Schweiz und ſetzten den Kaſſenſchrank unbeanſtandet in Zürich nieder. (Heiterkeit.) Wir waren nicht wenig erſtaunt über die Summen, welche ſich uns darboten und wir ſchwelgten einen Augenblick in dem Gefühl, auch einmal Kapitaliſten zu ſein. (Heiterkeit.) Dieſes Gefühl wich aber bald einem andern. Dieſe Zahlen, welche Bebel vorgetragen, beweiſen, daß die Sozialdemokratie nicht nur eine ſtarke Stirn und einen kräftigen Nacken, ſondern auch ein Herz im Leibe hat, das in Liebe ſchlägt, denn dieſe Zahlen athmen Liebe gegenüber den Verfolgten und Gemaßregelten; in dieſer Beziehung können uns diejenigen, welche die chriſtliche Liebe gepachtet haben, durchaus nicht das Waſſer reichen. Die Prüfung der Kaſſe war keine leichte Aufgabe. Es iſt auch ſelbſtverſtändlich, daß bei den Verhältniſſen, unter denen die Kaſſe geführt werden mußte, dies oder jenes nicht ſo klappen konnte, wie es vielleicht auf den erſten Blick hätte klappen ſollen. Wir haben einige Ungenauigkeiten und Irrthümer in den Büchern gefunden und richtig geſtellt und können nun den Antrag ſtellen, daß der Parteitag dem Parteirechner Decharge ertheile und ihm die Anerkennung ausſpreche, daß er als Kriegsminiſter und

Kasseninhaber es gut verstanden hat, die Kasse vor dem Feinde stets sicher zu stellen. (Heiterkeit und Beifall.)

In der nunmehr eröffneten Diskussion über den Bebel'schen Bericht lenkt Trautwein-Quedlinburg die Aufmerksamkeit des Parteitages auf die schlimme Lage der ländlichen Arbeiter unter der jetzigen Gesindeordnung, deren Beseitigung die Fraktion in erster Linie anstreben müsse. (Beifall.)

Schmidt-Berlin beantragt eine Kommission von 9 Mitgliedern zu wählen, welche die Streitigkeiten zwischen der Fraktion und den Berliner Parteigenossen zu regeln hat. Es ist nicht nothwendig, daß wir diese Angelegenheiten im Plenum, vielleicht zum Gaudium unserer Feinde, besprechen. Aber es muß über die Sache Klarheit geschaffen werden; das geschehe aber am besten in einer Kommission.

Der Vorsitzende hält es für zweckmäßiger, diesen Antrag an der Stelle zu berathen, wo die Anträge aus der Mitte des Parteitages zur Berathung kommen. In diesem Stadium der Verhandlung können nur etwaige Bedenken gegen die Parteileitung zur Sprache kommen, nicht aber persönliche Streitigkeiten. Der Antrag Schmidt könne nur als selbstständiger Antrag behandelt werden.

Schmidt hält seinen Antrag aufrecht. Von Seiten der Parteileitung und der Fraktion ist der Vorwurf erhoben worden, daß ein großer Theil der Genossen sozusagen mit der Polizei in Verbindung steht (große Unruhe; Glocke des Präsidenten).

Vorsitzender: Ich kann nicht zugeben, daß dieses Thema in der Breite hier verhandelt wird. Will aber der Genosse Schmidt nicht Abstand nehmen, so mag er seinen Antrag schriftlich einreichen. Der Antrag wird dann geschäftsordnungsmäßig erledigt werden.

Schmidt: Dies wird sofort geschehen.

Wilschke-Berlin (zur Geschäftsordnung): Man sollte doch die Vorurtheile gegen die Berliner Genossen fallen lassen. Wenn wirklich von den Berliner Genossen ein Bock geschossen worden ist....

Vorsitzender: Das gehört nicht zur Geschäftsordnung.

Wilschke: Ich wünsche nur, daß Redewendungen, wie vorhin gegen Gen. Werner, welche persönliche Zwistigkeiten oder Störungen hervorrufen könnten, vom Bureau unterdrückt werden.

v. Vollmar bittet dem Antrage Schmidt statt zu geben. Es werde damit vermieden, daß diese Angelegenheiten mit der eigentlichen Debatte über den Bebel'schen Bericht verquickt werden. Es werde damit der Sache die persönliche Spitze abgebrochen, und er zweifle nicht, daß sie in der Kommission befriedigend erledigt werden. (Zustimmung.)

Bebel: Es thut mir leid, daß ich dem Gen. Vollmar entgegentreten muß, weil ich auch beim besten Willen nicht zu sehen vermag,
was der Berliner Freund will und warum er Ursache hat, sich zu
beschweren. Eine Animosität gegen die Berliner liegt nicht vor,
sie sind ja auch hier genügend vertreten. Ebenso weiß ich nichts
von persönlichen Streitigkeiten zwischen der Parteileitung und den
Berliner Genossen. Ich bestreite, daß Schmidt da im Namen der
Berliner Genossen sprechen kann. Hat das eine oder andere Fraktionsmitglied Berliner Genossen beleidigt oder verletzt, dann möge man
bestimmte konkrete Thatsachen und Personen anführen, und dann
wollen wir die Kommission wählen. Wir können aber keine
Kommission wählen, wo wir gar nicht wissen, was in dieser
Kommission verhandelt werden soll. Bis jetzt liegt nichts vor, was
bei den nächstfolgenden Punkten der Tagesordnung nicht hier vor
offenem Plenum verhandelt werden wird. Es sind das Kontroversen in
Bezug auf die Parteitaktik, die parlamentarische Thätigkeit der
Fraktion u. s. w. Da wird die Fraktion Rede und Antwort stehen.
Eine solche Kommission müßte die Fraktionsmitglieder als Angeklagte
oder Zeugen vernehmen, und was kommt schließlich heraus? Ich
weiß es nicht, denn soweit es sich um allgemeine Angelegenheiten
handelt, gehören sie überhaupt vor den Parteitag, soweit es sich
aber um persönliche Reibereien handelt, müssen diese hier kurz angeführt werden, damit der Parteitag genau entscheiden kann, ob
es der Mühe werth ist, eine solche Kommission zu wählen.

Stolle-Gesau glaubt, daß nur solche Anträge angenommen
werden dürfen, welche mit dem Punkt der Tagesordnung direkt
zusammenhängen.

Der Antrag Schmidt-Berlin wird hierauf mit großer Mehrheit
abgelehnt.

Die Diskussion wendet sich wieder zu dem Bebel'schen Bericht.

Haburg-Potsdam wünscht ein möglichst billiges Parteiblatt
für die ländlichen Arbeiter. Es sei dankbar anzuerkennen, daß die
großen Städte, namentlich Berlin, die Agitation in den ländlichen
Kreisen unterstützt hätten, es sei aber sein, des Redners, Wahlkreis
dabei nicht berücksichtigt worden.

Werner-Berlin: Parteigenossen! Als die große Versammlung
in der Lips'schen Brauerei in Berlin stattfand, wandte ich mich zum
Schlusse derselben an Genossen Singer mit der Frage: soll hier
durch diese Resolution die Meinung der Berliner Genossen irgendwie in Frage gestellt, den Berliner Genossen ein Maulkorb umgelegt
werden? Da erklärte Singer, nein, dies wird nie und nimmermehr
stattfinden. Den Genossen Bebel bat ich in derselben Versammlung,
er möge der vermeintlichen Opposition doch wenigstens Gehör
schenken — sonderbarer Weise stand an den Litfaßsäulen: große

Volksversammlung, erster Punkt der Tagesordnung Referat von August Bebel. Der Name in ziemlich großen Lettern. In dieser Versammlung sind viel mehr Leute erschienen, die mal den Abgeordneten Bebel wollten sprechen hören; Singer und Bebel wissen aber sehr gut, daß die Berliner Parteigenossen doch auch noch ein anderes Forum hatten unter dem Sozialistengesetz, wo sie sich viel eingehender und genauer mit diesen Parteifragen beschäftigen konnten — ich sagte: „die Leute geben etwas auf Ihren Namen, schaffen Sie den Leuten wenigstens Gehör, damit die Zuschauer wenigstens ein objektives Urtheil gewinnen können. Wir wollen sagen, daß die Berliner Opposition nicht aus reiner Lust zur Opposition Opposition macht" (Unruhe). Als ich nun Bebel bat, er möchte wenigstens ein Wort einlegen und Ruhe stiften, ein Wort von ihm würde genügen, da zuckte er die Achsel und sagte, das geht mir nichts an. Das ist nicht die richtige Art und Weise, aufzutreten und der Objektivität die nöthigen Bahnen zu ebnen.

Der Rechenschaftsbericht Bebel's war viel zu einseitig. Ueber die Thätigkeit der Parteileitung in der Frage des 1. Mai hat Bebel nichts gesagt. Ich mache der Parteileitung nicht den Vorwurf, daß sie sich in diese Frage eingemischt hat, sondern daß sie den Aufruf zu spät erlassen hat. Man hat erst ein halbes Jahr in Deutschland Beschlüsse fassen lassen, ehe man sich darüber in der Parteileitung einigte.

In der Unterstützung der Freisinnigen bei den Stichwahlen hat die Parteileitung dem Beschlusse des St. Gallener Parteitages zuwider gehandelt. Sie hat diesen Beschluß einfach wegdekretirt und gesagt, die politischen Verhältnisse haben sich geändert, ergo müssen wir jetzt für unseren Erbfeind, dem Freisinn, doch noch unsere Stimmen abgeben.

Es giebt keinen Unterschied zwischen Parteigenossen erster und zweiter Güte, ich verlange für jeden einzelnen Parteigenossen das gleiche Recht, und deshalb bin ich für die Prüfung dieser Angelegenheit in einer Kommission. Wir Opponenten werden Gelegenheit haben müssen, Ihnen das Material zu geben, warum wir Opponenten sind. Wir wollen der Versumpfung in der Partei entgegentreten (lebhaftes oho! fortdauernde Unruhe) ... nun, ich will den Ausdruck „Versumpfung" zurücknehmen, ich will sagen, wunder Fleck, der schließlich zu einer Krankheit ausarten könnte (lebhafter Widerspruch). Sie wissen, daß ich mit Grillenberger einen Streit hatte. Ich will Ihnen zeigen, wie uns gegenüber eine Abschlachtung vor sich geht. Grillenberger, den ich nur oberflächlich gesehen und dem ich nur einmal guten Abend gesagt, über den ich vorher kein Wort gesprochen und den ich nachträglich in einer Versammlung sogar in Schutz genommen gegen einen nicht anständigen Angriff — er hat mich in Nürnberg des Geschäftssozialismus beschuldigt. Ich habe jeder Zeit auf dem Posten, wo ich stand, meine Schuldigkeit gethan (Zustimmung bei einem Theil der Berliner Delegirten). Ich glaube auch nicht, daß der Abgeordnete Grillenberger schuld ist, sondern es hat sich eine Zwischenperson zwischen die Parteileitung und die Berliner Genossen eingedrängt, wofür ich den Beweis bringen werde. Diese Zwischenperson hat sich nur ein gutes Ansehen geben wollen, um die Berliner Genossen bei der Parteileitung in Mißkredit zu bringen. Ich werde diese Person nachher in der Kommission namhaft machen. Nun ein Wort über meinen „Geschäftssozialismus". Als ich wegen meiner Agitation aus allen meinen Stellungen in Berlin entlassen wurde, wandte ich mich an das Berliner Volksblatt um die Stelle als Maschinenmeister. Die Stelle war frei, ich wollte Niemand verdrängen. Da wurde mir gesagt, Ihre Ansprüche sind um 3 Mark zu hoch, das kann das Parteiblatt nicht tragen (große Unruhe; Rufe: Unwahrheit! Lüge!). Ich rufe den Herrn Bading, als Drucker des „Volksblatt", zum Zeugen an, mit dem ich eine Unterredung gehabt, daß das keine Lüge ist. Ich war nun genöthigt, mich selbständig zu machen, weil ich dort keine Arbeit bekam. Nach kurzer Zeit stand in der „Fränkischen Tagespost" eine Briefkastennotiz: „leider ist es nur zu wahr, daß es in Berlin Geschäftssozialisten giebt; die Adresse des Briefschreibers, der uns dies mittheilt, steht zur gefälligen Verfügung". Ich wandte mich an Grillenberger mit dem höflichen Ersuchen, er möchte mir die Adresse des betreffenden Parteigenossen mittheilen. Darauf erhielt ich folgende Karte: „Die bewußte Adresse steht für Parteigenossen zur Verfügung, für Sie nicht." (Rufe: Pfui!) Es sollte nicht in der Partei die Gewohnheit Platz greifen, Andere mit Schmutz zu bewerfen. Ich habe der Parteileitung noch ganz andere Dinge vorzuwerfen. (Bebel: heraus damit!) Sie Alle wissen, wie gegen den jetzigen Abgeordneten Schippel, früherem Parteigenossen zweiter Güte, vorgegangen wurde. Einige hervorragende Parteigenossen haben sich nicht entblödet, die Berliner Volkstribüne als Polizeiblatt hinzustellen. (Sehr richtig!) Sie haben die Person des Redakteurs beschimpft. Wenn man diesen Terrorismus weiter gehen läßt, dann ist es schade um unsere Partei. Diese Abschlachtung durch einzelne Abgeordnete und durch die Parteileitung dürfen wir nicht noch länger dulden. Wir müssen uns darüber beschweren, daß unsere Abgeordneten zur ausländischen Presse gehen und in derselben Jeden, der es wagt, ihnen Opposition zu machen, heruntermachen, daß sie von unsauberen Elementen in der „Volkstribüne" sprechen u. f. w. Ein Abgeordneter hat in einer Arbeiterzeitung geschrieben: seht Euch diese Leute einmal an, sie haben die bekannten Beziehungen zum Molkenmarkt. Ich fordere die Parteigenossen auf, uns zu beweisen, daß wir Schurken und erkaufte Verräther unter uns haben. Wir protestiren ganz energisch gegen ein derartiges Gebahren einzelner Abgeordneten. Die Parteileitung hätte dagegen eintreten müssen. Ich werde die vorhin erwähnte Karte, damit ich nicht der Fälschung geziehen werde, hier zirkuliren lassen.

Leutert-Apolda: Die Genossen aus der Provinz haben gar kein Interesse daran, daß auf dem allgemeinen Parteitag persönliche und lokale Fragen in verletzender und beleidigender Form erörtert werden. Darüber mag eine Kommission entscheiden. Dies Forum ist zu heilig, als daß wir damit unsere Zeit vergeuden.

Theiß-Hamburg: Ich halte es den persönlichen Gefühlen der Berliner Genossen zu Gute, wenn sie in recht derber und aufgeregter Weise ihre Angelegenheiten erörtern. Es wird doch nicht so ohne Weiteres möglich sein, über diese Dinge hinwegzukommen, wie der letzte Redner meinte. Ich habe hier insbesondere die Postkarte Grillenbergers im Auge. Immerhin gehört doch der durch dieselbe schwer gekränkte Berliner Genosse zu uns, sonst hätte man ihn nicht nach hier gesandt. Er muß also das Vertrauen der Genossen genießen. Ich möchte aber bitten, daß wir diesen leidenschaftlichen, förmlich gehässigen Ton zu vermeiden suchen. Kehren wir mehr den Genossen heraus! Schließlich möchte auch ich um Aufklärung bitten, weshalb die Fraktion in der Frage des ersten Mai so spät das Wort ergriffen hat.

Wilschke-Berlin: Den Vorwurf, den Werner Bebel wegen der Lips-Versammlung machte, muß ich entschieden zurückweisen. Wäre eine Versammlung aus dem Kreise der internen Genossen einberufen worden, so hätte man denselben Vorwurf erhoben wie in Dresden, wo durch Zirkular eingeladen war. Alle, welche in jener Versammlung und in der Nähe Bebels waren, werden den Eindruck gewonnen haben, daß er eine Schlichtung herbeizuführen suchte.

Betreffs der Thätigkeit des Parteivorstandes zum 1. Mai muß ich dem Genossen Werner beipflichten. Durch die Erklärung der Fraktion wurden die großen Hoffnungen, die man auf den 1. Mai gesetzt und zu denen man schon Vorbereitungen getroffen hatte, zunichte gemacht. Die Aufregung darüber war in den Berliner Gewerkschaften eine sehr große. Ebenso verhält es sich mit der Haltung der Parteileitung in der Frage der Stichwahl. Auf dem St. Gallener Parteitage und auch bei anderen Gelegenheiten ist die freisinnige Partei mit den anderen bürgerlichen Parteien als die eine reaktionäre Masse bezeichnet worden; wir hatten deshalb kein Urfache, dieser Partei eine Begünstigung zu Theil werden zu lassen und für sie einzutreten.

Von einer Versumpfung der Partei kann darum jedoch kein Rede sein. Tritt eine Versumpfung ein, dann ist nicht der Partevorstand oder die Parteileitung schuld, sondern es sind diejenige Genossen schuld, die sie eintreten lassen. Einzelne Fehler las sich leicht korrigiren; dagegen muß ich allerdings Verwahrung einlegen, daß man, wie es von dem Leipziger „Wähler" geschehen ist, unsern Freund Schippel als Anarchisten oder dergleichen bezeichnet. Wenn wir Freunde Schippels sind, nun, ist das ein Fehler? Ich bin noch heute sein Freund. — Die Ausführungen Werner's zeigen, daß es unbedingt nothwendig ist, eine Kommission zur Prüfung der ganzen Angelegenheiten niederzusetzen.

Inzwischen ist folgender Antrag eingegangen:

Die Versammlung wolle eine Kommission, bestehend aus neun Personen, einsetzen zur Untersuchung der vom Genossen Werner vorgebrachten Beschwerden

a) gegen den Genossen Grillenberger,

b) gegen das von ihm der Kommission zu benennende Mitglied, das sich zwischen die Parteileitung und Berlin gedrängt haben soll,

c) gegen seine Behandlung bei Bewerbung um Anstellung im „Volksblatt",

d) gegen zu scharfes Vorgehen gegen Genosse Schippel,

e) gegen ungerechte Bezeichnung Berliner Genossen als Spitzel.

Arthur Stadthagen.

Unterstützt durch Wilschke, Klein, Janiszewski, Porges, Hirsch, Plasse, Wurm.

Emmel-Frankfurt a. M.: In Bezug auf die Maifeier ist der Fehler gemacht worden, daß die Fraktion nicht sofort Stellung nahm, als in den großen Versammlungen in Berlin und Hamburg beschlossen wurde, am 1. Mai zu feiern. In der Resolution der Fraktion war freilich gesagt worden, daß man am 1. Mai feiern könnte, aber der moralische Eindruck konnte nicht erzielt werden, wenn die Demonstration nicht großartig ausfiel. Daran war aber nach Bekanntwerden der Resolution der Fraktion nicht mehr zu denken. Es wird darauf zu sehen sein, eine derartige unsichere Haltung in Zukunft zu vermeiden.

Wenn die Fraktion in der letzten Stunde vor den Stichwahlen für den freisinnigen Kandidaten zu stimmen anrieth, so billige ich das prinzipiell eigentlich auch nicht. Es war ein Verstoß gegen den St. Gallener Beschluß. Es ist aber zu berücksichtigen, daß die Wähler in den einzelnen Kreisen bei den Stichwahlen doch für den Freisinnigen gestimmt hätten. Daß wir offen als Partei eintreten für eine andere Partei, würde ich entschieden mißbilligen; wenn aber die Genossen einmal wählen, dann mögen sie wenigstens für einen Kandidaten stimmen, der nicht mit der Regierung durch Dick und Dünn geht. So wollen wir es auch künftig halten; aber wir beanspruchen keine Gegenleistung, wir verzichten auf alle Kompromisse.

Die Gründung eines Organs für die ländlichen Arbeiter würde ich mit Freude begrüßen. Es müßten aber schon vorher, sobald wie möglich, Flugblätter für die Landleute und besonders für die katholischen Gegenden zur Bekämpfung der Zentrumspartei massenhaft verbreitet werden.

Schulze-Erfurt: Wir müssen Alle wünschen, daß der Streit zwischen den Berliner Genossen und der Fraktion endgiltig gelöst werde. Die Ursache des Streits liegt darin, daß ein Theil der Genossen sich noch nicht in die neuen Verhältnisse nach dem Sozialistengesetz hat finden können. Wenn der Parteitag erst gesprochen hat, dann werden alle Mißverständnisse schwinden.

Auch ich kann es nicht billigen, daß in Bezug auf die Maifeier von der Fraktion abgewinkt ist. Wäre sie großartig und unbeeinflußt vor sich gegangen, die Maßregelungen wären mindestens nicht größer gewesen als es der Fall war. Aus unserem Zwiespalt schöpften unsere Gegner den Muth, um gegen die Arbeiter, die trotzdem feierten, Front zu machen. Wäre in ganz Deutschland gefeiert worden, wo hätte man die Streikbrecher für Hamburg herbekommen? Doch denken wir lieber an die Zukunft. Da möchte ich Ihnen zur Erwägung anheimgeben, ob es nicht zweckmäßig wäre, auch ein Blatt für Arbeiterinnen herauszugeben, welches der Provinzialpresse zum Herstellungspreis als Sonntagsbeilage überlassen werden könnte.

Was die Agitation betrifft, so müssen besonders das Land und die Industriedörfer berücksichtigt werden.

Zapay-Marburg: Auch wir in Hessen sind der Ueberzeugung, daß für die ländliche Bevölkerung etwas geschehen muß, wenn anders wir Böckels Agitation gegenüber nicht in einzelnen Distrikten zurückweichen sollen.

Was den 1. Mai betrifft, so war es sehr gut, daß die Fraktion abwiegelte, denn unsere Gegner haben nur auf einen Vorwand zu Maßregelungen gelauert. Deshalb war es gut, daß es in das freie Ermessen der Arbeiter gestellt wurde, zu feiern oder nicht. Ich bin von Marburg besonders beauftragt worden, dies hier zu erklären. Außerdem bin ich beauftragt worden, dahin zu wirken, daß in dem Programm die Bestimmung stehen bleibt: Die Religion ist Privatsache.

Frau Ihrer: Die Vorbereitungen zur Herausgabe einer Frauenzeitung sind nahezu abgeschlossen; es bedarf nur noch der Zustimmung meiner Genossinnen. Beilagen in der Form von Unterhaltungsblättern haben gar kein Resultat erzielt, sie dienen nur zur Unterhaltung der Frauen, wie viele andere Klatschblättchen auch. Uns thut eine wirkliche Frauenzeitung noth, und nach den mir gewordenen Mittheilungen bin ich sicher, daß die Frauen diese Zeitung auf der Höhe der Zeit erhalten werden (Bravo), vorausgesetzt, daß die

Genossen uns in der Weise unterstützen, daß sie ihre eigenen Frauen dafür anregen. (Heiterkeit und Beifall.) Wenn der Mann seiner Frau sagt, wir halten ja schon eine Zeitung, dann ist alle unsere Mühe vergebens. Auf dem Pariser Congreß sind alle Genossen verpflichtet worden, die Frauenbewegung in jeder Weise, also geistig und materiell, zu unterstützen. Was ist bisher geschehen? Von Seiten der Männer, mit wenigen, rühmlichen Ausnahmen, so gut wie nichts. Wir Frauen haben noch keine Fonds, und man hat uns gesagt: Ihr könnt nicht zum Parteitag entsandt werden, weil Ihr keine materiellen Mittel habt. Ja, da hättet Ihr Männer die Pflicht, für uns einzutreten. Wir wollen keine Extrabewegung für die Frau, keinen Sport; wir wollen nur die allgemeine Arbeiterbewegung unterstützen, rechnen dann aber auch auf Eure Unterstützung. Also behandeln Sie uns nicht so kühl abweisend, und unterstützen sie uns materiell. Wir haben ein Recht darauf, von Ihnen als vollberechtigte Genossinnen behandelt zu werden. Unterstützen Sie uns materiell und geistig, das wird seine Früchte tragen. Es handelt sich hier nicht um Spielereien, sondern um den vollen Ernst der Zeit! (Lebhaftes Bravo und Händeklatschen.) Hierauf wird die Sitzung abgebrochen. Schluß 1 Uhr.

Nachmittagssitzung.

3 Uhr. Den Vorsitz führt Dietz, welcher die Schriftführer Ernst-Berlin, Schwartz-Lübeck und Oertel-Nürnberg auf das Büreau beruft.

Die Diskussion über Punkt 1 der Tagesordnung wird fortgesetzt. Es sind ca. 40 Redner gemeldet.

Germer-Groitzsch: Mit Freuden begrüße ich, daß unsere Agitation jetzt die ländlichen Kreise kräftiger in Angriff nehmen soll. Es muß dort in der That in Zukunft viel mehr geschehen. Populär gehaltene Flugblätter müssen die Vorarbeit besorgen. Wir dürfen nicht hoffen, daß das Organ, welches wir für die ländlichen Arbeiter erscheinen lassen, von denselben auch sofort gehalten wird; im Sommer haben die Leute kaum Zeit zum Lesen, und wenn sie dafür noch Geld ausgeben sollen, thun sie es erst recht nicht. Also muß für unentgeltliche Lektüre gesorgt werden, zunächst auch auf dem von Berlin empfohlenen Wege, die gelesenen Blätter aufs Land zu schicken und so den Landarbeitern Gelegenheit zu geben, sie zu studiren. Auf dem flachen Lande, wo Industrie fehlt, ist die Agitation besonders schwierig; dort hat man stellenweise unsere Genossen fürchterlich mißhandelt. Auch hier muß besonders in der ersten Zeit durch Flugblätter vorgearbeitet werden.

Ein inzwischen eingelaufener Antrag Guttenstein und Genossen, die Differenzen der Berliner Genossen vollständig von der Diskussion zu trennen, wird zurückgezogen, nachdem der Vorsitzende darauf verwiesen, daß der Antrag Stadthagen ausdrücklich mit zur Debatte gestellt ist.

Metzner-Berlin I: In den beiden Fragen des Verhaltens der Fraktion zum 1. Mai und betreffs der Stichwahlen habe ich klarzustellen, daß die von Werner als Berliner vertretene Anschauung nicht von allen Berliner Genossen getheilt wird. Im I. Wahlkreise, und auch in mehreren anderen, ist man mit dem Für und Wider kurz vor dem 1. Mai nicht einverstanden gewesen; aber darin, ob der Fraktion lediglich die Schuld hierfür beizumessen sei, gingen die Ansichten weit auseinander. Ein großer Theil der Genossen stand und steht auf dem Standpunkt, daß der erste Schritt zum Auseinandergehen der Anschauungen von der „Berliner Volkstribüne" gethan worden ist. Sie meinen, dieses Blatt hätte sich vorher näher bei der Fraktion informiren müssen. Ein Fehler ist damit begangen worden, daß das Protokoll des vorjährigen Pariser Kongresses, welches den bezüglichen Beschluß enthielt, so spät an die Oeffentlichkeit gelangt ist. Denn aus diesem Protokoll hätte mit Leichtigkeit ersehen werden können, daß der Beschluß nicht so strikte auf allgemeines Feiern lautete. Auch bezüglich der Stichwahlen waren in Berlin die Meinungen sehr getheilt. Vielfach aber hat die Ansicht vorgeherrscht, daß in der Aufforderung der Fraktion ein Verstoß gegen den Beschluß von St. Gallen nicht gefunden werden kann. Auch ich habe dieses taktische Vorgehen dahin aufgefaßt, daß möglichst das Kartell gesprengt werden sollte. Lautet das Urtheil jetzt anders, weil wir wiederum vor einem Kartell stehen, so ist das Urtheilen nach vollzogenen Thatsachen bekanntlich leichter, als vorher. Man ist stets klüger, wenn man vom Rathhause kommt. Ich bestreite nun aber entschieden, daß gerade diese beiden Punkte die Opposition in Berlin hervorgerufen haben. Die Opposition ist viel älteren Datums, sie ist Jahre lang früher schon vorhanden gewesen; schon vor 4 Jahren hat sie sich breit gemacht, indem sie dem St. Gallener Beschluß eine ganz andere Auslegung gegeben hat, als er sie zuläßt. Die Opposition ist damals schon gegen die Stadtverordnetenwahlen mit einem gewissen Terrorismus aufgetreten. Ebenso in jüngster Zeit, wo große Versammlungen mit erdrückender Mehrheit für die Betheiligung entschieden, erklärte Werner gerade heraus, er füge sich nicht; für dieses Mal allenfalls noch, aber im Allgemeinen müsse er auf seinem Standpunkte beharren. Die Opposition hatte sich also gewissermaßen in Permanenz erklärt; sie benutzt die erwähnten beiden Beschwerdepunkte nur als Vorwand. Der Kommission muß das Material, wenn sie gründlich prüfen soll, auch vollständig geliefert werden. Wenn hier gefolgert worden ist, daß der Zwiespalt des 1. Mai die wesentliche Ursache der späteren Maßregelungen geworden sei, so gebe ich zu bedenken, daß, selbst wenn die Fraktion die Parole „allgemeine Feier" ausgegeben hätte, dieselbe doch den gewünschten imposanten Charakter nicht würde getragen haben, weil die gewerkschaftliche Organisation noch nicht so weit gekräftigt ist, um jeden Einzelnen, mindestens aber die große Masse vor Maßregelungen zu schützen. Ich besorge leider, daß, wenn der Parteitag entschieden Stellung gegen die Opposition nimmt, diese nicht nur nicht aufhören, sondern neue Anknüpfungspunkte finden wird. In der Sache selbst bitte ich die Einsetzung einer Kommission zu beschließen, und diese Kommission möge unparteiisch und streng prüfen! (Lebhafter Beifall.)

Volderauer-Karlsruhe: Das Referat Bebels ist mit Unrecht als einseitig bezeichnet worden. Was uns Bebel über die Vorgänge in der Partei während 12 Jahre in einer Stunde berichtet hat, war nicht einseitig, sondern sehr vielseitig, namentlich was unsere Aufgaben für die Zukunft betrifft; und damit haben wir uns doch vor allem zu befassen. Bezüglich des Vorwurfs der zu späten Ausgabe der Parole zum ersten Mai meine ich, die Parteileitung hat sich zunächst über die Verhältnisse im ganzen Lande, über die Stimmung in den einzelnen Gewerkschaften orientiren wollen; die Parole, so spät sie kam, war die einzig richtige. Man darf die Berliner Gewerkschaften nicht mit denen bei uns im Süden vergleichen. — Bei den Stichwahlen ist es uns in Baden gerade durch die angerathene Taktik gelungen, den Liberalismus völlig aus dem Felde zu schlagen; selbst den Wahlkreis Karlsruhe haben wir uns näher gebracht. Seit dem St. Gallener Kongreß haben sich eben die Verhältnisse, und mit ihnen die Ansichten, erheblich geändert. Die Thätigkeit der Parteileitung bitte ich in Zukunft dahin zu lenken, daß alle Kraft auf die Wahlkreise verwandt wird, wo die Genossen am Platze zu schwach sind. In diesem Punkte hätten wir Grund zu klagen; wir machen aber doch keine Opposition, denn wir wissen, daß die Leitung alles thut, was irgend in ihrer Macht steht. Die Berliner würden ihrer Sache viel mehr dienen, wenn sie sie mit größerer Ruhe und ohne alles Hereinziehen persönlicher Momente vorbringen würden. Ich muß mich ganz entschieden gegen solche Zeitvergeudung erklären. (Beifall.)

Grenz-Chemnitz: Auf die beiden taktischen Fragen wird Bebel wohl noch näher eingehen. Ich denke über dieselben ähnlich wie Werner; aber dieser würde seiner Sache mehr Sympathieen erwerben, wenn er nicht immer auf die Fraktion hinwiese, als auf den Bösewicht, der da wieder diese oder jene große Sünde begangen habe. Auch die Parteileitung ist nicht unfehlbar. Wie gerade die Berliner die Schuld für den ersten Mai der Parteileitung zuschreiben wollen, verstehe ich nicht. Diese tüchtigen

4*

Berliner Genossen hätten doch selbstständig etwas Verständiges
leisten können. Aber wenn sie nicht geführt werden, gehen sie um-
her wie die irrenden Schafe (Heiterkeit); das zeigt, daß sie der
Führung und Leitung noch sehr bedürftig sind. Im sächsischen
Erzgebirge sind wir verständiger vorgegangen. Wenn in Versammlungen die Inscenirung großer Streiks beschlossen wird, so
genügt uns das nicht; wir haben Fragebogen an alle Arbeiter
verschickt, wodurch wir einmal Zeit gewinnen, und dann auch die
wahre Meinung der Arbeiter erfahren wollten. Es ergab sich, daß
zwei Drittel aller Arbeiter gegen die Feier waren. So hätten sich
doch die Berliner Genossen, welche sonst so sehr vorneweg sind,
auch einmal ohne den Rath der Fraktion behelfen können! Für
das Vorgehen der Fraktion bezüglich der Stichwahlen glaube ich
herausgefunden zu haben, was sie uns hat sagen wollen: Wenn
wir über einen recht sumpfigen Graben hinüberspringen wollen und
nicht mit einem Satz hinüberkommen können, dann sollen wir erst
einmal in der Mitte festen Fuß fassen; wir können die Arbeitermassen nicht sofort zur Sozialdemokratie hinüberziehen, sondern
müssen unter Umständen auch einmal unter den bürgerlichen Parteien
das kleinere Uebel, z. B. die Freisinnigen, wählen. Schippel ist
leider von verschiedenen Seiten ganz gefährlich verdächtigt worden.
Von einigen Freunden aus dem hohen Norden ist wörtlich gesagt
worden: „Paßt mal auf, was das werden wird!" Auf Grund der
Schreibweise der „Volkstribüne" ist ihm zur Last gelegt worden,
daß er irgendwie mit einer anderen Gesellschaft zusammenhängen
müsse und dergleichen. Schippel hat, glaube ich, gezeigt, daß er
zu uns gehört; er hat so agitirt, daß ihm die Agitation neun
Monate eingebracht hat. Die Klagen der Berliner über die schwere
Arbeit, die sie hätten, sind unberechtigt. Sie sollten mal in die
Bezirke gehen, wo nicht immer 2000 Mann in einer Versammlung
anwesend sind, wo die Leute einzeln bekehrt werden müssen. — Redner
spricht sich weiter für eine rege Landagitation und für eine eigene
Frauenzeitung aus.

Franz Berndt-Berlin IV: Genosse Metzner hat schon zutreffend
bemerkt, daß man nicht glauben solle, es ständen alle Berliner
Parteigenossen durchgehends zu der Ansicht von Werner und Wildberger. Ich bestätige hier, daß ich trotz meiner abweichenden Ansichten mit der größten Majorität gewählt worden bin. Ich muß
auch dagegen protestiren, daß Werner so thut, als spräche er hier
für die gesammten Berliner. Er ist nicht in Berlin, sondern
in Teltow-Beeskow gewählt. Hört man ihn, so muß man
meinen, in Berlin sei nur Pech und Schwefel vorhanden, dort
alles gewillt, gegen die Fraktion zu gehen. Wenn Werner sagt
die Berliner leiden an Oppositionswuth, so sage ich aus voll
Ueberzeugung: zum Theile trifft das zu; aber die Berliner Oppositi

ist eine künstlich erzeugte, erzeugt von einigen wenigen Personen (Zurufe), diese Ueberzeugung kann mir niemand aus dem Herzen reißen (sehr gut! und Beifall). Berlin ist keineswegs das Heerlager der Opposition. Man sollte diesen Leuten tiefer ins Herz, in die Augen sehen, ihre Intelligenz prüfen. Wenn ich oder ein anderer mit der Fraktion sich einverstanden erklärt, muß es da nicht sehr unangenehm berühren, wenn es dann immer heißt: man tutet in das Horn der Fraktion mit hinein? Versammlungen, die zu demselben Resultat kommen, spricht man Urtheil und Verständniß ab, nennt sie nach der Theorie des Herrn Wille eine Hammelheerde! Dagegen protestire ich; ich folge der Vernunft! (Bravo!) Bezüglich der Stichwahlen hat nicht die Fraktion, nicht die Parteileitung einen Fehler gemacht, sondern die Genossen, welche auf dem St. Gallener Parteitage den Enthaltungsbeschluß faßten. Unsere Taktik muß sich den jeweiligen Verhältnissen anpassen; wir sind eine Partei der Entwicklung. Thoren wären wir gewesen, wenn wir angesichts der Ergebnisse des 20. Februar nur an dem alten Grundsatz hätten festhalten wollen. Das Vorgehen der Parteileitung war also völlig motivirt. Was den 1. Mai betrifft, so sollte Genosse Werner doch mal selbst in sich gehen. Heute war der Kongreß in Paris geschlossen, übermorgen schon fanden in Berlin Versammlungen statt, in denen sofort beschlossen wurde, den 1. Mai zu feiern, ohne genau zu wissen, wie denn der Kongreßbeschluß eigentlich lautete. Das wirkte epidemisch; überall ging der Antrag durch, den 1. Mai zu feiern. Man war förmlich wild. Vielen andern aber kam auch schon damals der Gedanke, ob ein gemeinsames Feiern am 1. Mai nicht zu Scenen führen könnte, die der Einzelne dann schwer verantworten müßte. Das ist meine und zahlreicher Genossen Ueberzeugung, die Ueberzeugung der Majorität der Berliner Genossen, die spreche ich aus und bitte deshalb, nicht von uns zu sagen, das sei blos eine Horntuterei gewesen. (Lebhafter Beifall.)

Es wird von zwei Seiten der Schluß der Debatte beantragt und ausreichend unterstützt.

Nachdem Pittak für und Horn-Löbtau gegen den Schluß gesprochen, wird der Antrag abgelehnt.

Gewehr-Elberfeld: Diese unerquicklichen Streitereien sind auch eine Folge des Ausnahmegesetzes, welches das Spitzelsystem großgezogen hat. Berechtigte Beschwerden und persönliche Häkeleien werden mit einander vermengt. Viele Parteigenossen glauben, es sei Manchem blos darum zu thun, dieses oder jenes Mitglied der Fraktion zu stürzen. Nur ein Vorwurf gegen die Fraktion ist nicht so ganz unbegründet, das betrifft den 1. Mai. Thatsächlich ist der Vorschlag der Fraktion zu spät gekommen. Dagegen kann ich im Verhalten der Fraktion zu der Stichwahlfrage einen Fehler nicht

jener Adreffe! Da schrieb ich ihm, was hier verlesen worden ist. Ich beanspruche als mein Recht, Diesen oder Jenen als würdig anzuerkennen, Parteigenosse zu sein. So wenig ich Stöcker oder Most als Parteigenossen anerkenne, so wenig lasse ich mir oktroyiren, Werner als würdigen Genossen anzuerkennen. Es liegen noch andere Dinge gegen ihn vor (Werner: heraus damit!) in allgemein menschlicher Beziehung, für die ich auch der Kommission Beweise bringen werde. (Andauernder Beifall und Zischen; fortdauernde Bewegung.)

Stolle-Gesau: Es ist das Recht des Parteitages, an der Parteileitung Kritik zu üben; aber Werner ist weit über dieses Recht hinausgegangen. Er hat seine Kritik mit Persönlichkeiten vermischt, die absolut nicht hierhergehören. Was hat die Parteileitung mit der „Volkstribüne" zu thun gehabt? Nichts! Was gehen Werner's persönliche Angelegenheiten mit dem Drucker des „Volksblatt" den Parteitag an? (Sehr richtig.) Alle diese Privatsachen sind in der Komission auszufechten. Wenn endlich der Leipziger „Wähler" Stellung genommen hat gegen die „Tribüne", mag sie scharf gewesen sein oder nicht, so geht das wiederum die Parteileitung gar nichts an. Wir haben ja noch den Punkt „Presse" auf der Tagesordnung; sehen wir also jetzt davon ab. Auch Werner soll beweisen, daß ihm die Parteiangelegenheiten höher stehen, als seine eigenen. (Beifall.)

Liebknecht: Ich werde das Persönliche möglichst vermeiden und mich auf die Kritik der gegen die Parteileitung und Fraktion von der Opposition erhobenen Angriffe beschränken. Zunächst bin ich selbst hier herangezogen worden im Zusammenhang mit einem Artikel des „Wähler." Mein Name ist zwar nicht genannt, der Artikel ist aber von mir, ich bekenne mich zur Autorschaft. In jenem Artikel sollen die Berliner Genossen anarchistischer Taktik beschuldigt worden sein. Das ist beiläufig nicht der Fall; früher, so heißt es in dem Artikel, als noch anarchistelnde Elemente in Berlin vorhanden waren, wäre diese Taktik der Wahlenthaltung auf fruchtbaren Boden gefallen, — und das ist gewiß richtig, ich habe ja ihre Flugblätter selbst in Händen gehabt. Das Ganze ist aber schon verschiedene Jahre her; der Artikel trifft keinen der jetzigen Leute; man sieht, mit welchen Mitteln hier gearbeitet wird. Die Berliner Genossen aber schieben diese Opposition von den Rockschößen; in 5 Versammlungen, die ich dieses Jahr in Berlin abgehalten habe, ist sie mir niemals entgegengetreten. Da habe ich denn gefunden, daß diese sog. Opposition eine verschwindende Minorität ist, die ich bis jetzt noch nicht zu Gesicht bekommen habe. Ist es nun nicht eine anarchistische Kampfesweise, wenn ich allen Parlamentarismus, die Betheiligung an jeder Thätigkeit auf gesetzlichem Wege für verwerflich erkläre? Was bleibt uns dann

noch übrig? Diese jetzt so unreif vertretene Theorie ist ja schon
früher, und zwar viel klarer und viel logischer, von Most gepredigt
worden; das sind ja für uns alles „olle Kamellen". Der Fraktion
vorwerfen, daß sie nicht mit dem Kopf durch die Wand gerannt ist,
heißt ihr das Zeugniß ausstellen, daß sie vernünftig gehandelt hat.
Den letzteren Weg gehen vernünftige Menschen, den ersteren gehen
Narren! (Bravo.) Wir verwerfen die rohe Gewalt. Und doch
ist unsere Partei eine Partei der Revolution, das haben wir
niemals verleugnet. Wir wollen die heutige Produktionsform
umgestalten; das unterscheidet uns von allen übrigen Parteien. Aber
in der Anwendung der Gewalt sind uns doch die Gegner über.
Was uns unsere Kraft giebt, ist jene Agitation, welche an die
Massen appellirt: unsere Taktik muß ihnen beweisen, daß wir in
vernünftiger Weise nach Macht streben, um unsere Ziele zu verwirklichen. Was ist aus dem Appell an die Gewalt geworden?
In einem Monat vollendet sich das dritte Jahr, daß die Märtyrer
von Chicago am Galgen ihr Leben endeten. Was hat sie an den
Galgen geliefert? Die Theorie, welche Gewalt der Gewalt entgegen-
setzen wollte! Wenn wir uns auf den Boden stellen wollten, dann
sind wir verloren. Wenn wir auch stark sind, wohlan, gegen uns
stehen 80% der Bevölkerung; wenn wir proklamiren, wir wollen
nicht durch Gesetz, sondern durch Zertrümmerung des Gesetzes unser
Ziel erreichen; nun wohlan, wir haben 20%, unsere Gegner 80,
sie haben die Armee, die Kanonen und die Polizei, sie stecken uns
ins Zuchthaus oder besser noch ins Narrenhaus, denn dahin gehörten
wir! Gehen wir fort, wie wir begonnen haben, dann wird es
besser werden; mit jedem Schritt vorwärts wächst unsere Macht.
Wir repräsentiren eine Kraft, und wollen sie nicht durch thörichte
Maßregeln einfach verpulvern. Wir wollen nicht für unsere Gegner
arbeiten! — Was nun die Correspondenz in einem ausländischen
Blatte betrifft, so habe ich die Sache in einer Notiz in einem
dänischen Blatte berührt. In der ausländischen Presse war gesagt
worden: Jetzt sind diese Parlamentarier alt geworden; das Proletariat,
welches sie erweckt haben, drängt sich vor, die „Jungen" fressen mit Haut
und Haaren diese Alten auf. Solche Hanswurstiaden glaubten ja unsere
Genossen nicht; aber unsere Genossen im Auslande und auch die Gegner
mußten über die Lügenhaftigkeit solcher Berichte aufgeklärt werden. Und
da frage ich: Ist es ehrenhaft, einen Mann, der unter dem Sozialistengesetz für ein auswärtiges Blatt schreibt, als Korrespondent dieses
Blattes zu nennen, das nicht unter deutscher Zensur und nicht
unter dem Ausnahmegesetz erscheint? Das ist einfach eine Denunziation! (Sehr richtig!) Dann hieß es noch im Anschluß an diese
paar Zeilen, in denen ich die Opposition solchermaßen charakterisirt
habe, ich hätte ein Preßbureau. Ich habe mein Urtheil einem auswärtigen Freunde, ich glaube es war Lafargue, geschrieben. Auf

dieſes mein Urtheil nahm ſpäter ein Artikel im „Temps" Bezug; ich ſelbſt habe aber für dieſes Blatt keine Zeile geſchrieben. Auch nicht nach Oeſterreich für das Wiener Parteiorgan. Der Genoſſe, der in dieſes Blatt ſchrieb, hat ſich mit ſeinem Namen als Verfaſſer des Artikels bekannt. Soll man ſich denn, ohne das Recht der Vertheidigung, die Vorwürfe von Korruption und Verſumpfung einfach gefallen laſſen? War das ein einfacher Scherz von Ihnen? — für ſo ſcherzhaft, wie ſie ſelbſt ſich nehmen, nehme ich ſie nicht! Jeder ehrliche Parteigenoſſe hat ſelbſtverſtändlich das Recht der freien Kritik. Räſonniren Sie, ſchimpfen Sie, kritiſiren Sie meine Perſon, es iſt mir egal; aber ſchänden Sie die Partei nicht. Reden Sie nicht von Korruption einer Partei gegenüber, welche alle corrupten Elemente beſeitigte, und welche gerade hier den Beweis liefert, daß ſie keine unreinen Elemente haben will. Ich halte den nicht für einen wirklichen Parteigenoſſen, der die Partei derartig ſchädigt. Man ſoll nach dem Feinde ſich richten; als die Herren von der Oppoſition ſahen, wie die gegneriſche Preſſe ihre Oppoſition aufnahm, da mußten ſie ſtutzend ſich fragen: Haben wir recht gethan? Haben wir uns nicht an der eigenen Partei vergangen? Wer ſich das nicht geſagt hat, der iſt in meinen Augen allerdings kein Parteigenoſſe, der ſteht mit dem Herzen außerhalb, der iſt ein Feind! (Lebhafter Beifall.)

Heppner-Dresden Land: Redner erklärt die Haltung der Fraktion in der Fage des 1. Mai für ganz korrekt. Wollen einzelne Gewerkſchaftsführer die Fraktion für den Wirrwarr verantwortlich machen, ſo vergeſſen erſtere, daß ſie ſich erſt, bevor ſie die Loſung für den allgemeinen Feiertag ausgaben, mit der Fraktion hätten verſtändigen ſollen.

Bebel: Einer unſerer Genoſſen hat den bisher nicht erörterten Antrag geſtellt, es möchten in Rückſicht auf die günſtigen Kaſſenverhältniſſe der Partei die noch ungedeckten Wahlſchulden aller Kreiſe aus der Parteikaſſe beſtritten werden. Dieſen Antrag anzunehmen, iſt ganz unmöglich, weil wir gar nicht überſehen können, ob die Kaſſe dazu ausreichen würde. Außerdem können wir nicht wiſſen, ob nicht manche dieſer Kreiſe dennoch ihre Schuld allmählich werden abtragen können. Auch haben wir diesmal den Wünſchen der Parteigenoſſen in dieſer Richtung viel mehr als früher entgegenkommen können; kaum eine Forderung iſt verkürzt, viele ſind über den geforderten Betrag hinaus berückſichtigt worden. Wenn nun noch einige Wahlkreiſe mit Schulden vorhanden ſind, ſo mögen dieſe ſich einzeln an die neu zu wählende Parteileitung wenden, dieſelbe wird dann prüfen und thunlichſt jedem Wunſche gerecht werden. — Ich habe vorhin den Antrag auf Niederſetzung einer Kommiſſion deshalb bekämpft, weil nicht genügend konkretes Material vorhanden ſei. Nachdem nun aber der formulirte Antrag Stadthagen einge-

gangen ift, erfläre ich meinerfeits, daß ich nunmehr die Wahl einer
folchen Kommiffion befürworte. Werner ift heute mit fehr heftigen
perfönlichen Vorwürfen aufgetreten, die fich zum Theil durch ihre
Kläglichkeit auszeichnen. Ein Mann von feiner Intelligenz hätte
fich doch fragen follen, ob es fich fchickt, einen Parteitag von
400 Mann mit folchen Dingen zu behelligen. Ich foll ihm, nach
feiner Meinung, in der Verfammlung bei Lips nicht geholfen haben,
der Oppofition genügend Gehör zu verfchaffen; Herr Bading hat
ihn nicht als Mafchinenmeifter eingeftellt; eine Zwifchenperfon foll
durch ihren Einfluß Fraktion und Berliner Genoffen unter einander
verhetzt haben. In einem Kaffeeklatfchkränzchen würde ich folche
Gefchichten begreifen; aber das ift noch nicht dagewefen, hier vor
der ganzen Welt fo etwas als ernfthaften Grund für eine Oppofition
vorzubringen. Das ift den Herren von der Berliner Oppofition zum
erften Male geglückt. Sind das die Beweife für die Korruption,
von der Sie Monatelang gefprochen haben? Ueber jene Lips'fche
Verfammlung verliere ich kein Wort. Intereffant war mir, daß
Werner, er, der fortgefetzt unter den niedrigften, gehäffigften, ver-
werflichften Angriffen auf meine Perfon gegen die Fraktion gehetzt
hatte, er, der heute hier als Gegner des Perfonen- und Autoritäten-
kultus fich auffpielt, dort mich als Autorität anrufen wollte, um
ihm und feinen Freunden Gehör zu fchaffen. Nun, ich fagte damals,
ich thue das nicht; Zubeil ift ja gewählt, die Verfammlung zu leiten.
Und da will ich bemerken, daß Zubeil feine Aufgabe als Vorfitzender
mufterhaft gelöft und fein Amt ebenfo ernft als unparteiifch führte.
Er hatte vieren von der Oppofition gegen drei von uns das Wort
gegeben. Das war durchaus loyal. Wenn Werner ferner behauptet,
die Befucher jener Verfammlung feien nicht Berliner Genoffen gewefen,
fondern folche Leute, die einmal Bebel hätten hören wollen, fo kann
ich das nicht kontrolliren; aber die Berliner Genoffen werden diefen
Punkt klarftellen können. Leute, die blos einen von uns hören
wollen, machen nicht um 2 Uhr Mittags Feierabend, bringen folche
Opfer nicht. Keiner in der Oppofition hat uns mit gehäffigeren,
niedrigeren, verwerflicheren, unwürdigeren Mitteln bekämpft, wie
Herr Werner, und ich bitte die Kommiffion, mich zu vernehmen, da werde ich beweifen, daß ich mit vollftem Recht diefe
Befchuldigung ausfprechen durfte. Nach den heutigen Erfahrungen
erkläre ich, daß ich, gleich Grillenberger, Herrn Werner nicht
als Genoffen anfehe. (Hört, hört!) Er hat dann weiter auf
Schippel Bezug genommen. Glaubte Schippel, ihm fei von der
Fraktion oder einzelnen Mitgliedern derfelben Unrecht gefchehen,
oder daß das ihm widerfahrene Unrecht nicht in den Fraktions-
verhandlungen genügend gefühnt worden fei, fo würde er doch felbft
an den Parteitag kommen; ich ftaune, daß Werner es ift, der fich
zu feinem Vertheidiger aufwirft. Alle diefe Schippeldinge find drei,

viermal in der Fraktion ausführlichst behandelt worden; schon zu
einer Zeit, wo Schippel noch gar nicht in der Fraktion war; er ist
davon durch mich genau unterrichtet. War er noch nicht befriedigt,
so hatte er gewiß den Muth und das Pflichtgefühl, seine Angelegenheiten vor den Parteitag zu bringen, und brauchte er die
Anwaltschaft des Herrn Werner nicht. Das Auftreten der Opposition
hat die Partei schwer geschädigt. Meinungsverschiedenheiten sind
begreiflich. Glauben Sie nur nicht, daß in der Fraktion lauter
Friede und Einigkeit herrschen; wir gerathen auch dort hinter-
einander. Es stehen sich aber nicht die Alten und die Jungen
gegenüber, sondern in der Regel sind es die „Alten" selbst, die am
heftigsten aufeinanderplatzen. Aus mehr als einem Munde eines
jüngeren Kollegen habe ich es in der letzten Session vernommen:
Daß Ihr Alten Euch dermaßen in die Haare geriethet, hätten wir
nicht für möglich gehalten; aber es freut uns doch, daß da ehrlich
gearbeitet wird! Auf den 1. Mai und unseren Aufruf zu den
Stichwahlen komme ich im Schlußwort zurück; ich habe diese Punkte
im Referat nicht erwähnt, weil ich wußte, daß sie in der Diskussion
doch kommen würden, und weil ich mit der mir zugemessenen
knappen Redezeit haushalten mußte. (Andauernder, lebhafter Beifall.)
Wiederum liegen vier Schlußanträge vor, die aber sämmtlich
abgelehnt werden.

Gottschalk-Hamburg: Bebels Bericht kann uns nur mit Befriedigung erfüllen. Nothwendig und erforderlich ist es, jetzt mit
der Agitation aufs Land hinauszugehen. Auch in Hamburg II ist
der Vorwurf erhoben worden, die Parole für den 1. Mai sei zu spät
ausgegeben; man sagte sich, die Fraktion wolle wohl gar nicht
Stellung dazu nehmen. Das Pariser Protokoll kam zu spät heraus;
um so mehr war die Fraktion verpflichtet, mitzutheilen, was denn
eigentlich auf dem Kongreß beschlossen war. Deshalb behaupte ich
entschieden, daß die Fraktion einen Fehler mit dieser Zögerung begangen hat, wodurch speziell den Hamburgern ein böser Schlag
versetzt worden ist. Die Hamburger hatten schon zu viel Vor-
kehrungen getroffen, sie konnten nicht im letzten Augenblicke Kehrt
machen, und das benutzten die Arbeitgeber. So kam es in Hamburg
zu der furchtbaren Niederlage in dem großen Streik. Unbedingt
wäre das nicht gekommen, hätte die Fraktion rechtzeitig gesprochen.
Bezüglich der Stichwahlen erklärt Redner am St. Gallener Beschluß
festhalten zu wollen.

Hillmer-Hamburg: Ich kann nicht umhin, die ganze Behand-
lungsweise, welche wir in Hamburg seitens der Fabrikanten zu erleiden hatten, zum großen Theil auf den verspäteten Beschluß der
Fraktion zurückzuführen (Zustimmung und Widerspruch). Ich weiß
sehr wohl, daß in Paris nicht beschlossen worden ist, einen allgemeinen Feiertag einzuführen, sondern daß die Art der Demon-

ſtration jedem Lande überlaſſen wurde. Nun, die Hamburger beſchloſſen, da die Fraktion für die deutſchen Arbeiter nicht die
Initiative ergriff, auf ihre eigene Hand den 1. Mai als Feiertag
zu begehen. Unſere Demonſtration hätte auch Erfolg gehabt, wenn
der Fraktionsbeſchluß nicht hinterher gekommen wäre. Das haben
die Hamburger Arbeitgeber benutzt, und da auch ein ganz kleiner
Bruchtheil der Arbeiter uns opponirte, ſo war Zwieſpalt in unſeren
Reihen. Dieſen Zwieſpalt benutzte der Fabrikantenbund, der ſich
dort gebildet, um gegen uns vorzugehen. Wir haben nun zwar die
Schläge parirt, aber ich möchte für künftige Fälle die Bitte ausſprechen, daß dann, wenn wieder eine ſolche allgemeine Demonſtration
inſcenirt werden ſoll, die leitenden Perſönlichkeiten nicht zu ſpät
auftreten, ſondern frühzeitig auf dem Poſten ſind.

In Bezug auf die Angelegenheit des Herrn Schippel iſt that-
ſächlich ſeitens einzelner Fraktionsmitglieder in einer unerhörten Weiſe
vorgegangen worden (hört! hört!). Die Berichte über angebliche
Korruption in den Reihen der Berliner Sozialdemokratie veranlaßten
einen Theil der Hamburger Genoſſen, eine Kommiſſion zweimal
nach Berlin zu ſenden, um die Sache zu prüfen, reſpektive um mit der
Fraktion Rückſprache zu nehmen. Ferner haben wir uns noch nach
Chemnitz, nach dem Wahlkreis Schippels gewendet; in beiden Fällen
aber ohne Erfolg. Deshalb halte ich Unterſuchung durch eine
Kommiſſion für ſehr nothwendig, damit die Uneinigkeit aus unſeren
Reihen ausgemerzt werde.

Es wird wieder Schluß der Debatte beantragt, derſelbe aber
abgelehnt.

Werner konſtatirt zur Geſchäftsordnung, daß er zur perſön-
lichen Bemerkung das Wort verlangt hätte, wenn der Schluß angenommen worden wäre.

Slomke-Bielefeld wendet ſich gegen die Doppelkandidaturen.
Vollmar habe ſich in München und Magdeburg als Reichstags-
kandidat aufſtellen laſſen — zwei ausſichtsvolle Wahlkreiſe — und
dieſe Doppelwahl habe viel Arbeit und Geld gekoſtet. Dazu müſſe
der Parteitag Stellung nehmen.

Zubeil: Werner hat keine gute Bahn damit beſchritten, daß
er die Verſammlung bei Lips herabzuſetzen ſucht. Ich habe den
Eindruck gehabt, daß ſämmtliche Parteigenoſſen Berlins zu jener
Verſammlung eingeladen waren. Redner konſtatirt nun, daß Bebel
erſt mit dem Referat betraut wurde, nachdem die Polizei Singer
die Verſammlung verboten hatte. In Bezug auf die Maiſeier kann
er Berndt nicht zuſtimmen, wenn dieſer meinte, man habe ſich in
die Agitation geſtürzt, ohne die Pariſer Beſchlüſſe genau zu kennen.
Die Arbeiter der meiſten Berliner Fabriken waren für die Maiſeier,
und dieſe wäre ſo großartig geworden, wie wir eine ähnliche
Demonſtration in Berlin noch nicht erlebt haben. Da mit einem

Male kam der Erlaß der Fraktion. Man trat uns nun in den Fabriken entgegen und sagte, in welcher Weise habt Ihr uns hinter das Licht geführt! So hat die ganze Berliner Gewerkschafts-bewegung durch jenen Fraktionsbeschluß einen Schlag erhalten, den wir noch Jahre lang empfinden werden. Diese Schuld kann die Fraktion nicht von sich abwälzen. Redner spricht sich auch gegen den Stichwahlerlaß aus und erklärt, es sehr vermißt zu haben, daß nicht eine öffentliche Einladung der Frauen zu diesem Parteitage erfolgt sei (sehr richtig! bei den Frauen). Man darf der Frauen-bewegung nicht entgegentreten, wie es so vielfach geschehen ist. In den meisten Textilstädten ist kein Lohnkampf ohne die Frauen durch-zuführen. Die Frauenfrage ist ein wesentlicher Theil der sozialen Frage.

In vielen Punkten theile ich die Ansichten und die Opposition Werner's nicht. Oft haben wir aber auch Grund zu berechtigter Beschwerde, und man sollte nicht über die gesammten Berliner Parteigenossen den Stab brechen. Wir Berliner haben unter den schwierigsten Verhältnissen vom Anfang des Ausnahmegesetzes bis zum Ende furchtlos und unverzagt gearbeitet und wir werden dies auch in Zukunft thun. (Beifall.)

Singer: Ich werde mich auf die gegen einzelne Mitglieder der Fraktion gerichteten Angriffe in diesem Moment nicht einlassen. Ich habe die Ueberzeugung, daß es den Mitgliedern der Fraktion nur angenehm sein kann, wenn in einer Kommission diese Angriffe untersucht werden. Der Kommissionsbericht wird ja ergeben, in-wieweit die sogenannte Opposition in Berlin berechtigt war, von einer Korruption in der Fraktion zu sprechen.

Für viel wichtiger halte ich die vorgebrachten Bedenken gegen die Haltung der Parteileitung bezüglich der Stichwahlen und der Feier des 1. Mai. Ich konstatire, daß dies überhaupt die einzigen sachlichen Bedenken sind, welche als gegen die Parteileitung ge-richtet betrachtet werden können und die eine Diskussion verlohnen.

Als in St. Gallen der Beschluß gefaßt wurde, den Partei-genossen zu empfehlen, sich bei den Stichwahlen der Abstimmung zu enthalten, gehörten Bebel und ich zu denjenigen, die diesen Beschluß auf das Lebhafteste befürworteten, und es ist charakteristisch, daß Bebel in St. Gallen diesen Antrag gestellt hat. Wir sind damals zu dem bekannten Beschluß gekommen, weil absolut keine Veranlassung war, zu glauben, daß das Sozialistengesetz aufgehoben werden könnte. Wir mußten annehmen, daß es verewigt werden würde und daß wir uns darauf dauernd einrichten müßten. Wir waren in Bezug auf die ökonomische Entwickelung derselben Ansicht wie heute, nämlich, daß unserer Forderung gegenüber auf die Umwandlung der Produktionsweise alle bürgerlichen Parteien eine reaktionäre Masse bilden.

Nun trat aber etwas Unerwartetes ein. Als uns der Ausfall des Wahlresultats vom 20. Februar nicht nur die Möglichkeit, sondern fast die Sicherheit brachte, daß die Fortdauer des Sozialistengesetzes fraglich sei, als jedenfalls das feststand, daß der Ausweisungsparagraph fallen würde, da mußten wir uns fragen, ob wir nicht einen Verrath gegen die Partei, einen politischen Selbstmord begehen würden, wenn wir durch die Parole auf Stimmenthaltung bei den Stichwahlen die Möglichkeit schafften, daß schließlich doch noch eine Majorität für die Verlängerung des Sozialistengesetzes zu stande käme. Aus diesen Gründen und entsprechend den Anregungen, die uns aus vielen, vielen Wahlkreisen gekommen sind, hat das Zentralwahlkomitee damals einstimmig beschlossen, trotz des St. Gallener Beschlusses den Genossen zu empfehlen, für die Kandidaten der Opposition zu stimmen. Wir waren uns bei diesem Beschluß vollkommen bewußt, daß wir dem nächsten Parteitag Rechenschaft würden ablegen müssen; aber wir glaubten nicht Leidenschaftlichkeit, sondern kühle Abwägung der Parteiinteressen walten lassen zu sollen. Wer in der Wahlagitation viel herumgekommen ist, weiß ganz genau, daß in weiten Parteikreisen die Nothwendigkeit anerkannt worden ist, bei der Wahl zwischen einem Konservativen und einem Zentrumsmann, oder zwischen einem Nationalliberalen und einem Freisinnigen, die Stimme auf den Kandidaten der Opposition zu lenken. Nach unserer Ueberzeugung wäre es gradezu ein Verrath an der Partei gewesen, wenn wir die Hand dazu geboten hätten, den Strick, den man uns um den Hals gelegt hatte, selbst noch zu verlängern. Ich bin überzeugt, daß der Parteitag bei ruhiger, leidenschaftsloser, politischer Erwägung in seiner großen Majorität anerkennen wird, daß die damalige Situation eine derartige Entscheidung geboten hat. (Zustimmung.)

Was die Frage des 1. Mai betrifft, so will ich ohne Weiteres sehr gern zugeben, daß es viel besser gewesen wäre, wenn die Fraktion früher vor die Partei getreten wäre. (Sehr richtig!) Ich muß aber bestreiten, daß die Parteigenossen den Sinn der Pariser Resolution nicht gekannt haben. Denn unmittelbar nach Schluß des Pariser Kongresses war im Berliner Volksblatt die Resolution abgedruckt, und darin stand kein Wort, daß die Manifestation am 1. Mai geführt werden solle durch allgemeines Ruhenlassen der Arbeit. Diese Interpretation haben erst die Versammlungen hineingelegt, und der Vorwurf, daß die Fraktion zu spät gekommen, wird sehr gemildert, wenn man sich in die damaligen Verhältnisse zurückversetzt. Es war unmittelbar vor den Wahlen. Die ganze Kraft der Partei war in Anspruch genommen durch die Wahlagitation. Auch die Fraktionsmitglieder hatten keine Zeit und Gelegenheit, sich um andere Dinge zu kümmern. Allgemein war

die Ansicht verbreitet, der Reichstag würde Anfangs März zusammenberufen werden, und wir konnten uns also sagen, daß es
dann noch reichlich Zeit sei, die Frage wegen der Maifeier zu
erledigen. Dazu kommt, daß die Fraktion damals nur aus elf
Mitgliedern bestand, deren Mandate nur noch wenige Wochen
galten, und die die Verantwortung nicht auf sich nehmen konnten,
angesichts einer so wichtigen Frage, die Parteiaktion für die
Zukunft festzulegen. Die Auffassung, daß, wenn die Fraktion ihren
Rath nicht gegeben hätte, die Arbeitsruhe ohne wirthschaftliche Nachtheile erfolgt wäre, kann ich persönlich nicht theilen. Es wären in
diesem Falle außer den Hamburgern vielleicht Hunderttausende von
Genossen in Deutschland aufs Pflaster geworfen worden. (Sehr
richtig!) Aber ich will darum nicht streiten. Sicher ist, daß nur
die großen Städte, wie Berlin und Hamburg, in denen große und
starke Arbeiterorganisationen vorhanden sind, im Stande sind, einen
solchen Kampf zu führen. Die Fraktion ist aber gewählt zur Vertretung der gesammten Partei, des ganzen Reiches, und wenn
fünfunddreißig Männer zusammengekommen sind aus allen Theilen
des Reichs und einstimmig erklärt haben, die Maifeier muß im
Interesse der Partei in der vorgeschlagenen Weise abgehalten werden,
so muß diesen Leuten doch ein sachverständiges Urtheil zuerkannt
werden. (Glocke des Präsidenten.) Ich werde eben angeläutet
(Heiterkeit) und muß schließen. Es lag mir nur daran, die Gründe
anzuführen, welche für die beiden angefochtenen Erlasse der Fraktion
bestimmend waren. (Lebhaftes Bravo!)

Von Liefländer-Potsdam ist ein Antrag eingegangen, der zur
Untersuchung und Schlichtung der Berliner Beschwerden zu ernen-
nenden Kommission auch andere als im Antrag Stadthagen be-
zeichneten Beschuldigungen zu überweisen.

Dieser Antrag wird nicht genügend unterstützt und gelangt also
auch nicht zur Verhandlung.

Sittig-Hannover: Der „Hannoversche Courier", das Leibblatt
des „großen" Rudolf von Bennigsen, jammerte kurz nach dem
1. Mai, das Sozialistengesetz habe durch den 1. Mai den Todesstoß
erhalten. Das ist richtig, und deshalb war auch die Taktik der
Fraktion eine vollkommen korrekte. Hätten wir, wie die Berliner
Genossen es wünschen, den 1. Mai in der Art und Weise begangen,
wie es von ihnen verlangt wurde, dann hielten wir vielleicht nicht
diesen Parteitag ab. Die ganze reaktionäre Masse hat sich auf den
1. Mai gespitzt und gehofft, daß nicht blos Arbeitseinstellungen und
kleine Anrempeleien vorkommen würden; nein, man hoffte auf einen
großen Aufruhr, um dann das Sozialistengesetz zu verschärfen und
dauernd einführen zu können. Wir sind deshalb der Fraktion zu
Dank verpflichtet, daß sie uns davor behütet hat, unseren schlimmsten
Gegnern einen Gefallen zu erweisen.

Schmidt-Berlin: Die Opposition in Berlin ist absolut nicht mit allem einverstanden, was von Wille und Werner gesagt worden ist; aber sie hat allerdings zu verschiedenen Malen mit der Reichstagsfraktion in Widerspruch treten müssen, und es ist richtig bemerkt worden, daß schon lange eine gewisse Unzufriedenheit oder Opposition vorhanden war. Ich möchte aber statt Opposition lieber Neigung zur Kritik sagen. Daran, daß diese Kritik eintrat, war einzig und allein das Sozialistengesetz schuld, das uns eben nicht gestattete, unsere Meinung in der Oeffentlichkeit zu vertreten; so konnten leicht Mißverständnisse entstehen. Berücksichtigen Sie auch, daß die Berliner Genossen am schwersten mit dem Polizeibüttel zu kämpfen hatten. Berlin ist die Metropole der Polizei. Ein großer Theil unserer Parteigenossen, welche früher an der Spitze waren, saßen im Gefängniß oder waren ausgewiesen, konnten also nicht mitarbeiten, wo ihr Rath und Hilfe so sehr vonnöthen war. Alles dies hat eine Verbitterung herbeigeführt und die eigenthümlichen Verhältnisse gezeitigt, die auch ihren Ausdruck gefunden haben bei dem Streit um Stadtverordnetenwahlen, auf welche später zurückzukommen wir uns vorbehalten.

Wieder sind von mehreren Seiten Schlußanträge gestellt, die aber abgelehnt werden, nachdem Molkenbuhr ausgeführt, daß, da die gegnerische Presse so viel von schmutziger Wäsche, die gewaschen werden soll, zu schreiben gewußt habe, man nicht soll sagen können, daß einem einzigen Vertreter der Opposition das Wort abgeschnitten worden sei.

Täterow-Berlin: Ich konstatire, daß eine Zeit lang ein gewisser Muth dazu gehörte, in Berlin Sachen in Schutz zu nehmen, welche der Fraktion als Sünden angerechnet wurden. Ich persönlich bin ja schon längst als „Fraktionszuhalter" hingestellt worden. Ich kenne das Parteileben ziemlich genau und bin zu der Ueberzeugung gekommen, daß wohl niemand ehrenhafter vor den Parteitag treten kann, wie gerade die Fraktion. In schweren Kämpfen hat sie das Banner hochgehalten, und wenn sie geirrt hat, so ist das eine natürliche Sache. Es hat Jeder mal einen Fehler begangen. Aber diese Fehler müssen nicht aufgebauscht werden. Die Berliner Opposition hat aber längst den Rahmen der sachlichen und loyalen Kritik überschritten. Nun, wir kennen unsere Pappenheimer und wissen, was davon zu halten ist. Metzner hat schon nachgewiesen, was Berliner Genossen sind. Es sind nicht die einzelnen Schreier, sondern diejenigen, welche die Partei zu dem gemacht haben, was sie in Berlin ist. Es haben sich dort Leute eingedrängt, welche uns persönlich verhetzt haben, und in erster Linie die Fraktion. Wenn der 1. Mai nicht zu dem geworden ist, was er sein sollte, so sind die Genossen selbst schuld. Die Fraktion hatte die Pflicht, die Arbeiterschaft mit zu hören, in welcher Weise sie sich betheiligen

5

wollte, und sie mußte sich sagen, daß wohl die Arbeiterschaft der großen Städte, aber nicht die in kleinen Städten und ländlichen Bezirken dem Unternehmerthum entgegentreten konnte.

Redner spricht sich auch für den Stichwahlerlaß aus.

Es wird abermals der Schluß der Diskussion beantragt. Es sind noch 30 Redner vorgemerkt.

Pfannkuch-Cassel spricht gegen den Schluß, bittet aber die folgenden Redner, sich möglichst kurz zu fassen, um Werner zum Wort kommen zu lassen.

Der Schlußantrag wird abgelehnt.

Joest-Mainz: Aehnliche Streitigkeiten wie heute haben schon die Kongresse in Wyden, Kopenhagen und St. Gallen beschäftigt. Gewissen Berliner Elementen ist einfach nichts recht zu machen. Ich möchte darum aber nicht der Allgemeinheit der Berliner Genossen Vorwürfe machen. Wenn wirklich während der 12 Jahre Sozialistengesetz Mißstände in der Fraktion oder sonstwo entstanden wären, dann hätten die ehrlichen Genossen einen anderen Ton der Oeffentlichkeit gegenüber anzuschlagen, als wie es Berliner Genossen gethan haben. Die Art und Weise, wie sie den Kampf geführt, sagt mir, daß ich diesen Elementen nicht trauen darf. Ich habe zwar keine objektiven Beweise in der Hand, dafür giebt es in den meisten Fällen überhaupt keine objektiven Beweise, aber subjektiv bin ich überzeugt, daß wir diesen Leuten gegenüber Vorsicht üben müssen; die Verhältnisse in Berlin mahnen in der That zur Vorsicht. Am Vorabend des Todestages des Sozialistengesetzes ist in Berlin eine Agitation gegen die Parteileitung ins Leben gerufen worden von Leuten, die noch nicht soviel Jahre für die Partei thätig gewesen sind, als die Angegriffenen für dieselbe bereits im Gefängniß gesessen haben. Das Unheil droht uns nicht von den Feinden, sondern von den Freunden dort. (Zustimmung.)

In St. Gallen ist gar nicht beschlossen worden absolute Wahlenthaltung bei Stichwahlen zwischen unseren politischen Gegnern; es ist vielmehr gegen eine Stimme beschlossen worden, daß im allgemeinen die Wahlenthaltung nicht bindend sein solle für jeden einzelnen Wahlkreis, und die Fraktion hat sich ganz im Rahmen dieses Beschlusses bewegt. Die Erfahrung hat außerdem gelehrt, daß in dieser Angelegenheit die schärfsten Beschlüsse nicht respektirt werden. Man wählt eben lieber bei den Stichwahlen einen Demokraten oder Freisinnigen, als einen Nationalliberalen, der für das Sozialistengesetz gestimmt hat. Hier entscheiden persönliche Gefühle.

Was den 1. Mai betrifft, so können wir froh sein, daß die Fraktion, wenn auch spät, ihren Beschluß gefaßt hat. Die schlauen Berliner, die zwar immer die Autorität bei anderen bekämpfen selbst sie aber verlangen, wir sollen ihnen alles glauben, wir sollen alle ihre Sätze, weil sie sie aufstellen, für richtig anerkennen, sie sind für uns eben nichts weniger als Autoritäten. Wären sie aber wirklich eine solche, dann müßten sie wissen, daß man wohl in Berlin und Hamburg die Maifeier durchsetzen könnte, aber nicht in den übrigen Städten. Die Herren von der Berliner Opposition sind kurzsichtig, ihr Gesichtskreis reicht nicht weiter als wie das Weichbild der Stadt Berlin. Graben wir den Herren den Boden in der deutschen Sozialdemokratie ein für alle Mal ab! (Beifall.)

Schippel: Zwei Erklärungen lassen Sie mich abgeben. Die erste bezieht sich auf das, was Liebknecht über die „Berliner Volkstribüne" sagte. Die „Berliner Volkstribüne" hat die Notiz wegen der Korrespondenz Liebknecht's im dänischen „Sozialdemokrat" zu einer Zeit gebracht, wo ich mit der Redaktion nichts mehr zu thun hatte. Aber auch in Bezug auf die Person des jetzigen Redakteurs kann ich die Versicherung abgeben, daß ihm bei der Aufnahme dieser Notiz eine böse Absicht vollständig fern gelegen hat.

Ferner muß ich erklären, weil ich durch Bebel dazu provozirt bin, daß ich mit der Kommission betr. den Herrn Werner gar nichts zu thun habe. Ich würde selber nicht dafür sein, daß eine derartige Kommission eingesetzt werde, denn es kommt doch nichts dabei heraus, ich kann aber auch nicht dagegen sein, sonst würde es wahrscheinlich heißen, der Schippel hat sich vor irgend etwas zu geniren. Wer bis zum heutigen Tage noch nicht eingesehen hat, daß diese Beschuldigungen wegen der Verbindung mit der preußischen Regierung verrückt sind, dem wird es auch die Kommission nicht beibringen, und es hat keinen Zweck, alte Dinge nur aufzurühren, um sie aufzurühren. Sie sind nun einmal geschehen und können für mich auch durch den günstigsten Beschluß der Kommission nicht ungeschehen gemacht werden.

Hug-Bant verzichtet aufs Wort. (Bravo!)

Klein-Berlin schließt sich den Ausführungen Zubeils an.

Wesch-Crefeld hat den Beschuldigungen gegen die Fraktion niemals Gewicht beigelegt, ist aber doch für eine Prüfung der Sache.

Grothe-Halle: Ich glaube um so mehr berechtigt zu sein, hier zu sprechen, als ich auf den Namen Berliner Anspruch machen kann. Bevor ich aus Berlin ausgewiesen wurde, vor ca. 8 Jahren, war in Berlin doch ein anderer Zusammenhalt vorhanden, als in der jüngsten Zeit. Wer wie ich 7 Jahre im Exil gelebt hat, konnte nur mit aufrichtigem Schmerz und Bedauern die Berliner Bewegung der letzten Jahre verfolgen (Zustimmung). Eine Hauptschuld an n Verdächtigungen trägt freilich das Sozialistengesetz. Das snahmegesetz war ein Knebel, der verhinderte, daß wir offen vor er Welt hintreten und die Dinge aufklären konnten. Grillenger hat ganz Recht: es hat eine Zeit in Berlin gegeben, wo die tzel sich massenhaft in die Reihen der Genossen drängten und halb allgemeine Unsicherheit unter diesen selbst herrschte. Aus der Stadtverordnetenbewegung hat die Partei gerade frisches Blut bekommen. So stehen die Aktien! Genosse Werner hat damals keinen Blick in die Bewegung gehabt, er hat die Bewegung nicht mitgemacht. Die Stadtverordnetenwahlen waren die Pionierarbeit für die Reichstagswahlen. Gestehen Sie (zu den Berlinern) doch ehrlich zu, daß Sie da einen Fehler gemacht haben. Ich will ja auch nicht zu Allem Ja und Amen sagen, was die Fraktion gethan. Die Fraktion wird vielleicht bis kurz vor dem 1. Mai sich selbst nicht einig gewesen sein, deshalb hat sich die Sache in die Länge gezogen. Ich möchte die Berliner sogenannte Opposition bitten, nun endlich den Streit ruhen zu lassen. Es giebt in der Bewegung noch ungeheuer viel zu thun. Beherzigen Sie das Wort Bebel's: Vorwärts, vorwärts und immer vorwärts!

Betreffs meiner Stellung zu den Stichwahlen bin ich im fünften Wahlkreis scharf angegriffen worden. Ich bat Herrn v. Richthofen schriftlich um die Erlaubniß, in Berlin erscheinen zu dürfen, um mich vertheidigen zu können. Leider wurde das Gesuch abgeschlagen. Hätte aber Richthofen das Gesuch genehmigt, so hätte man womöglich in Berlin gesagt, das kann nicht richtig sein, Grothe steht mit der Berliner Polizei in Verbindung. Ich weiß ja, daß das Ausnahmegesetz schuld ist, wenn der eine oder der andere verleumdet wird. (Glocke des Präsidenten.) Ordnen Sie die Person der Sache unter, begraben Sie die alten Geschichten und blicken Sie in die Zukunft. (Bravo!)

Eine weitere Anzahl von Genossen verzichtet aufs Wort. (Bravo!)

Schiel-Koblenz hält es für angemessener, zu untersuchen, wie man die ländliche ultramontane Bevölkerung für die Sozialdemokratie gewinnen kann, als mit unnützen Streitigkeiten die Zeit zu vergeuden (Beifall).

Dr. Rüdt-Heidelberg: Ich hätte nicht geglaubt, daß sich an den wirklich großartigen Bericht Bebel's eine so kleinliche Debatte von gegnerischer Seite knüpfen würde, die geradezu einen gehässigen Eindruck machen mußte. Unsere altbewährten Führer sind so gut Menschen wie wir und können Fehler machen. Aber es ist hier nicht der Platz, vor ganz Europa, ja vor der ganzen Welt uns zu blamiren, es ist nicht nöthig, unsere Führer überall herumzuläftern und die Bourgeoisie aufzufordern, ebenfalls mitzuläftern. Der Fehler kann nur dadurch gut gemacht werden, daß das zurückgenommen wird, was gegen die bewährten Führer unserer Partei vorgebracht worden ist. (Sehr richtig!) Meine Auftraggeber — das erkläre ich im Namen von 4 Wahlkreisen — haben nie das geringste Mißtrauen gegen die Parteiführer gehabt. (Bravo!) Im Interesse unserer internationalen Bewegung muß ein Laster ausgerottet werden, das Laster der Verleumdung! (Sehr richtig!) Das ist der Krebsschaden der Partei. Die Welt kann nicht bewundernd auf uns

schauen, wenn wir selbst so kleinlich und elend sind, uns ins An-
gesicht zu schlagen und uns zu verleumden. Das, meine lieben
Freunde, ist meine Ansicht. (Lebhaftes Bravo!)

Krewinkel-Aachen: Wollten wir den Landleuten mit den
Berliner Ideen kommen, man würde sagen, die Kerle kommen
aus dem Narrenhaus. (Große Unruhe.) Wir in Aachen können
kein Blatt halten; man erwäge, ob nicht doch aus der allgemeinen
Parteikasse Unterstützungen für die Lokalpresse gewährt werden
können.

Bremer-Magdeburg: Die Opposition behauptet, sie hätte
nicht aus unlauteren Gründen opponirt. 1885 erschien eine Schrift:
„Das wahre Gesicht der Sozialdemokratie", und wer waren die
Verbreiter? Es waren auch damals die Leute, die sich als Parteigenossen geberdeten, und diese Schandschrift verbreiteten aus wahrer
Schand- und Schmähsucht gegen Hasenclever. Wenn solche Streitigkeiten unter uns herrschen, dann ist es kein Wunder, wenn die
ländliche Bevölkerung nichts von uns wissen will. Werner kam
nach Magdeburg, nicht um den Organisationsentwurf zu beleuchten,
ihn zu kritisiren und zu verbessern, sondern um die Streitigkeiten
aufzurühren, um seinen ganzen Geifer gegen die Fraktion zu ver-
spritzen. Und nun spielt er den Beleidigten, wenn die Angegriffenen
ihm die gebührende Antwort geben. Werner mag sich ja vertheidigen. Er erzählte da von Fraktionsmitgliedern, welche sich für
900 Thaler Wohnung mietheten u. s. w. in der Hoffnung, daß
davon etwas sitzen bliebe. Glaubt er selbst nicht daran, dann muß
er es nicht in die Welt hinaustragen. (Bravo.)

Nachdem noch eine ganze Reihe von Rednern verzichtet haben,
erhält das Wort

Werner-Berlin: M. H.! ich weiß nicht, ob ich noch Parteigenossen sagen darf. Bebel meinte, „sie sehen das wahre Gesicht
der Opposition, das ist der reine Kaffeeklatsch". Ich habe aber
nicht diesen Kaffeeklatsch und diese Kleinigkeiten hier gebracht, um
sie vielleicht zur Entscheidung des Parteitages zu stellen, sondern
ich habe nur damit bezweckt, daß die vorhin ins Wasser gefallene
Kommission gewählt werden sollte und daß dann die Streitigkeiten
sollten begraben sein (aha), in Folge der Aufklärungen der Kommission. Allerdings führen wir ja nicht große Namen; jede Opposition
fängt klein an, und daß sie in der Minorität bleiben würde, war
bstverständlich. (Große Unruhe.) Ich habe wiederholt in Ver-
mmlungen erklärt, wenn der Parteitag gesprochen, dann ist die
reitart begraben (Zurufe und fortdauernde Unruhe), und ich
nte, verehrte Anwesende, alle Gründe, die ich vorzubringen
te für die vermeintliche Opposition, konnten in öffentlichen Volks-
mlungen, wenn man die Partei nicht schädigen wollte, einfach
t verhandelt werden. (Hört!) Es ist auch vollständig falsch,

wenn man meint, die Opposition wäre zentralisirt. Diese Opposition, ich sage Ihnen das hier auf mein Ehrenwort .... (Lachen), ich überlasse es Ihnen, mir zu glauben oder nicht. Also ich sage, die Streitigkeiten waren nicht etwa vorher vorbereitet, sondern es hat Jeder für sich Opposition gemacht, der Eine aus diesem Grunde, der Andere aus jenem. Ich für meine Person stehe zur Opposition, weil nach meiner Meinung — ich kann mich ja auch irren — ein System in dieser Abschlachtung liegt. (Lebhafter Widerspruch.) Ich meine, und nur im guten Glauben, die Partei damit vorwärts zu bringen, daß nicht nolens volens Jemand, der eine andere Meinung hat, mit Schlagworten, wie Anarchist, Polizeispitzel und unberechtigte Opposition einfach beseitigt wird. Wenn man diese Theorie verfolgt, dann wird das sonst frisch pulsirende Blut dick, und die Diskussion, die Meinungsverschiedenheit, die Belehrung untergraben werden. Dann werden einzelne Parteigenossen sich nicht mehr getrauen, irgend noch einmal Opposition zu machen. (Oho!) Es würde nicht mehr frisches Blut in den Adern rollen, und diesen wunden Punkt glaube ich in der Partei entdeckt zu haben (Gelächter) und im Interesse der Partei glaube ich als Sozialdemokrat meine Schuldigthun zu müssen.

Metzner sagte, die Opposition wäre schon lange in Berlin. Ja wohl, seit 1885. Da war allerdings Genosse Grothe nicht mehr in Berlin. Es wurde uns Berliner Parteigenossen angesonnnn, wir sollten den Anarchisten Vorspanndienste leisten und da war ich der energischste Bekämpfer dieser Opposition, dieses Hineintragens der anarchistischen Elemente in unsere Organisation in Berlin. Deshalb erkläre ich auch hier, daß ich nicht Anarchist bin und daß ich auf die Gefahr hin, nicht mehr als Sozialdemokrat thätig sein zu können, Sozialdemokrat für mich allein bleiben werde. (Sehr gut.)

Metzner sprach von den Stadtverordneten-Wahlen von 1885. Ja, da spielten die örtlichen Verhältnisse eine ganz bedeutende Rolle. Da hatte jeder Genosse drei geheime Agenten hinter sich, und da haben die Parteigenossen, die einen besseren Einblick in die Verhältnisse hatten, in ihrer Mehrzahl sich gegen die Betheiligung an den Stadtverordnetenwahlen ausgesprochen. Nachdem aber im vorigen Jahre die Majorität der Berliner Sozialdemokraten für eine Betheiligung eingetreten, ist es keinem Einzigen von uns eingefallen, noch länger dagegen zu opponiren in öffentlichen Versammlungen. Ich bin selbst zur Wahl gegangen und habe einen sozialdemokratischen Stadverordneten gewählt, weil mich die Disziplin als Sozialdemokrat den Beschlüssen einer großen öffentlichen Volksverfammmlung unterwarf. Daß ich nachher doch meine Opposition nicht aufgegeben, ist selbstverständlich. Ich kann doch öffentlich hier nicht anders sprechen, als wie ich innerlich denke. Das kann doch der Beschluß einer großen Versammlung nicht aus meinem Innern herausreißen. Ich kann doch nicht zum Gesinnungslump werden.

Der Genosse Berndt hat sicher nicht im Interesse und Sinne derjenigen Genossen gesprochen, die ihn hierhergeschickt haben (lebhafte Unruhe). Es hat in Berlin eine Auseinandersetzung stattgefunden, in der das Vorgehen Grillenbergers scharf gerügt wurde. Dieser starken Rüge entsprechend, sollte der Delegirte Berndt gegen das Gebahren Grillenbergers auf dem Parteitag protestiren; das ist aber nicht geschehen.

Die Sache mit der Maschinenmeister-Stelle ist allerdings nur eine kleinliche; ich wollte damit nur dokumentiren, warum ich selbstständiger Geschäftsmann geworden bin, und daß ich nicht selbstständig geworden wäre, wenn ich beim „Volksblatt" angestellt worden wäre.

Eine „Schmach" für die Partei kann es nicht sein, wenn man seine Meinung offen ausspricht. Die letzten Vorgänge haben aber gezeigt, daß es nicht so leicht ist seine Meinung mit in die Wagschale zu legen. Es hätte nicht geschadet, wenn die Redakteure des „Sächsischen Wochenblatts" und der „Magdeburger Volksstimme" noch bis zum Parteitag in ihren Stellungen geblieben wären. Wir haben mit unseren Entgegnungen in unserem „Berliner Volksblatt" sehr trübe Erfahrungen gemacht, es sind dieselben nicht alle aufgenommen worden.

Man hat gesagt, die schlauen Berliner sollten sich ein Bischen um die ländlichen Wahlkreise bekümmern. Nun, ich habe ländliche Distrikte sehr wohl durchgearbeitet; ich bin Tag für Tag auf den Füßen gewesen; nicht der Anerkennung wegen, sondern aus Pflichtgefühl.

Was nochmals unsere Opposition betrifft, so sind wir durchaus nicht in allen Fragen einer Meinung. Ich huldige nicht allen Ansichten des Dr. Wille über den Parlamentarismus, auch Wildberger und Baginski sind nicht in Allem seiner Meinung, und so trennen auch uns drei wieder verschiedene Punkte. Meine Opposition beruht darauf: ich befürchte, daß die freie Meinung etwas umschnürt und abgeschnitten wird, und diese Befürchtung darf ich doch wohl auf dem Parteitag aussprechen.

Was den 1. Mai betrifft, so wird mir Singer zugeben müssen, daß die Beschlüsse in Paris wirklich nicht derartige waren, daß sie vorher konnten überlegt werden. Es war dort beantragt worden, daß sämmtliche Anträge und Resolutionen vom Bureau zu einer einheitlichen Resolution zusammengefaßt werden sollten. Kein einziger Redner hatte davon gesprochen, den 1. Mai als internationalen Feiertag zu betrachten. Erst in der letzten Sitzung, am Sonnabend, wurde eine große, lange Resolution verlesen, wo man den ersten Punkt vergaß, bis der dritte verlesen war. Nachdem diese Resolution verlesen war, wurde gesagt, erst wird abgestimmt und nachher diskutirt. Der Kongreß muß heute Abend geschlossen werden. Nun waren aber sämmtliche Delegirten, mit Ausnahme des Bureaux, über jenen Punkt nicht richtig informirt. Es wurde nicht einmal nachgesehen, auf welchen Tag der 1. Mai fällt. Auf Anfrage hieß es schließlich, er fällt nach dem Bußtag. Darauf kamen die deutschen Delegirten und setzten eine Propaganda in Scene. Verschiedene Versammlungen großer Städte beschlossen eine Demonstration. Von Anfang August bis zum Februar war doch wahrlich eine lange Zeit, in der die Fraktion aufklärend wirken konnte. Ich bin erstaunt, wie der Genosse Täterow, der selbst in solchen Versammlungen die Beschlüsse mit gefaßt hat, nun mit einem Male von diesen Beschlüssen nichts wissen will. Unsere Presse hätte, sobald eine derartige Resolution bekannt wurde, hervortreten und sagen müssen, das geht nicht, unterlaßt in Zukunft derartige Beschlüsse. Erst als im April die bekannte Erklärung in der „Berliner Volks-Tribüne" erschien und das „Berliner Volksblatt" dieselbe abdruckte, da gab es schon am nächsten Tage ganz gehörig etwas auf die Finger. Der Zweck dieser Erklärung war lediglich der, daß die Fraktion wenigstens mit der Sprache herauskomme. Ich will zugestehen, daß wir vielleicht einen Fehler gemacht haben; wir hätten uns vielleicht erst einmal an die Parteileitung wenden sollen (Bebel: sehr richtig!). Aber da es schon April war, so glaubten wir bestimmt, daß die Parteileitung mit unserem Vorgehen einverstanden wäre. Wenn Singer auf die wirthschaftlichen Nachtheile hinwies, so sage ich, dann dürfen wir nicht Sozialdemokraten sein und den Arbeitern in den ländlichen Distrikten zumuthen, daß sie für unsere Ideen Propaganda machen. Jede Agitation hat unbedingt wirthschaftliche Nachtheile im Gefolge. . . .

Vorsitzender: Ich habe Sie bereits die doppelte Zeit, die Ihnen zusteht, sprechen lassen. Ich bitte Sie, sich etwas kürzer zu fassen.

Werner (fortfahrend): Die verspätete Erklärung der Parteileitung hat thatsächlich der Gewerkschaftsbewegung in Berlin geschadet. Die Leute wagen sich gar nicht mehr in die Gewerkschaftsversammlungen (große Unruhe; Rufe: Schluß!) Bebel meinte, meine Worte über die Lips-Versammlung werden auch in Berlin gehört werden. Ja, meine Herren! ich bin mir dessen sehr wohl bewußt. Aber ich habe keine andere Auffassung von den Versammlungen, als wie Bebel selbst, als er sagte, was sind denn Versammlungen? Die Beschlüsse derselben können irgendwie hervorgerufen werden. Auch jene Worte von Bebel werden gehört werden: „ein Theil der Streiks sind Ausgeburten des Machtkitzels der Arbeiter vom 20. Februar." Diese Worte sind auch von den Gegnern gehört worden. Denn überall brachten die Innungsmeister jene Erklärung den Arbeitern

und sagten: „Eure Führer sehen in den Streiks nur Frivolitäten."
Bremer hat mich beschuldigt, ich hätte versucht, Parteigenossen
in Mißkredit zu bringen. Ich rufe die Genossen Klees und Schulze
zu Zeugen an, ob ich nicht erklärt habe, ich wüßte, wie leicht das
Mißtrauen in unsere Reihen gebracht sei. Ich sagte, Sie sehen,
wie leicht es ist, Mißtrauen in Geldangelegenheiten hervorzurufen,
indem man so albernes Gewäsch, dem wir selbst entgegengetreten
sind, vorbringt, als ob sich ein Fraktionsmitglied eine Wohnung
für 900 Thaler gemiethet hat." War das wirklich strafbar für
mich, dann bitte, verurtheilen Sie mich, ich bin sehr gern bereit,
jede Konsequenz meiner Handlungen zu tragen.

Schließlich bitte ich Sie, daß Sie in die Kommission Leute
hineinwählen, die ganz objektiv urtheilen. Ich sehe dem Material
über meine Person mit größter Ruhe entgegen, mit der allergrößten
Ruhe. Wenn die Kommission ihr Urtheil gefällt, dann werden Sie
sehen, ob ich Sozialdemokrat bin oder nicht, dann werden Sie entscheiden können, ob ich gegen die sozialdemokratischen Prinzipien
verstoßen habe, ob ich nicht in guter Absicht gehandelt habe, als
ich in der Meinung, einen wunden Fleck in unserer Fraktion entdeckt
zu haben glaubte, Opposition machen zu müssen. (Vereinzeltes Bravo!)

Die Diskussion wird nunmehr mit großer Mehrheit geschlossen,
und nach einer Reihe persönlicher Bemerkungen erhält Bebel, als
Referent das Schlußwort.

Bebel: Genossen! Ich möchte vorweg empfehlen, die beantragte
Kommission nicht schon heute, sondern erst morgen früh zu wählen,
da doch vorsichtige Auswahl getroffen werden muß. Es gilt,
Männer zu wählen, die an den Dingen gar nicht betheiligt sind,
sondern ihnen völlig objektiv gegenüberstehen, die Dinge objektiv
beurtheilen können. Dazu müssen die Genossen erst Rücksprache
unter sich nehmen. Indem ich nun kurz auf Herrn Werner's Ausführungen eingehe, konstatire ich im Voraus, mit welchem Pathos,
mit welcher Lungenkraft Herr Werner auch jetzt wieder seine Sätze
in den Saal hinausgestoßen hat. Aus dem ganzen ersten Theil
seiner Rede ist nichts, aber auch gar nichts zu ersehen, aus dem
sich schließen ließe, was seine monatelange, fortgesetzte Opposition
gegen die Leiter der Partei rechtfertigt. (Sehr wahr!) Nachdem
Sie, Genossen, fast ein halbes Dutzend Male den Schluß der Debatte
abgelehnt haben, um Herrn Werner zur Rechtfertigung Gelegenheit
zu geben, hat er nichts vorzubringen vermocht, was einer Rechtfertigung ähnlich sieht, das konstatire ich hiermit ausdrücklich. Zu
den Punkten, bei denen er thatsächliche Ausführungen gemacht hat,
zur Frage des ersten Mai und der Stichwahlen, haben auch zahlreiche andere Redner gesprochen; das sind Fragen, in denen
Meinungsverschiedenheiten sich ergeben können, und hätte die Berliner Opposition nur solche Punkte in den Kreis ihrer Erörterungen

in den Versammlungen gezogen, niemals hätte die Opposition den gehässigen Charakter annehmen können, den sie angenommen hat. Wenn statt dessen die Opposition mit gehässigen persönlichen An- griffen kommt, wie die, daß sie die ganze Fraktion beschuldigt, die Korruption zu kultiviren, dann kann sie nicht mehr auf Sachlichkeit Anspruch machen, dann ist sie auch vor allem verpflichtet, ihre An- schuldigungen zu beweisen. (Sehr wahr!) Dieser Beweis ist bis jetzt von ihrer Seite noch nicht erbracht, ja nicht einmal zu erbringen versucht worden. Herr Werner begründet seine kleinliche Opposition mit hygienischen Rücksichten, er habe sie im Hinblick auf das Wohl der Partei gemacht. Wir brauchen solche Pferdekuren am Partei- körper nicht, um uns wohl zu befinden. Wäre der Parteikörper nicht so urgesund, er könnte leicht zu Tode kurirt werden. Eine Opposition um jeden Preis verbitten wir uns recht sehr; denn sie kann nur darauf ausgehen, das Parteiinteresse zu schädigen. Auch bezüglich der behaupteten unehrenhaften Handlungen Einzelner ist Herr Werner keinerlei Beweise vorzuführen im Staude.

Der ganze Streit, d. h. der wirklich sachliche Theil der Oppo- sition, dreht sich in erster Linie darum, daß das Centralwahlkomitee, in Widerspruch mit dem Beschluß von St. Gallen, kurz vor den Stichwahlen einen Aufruf erließ, in dem es die Parteigenossen auf- forderte, bei den bevorstehenden engeren Wahlen, insoweit ihre Stimmen in Frage kommen und den Ausschlag geben könnten, unter allen Umständen solche Kandidaten, welche gegen jede Ver- längerung und Verewigung des Ausnahmegesetzes sich erklärten, zu unterstützen. Damit soll ein Kardinalverbrechen an der Partei be- gangen worden sein. Den Rednern, die darüber voll sittlicher Entrüstung sind, gebe ich zunächst zu erwägen, daß diese Frage keine Frage des Prinzips, sondern der Taktik ist, die schon seit 18 Jahren vor St. Gallen stets in dem Sinne beantwortet wurde, daß derjenige Kandidat bei engeren Wahlen unsere Stimmen be- kommen solle, welcher gewisse und besonders wichtig scheinende Forderungen der Partei zu unterstützen sich verpflichtete. Dies ist bis 1887 auf allen Parteitagen beschlossen worden. In dem, was hier über das Wesen der bürgerlichen Opposition gesagt wurde, hat uns niemand etwas Neues gesagt. Ich habe seit 20 Jahren in Schrift und Wort klarzulegen versucht, wie wir zu den bürgerlichen Parteien stehen und stehen müssen, was uns aber nicht abgehalten hat, so zu verfahren, wie die Taktik gebot. Auf dem Parteitag in St. Gallen trat nun wieder die Frage an uns heran, wie wir uns künftig verhalten sollten. Ein Theil der Redner verwarf die bis- herige Taktik deswegen, weil die Hoffnungen auf die Fortschritts- partei bei den engeren Wahlen sich nicht verwirklicht hatten. Gerade dagegen trat ich auf und erklärte: Die gegnerischen Parteien sind Bourgeoisparteien; sie werden stets, namentlich wenn besonders

wichtige Fragen des Klasseninteresses im Vordergrunde stehen, lieber
einem der ihrigen, stehe er politisch wo er wolle; als einem Sozialdemokraten ihre Stimme geben; darauf dürfen wir also nicht
rechnen, daß sie sich für uns ins Zeug legen. Das ist aber für
unsere Haltung auch gar nicht maßgebend; für uns steht die Frage
im Vordergrund: Bereiten wir uns den Boden für unsere Operationen
möglichst ungünstig, wenn wir durch Stimmenthaltung den aus-
gesprochensten gegnerischen Parteien in die Hände arbeiten? Nun
waren wir damals der Meinung, und ich habe das ausdrücklich
ausgesprochen, daß, wie damals die Dinge lagen, gar kein Gedanke
daran sei, daß wir je einmal wieder in die Lage kommen würden,
daß uns daran liegen könne, ob wir ein Dutzend entschieden Liberaler
mehr oder weniger im Reichstage hätten. Ich habe mich damals
in diesem Punkt geirrt, wie schon manchmal in meinem Leben, und
wenn das geschieht, so gestehe ich das auch offen ein. (Bravo!)
Nach drei Jahren lag eben die Frage anders; jetzt lautete sie, was
damals niemand voraussehen konnte: Sollen wir durch Stimmenthaltung bei den engeren Wahlen, entsprechend dem St. Gallener
Beschluß, möglicher Weise dazu beitragen, eine reaktionäre Majorität
in den Reichstag zu bringen, die das Ausnahmegesetz verewigt?
Dies war eine Kardinal- und Lebensfrage für uns, darüber kann
kein Zweifel sein. Da bin ich es wieder gewesen, der in dem
Central-Wahlkomitee den Antrag stellte, so zu verfahren, wie
schließlich bei den Stichwahlen verfahren worden ist. Ich führte
aus: Wir haben dazumal in St. Gallen den Beschluß Stimmenthaltung gefaßt, ich selbst habe dafür gestimmt; heute stehen wir
in einer Situation, die damals kein Mensch voraussehen konnte.
Wenn wir nach jenem Beschluß handelten, würden wir nicht nur
für den Augenblick, sondern auf unabsehbare Zeit hinaus das
Parteiinteresse schwer schädigen, auch hätten wir in diesem Augenblick für den alten Beschluß nicht einmal die Majorität der Partei
hinter uns, die denkt eben anders als zur Zeit in St. Gallen. Ich
schlug dann weiter vor, wir sollten durch Cirkular die Meinung
der Parteigenossen der größeren Orte hierüber in Erfahrung zu
bringen suchen. Da wurde mir aber mit Recht entgegnet, dazu sei
nicht mehr Zeit, dieser Modus würde zu lange Zeit erfordern und
überdies unter die Genossen eine Streitfrage werfen, die Angesichts
der Wahlen allerlei Zerwürfnisse herbeiführen könnte — kurz, besser
sei es, auf eigene Verantwortung zu handeln. Da haben wir denn
einstimmig beschlossen, den Parteigenossen zu empfehlen, in Rücksicht auf die besonderen obwaltenden Verhältnisse die bekannte Parole
für die engeren Wahlen auszugeben. Daß damit gegen den St. Gallener
Beschluß verstoßen wurde, dessen waren wir uns voll bewußt; wir
haben auch ausdrücklich damals öffentlich erklärt, daß wir, trotz des
St. Gallener Beschlusses, durch die gegenwärtige Lage Deutschlands

und der Partei uns veranlaßt sähen, diese Rathschläge zu geben. Und daß wir recht gehandelt, zeigte sich sofort; denn noch vor der Veröffentlichung unseres Beschlusses kamen bereits am 21. und 22. Februar aus zahlreichen Wahlkreisen an uns die Briefe, alle mit der Erklärung, man könne in Rücksicht auf die Lage dem Beschlusse von St. Gallen unmöglich nachkommen, man müsse dem entgegen für den oppositionellen Kandidaten, den Gegner des Ausnahmegesetzes, eintreten. Wir gewannen so schon damals die Ueberzeugung, daß für unsern Schritt die sehr große Mehrheit der Partei hinter uns stehe. Das verflossene Central-Wahlkomitee hat aber ein großes Interesse daran, zu wissen, ob der Parteitag nachträglich diese seine Taktik billigt. Ich hätte gewünscht, es wäre von der Opposition ein Mißtrauensvotum beantragt worden, damit der Parteitag zu dieser Frage Stellung nehmen kann. Da das nicht geschehen ist, beantrage ich die Abstimmung über folgende Resolution:

Der Aufruf des Centralwahlkomitees bezüglich der engeren Wahlen entsprach der politischen Lage zur Zeit der Wahlen, und spricht der Parteitag nachträglich seine Billigung zu dem Vorgehen des Central-Wahlkomitees aus.

Nun noch eins. Ich habe in Berlin, wo ich mit Genossen über diese Dinge privatim sprach, nicht nur einmal, sondern mehrmals die Antwort gehört: Wenn ihr damals im Zentralkomitee diese Parole nicht ausgegeben hättet, würden wir in einem bestimmten Wahlkreise Berlins und in der Umgegend gesiegt haben, denn dann hätten die Konservativen für uns gestimmt. (Ruf: Stimmt.) Nun da ist einem Theile dieser Opposition ein ganz merkwürdiger Beigeschmack gegeben; man war Opponent gegen die Erklärung des Zentralkomitees, weil man ohne dieselbe konservativen Stimmenfang glaubte treiben zu können. Damit ist für mich diese Frage abgethan.

Was nun den 1. Mai betrifft, so kann ich mich kurz fassen. Herr Werner hat auch hier nach seiner Art die Dinge auf den Kopf gestellt; erst am 20. April habe die Erklärung der Fraktion erscheinen können. Nicht am 20., sondern am 6. April sind wir hier in Halle zusammengekommen, und die Erklärung von mir im „Volksblatt" ist nicht im April, sondern Anfang März erfolgt; ich sah mich zu dieser Erklärung veranlaßt, weil allerdings der Aufruf der Berliner auf nichts anderes hinausging, als der gesammten Partei die Direktive vorzuschreiben. Dagegen habe ich zunächst Opposition gemacht. Bedenken Sie doch in Ihrer Kritik die damalige Situation. Man spricht hier immer von der Fraktion als Parteileitung, und will sie für alles verantwortlich machen, und doch hat die Fraktion fast nie von den Schritten des Parteivorstandes Kenntniß nehmen oder ihnen zustimmen können, weil eine Verständigung in den wichtigsten Fragen ungeheuer schwer war; das

war selbst schon dem Fraktionsvorstand schwer, der zwar nur aus
5 Personen bestand, die aber an 4 oder 5 verschiedenen Orten wohnten,
sodaß immer erst viel Aufwand an Zeit und Mühe verloren ging,
ehe man sich über ein geschlossenes Vorgehen verständigen konnte.
Diese Schwierigkeiten haben es ganz wesentlich mit verschuldet, daß
in so manchen wichtigen Fragen erst spät eine Verständigung unter
den Leitern der Fraktion herbeigeführt werden konnte.

Nun meine ich, die Berliner Genossen hätten vor der Veröffentlichung ihres Aufrufs erst an uns eine Anfrage richten sollen,
ob wir etwas zu thun gedächten. Gaben wir eine unbefriedigende
Antwort, dann hatten sie ein Recht zu ihrem Vorgehen. Daß sie
das nicht thaten, erregte bei uns Mißstimmung, und ich nahm zu
der Volksblatterklärung das Wort, die ja, wie ich begreife, verschiedentlich verletzt hat. Es heißt, die Fraktion hätte früher
reden sollen. Sie hätte unter gewissen Umständen früher reden
zönnen, wenn nicht allgemein geglaubt worden wäre, wir, die
35 neu Gewählten, kämen bald in Berlin zum Reichstage zusammen.
Dieser Umstand verhinderte uns zunächst, die Entscheidung so frühzeitig, wie vielleicht wünschenswerth war, zu treffen. Aber selbst
wenn wir zu Anfang oder Mitte März eine Erklärung erlassen
hätten, so war doch vielfach schon längst vorher in den großen
Städten Stellung genommen, und die Sache lag um kein Haar
breit anders. Wir haben gehandelt, wie wir nach bester Einsicht
handeln mußten, und wie kamen nun die Dinge? Die Hamburger
haben den Kampf aufgenommen; nirgends ist die Arbeiterklasse so
gut organisirt, so reich an Geldmitteln, wie in Hamburg; man hat
den Kampf aufgenommen und ist unterlegen. Aehnlich ist es anderwärts gegangen, und es konnte nicht anders kommen. Nun will
man einen Sündenbock haben, und der soll die Fraktion sein. Und
doch ist in Hamburg nur der kleinste Theil der Arbeiter der Fraktion
gefolgt. Was aber hat denn in Wahrheit die Niederlage herbeigeführt? Die ungünstige ökonomische und industrielle Lage zahlreicher Gewerbe! Die Bourgeoisie würde nirgends gewagt haben,
gegen uns den Kampf aufzunehmen, wenn sie die Arbeiter jeden
Tag haben mußte. Das war aber nicht der Fall, und daß unsere
Genossen in den großen Städten das übersehen haben, war der
große Fehler, der von ihnen gemacht worden ist. Mußten nicht
schon im März unsere Genossen in Berlin, Hamburg und andere-
orts ganz genau wissen, daß in erster Linie wir ein ganz miserables
Baujahr haben würden? Und in anderen Fabrikationszweigen war
es nicht besser. Mit Vergnügen warf daher die Bourgeoisie Tausende
auf das Pflaster, weil es ihr eben paßte; sie gebrauchte sie nicht.
Es war wenig oder keine Arbeit vorhanden, es war faule oder
halbfaule Zeit für die Fabriken; darum wagte sie so gegen die
Arbeiter zu handeln. Die Bourgeoisie mag die Erklärung der

Fraktion nicht unangenehm gewesen sein; aber man vergesse nicht, daß bereits im März überall in den großen Städten, Leipzig, Dresden, Berlin, Hamburg u. f. w., die Parole ausgegeben war, daß, wenn die Arbeiter am 1. Mai feierten, sie in den ersten 4, 5 Tagen nicht in die Werkstätten und Fabriken kommen dürften. Dieses sehr wesentliche ökonomische Element für unsere Haltung konnten wir nicht an die große Glocke hängen; aber es hat uns in unserer Haltung wesentlich mitbestimmt. Dazu kam ferner, daß wir der Bourgeoisie in Rücksicht auf die kurz zuvor getroffenen Entschließungen der Reichsregierung bezüglich des Sozialistengesetzes gar keinen größeren Gefallen hätten thun können, als wenn wir dem Wunsche eines Theiles unserer Genossen in den großen Städten, zum Feiern aufzufordern, gewillfahrt hätten. Und hatten wir denn übrigens das Feiern verboten? Ueberall da, erklärten wir, wo die Feier ohne wirthschaftliche Schädigung stattfinden könnte, sollte es geschehen; in dieser Einschränkung uns zu erklären, das waren wir unseren Parteigenossen schuldig. Das Feiern war kaum in den großen Städten zu erwarten, nimmmermehr aber in den kleinen Städten und in den ländlichen Industriebezirken. Schippel war am energischsten für die Feier eingetreten, und Niemand ist durch seine eigenen Wähler mehr desavonirt worden, als er; denn in Chemnitz und Umgegend hat kein einziger Arbeiter gefeiert; auch dort kamen die ökonomischen Verhältnisse in Frage, und das hatten die Arbeiter begriffen. Wollen wir in Zukunft ähnliche Demonstrationen wiederholen, so werden wir wiederum alle diese Momente zu berücksichtigen haben. In Rücksicht auf die ökonomische Krise, in deren Anfang wir stehen, und welche im kommenden Winter und im nächsten Jahre sich immer mehr ausdehnen wird, können wir, meiner Meinung nach, unmöglich auf einem Beschlusse fernerhin beharren, der nothwendig zahllose Freunde in die übelste Lage brächte. Lieber wollen wir Alles aufbieten, um den Beschluß dahin zu formuliren, nicht den 1. Mai, sondern den ersten Sonntag im Mai als Demonstrationstag zu setzen, wenn der internationale Kongreß sich im nächsten Jahre mit der Frage wieder beschäftigt.

Es waren also die ernstesten, sorgfältigsten Erwägungen, welche die Fraktion veranlaßten, den Aufruf, wie geschehen, zu erlassen. Wir sind damals hier in Halle auch in dieser Frage sehr heftig auf einander geplatzt und haben uns gründlich ausgesprochen, aber schließlich wurde, gegen eine oder zwei Stimmen, der Beschluß so gefaßt, wie er veröffentlicht wurde. Ich möchte, daß auch in dieser Frage der Parteitag Veranlassung nähme, seine Meinung der Fraktion gegenüber zu äußern, und schlage vor, der Parteitag wolle erklären:

Die Motive, welche die Fraktion veranlaßten, den bekannten Aufruf für die Demonstration am 1. Mai zu erlassen, fanden in

der allgemeinen ökonomischen und politischen Lage ihre Rechtfertigung.

(Andauernder lebhafter Beifall.)

**Beide Resolutionen werden mit sehr großer Majo-
rität angenommen;** eine dritte, inzwischen eingelaufene Resolution
von Dr. Rübt, welche einen scharfen Tadel der Opposition der sogenannten „Jungen" ausspricht, wird einstweilen zurückgezogen.

**Auf Antrag von Geck-Offenburg wird dem Genossen Bebel
für die Kassenführung einstimmig Decharge ertheilt.**

**Der Antrag Stadthagen, auf Einsetzung einer Kommission, wird
ebenfalls mit großer Mehrheit genehmigt.** Die neun Mitglieder der
Kommission sollen morgen Vormittag gewählt werden. Während
der Debatte sind bereits beim Bureau eine Anzahl Delegirten für
die Kommission in Vorschlag gebracht worden. Der Vorsitzende
verliest die Namen derselben, worauf Meister-Hannover gegen
diese „hinterrücks" gemachten Vorschläge protestirt, und deren
Annullirung beantragt, da ihm die Sache zu sehr als gemacht
erscheine.

Vorsitzender Dietz verwahrt das Bureau gegen solche grund-
losen Angriffe. Unter solchen Verhältnissen bleibe nichts übrig, als
morgen durch Stimmzettel zu wählen.

Meister hat nicht dem Bureau irgend welchen Vorwurf machen,
vielmehr nur rügen wollen, daß das Bureau mit solchen Vorschlägen
bereits bestürmt worden sei, ehe noch feststand, ob eine Kommission
eingesetzt würde oder nicht.

Nachdem der Vorsitzende noch mitgetheilt, daß die Präsenzliste
nicht vor Beendigung der Arbeiten der Mandats-Prüfungskommission,
das heißt nicht vor zwei Tagen, werde erscheinen können, wird die
Sitzung um acht Uhr geschlossen.

Zweiter Verhandlungstag.

Dienstag, den 14. Oktober, Vormittags 9½ Uhr.

Vorsitzender Dietz eröffnet die Sitzung.

Der Vorsitzende theilt mit, daß die Mandats-Prüfungskommission ihre Arbeiten im Laufe des Vormittags beenden wird.
Vorläufig ist festgestellt, daß, außer den Abgeordneten, 410 Delegirte,
darunter drei Frauen, auf dem Parteitage anwesend sind.

Vor Eintritt in die Tagesordnung erklärt Berndt-Berlin, in
seiner Eigenschaft als Vorsitzender der betreffenden Versammlung
im V. Berliner Wahlkreis, daß dort in keiner Weise Grothe-Halle,
als in Beziehungen zur Polizei stehend, geschildert worden sei.

Vom Redakteur der „Berliner Volkstribüne", Konrad Schmidt,

ift nachfolgendes Schreiben eingegangen, das verlesen wird. Dasselbe lautet:

Ein Nichtmitglied des Parteitages ersucht den geehrten
Vorsitzenden, um jedes Mißverständniß zu beseitigen, folgende
Berichtigung zu verlesen:

Genosse Liebknecht hob gestern die Gefahr hervor, die
eventuell durch seine Namhaftmachung als Korrespondent des
„Dänischen Sozialdemokrat" für ihn hätte entstehen können.
Daß die „Volkstribüne" sich erst gegen jene Korrespondenz
gewandt habe, nachdem L. öffentlich als Urheber derselben
genannt war, und daß der Vorwurf einer Denunziation das
Blatt schon aus diesem Grunde nicht treffen köune, hat L.
selbst bereitwilligst konstatirt. Er fügte aber hinzu, daß jene
Korrespondenz, gewissermaßen gegen den Willen des Redakteurs,
unter dem zwingenden Druck gewisser Hintermänner in die
„Tribüne" lanzirt sei. Das ist ein Irrthum. Ich bin dabei
durchaus selbstständig vorgegangen und muß die volle Verantwortung für die polemische Erwähnung der Liebknecht'schen
Korrespondenz in der „Tribüne" übernehmen.

Konrad Schmidt.

Für die Wahl der gestern beschlossenen Neunerkommission wird
auf Vorschlag Bebel's bestimmt, daß eine Vorschlagsliste gedruckt
und um 1 Uhr vertheilt werden soll. Den Abstimmenden soll es
frei stehen, Aenderungen resp. Ergänzungen in dieser Liste vorzunehmen. Diese Liste gilt als Stimmzettel. Die Mandats-Prüfungskommission wird beauftragt, die Zettel zu sammeln und das Wahlresultat festzustellen.

Ein Antrag von Zubeil, das Prinzip der Schließung der
Rednerliste einzuführen, wird, nachdem Singer sich dagegen erklärt,
abgelehnt.

Der Parteitag tritt nunmehr in die Tagesordnung ein:

Punkt 3. **Bericht über die parlamentarische Thätigkeit
der Fraktion.**

Berichterstatter Singer: Parteigenossen! Es kann nicht meine
Aufgabe sein, Sie mit den einzelnen Fragen, welche im Laufe der
letzten drei Jahre im Reichstag verhandelt worden sind, eingehend
zu beschäftigen. Sie stehen Alle im öffentlichen Leben, haben die
parlamentarische Thätigkeit der Fraktion aufmerksam verfolgt und
werden sich wohl bereits selbst ein Urtheil darüber gebildet haben,
ob die parlamentarische Thätigkeit der Fraktion dem Interesse der
Partei entsprochen, oder ob die Partei Veranlassung hat, sich mit
dieser Thätigkeit nicht einverstanden zu erklären. Ich möchte nur
in großen Zügen die Reichstags-Thätigkeit der Fraktion beleuchten
und daran eine Betrachtung knüpfen, ob die Nothwendigkeit vor-

liegt, wie behauptet worden, in der parlamentarischen Taktik und
Thätigkeit der Partei eine Aenderung vorzunehmen.

In Bezug auf die Behandlung der Reichshaushaltsetats
hatte die Fraktion keine Veranlassung, von der Taktik, welche sie,
solange es Sozialdemokraten im deutschen Reichstage giebt, befolgt,
abzuweichen. Wir haben aus prinzipiellen Gründen gegen die Etats
gestimmt, weil die durch den Etat geforderten Summen wesentlich
aufgebracht werden zur Unterhaltung des Militarismus, dem wir
feindlich gegenüberstehen. Wir haben mit unserer Ablehnung des
Etats Protest eingelegt gegen das System Bismarck, welches zwar
in seinem bisherigen Träger gefallen ist, welches aber der That
nach immer noch besteht und regiert. Wir mußten mit unserer Abstimmung dokumentiren, daß die von uns vertretenen Wähler, die
politisch in der Sozialdemokratie organisirte Arbeiterklasse, dem
herrschenden System, welches zu Gunsten des Militarismus ungeheure, das Mark des Volkes aufsaugende Summen fordert, feindlich gegenübersteht. Wir betrachten den Völkerfrieden als eine
unerläßliche Vorbedingung der Bessergestaltung der sozialen Verhältnisse und stimmen gegen die Ausgaben für den Militarismus,
in der Ueberzeugung, daß den steten Rüstungen, der fortwährenden
Vermehrung der Mordmittel ein Ende gemacht werden muß, daß
es der zivilisatorischen Aufgabe der Völker widerspricht, wenn sie,
gewaffnet bis an die Zähne, gleich wilden Thieren nur auf den
Moment lauern, wo sie sich zerfleischen können. (Beifall.)

Selbstverständlich haben wir auch die für jene Militärzwecke
geforderten indirekten Steuern abgelehnt. Wir sind der Ansicht, daß die Mittel, welche die heutige Gesellschaft für den Militarismus braucht, getragen werden sollen von den Bevölkerungs-
klassen, zu deren Schutz eventuell das Militär in Aktion tritt; die
heutige Gesellschaft muthet der Arbeiterklasse zu, nicht nur mit
ihrem Leben und Gesundheit, im Falle eines Krieges, das Vaterland
und den Besitz der herrschenden Klassen zu vertheidigen, sondern
belastet auch noch in den indirekten Steuern und der dadurch herbei-
geführten Vertheuerung der nothwendigsten Lebens-
bedürfnisse die wirthschaftlich schwachen breiten Volksmassen mit
den Kosten für den Militarismus.

Wir haben in einer der früheren Sessionen einen Antrag eingebracht auf Aufhebung der Getreidezölle, der nicht über die erste
Berathung im Reichstage hinausgekommen ist. Denselben Antrag
haben wir in der laufenden Session gestellt. Wir werden bei der
Berathung dieses Antrages Gelegenheit haben, nachzuweisen, wie
verheerend die Getreidezölle gewirkt haben; während dieselben das
nothwendigste Lebensmittel im Preise steigern, zieht ein Theil der
besitzenden Klassen, namentlich die Großgrundbesitzer, bedeutende
materielle Vortheile aus den durch die Zölle erhöhten Getreidepreisen

und das arbeitende Volk zahlt den Gewinn der Agrarier mit der Vertheuerung des Brotes. (Sehr richtig.)

Wir haben uns weiter zu beschäftigen gehabt mit dem Sozialistengesetz. Zweimal ist dasselbe im Laufe der letzten drei Jahre im Reichstage zur Verhandlung gekommen. Erstens, als es sich darum handelte, die bekannten Puttkamerschen Verschärfungen in das Gesetz aufzunehmen. Sie kennen unsere Enthüllungen, welche der Welt nachwiesen, wie korrumpirend das Sozialistengesetz gewirkt hat und wie durch das Sozialistengesetz das Spitzelthum und das Agent-provocateurthum gezüchtet worden ist. Nach diesen, auf amtliche Aktenstücke gestützten Enthüllungen hatte die Majorität des Reichstages noch so viel Schamgefühl, daß sie die von der Regierung beantragten Verschärfungen, die Erhöhung der Gefängnißstrafen, das Verbot der Versammlungen im Auslande, die von Herrn v. Puttkamer geforderte Expatriirung c. ablehnte und nur für die einfache Verlängerung des Sozialistengesetzes auf zwei Jahre stimmte. Das zweite Mal beschäftigte sich der Reichstag mit dem Sozialistengesetz kurz vor den letzten Wahlen, bei welcher Gelegenheit die Verewigung des gegen uns gerichteten Ausnahmegesetzes gefordert wurde. Neben einigen angeblichen Milderungen forderte der Bundesrath die Aufhebung der Fristdauer und die Beibehaltung der Ausweisungen. Diese Vorlage ist bei der Gesammtabstimmung abgelehnt worden. Die Nationalliberalen hatten sich in Rücksicht auf den bevorstehenden Wahlkampf, und weil sie glaubten damit Stimmen fangen zu können, entschlossen, gegen die Ausweisungen zu stimmen und die Verewigung des Sozialistengesetzes von der Beseitigung des Ausweisungsparagraphen abhängig zu machen. Die Kommission kam zu keinem definitiven Resultat, und selbst während der zweiten und dritten Berathung im Plenum hatte sich noch keine feste Mehrheit gebildet. Das Kartell — damals hatte es noch die Majorität im Reichstage — wartete auf das erlösende Kommando seines Abgottes in Friedrichsruhe; aus dem Umstande, daß Fürst Bismarck seinen Mamelucken keine Befehle ertheilte, glaubten die Konservativen des Reichstages schließen zu sollen, daß die Regierung auf die Annahme des Gesetzes ohne die Ausweisung keinen Werth legen würde, und weil der rechten Seite des Reichstages das Gesetz überhaupt nicht scharf genug war, fand sich bei der Gesammtabstimmung keine Majorität für eine nochmalige Verlängerung desselben. So ist denn am 1. Oktober dieses Jahres das Sozialistengesetz gefallen, während dem Urheber sowohl als dem Hauptvollstrecker desselben bereits früher das verdiente Loos zu Theil geworden ist; das Ausnahmegesetz, unter dessen Herrschaft wir stetig an innerer und äußerer Kraft gewachsen sind, jenes Monument der Schande liegt im Staube, zertrümmert von der Partei, zu deren Vernichtung es errichtet wurde. (Lebhafter Beifall.)

Was den Arbeiterschutz betrifft, so wissen Sie, daß wir bereits im Jahre 1884 einen Arbeiterschutz-Gesetzentwurf im Reichstage eingebracht haben, der damals nicht vollständig zur Verhandlung kam. In der Legislaturperiode 1887/90 konnten wir diesen Antrag nicht wieder einbringen, weil wir nicht die dazu geschäftsordnungsmäßig erforderliche Zahl von 15 Mitgliedern, sondern nur 11 Abgeordnete hatten. In dieser Session haben wir unseren Arbeiterschutz-Gesetzentwurf auf's Neue eingebracht und es wird nach dem Wiederzusammentritt des Reichstages eine Verhandlung darüber stattfinden. Die anderen Parteien haben seit mehreren Jahren, um uns den Wind aus den Segeln zu nehmen, ein Wettrennen um die Gunst der Arbeiter veranstaltet; die Herren leben in dem naiven Glauben, daß die Arbeiterbevölkerung ihnen bei den Wahlen folgen werde, wenn derselben in Bezug auf die Arbeiterschutz-Gesetzgebung Versprechungen gemacht werden; sie haben deshalb Anträge auf Arbeiterschutz eingebracht, und es ist charakteristisch, daß diesen an sich durchaus ungenügenden und ganz schwächlichen Anträgen bis zu dieser Session die Bundesregierungen ablehnend gegenübergestanden habe. Der Antrag auf Verbot der Sonntagsarbeit, auf Verbot der Kinderarbeit, auf Verbot der Nachtarbeit für jugendliche Arbeiter und Frauen — Dinge, die sich in einem civilisirten Staate eigentlich von selbst verstehen müßten — wurden seitens der verbündeten Regierungen mit dem Hinweis darauf abgelehnt, daß die Nothwendigkeit einer Aenderung der Gesetzgebung auf diesem Gebiete nicht nachgewiesen sei; der damalige Träger der Politik der herrschenden Klassen, Fürst Bismarck, war es, welcher meinte, es müsse erst durch eine Enquete festgestellt werden, ob z. B. ein Verbot der Sonntagsarbeit nothwendig und den Arbeitern nützlich sei; trotzdem nun bei diesen Erhebungen die übergroße Mehrzahl der befragten Arbeiter und eine große Anzahl von Unternehmern sich für das Verbot der Sonntagsarbeit ausgesprochen, haben die verbündeten Regierungen sich damals nicht entschließen können, in dieser Beziehung mit Vorlagen an den Reichstag zu kommen, und wir sind erst jetzt, im Laufe dieser Legislaturperiode, in der Lage, den Gesetzentwurf, welchen die Regierung behufs Abänderung der Gewerbeordnung eingebracht hat, zu berathen. Unsere Fraktion hat bei der ersten Berathung dieses Gesetzentwurfes, welcher die „neue Aera" einleiten soll, ihren Standpunkt bereits zum Ausdruck gebracht. In der Kommission, welcher dieser Gesetzentwurf zur Vorberathung überwiesen ist, haben unsere drei Vertreter die Einfügung der Bestimmungen unseres Arbeiterschutzgesetzes in die Regierungsvorlage beantragt. Die Berathungen über die Vorlage sind noch lange nicht abgeschlossen, und es wird sich in der Presse und in Versammlungen noch oft Gelegenheit finden, über die vorgelegte Gewerbeordnungsnovelle zu verhandeln. Das aber erkläre ich schon

jetzt: Wir werden im Reichstage dem mit dem Arbeiterschutz ver-
quickten Arbeitertrutz in Bezug auf die Koalitionsfreiheit nicht
nur nicht zustimmen, sondern wir werden an diesen arbeiterfeindlichen
Bestimmungen die gänzliche Inhaltlosigkeit des offiziellen Arbeiterschutzes nachweisen. (Bravo!) Wir werden zeigen, in welch'
heuchlerischer Weise die herrschenden Klassen ihre sogenannte
Arbeiterfreundlichkeit zum Ausdruck bringen, und beweisen, daß dieselben sich die überaus winzigen Bestimmungen zum Schutz der
Arbeiter mit der Vernichtung des letzten Restes des Koalitionsrechtes bezahlen lassen wollen. Die Sozialdemokratie, welche unter
der Herrschaft des Ausnahmegesetzes das Zuckerbrot der Versicherungs-
gesetzgebung zurückgewiesen und die Peitsche des Sozialistengesetzes
verlacht hat, sie wird sich auch nicht dazu herbeilassen, um des in
der Vorlage gebotenen winzigen Arbeiterschutzes willen auf das
wichtigste Recht der Arbeiterklasse, auf die volle Koalitionsfreiheit,
zu verzichten. Das Koalitionsrecht der Arbeiter muß nicht nur in
dem jetzigen Umfange erhalten werden, nein, es muß so ausgestaltet
werden, daß kraft desselben die Arbeiter im Stande sind, sich, von
der Gesetzgebung gegen die Brutalität der Unternehmer geschützt,
menschenwürdige Lohn- und Arbeitsbedingungen zu erkämpfen.
Wir werden beantragen, die Unternehmer unter Strafe zu stellen,
wenn sie es wagen, das durch die Bestimmungen des Koalitions-
gesetzes verbriefte Recht der Arbeiter anzutasten. Gegenüber den
Unternehmerkartellen, den Industrieringen, den Bestrebungen der
herrschenden Klassen, die Arbeiter wirthschaftlich auszubeuten und
politisch zu unterjochen, diejenigen von ihnen aufs Pflaster zu
werfen, welche für die Arbeitsgenossen eintreten, werden wir gesetzliche Bestimmungen verlangen, welche diese unwürdigen und grau-
samen Zustände beseitigen; wir werden Strafbestimmungen nicht
für die um ihr Menschenrecht kämpfenden Arbeiter, sondern für die
ihre wirthschaftliche Gewalt mißbrauchenden Unternehmer fordern.
(Lebhaftes Bravo!) Ich brauche Ihnen nicht erst zu sagen, daß
wir uns vollkommen klar darüber sind, daß durch die Arbeiterschutz-Gesetzgebung die Ziele, denen die Sozialdemokratie zustrebt
nicht erreicht werden, daß durch eine noch so gute Arbeiterschutz-
Gesetzgebung das heutige Produktionssystem, unter welchem die
Arbeiterklasse immer mehr und mehr verelendet, in keiner Weise
geändert wird. Die Sozialdemokratie kämpft für die Beseitigung
des Lohnsystems, für die Aufhebung der privatkapitalistischen
Produktionsweise, und weiß, daß nur durch Konstituirung der
sozialistischen Gesellschaft die Möglichkeit zur Schaffung wahrhaft
menschenwürdiger Zustände gegeben ist. Die Sozialdemokratie,
welche die jetzige Gesellschaftsordnung von Grund aus umändern
will und daher ihrer prinzipiellen Stellung nach eine durchaus
revolutionäre Partei ist, weiß ganz genau, daß ihre Ziele nicht

auf dem Wege der Arbeiterschutz-Gesetzgebung zu erreichen sind. Wir wissen aber auch, daß wir unsere Ziele erheblich früher erreichen werden, wenn wir die Soldaten, die in dem Befreiungskampfe für die Menschheit ihre Pflicht thun sollen, in bessere Lebensverhältnisse bringen, und das geschieht, indem wir den verheerenden, degenerirenden Wirkungen des heutigen Gesellschaftssystems möglichst einen Riegel vorschieben; dazu ist die Arbeiterschutz-Gesetzgebung bestimmt. Die Arbeiterschutz-Gesetzgebung, in unserem Sinne durchgeführt, wird es der Arbeiterklasse möglich machen, in Lebensbedingungen zu kommen, in welchen es ihr ermöglicht sein wird, an dem großen Befreiungskampfe der Menschheit thatkräftigen und erfolgreichen Antheil zu nehmen. Durch entsprechende Verkürzung der Arbeitszeit, durch ein Verbot der Nachtarbeit, namentlich durch Feststellung eines Normalarbeitstages, durch ein ausreichendes Fabrikinspektorat, durch Errichtung von Arbeiterkammern zur Ueberwachung der gesundheitlichen Verhältnisse in der Industrie wird es möglich sein, Zustände zu schaffen, in denen die Arbeiterklasse nicht mehr gezwungen ist, sich in dem Maße abzurackern und sich so elend zu ernähren, wie es heute der Fall ist. Je höher die Lebensbedingungen der Arbeiter, desto schneller wird unsere Armee wachsen und immer thatkräftiger, zielbewußter und schlagbereiter werden. (Lebhafter Beifall.)

Weiter hatten wir Stellung zu nehmen zur Kolonialpolitik des Reiches. Wir sind Gegner dieser Politik, weil ihre Wirkungen wiederum nur den besitzenden Klassen zu Gute kommen, und weil es keine Kulturaufgabe für Deutschland ist, seine Bürger nach Afrika zu schicken, um sie unter den dortigen ungünstigen klimatischen Verhältnissen elend zu Grunde gehen zu lassen. Die Sklaverei gilt es auch in Deutschland zu beseitigen, und die Antisklavereibestrebungen sind nur eine Maske, unter welcher ein kleiner Kreis von großen Handelsfirmen den Löwenantheil aus dem Nutzen der Kolonialpolitik zieht.

Ferner ist verhandelt worden über ein Gesetz, welches die Einschränkung der Oeffentlichkeit bei Gerichtsverhandlungen weiter ausdehnte. Wir haben dabei die Forderung vertreten, daß die Gerichtsverhandlungen öffentliche sein müssen. Die Oeffentlichkeit der Gerichtsverhandlungen ist ein Grundpfeiler einer geordneten und guten Gerichtsbarkeit. In demselben Maße, wie, namentlich bei politischen Prozessen, die Oeffentlichkeit eingeschränkt wird, wächst die Möglichkeit, Tendenzprozesse zu führen, und wir haben in dieser Beziehung bei den Geheimbundprozessen recht viele Erfahrungen gemacht.

Das Alters- und Invaliditätsgesetz wurde von der Regierung als „Krönung der Sozialreform" bezeichnet; dasselbe ist mit einer kleinen Majorität von 20 Stimmen vom Reichstag angenommen worden. Wir haben gegen dieses Gesetz gestimmt, weil es uns zu wenig für die Arbeiter geboten hat. Das Bettelgeld, welches in Form einer Rente den durch Alter und Invalidität erwerbsunfähig gewordenen Arbeitern gegeben wird, meinten wir, hätte Deutschland sich schämen sollen, der Arbeiterklasse anzubieten. (Sehr richtig!) Wir konnten in diesem Gesetze nichts weiter sehen, als eine, nicht einmal verbesserte, sondern nur veränderte Armengesetzgebung, und wir haben nachgewiesen, daß die Armenunterstützungen in vielen Orten Deutschlands erheblich höher sind, als die Renten, welche auf Grund dieses Gesetzes als „wohlerworbene Rechtsansprüche" den alten und invaliden Arbeitern gezahlt werden. Wir haben das Invaliditäts- und Altersversicherungsgesetz abgelehnt, weil das den Arbeitern darin Gebotene durchaus unzulänglich ist und in keiner Weise den Namen verdient, welchen das Gesetz trägt. Wir haben uns mit dem Grundgedanken des Gesetzes einverstanden erklärt, wir haben aber die Ueberzeugung, daß der Gewinn, welchen die Unternehmer aus der Ausbeutung ihrer Arbeiter ziehen, sie in die Lage versetzt, in weit höherem Maße die materiellen Lasten eines solchen Gesetzes auf sich zu nehmen. Wir haben zu diesem Gesetz zahlreiche Amendements eingebracht, weil wir, wenn es uns gelungen wäre, das Gesetz so zu gestalten, daß es den Minimalforderungen der Arbeiterklasse entsprochen hätte, dafür gestimmt haben würden. Nachdem aber im Reichstage unsere so sehr bescheidenen Forderungen abgelehnt worden sind, mußten wir gegen das Gesetz stimmen; wie recht wir damit hatten, wie wenig die Prophezeihungen der Minister und der Majorität, daß nach unserer Ablehnung des Gesetzes die Arbeiter sich von uns abwenden würden, begründet waren, das hat der 20. Februar, das haben die Wahlen auf das Allerglänzendste bewiesen. (Sehr richtig; Bravo.)

Wir haben uns in dieser Session zu beschäftigen gehabt mit einer Vorlage der Reichsregierung, welche die Erhöhung der Friedenspräsenzstärke des Heeres um 18 000 Mann verlangte. Dabei war das Merkwürdige, daß dieselbe Regierung, welche vor wenigen Jahren erklärt hat, sie könne ohne Septennat nicht auskommen, in dieser Session selbst mit dem Septennat gebrochen, und eine Erhöhung der Friedenspräsenzstärke gefordert hat. Wir haben selbstverständlich gegen die Vorlage gestimmt, gegen die Erhöhung des stehenden Heeres um 18 000 Mann sowohl, als auch gegen die neuen damit verbundenen Heeresformationen. Aber wir haben auch gegen die vom Zentrum bei dieser Gelegenheit eingebrachten Resolutionen gestimmt, weil wir uns verpflichtet fühlten, gegen Herrn Windthorst, welcher durch die Einbringung solch' nichtssagender Resolutionen dem Volke nur Sand in die Augen streuen wollte, Stellung zu nehmen. Wir machen die Komödie nicht mit, in demselben Augenblick, wo man 40 Millionen für die Erhöhung des Heeresstandes bewilligt, die Regierungen aufzufordern, in ernste Erwägung zu nehmen, ob die durch den Militarismus dem Volke auferlegten Lasten nicht verringert werden könnten. Der Militarismus gereicht den Völkern zum Unheil, seine Lasten können auf die Dauer nicht getragen werden, die Völker brechen unter den Wirkungen des heutigen Militärsystems wirthschaftlich zusammen; darum wollen wir den Militarismus beseitigen und, ohne die Wehrhaftigkeit des Landes zu schwächen, durch Schaffung eines Milizheeres, durch Einführung der wirklichen allgemeinen Wehrpflicht dafür sorgen, daß Deutschland etwaigen Feinden gegenüber gewappnet ist. Der heutige Zustand dagegen ist unerträglich; aus ihm entstehen die sich stets vermehrenden Rüstungen, und schließlich führt er die Zeit herbei, in welcher der Krieg ausbrechen muß, weil die Aufrechterhaltung des heutigen bewaffneten Friedens auf die Dauer unmöglich ist. (Bravo!)

Sodann die Vorlage der Gewerbegerichte. Auch hier haben wir Amendements eingebracht, deren Annahme uns das Gesetz acceptabel gemacht hätte, weil wir glauben, daß die Schaffung solcher Gerichte in Deutschland im Interesse der Arbeiter liegt. Aber auch hier zeigte sich wieder, was man auf der andern Seite unter „Sozialreform" versteht. Alle hierher gehörigen Gesetzvorlagen, und also auch diese, sind von einem Geist des Mißtrauens gegen die Arbeiterklasse durchtränkt, der uns selbstverständlich nicht veranlassen konnte, für die Vorlage zu stimmen. Wir haben bekanntlich schließlich das Gesetz abgelehnt, weil die Theilnahme an den Wahlen an eine viel zu hohe Altersgrenze gebunden war, weil den Arbeiterinnen das Stimmrecht nicht gewährt wurde, weil bei der Organisation und Verwaltung die Mitglieder der freien Hilfskassen völlig übergangen wurden, und weil alles in allem das Gesetz den Zustand in den Städten, wo solche Gerichte bereits bestehen, wesentlich verschlechtert. Die Statuten der Gewerbegerichte in Frankfurt, Nürnberg, Leipzig u. s. w. sind für die Arbeiter viel besser, als die auf Grund des Gesetzes zu erlassenden ausfallen werden; und zu einer Verschlechterung konnten wir natürlich unsere Hand nicht bieten.

Wir haben ferner selbstständige Anträge eingebracht. Schon in der vorigen Session hatten wir bei der Etatsberathung auf einige Lücken und Mängel des Unfallversicherungsgesetzes hingewiesen; damals aber waren wir nicht in der Lage, selbstständig mit Abänderungsanträgen vorzugehen; im Laufe der letzten Session haben wir das gethan, indem wir die Aufhebung der 13wöchentlichen Karenzzeit verlangten und noch einige andere Bestimmungen des Unfallversicherungsgesetzes verbessern wollten. Bei der Verhandlung dieses unseres Antrags hat die Regierung erklärt, noch im Laufe der Session eine Novelle zum Unfallgesetz vorlegen zu wollen. Wir werden ja bald in der Lage sein, be-

urtheilen zu können, inwieweit darin unsere Forderungen berücksichtigt sind.

Wir haben sodann Anträge auf Erhöhung und Verbesserung
des Einkommens der unteren Beamten gestellt, Anträge, welche
bereits in der vorigen Session in Aussicht genommen waren und
dazu geführt haben, daß die Regierung einen Nachtragsetat vorgelegt hat. Wie sehr der Militarismus in Deutschland alles be-
herrscht, zeigte sich auch hier wieder, dadurch, daß diese Vorlage
mit einer Erhöhung der Offizierseinkommen verquickt wurde. Nach
Ablehnung dieser Forderung wurde beschlossen, den durch die Vertheuerung der Lebensmittel in äußerst ungünstige Verhältnisse
gerathenen unteren und mittleren Beamten, Briefträger u. s. w. eine
Gehaltserhöhung zu gewähren.

Wie ich schon anführte, haben wir dann den Antrag auf
Aufhebung der Lebensmittelzölle gestellt, der noch verhandelt
werden wird, und schließlich eine Verfassungsänderung dahin-
gehend beantragt, daß dem Reichstage das Recht auf Einsetzung von Untersuchungskommissionen mit der Befugniß
selbstständiger Erhebungen, der eidlichen Vernehmung von Zeugen u. s. w.
verliehen wird. Wir sind hierzu gekommen, weil durch die Art
und Weise der amtlichen Untersuchungen uns zur Gewißheit geworden
ist, daß die Arbeiterkreise fast gar nicht befragt werden, obgleich
angeblich in ihrem Interesse die Erhebungen vorgenommen werden.
Wir wollen dem deutschen Parlament, ähnlich wie es in England
der Fall ist, das Recht gewährt wissen, Untersuchungsausschüsse
einzusetzen; wir wollen, daß das Parlament die verbesserungs-
bedürftigen Verhältnisse selbstständig untersuchen kann. Dieser Antrag
ist noch nicht verhandelt, das wird erst im Laufe der Session
geschehen.

Ich komme nun zu der Frage: Sind die Interessen der Partei
durch die parlamentarische Thätigkeit gefördert worden? Ich habe,
gegenüber den wiederholten Manifestationen innerhalb der Partei,
nicht den geringsten Zweifel, daß die Partei nicht nur mit der
Thätigkeit der Fraktion einverstanden ist, sondern in ihrer übergroßen Mehrheit auch damit einverstanden ist, daß die parlamentarische Thätigkeit überhaupt für die Partei eine unbedingte Nothwendigkeit ist. Es hieße auf eins der wirksamsten Agitationsmittel
verzichten, wenn jener, in vereinzelten Kreisen laut gewordenen
Auffassung gemäß die Partei sich entschließen wollte, diese Thätigkeit
aufzugeben oder wesentlich einzuschränken. In der übergroßen
Majorität der Parteigenossen wird kein Verständniß dafür vorhanden
sein, daß zwar gewählt werden soll, daß aber die Gewählten nachher nicht arbeiten brauchen. Die Partei hat ein volles Recht, zu
verlangen, daß ihre Vertreter im Parlament die Forderungen aufstellen, deren Erfüllung sie von der heutigen Gesellschaft verlangt;

die Befürchtung, daß durch die parlamentarische Thätigkeit eine
Versumpfung der Partei eintreten könnte, daß wir zu einer Possi-
bilistenpartei werden könnten, hat in den Ergebnissen der bisherigen
parlamentarischen Bethätigung keinen Boden. Auf allen Parteitagen
ist bisher erklärt worden, von allen Rednern ist betont worden,
daß wir den Parlamentarismus wesentlich als Agitationsmittel
betrachten; um dieses Mittel aber zu voller Wirkung zu bringen,
dürfen wir nicht nur für die Wahlen agitiren, sondern müssen auch
die Parlamentstribüne zur Stellung unserer Forderungen, zur
Kritisirung des Bestehenden, zur Aufklärung und Belehrung benutzen.
Diese agitatorisch-parlamentarische Thätigkeit kann nicht dahin verstanden werden, daß man einzelne Reden im Reichstage hält, daß
von Zeit zu Zeit ein Fraktionsmitglied eine allgemein gehaltene
Darstellung unseres Programms giebt, sondern daß unabläßig und
ernsthaft, selbstredend keinen Schritt vom Programm abweichend,
und niemals zu Kompromissen geneigt, bei jeder Gelegenheit dafür
gesorgt wird, daß die Agitation für unsere Zwecke und Ziele
gefördert wird und daß bei der Nachweisung der Schäden im
Einzelnen durch Stellung von Verbesserungsanträgen die Forderungen
der Partei in immer weitere Kreise hineingetragen werden. Wer
da glaubt, daß dadurch die prinzipielle Stellung der Partei verwischt
wird, der beurtheilt ihre Intelligenz zu niedrig, ihre prinzipielle
Festigkeit zu gering. Es hieße, eins der schneidigsten, wirksamsten
Mittel, die uns zum guten Theil zu dem gemacht haben, was wir
sind, in die Ecke werfen, wenn wir anders handeln würden. Die
Reichstagstribüne mußte, wie alle Agitationsmittel, wirksam benutzt
werden und wird weiter benutzt werden müssen; durch eine
prinzipielle und zielbewußte Thätigkeit im Parlament können wir
der Partei große Dienste leisten. Ich glaube, daß die parlamentarische Thätigkeit, so wie sie von uns geübt worden, dem Interesse
der Partei sowohl in prinzipieller, wie in taktischer Beziehung
entspricht. Wir sind verpflichtet, überall da, wo es möglich ist, für die
Arbeiterklassen das denkbar Beste herauszuschlagen, und wenn wir der
Regierung die Anerkennung der Nothwendigkeit des Arbeiterschutzes
aufgezwungen haben, wenn wir den herrschenden Klassen die Ueberzeugung beigebracht haben, daß die jetzige Ausbeuterwirthschaft für
die Dauer unhaltbar ist, wenn wir durch unsere unabläßige Agitation
im Volk und im Parlament einen Erfolg errungen haben, der sich
darin dokumentirt, daß selbst die herrschenden Klassen daran gehen
müssen, die Erfüllung unserer Forderungen in Angriff zu nehmen,
dann hieße es in der That thöricht handeln, wenn wir darauf
verzichten wollten, in diesem Sinne weiter zu arbeiten. (Lebhafte
Zustimmung.) In der Diskussion wird sich innerhalb des Parteitages mit Nothwendigkeit die Ueberzeugung Bahn brechen, daß auch
im Parlament ein Boden für unsere Thätigkeit gegeben ist und daß

wir auch dort erfolgreich zu kämpfen im Stande sind. (Sehr richtig!) Ich schließe in der Hoffnung, daß der Parteitag aus dem Mitgetheilten die Ueberzeugung gewinnen wird, daß die parlamentarischen Vertreter der Sozialdemokratie es mit ihrer Aufgabe ernst genommen haben, daß sie bestrebt gewesen sind, den Interessen der Partei zu dienen und daß sie somit für die Sozialdemokratie Deutschlands, zugleich aber auch für die Arbeiterklasse aller Länder das, was sie thun konnten, geleistet haben. (Andauernder stürmischer Beifall und Händeklatschen.)

Es ist zu diesem Gegenstande der Tagesordnung folgende Resolution von Fischer-London und Oertel-Nürnberg eingebracht worden:

Der Parteitag erklärt, daß die parlamentarische Thätigkeit der Fraktion sowohl den Beschlüssen des St. Gallener Parteitages entsprach, als auch die aus der Aenderung der politischen Parteigruppirung für die deutsche Sozialdemokratie erwachsenen Verpflichtungen völlig erfüllt hat.

Der Parteitag fordert die Fraktion deshalb auf, wie bisher die prinzipiellen Forderungen der Sozialdemokratie gegenüber den bürgerlichen Parteien und dem Klassenstaat rücksichtslos zu vertreten; ebenso aber auch die auf dem Boden der heutigen Gesellschaft möglichen und im Interesse der Arbeiterklasse nöthigen Reformen zu erstreben, ohne über die Bedeutung der Tragweite dieser positiven gesetzgeberischen Thätigkeit für die Klassenlage der Arbeiter in politischer wie ökonomischer Hinsicht Zweifel zu lassen oder Illusionen zu wecken.

Diese Resolution wird mit zur Debatte gestellt.

Fischer-London: Wiewohl ich die feste Ueberzeugung habe, daß innerhalb des Parteitages über die Thätigkeit der Fraktion und unsere allgemeine Stellung zur parlamentarischen Thätigkeit absolut keine Meinungsverschiedenheit existirt, halte ich doch für nothwendig, daß der Parteitag eine bestimmte Meinung bekunde, und zwar angesichts der aus den Reihen der sogenannten Opposition wiederholt hervorgegangenen Beschuldigung, daß die bisherige Thätigkeit unserer Abgeordneten zum Possibilismus hinneige, ja bereits die Gefahr einer Versumpfung in sich schließe. Eine Stellungnahme des Parteitages ist auch nothwendig angesichts des Umstandes, daß die bürgerliche Presse diese Ansicht als die Meinung eines großen Theils der deutschen Genossen dargestellt hat. Wir müssen klipp und klar erklären, daß in dieser Beziehung unsere Meinung dieselbe geblieben ist. Wir müssen das bekunden dem wiederum aus den Reihen der sogenannten Opposition hervorgegangenen Bestreben gegenüber, einen „Radikalismus" zu kultiviren, der eigentlich nur die politische Impotenz bedeutet und in seiner Konsequenz zum Anarchismus führt, gegen den schon in Wyden und auch später bei jeder passenden Gelegenheit

Stellung genommen worden ist. Mit dem zweiten Theil unserer
Resolution wollen wir den Einwurf der Opposition begegnen, als
ob die Sozialdemokratie irgendwie Anlaß zu der Annahme gegeben
hätte, von den in der sogenannten neuen Aera versprochenen Reformen
etwas Durchgreifendes zu erwarten. Wir haben eine viel zu gute
Meinung von der Arbeiterschaft überall, um auch nur einen Augenblick in dieser Richtung Zweifel zu hegen. Auf Einzelheiten glaube
ich nicht eingehen zu sollen; die Resolution faßt Alles zusammen,
sodaß ich lediglich mich in Wiederholungen ergehen müßte. Eins
aber muß ich noch besonders betonen: es ist die Stellung der verschiedenen ausländischen Bruderparteien zu der von der Fraktion
eingenommenen Haltung. Wenn wir in allen Ländern das Bestreben
sehen, die deutsche Sozialdemokratie in Taktik und Kampfmitteln zum
Muster zu nehmen, so sollte uns diese Wahrnehmung doch dahin
belehren, daß wir auf dem richtigen Wege sind. Die Resolution ist
aber auch deshalb nothwendig, weil die Sozialdemokratie alle Ursache
hat, sich dessen zu freuen, daß sie eine solche Fraktion besitzt. Die
beste Armee wird durch schlechte Führung desorganisirt und zu
Niederlagen geführt. Unter der Führung dieser Fraktion aber hat
es die deutsche Sozialdemokratie dahin gebracht, daß wir wieder
hier in Halle auf deutschem Boden uns zu unseren Geschäften vereinigen konnten; die Fraktion hat uns im Kampf von Sieg zu Sieg
geführt. Wir haben alle Ursache, uns dessen zu freuen, daß die
politische Situation so klug ausgenutzt worden ist, ohne dabei
unserer Würde irgend etwas zu vergeben. Wie wir für unsere
Pflichterfüllung Anerkennung beanspruchen, hat auch die Fraktion
das Recht auf Anerkennung, wenn ihre Thätigkeit für uns ersprießlich
und erfolgreich gewesen ist! (Allseitige Zustimmung und Händeklatschen.)

Dr. Rüdt: Es hieße Eulen nach Athen tragen, wenn man der
Thätigkeit der Fraktion auf diesem Parteitage noch mehr Anerkennung und Lob zuerkennen wollte; ist doch beides seit Jahren
in Tausenden von Versammlungen von den Parteigenossen ausgesprochen worden, hat doch namentlich das sachliche Verhalten der
Fraktion im Reichstage zu der großen Begeisterung der Partei und
zur Ergreifung aller der Mittel, welche den großen Sieg garantiren
mußten, beigetragen! Auch die Feinde haben anerkannt, daß unsere
parlamentarischen Vertreter nicht uns das Parteiinteresse würdig
vertreten, sondern daß sie stets auf der Höhe der Zeit gestanden
haben. So sehr wir als Sozialdemokraten Gegner des Parlamentarismus als einer Schöpfung des Bourgeoisie-Staates sind, so
müssen wir doch zugestehen, daß von unseren Vertretern alles geschehen ist, was unter solchem Regime geleistet werden konnte.
Namentlich ist das Schandgesetz, welches 12 Jahre lang die Sozialdemokratie in Fesseln schlug, dadurch unmöglich geworden, weil die

Fraktion es durch die Enthüllung der Polizeispitzelei, durch die Aufdeckung der in seinem Gefolge selbst von gewissen Gerichten und seitens der Polizei in Deutschland begangenen Ungerechtigkeiten und Schändlichkeiten schon vor zwei Jahren an den Wurzeln untergrub. Dadurch hat sich auch der herrschenden Bourgeoisie gewissermaßen ein moralischer Ekel vor solchen Machinationen bemächtigt, und so ist das Gesetz gefallen. Ueberall, auch im Auslande, hat die Fraktion für ihre Haltung, ihre Thätigkeit, ihre Energie, für ihre begeisterte Vertretung der Interessen des arbeitenden Volkes Anerkennung gefunden, und diese Haltung hat es vor Allem auch dahin gebracht, daß unsere Partei so mächtig, so gefürchtet in Deutschland geworden ist. Die auf sie gemachten Angriffe waren im Wesen und in der Form völlig unbegründet und unzulässig. (Lebhafter Beifall.)

Hug-Wilhelmshaven: Ueber die Thätigkeit unserer Abgeordneten will ich kein Wort verlieren; hätten sie eine andere Taktik befolgt, so wären wir einfach auf dem Wege zur Anarchie. Die großen Worte, die tönenden Phrasen der kleinen Berliner Klique haben nirgendwo ein Echo gefunden. Ich lenke nur die Aufmerksamkeit der Fraktion auf den Umstand, daß in Deutschland einige Tausend Arbeiter in Staatswerkstätten noch immer unter einem Ausnahmegesetz stehen, obwohl das Sozialistengesetz gefallen ist. In den Arbeitsordnungen jener Werkstätten sind die bekannten Bestimmungen, welche von sozialdemokratischen, sozialistischen und kommunistischen Bestrebungen sprechen, nach wie vor enthalten. Die Fraktion sollte das sofort im Reichstage bei den Marinewerkstätten zur Sprache bringen und, soweit sie kann, dafür Sorge tragen, daß diese Bestimmungen hinauskommen. Gerade unsere Nordwestecke bedarf in dieser Beziehung der Hilfe; ich habe dort 12 Jahre gearbeitet und gesehen, wie alle und jede politische Bewegung eingeschränkt und verboten wurde; heute ist das Gesetz fort, und trotzdem kann man sich nicht rühren. Nicht einmal an einer gewerkschaftlichen Versammlung können die Arbeiter der Staatswerkstätten theilnehmen, ohne zu riskiren, entlassen zu werden.

Zur Geschäftsordnung beschwert sich Genosse Hermann, daß Ausdrücke wie „Berliner Klique" gebraucht werden; man solle alles Persönliche vermeiden.

Ebenfalls zur Geschäftsordnung wünscht Genosse Schulze-Erfurt, daß doch diejenigen, welche zu Gunsten der Parteileitung und der Fraktionsthätigkeit sprechen wollen, auf das Wort verzichten möchten, man wolle lieber die Gegner hören.

Herbert-Stettin: Die Angriffe auf die Fraktion kommen von Seiten Derer, die in den großen Städten sitzen und sich nicht die Mühe geben, aufs Land zu gehen und dort die ungleich schwerere Agitation zu betreiben. Dort fragt man uns zunächst immer: Was

habt ihr bereits gethan? und kann man keine positive Antwort
geben, dann ist es nichts mit dem Erfolg. Die Landbevölkerung
ist bisher von uns noch nicht genügend berücksichtigt worden, auch
bei den Arbeiterschutzanträgen. Wir müssen darauf hinarbeiten,
daß auch den Landarbeitern das Koalitionsrecht gegeben wird. Ich
habe während der Zeit meiner Ausweisung aus Stettin manches
auf dem platten Lande in der so verrufenen Provinz Pommern
erreicht; aber weit mehr würde man dort den neuen Ideen zu-
jauchzen, wenn die Führer und bewährten Kräfte mehr von den
Städten hinausgingen, wenn nicht so oft der mit Mühe gewonnene
Referent im letzten Augenblicke wieder abschriebe. Es wäre doch
die größte Ruhmesthat, gerade Pommern zu gewinnen. Griffe
hier die Fraktion ein, sie würde sich den besten Dank erwerben.

Bremer-Magdeburg (sehr schwer zu verstehen): In letzter Zeit
ist die Behauptung, unsere Theilnahme am Parlamentarismus sei ein
Unrecht, mit derartigen Argumenten durch die Opposition vertreten
worden, daß ich dagegen doch protestiren muß. In einem von
jener Seite ausgegangenen Artikel heißt es u. A. sogar: Wer den
Arbeitern sagt, er will ihnen mit dem Parlament helfen, begeht
einen Schwindel, einen Betrug! — Wir haben doch unser Parteiprogramm und solange das nicht geändert ist, so lange es uns
anweist, die alten demokratischen Forderungen zu erheben, deren
Verwirklichung auf dem Felde des Parlamentarismus liegt, solange
erkenne ich nur den als Parteigenossen an, der sich auf dieses
Programm stellt. Ich gewähre die weitgehendste Freiheit in der
Diskussion, aber Unterschiebung von Lüge und Betrug verbitte ich
mir. Aus der Diskussion darf nicht Gehässigkeit hervorgehen, durch
sie darf auch die Parteidisziplin nicht untergraben werden!

Kunert beschwert sich zur Geschäftsordnung über störende
Unruhe an den Saalausgängen; Riemann-Chemnitz führt über
die vorhandene Zugluft Klage.

Es läuft von Vollmar und Genossen folgende Resolution ein:

Der Parteitag wolle beschließen:

Die Partei hat für die nächste Zeit eine hauptsächliche Wirksamkeit dahin zu richten, daß das vorhandene Koalitionsrecht
nicht nur im ganzen Umfange aufrecht erhalten und gegen jede
wie immer geartete Beeinträchtigung thatkräftig geschützt, sondern
weiter bis zur vollen Versammlungs- und Verbindungsfreiheit
entwickelt wird. Als ein nothwendiges Mittel zum Schutze des
Koalitionsrechtes der Arbeiter gegen die unterdrückerischen Bestrebungen des Unternehmerthums ist ein Gesetz anzustreben,
welches jeden Versuch, das Koalitionsrecht oder die sonstige Ausübung der gesetzlichen Rechte zu hindern oder zu erschweren,
unter nachdrückliche Strafe stellt.

Kloß-Stuttgart wünscht, daß diese Resolution bis zu Punkt 8 der Tagesordnung zurückgestellt werde.

Vollmar: Mein Antrag zielt nicht nur auf das gewerbliche Koalitionsrecht, sondern auf jedes Koalitionsrecht, und wir können unmöglich die Materie derart theilen, daß wir einen Theil erst bei Punkt 8 behandeln; das Koalitionsrecht ist ein politischer Faktor, der gerade nur hier erledigt werden kann, wo es sich um unsere parlamentarische Bethätigung handelt. Wir fordern bekanntlich für alle Deutschen, ob Männer oder Frauen, das gleiche, vollkommen freie Vereinigungs-, Versammlungs- und Verbindungsrecht nach jeder Richtung, darüber brauchen wir nicht zu reden; nur scheint es mir taktisch an der Zeit, jetzt uns dieses Rechtes besonders anzunehmen. Sowohl von Seiten der Regierungen wie des Unternehmerthums wird jetzt bereits der Versuch gemacht, das Vereinsrecht zu beeinträchtigen; weitere Versuche werden, wenn wir von unseren Rechten unter dem jetzt zurückgewonnenen gemeinen Recht wollen Gebrauch machen, gar nicht auf sich warten lassen. Wir müssen bedenken, die Leute sind wenig durch die bisherigen Verhältnisse an die öffentliche Diskussion gewöhnt, und wenn erst die Lawine von Versammlungen, Preßerzeugnissen, Reden u. s. w. über sie ergehen wird, dann werden die Spießbürger erst recht wieder nach Polizei schreien. Deshalb sollte nach meiner Ansicht der Parteitag hier ansetzen, nicht nur mit dem Verlangen der Ausdehnung des Rechtes, sondern auch mit der Forderung nachdrücklicher Strafen für jeden, der diese gesetzliche Freiheit zu beeinträchtigen versucht. In dem Arbeiterschutz-Gesetzentwurf der Fraktion ist die Sache insofern berührt, als dort die Unternehmerkartelle und die schwarzen Listen als strafbar hingestellt werden, nicht nur civilrechtlich, sondern auch durch Verwirkung von Konventionalstrafen und dergleichen. Die Sache hat damals großen Krakehl hervorgerufen und alle guten Bürger in furchtbare Wuth versetzt, daß wir ihnen ihre Freiheit, uns zu unterdrücken, verbieten wollen. Aber gerade der Ach- und Wehescrei der Bourgeoisie hat uns den rechten Weg gezeigt; wir dürfen nicht zurück, sondern müssen weiter gehen, und das soll durch meinen Antrag geschehen. Derselbe ist nicht etwas noch nie Dagewesenes, sondern sein Inhalt ist in Frankreich z. B. bereits Gesetz; es werden dort solche Zuwiderhandlungen unter eine Geldstrafe von 200 bis 1000 Franks und unter die Androhung von Gefängniß bis zu drei Monaten gestellt. Ich bitte den Parteitag, sich möglichst einstimmig für den Antrag zu erklären, um der Fraktion gebundene Marschroute zu geben, daß sie bei der ersten Gelegenheit denselben im Reichstage einbringt.

Fleischmann-Frankfurt a. M. Sie werden sich Alle sehr wohl zu erinnern wissen, daß es eine Zeit gab, wo es fast ein moderner Sport geworden war, etwas revolutionär zu renommiren. Wir haben dieses Treiben fast überall wahrnehmen können. Man renommirte einerseits beständig mit der Behauptung, die parlamentarische Thätigkeit führe uns nicht zum Ziel, und andererseits wurde immer auf den sog. großen kommenden Tag hingedeutet, welcher die Menschheit mit einem Schlage erlösen sollte. Derartige Leute giebt es noch hier und da in unseren Reihen; ich habe keine Veranlassung, Namen zu nennen, aber auch ich halte für nothwendig, daß wir uns in einer bestimmten Richtung ganz entschieden äußern und den von uns zu gehenden Weg bezeichnen. Wir wollen und müssen bestrebt sein, das Klasseninteresse der großen indifferenten Masse zu wecken, dann wird sich schon zeigen, wie weit wir unseren Zielen uns nähern. Ich bin nicht gerade ein Freund des Boykotts, aber ich bin entschieden für den Boykott des Militarismus. Boykottiren wir ihn, geben wir ihm keine Gelegenheit, von seinen Schießwaffen Gebrauch zu machen. Geben wir ihm keine Gelegenheit zum Einhauen auf die Massen, dann haben wir im Interesse der Fortentwicklung unserer Bewegung mehr gethan, als mit aller Revolutionsmacherei und mit dem Hindeuten auf jenen großen Tag, auf Putsche u. dgl. Die große Masse ist zum Klassenbewußtsein zu bringen, alles andere sind nebensächliche Fragen.

Liebknecht: Genossen! Ich hätte eigentlich erwartet, daß die Opposition sich melden würde. Dem Genossen Vollmar wollte ich zunächst sagen, daß das Koalitionsrecht von uns in seiner Bedeutung voll erkannt wird. Wir wissen genau, daß das Wahl- und das Koalitionsrecht die bedeutendsten Rechte sind, die wir zu vertheidigen haben werden. Uebrigens ist das, was Vollmar beantragt und von ihm hier befürwortet wurde, bereits geschehen. — Da nun hier kein Ansturm gegen den Parlamentarismus bisher gekommen ist, muß ich mich gegen einiges in der Presse Gesagte wenden. Der ganze Ansturm läuft auf eine Verwechselung dessen hinaus, was man unter Parlamentarismus versteht. Früher verstand man darunter — in Frankreich unter Louis Philipp und in England — unter Parlamentarismus nicht das Wahlrecht im Allgemeinen, sondern bloß das Wahlrecht einer Minorität, nämlich der besitzenden Klassen. Dieses ganze System ist uns als ein Schwindelsystem erschienen. Wo aber ein allgemeines Wahlrecht besteht, kann davon keine Rede sein. Die 45 Millionen Deutsche können doch nicht an einem Tage zusammenkommen und über jedes Gesetz berathen; wir müssen also eine Vertretung haben. Wessen Schuld ist es, wenn die Volksvertretung nichts taugt? Schuld daran ist doch nicht das allgemeine Wahlrecht, sondern der Unverstand der Massen, die leider noch allzu oft ihre eigenen Feinde wählen. Da zeigt sich, wo wir den Hebel anzusetzen haben. (Sehr richtig!) Von den 80 Prozent, die gegen uns sind, würden mindestens noch neun Zehntel zu uns gehören, wenn sie ihr Interesse verständen. Diese bis jetzt indifferente Masse müssen wir erobern; haben wir sie erobert, so haben wir den Sieg. Das war gerade das Gefährliche jener Opposition, womit sie den Gegnern einen ungeheuren Dienst geleistet hätte, wenn es ihr gelang, diese indifferente Masse gegen uns aufzubringen. In die Partei schlagen sie damit keinen Keil hinein, die schüttelt solche Dinge mit Leichtigkeit ab (Zustimmung), aber jene mögliche Wirkung des Auftretens der Opposition ist der Hauptfehler gewesen. Man hat alles gethan, den Parlamentarismus zu diskreditiren, so daß ein Abgeordneter fast als ein Feigling erscheinen mußte. Die Herren haben auf die Brust geschlagen, als wären sie die einzig Thätigen in der Partei. Was haben sie gethan? Ein Paar Reden gehalten. Eine Bombe werfen kann einmal jeder Esel. (Sehr richtig.) Schon früher habe ich auf die anarchistische Bewegung hingewiesen; sie ist zurückgeworfen worden, während wir in Deutschland eine Macht geworden sind. — Kompromisse sollen nicht geschlossen, unser revolutionärer Charakter muß stets scharf aufrecht erhalten werden. Im Parlament ist es oft sehr schwierig, die Grenzlinie zu ziehen; da wird unter Umständen ein klein bischen zu weit nach rechts oder nach links gegangen; wenn man aber das Ziel fest vor Augen hat, wird man diese Linie stets im Ganzen richtig innehalten, und das ist unsererseits geschehen. Die ungeheure Bedeutung des Wahlrechts wird Ihnen ja durch unsere ausländischen Genossen bezeugt. In Belgien, Oesterreich, in den Niederlanden, überall kämpft man um das allgemeine Wahlrecht, das gewaltigste Agitations- und Erziehungsmittel für die Massen, welches existirt. Trotz aller Unterdrückung, die wir erlitten haben, sind dadurch die Volksmassen bis ins Innerste aufgerüttelt worden. Wenn Sie heute den politischen Bildungszustand auf dem Lande mit dem zur Zeit vor dem allgemeinen Wahlrecht vergleichen, werden Sie erklären müssen, daß die erzieherische Wirkung dieses Wahlrechts garnicht hoch genug geschätzt werden kann, und darum müssen wir es benutzen. Fürst Bismarck, der zwar kein Staatsmann war, aber ein Demagoge, wie er im Buche steht, hat den Wählerfang gründlich betrieben. Das thun wir auch, aber wir schwindeln den Leuten nichts vor, was wir nicht erfüllen können. Früher haben wir ja theilweise eine ganz andere Taktik verfolgt. Taktik und Prinzip sind zwei verschiedene Dinge. Ich habe 1869 in einer Rede in Berlin den Parlamentarismus verurtheilt. Das war damals. Die politischen Verhältnisse waren ganz andere; der Norddeutsche Bund war eine Mißgeburt, ein Deutsches Reich gab es nicht. Niemand konnte die Wendung voraussehen, die so bald eintrat. Sie kennen die Geschichte. Der österreichische Oberkriegsrath gab seine ausgearbeiteten Schlacht- und Siegespläne den Feldherren in die Hand, und sie wurden geschlagen; den französischen Heerführern sagte man nur: Ihr habt

zu siegen, und sie siegten. Und das müssen auch Sie der Partei-
führung sagen: Ihr müßt siegen, Ihr habt unsere Interessen zu
vertreten! Die Taktik ist Sache der Umstände, aber Ihr müßt siegen!
(Stürmischer Beifall.)

Werner-Teltow (zur Geschäftsordnung): Ich habe sofort, als
der Berichterstatter begann, einen Zettel mit meiner Meldung hinauf-
geschickt; ich bewundere, daß der Zettel weggekommen ist. . . .

Vorsitzender Dietz: Der Zettel ist nicht verloren gegangen,
Genosse Werner bekommt jetzt das Wort.

Werner-Teltow: Ich hätte zunächst gewünscht, daß vom
Bureau der Ausdruck „Berliner Clique" gerügt worden wäre, wie
das schon der gewöhnliche parlamentarische Anstand erheischt . .
(Glocke des Präsidenten.)

Vorsitzender Dietz: Ich kann dem Genossen Werner nicht
gestatten, das Bureau zu kritisiren; ich werde aber auch beleidigende Ausdrücke, gleichgiltig von welcher Seite sie kommen,
zurückweisen.

Werner (fortfahrend): Dann hat der Vorsitzende das über-
hört. — Ich stehe in der Frage des Parlamentarismus auf dem
Standpunkte, daß man das Agitationsmittel der Wahl für unsere
Partei unbedingt zu inscenniren und anzuwenden hat, da man dadurch
in die entlegensten Kreise der noch indifferenten Bevölkerung
Deutschlands hineindringen kann. Aber mit der Resolution Fischer,
die ja ähnlich auch schon in Kopenhagen und St. Gallen angenommen ist, kann ich mich nicht einverstanden erklären. Ich spreche
unseren Abgeordneten garnicht ab, daß sie ihre Thätigkeit im Reichstage entwickelt haben; viel zu rührig sind sie gewesen; aber
ob diese Rührigkeit am rechten Ende angewandt worden ist, ist eine
zweite Frage. Unsere Reichstagsfraktion muß im Parlament mehr
propagandistisch, mehr agitatorisch wirken für die Ideen der Sozialdemokratie. Wir wollen doch das Parlament nicht betrachten als
Selbstzweck, sondern als Mittel zum Zweck! Nun sagt Singer, wir
müssen uns die Soldaten erziehen, damit, wenn die heutige Anschauung fällt, die große Masse soweit ist, daß sie weiß, welches
die sozialdemokratischen Prinzipien sind und daß auf Grund derselben die neue Weltordnung aufgebaut wird. Auf diese Weise
kann ich aber Soldaten nicht erziehen, wenn ich die Zweckmäßigkeit
der Arbeiterschutzgesetzgebung in der heutigen Gesellschaft so in den
Vordergrund stelle. Was heißt es denn, wenn heute die Verkürzung
der Arbeitszeit so sehr betont wird? Ich betrachte die Kaiserlichen
Erlasse, die ja von Einzelnen bei uns gelobt worden sind als erster
Anstoß zu einer neuen Aera, dahin: der Regent wollte die Bourgeoisie,
das Kapital, darauf hindrängen, zu sagen, die anstürmende Gefahr
der Arbeiterbewegung ist vorhanden, verbrüdert euch international,
damit ihr jene sozialen Forderungen, die von Seiten der Arbeiter-

7

vertreter erhoben werden, Verkürzung der Arbeitszeit, welche Erhöhung des Lohnes nach sich ziehen muß, regeln könnt; denn wenn
ihr auf dem Weltmarkt vollständig einig seid, dann kann das Produkt
diese Lohnerhöhung durch die verkürzte Arbeitszeit sehr wohl tragen.
Betrachten wir doch die Sache ruhig. Bei zehnstündiger Arbeitszeit wird bei der heutigen Wirthschaft ein Quantum von Arbeit
fertig (Unterbrechungen) .. ich glaube, ich erzähle Ihnen nichts
Neues. (Heiterkeit, Rufe: Sehr richtig!) Wenn durch die Verkürzung der Arbeitszeit und den erhöhten Arbeitslohn das gelieferte
Quantum jetzt ein geringeres wird, muß doch ganz naturgemäß das
einzelne Produkt im Preise steigen. (Zwischenrufe: Das wissen wir!)
Es ist aber wesentlich, daß ich das heute hier konstatire. (Große
Heiterkeit). Sie werden mich heute nicht aus der Fassung bringen.
Die Lage der Bevölkerung wird nicht gehoben, wenn durch die
Vertheuerung der Produkte eine Steigerung des Lohnes stattfindet.
und wenn durch die Bestimmungen des ehernen Lohngesetzes die
arbeitende Bevölkerung auf dem niedrigsten Niveau der Selbsterhaltung ihre Forderungen von der Kapitalistenklasse erfüllt bekommt.
Wenn heute der Lohn zwei Mark ist und die Waare kostet auch
zwei Mark, so ist das doch gleichbedeutend, ob der Lohn fünfzig
Mark ist, wenn die Waare auch fünfzig Mark kostet. Das ist doch
ganz klar. (Lachen und fortgesetzte Unterbrechungen.) Ich wollte
dies Beispiel hier nur anführen, um zu konstatiren, daß unsere
Reichstagsabgeordneten darauf hindrängen sollten, daß die Kapitals-
wirthschaft unbedingt weg muß. Diese Flickerei durch Arbeiterschutz-
gesetzgebung an der heutigen Wirthschaftsordnung wird niemals eine
Hebung der materiellen Lage der arbeitenden Klassen mit sich bringen.
Geistig kann die Arbeiterklasse durch die verkürzte Arbeitszeit sehr
wohl gehoben werden. (Rufe: Aha! Andauernde Unruhe.) Das
ist der einzige Grund, aber eine materielle Hebung möchte ich sehr
stark bezweifeln, und deshalb kann ich Singers Ausführungen nicht
zustimmen, wonach auch eine bessere Ernährungsweise dadurch
erzielt werden soll. Die Arbeiter werden immer auf dem niedrigsten
Niveau stehen. (Fortgesetzte Unruhe.)

Vorsitzender Dietz: Die zehn Minuten sind vorüber. (Werner
bittet um weiteres Gehör. Stürmischer Widerspruch. Bebel ruft:
Gebt ihm noch zehn Minuten! G. Schulz-Berlin: Geben Sie
Herrn Werner noch zehn Minuten mehr! Jeder blamirt sich, so gut
er kann! Stürmische Heiterkeit und Lärm.)

Auf die Anfrage des Vorsitzenden beschließt der Parteitag ohne
Widerspruch, den Redner weitersprechen zu lassen.

Vorsitzender: Herr Werner hat das Wort. Ich bemerke aber,
daß dies kein Präjudiz sein soll. Jeder folgende Redner darf unbedingt nur 10 Minuten sprechen.

Werner (fortfahrend): Ich danke zunächst Herrn Schulz für

die Zensur, die er mir gegeben; wir werden in Berlin mit ihm darüber weiter sprechen. Vor dem Sozialistengesetz wehte in den Reden unserer Abgeordneten ein frischer, belebender Hauch; das sprach zum Herzen; da sah die Masse, daß sie von unserer heutigen bürgerlichen Gesellschaft nichts zu erwarten hat und daß die Prinzipien der Sozialdemokratie einzig und allein die richtigen seien. Aber jetzt hat im Reichstage der Abgeordnete Bebel in einer Kommission erklärt, und ich möchte darüber von ihm Auskunft haben, wie er das gemeint hat, man müsse einer jeden Regierung Vertrauen entgegenbringen (Lachen). Bebel wird mir das beantworten. Ich möchte diesen Ausspruch nicht näher ausmalen. Ferner hat Bebel in seiner letzten Militärrede etwas ausgeführt, was ich nicht unterschreiben kann und was ich als Sozialdemokrat auch nicht verstehe. Ich bin ja ein ziemlich beschränkter Mensch. (Zustimmung und Heiterkeit.) Ich habe ja keine Gymnasialbildung. — Der Abgeordnete Bebel hat bei der Militärvorlage im Reichstage gesagt, er sehe ein, daß die Abrüstung nicht möglich sei und daß von der bürgerlichen Gesellschaft nicht zu erwarten sei, daß sie die Kraft aus den Händen gebe. (Redner citirt den stenographischen Bericht.) Bebel erklärte sich sogar eventuell bereit, dazu Mittel zu bewilligen, um die Uniformen umzuändern. Ich kann mich nicht damit einverstanden erklären, daß man der Regierung in dieser Weise Konzessionen von unserer Seite macht. Wenn wir die internationale Abrüstung verlangen, so muß immer und immer wieder betont werden, daß der Militarismus etwas Kulturfeindliches ist. Ich bin zufrieden, wenn mich Bebel in dieser Beziehung eines Besseren belehren kann, aber ich konnte das, von meinem Standpunkte aus nicht gutheißen.

Im deutschen Reichstage sind unsere Vertreter mit Recht gegen das Alters- und Invaliditätsgesetz aufgetreten. Es wurde gesagt, das Gesetz sei nur eine verschobene, nicht verbesserte Armenpflege, und darum könne man ihm nicht zustimmen. Es ist mir aber erinnerlich, daß von der Fraktion der Antrag gestellt wurde, daß das kleine Bürgerthum, der Handwerkerstand, auch solle der Wohlthaten des Gesetzes theilhaftig werden. Ferner sagten die Abgeordneten im Reichstage: wir sind gegen jede veränderte Armenpflege, wir wollen keine derartige Armenpflege, — und dann kommen unsere Leute in der Stadtverordnetenversammlung und sagen: hier in der Stadtverordnetenversammlung müssen wir einmal anfangen, die Armenpflege ein bischen zu reformiren, und müssen einmal sehen, ob wir hier einen Pfennig der einen oder anderen Familie mehr geben können. Das ist gefährlich. Ich bin für die Thätigkeit der Fraktion im Reichstage, aber sie muß propagandistisch, agitatorisch, von unseren Gesichtspunkten, von sozialdemokratischen Zielen aus immer zündend zur Masse sprechen.

7*

Ferner muß ich auf etwas aufmerkjam machen, was zu un-
liebjamen Auseinanderjetzungen in der Preſſe geführt hat. Im
Wahlkreiſe des Abgeordneten Stadthagen, bei der Hauptwahl, ver-
theilten die Freiſinnigen illuſtrirte Flugblätter, und bei der Stichwahl kam unſere Partei und vertheilte dieſelben illuſtrirten Flugblätter. Es handelte ſich in denſelben um die indirekten Steuern.
Wir ſehen aber doch die Zölle von ganz anderen Geſichtspunkten
an, als die bürgerlichen Parteien. Die Freiſinnigen ſind allerdings
auch gegen die indirekten Steuern, aber nur, weil ſie das Privat-
kapital in ſeiner Beweglichkeit nicht einſchränken wollen. Wir dagegen ſind gegen die Getreidezölle, weil wir, wie Karl Marx auf
dem Brüſſeler Kongreß ausführte, einen revolutionären Standpunkt
einnehmen, weil die große Maſſe der arbeitenden Bevölkerung einfach ihre Lebensmittel vertheuert bekommt und weil der Freihandel
eher zum Zuſammenbruch der privatkapitaliſtiſchen Produktionsweiſe
führt. Auf dieſem Standpunkte ſtehe ich auch; der Parlamentarismus iſt nicht Zweck, ſondern Mittel zum Zweck. Er muß agita-
toriſch, propagandiſtiſch ſein, um ſo die Maſſen aufzuklären. Das
Koalitionsrecht, das Vereins- und Verſammlungsrecht, die politiſchen
Fragen müſſen mehr in den Vordergrund geſtellt werden als bis
dato, die Arbeiter müſſen vor dem Terrorismus der Arbeitgeber
geſchützt werden.

Löwenſtein-Nürnberg: Jede agitatoriſche Thätigkeit unſerer
Fraktion muß für unſere Partei zugleich eine praktiſche ſein. Werner
aber faßt die Thätigkeit der einzelnen Abgeordneten in dem Sinne
auf, wie z. B. Haſſelmann und Moſt dies thaten, als ſie — nicht
mehr Abgeordnete waren. Das iſt der Kernpunkt ſeiner ganzen
Ausführungen: es ſollen anarchiſtiſche Auffaſſungen ins Volk hineingetragen werden. Daß wir aber damit nichts wollen zu thun
haben, brauche ich nicht auseinanderzuſetzen. Nach Werners Meinung korrumpirt die parlamentariſche Thätigkeit. In gewiſſem
Sinne iſt das ja auch richtig. Daſſelbe läßt ſich aber ebenſo gut
von jeder Theilnahme an der Politik überhaupt ſagen. Es werden
nur Diejenigen korrumpirt, die nicht geſinnungstreu
ſind, die keine Prinzipien haben, die nicht opferwillig
ſind, die nicht die Allgemeinheit, ſondern nur perſön-
liche Intereſſen im Auge haben. Für die Charaktere iſt die
parlamentariſche Thätigkeit eine Schule, und wer da charakterfeſt
hervorgeht — und das iſt bei der Thätigkeit unſerer Fraktion in
vollſtem Maße der Fall —, bei dem iſt von Korruption keine Rede.
Ich bin der Meinung, daß unſere Vertreter, weil auf die agitatoriſche
Thätigkeit der Hauptwerth zu legen iſt, hauptſächlich in den großen
Prinzipienfragen, alſo zunächſt in den ſozialpolitiſchen Fragen, arbeiten müſſen und nicht in Kleinigkeiten ihre Kraft zerſplittern ſollen.
Ich wünſche aber auch, daß unſere Abgeordneten mehr als bisher

— ich will ihnen damit keinen Vorwurf machen —, ähnlich wie seiner Zeit der leider viel zu früh gestorbene Abgeordnete Kayser, beim Budget die vorhandenen Mißstände zur Sprache bringen; das kann uns nur Anhänger gewinnen.

Bebel: Sie werden von mir nicht erwarten, daß ich mich auf die sogenannten nationalökonomischen Auseinandersetzungen des Herrn Werner einlasse. (Sehr richtig; Heiterkeit.) Ich wäre auch gar nicht dazu im Stande; nicht weil ich mich zu unwissend halte, sondern weil ich, was er ausführte, nicht habe verstehen können. Ein solcher Wirrwarr von verschiedenartigen Gedanken, eine solche geistige Konfusion ist mir bei einem Parteigenossen, der sich öffentlich um ein Reichstagsmandat beworben hat, noch nie begegnet. (Lebhafte Zustimmung.) Wenn ich früher den lebhaften Wunsch gehabt habe, in Rücksicht auf die Rolle, welche Werner in der Berliner Bewegung gespielt hat, daß er bei den Wahlen des 20. Februar oder bei der Nachwahl als Abgeordneter gewählt werde, so muß ich erklären, nachdem ich heute seine Rede gehört, freue ich mich außerordentlich, daß er nicht mein Reichstagskollege geworden ist. (Sehr gut!) Wäre er gewählt worden, fürchte ich sehr, daß wir in seiner Person eine ganz ungeheure Blamage im Reichstage uns zugezogen hätten. (Bravo!) Hätte Werner seine heutige Rede im Reichstage gehalten, wo jedes Wort durch den stenographischen Bericht festgenagelt wird, ich wäre schamroth geworden über den Effekt in der Presse. Die Auseinandersetzungen, die er bezüglich der indirekten Steuern zum Besten gegeben, und bei denen er, ein Bekämpfer der Autorität, sich auf die Autorität von Karl Marx bezog, beweisen, daß er nicht einmal die wesentlichen Grundbegriffe unseres Parteiprogramms kennt. In dieser Hinsicht genügt sein Wissen nicht einmal den bescheidensten Anforderungen. Auch die von ihm zitirte Rede, die Marx auf dem Brüsseler Kongreß gehalten, hat er nicht verstanden. Würde einer von uns im Reichstag in einer Rede über die Aufhebung der Getreidezölle u. s. w. ähnliche Ausführungen machen, wie wir sie heute von Werner gehört haben, ein gründliches Fiasko wäre die nothwendige Folge. Ich sage aber mehr. Hätte Herr Werner die Ausführungen, die er heute hier über die parlamentarische Thätigkeit der Fraktion und über seine Stellung zu den indirekten Steuern zum Besten gegeben hat, auch bei der Wahlagitation vor seinen Wählern gemacht, ich bin fest überzeugt, daß er nicht den dritten Theil der Stimmen bekommen hätte, die er thatsächlich bekommen hat. (Sehr richtig!) Dieselben Herren, die heute fortgesetzt gegen die parlamentarische Thätigkeit der Fraktion vorgehen und nicht genug heftige Worte finden, um sie zu verurtheilen, haben bei der Wahlagitation vor 6 Monaten genau in derselben Weise, wie wir Alle, für ihre Kandidaturen gewirkt. Damals hörte man von ihrer jetzt zur Schau

dem Sinne handhabt, daß sie den Fabrikinspektoren die dem jeweiligen Stande der Technik entsprechenden Anweisungen zur Kontrole der Fabriken giebt. Also auf dem Wege der Verwaltung, wenn eine Aenderung des Produktionsprozesses eintritt, muß die Regierung die Möglichkeit haben, heute so, morgen so zu operiren. Jede andere Regelung würde zum Schaden der Arbeiter selbst ausschlagen. Da ist es egal, wer augenblicklich in der Regierung sitzt. Wir müssen uns eben darauf verlassen, daß sie die getroffenen Bestimmungen in deren Geiste handhabt. Das ist der Sinn meiner Worte

Ich soll mich dann, entgegen unserer sonstigen Auffassung, gegen die Abrüstung erklärt haben. Das ist auch wieder eine der Wortverdrehungen, an denen kein Mensch in der Partei reicher ist, als Werner. So oft ich auch Gelegenheit gehabt habe, mit diesem Herrn zu disputiren, habe ich gefunden, daß es keinen größeren Meister in der Entstellung und Verdrehung der Worte des Gegners giebt, als ihn. Ich muß erklären, das ist ein Verfahren, das ich mit dem Begriff der Ehrlichkeit und Anständigkeit eines Mannes nicht vereinbaren kann (Bravo!). Ich habe ausgeführt, ich halte die Bestrebungen der sogenannten Friedensfreunde auf allgemeine Abrüstung für aussichtslos, weil es überhaupt nicht denkbar ist, daß die rivalisirenden Militärstaaten dazu übergehen können, gesetzliche Bestimmungen über die Abrüstung zu vereinbaren; aber selbst, wenn derartige Bestimmungen getroffen würden, dann wird mit Nothwendigkeit jede Regierung heimlicherweise dieselben zu umgehen suchen, um im Kriegsfalle dem Gegner mit größerer Macht gegenübertreten zu können. Der Krieg und die Nationalitätenfeindschaft, so führte ich aus, ist ein nothwendiges Produkt der bürgerlichen Gesellschaft und der in ihr existirenden Klassengegensätze. Sie kann keine Verbrüderung der Nationalitäten wollen, sie muß nothwendig auf die Völkerverhetzung hinarbeiten. Die Kriege sind heute schon nothwendig, damit gewisse Machthaber jeden Augenblick ein Mittel zur Hand haben, die Aufmerksamkeit der Massen von den inneren Angelegenheiten und den sozialen Mißständen abzulenken. Weiter sind die stehenden Heere ein sehr probates Mittel, um die überflüssigen Söhne der Bourgeois in fett dotirte Offizierstellen unterzubringen (Bravo!). Wenn Ihr aber einmal diese stehenden Heere für nothwendig haltet, so führte ich den Freisinnigen gegenüber, speziell gegen die sich so breit machende Richter'sche Scheinopposition aus, dann trefft wenigstens Einrichtungen, daß der aus den ungeheuren Verbesserungen in der Technik der Kriegführung entspringenden Massenhinschlachtung nach Möglichkeit gesteuert wird. Ich habe darauf hingewiesen, daß bei der Anwendung des rauchlosen Pulvers und der gegen früher ungeheuren, gesteigerten Treffsicherheit der Gewehre, die jetzigen Uniformen mit ihren blitzenden

Metallknöpfen und grellen Farben ein geradezu Verderben bringendes Zielobjekt für die Feinde seien. Müßten sich unsere Brüder, Söhne und Väter schon einmal auf das Schlachtfeld schleppen lassen, dann kleide man sie wenigstens so, daß sie nicht geradezu das Auge des feindlichen Schützen herausfordern. (Bravo!) Und nun frage ich Euch Alle, die Ihr verpflichtet seid, gegen den auswärtigen Feind die Waffen zu tragen: als Liniensoldaten, Reservisten, Landwehrmänner oder Landsturm, wenn ich verhindern will, daß Ihr durch äußere Kennzeichen eine bequeme Zielscheibe für die Feinde werdet, habe ich damit irgend etwas gethan, was vom Parteistandpunkt aus verwerflich wäre? (Rufe: nein!) Wenn ich aber weiter erklärte, ich bin bereit, die Mittel für weniger sichtbare Uniformstücke zu bewilligen, dann habe ich damit nichts weiter gethan, als meine Bereitwilligkeit ausgedrückt, dafür zu sorgen, daß im nächsten Kriege nicht Zehntausende unserer eigenen Genossen durch die Ungeschicklichkeit unserer Militärverwaltung zwecklos auf die Schlachtbank geführt werden. Ich habe die Genugthuung gehabt, daß jetzt nach den Manövern in allen Zeitungen und Militärblättern diese Frage erörtert wird. Es wird da ausgeführt, daß es mit der bisherigen farbenschillernden Montirung nicht mehr geht, wenn unsere Soldaten vor der massenhaften Hinschlachtung bewahrt bleiben sollen. Nie in meinem Leben habe ich in einer Frage ein besseres Gewissen gehabt, wie in dieser. Damit bin ich mit Werner fertig. (Heiterkeit).

Was den Antrag Vollmar betrifft, so ist derselbe thatsächlich in unserem Entwurf bereits wörtlich enthalten. Es ist also garnicht nothwendig, daß uns der Parteitag in dieser Beziehung erst eine gebundene Marschroute vorschreibe. Wenn die Bestimmungen, wie sie unser Antrag enthält — woran freilich nicht zu denken ist, — vom Reichstag acceptirt würden, dann stände in der That das Vereins- und Koalitionsrecht der deutschen Arbeiter auf so festem Grund und Boden, wie in keinem andern Lande der Welt (stürmisches Bravo!)

Die Diskussion wird geschlossen.

Persönlich bestreitet Gen. Schibolsky-Nieder-Barnim die Behauptung Werners bezüglich der Flugblätter im Wahlkreise Niederbarnim.

Stadthagen: Werner hat behauptet, ich hätte Flugblätter, die bei den Hauptwahlen für die Freisinnigen verbreitet waren, bei den Stichwahlen als sozialdemokratische verbreitet. Das ist unrichtig. Ich habe selbstverständlich lediglich sozialdemokratische Flugblätter verbreitet. Ich habe allerdings dieselben nicht bei Werner drucken lassen. (Heiterkeit.) Ich habe sie aber auch bei einem anderen sozialdemokratischen Genossen nicht drucken lassen können, weil dieser sein Wort nicht hielt. Ich habe sie dann allerdings bei einem Freisinnigen drucken lassen — ich hätte sie ebenso bei einem Konservativen drucken lassen können. Der Inhalt dieses Flugblattes ist ein lediglich sozialdemokratischer gewesen. Nun waren Bilderbogen, auf denen dargestellt war, wie die Lebensmittelzölle das Volk auspressen, im Mossesschen Verlage erschienen. Von diesen suchten wir welche zu bekommen, um auf der Rückseite unser Flugblatt zu drucken. Wir bekamen sie zu spät und haben sie mit dem Zusatz verbreitet: „Der Gegenkandidat hat für diese Zölle gestimmt, wir wünschen die Abschaffung der Getreidezölle." Das ist das „freisinnige Flugblatt," demgegenüber ein Genosse den Muth hat, von einer Korruption der Partei zu sprechen. Ich bedaure, sagen zu müssen: ich glaube nicht, daß Werner im allgemeinen an Mangel an Verständniß leidet. Soweit seine prinzipiellen Auseinandersetzungen in Betracht kommen, mag das ja zutreffen; das leuchtet aus seinen sachlichen Ausführungen hervor; was aber seine persönlichen Angriffe betrifft, so weiß er nur zu gut, daß dasjenige, was er sagt, der Wirklichkeit nicht entspricht. (Bravo!)

Werner: Bebel sagte, ich hätte den Standpunkt, den er in seiner Reichstagsrede über die Militärvorlage vertreten, für verwerflich für die Partei gehalten. Ich habe ihn aber nur um Auskunft gebeten, wie er das, was er in der Kommission gesagt, gemeint habe. Ich glaube, Sie Alle werden das so verstanden haben. Aber es scheint, daß meine Gegner hier eine sehr sonderbare Kampfesweise gegen mich zur Anwendung bringen wollen. (Gelächter.) Stadthagen habe ich persönlich überhaupt nicht vorgeworfen, daß er die Flugblätter hätte verbreiten wollen. Ich habe nur gesagt, in dem Wahlkreise, in dem Stadthagen aufgestellt war, sind diese Flugblätter gedruckt und verbreitet worden. Ich werde sofort nach Berlin telegraphiren und mir ein Exemplar senden lassen. Auf den Flugblättern steht: „Wer nicht will, daß es so werden soll, der wähle den sozialdemokratischen Kandidaten Stadthagen." (Unruhe.) Ich meine, wenn diese Flugblätter erst von freisinniger und dann von sozialdemokratischer Seite verbreitet werden, so bringt das eine Verwirrung unter die Massen. Schließlich möchte ich doch ersuchen, daß derartige Unterschiebungen nicht vorkommen, wie die von Stadthagen, ich sei darum gegen die Flugblätter, weil sie nicht in meiner Druckerei gedruckt seien. Das ist unanständig!

Vollmar: Mein Antrag ist keineswegs überflüssig; denn er will nicht nur die Unternehmer bestraft wissen, wenn sie die Arbeiter von Gewerkschaften, von Streiks abhalten und sie maßregeln wollen, sondern auch, wenn sie sie abhalten wollen von der Ausübung sonstiger politischer Rechte.

Bebel erklärt, daß, wenn Vollmar seinen Antrag aufrecht erhalte, selbstverständlich Niemand gegen denselben stimmen werde.

Der Vorsitzende ruft den Genossen Stadthagen wegen der eben von Werner erwähnten Aeußerung, die im Bureau wegen der herrschenden Unruhe nicht gehört worden war, nachträglich zur Ordnung.

Stadthagen: Ich habe lediglich Thatsachen aneinandergereiht und garnicht geäußert, was mir vorgeworfen wird. Wenn aus diesen Thatsachen ein Schluß gezogen wird, so kann ich das nicht ändern; ich habe es nicht gethan.

Das Schlußwort als Berichterstatter erhält Singer: Genossen! Ich werde mich ganz kurz fassen, denn unsere Zeit ist gemessen, in der Sache sind wir alle, mit einer einzigen Ausnahme, vollkommen einig; da aber von den übrigen Berliner Genossen leider keiner dazu kam, in der Diskussion diesen Punkt hervorzuheben, so möchte ich als Berliner Abgeordneter sowohl, wie auch als Berliner, Namens der Berliner Partei dagegen protestiren, daß Werner sich immer wieder herausnimmt, hier für die Berliner Parteigenossen zu sprechen. (Sehr richtig!) Die sogenannte Opposition ist in Berlin in den Kreisen der Parteigenossen gerade so vereinzelt, wie die Opposition Werner's hier auf dem Parteitage. (Sehr richtig!) Die Berliner Genossen haben zu butzend Malen in den letzten Jahren ihr volles Einverständniß mit der parlamentarischen Thätigkeit der Fraktion ausgesprochen. Gerade in Bezug auf das Arbeiterschutzgesetz, das Werner als so nebensächlich hinstellt, haben sich eine sehr große Anzahl von Berliner Versammlungen entschieden für das Vorgehen der Fraktion ausgesprochen. Ich bin überzeugt, die Berliner Genossen werden es sich nicht gefallen lassen und dagegen remonstriren, wenn man annimmt, sie seien hier durch Werner vertreten. Wäre Werner ein ehrlicher Kämpfer, so hätte er immer sagen müssen: „Es sind einige Genossen in Berlin, die meine Auffassung theilen und in deren Namen ich spreche." Werner meinte, er würde mit seinen Aeußerungen nichts Neues sagen; ja, wenn er nur etwas Gescheutes gesagt hätte! (Heiterkeit; Zuruf: Ist nicht parlamentarisch!) Die national-ökonomischen Ausführungen Werner's kann ich nicht wiederlegen, denn ich habe dieselben nicht verstanden; er sagt, im Reichstag müsse alles agitatorisch, propagandistisch, zündend wirken. Wir wirken, soweit unsere Kräfte reichen, in diesem Sinne im Reichstag. Wir thun das, indem wir die Haltlosigkeit der bestehenden Ver-hältnisse nachweisen, den herrschenden Klassen die Maske vom Antlitz reißen und unserem Prinzip entsprechende Anträge einbringen; damit wirken wir tausendmal agitatorischer und zündender als wie es etwa durch eine Rede à la Werner geschehen würde. (Lebhaftes Bravo!)

Zur Charakterisirung der sogenannten Opposition, vertreten einzig durch Werner, verweise ich auf den eigenthümlichen Umstand, daß jedes Mal, wenn eine Erwiderung seitens des Angegriffenen erfolgt, Werner kommt und sagt: „Ich habe Niemand angreifen wollen; ich habe das auch nicht geglaubt und ich bin erfreut, die Aufklärung bekommen zu haben." So hat er es auch heute wieder gegen Bebel gemacht. Wenn Werner von „sonderbarer Kampfesweise" spricht, dann gilt dies Wort von ihm in erster Linie. Er ist es, der erst verdächtigt und verleumdet, und dann, wenn die Unwahrheit der Angriffe nachgewiesen ist, sagt, ich wollte ja blos Aufklärung haben, ich wollte nur hören, ob das, was ich nicht glauben kann, wahr ist. So hat er es in Volksversammlungen, so hier gemacht; so handelt aber kein ehrlicher Parteigenosse; der fragt vorher, wenn ihm etwas nicht in Ordnung scheint, verläumdet und verdächtigt aber nicht frisch darauf los um sich nachher hinter die Redensart zu verschanzen „ich habe nur aufklären wollen." (Bravo!) Ich bin überzeugt, daß dieser Parteitag Aufklärung verbreiten wird über den Werth der Opposition, wie sie von Herrn Werner und den ihm Gleichgesinnten betrieben wird. (Sehr richtig!) In sofern können wir auch den Genossen aus dem Wahlkreise Werners nur dankbar sein, daß sie ihn hierher geschickt haben. (Sehr gut!) Ich glaube aber auch, daß die Zahl der übrigen Berliner Genossen, die bisher noch sachlich in einigen Punkten mit Werner übereinstimmten, nach seinen heutigen Ausführungen auf Null schwinden wird. Ich konstatire nochmals, daß alles dasjenige, was an persönlichen, kränkenden, verleumderischen Aeußerungen vorgebracht worden ist, einzig und allein Privateigenthum des Herrn Werner und der wenigen Anhänger, die er um sich geschaart hat, bleibt. Die ungeheure Mehrzahl der Berliner Genossen ist ebenso treu, brav, intelligent und kampfbereit, wie die Genossen in ganz Deutschland und hat ein Recht darauf, nicht mit Herrn Werner indentificirt zu werden. Das muß vom Parteitag anerkannt werden. (Lebhaftes Bravo!) Den Antrag Vollmar bitte ich anzunehmen, obgleich wir bereits eine derartige Bestimmung im Reichstage beantragt haben. Ueber die Resolution Fischer will ich, als Fraktionsmitglied, kein Wort sagen, aus dem Grunde, weil sie eine Anerkennung für uns enthält, hierüber müssen die Parteigenossen allein entscheiden. (Stürmisches Bravo!)

Die Resolution Fischer wird einstimmig angenommen. Werner enthält sich der Abstimmung.

Die Resolution Vollmar wird gegen 2 Stimmen angenommen.

Damit ist der dritte Punkt der Tagesordnung erledigt.

Vom Lokalkomitee in Halle ist ein Schreiben eingegangen, durch welches die Delegirten und Gäste zu einem Kommers auf heute Abend 8 Uhr im Saale des „Prinzen Karl" eingeladen werden.

Um 12¾ Uhr werden die Verhandlungen abgebrochen.

Nachmittagssitzung.

8¼ Uhr. — Den Vorsitz führt Singer.

Nachdem die Wahlhandlung zur Neunerkommission für geschlossen erklärt und die Mandatsprüfungskommission mit der Feststellung des Resultats und der Berichterstattung über dasselbe beauftragt worden ist, begrüßt der Vorsitzende die neu erschienenen ausländischen Gäste: Frau Eleanor Marx-Aveling (lebhafte Akklamationen), die Tochter von Karl Marx, als Vertreterin der Gasarbeiter Londons und der allgemeinen Arbeitervereinigung von Großbritannien und Irland, ferner die Herren Jules Guesde und Ferroul aus Paris, als Delegirte des Nationalkongresses der französischen Arbeiterpartei zu Lille (stürmische Beifallsbezeugungen) und des Genossen Wullschleger-Basel, Mitglied des Komitees zur Vorbereitung des nächsten internationalen Kongresses und Redakteur des Journals „Der Achtstundentag". Der Vorsitzende heißt auch diese ausländischen Genossen namens des Parteitages herzlich willkommen; ihre Ankunft sei ein neuer Beweis der Solidarität des Proletariats aller Länder; er wünsche, daß sie von Halle die Ueberzeugung mitnehmen mögen, daß der Kongreß aufs Ernsteste bemüht sei, die Interessen der Arbeiterklasse aller Länder zu pflegen und zu fördern. Ihre Anwesenheit sei für den Kongreß eine Ehre. (Lebhafte Zustimmung.)

Darauf richtet Jules Guesde in französischer Sprache eine begeistert aufgenommene Ansprache an die Versammlung. Die Ausführungen des Redners werden von Liebknecht übersetzt; sie lauten im Wesentlichen wie folgt:

Bürgerinnen und Bürger! Ich bin glücklich und stolz, hier vor Ihnen stehen zu können. Die französische Arbeiterpartei und der Kongreß von Lille, in deren Namen ich hier spreche, senden dem Kongreß der deutschen Arbeiter vereint ihren Gruß, ihre Sympathie; ihre Bewunderung. Die französischen Arbeiter haben von Anfang an, seit dem Beginn des Ausnahmegesetzes, Euren heldenmüthigen Kampf gegen Polizeimacht und Despotismus mit der größten Aufmerksamkeit verfolgt; Eure Taktik, die auf jeden Zug der Gegner mit einem Gegenzuge antwortete, hat bewirkt, daß alle Waffen des Feindes gegen den Feind gewendet wurden; sie hat bewerkstelligt, daß dieser Kampf ein Zeugniß wurde für den Despotismus in seiner schlimmsten Gestalt, aber auch ein Zeugniß für die Ohnmacht des Despotismus, dessen Waffen alle zerbrochen sind an der ehernen Rüstung der Sozialdemokratie. Von Frankreich kommend, finde ich hier denselben Geist, der den Internationalen Kongreß in Paris beseelte — den Geist des großen Denkers, dessen Bildniß auf dem Kongreß zu Paris im vorigen Jahre auf uns herniederstrahlte essen Spruch: „Proletarier aller Länder vereinigt Euch!" auch in

unſerem Herzen, wie in dem aller Arbeiter der Welt, Widerhall gefunden hat. Das Ziel der Arbeiter aller Länder iſt das gleiche:
Die Umgeſtaltung der Produktionsverhältniſſe, die Verwandlung
des Klaſſenſtaats in einen ſozialiſtiſch organiſirten Staat. In
Frankreich wie in Deutſchland giebt es für den Sozialismus keine
Grenzen; unſere Heimath iſt die Welt, die Erlöſung der Menſchheit
unſer Ziel. Wir in Frankreich haben daſſelbe Programm, wir
verfolgen dieſelbe Taktik, und freudig bewegt ſind wir, daß wir
gerade noch rechtzeitig hierher gekommen ſind, um zu ſehen, wie
die von der Bourgeoiſie auch in der franzöſiſchen Preſſe verbreitete
Lüge, daß die deutſche Sozialdemokratie durch innere Spaltung
Selbſtmord begehen werde, in ihr Nichts zerronnen iſt. Wir ſind
Zeugen geworden, daß die deutſche ſozialdemokratiſche Partei niemals einiger geweſen iſt als heute, und wenn wir nach Frankreich
zurückgekehrt ſind, werden wir den Genoſſen ſagen, daß die Spaltungs-
nachricht eine infame Lüge der Bourgeoispreſſe war. Deutſchlands
Proletariat iſt das am großartigſten organiſirte, es ſteht an der
Spitze des Welt-Proletariats mit ſeinem Programm, ſeiner Organiſation und ſeinen Erfolgen. Wir in Frankreich benutzen das allgemeine Wahlrecht, wie Ihr in Deutſchland, zur Agitation bei
allen Wahlen, ohne dabei auch nur einen Augenblick das Endziel
aus den Augen zu verlieren. In Frankreich iſt der internationale
Gedanke nicht erſt neueren Datums: ſchon die Junikämpfer fochten
1848 unter dem rothen Banner; die Kommune kämpfte für das
Proletariat der ganzen Welt. Und der deutſchen Sozialdemokratie
werden wir es nie vergeſſen, daß ſie in dem Moment, wo die
Kommune, im Blut erſtickt, am Boden lag, ſich mit ihr ſolidariſch
zu erklären den Muth hatte. Das Proletariat hat nur einen Feind:
ſich ſelbſt; iſt es einig, ſind die Arbeiterklaſſen der verſchiedenen
Länder zu einer Armee geſchloſſen, dann kann ihm keine Macht der
Erde widerſtehen! — Zum Schluſſe liegt mir noch daran, das
Mißverſtändniß zu zerſtreuen, als ob in Frankreich Sympathieen
beſtänden für das despotiſche Rußland; der franzöſiſche Arbeiter
haßt in Rußland das Rückgrat des europäiſchen Despotismus.
Der Kongreß in Lille hat es durch einen beſonderen Beſchluß an
den Pranger geſtellt und hat die Bourgeoiſie der Verachtung ge-
weiht, die in ihrer Angſt vor dem Proletariat in dem Bündniß
mit Rußland Hilfe ſucht. Hoch das ſozialiſtiſche Deutſchland!

Hiernach richtet Genoſſe Liebknecht Dankesworte in franzöſiſcher
Sprache an den Vorredner, und fordert dann den Parteitag auf, ein
dreifaches Hoch auf das ſozialiſtiſche Frankreich, auf das Frankreich
der Arbeit und ebenſo auf die internationale Sozialdemokratie aus-
zubringen. „Vive la France ouvrière, vive la France socialiste! Und hoch
die internationale Sozialdemokratie!“ Begeiſtert ſtimmen die An-
weſenden, die ſich von den Plätzen erhoben haben, in die Hochrufe ein.

Mit lebhaftem Beifall begrüßt, richtet darauf auch Ferroul, Mitglied der französischen Kammer und der sozialistischen Fraktion derselben, in französischer Sprache einige Begrüßungsworte an die Versammlung, welche ebenfalls von Liebknecht verdeutscht werden. Er bringe die Grüße seiner Fraktion und ebenso, wie Guesde, die des Liller Kongresses. Die französischen Arbeiter haben im Geiste mitgekämpft den Kampf der deutschen Brüder gegen die Unterdrückung; sie haben den Sieg vom 20. Februar auch als den Sieg der französischen Arbeiter, als den Sieg des Proletariats der ganzen Welt angesehen. Er habe der deutschen Arbeiterschaft die Anerkennung auszusprechen für ihre Ausdauer im Kampf, wie für die Tüchtigkeit ihrer Organisation, die unter den Schlägen der Gegner, statt zertrümmert zu werden, immer härter gehämmert worden sei. Das französische Volk wolle keine Allianz der Diplomaten, die sich gegen die Völker wende, sondern nur eine Allianz der Völker gegen die Despoten, gegen die internationale Bourgeoisie. Redner schloß: „Vive l'internationale ouvrière en guerre ouverte et en guerre acharnée contre l'internationale capitaliste et despotique!" „Es lebe die Internationale der Arbeiter, die in offenem und unablässigem Kampfe steht gegen die Internationale des Kapitalismus und Despotismus!" (Stürmischer Beifall.)

Auch an diesen Vertreter der französischen Arbeiter richtet Genosse Liebknecht Dankesworte in französischer Sprache.

Der Vorsitzende macht Mittheilung von dem Eingang einer weiteren Reihe von Begrüßungstelegrammen und Zustimmungsadressen an den Parteitag aus dem In- und Auslande.

Vor der Tagesordnung wird dann der

Bericht der Mandatsprüfungskommission

erstattet.

Berichterstatter Pfannkuch-Kassel: Die Kommission hat an den Mandaten sehr wenig auszusetzen gehabt. Nur in einem Falle wird die Ungiltigkeitserklärung beantragt. — Es sind anwesend 410 Delegirte, welche 235 Wahlkreise vertreten. Außerdem sind 2 Mandate resp. Ausweise von schweizerischen und dänischen Genossen der Kommission überwiesen worden. Diese Ausweise sind aber nicht als Mandate für den Kongreß anzusehen. Ferner sind 3 Mandate für Arbeiterinnen nicht von Wahlkreisen, sondern von Arbeiterinnenversammlungen ausgestellt. Das Mandat der Frau Gundelach ist vom Delegirten Bremer-Magdeburg angefochten worden, da Frau Gundelach bei der ursprünglichen Wahl nicht gewählt wurde. Erst als die gewählte Frau Großendorf das Mandat nicht auszuüben im Stande war, habe letztere dann kurzer Hand Frau Gundelach, unter Ueberweisung des Mandats und des Geldbetrages, mit der Vertretung beauftragt. Außerdem ist n der Kommission ein Mandat des Genossen Lutz aus Baden-

Baden für ungiltig erklärt; seine Qualifikation als Delegirter wird dadurch aber nicht berührt, da er im Besitz anderweiter giltiger Mandate sei. In dem Protest gegen die Lutz'sche Wahl wird behauptet, daß Lutz in der betreffenden Wahlversammlung alle Diejenigen, welche anderer Meinung waren als er, nicht zum Worte hat kommen lassen. Außerdem soll er Wähler, die ihn bereits in Gaggenau gewählt hatten, nochmals zu dieser Versammlung kommandirt haben. Die Kommission hat das nicht für korrekt befunden und deshalb dies Mandat für ungiltig erklärt. Ein Monitum liegt ferner vor gegen die Wahl von Wesch-Crefeld. 15 dortige Genossen drücken in einem Schreiben an den Kongreß ihre Unzufriedenheit mit seiner Wahl aus, gestehen aber gleichzeitig zu, daß die Wahl ordnungsmäßig vor sich gegangen ist. Ferner wird das Mandat von Gotthelf von Wietersheim — Hamm-Soest beanstandet, weil es nicht von den Genossen des dortigen Wahlkreises, sondern von Spezialbranchen, den Hut- und Bergarbeitern, aufgestellt ist, der Form der Einladung zum Parteitag also nicht Genüge geschehen ist. Ebenso wird die Wahl des Genossen Plorin-Halle insoweit beanstandet, als in dem dem Mandat beigefügten Schreiben nur gesagt ist, daß der hier in Halle in der Wahlversammlung gewählte Krüger nicht in der Lage sei, sein Mandat auszuüben, und man daher Plorin mit der Vertretung beauftragt habe. Dann ist gegen die Wahl des Delegirten in Meerane ein Schreiben eingelaufen, welches denselben seiner Schulden halber als nicht berechtigten Theilnehmer bezeichnet. (Heiterkeit.) Die Kommission war aber der Ansicht, wenn das ein Grund für die Anfechtung sein sollte, daß dann wohl gar zu viele der Anwesenden ihre Mandate verlieren müßten. (Große Heiterkeit.)

Außerdem ist gegen die Wahl von Alwin Kerrl aus Lemgo ein Schreiben eingelaufen, über dessen Natur die Kommission zu keinem Urtheil gelangen konnte, indem die Aeußerungen darauf basiren, daß er von einem Verein der neuen Aera gewählt sei und diese Neugründung sich mit dem vorhandenen Arbeiterverein nicht in Verbindung gesetzt habe. Eine Ausstellung haben wir daran nicht zu machen. Auch ein ziemlich umfangreicher Protest gegen die Münchener Wahl liegt vor; des Pudels Kern ist die Behauptung, daß die Wahlen für München I und II in einem combinirten Wahlgang gleichzeitig vorgenommen; 6 Genossen seien dort gewählt und man wisse nicht, wer München I, wer München II vertrete. Die Protesterheber scheinen damit unzufrieden, daß ein Genosse Wambsgans, den sie mit der Delegation betrauen wollten, nicht gewählt worden ist. Einen Antrag knüpft die Kommission auch an diesen Protest nicht.

Ueber die Proteste wird nach der Reihenfolge des Berichts verhandelt.

Kloß-Stuttgart theilt mit, daß soeben noch ein Mandat ein-geliefert ist für Frau Helene Steinbach in Hamburg, gewählt in Gera von einer Versammlung von Frauen und Männern.

Die Mandate für Frauen werden ohne Diskussion für giltig erklärt. Vorsitzender Singer spricht seine Freude darüber aus, daß die Arbeiterinnen Deutschlands sich der Pflicht bewußt gewesen sind, ihre Interessen hier vertreten zu lassen.

Bezüglich des Mandats der Frau Gundelach theilt Köster-Wanzleben mit, daß, nachdem sich für die Magdeburger Frauen die Unmöglichkeit ergeben hatte, Frau Großendorf zum Kongreß zu senden, die Frauenkommission sich mit Frau Gundelach in Ver-bindung gesetzt und ihr einstimmig das Mandat übertragen habe.

Das Mandat wird mit großer Mehrheit für giltig erklärt.

Zur Frage der Giltigkeit seines Baden-Badener Mandats nimmt Lutz selbst das Wort. Es beständen dort zwei Arbeiter-Wahlvereine; ein älterer mit sieben Mitgliedern und ein jüngerer, dessen Vor-sitzender der Redner selbst ist. Die für die Wahl auf den 5. Oktober aus-geschriebene Volksversammlung sei gut besucht gewesen, während sonst die Arbeiter in Baden-Baden lieber zum Pferderennen als in die Versammlungen gehen. Bei der Gegenprobe sei Niemand auf-gestanden. Jene sieben aber haben für sich ihren Delegirten in der Person des Herrn Geck-Offenburg erwählt und protestiren nun gegen meine ganz loyal erfolgte Wahl.

Ohne weitere Debatte wird auch diese Wahl für giltig erklärt.

Für die Giltigkeit der Wahl des Genossen v. Wietersheim treten letzterer persönlich und Zwiener-Bielefeld ein. Bei der in den dortigen Industriebezirken herrschenden Verfolgungswuth der Arbeitgeber habe man zu dem Deckmantel von Fachversammlungen greifen müssen, um eine Delegirtenwahl zu ermöglichen; sonst wäre weder ein Lokal zu haben, noch eine Versammlung zu veranstalten gewesen.

Einstimmig wird auch dieses Mandat für giltig anerkannt.

Das Mandat von Plorin-Halle bittet Schulze-Erfurt für ungiltig zu erklären. Thatsächlich sei Krüger gewählt; das Komitee habe aber nach Schluß der Versammlung diese Wahl eigenmächtig annullirt. Das sei, aus Achtung vor dem demokratischen Prinzip und auch des Präjudizes halber, nicht zulässig.

Kaulich-Halle: Es sind zunächst 3 Genossen für Halle gewählt worden, demnächst 3 Stellvertreter, unter letzteren befand sich Plorin. Krüger ist, seiner Arbeitsverhältnisse halber, an der Ausübung des Mandats behindert und Plorin rechtmäßig als sein Vertreter hier erschienen.

Auch dieses Mandat wird mit großer Mehrheit für giltig erklärt.

In Betreff der Münchener Wahl erklärt Vollmar, daß seit Menschengedenken München keine Versammlung wie jene Wählerversammlung gesehen habe; zwischen 6- und 7 000 Mann wären zugegen gewesen. Bei der Fülle des Besuchs war die Wahl durch Stimmzettel einfach unmöglich. Nach dem stenographischen Bericht über die Versammlung (den Redner verliest) sei alles ordnungsmäßig zugegangen. Wambsgans sei bei der Wahl durchgefallen, was für ihn um so unangenehmer war, als er zweiter Vorsitzender in der Versammlung war. Daher der Protest.

Auch über diesen Protest wird hinweggegangen.

Das Mandat von Wesch-Crefeld wird für giltig erklärt, nachdem der Referent Pfannkuch noch darauf aufmerksam gemacht, daß die 15 Crefelder gegen die ordnungsmäßige Wahl von Wesch überhaupt keinen Einspruch erhoben haben.

Lichtenberg-Crefeld meldet sich zum Worte. (Rufe: Ist kein Delegirter!)

Vorsitzender Singer: Dann habe ich nur zu bedauern, daß die an den Thüren postirten Genossen Leute hereingelassen haben, die nicht im Besitze eines Mandats sind. (Zu Lichtenberg:) Haben Sie ein Mandat?

Lichtenberg: Ja!

Vorsitzender Singer: Haben Sie es der Kommission übergeben?

Lichtenberg: Ja!

Referent Pfannkuch: Das Mandat ist ordnungsgemäß ausgestellt.

Grimpe-Elberfeld: Wenn wir das Mandat für Lichtenberg anerkennen wollen, müssen wir doch erst prüfen, ob die Versammlung, in der er gewählt, ordnungsgemäß berufen war. Es sollte in öffentlicher Versammlung gewählt werden; dort ist Wesch nahezu einstimmig delegirt worden. Ausdrücklich wurde beschlossen, nur einen Delegirten zu wählen.

Vorsitzender Singer: Dann schlage ich vor, diese Sache zur Klarstellung der Verhältnisse an die Mandatsprüfungskommission zurückzuverweisen.

Der Parteitag beschließt demgemäß.

Schulze-Erfurt beantragt, die Wahl des Delegirten Giertz-Weimar für ungiltig zu erklären. Der Antrag wird ausreichend unterstützt, und nachdem der Antragsteller und Leutert-Apolda für Ungiltigerklärung und Reißhaus-Erfurt dagegen gesprochen, das Mandat Giertz für giltig erklärt.

Frau Ihrer (zur Geschäftsordnung): Ich wollte den anwesenden Delegirten nur im Namen meiner Genossinnen und derer, die uns gewählt haben, unseren Dank aussprechen dafür, daß Sie abgegangen sind von der veralteten Methode des Ausschlusses der

Frauen.*) Ich spreche Ihnen unseren wärmsten Dank dafür aus. Sie haben uns dadurch für die Zukunft vieles erleichtert. Wir werden jederzeit unser Theil an der sozialen Arbeit gründlich zu erledigen suchen. (Beifall.)

Vorsitzender Singer: Damit ist dieser Gegenstand erledigt. Ich glaube, die Partei kann stolz sein auf das Resultat, daß sie ihren ersten Parteitag in der neuen Aera mit 413 Delegirten beschickt hat. Sie darf sich freuen, wieder einmal ihre Kraft, Einheit und Stärke auf diese Weise bewiesen zu haben.

Danach geht der Parteitag über zu Punkt 4 der Tagesordnung:

Die Organisation der Partei,

(Wortlaut des Entwurfs siehe Anhang.)

Berichterstatter Auer: Werthe Genossen! Unsere bisherigen Verhandlungen haben sich hauptsächlich mit den Aktionen der Vergangenheit und speziell der letzten Zeit befaßt. Nachdem wir damit fertig, gehen wir dazu über, die Basis zu schaffen, auf welcher wir unsere weiteren Aktionen unternehmen, die Schlachten der Zukunft schlagen wollen. Es handelt sich jetzt darum, uns eine neue Organisation zu geben, nachdem es uns wieder möglich geworden ist, frei und offen aufzutreten. Nicht zum ersten Mal schaffen wir uns eine Organisation; schon vor dem Sozialistengesetz haben wir uns mehrere Male mit der gleichen Aufgabe beschäftigt. Ich halte es deshalb für nothwendig, bevor ich auf den jetzigen Entwurf näher eingehe, auf unsere frühere Organisation einen Rückblick zu werfen. Ich will dabei die älteren Organisationen, das Vereinsstatut des Allgemeinen Deutschen Arbeitervereins und das Statut der sogenannten Eisenacher Partei nicht heranziehen, sondern nur auf die nach der Vereinigung auf dem Gothaer Vereinigungskongreß von 1875 geschaffenen Einrichtungen eingehen. Nicht 1876, wie hier über meinem Haupte (auf einer der zahlreich im Sitzungssaale angebrachten Gedenktafeln) zu lesen ist, fand dieser Kongreß statt; denn 1876 hatten wir die Organisation schon nicht mehr, die wir 1875 im Mai geschaffen hatten. Warum wir sie nicht mehr hatten, das bitte ich Sie auch bei der jetzigen Berathung nicht außer Acht zu lassen. Nicht wir waren daran Schuld; sondern daß unsere damalige Organisation nur eine so kurze Lebensdauer hatte, es kam davon, daß in der Organisationsfrage Mächte mitzureden haben, auf die, einen Einfluß auszuüben, wir nicht in

---

*) Es mag bemerkt sein, daß auf keinem der Parteikongresse, weder vor dem Sozialistengesetz, noch während der Giltigkeit desselben, Frauen, welche sich zur Theilnahme gemeldet hatten, von den Kongressen oder Parteitagen ausgeschlossen wurden. Es haben sich nur leider sehr selten Frauen gemeldet.

der Lage sind. Die Organisation kann und wird nicht so von uns geschaffen werden können, wie wir sie unserer Ueberzeugung nach für am geeignetsten und besten halten; sondern wir müssen dabei auf die eben angedeutete Mächte Rücksicht nehmen. Daß wir 1876 nicht mehr zusammentreten konnten als Kongreß der sozialistischen Arbeiterpartei Deutschlands, wie wir uns 1875 nannten, sondern daß 1876 ein allgemeiner Sozialistenkongreß berufen werden mußte, lag daran, daß, nachdem wir im Mai 1875 uns konstituirt hatten, im März 1876 unsere Partei für Preußen bereits „vorläufig" geschlossen worden ist. Als wir 1876 zusammentraten, mußte der damalige Berichterstatter des früheren Parteiausschusses die Erklärung abgeben, daß für Preußen die Parteiorganisation ungiltig gemacht und daß wegen der vorläufigen Schließung der Partei es unmöglich gemacht sei, die Organisation in der früheren Form weiter zu handhaben. Wir haben deshalb 1876 keinen Parteivorstand mehr gewählt, sondern, da die Wahlen in Aussicht standen, ein Central-Wahlkomitee eingesetzt mit dem Sitze in Hamburg. Es wurde von Otto Capell der Antrag gestellt, zur permanenten Leitung der sozialistischen Wahl- und Parteiagitation möge der Kongreß ein ständiges Central-Wahlkomitee aus 5 Personen wählen, dessen Amtsthätigkeit sich bis zum nächsten Kongreß zu erstrecken habe; diesem Komitee sollte in allen Agitations- und Parteiangelegenheiten diktatorische Gewalt übertragen werden. Zur Kontrole dieser Centralbehörde solle weiter eine Revisions- und und Beschwerdekommission, bestehend aus sieben Personen, eingesetzt und gewählt werden von den Genossen des Ortes, wo die Kommission ihren Sitz hat.

Dieser Antrag ist einstimmig angenommen worden, trotz der heute wohl für manche Ohren schrecklichen Worte „diktatorische Gewalt". Es folgten die Wahlen von 1877 mit ihren bedeutenden Erfolgen für uns. Wir traten nach den Wahlen wieder zusammen im allgemeinen Sozialistenkongreß zu Gotha 1877. Dort war eine der ersten Handlungen die Konstituirung einer sogenannten Organisationskommission, welche die Frage der Neuorganisation zu prüfen hatte. Diese Kommission trat unter dem Vorsitze unseres Altmeisters der Organisation, dem in Organisationsfragen so oft bewährten Genossen C. W. Tölcke, der auch jetzt, trotz geschwächter Kräfte, es sich nicht hat nehmen lassen, unter uns zu erscheinen, und dem ich den freundlichsten Gruß der Versammlung entgegenbringe (allseitige freudige Zustimmung), zusammen und das Resultat ihrer Berathungen war, dem Kongresse zu empfehlen, von irgend einer formellen Organisation Abstand zu nehmen. Die Kommission sei, so führte der in ihrem Namen sprechende Genosse Tölcke damals aus,

„zu der Ueberzeugung gelangt, daß der Kongreß von der Schaffung einer Organisation Abstand nehmen müsse; nicht deshalb, weil eine solche etwa nicht mit den Vereinsgesetzen in Einklang zu bringen wäre, sondern, weil nach der ausdrücklichen Erklärung des Staatsanwalts Tessendorf keine wie immer gestaltete Organisation der Sozialisten in Preußen geduldet werden dürfe, so lange das jetzige Vereinsgesetz in Preußen existire. — Man dürfe Tessendorf den Gefallen nicht thun, ihm durch Herstellung einer neuen Organisation Gelegenheit zu geben, die Sozialisten in Preußen durch erneute Strafanträge verfolgen zu können. — Uebrigens sei eine formelle Organisation nicht mehr nöthig, wie das Resultat der Reichstagswahl und die trotz des Mangels einer Organisation fortwährend steigernde sozialistische Propaganda genügend beweisen. Die Kommission schlug dem Kongresse vor, in einer Resolution zu erklären: „Mit Rücksicht auf die von preußischen Behörden förmlich proklamirte völlige Rechtlosigkeit sozialistischer Vereine in Preußen nimmt der Kongreß von der Herstellung irgend einer Organisation der Partei Abstand, auf welche die in Deutschland, besonders in Preußen, bestehenden Vereinsgesetze angewendet werden können; der Kongreß überläßt es den Parteigenossen an den einzelnen Orten, sich je nach den örtlichen Verhältnissen und Bedürfnissen zu organisiren."

Diese Resolution fand ohne weitere Debatte einstimmige Annahme. Daneben wurde die Wiedereinsetzung des Centralkomitees und außerdem die Wiedereinsetzung einer Art Kontrollkommission beschlossen.

So standen die Dinge vor dem Sozialistengesetz unter dem gemeinen Recht. Bemerken will ich, daß nach der Zeit, wo in Gotha diese Resolution angenommen wurde, außer in Preußen, auch in Bayern und Sachsen die Schließung der Partei erfolgte.

Die Beschlußfassung über diesen Punkt der Tagesordnung hängt also, wie Sie sehen, durchaus nicht davon ab, was wir wohl für das Richtigste und Beste für die Partei halten, sondern wir haben auf Verhältnisse Rücksicht zu nehmen, die wir allerdings am liebsten davon fernhalten möchten. Ich betone, daß dieselben gesetzlichen Bestimmungen, auf Grund deren vor dem Sozialistengesetz die Organisation aufgelöst wurde, auch heute noch existiren. (Sehr richtig!). Niemand wird nun so naiv sein, zu glauben, daß man heute uns gegenüber eine mildere Praxis anwenden wird, als 1876/77. Wir werden deshalb ungemein vorsichtig sein und bei unseren Beschlüssen uns stets gegenwärtig halten müssen: es sieht uns Jemand über die Schultern, bei dem es bei dem geringsten Versehen unsererseits, blos eines Federstriches bedarf, um unser ganzes Werk über den Haufen zu werfen.

Was nun thun? Wir haben Ihnen einen Organisations-entwurf vorgelegt. Ueber diesen Entwurf ist seit seiner Veröffent-

lichung in der Parteipresse sowohl wie auch in Versammlungen eine
außerordentlich erregte Diskussion geführt worden. Ich muß bedauern, daß gelegentlich dieser Diskussion Angriffe erfolgt sind, die
bei näherer Kenntniß der Sache vielleicht weniger scharf ausgefallen
wären. Der Entwurf trägt die Unterschrift der 35 Mitglieder der Fraktion. Wenn nun das eine oder andere Mitglied durch persönliche Gründe verhindert war an der Berathung
und Mitarbeiterschaft theilzunehmen, so konnte man doch voraus-
setzen, daß es durch seine Abwesenheit bereits bekunde, daß es überzeugt sei, daß die Anwesenden, soweit es in ihren Kräften steht,
das Möglichste und Beste thun würden. Wenn wider Erwarten
aber auch von dieser Seite her noch scharf kritisirt worden ist, so
steht ja das Recht der Kritik zweifellos jedem Genossen offen; nur
darf ich im Namen aller derjenigen, die sich den Kopf über den
Organisationsentwurf zerbrochen, die Arbeit geleistet und die nicht
selten gegentheiligen Anschauungen mit aller Schärfe betont und vertreten haben, das Bedauern aussprechen, daß es denjenigen Fraktionsgenossen, die nachher durch ihre Kritik ein so hohes Interesse an
dem Entwurf bekundet haben, nicht möglich gewesen ist, an den
Berathungen und den Arbeiten in der Fraktion theilzunehmen. Es
wäre uns dann vielleicht die etwas unangenehme Erscheinung er-
spart geblieben, daß Personen, deren Namen selbst unter dem Ent-
wurfe standen, nachher zum Gaudium der Gegner sich zu einer solch'
scharfen Kritik desselben veranlaßt gesehen haben.

Die Kritiker hätten überhaupt mehr berücksichtigen sollen, daß es
doch auch Genossen sind, die diesen Entwurf verfaßt haben. Wir
sind ja unter uns gewohnt, uns nicht gerade all zu sanft zu behandeln; aber von Fraktionsherrschaft, Diktatur, ja sogar Partei-
päpsten und Aehnlichem zu reden und zu schreiben, schien uns doch etwas
über das Erlaubte hinauszugehen. (Sehr richtig!) Es muß doch
nicht immer der schlimmste Ausdruck gebraucht werden (Heiterkeit),
wenn man Jemandem sagen will, daß man mit ihm nicht einverstanden ist. Man muß nicht gleich mit der Thür ins Haus fallen.
(Heiterkeit). Ich muß weiter sagen, daß ich beim Lesen und Hören
der verschiedenen Urtheile recht oft die Empfindung hatte, daß die
guten Leute, die am schärfsten kritisirten, sich in ihrem Urtheil durch
Sachkenntniß recht wenig beengt fühlten und gerade deshalb so gar
ungenirt raisonniren konnten. (Heiterkeit).

Das Recht der Kritik steht gewiß Jedem offen, und ich kann
Ihnen ruhig mittheilen, daß der Entwurf, so wie er Ihnen vorliegt,
auch nur das Produkt eines Kompromisses ist. In der Fraktion war
nicht ein Einziger, der an dem Entwurf nicht das eine oder das
andere auszusetzen hatte. Es zeigt überhaupt von wenig Scharfsinn
und noch weniger Kenntniß der thatsächlichen Verhältnisse, von
Fraktionsherrschaft bei uns zu reden. Die Fraktion, welche als

Parteipapst geherrscht haben sollte und angeblich noch herrscht, wechselt doch in ihrem Personenbestande fortwährend. Unter den 35 heutigen Fraktionsmitgliedern ist nicht ein Einziger, der während der ganzen 13 Jahre der Herrschaft des Sozialistengesetzes der Fraktion dauernd angehört hat. Selbst unser dauerhaftester Abgeordneter, Genosse Bebel, hat bei der Wahl von 1881 einen Durchfall erlebt. (Bebel: Trotz 37 Kandidaturen! Heiterkeit). Sie sehen, der Fraktionspapst ist nur ein Gespenst ohne Fleisch und Körper. Außerdem hat Bebel gestern, so drastisch wie nur er zu schildern vermag, bereits über die einzelnen Vorgänge in der Fraktion, die ich Ihnen gar nicht so offen eingestanden hätte (Heiterkeit.) Mittheilung gemacht. Also auch unter den Fraktionsmitgliedern giebt es Meinungsverschiedenheit und es wird dort ebenso per majora abgestimmt, wie hier. Dabei soll nicht gesagt werden, daß man nachher keine eigene Meinung mehr haben darf. Speziell aber bei dem vorliegenden Entwurf handelt es sich gar nicht um endgiltige Bestimmungen, die sollen Sie ja hier erst schaffen. Man hätte bei der Kritik berücksichtigen sollen, daß man ein Produkt von Genossen und nicht einen Gesetzentwurf des Bundesraths vor sich hatte. (Große Heiterkeit). Der Bundesrath ist außerdem in viel günstigerer Lage; für ihn treten die Staatsanwälte ein, während wir hilflos dastanden. (Heiterkeit.)

Indem ich nun auf den Entwurf selbst eingehe, will ich zunächst hervorheben, daß auch für die Fraktion die Frage im Vordergrund stand: können wir es riskiren, einen „Verein der sozialdemokratischen Arbeiterpartei" für ganz Deutschland zu gründen, oder müssen wir uns konstituiren als Partei, der möglichst der Charakter eines Vereines nicht aufgedrückt werden kann? Diese Frage ist sehr scharf diskutirt worden, wir sind aber zu keiner Entscheidung gekommen, und zwar deshalb nicht, weil die Mehrheit der Fraktion, auf Grund der früheren schlimmen Erfahrungen, unter dem Eindruck stand: es ist ja absolut gleichgiltig, wie wir die Paragraphen fassen, wir werden ja doch wieder aufgelöst. Andererseits fühlten wir uns moralisch verpflichtet, sowohl den Genossen wie der Oeffentlichkeit gegenüber, uns wieder eine formelle Organisation zu geben. Wird sie später wieder aufgelöst, nun — dann geht's auch so weiter (Heiterkeit). Aus der Welt sind wir bisher nicht geschafft worden, trotz aller Auflösungen; erfolgt eine neue, so haben wir einen größeren Spielraum (Heiterkeit).

Auf alle Einzelheiten der Vorlage kann ich nicht eingehen; es ist auch nicht nothwendig. Zunächst ist eine Aenderung des Namens vorgeschlagen; wir sollen uns von jetzt ab sozialdemokratische Partei nennen. Bisher war der offizielle Parteititel: Sozialistische Arbeiterpartei. Bei der seinerzeitigen Wahl dieses Namens wurde von einflußreichen Genossen auseinandergesetzt, daß eine sozialistische

Partei eo ipso eine demokratische sein müsse. Diese Auffassung läßt sich heute, wo alle Welt in Sozialismus macht, wohl nicht mehr gut aufrecht halten. Doch das sind Formsachen; wir bleiben, gleichgiltig wie wir uns nennen, was wir waren.

Besonderen Anstoß hat es erregt, daß wir die Mitgliedschaft an der Partei von der dauernden materiellen Unterstützung derselben abhängig machen wollen. Ich mache darauf aufmerksam, daß alle früheren Organisationsstatuten ausnahmslos Bestimmungen enthielten, worin sogar ein bestimmter Beitrag festgesetzt war und worin es hieß, wer nach Verlauf einer bestimmten Frist diesen Beitrag nicht geleistet hat, kann nicht mehr als Parteigenosse im engeren Sinne, d. h. als Angehöriger der organisirten Partei, betrachtet werden. Von einer Vergewaltigung gegenüber den Arbeitern und Genossen kann also bei unserem Vorschlag gar keine Rede sein. Diese Bestimmung ist auch früher nicht so schlimm aufgefaßt worden; Sie finden auch ein Analogon in allen unseren Wahl- und Arbeitervereinen. Man hat gesagt, wer nicht mehr bezahlt, würde von uns nicht mehr als Sozialdemokrat betrachtet werden. Das ist einfach thöricht. Ebenso falsch ist, wenn andererseits gesagt wird, die Zugehörigkeit zur Partei bekunde doch die für uns erfolgte Stimmabgabe. Wir haben ja gar keine Kontrole, wer für uns stimmt, und die betreffenden Genossen werden doch wohl nicht Puttkamer entgegenkommen und das geheime Wahlrecht aufheben wollen. Trotzdem also diese Einwürfe unbegründet sind, so darf ich doch im Namen meiner Auftraggeber, der Fraktion, erklären, daß wir bereit sind, die Worte „dauernde materielle Unterstützung" fallen zu lassen. Wir sind nämlich von hervorragender juristischer Seite darauf aufmerksam gemacht worden, daß das Verlangen einer fortgesetzten pekuniären Leistung schon genüge, uns als einen Verein zu erklären.

Dagegen müssen wir unter allen Umständen im Parteiinteresse wünschen, daß man daran festhält, daß zur Partei nicht gehört, wer sich nicht zu den Grundsätzen des Parteiprogramms bekennt und wer sich ehrloser Handlungen schuldig gemacht hat. Unsere Partei muß rein bleiben von zweifelhaften Elementen. Ich bemerke, daß wir nicht gerade an ehrlose Handlungen gedacht haben, wo der eine oder der andere durch Zufälligkeit, Leichtsinn, Noth u. s. w. in Konflikt mit dem Strafgesetzbuch gekommen ist; nein, es giebt ehrlose Handlungen, die kein Strafgesetzbuch der Welt verurtheilt und die doch schlimmer sind als die gemeinsten Verbrechen. (Sehr richtig!)

Ich möchte wünschen, daß wir uns mit Ausschließungen gar nicht mehr zu beschäftigen haben; aber die Möglichkeit, unsaubere Elemente uns von den Rockschößen zu schütteln, müssen wir haben und dafür eine Form festsetzen.

Was die Vertrauensmänner betrifft, so wird die glückliche Lösung der Frage, wie wir die für die Parteileitung absolut noth-

wendigen Korrespondenten und Vertrauensmänner in den verschiedenen Wahlkreisen Deutschlands schaffen werden, sehr schwer sein.
Werden bessere Vorschläge gemacht, als unsere sind, so werden wir
sie mit Vergnügen entgegennehmen. Die Bestimmung des § 3:
„Insofern der Wahlkreis durch einen Ort oder durch Theile eines
Ortes gebildet wird, ist nur ein Vertrauensmann zu wählen", bedarf
eines Zusatzes. Es giebt Wahlkreise, die nur den Theil eines Ortes
bilden, aber trotzdem sehr umfangreich und groß sind und innerhalb
deren Parteigenossen in sehr großer Zahl vorhanden sind. Ich
exemplifizire nur auf Berlin VI und IV. Es wird also heißen
müssen, daß da in der Regel nur ein Vertrauensmann zu
wählen sei.

Daß alljährlich ein Parteitag stattzufinden habe, ist von keiner
Seite angegriffen worden; daß die Einberufung des Parteitages
von der Parteileitung zu erfolgen habe, ist ebenso selbstverständlich,
und die Frage dreht sich nur um das Recht der Vertretung auf
demselben. Da haben wir nun vorgeschlagen, daß zur Theilnahme
am Parteitage berechtigt sind die Delegirten der Partei aus den
einzelnen Wahlkreisen, mit der Einschränkung, daß kein Wahlkreis
durch mehr als 3 Personen vertreten sein darf. Diese letztere Bestimmung ist scharf angegriffen worden. Nun ist es aber selbstverständlich, daß Wahlkreise, die gar kein Parteileben haben, die bei
den allgemeinen Wahlen mit 90 oder 150 für uns abgegebenen
Stimmen auftreten, sich nicht durch 3 Delegirte vertreten lassen
werden. Dazu fehlen ja den Genossen jener Kreise schon die Mittel.
So konnte unser Vorschlag nicht verstanden werden. Es hat uns
vollständig fern gelegen, wie uns vorgeworfen wurde, durch diese
Bestimmung die Intelligenz der großen Städte vom Parteitag fernzuhalten. Wie hat sich denn die Sache in Wirklichkeit gemacht?
Nun, Berlin IV und VI und — Weimar haben je 4 Delegirte hierher geschickt, also mehr, als unser Entwurf festsetzt. Ob die
Berliner Delegirten das Berliner Parteileben nicht repräsentiren,
weiß ich nicht. Ich weiß auch nicht, ob durch jene Einschränkung
die Intelligenz innerhalb der Berliner Genossenschaft zu kurz gekommen
ist; ich glaube es nicht; denn wir haben gesehen, daß die Berliner
Delegirten — natürlich Werner nicht, er ist ja kein Berliner
Delegirter — es sehr wohl verstanden haben, ihre Sache hier zu
vertreten.

Persönlich bin ich übrigens der Ansicht, man macht in der
Organisation gar keine Vorschriften darüber und überläßt es dem
Taktgefühl der einzelnen Orte und Wahlkreise, wie sie sich auf dem
Parteitag vertreten lassen wollen. Mit dieser meiner Ansicht bin
ich aber nicht durchgedrungen. Man meint, eine gewisse Abgrenzung
i nothwendig. Man will sich nicht dazu entschließen, den kleineren
ahlkreisen dasselbe Recht, wie den größeren, zu geben. Ja, wo

soll uns dies Bedenken hinführen; das stellt uns ja gegenseitig auf den Kriegsfuß! Die Genossen in Greiz ältere und jüngere Linie sind zweifellos so brav und tüchtig, wie die Parteigenossen in den großen Wahlkreisen. Wir sind doch hier nicht eine Aktiengesellschaft, die zusammenkommt, um auf Heller und Pfennig zu rechnen, daß keiner zu viel kriegt, oder welche Dividende herauskommt. Hier giebt's überhaupt nichts zu theilen. Die 170 000 Mark in der Parteikasse sind wohl aufgehoben, nicht einmal die Polizei kann an sie heran (Heiterkeit). Es gilt nur das Interesse der Partei nach allen Richtungen zu wahren. Die Parteitage haben vor allem den hohen Werth, daß sie uns moralisch heben; daß die Genossen, ob sie nun in Memel oder in Konstanz oder sonstwo wohnen, frisch, froh und muthig auf demselben erscheinen, und nachdem die Partei- angelegenheiten geordnet sind, alle mit neuer Lust, mit der Ueber- zeugung nach Hause gehen, daß wir Alle der Sache treu bleiben wollen bis in den Tod. (Lebhaftes Bravo!) Wie viel Vertreter da aus einem Kreise anwesend sind, ist ziemlich gleichgiltig. Die Ber- liner sind mit 20 Mann hier, die Hamburger mit 9. Will nun Jemand behaupten, Berlin und Hamburg sei hier nicht entsprechend vertreten? Gewiß kann man über die geeignetste Form der Ver- tretung verschiedener Meinung sein; aber dessen können Sie ver- sichert sein: der Fraktion lag nichts ferner, als den großen Städten einen Kappzaum anzulegen.

Daß den Mitgliedern des Parteivorstandes das Recht der Theil- nahme am Parteitage eingeräumt werden soll, ist eigentlich mehr eine Formalität. Solange wir einen Parteivorstand haben werden, wird auch verlangt werden, daß Mitglieder desselben da sind, um Bericht zu erstatten über dessen Thätigkeit. Was weiter die Theil- nahme der Reichstagsabgeordneten betrifft, so müßte das ja ein jämmerlicher Kerl von Reichstagsabgeordneter sein, der, wenn ihm daran liegt, auf den Parteitag zu kommen, sich kein Mandat an- zuschaffen wüßte. Die Anwesenheit eines Abgeordneten ist aber unter Umständen sogar sehr nothwendig. Taugt einer davon nichts in der Partei, dann soll er erst recht auf dem Parteitag sein, damit man ihm sagt, du bist nichts werth, du hast dein Mandat nieder- zulegen; ist er gar ein Verräther, so wäscht man ihm den Kopf und schmeißt ihn hinaus. Da es aber nothwendig ist, daß unsere Abgeordneten nach den Parteitagen kommen, so dürfen wir sie nicht in die Lage bringen, eventuell um ein Mandat betteln zu müssen. Wir schlagen also vor, den Reichstagsabgeordneten das Recht zu geben, auf dem Parteitage anwesend zu sein, mit der Einschränkung, — die ich übrigens nicht einmal für richtig halte — über ihre parlamentarische Thätigkeit u. s. w. nur eine berathende Stimme zu haben. Mit der Anerkennung, daß die sozialdemokratischen Ab- geordneten das Recht haben, auf dem Parteitag zu erscheinen, ist aber — ich hebe das hervor — noch nicht ausgesprochen, daß die Partei die Verpflichtung hat, auch für die Mittel zu sorgen, daß sie auf dem Parteitag erscheinen können. Ob das ausgesprochen werden soll, lasse ich dahingestellt. In dem Entwurf ist diese Verpflichtung nicht, und von den Verfassern ist deren Aufnahme sogar abgelehnt worden.

Nach § 10 kann ein außerordentlicher Parteitag einberufen werden durch den Parteivorstand, auf Antrag der Reichstagsfraktion und auf Antrag von 15 Wahlkreisen und durch die Namensunterschriften von mindestens 10 000 Parteigenossen. Es wird allerdings außerordentlich schwierig sein, diese 10 000 Unterschriften zu kontrolliren. Im Uebrigen hat diese Bestimmung wohl auch nur einen mehr dekorativen Werth. Nach dem Entwurf soll jedes Jahr ein Parteitag stattfinden. Der Termin ist also möglichst kurz gesetzt. Die Parteibehörden haben außerdem absolut keine Exekutivgewalt, durch die sie die Genossen zu etwas zwingen könnten, was diese, freiwillig zu thun, sich weigern. Auch die Fraktion wird ja doch immer aus Parteigenossen bestehen, die in Bezug auf Parteigüte, persönliche Ehrenhaftigkeit, Tüchtigkeit und Mannhaftigkeit nicht unter dem Durchschnitt der Genossen stehen werden, so daß alle Garantieen vorhanden sind, daß, wenn sich ein Parteitag innerhalb des Verlaufs eines Jahres nothwendig machen wird, derselbe, ohne daß das Mittel einer Abstimmung erst in Anwendung zu kommen braucht, — berufen werden wird.

Die Bestimmung, daß die Mitglieder des Parteivorstandes für ihre Thätigkeit eine Besoldung beziehen können, und daß die Höhe derselben durch die Reichstagsfraktion festgestellt wird, hat zu vielen Aussetzungen Anlaß geboten. Die Kritik hat geradeheraus bei diesem Punkt hier und da sehr über die Schnur gehauen. Es hätten Fernerstehende wirklich zu dem Glauben gelangen können, daß der Parteivorstand den Fraktionsmitgliedern Prozente vom Gehalt geben wird. Diese Art Vorwürfe sind denn doch etwas schlimmer, als einfach lächerlich. Es ist doch für die Höhe der Gehälter wirklich gleichgiltig, ob der Parteitag die Gehälter festsetzt, oder nicht; darüber redet kein anständiger Mensch. Uns hat ein praktischer Fall zu dieser Bestimmung geführt. Als wir 1875 auf dem Vereinigungskongreß den Parteivorstand erwählten, wählten wir uns auch einen vollständig besoldeten Vorsitzenden in der Person des verstorbenen Genossen Hasenclever. Es stellte sich aber in kürzester Frist heraus, daß in diesem Amt keine volle Beschäftigung für ihn da war. Hasenclever sah dies selbst ein; er widmete deshalb seine Thätigkeit der Presse, und wir haben ihn ersetzt durch einen Vorsitzenden, der monatlich blos 15 Thaler erhielt. Weil wir nun auch heute nicht wissen, wie in Zukunft die Thätigkeit des zukünftigen Vorstandes sein wird, so haben wir die Frage der Höhe der Besoldung offen gelassen. Dem Parteitag wird ja Rechnung zu legen sein. Der Vorwurf, daß man mit in der Fraktion Techtel= mechtel machen werde, um sich möglichst hohe Gehälter heraus= zuschlagen, ist gehässig, undelikat, und ich bedaure, daß es Genossen giebt, die solche Vorwürfe erheben. Wenn solche Schofels unter uns wären, dann wäre es schlimm. Nachdem aber einmal solche Vorwürfe erhoben sind, mögen Sie anders beschließen. Aber ich glaube, so tief sind wir wirklich nicht gesunken, wie man uns unter= stellt. (Zuruf Bebels). Nein, wir sind garnicht gesunken, wir sind ganz nette Kerls! (Große Heiterkeit.)

Die Bestimmung des § 14, daß der Parteivorstand auch die prinzipielle Haltung der Parteiorgane zu kontrolliren hat, hat zu der irrigen Annahme geführt, der Vorstand werde in einem fort in die Redaktion hineinreden. In einem gegnerischen Blatte hieß es in Bezug auf diese Bestimmung sogar „man spricht dort schon", nämlich in der Opposition, „offen von Geschäftssozialismus, namentlich durch die Centralisirung der Presse in den Händen zu= verlässiger Genossen will man diesen auf Kosten der Arbeiter eine seine, bourgeoismäßige Existenz schaffen. Die finanzielle Kon= kurrenz allein, welche die neuauftauchenden Arbeiterblätter ihnen machen wollen, ist ein Grund des heftigen Auftretens der Partei= päpste gegen dieselben, und man wird sich auf heftige Debatten auf dem Kongreß gefaßt machen müssen" 2c. Ich will mich bei dieser Auslassung nun nicht weiter aufhalten, und verweise Sie nur auf § 18 unserer alten Organisation. Derselbe lautete:

„§ 18. Zur Begründung von lokalen Parteiblättern ist die Zustimmung des Vorstandes, der Kontrolkommission und des Ausschusses, welchen über die bezüglichen örtlichen Verhältnisse rechtzeitig und ausführlich berichtet werden muß, erforderlich. Nur solche Blätter, welche mit Zustimmung genannter Partei= behörden ins Leben treten, sind als Parteiorgane zu betrachten und können die moralische und materielle Unterstützung der Partei beanspruchen. Die lokalen Parteiblätter haben sich in prinzipiellen Fragen an das Parteiprogramm zu halten, und sind, gleich den beiden in § 14 genannten Organen, in taktischen Partei= fragen dem Vorstand unterstellt."

Das war früher Parteigesetz! Und nun frage ich die älteren Parteigenossen, ob früher wirklich von Seite der Parteileitung irgend ein unberechtigter Einfluß auf die lokale Presse ausgeübt worden ist? Gewiß nicht! das wäre auch eine Thorheit gewesen. Es wär aber nicht blos eine Thorheit, sondern auch eine Unmög= lichkeit. Wie uns Genosse Bebel in seinem Bericht mitgetheilt, existiren zur Zeit in Deutschland über 100 sozialdemokratische Blätter. Wie soll ein Parteivorstand, und mag er noch so zahlreich sein, es fertig bringen, diese gesammte Presse zu kon=

trolliren und event. zu zensiren? Ein Vorstand, der sich so etwas herausnähme, würde einfach „hinausfliegen."

Andererseits ist freilich auch festzuhalten, daß, jemehr die Partei sich ausbreitet, je größer die Zahl unserer Blätter wird, und vor allem, jemehr es nach und nach anfängt, profitabel zu werden, Blätter mit sozialdemokratischer Tendenz herauszugeben, irgend ein Organ in der Partei da sein muß, welches feststellt, ob dieses oder jenes Blatt auch wirklich befähigt und berechtigt ist, im Namen der sozialdemokratischen Partei zu schreiben und zu sprechen. (Sehr richtig!) Wollen Sie den Vorstand nicht mit dieser Aufgabe betrauen, so müssen Sie eben irgend ein anderes Organ schaffen.

Zwar sagt Werner: die Genossen am Ort werden das schon machen. Ich aber behaupte, die Genossen am Ort werden nicht verhindern können, daß derartige Organe doch erscheinen, selbst wenn erstere nicht abonniren. Solche Organe können aber der Partei schwere Verlegenheiten bereiten. Diese Blätter können und werden mit einzelnen Artikeln Unfrieden in die Partei bringen und unter dem Scheine, daß ihre Tendenz sonst ein gute ist, als enfants terribles die Partei blamiren.

Ich komme nun zur Kontrollfrage. Wenn es möglich ist, was ich augenblicklich noch bezweifle, eine Form zu finden, die uns ein Kontrollsystem, wie wir es früher gehabt haben, erlaubt, ohne dabei an den Klippen der Gesetzgebung zu scheitern, so bin ich beauftragt, im Namen meiner übrigen Fraktionsgenossen, welche den Entwurf ausarbeiteten, zu erklären, daß wir gar nicht darauf bestehen, daß die Kontrolle der Fraktion übertragen wird. Wir sind nur aus rein praktischen Erwägungen dazu gekommen, die Fraktion mit dieser Aufgabe zu betrauen. Es liegt aus der Mitte der Delegirten ein Antrag vor, der nicht den Entwurf anerkennen, sondern nur eine Parteispitze ausbilden will. Wenn man überhaupt dieser Ansicht huldigt — und sie ist mir am sympathischsten — dann begreife ich nicht, wie man dem gesetzlich am meisten geschützten Faktor, nämlich der Fraktion, mit einer Art, ich will nicht sagen Mißtrauen, aber doch Bedenken, entgegentreten kounte. Wären wir frei in Bezug auf unsere organisatorische Gestaltung, so würden wir gar nicht davon geredet haben, die Fraktion mit besonderen Befugnissen auszustatten; da wir aber nicht frei sind, so halte ich es für meine Person allerdings nicht für taktisch klug, demjenigen Organ, das hervorgegangen ist aus dem Vertrauen der Partei und in seiner Gesammtheit gewiß auch die Parteiintelligenz und Tüchtigkeit repräsentirt, nicht diejenigen Aufgaben zuzuweisen, die in anderen Händen vielleicht schwer zu erfüllen sind.

Also nicht die Sucht, der Fraktion die Herrschaft zu sichern, hat uns zu dem Vorschlage gebracht, sondern der Glaube, daß es dadurch möglich sein wird, die vereinsgesetzlichen Klippen zu um-schiffen. Ich gebe aber gern zu, eine angenehme, eine willkommene Lösung dieser Schwierigkeit ist unser Vorschlag nicht; ich kann aber, bis etwas Besseres bekannt gemacht wird, für meine Person von demselben nicht abgehen.

Als Parteiorgan schlagen wir Ihnen vor, das „Berliner Volksblatt", das am stärksten verbreitete, zweifellos gut redigirte und in Zukunft wo möglich noch besser redigirte Blatt der Partei zu wählen. Dieser Vorschlag bricht mit der bisherigen Tradition, ein wöchentlich nur zwei oder drei Mal erscheinendes Blatt, das ganz frei vom Charakter eines Lokalorgans ist, zum Zentralorgan zu haben. Wir haben früher als Centralorgan gehabt: im Allg. deutschen Arbeiterverein den „Neuen Sozialdemokrat", bei den Eisenachern den „Volksstaat" und später den „Vorwärts".

Bei unserem Vorschlage haben uns wieder nur rein praktische Gesichtspunkte geleitet. Hätten nicht Hödel und Nobiling geschossen und wäre der „Vorwärts" nicht verboten worden, so wäre an uns wahrscheinlich schon 1878, sicher aber 1879 die Frage herangetreten, ob der „Vorwärts" nicht eingeschränkt werden müsse. Denn dieses Blatt — und das ist für Viele von Ihnen gewiß neu es zu hören — war in der kurzen Zeit seiner Existenz von 12 000 bis auf 7 000 Abonnenten zurückgegangen, und diesem Zurückgehen ließ sich nicht steuern, trotz unseres ganzen Parteiapparats. Wo Lokalblätter entstanden, ging der „Vorwärts" zurück. Dazu kam die Konkurrenz der „Berliner Freie Presse". Man sagte sich in der Provinz, der „Vorwärts" bringt alles 2—3 Tage später als die „Freie Presse". Die „Freie Presse" nahm an Abonnenten fortwährend zu, der „Vorwärts" ging zurück. Es war thatsächlich damals bereits so weit, daß die Parteileitung, die Fraktion zc. sich genöthigt sahen, sehr oft mit ihren Erlassen und Bekanntmachungen sich zunächst an die „Freie Presse" zu wenden, so daß das offizielle Organ erst nachhinkte. In eine ähnliche Situation würden wir heute wieder gerathen, wenn wir ein Wochenblatt als Centralorgan ins Leben riefen. Mit einem Blatt nach Art des „Vorwärts" würden wir also unseren Zweck nicht erreichen, sondern wahrscheinlich damit der Partei nur ein nicht unerhebliches Defizit aufladen. Die ebenfalls laut gewordene Befürchtung, daß das „Volksblatt" der Lokalpresse Konkurrenz machen würde, ist vollständig unbegründet. Das würde im Gegentheil viel mehr bei einem neuen Wochenblatt als Centralorgan der Fall sein. Die Vertrauensmänner werden ja allerdings das „Volksblatt" halten müssen, das macht aber der Lokalpresse keine Konkurrenz. Es ist aber auch gar kein Bedürfniß nach einem neuen Wochenblatt als Centralorgan. Wir haben bereits drei Blätter, welche ihrer ganzen Haltung und ihrem Inhalt nach nicht blos für enge lokale und provinzielle Kreise wirken, sondern für die ganze Partei bestimmt sind: die „Arbeiterchronik" in Nürnberg, die „Volkstribüne" in Berlin und die „Nordwacht". Die „Berliner Volkstribüne" wird mit großem Geschick redigirt, das kann ruhig anerkannt werden, wie ja unsere Presse im Großen Ganzen sehr gut ist, und die Proletarierpresse weit erhaben über dem gewöhnlichen Preßklatsch steht. Gewiß hat die „Volkstribüne" schon ab und zu kleine Nebensprünge gemacht, aber das schadet nichts. Die „Nordwacht" und die „Arbeiterchronik" haben stets ihre Pflicht gethan und sind in ihrer Art nicht minder gut gehalten, als die „Volkstribüne". Gründen wir nun ein Wochenblatt als Centralorgan, so werden die drei bestehenden ruinirt, oder wir haben vier Blätter, von denen keines sich deckt. Nun sind die drei bestehenden Blätter keineswegs Privatunternehmungen. Zwei von ihnen, die „Nordwacht" und die „Arbeiterchronik" standen bereits bisher in Bezug auf ihre finanziellen Erträge der Partei zur Verfügung, und die „Berliner Volkstribüne" wird sich keinen Augenblick weigern, wenn es verlangt wird, in ganz dasselbe Verhältniß zur Partei zu treten. Es ist doch nun entschieden besser, die bereits existenzfähigen Blätter in diesem Zustande zu erhalten und sie wo möglich zu Ertragsquellen für die Partei auszubilden, als ein viertes Konkurrenzorgan zu gründen, welches die bestehenden Blätter ruinirt oder gar Zuschüsse erfordert. Unsere Zeitungen werden in Zukunft wesentlich dazu dienen müssen, in pekuniärer Hinsicht das Rückgrat der Partei zu bilden. Von Beiträgen allein kann die Partei nicht mehr existiren, wir bedürfen dazu der Erträge aus der Presse. Nun haben allerdings unsere ausländischen Genossen mit großem Bedauern das Eingehen des „Sozialdemokrat" empfunden. Auch wir bewahren dem Londoner „Sozialdemokrat" und seiner ebenso tapferen als geschickten Vertheidigung der Parteiinteressen ein sehr gutes Andenken. (Bravo!) Aber er mußte eingehen, es war das ein Gebot der politischen Ehrlichkeit, und in dieser Beziehung giebt es für uns kein Wanken und kein Schwanken. Wir kämpfen immer mit offenem Visir, wenn man uns nur die Möglichkeit dazu offen läßt. Einen Ersatz für den „Sozialdemokrat" zu schaffen, ist allerdings schwer, ja unmöglich. Ein „Sozialdemokrat" mit dem Inhalt, wie er in London und in der Schweiz erschien, kann vorläufig in Berlin noch nicht erscheinen (Heiterkeit). Sie bedauern dies gewiß mit mir, denn man liest gern, was man sich sonst denken muß. Die ausländischen Genossen können sich aber aus den Wochenblättern und der „Neuen Zeit" zur Genüge über die Vorgänge in Deutschland informiren. Konnten wir also einen vollen Ersatz für den Londoner „Sozialdemokrat" unmöglich schaffen, so glaubten wir nichts Besseres thun zu können, als das größte in Deutschland, im Centralpunkt des politischen Lebens erscheinende sozialdemokratische Tageblatt zum Centralorgan zu erwählen. Ob Sie den Titel des Blattes ändern wollen oder nicht, ist gleichgiltig.

Ich gebe auf Förmlichkeiten nichts. Dieses Blatt darf aber auch seinen lokalen Charakter nicht verlieren. Das schadet auch nichts. Wer den lokalen Theil nicht lesen will, für den bringt der politische Theil immer noch mehr, als das größte und bestredigirte Wochenblatt. Soll das „Berliner Volksblatt" überhaupt seine Aufgabe erfüllen, dann muß es das Organ besonders der Berliner Genossen bleiben. Dies zu ihrer Beruhigung. Für draußen wird es nur das Centralblatt der Partei sein, das in Berlin erscheint und in einzelnen Orten in einzelnen Exemplaren gelesen wird. An eine Massenverbreitung, wie mit dem „Neuen Sozialdemokrat", ist natürlich bei einem wöchentlich sechs Mal erscheinenden Blatt nicht zu denken. Das ist aber auch heute nicht mehr nothwendig. Unsere Lokalpresse verdient heute schon das Prädikat „gut" und ich hoffe, daß sie in kürzester Zeit sehr gut werden wird. Deshalb können wir diese Sache ganz ruhig der Zeit und der Entwicklung überlassen. Sollte sich aber wirklich nach Verlauf eines Jahres die Nothwendigkeit eines besonderen Wochenblattes herausstellen, gut, dann schaffen wir es.

Damit bin ich mit meinen allgemeinen Ausführungen zu Ende. Was nun die geschäftliche Behandlung unseres Entwurfes betrifft, so halte ich es für das Beste, wir treten jetzt in eine Generaldiskussion ein, in der wir uns über die allgemeinen Gesichtspunkte aussprechen, und setzen dann eine Kommission von 25 Mitgliedern ein, der wir das gesammte Material, alle zu diesem Gegenstande eingegangenen Anträge und die in der Generaldiskussion zu Tage getretenen Wünsche und Anschauungen mitgeben. Wir können dann vielleicht schon übermorgen endgiltig über die Organisationsfrage entscheiden. (Stürmisches Bravo!)

Der Parteitag erklärt sich mit der vom Referenten vorgeschlagenen Art der geschäftlichen Behandlung einverstanden und vertagt die Generaldiskussion auf Mittwoch 9 Uhr.

Schluß 6½ Uhr.

Dritter Verhandlungstag.

Mittwoch, den 15. Oktober 1890.

Vormittagssitzung.

Vorsitzender Singer eröffnet die Sitzung um 9¼ Uhr und giebt vor Eintritt in die Tagesordnung das Wort dem als Gast des Parteitages anwesenden

Genossen Wullschleger-Basel: Werthe Genossen und Freunde! Ich wollte nicht ermangeln, Ihnen auch an dieser Stelle die Grüße Ihrer schweizerischen Gesinnungsgenossen zu überbringen. Das

Parteikomitee der sozialdemokratischen Partei der Schweiz hat es für nothwendig erachtet, angesichts der großen Bedeutung, welche Ihre, die deutsche Partei, innerhalb der Arbeiterbewegung aller Länder einnimmt, und angesichts der Wichtigkeit Ihrer Traktanden einen Abgeordneten an Ihren Kongreß zu schicken. Ich danke Ihnen für die freundliche Aufnahme, die Sie auch mir, als auswärtigem Gaste, haben zu Theil werden lassen. Ich vertrete zwar hier ein kleines Land, und mit gemischten Gefühlen .stehe. ich hier vor Ihnen. Denn Sie erinnern sich, daß vor noch nicht langer Zeit einigen Ihrer besten Genossen in unserm Lande schwere Unbill widerfahren ist. Es ist allerdings unsere Partei daran nicht schuld; es trägt überhaupt daran das Schweizervolk in seiner Gesammtheit keine Schuld, sondern, wenn überhaupt Schweizern eine Schuld daran beizumessen ist, so sind es vor allem unsere Behörden gewesen. Freilich muß man auch diese von einem Theile der Schuld freisprechen; Sie wissen es, unter welchem ungeheuren Drucke unser kleines Land gestanden hat. Es ist ja nur zu richtig, was Engels im Londoner „Sozialdemokrat" über die kleinen Staaten geschrieben hat: „es ist schwierig für ein kleines Land, sich allen Anforderungen zu widersetzen, die die fremde Diplomatie stellt." Ich kann Sie aber versichern, daß unter den heutigen Verhältnissen eine Ausweisung wie damals nicht mehr beschlossen würde; ich glaube annehmen zu können, daß unsere Behörden selbst jene Vorgänge ihrerseits bedauern, wenn sie auch natürlich es nicht wagen, dies öffentlich einzugestehen.

Ich stehe aber hier mit gemischten Gefühlen auch deshalb, weil unsere Arbeiterbewegung in der Schweiz im allgemeinen und die sozialdemokratische im besonderen noch sehr jungen Datums ist. Während Sie in Deutschland bereits eine mächtige Partei sind, verfügen wir erst über die Anfänge einer solchen. Unsere ganze Bewegung ist noch im ersten, höchstens erst im zweiten Stadium der Entwickelung. Eine eigentliche sozialdemokratische Partei haben wir erst seit zwei Jahren, seit den bekannten Vorgängen gegen ihre damals bei uns ausgewiesenen Landsleute, und es ist diesem Gewaltstreich vornehmlich zuzuschreiben, daß die Schweizer Bürger sozialdemokratischer Richtung sich zu einer eigenen Organisation zusammengethan haben. Auch da hat sich das Sprichwort bewährt: „Kein Unglück ist so groß, es ist ein Glück dabei."

Wir laufen in der Schweiz innerhalb unserer Richtung hauptsächlich zwei Gefahren. Entweder wir tragen dem nüchternen Charakter des Schweizervolks allzusehr Rechnung, nehmen Umgang von theoretischer Propaganda und betheiligen uns bloß an den jeweiligen Fragen der Tagespolitik: auf diese Weise wird es uns allerdings gelingen, da und dort Erfolge zu erzielen und unserer

9

Partei, äußerlich wenigstens, eine gewisse Bedeutung zu sichern; aber wir würden dabei Gefahr laufen, in einen kleinbürgerlichen Possibilismus auszuarten, der dann schließlich von den Grundprinzipien der Sozialdemokratie nichts mehr wissen will. Die andere Gefahr ist, daß wir unserem nüchternen Volkscharakter zu wenig oder gar nicht Rechnung tragen, daß wir uns vorzugsweise oder ausschließlich mit theoretischer Propaganda befassen; dann werden wir vielleicht ein kleines Häuflein von Gesinnungsgenossen um uns schaaren, aber auf die Masse des Volks keinen Einfluß haben. Da gilt es, die richtige Mitte zu treffen, beides richtig zu verbinden. — Für uns in der Schweiz ist es eine gegebene Sache, uns am politischen Leben zu betheiligen, darüber können bei uns eigentlich keine Meinungsverschiedenheiten entstehen. Ein Gegner der Betheiligung am praktischen politischen Leben ist für uns einfach ein Anarchist. Die ganze politische Entwicklung des Landes, seine politisch demokratischen Institutionen bringen es mit sich, daß alle Parteischattirungen sich am praktisch politischen Leben zu betheiligen haben, und diese Betheiligung mit der Propaganda für die sozialdemokratischen Ideen richtig zu vereinen, das ist unsere Aufgabe. In dieser Richtung haben wir uns in neuester Zeit sehr bethätigt und gedenken das in der Folge noch sehr viel umfangreicher zu thun. Insbesondere kann ich Ihnen mittheilen, daß wir in nächster Zeit bei den Wahlen zur schweizerischen Volksvertretung, zum Nationalrath, in verschiedenen Wahlkreisen, wo unsere Genossen in größerer Zahl vorhanden sind, als eigene sozialdemokratische Partei vorzugehen und eigene Kandidaten aufzustellen gedenken. (Beifall.) Wenn wir auch vor der Hand damit noch keinen großen Erfolg erzielen werden, so ist doch ein Anfang zu selbstständigem politischem Vorgehen geschehen, und die Anfänge sind am Ende die Hauptsache, aus ihnen wird sich dann das Weitere von selbst ergeben.

Wenn auch da und dort in Ihrem Lande die Anschauung verbreitet ist, unsere Entwicklung sei eine zu konservative, so bitte ich Sie doch zu bedenken, daß nur der Schein, die äußere Form, diesen Glauben erwecken kann. Wir Deutschschweizer sind ja ungeheuer nüchtern und unsere ungeschliffenen Manieren lassen noch durchblicken, daß wir dem Wesen nach immer noch mehr ein Volk von Bauern sind. Allein nichtsdestoweniger ist die radikale Gesinnung auch unter uns verbreitet und die Verhältnisse sorgen ja reichlich dafür, daß der Radikalismus in unserem Sinne auch im Schweizervolk von Tag zu Tag mehr um sich greift. Die wirthschaftliche Entwicklung hat auch in der Schweiz in den letzten Jahren den Gang genommen, wie anderswo, daß die Kleinbetriebe nach und nach absorbirt werden. Diese Entwicklung wird manchem Blinden die Augen öffnen und ihn in die Reihen der Sozialdemokratie überführen. Die Parole der schweizerischen Sozialdemokraten ist die-

jenige der Sozialdemokraten aller Länder: Nieder mit der Lohn-
sklaverei! (Lebhafter Beifall.)

Vorsitzender S i n g e r theilt mit, daß zu den ausländischen Gästen
noch hinzugekommen ist der Präsident des Grütlivereins der Schweiz,
Fürsprech S c h e r r e r, den diejenigen Delegirten, welche den Parteitag
in St. Gallen mitgemacht haben, persönlich kennen gelernt und
dem sie das beste Andenken bewahrt haben. (Beifall.)

Eine weitere Reihe von Telegrammen und Zuschriften ist eingelaufen. Es liegt ein Geschäftsordnungsantrag vor, eine Liste
aller dieser Schriftstücke dem Protokoll einzuverleiben. Das Bureau
wird diesem Wunsche nachkommen.

Das R e s u l t a t   d e r   W a h l   z u r   N e u n e r - K o m m i s s i o n
ist festgestellt und wird verkündet. Abgegeben sind 372 Stimmzettel,
davon sind 17 ungiltig, weil sie mehr Namen enthalten, als Personen
zu wählen waren; es haben erhalten: Kloß-Stuttgart 181, Pfannkuch-
Kassel 180, Müller-Darmstadt 171, Kaden-Dresden 147, Reißhaus-
Erfurt 135, Geck-Offenburg 119, Grimpe-Elberfeld 106, Meist-
Köln 103, Ewald-Brandenburg 90 Stimmen.

Die übrigen zersplitterten Stimmen, die dem Ermittelungs-
protokoll angehängt sind, kommen nicht zur Verlesung. Die
Kommission wird vom Vorsitzenden ersucht, sich zu konstituiren; das
bezügliche Material wird ihr sofort zugehen.

Darauf tritt der Parteitag in die Tagesordnung ein: G e n e r a l -
d i s k u s s i o n   d e s   O r g a n i s a t i o n s e n t w u r f s.

V o l l m a r: Parteigenossen! In dem ausführlichen Vortrag
Auers von gestern sind manche Punkte enthalten gewesen, mit denen
ich mich einverstanden erklären kann, nicht wenige aber auch, mit
denen ich nicht einverstanden bin. Insbesondere muß ich beanstanden,
daß Genosse Auer sich nicht dazu hat entschließen können, die Sache
absolut ruhig und kühl sachlich zu behandeln, sondern daß er dem
polemischen Ton, der leider zu lange während des Sommers in
der Partei geherrscht hat, auch hier noch einen Nachklang gegeben
hat. Sie haben während der vergangenen Tage hinreichend Ihre
Ansicht über Gedanken und Kampfesweise der sogenannten Opposition ausgesprochen. Ich bin gewiß der allererste, der eine Kampfesweise der Opposition, die Gehässigkeit in die Sache trägt, verurtheilt;
andererseits aber müssen wir vollkommen gerecht sein und zugeben,
daß auch von der andern Seite dieser polemische Ton die Sache
nicht wenig zugespitzt hat. Wir sind doch nicht hier, um uns
Schmeicheleien zu sagen, auch nicht dazu, Leichenreden zu halten;
aber wenn wir irgendwo einen Fehler, eine Unart entdecken, sollen
wir doch an uns selbst Kritik üben und zusehen, wie es besser zu
machen ist. Ein Erfurter Genosse hat am ersten Tage ein sehr
wahres Wort gesprochen; er meinte, daß wir noch nicht genügend
aus dem Ausnahmezustand herausgekommen sind, uns noch nicht

genug an die frühere öffentliche Kritik und Diskussion gewöhnt haben. Das beruht durchaus auf Gegenseitigkeit, und ich möchte ersuchen, von nun an diesen polemischen Ton, der auf alle Fälle nur verletzend wirken kann, fahren zu lassen und rein sachlich zu verhandeln. Daß das von Auer nicht geschehen ist, haben Diejenigen, die die Verhältnisse etwas näher kennen, schon gestern gehört. Auer hat meinen Namen nicht genannt; aber Jeder, der Augen und Ohren hat, wußte, wer gemeint war; diese mehreren, welche nicht in der Fraktion anwesend waren, bin ich. Die Sache ist ja vollkommen richtig. Wer die Blätter liest, weiß, daß ich auf Grund eines Gesuchs aus Gesundheitsrücksichten beurlaubt worden bin, nachdem ich einen Theil der Reichstagssitzungen mitgemacht hatte. Was ich, wenn ich weiter geblieben wäre, gesagt haben würde, kann ich nicht wissen ist jetzt auch gleichgiltig; jedenfalls behielt ich der Partei gegenüber das volle Recht der Kritik. Nun heißt es, jeder hat das Recht der Kritik; aber wenn man es anwenden will, liegt die Sache anders. Sonst würde ich mir das Urtheil über die von mir veröffentlichten Artikel nicht erklären können. Kein Mensch soll sein eigener Lobredner sein; aber ich fordere die Leser jener Artikel auf, Zeugniß darüber abzulegen, ob eine ruhigere, sachlichere, rücksichtsvollere, höflichere Art der Kritik möglich ist, als die meinige. Wenn nun eine solche Kritik geübt wird, soll man in einer Partei wie der unsrigen froh sein, daß sie so geübt wird, denn jedes kritisirende Wort kann nur zur Aufklärung beitragen; aber man soll sich nicht formell dahinter verschanzen, daß es besser gewesen wäre, die Kritik zu unterlassen. Ich bin nur gezwungen und herausgefordert worden; ich wollte schon früher hier das Wort ergreifen, habe aber angesichts der frieblichen, guten Stimmung darauf verzichtet, und habe auch meine wenigen Bemerkungen nur gemacht, weil ich herausgefordert war.

Nun zu dem Entwurf selbst. Wenn etwas meine ursprüngliche Meinung, daß er nicht auf richtigen Grundsätzen aufgebaut ist, verstärkt hat, so ist es der gestrige Vortrag Auers. Er sagte uns geradezu, wir haben unausgesetzt in dem Gedanken gearbeitet, daß die Arbeit doch für nichts ist. Wenn ich die deutschen Polizeiverhältnisse mir ansehe, glaube ich das auch; es ist traurig, aber es ist so. Sie können die Organisation beschließen, wie Sie wollen, wir in Bayern werden sie nicht ausführen, weil wir es nicht können. Der ganze Absatz von den Vertrauensmännern ist in Bayern, nach oberster gerichtlicher Auslegung, hinfällig; es ist schon eine ganze Anzahl Genossen daraufhin zu drei, vier Monaten Gefängniß verurtheilt worden wegen Geheimbündelei. Dadurch fällt schon diese Art der Organisation für einen nicht kleinen Theil des deutschen Reiches hinweg; in Preußen, sagt man mir, wird ganz ähnlich verfahren. Ob es dann noch der Mühe werth ist, solche wesentliche Bestimmungen für Thüringen, Baden, die freien Städte aufrechtzuerhalten, das überlasse ich gänzlich dem Parteitag. Mit Recht hat Auer gestern den 1877er Beschluß angezogen, in dem es heißt, wir bedürfen einer formellen Organisation im früheren Sinne nicht; die Verbindung wird den Genossen in den einzelnen Städten und Ländern, je nach den Verhältnissen, überlassen. Wenn wir damals mit Recht erklären konnten, daß dieser ideelle, nicht formelle Zusammenhang vollkommen aufrecht erhalten worden ist, so sehe ich garnicht ein, weshalb wir heute andere Grundsätze acceptiren wollen. Noch eins. Die heutige Partei ist etwas himmelweit Verschiedenes von der Partei vor zwölf Jahren. Damals war sie klein, jetzt ist sie die größte. Je größer die Partei wird, desto unmöglicher wird es, eine irgendwie an Vereinswesen erinnernde Organisation zu schaffen und aufrecht zu erhalten, desto mehr muß sie ähnlich gemacht werden der anderer großen Parteien. Mit einem Worte: nicht nur aus gesetzlichen, sondern auch aus praktischen Gründen sollten wir alles, was irgend an eine vereinsähnliche Organisation erinnert, nach Möglichkeit von uns thun und immer daran denken, daß wir nicht einen Verein, sondern eine gewaltige politische Partei organisiren sollen. Jedem einzelnen Ort ist die Organisation selbst zu überlassen und als gemeinsames Band giebt es, außer der Fraktion, nur drei Dinge: Parteivorstand, Kontrollausschuß und Centralorgan. Das ist völlig genügend.

Damit komme ich auf den Kontrollausschuß, den ich auch schon in meinen Veröffentlichungen hauptsächlich besprochen habe. Ich brauche wohl nicht dagegen zu sprechen, daß der Fraktion Herrschaftsgelüste untergeschoben werden. Soweit ich es verfolgt habe, sind sie ihr auch nicht untergeschoben worden, sondern es ist gesagt worden, daß eine derartige Organisation dazu benutzt werden könnte. Das ist ein himmelweiter Unterschied. Ich bin im Gegentheil sicher, daß die Fraktionsmitglieder herzensfroh sind, daß man ihnen nicht mehr aufladet; trifft man aber derartige Bestimmungen, so müssen sie dem Charakter der Partei entsprechen und dürfen nicht gemißbraucht werden können von Leuten, die wir noch gar nicht kennen. Der Vorschlag, daß die Fraktion die Kontrolle über den Parteivorstand ausüben soll, ist nach meiner aufrichtigen Meinung unannehmbar, deswegen, weil er Fraktion wie Parteivorstand in die denkbar schieffste Lage bringt. Nach dem Entwurf soll die Fraktion die Gehälter der Vorstandsmitglieder festsetzen, sie hat das Recht, die Kasse und die Geschäftsführung zu untersuchen, sogar das Recht, Vorstandsmitglieder abzusetzen; der Vorstand dagegen soll die Kontrolle über die prinzipielle Richtung der Parteiblätter haben. Nun sind bekanntlich die meisten Fraktionsmitglieder entweder direkte Leiter und Redakteure von Parteiblättern, oder stehen als Reporter u. dgl. mit ihnen in Verbindung. Ich verweise lediglich auf Berlin.

Nach dem Entwurf ist nun der Vorstand berechtigt und verpflichtet, die Fraktionsgenossen in ihrer Eigenschaft als Redakteure oder Herausgeber auf ihre Haltung zu kontrolliren, hat aber nicht das Recht, sie abzusetzen, wohl aber kann die Fraktion die Kontrolleure absetzen. Da vermag ich mich nicht herauszufinden; ich würde unter keiner Bedingung solche Kontrolle annehmen, weil die Lage unbedingt eine schiefe ist, weil Mißhelligkeiten zwischen beiden dazu führen können, daß die betr. Vorstandsmitglieder sich als unterdrückt ansehen. Der Parteitag hat das endgiltige Urtheil; aber der „Himmel ist hoch und der Zar ist weit". Er tritt einmal im Jahre zusammen; da häuft sich so viel Stoff, daß, wenn nicht gerade die Streitfrage der Zeit nach unmittelbar vor den Kongreß fällt, neuere Dinge die alten Streitigkeiten vollständig zudecken und der Kongreß davon gar nichts mehr hören mag. Auch in dieser Beziehung bin ich für die frühere Einrichtung. Auer sagt, der Kontrollausschuß könne gemaßregelt werden. Ja, vor dem Sozialistengesetz und als Tessendorff schon da war und uns verfolgte, hat drei Jahre lang ein Kontrollausschuß bestanden, ohne behelligt zu werden. Möglich, daß das jetzt anders werden kann, aber wir müssen es versuchen, und Mittel und Wege werden sich finden, diesen Ausschuß von solchen Maßregelungen ziemlich unabhängig zu stellen. Täusche ich mich, dann müssen wir auf andere Einrichtungen sinnen; die vorgeschlagene ist im Interesse der Partei und der Fraktion unannehmbar.

Gegen die Kontrolle der Parteiorgane, so wie sie im Entwurf steht, habe ich nichts einzuwenden. Zweifellos muß, wenn ein Blatt nicht auf dem prinzipiellen Boden der Partei steht, irgend eine Stelle zu der Erklärung befugt sein, daß das Blatt nicht zu uns gehört. Aber im Gegensatz zu Auer meine ich, für diese Kontrolle reichen die Parteigenossen des Ortes vollkommen aus. Wir sollen es nicht verhindern können, meinte Auer, daß ein solches Blatt trotzdem weiter besteht. So liegen die Dinge nicht. Die Genossen jedes wohlorganisirten Parteiortes können ein solches Blatt ohne weiteres todt machen, dazu genügt eine einzige Versammlung, in der man die Thatsachen erzählt und vor dem Blatte warnt. Bleibt die Bestimmung bestehen, so werde ich sie nicht groß bekämpfen, aber Auer's Aeußerungen haben mich doch bedenklich gemacht. Er meinte, es handle sich darum, daß Blätter, die an sich gut sein können, auf unserm Programm stehen, aber hintenherum eine abweichende Ansicht vertreten, Feindseligkeiten hereintragen, desavouirt werden sollen. Hier hat's ein Ende; wenn solche Auslegung gelten soll, dann haben wir keine freie Presse mehr. Ueber die Abweichung von der prinzipiellen Haltung ist leicht zu entscheiden; aber wer entscheidet darüber, ob ein sonst im allgemeinen ausgezeichnet gehaltenes sozialdemokratisches Blatt vielleicht einmal bei einer Frage der auswärtigen Politik oder dergleichen sich verfehlt und den Anschein erweckt, als ob es Unfrieden stiftet? Das alles ist dem Parteivorstand in die Hände gegeben, und ich möchte mich in solche Hände nicht geben.

Ein offizielles Parteiorgan wünsche auch ich. Für eine Partei wie die unsrige, welche jeden Tag im politischen Leben zu kämpfen hat, muß tagtäglich ein Centralorgan am Sitze der Macht in Berlin selbst, wohl bedient von leitenden Persönlichkeiten, seine Stimme ertönen lassen können; ohne ein solches können wir nicht auskommen. Dafür soll aber auch die übrige Presse vollkommen frei sein. Gewiß hat keiner der Genossen sie unterdrücken wollen, aber wir müssen unsere Bestimmungen so treffen, daß nicht in Zukunft eine andere Auslegung möglich wird.

Was die Beschickung des Parteitages anbetrifft, so bin ich mit Auer gegen jede Beschränkung der Delegation. Wir haben früher damit die besten Erfahrungen gemacht; wir sind doch alle miteinander Sozialdemokraten. Soll aber eine Beschränkung eintreten, so bin ich gegen die mechanische Feststellung von drei Mann, sondern würde ein Proportionalsystem vorziehen.

Alles übrige läßt sich auf diese drei Hauptpunkte zurückleiten. Ich beantrage, die ganze Stelle, welche von der Kontrolle des Parteivorstandes durch die Fraktion handelt, zu beseitigen und dafür, wie früher, einen Kontrollausschuß zu setzen, so zwar, daß der Kongreß einen Ort bestimmt, dessen Parteimitglieder die Kontrollkommission wählen. Ich bitte Sie, in diesem Sinne zu beschließen. (Beifall.)

Werner-Teltow: Ich freue mich, daß endlich einmal einer der Parteigenossen erklärt hat, es möge hier streng sachlich vorgegangen werden. Wenn Jemand eine irrige Ansicht gehabt hat, soll man ihn sachlich zu belehren versuchen. Ich habe mir noch nicht angemaßt, für die gesammten Berliner hier zu sprechen; ich bin Delegirter von Teltow-Beeskow-Storkow-Charlottenburg und spreche meine eigene Meinung aus. Das System, welches hier Platz zu greifen schien, war nicht sehr schön. Ich bin einer Derjenigen, welche auch in Opposition gestanden haben gegen die Auffassung der Organisation im Entwurf. Ich habe an den verschiedensten Orten auch darüber referirt und muß hier gleich erklären, daß man mir niemals nachsagen konnte, daß ich ihn nicht vollständig objektiv behandelt habe. Die mir bezüglich Magdeburgs gemachten Unterstellungen sind nicht wahr. Ich theile die Meinung Vollmars hinsichtlich der Kontrolle durch die Fraktion vollständig; ich meine auch, daß unsere Abgeordneten gerade an der Parteipresse beschäftigt sind, und weil ich annehme, daß die Reichstagsfraktion eine Körperschaft ist, die in der Auffassung der Dinge schließlich eine einheitliche Meinung hat, wonach die ganze Presse in Deutschland von diesem Gesichtspunkte aus bearbeitet wird, und daß in Folge dessen, wenn Jemand, wie es uns in Berlin gegangen ist, wenn wir in dem Organ eine Aufnahme in Anspruch nahmen, uns unsere Entgegnung, die dem Blatte nicht lieb war, einfach abge- schnitten wurde, oder man frug erst in Dresden an, ob auch diese oder jene Notiz wirklich ins „Volksblatt" hinein soll. Parteigenossen! Darum sage ich, kann die Fraktion nicht als Kontrollkommission fungiren, nicht weil ich ihr unterschieben will, daß ich irgend welche Unehrlichkeit der Fraktion zutraue, oder behaupten will, sondern weil ich sage: die Wähler zum Reichstage wählen doch nicht die Fraktionsgenossen, daß sie die Parteileitung in die Hand nehmen sollen, sondern die Fraktion untersteht der Kontrolle der Partei- genossen, sie soll agitatorisch thätig sein. Wenn nun die Partei- genossen an irgend einem Orte etwas gegen die Fraktion haben, wenden sie sich an den Vorstand, und der Vorstand giebt diesem Drucke nach und die Fraktion, als Kontrollkommission, sitzt oben als oberste Richterin wie in Paris auf dem Eiffelthurm, in der Glas- hütte, und überschaut so den ganzen Bau, dann kann die Fraktion, wenn sie angeklagt ist, nicht als Richter über sich fungiren. Darum habe ich mich, auch aus praktischen Gründen, zuerst dagegen gewendet. Der Auer'schen Erklärung, daß das Vereinsgesetz eine öffentliche Kontrollkommission zu wählen verbietet, steht § 8 des Vereinsgesetzes entgegen; ja, ich glaube, daß die Fraktion als Kontrollkommission, wenn letztere als politischer Verein betrachtet wird, in der Zeit der Unterbrechung der Sitzungen ganz ebenso antastbar und unter Anklage zu stellen ist, wie mit einander in Verbindung tretende politische Vereine. Darum habe ich — ich stehe nicht auf dem Standpunkte, daß ich jeder Regierung Vertrauen schenke — mit einem Theil der Berliner Genossen den Antrag eingebracht, daß der Parteitag einen Vorstand von 20, 18, 16 — die Zahl ist ja egal — wählt; diese wählen unter sich eine Körperschaft zur Führung der Geschäfte, und die andern sollen die Kontroll-Kommission und Beschwerde- instanz bilden. Dadurch glauben wir, ist das Inverbindungtreten zweier politischer Vereine völlig illusorisch gemacht. Schon Vollmar hat gesagt, es sei fraglich, ob der Aufbau der Organisation im Entwurf nicht mit den Bestimmungen des preußischen Vereins- gesetzes kollidire. Ich frage, ist es möglich, daß man an jedem Ort, wenn ein Wahlkreis aus mehreren Orten besteht, den Vertrauens- mann, der die Beiträge der zahlenden Parteigenossen annimmt und abliefert, mit diesen Genossen als politischen Verein konstruirt? Sollte nicht ein Staatsanwalt dies als einen Verein am Orte be- trachten können, der durch den Vertrauensmann mit dem Vorstand in Verbindung tritt? Ich bin nicht Rechtsgelehrter genug, das zu entscheiden. Und wie, wenn nach Vollmars Vorschlag die Genossen sich an jedem Orte selbst organisiren und um an den Parteivorstand die Gelder abzuliefern, einfach in Versammlungen beschließen, zu dem und jenem Zweck bewilligen wir diese Summe, sie gewissermaßen schenken? Wie gesagt, ich überlasse das den Rechtsgelehrten. — In dem wichtigsten Punkt, dem des Centralorgans, kann ich mit Vollmar nicht einverstanden sein. Für das (für einige Berliner Genossen leidige) „Volksblatt" wäre besser eine Korrespondenz, auf hektographischem Wege hergestellt, alle offiziellen Bekanntmachungen und Mittheilungen an die Redaktionen der Provinzpresse enthaltend, je nach Bedürfniß versandt; die lokalen Redaktionen müßten zur Erhaltung dieser Korrespondenz einen Abonnementsbeitrag leisten, und dadurch wären auch diejenigen Sozialdemokraten, welche nicht in der Lage sind, das Centralorgan halten zu können, in ihrem Organ über die Absichten der Parteileitung vollständig informirt. Denn was jedem Orte recht ist, ein Lokalblatt zu besitzen, das ist doch den Berliner Parteigenossen wahrhaftig billig. Sie haben es verstanden, den Abonnentenstand des „Volksblatt" in 3 Wochen von 12 000 auf 30 000 zu bringen, allerdings mit den Mitteln des Boykotts. Sie müssen doch diesen Berlinern Rechnung tragen. Wenn das „Volksblatt" Centralorgan wird, werden ewige Streitig-keiten vorhanden sein, weil wir dort eine entwickelte Gewerkschafts-organisation haben und jede Gewerkschaft das Blatt auch gleich-zeitig als Agitationsorgan für ihren Beruf benutzen will, und da sollen nun die ellenlangen Berichte ins Centralorgan kommen? Die kommen dann zu spät oder werden hinter wichtigeren Dingen zurück-gestellt; und die Gewerkschaftsführer werden dann sagen: Da seht ihr für unsere Agitation wird gar nichts gethan. Dadurch wird ein Unwille in die Gewerkschaften getragen, wie er jetzt schon that-sächlich existirt. Das „Berliner Volksblatt" ist ein sehr wunder Punkt in der Berliner Bewegung; die Mehrzahl der Berliner Ge-nossen verlangt da einen Einblick in die Verhältnisse des Blattes. Die Gewerkschaftsbewegung darf darunter nicht leiden, darum soll man das Blatt den Berlinern nicht nehmen, sondern ein neues Centralorgan gründen, wenn durchaus eins sein soll. Macht man das „Volksblatt" dazu, so wird das dauerndes Zerwürfniß erzeugen und das Blatt ein ewiger Zankapfel der Berliner Sozialdemokraten sein. Auch bezüglich der Festsetzung der Gehälter theile ich Vollmar's Ansicht. Ich bitte Sie, unbedingt den Parteivorstand so zu wählen, wie wir es vorschlagen.

Müller-Schkeuditz: Redner meint, daß die geübte Kritik, wenn sie auch zum Theil als schon nicht mehr anständig bezeichnet werden mußte, doch soviel ergebe, daß der Entwurf Mängel hat, die zu beseitigen sind. Es müssen vor allem Formen gefunden werden, welche uns vor der Gefahr behüten, mit dem Vereinsgesetz in Konflikt zu kommen. Die Zugehörigkeit zur Partei soll man nicht an einen bestimmten, laufenden Betrag binden; das kann von unseren ländlichen Bezirken, bei der Natur ihrer Lohn- und Arbeits-verhältnisse, nicht verlangt werden. Man soll nicht zu strikte Vor-

schriften aufnehmen, oder doch wenigstens Milderungsgründe zulassen, wie Arbeitslosigkeit oder Krankheit, die von der Zahlung zu
entbinden hätten. Mit der Vertretung auf dem Parteitage nach
dem Entwurf ist Redner einverstanden. Agitatorisch ist gerade
möglichst starke Vertretung der Kreise mit wenigen Parteigenossen
erforderlich, da diese auf dem Parteitag lernen und die erworbene
Kenntniß in ihre Kreise tragen und sie dort verwerthen sollen.

Metzner-Berlin 1: Ich schließe mich dem Wunsche Vollmars
an, daß die Diskussion möglichst leidenschaftslos geführt und jede
verletzende Aeußerung bei Seite gelassen werden möchte, meine aber,
daß dieser Wunsch von Allen beachtet werden sollte und bedaure,
daß der nachfolgende Redner es sofort hat über sich gewinnen
können, die Redewendung zu gebrauchen: er stehe nicht auf dem
Standpunkte, daß er jeder Regierung Vertrauen schenke. Das ist
eine Anknüpfung an Dinge, die gestern erörtert und völlig klargestellt worden sind; sie heute wieder hereinzuziehen, kann nur in der
Absicht geschehen sein, sich der verletzenden Ausdrücke nicht begeben
zu wollen. (Sehr richtig!) — Nun hören wir von Auer wie von
Vollmar, daß wir möglicherweise verfolgt werden, welcher Art
auch die Organisation sei, die wir uns geben; daß wir vor An-
fechtungen in keinem Falle ganz sicher sind. Andererseits steht fest,
daß wir, trotzdem uns jede Möglichkeit der Organisation fehlte,
uns nicht nur zusammengefunden, sondern auch zusammengehalten
und verstärkt haben. Sollen wir nun, um uns vor jeder Anfechtung
zu bewahren, jede Organisation bei Seite lassen, oder sollen wir
uns, nachdem wir dem Anschein nach wieder unter das gemeine
Recht gestellt sind, dementsprechend in irgend einer Weise organisiren?
Da meine ich, daß die ganz überwiegende Ansicht auf letzteres geht.
Auf die Form müssen wir freilich näher, bis ins Einzelne, eingehen,
denn gerade diese Frage ist es nothwendig, streng sachlich zu erörtern.
Es ist vorgeschlagen worden, der Partei vom Parteitag einen Vorstand von 20 Personen geben zu lassen, um allen Widerwärtigkeiten
zu entgehen. Thun wir etwas in dieser Richtung — nun, die
Tessendorff's sind noch nicht alle geworden; sie werden im Auslegen
erfinderisch sein und auch in der allerharmlosesten Form etwas
finden, was sie anfechten können. Ich meine deshalb, wir müssen
den Entwurf, wie er vorliegt, unter allen Umständen als Grundlage
in Betracht ziehen. Von den Einzelfragen ist die: ob dauernder
Beitrag oder nicht, auch in Berlin vielfach behandelt worden, man
ist aber darüber nicht zur Klarheit gekommen, weil sich Theori
und Praxis, Wünsche und Erfahrungen gegenüberstehen, so daß die
Kommission, für deren Einsetzung ich ganz entschieden bin, mit den
Erfahrungen, die auf diesem Gebiete bereits gemacht worden sind,
ganz besonders zu rechnen haben wird. Ich bin fest überzeugt,
wenn allseitig der gute Wille vorhanden ist, uns ein Band zu geben,

das möglichst den Wünschen Aller entspricht, dann ist auch der scheinbare Widerspruch gelöst, der in den Ausführungen Auer's gefunden wurde, daß wir uns eine Organisation geben müssen und daß wir doch wahrscheinlich vergeblich arbeiten. Ich empfehle die Wahl einer Kommission von ganz besonders erfahrenen Männern aus möglichst allen deutschen Staaten.

Theiß-Hamburg ersucht zur Geschäftsordnung, die nachfolgenden Redner möchten nicht auf provokatorische Aeußerungen des Vorredners derart, wie eben geschehen, eingehen. Man kenne doch Werner's Art und solle nicht auf seine Versuche, Jemandem eins auszuwischen, immer wieder anbeißen. Das Beste sei, ihn gar nicht zu beachten.

Vorsitzender Singer: Ich bin nicht im Stande, einem Redner, wenn er sonst sachlich ist, aus solchem Grunde das Wort zu entziehen.

Keßler-Bernburg: Ich schließe mich ebenfalls der Mahnung Vollmar's durchaus an und werde mich freuen, wenn die Diskussion ferner sachlich geführt wird. Ich werde den Frieden nicht brechen, aber: wie man in den Wald hineinschreit, schallt es auch wieder heraus. Ich möchte das preußische Vereinsrecht etwas näher beleuchten. Liebe Genossen! Dieses preußische Recht gilt für den größten deutschen Staat, und wenn es auch höchst reaktionär ist, so bietet es doch den großen Vortheil, daß dem polizeilichen Einschreiten ein richterlicher Spruch folgen muß. Wenn Tessendorff gesagt hat, er würde alle Vereine vernichten, wir könnten uns nicht organisiren, so haben wir den Kampf aufgenommen und gezeigt, daß es dennoch Formen giebt, in welchen man sich in Preußen organisiren kann, die für Staatsanwalt und Polizei völlig unangreifbar sind. Diese Formen sind aber in dem Entwurf nicht dargestellt; der Entwurf bietet vielmehr dem Vereinsgesetz die allergrößte Angriffsfläche dar. Ich habe mich darüber gewundert, da ich aus Auer's Worten vernahm, daß man mit einem solchen Entwurf schon früher ein sehr schlechtes Geschäft gemacht habe. Man hat aber in dem neuen Entwurf die Angriffsfläche des vorigen noch vergrößert. Ein Vergleich des § 1 des Gothaer und des jetzigen Entwurfs zeigt, daß im letzteren der Begriff eines Vereins noch viel deutlicher und bestimmter zum Ausdruck kommt. Mit Interesse habe ich von dem Beschlusse gehört, den der Kongreß von 1877 gefaßt hat, der darin gipfelte, überhaupt keine Organisation zu schaffen; ich bin fest überzeugt, wenn unsere diesmalige Kommission sachgemäß und ernst verfährt, wird sie auch zu keinem anderen Resultat kommen, denn die Verhältnisse sind ganz dieselben wie früher, wir stehen unter denselben Gesetzen und der gleichen Handhabung dieser Gesetze wie früher. Will man in Preußen eine Organisation gründen, dann muß man von vornherein wählen, ob eine politische oder eine unpolitische; eine gemischte Form giebt es nicht. Wählt man die unpolitische Form, so verzichtet man von vornherein darauf, politische Angelegenheiten in Versammlungen zu verhandeln; nimmt man die politische Form, dann kann man zwar verhandeln, was man will, aber was wie ein Verein aussieht oder durch Richterspruch dafür erklärt ist, darf unter keinen Umständen mit einem andern Verein in Verbindung treten. Wenn Werner meint, die Vereine könnten Gelder sammeln und an eine Central-stelle abliefern, so ist das ganz unmöglich; es würde sofort eine neue Vereinsbildung konstatirt werden und die Auflösung müßte erfolgen. Denn politische Vereine dürfen absolut nicht zu gemein-samen Zwecken, auch nicht einmal zu einer Fahnenweihe, in Ver-bindung treten. Nach dem Reichsgerichts-Erkenntniß vom 2. No-vember 1888 in dem großen Maurerprozeß ist die Kommission, die von einer größeren Versammlung gewählt ist, wenn diese letztere sich auflöst und die Kommission übrig bleibt, ein Verein; ein Vor-stand, den wir einsetzen, wäre eine solche Kommission, und man könnte nur fragen: Sind schon zwei eine Mehrheit oder erst drei? Wählen wir noch eine Kontrollkommission, heiße sie wie sie will, so ist das wieder ein Verein, treten beide in Verbindung, dann klappt die Falle zu; beide werden aufgelöst und sind dem Gesetz verfallen. So bleibt denn nur der Vorschlag des Berliner Entwurfs, mit dem ich sonst nicht einverstanden bin: eine größere Kommission zur Führung der Verwaltung, welche aus sich heraus einen Vor-stand für die Kommission wählt, der zugleich Parteivorstand ist. Es sind also sehr große Schwierigkeiten zu überwinden; in dieser Form geht es aber, wenn von allen Seiten klug und umsichtig ver-fahren wird. Ich bedauere, daß man die Sache immer von dem Gesichtspunkte betrachtet: wir würden in jedem Falle angefochten werden; gewiß, aber wir sollten diesem Pessimismus nicht Raum geben. In Sachsen und Bayern wird es so nicht durchzuführen sein, für Preußen aber läßt sich diese Form verwirklichen. — Im Einzelnen kann ich nur unterschreiben, was Vollmar gesagt hat. In die Fraktion setze ich kein Mißtrauen; wir können weder an der persönlichen Haltung der Einzelnen, noch an der prinzipiellen Haltung der Gesammtheit etwas aussetzen. Volle Preßfreiheit wünsche und vertrete auch ich. Die Kontrolle muß sich selbstredend auf alle von der Partei begründeten und verwalteten Blätter be-ziehen; die Auslegung Auers aber, wonach sogar ein einzelner Artikel schon zum Einschreiten Veranlassung gäbe, führt zur Auf-hebung jeder Preßfreiheit. Das wäre eine Präventivzensur, und — vestigia terrent! Wie gegen die Dresdener und Magdeburger Zeitungen verfahren ist, das hat mich abgeschreckt. Ich bitte Sie, die Preßfreiheit zu sichern.

Stolle-Gesau: Als wir in der Fraktion den Entwurf be-riethen, waren wir alle fest davon überzeugt, daß wir, wie er auch

ausfalle, nicht unangefochten bleiben würden. Es ist ja auch nur
natürlich, daß die Parteigenossen von überall her aus dem großen,
weiten Reich ihre besonderen Ansichten zur Geltung zu bringen
versuchen würden. Doch sind immerhin nicht viele prinzipielle
Aenderungen vorgeschlagen worden; die meisten der zahlreichen Anträge sind formeller Natur. Ueber die prinzipiellen haben die meisten
sächsischen Delegirten sich in einer Vorbesprechung geeinigt und
werden in deren Namen nur zwei Redner, Kaden und ich, sprechen.
Für uns in Sachsen, dem klassischen Staat der Polizeigesetze, der
klassischen Polizeiwillkür, ist die Gestaltung der Organisation von
der allergrößten Wichtigkeit, namentlich ist dies die Frage, wer in
Zukunft öffentlich der Partei als Genosse angehören darf. In
Sachsen besteht das Vereinsgesetz von 1849, welches nach der Nieder-
werfung der Revolution gemacht wurde und eigentlich ein Ausnahmegesetz in Permanenz ist. Wir stehen da viel schlechter als unter dem
Sozialistengesetz. In dem kurzen Zeitraum seit dem Verfall dieses
Gesetzes sind mehr Versammlungen verboten worden, als jemals
zuvor im gleichen Zeitraum. Wenn wir die Parteigenossenschaft
erlangen sollen, ohne Gefahr zu laufen, diesem Vereinsgesetz zu verfallen, so darf die Forderung der „dauernden" Unterstützung der
Partei nicht erhoben werden. Ich habe sie schon in der Fraktion
bekämpft und bin erfreut, daß der Vorstand nicht mehr darauf besteht. Auch in Anbetracht unserer ökonomischen Verhältnisse war
diese Forderung falsch. Ein großer Theil unserer armen, namentlich
der ländlichen Bevölkerung wird nicht in der Lage sein, dauernd
zahlen zu können. Aber nicht blos durch das Landesgesetz, sondern
vielfach auch durch lokale Gesetze jeder einzelnen Stadt, durch Polizei-
strafen ist es bei uns verboten, irgendwie einen Beitrag zu leisten.
So sind noch in den letzten Wochen Polizeiverfügungen erlassen
worden, welche bei 50 oder 100 Mark Strafe die Leistung eines
Beitrags oder die Abhaltung einer Tellersammlung verbieten, ja
welche das Darreichen von Almosen an Arme untersagen. Die
„dauernde" materielle Unterstützung wäre also für uns eine große
Gefahr, und wir beantragen daher einstimmig, sie zu streichen. —
Was den Wahlmodus betrifft, so kann doch im Ernst von der Verletzung des demokratischen Prinzips nicht die Rede sein. Wenn
noch die Verhältnisse in den großen und kleinen Städten und auf
dem Lande die gleichen wären! Zudem hat der Fraktionsvorschlag
agitatorisch den großen Vortheil, daß er die Möglichkeit erleichtert,
unsere Bestrebungen in die Kreise zu tragen, wohin die Kenntniß
von uns und unseren Zielen noch wenig gedrungen ist. Aus diesen
Kreisen, die noch im Dunkel liegen, am Rhein, in Bayern, im
preußischen Osten u. s. w., müssen die Parteigenossen möglichst zahlreich den Parteitag besuchen, um, zurückgekehrt, reichlicher den Samen
für unsere Parteiziele ausstreuen zu können. In Berlin, wo sich

Tausende in Folge der ökonomischen Verhältnisse selbst zu Sozial-demokraten ausbilden, kann man sich leicht selbst helfen, und man soll daher nicht sagen, es sei undemokratisch, wenn auch ein Wahl-kreis mit nur 70 oder 100 sozialdemokratischen Wählern einen Dele-girten schickt. — Die Kontrollfrage ist im Entwurf so geregelt, weil uns eben diese Polizeigesetze abhielten, einen selbständigen Kontroll-ausschuß einzusetzen. Bis heute hat man noch nicht versucht, eine parlamentarische Fraktionskontrolle unter das Vereinsgesetz zu stellen. Die Zweifel an der Objektivität dieser Kontrole muß ich energisch abweisen. Sind denn die gewählten Abgeordneten so miserable, schlechte Charaktere, daß sie bei Dingen, die ihre Person betreffen, eine Einwirkung auf ihre Kollegen versuchen werden, ihr eigenes über das Parteiinteresse stellen werden? — Was das Centralorgan betrifft, so sind wir nach allen Verhandlungen der Meinung, daß wir heute nicht mehr mit einem „Volksstaat" oder „Vorwärts" nach früherem Muster kommen können. Wir müssen auf die gestiegene Ausdehnung der Partei und auf die Nothwendigkeit der täglichen Vertretung und Vertheidigung ihrer Prinzipien den Gegnern gegen-über Rücksicht nehmen. Darum stimmen wir dem Fraktionsvorschlag zu. — Von den selbstständigen Anträgen müssen wir denjenigen einiger Berliner Genossen entschieden bekämpfen, der dahin geht: „Betreffs Aufstellung von Kandidaten zu einer Gesetzgebungs- oder Verwaltungs-Körperschaft haben die Parteigenossen der einzelnen Wahlkreise oder Orte die Zustimmung vom Vorstand einzu-holen." Womit wollen Sie denn den Parteivorstand noch belasten? Ich bin erstaunt, daß gerade von der Seite ein solcher Antrag ausgeht. Das heißt doch, den Genossen alle Bewegungsfreiheit nehmen; in diesem Punkte haben die Männer in Berlin, so Gutes sie geleistet haben, kein größeres Recht, als bei uns die kleinste Land-gemeinde. (Sehr gut! Bravo!) Ich halte dafür, daß der Parteitag den Antrag einstimmig ablehnen wird. (Beifall.)

Thierbach-Königsberg in der Neumark: Auch wir sind für Streichung des Wortes „dauernd;" seine Aufrechterhaltung ist unter den heutigen Verhältnissen ein Ding der Unmöglichkeit. Von vielen Seiten sind sonstige Aenderungen vorgeschlagen, von Berliner Kollegen ist sogar ein vollständiger Gegenentwurf eingebracht worden. Ich stehe, zumal nach Vollmars und Werner's Ausführungen, auf dem Standpunkte, daß wir uns in Acht nehmen müssen, mit dem preußischen Vereinsgesetz in Konflikt zu gerathen, daß wir nach dem Berliner Antrag einen einzigen Vorstand aus 20 oder 16 Personen einsetzen müssen. In der Kontrollfrage bin ich aber anderer Meinung; ich hege kein Mißtrauen gegen die Fraktion und kann die in dieser Richtung geäußerten Befürchtungen nicht theilen. Ursprünglich war auch ich gegen das „Volksblatt" als Centralorgan; nach reiflicher Ueberlegung aber meine ich, Berlin, das zugleich noch ein Wochen-

blatt besitzt, kann sehr wohl das „Volksblatt" den Genossen Deutschlands übergeben. Den Gewerkschaftsinteressen wird das Blatt
sicherlich Rechnung tragen; es wird gewiß vom 1. Januar 1891 ab
diesen Interessen eine Extrabeilage zur Verfügung stellen, auch wohl
eine Erweiterung der Redaktion vornehmen, um diese Interessen
weiter, wie bisher, zu pflegen. Mit dem Vorschlag einer Kommissions-
berathung bin ich einverstanden.

Schönfeld-Dresden: Auch ich gehöre zu den Bösewichtern,
die mit dem Organisationsentwurf nicht ganz einverstanden sind.
Hätte man diesem Entwurf Motive beigegeben, dann hätte die Kritik
nicht die Schärfe angenommen, die Auer beklagte.

Die Verpflichtung zur materiellen Unterstützung der Partei sollte
man als moralischen Zwang festlegen, nicht aber die Mitgliedschaft
von der dauernden materiellen Unterstützung abhängig machen.
Ich bin aber mit dieser Ansicht in Dresden nicht durchgedrungen,
die Dresdener beantragen nur, daß Erwerbslosigkeit von jener
Verpflichtung entbinden soll.

In Bezug auf die Zugehörigkeit zur Partei beantragen wir,
daß ehrlose Handlungen gegen die Partei von der Partei ausschließen. Wir können nicht das, was heute der bürgerlichen Moral
als ehrlos gilt, auch für uns reklamiren. Wenn z. B. Jemand aus
Noth ein Stück Brod stiehlt, so kann uns das noch nicht bestimmen,
den Mann von uns zu weisen.

Bezüglich der Vertretung auf dem Parteitag stimmen wir dem
von Vollmar in der „Münchener Post" vorgeschlagenen System der
proportionalen Vertretung zu.

Hinsichtlich der Kontrolle über die prinzipielle Haltung der
Parteiorgane können wir dem Entwurf nicht zustimmen. In Dresden
war bekanntlich ein Zeitungsstreit in der Frage des 1. Mai. Die
„Sächsische Arbeiterzeitung" stand auf dem Boden der Dresdener
Genossen und beharrte auf demselben, nachdem in Halle die Fraktion
einen anderen Standpunkt eingenommen. Da nun anzunehmen ist,
daß in einem solchen Falle der Parteivorstand, die Parteikontrolle,
eingreifen und das Blatt verpflichten würde, in ihrem Sinn zu
schreiben, so ist die Bestimmung für mich unannehmbar. Ich gestehe den Genossen am Ort zu, die Kontrolle über die Zeitungen
auszuüben, aber nicht dem Parteivorstande, weil dann eine gewisse
schablonenmäßige Schreibweise bei der Presse eintreten müßte.

Das „Berliner Volksblatt" zum Centralorgan zu wählen, halte
ich für verfehlt. Ein Lokalorgan darf nicht zugleich Centralorgan
sein. Die Genossen außerhalb Berlins müßten den ganzen Ballast
des „Volksblattes" mit in den Kauf nehmen. Es müßte ein selbst-
ständiges Centralorgan geschafft werden, in dem der Parteivorstand
seine Ansichten geltend machen könnte.

Dietz übernimmt den Vorsitz.

Stengele-Hamburg: Wir Hamburger wünschen, daß die Fraktion verpflichtet, nicht berechtigt ist, auf dem Parteitag zu erscheinen. Die Mittel hierzu werden sich in irgend einer Weise beschaffen lassen.

Das „Berliner Volksblatt" als Centralorgan würde der Lokalpresse der kleineren Städte Abbruch thun. Der lokale Theil des Volksblatts, mit seiner breiten Schilderung der Berliner persönlichen Streitigkeiten, ist für das übrige Deutschland von gar keinem Interesse, ja in gewissem Sinne sogar schädlich.

Wir in Hamburg II. beantragen weiter, daß, sofern gesetzliche Hindernisse nicht im Wege sind, ein Parteiausschuß an Stelle der jetzt normirten Kontrollkommission der Reichstagsfraktion gewählt werde. Wir wünschen also, daß die Kommission selbstständig gewählt werde, und nicht die Fraktion als solche eine besondere Kommission bilde. Die Aufgaben der Fraktion und der Kontrollkommission sind sehr verschieden. Was nun die vereinsgesetzlichen Bedenken betrifft, so hat seiner Zeit das Hamburger Oberlandesgericht entschieden, daß die Mitglieder einer solchen Kommission nicht als Verein zu betrachten sind. Hiernach würde also der Gründung einer selbstständigen Kommission nichts im Wege stehen.

Liefländer-Osthavelland: Die Auer'sche Rede hat mich im Allgemeinen sehr erfreut, denn sie hielt sich, im Gegensatz zu anderen Fraktionsgenossen, in sachlichen Grenzen, und war nicht geeignet andere Parteigenossen, wenigstens indirekt, zu beleidigen.

Mit dem Organisationsentwurf, wie er von der Fraktion vorgelegt worden ist, kann ich mich nicht einverstanden erklären. Die „Abänderungsanträge zum Organisationsentwurf" von den Berliner Genossen sind entschieden vorzuziehen. Der Ausdruck „Genossen" in § 1 ist jedenfalls präziser, als der Ausdruck „Personen". In Bezug auf die Wahlen zum Parteitag muß eine bestimmte Grenze gezogen werden, und es dürfen nicht, wie gesagt worden, aus den Kreisen beliebig viel Delegirte hergeschickt werden.

Die Opposition hat gar kein Mißtrauen zur Fraktion insgesammt; wir wünschen ihr nur nicht noch größere Macht zu übertragen, als sie heute inne hat, und das ist in dem Berliner Antrag ausgesprochen. Es kann kein Mißtrauen darin erblickt werden, wenn wir beantragen, der Parteitag solle die Besoldung der thätigen Mitglieder des Parteivorstandes festsetzen. Der Parteitag ist doch die höchste Instanz, und es würde Mißtrauen hervorrufen, wenn die Parteifraktion einseitig die Besoldungen festsetzte. Die Kritik hat nicht das Gehässige gehabt, was man ihr zuschreibt. Auer hat auf die gegnerische Presse hingewiesen. Ja, seit wann kümmern wir uns um die gegnerische Presse? Hat sie nicht die Reden verdreht, hat sie nicht die Reden Bebel's benutzt, um gegen uns Propaganda zu machen? Warum jetzt diese Empfindlichkeit,

früher ist doch viel schärfere Opposition gemacht worden! Wir sind
doch nicht hierhergekommen, um uns Süßigkeiten zu sagen! Grade
die Parteigenossen, die an der Spitze der Leitung stehen, und denen
wir eine höhere Intelligenz zuschreiben müssen, sollten nicht ihre
Meinung in einer die Opposition verletzenden Weise zum Ausdruck
bringen und dadurch zu neuer Opposition Anlaß geben. (Sehr
richtig!) Es bekundet einen schwachen Standpunkt und eine schwache
Intelligenz, wenn man auf den groben Klotz einen noch gröberen
Keil setzt; das ist nicht der Weg zum Frieden. Vollmar stimme ich
völlig bei. Er hat das ausgeführt, was die sogenannte Opposition
in Berlin ausgeführt hat. Die „Opposition" beschränkt sich nicht
auf Berlin. Nein, wir sind auch in der Umgegend von Berlin
derselben Ansicht. Wir verurtheilen es, wenn von Berlin gehässig
vorgegangen wird, aber auch, wenn das von der anderen Seite
geschieht. Eine Partei, welche die Toleranz auf ihre Fahne geschrieben, muß zunächst selbst tolerant sein.

Die Vereinigung möchten wir möglichst lose gestaltet haben.
Als früheres Mitglied des Allgemeinen deutschen Arbeitervereins
wäre ich für eine möglichst straffe Centralisirung; aber da jede derartige Organisation aufgelöst werden wird, so möchte ich mich für
die lokale Organisation erklären.

In Bezug auf die Presse kann ich der Fraktion als solcher kein
Kontrollrecht einräumen. Es kann aus der Mitte des Parteitages
sehr wohl eine Kommission bestellt werden. Außerdem wissen die
Genossen am Orte am besten über die Haltung ihrer eignen Presse
ein Urtheil zu fällen.

Für ein Centralorgan bin ich selbstredend; aber ich wünsche
nicht, daß es täglich erscheint. Ein dreimal wöchentlich erscheinendes
Blatt könnten auch die ärmeren Parteigenossen in Ostpreußen,
Schlesien und anderswo halten. Das „Volksblatt" ist auch viel zu
theuer, und die Genossen haben gar nicht die Zeit, den ganzen
Ballast zu lesen. Ich habe beantragt, daß, wenn ein Centralorgan
geschaffen wird, es wenigstens völlig Eigenthum der Partei wird,
damit der Profit des „Berliner Volksblatt" und der anderen
Berliner Parteiblätter und aus dem Druck der Broschüren, der sich
auf 100 000 Mark belaufen wird, und der den Privatdruckern in
die Tasche fließen würde, der Partei wieder zugute komme. Dieser
Antrag mag Manchem unangenehm sein, aber ich werde ihn nachher vertheidigen.

Wilschke-Berlin: In Bezug auf § 3 Absatz 2, wo es heißt:
„Insofern der Wahlkreis durch einen Ort oder durch Theile eines
Ortes gebildet wird, ist nur ein Vertrauensmann zu wählen,"
wünschen meine Auftraggeber, daß in der Regel nur ein Ver-
trauensmann gewählt wird, je nach Lage und Stärke des Wahlkreises.
Im übrigen glaubt Redner, daß es genügte, wenn zu den

10

Parteitagen aus jedem Kreise ein Delegirter käme. Als Centralorgan erscheint ihm das „Volksblatt" nicht geeignet; wird es aber
doch dazu genommen, dann müsse es so billig als möglich abgegeben
werden.

Klein-Berlin: Als Parteigenosse sollte Jeder gelten, der das
Parteiprogramm anerkennt. Der Unterschied zwischen organisirten
und nicht organisirten Parteigenossen ist schwer durchzuführen. Bei
der Streikbewegung haben wir auch die unorganisirten Kollegen
mit in den Kauf nehmen müssen.

In Rücksicht auf die Vereinsgesetze giebt Redner anheim, ob es
nicht zweckmäßig wäre, sich eine ganz lose Organisation, nach Art
der einzelnen Gewerkschaften mit dem Vertrauensmännersystem, zu
geben. Die Einberufung eines außerordentlichen Parteitages sollte
man nicht allzu leicht, aber auch nicht zu schwierig machen.

Schmidt-Berlin: Die Bedenken Vollmar's gegen das Vertrauensmännersystem werfen, wenn sie berechtigt sind, die vorgeschlagene Form der Organisation über den Haufen.

Die Wahl einer besonderen Kontroll-Kommission ist nach den
Keßler'schen Ausführungen absolut unmöglich. In dieser Beziehung
bietet der Berliner Antrag auch dem sophistischsten Staatsanwalt
nicht die geringste Angriffsfläche dar. Stolle hat gesagt, die Erfahrung
habe uns bisher belehrt, daß Kommissionen, welche von der Fraktion
einer Partei eingesetzt werden, nicht als politische Vereine angesehen
werden und daß auch nicht die Gefahr bestehe, daß, wenn sie mit
einander in Verbindung treten, sie mit dem Vereinsgesetz kollidiren.
Wir müssen aber bedenken, daß die Sozialdemokratie bisher eine
solche Institution nicht gehabt hat, und die Erfahrung von anderer
Seite beweist für uns nichts. Was dem einen erlaubt, ist dem andern
verboten; das zeigt unsere Gewerkschaftsbewegung im Vergleich zur
Innungsbewegung und den sonstigen Unternehmerverbänden. Diese
können sich zusammenthun in Kongressen, Vereinen und Korporationen
und politische Angelegenheiten erörtern, wir nicht.

Die von uns vorgeschlagene und von Stolle angefochtene Bestimmung, daß der Vorstand befugt sein soll über die aufgestellten
Kandidaturen in den Kreisen ein Urtheil abzugeben, ist keineswegs
überflüssig und kleinlich. Die Genossen am Ort können nicht immer
wissen, ob der aufgestellte Kandidat auch das Vertrauen der Partei
verdient und ob er schon etwas für die Partei gethan hat. Bei
den Berliner Stadtverordnetenwahlen war Kandidatenmangel, und
es sollte ein Holzhändler als Kandidat aufgestellt werden, der nicht
einmal unser Programm anerkannte. So etwas muß vermieden
werden.

Der Wahl des „Berliner Volksblatt" zum Centralorgan haben
wir keine Veranlassung entgegenzutreten. Die Genossen in der
Provinz haben ja nicht die Verpflichtung, auf das Volksblatt zu

abonniren. Die Provinzialblätter können einfach sagen, der Parteivorstand hat im Centralorgan das und das veröffentlicht.

Es wird Schluß der Diskussion beantragt, aber abgelehnt.

Von einer Seite wird zur Geschäftsordnung bemerkt, es hätten
schon 5—6 Berliner Genossen gesprochen, ohne weitere Momente
anzuführen.

Vorsitzender Singer: Ich für meine Geschäftsführung kenne
weder Berliner, noch andere lokale Genossen, sondern nur Mitglieder des sozialdemokratischen Parteitages. (Sehr richtig!) Jeder hat
dasselbe Recht und kommt in der Reihenfolge zum Wort, in der
er sich gemeldet hat.

Faber-Frankfurt-Lebus: Die Berliner haben sich 5- bis 6mal
zu demselben Thema geäußert. Die einzelnen Kreise sollten sich
verständigen und nur einen Redner wählen.

Vorsitzender: Darüber können wir hier doch unmöglich beschließen!

Jochem-Danzig: Ich bin der Ansicht, daß eine feste Organisation nicht geschaffen werden kann. Der Entwurf hat auf mich
den Eindruck gemacht, als wenn er ein Statut eines Vereins wäre.
Die sozialdemokratische Partei ist so mächtig, daß sie auch ohne
eine eiserne Form bestehen kann. So war es nach dem Freiberger
Prozeß und warum nicht nach dem Fall des Sozialistengesetzes?
Soll aber eine feste Organisation geschaffen werden, so beantrage
ich zu § 1, daß Jeder Parteigenosse ist, der für die Partei thätig
ist. Die Parteigenossen werden zahlen, ob das hier steht oder nicht.
In Bezug auf die Vertretung zum Parteitag bin ich für das Proportionalsystem. Was das Parteiorgan betrifft, so habe ich mich
durch die Gründe Auer's für das „Berliner Volksblatt" umstimmen
lassen. Ein eigenes Centralorgan würde keine hohe Abonnentenzahl
haben und nicht gelesen werden. Ein Organ auch für Ost- und
Westpreußen zu schaffen, wäre falsch. Ein Parteiorgan soll keine
Agitationsschrift, sondern eine Zeitschrift sein, welche die Genossen
auf dem Laufenden erhält.

Randt-Rostock: Wir in unserer engeren Heimath können von
dieser ganzen Organisation absolut keinen Gebrauch machen, abgesehen vielleicht vom Parteivorstand. Indessen, ich spreche hier
auch für die Allgemeinheit; da meine ich, daß in § 1 unbedingt die
dauernden Beiträge wegfallen müssen. Wer einen bestimmten
Beitrag zahlt, muß nothwendiger Weise gebucht werden, und daraus
würde der Staatsanwalt mit Leichtigkeit die Existenz eines Vereins
konstruiren.

Redner schildert nun die bekannten politischen Zustände Mecklen-
burgs und erklärt, so pessimistisch geworden zu sein, daß es ihn
nicht mehr wundern würde, wenn er es eines Tages erleben sollte,
daß die Staatsanwaltschaft eine einzelne Person für einen politischen

10*

Verein hält. (Oh!) In der Interpretation und Konstruktion sind die Herren sehr findig, dagegen sind wir Kinder. Deshalb theile ich Auer's Meinung, daß uns alles zu Schanden gemacht werden wird.

Wir haben den Organisationsentwurf nicht in öffentlichen Versammlungen berathen können, wie Sie, sondern nur privatim. Wir haben uns aber dahin geeinigt, daß es nicht gut ist, das „Berliner Volksblatt" als Centralorgan zu wählen. Ein solches Organ ist uns zu theuer; auch interessirt es uns nicht, zu erfahren, was der Schuhmacher Müller oder der Schneider Schulze in einer Berliner Versammlung geredet haben. Meine Freunde sind für ein wöchentlich dreimal erscheinendes, neues Centralorgan.

Meyer-Frankfurt a. M.: Ohne eine Organisation werden wir zu unseren Wählern nicht zurückkehren dürfen. Der vorliegende Entwurf ist aufgebaut auf dem System der Vertrauensmänner. Obgleich ich nun allen Respekt vor der Findigkeit der preußischen Staatsanwälte habe, so gestehe ich, daß es mir bis dato nicht vorgekommen ist, daß ein Vertrauensmann als politischer Verein erklärt worden ist. Ich bin also im Prinzip für den Entwurf. Das Wort „dauernd" im § 1 muß gestrichen werden. Weiter bin ich dafür, daß die Einberufung des Parteitages, mit Rücksicht auf die ländlichen Kreise, nicht vier, sondern sechs Wochen vor der Abhaltung des Parteitages im Parteiorgan publizirt werden muß. Gegen ein täglich erscheinendes Centralorgan ließe sich nichts einwenden, man wird aber neben demselben nicht noch ein Lokalblatt halten können, und insofern würde allerdings die Lokalpresse verdrängt werden. Niemand von uns will den Berliner Lokalklatsch lesen, der kann vollständig in Berlin bleiben. Wird aber das „Volksblatt" gewählt, so mag es in einem Bogen für die Provinz erscheinen, das Uebrige aber kann in Berlin bleiben.

Emmel-Aschaffenburg: Ich bin mit der Ausführung des Vorredners einverstanden. Nachdem wir wieder dasselbe Recht haben, wie die anderen Parteien, müssen wir auch danach trachten, möglichst ähnliche Organisationen, wie die Gegner sie haben, für uns zu schaffen. Wird uns dies verwehrt, so gewinnen wir der Regierung gegenüber ein Agitationsmittel, welches wir nicht unterschätzen dürfen. Ohne Organisation werden dann unsere Genossen mehr leisten, als mit einer solchen, denn sie werden sich enger zusammenschließen. Aber der Versuch muß wenigstens gemacht werden. Ich bin für die Fraktion als Kontrollkommission. Ein Ausschuß, in einer Stadt gewählt, würde viel parteiischer sein als die Fraktion, deren Mitglieder über ganz Deutschland verbreitet wohnen. Dazu kommt, daß die Fraktion, nach dem Vereinsgesetz, noch nicht als Verein gilt und einen großen Theil des Jahres in Berlin zusammen ist. Am Besten wäre es wohl, wenn die Presse Eigenthum der

Partei würde. Ich fürchte aber nicht, daß die Fraktionsmitglieder, selbst wenn sie Leiter von Blättern sind, aus persönlichen Gründen, in ungerechtfertigter Weise, gegen ein Blatt vorgehen würden. Gegen ein solches Gebahren würde sich sofort eine Opposition erheben und ein außerordentlicher Parteitag einberufen werden. Ich habe keine Furcht, daß die Fraktion diktatorisch handeln könnte; denn nicht die leeren Formen machen die Demokratie aus, sondern der Geist der Demokratie, der in uns Allen lebt, muß den Ausschlag geben. (Bravo!) Das Centralorgan muß billig sein und möglichst verbreitet werden. Es wäre am einfachsten, wenn nur das Hauptblatt zu einem niedrigeren Preise nach außerhalb verschickt würde, die Berliner können auf die lokale Beilage besonders abonniren.

Schibolsky-Niederbarnim: Wir bitten Sie, dem zweiten Passus des § 4 folgende Fassung zu geben:

Die Vertrauensmänner haben ihre Wahl, mit Angabe ihrer genauen Adresse, sofort dem Parteivorstande mitzutheilen; in denjenigen Wahlkreisen, wo mehrere Vertrauensmänner in verschiedenen Orten gewählt werden, haben die gesammten Vertrauensmänner des Kreises aus ihrer Mitte einen Obmann zu wählen, der seine Adresse an den Parteivorstand abgiebt.

Die Debatte wird abgebrochen.

Bebel macht Vorschläge über die in die 25er Kommission zu wählenden Personen. Zunächst müßten alle diejenigen Richtungen in der Kommission vertreten sein, die hier während der Debatte ihre abweichenden Ansichten vertreten haben. Zweitens müßte Rücksicht genommen werden auf die verschiedenen Gegenden und Provinzen Deutschlands. Drittens müßten solche Personen gewählt werden, die auf Grund ihrer bisherigen Thätigkeit mit dem Organisationswesen genau vertraut sind. Viertens gehören in die Kommission einige Mitglieder der Fraktion, die theils durch ihre persönliche Stellung bei der Berathung in der Fraktion selbst, theils, wie Vollmar, außerhalb derselben sich veranlaßt sahen, gegen den Entwurf Stellung zu nehmen. In der Fraktion selbst — ich verrathe kein Geheimniß — standen sich Auer und meine Person in wesentlichen Dingen und Anschauungen gegenüber. — Bebel schlägt nun fünfundzwanzig Namen vor, darunter drei Abgeordnete.

Außerdem werden noch weitere Namen vorgeschlagen.

Ein Antrag von Zubeil-Berlin, die Bebel'sche Liste en bloc anzunehmen, wird abgelehnt, nachdem Stolle darauf hingewiesen, daß damit die freie Willensmeinung der Abstimmenden beschränkt wird.

Auerbach wünscht, daß in die Kommission auch eine Frau, zum Beispiel Frau Ihrer, gewählt werde.

Die Wahl der Kommission wird nach dem Vorschlage des Vorsitzenden in derselben Weise, wie bei der Neunerkommission morgen, vor Beginn der Sitzung, durch Stimmzettel erfolgen. Der Vorsitzende theilt schließlich auf Befragen mit, daß Dr. Rübt vom Bureau nicht beauftragt worden sei, auf dem Kommerse im Namen der Partei zu sprechen.

Schluß 1 Uhr 26 Minuten.

Nachmittagssitzung.

3¾ Uhr. — Den Vorsitz führt Dietz.

Vor der Tagesordnung berichtet:

Pfannkuch, als Referent der Mandat-Prüfungskommission, über das Ergebniß der nochmaligen Prüfung der Krefelder Mandate. Die Kommission beantragt, das Mandat von Carl Wesch, der als alleiniger Kandidat gewählt ist, für giltig anzuerkennen, dagegen das des Genossen Lichtenberg, der in einer fünf Tage späteren Besprechung etlicher Genossen mit der Vertretung der Krefelder betraut worden ist, für ungiltig zu erklären.

Ohne Debatte wird demgemäß beschlossen. Darauf setzt der Parteitag die Generaldiskussion über den Organisations-entwurf fort.

Gottschalk-Hamburg: Die Hamburger glauben darauf be-harren zu müssen, daß ein dauernder Beitrag durchaus nothwendig ist, um die Zugehörigkeit zur Partei zu verbürgen. Wenn die Partei als solche prosperiren soll, muß sie Geld haben, und das kann sie doch nicht aus dem Aermel schütteln, es kann auch nicht von Einzelnen hergegeben werden. Was die Vertretung auf dem Partei-tag anbetrifft, so würden die Hamburger auch mit zwei Delegirten zufrieden sein, da es für die Propaganda jedenfalls förderlicher ist, wenn die ländlichen Wahlkreise möglichst viel Vertreter entsenden. (Sehr gut!) Nehmen Sie auf 5000 Wähler einen Delegirten, dann würde Berlin deren 34 zu stellen haben. Was würde das der Partei nützen? Aus derselben Erwägung haben die Hamburger auch prinzipiell keine Abgeordneten gewählt; die Abgeordneten aber besitzen selbstverständlich unser Vertrauen nach wie vor. Wenn 15 Wahlkreise, oder die Unterschriften von 10 000 Parteigenossen als Voraussetzung für die Berufung eines außerordentlichen Parteitages hingestellt werden, so entsteht doch die Frage, wie sollen diese Unterschriften kontrollirt werden? Das ist einfach ein Unding. Die 15 Wahlkreise können ja bleiben, die Zahl ist besser als sechs oder sieben, wodurch es die Berliner leicht haben würden, einen Extraparteitag für sich einberufen zu lassen; die Bedingung der 10 000 Unterschriften aber wäre zu streichen. Daß der Parteitag die Höhe der Gehälter des Vorstandes festsetzt, wie die Berliner

Genossen beantragen, halten wir für unmöglich; das muß dem Ausschuß oder der Fraktion überlassen bleiben, die doch erst kontrolliren müssen, was für Arbeit erwächst. Dieser Parteitag kann das nicht übersehen; der nächste würde schon wenigstens annähernd dazu in der Lage sein. Die Kontrolle der Presse nehmen wir unbedingt für die Parteigenossen am Orte in Anspruch; im Falle einer Streitigkeit, ist der Ausschuß zur Entscheidung heranzuziehen. Einen solchen Ausschuß befürworten wir, und nicht etwa aus Mißtrauen gegen die Fraktion. Wir sind der Meinung, daß das Mißtrauen garnicht erst geweckt werden soll, daß wir die Fraktion vor solchen Anschuldigungen, inkorrekt zu handeln und dergleichen, bewahren müssen. Sonst sind wir eventuell auch dafür, daß der Vorschlag auf Einsetzung eines einzigen Ausschusses von zwanzig Personen mit einer aus sich heraus gewählten Exekutive von fünf Personen angenommen wird; wenn die fünfzehn andern, die kontrollirenden, zum Theil der Fraktion, zum Theil den Genossen des Parteitages entnommen werden, dann ist die Sache vollständig und glücklich geregelt. Der Vertrauensmännerfrage sollte nicht solches Gewicht beigelegt werden. Ein in öffentlicher Versammlung gewählter Vertrauensmann kann als Person mit anderen Personen in Verbindung stehen, da ist keine geheime Verbindung festzustellen; er kann auch Agitation treiben, ohne der Geheimbündelei beschuldigt zu werden. Die Organisation muß so eingerichtet sein, daß es auch möglich bleibt, sie aufrecht zu erhalten; darum sollten wir Genossinnen nicht aufnehmen, weil das gegen das preußische Vereinsgesetz verstößt.

Theiß-Hamburg: In meiner Stellung zum Organisationsplan haben mir meine Schleswiger Mandanten völlige Freiheit gelassen; meine Ausführungen dazu mache ich auf Grund der von mir gesammelten Erfahrungen. Die gegen den Entwurf lautgewordene abfällige Kritik ist mir von allem Anfang an ziemlich überflüssig erschienen, da doch bei allen darüber stattgehabten Diskussionen die Für- und Gegengründe nicht so eingehend untersucht werden konnten, als hier, wo uns Auer's Vortrag erst das vollständige Material zur Verfügung gestellt hat. Danach haben sich auch meine Anschauungen in manchen Punkten berichtigt. In einem Hauptpunkte aber muß ich bei meiner Meinung bleiben; ich halte nach wie vor für ganz verkehrt, daß, wie bisher, die Fraktion die Parteileitung haben soll. Es ist für die Zukunft die ganz spezielle Aufgabe unserer Fraktion, sozial-reformatorisch im Reichstag vorzugehen; darauf wird sie ihre ganze Kraft zu verwenden und gar keine Zeit haben, auch noch das Kontrollamt mit zu versehen. Redner acceptirt den Berliner Vorschlag über die Bildung des Partei-Vorstandes, verlangt aber volle Organisationsfreiheit für die einzelnen Kreise. In Bezug auf die Parteipresse tritt er den Ausführungen des Referenten bei, und giebt er dem Wunsche Ausdruck, daß die offiziellen Wochenblätter sich in Zukunft nicht mehr die Abonnenten wegzufischen suchen.

Auerbach-Berlin (zur Geschäftsordnung): schlägt vor, den Vormittags abgelehnten Vorschlag: Bebels Liste für die 25 er Kommission en bloc anzunehmen, nun doch zu acceptiren, da im andern Fall, das Wahlresultat erst Sonnabend festgestellt werden könne und die Verhandlungen sich bis in die nächste Woche hineinziehen würden. Nach kurzer Debatte für und wieder stellt der Vorsitzende Dietz die Unterstützungsfrage. Der Antrag wird genügend unterstützt und nachdem an Stelle der zurücktretenden Genossen Ehrhardt und Woldersky, die Frau Ihrer und Kandt-Rostock auf die Liste gesetzt sind, diese, entsprechend dem Antrag Auerbach, nun mit großer Mehrheit angenommen.

Der Vorsitzende theilt noch mit, daß auch Genosse Tölcke für die Kommission vorgeschlagen worden wäre, wenn man nicht bedacht hätte, daß dem alten Herrn die Anstrengung nicht gut thun würde. Tölcke werde aber eingeladen werden, der Kommission mit Rath und That, soweit angänglich, zur Seite zu stehen. (Bravo!)

Hierauf wird die unterbrochene Debatte wieder aufgenommen.

Schweer-Hamburg: Das Centralorgan muß ein täglich erscheinendes Blatt sein. Ich fürchte nicht, daß es deßwegen den Lokalblättern Konkurrenz machen wird. Erscheint es blos ein- oder zweimal in der Woche, so wäre der materielle Erfolg jedenfalls zweifelhaft und die Nothwendigkeit von Zuschüssen aus der Parteikasse wahrscheinlich. — Mein Wahlkreis hat mich beauftragt, hier dafür einzutreten, daß die Gehälter der festbesoldeten Vorstandsmitglieder vom Parteitag festgesetzt werden, nicht vom Parteivorstande. Man soll allen unangenehmen Eventualitäten aus dem Wege gehen; man soll nicht die Möglichkeit zulassen, daß gesagt werde, der Vorstand habe sich eine gute Besoldung angedeihen lassen. Auch dagegen müssen wir uns aussprechen, daß die Delegirten aus der Parteikasse Diäten beziehen sollen, wie beantragt ist; wir meinen, die Kosten für die Delegirten sollen einzig und allein von ihren Wahlkreisen aufgebracht werden.

Es sind 4 Schlußanträge eingegangen.

Liebknecht gegen den Schluß: Ich bitte Sie dringend, den Antrag abzulehnen. Der Entwurf ist schon vor Monaten vorgelegt worden, er ist in der Presse eingehend kritisirt worden; alle dort vorgebrachten Punkte müssen auch hier erörtert werden. Es ist behauptet worden, die Majorität, oder der Vorstand, wolle die Minorität vergewaltigen. Darum erst recht ist es nothwendig, daß Jeder zum Worte kommt, der an diesem Entwurf etwas auszustellen hat; denn es handelt sich hier um etwas, was auf längere Zeit für uns Gesetz sein soll. Ich warne davor, durch die Annahme des Schlußantrages auch nur den Schein zu erwecken, als wollten Sie die Minorität vergewaltigen. Glauben Sie nicht, daß durch den Schluß die Debatte abgekürzt wird. Diejenigen, denen das Wort jetzt abgeschnitten wird, werden alles versuchen, später doch mit ihrer Meinung zum Worte zu kommen, und es wird bei ihnen ein Gefühl der Unbefriedigtheit zurückbleiben. Lassen Sie es nicht dazu kommen. Die Kommission kann ja glücklicherweise schon heute zusammentreten und die Arbeiten des Kongresses werden dann bis zum Ende der Woche erledigt sein.

Meister-Hannover für den Schluß: Man scheint doch ein rascheres Tempo zu wollen. Schließen wir nicht, so bekommen wir doch alle diese Reden nachher bei der Berathung des Kommissions-berichtes noch einmal. Von einer Vergewaltigung wird man nicht sprechen können.

Der Schluß der Diskussion wird mit großer Mehrheit angenommen.

Das Schlußwort erhält

Referent Auer: Dem Wunsche, daß wir uns bei unseren Verhandlungen größerer Objektivität befleißigen möchten, schließe ich mich aus vollem Herzen an; auch meine Sache ist es nicht, Gegensätze besonders herauszukehren und was uns versöhnt und bindet zurückzudrängen. Wie aber die Dinge gekommen sind, nachdem man seit Wochen und Monaten die Verfasser des Entwurfs in der rücksichtslosesten Weise angegriffen hat, dürfen sie dem Referenten es nicht verdenken, wenn er sich dagegen im Namen der Verfasser vertheidigte. Ich bin für durchaus sachliche, von jeder Gehässigkeit freie Verhandlung. Schlägt man mir gegenüber aber einen anderen Ton an, wie es thatsächlich geschehen ist, dann halte ich es damit, daß die beste Deckung der Hieb ist, und setze auf einen Schelmen anderthalbe! So habe ich dieses Mal gehandelt, so gedenke ich es auch in Zukunft zu halten. Liefländer beanstandete, daß ich einen Satz aus der gegnerischen Presse zitirt hätte, und meinte, was kümmern uns die Gegner. Gerade die Gegner in dieser Frage unter unseren Parteigenossen haben aber zuerst die gehässigsten Urtheile aus der gegnerischen Presse in ihre Organe aufgenommen, um zu zeigen, wie gefährlich der Vorschlag sei. Aber auch unsere eigene Presse hat Leistungen aufzuweisen, die weit über das erlaubte Maaß der Kritik unter Genossen hinausgingen. Ich bringe dafür einen ganz kurzen Beleg. Der Punkt wegen Festsetzung der Höhe der Gehälter ist doch gewiß so nebensächlich wie nur etwas; und gerade in diesem Punkte wurden die gehässigsten Angriffe laut und zwar gegen Personen, welche durch ihr ganzes Thun und Handeln über jeden Verdacht nach dieser Richtung hin erhaben sein sollten. Die „Dresdener Arbeiter-Zeitung" enthielt in ihrer Nummer 102 vom 24. August einen „Der Organisationsentwurf" überschriebenen Artikel, in dem gegen Bebel polemisirt wird. Da heißt es: „Wird

Herr Bebel es nicht zugeben, daß es für die Wirkung vollständig gleichgiltig ist, ob das Geld, über das man im Uebrigen frei verfügen darf, einem selbst oder Jemand anderem gehört? Besonders überzeugend klingt so etwas nicht, und dieses Rechthabenwollen um jeden Preis ist nur geeignet, einem Betrachtungen nahezulegen, wie etwa: Was wohl die Herren der Fraktion veranlaßt, sich an Rechte und Befugnisse, trotzdem sie ihnen, wie Auer sagt, selbst nicht angenehm sind, so krampfhaft anzuklammern." Dieser Satz stand, wie gesagt, in einem parteigenössischen Blatte. Er ist aber so gehässig, und unterstellt so ordinäre Motive für unser Handeln, daß der bösartigste Gegner ihn nicht schlimmer hätte schreiben können. Dagegen muß man sich doch wohl wehren. Schönfeld, der dem Blatte ja nahe gestanden hat, stimmt gewiß diesem Satze auch nicht zu. Dieser Genosse meinte, wenn die Fraktion zu dem Entwurf Motive veröffentlicht hätte, so wäre manches Schlimme unterblieben. Dem gegenüber möchte ich die Frage stellen: wenn es den kritisirenden Genossen wirklich nur um Aufklärung zu thun war, warum haben sie sich dann nicht bei den paar Leuten, auf denen seit Jahren die ganze Arbeit der Parteileitung lastet, nach den Motiven erkundigt, bevor sie diese beleidigenden Angriffe losließen? Solchen Vorwurf hat der Genosse Bebel wirklich am allerwenigsten verdient. Andere die Arbeit machen lassen, schwierigen Entscheidungen aus dem Wege zu gehen und dann vom „demokratischen" Kothurn herab den Kritiker spielen, das ist sehr billig. — Sie wissen, was die Gegner daraus gemacht haben; aus unseren Reihen selbst, ist, wenn auch ohne Absicht, der gegnerischen Presse das Material geliefert worden, von der Spaltung, von „Alten" und „Jungen," und all dem übrigen Unsinn zu reden.

Auf das Weitere gehe ich nicht ein; ich wünsche, daß die persönlichen Kämpfe beseitigt sind. Ich werde immer objektiv sein, wenn ich objektiv kritisirt werde; ich kann aber, wenn es mir nothwendig scheint und die Umstände es erfordern, so saugrob sein, wie irgend Einer. (Heiterkeit.) Dem Genossen Keßler, der sich wunderte, warum der Entwurf, trotz unserer Erfahrungen, gerade so ausgefallen sei, antworte ich: Weil erst diese Verhandlung hier vorausgehen mußte, ehe die Partei, die eine große Masse junger, mit den früheren Vorgängen unbekannter Elemente unter sich hat, sich schlüssig machen kann. Wir mußten uns erst im persönlichen Meinungsaustausch gegenseitig überzeugen, daß dies oder jenes nicht geht, was in den einzelnen Köpfen spukt. Das ist der Grund dafür. Die meisten von uns haben sich darüber nicht getäuscht, daß der Entwurf so, wie er ist, nicht angenommen werden kann. Hätten wir aber den Entwurf nach Keßler's Wunsch gestaltet und vorgelegt, dann hätte ich erst einmal die Kritik hören mögen! In Bezug auf die Partei-beiträge sprach Stolle von Idealen, welche zur Bezahlung der Parteiagitation keinen Kurs haben. Er dachte dabei gewiß an das Wort des famosen Ritters Ofenheim von Pont Euxin: „Mit Idealen baut man keine Eisenbahnen!" Womit ja Beide auch ganz recht haben.

Wegen des Centralorgans seien Sie ganz ruhig. Sie werden doch dahin kommen, es so zu machen, wie es der Entwurf vorschlägt; es ist der Zwang der Thatsachen, was uns dahin bringt. Wir können das Centralorgan nicht wieder herstellen nach früherer Weise, es sei denn, daß wir einen großen Theil unserer Parteigelder zur Deckung des Defizits verwenden wollen. Hamburg ist ja zweifellos der kräftigste Parteiort, den wir haben, er war es auch schon vor dem Sozialistengesetz. Und in demselben Hamburg, das einen relativ gut genährten und bezahlten Arbeiterstand hat, wo die Arbeiter auch wirklich etwas für ihre Partei hingeben, das 22 000 Abonnenten für sein Lokalblatt hatte, wo die Genossen stets auf der Centralisation und auf der Nothwendigkeit eines Centralorgans bestanden, in diesem Hamburg hatte der „Vorwärts" in den zwei Jahren vor dem Sozialistengesetz einen fortgesetzten Rückgang zu verzeichnen. (Hört, hört!) Wollen Sie ein neues Centralorgan, das etwas anderes ist als die Wochenblätter, die wir schon besitzen, wollen Sie etwas Gediegenes und nur halbwegs den Wünschen der Genossen Entsprechendes — und wir dürfen doch keinen Schofel herausgeben —, dann kostet uns ein derartiges Organ solche Summen, daß Sie im nächsten Jahre, wenn wir die Rechnung vorlegen, sagen werden: Um Gotteswillen, bringt das Centralorgan wieder bei Seite! Niemand hat ein Interesse daran, es nicht zu schaffen; aber die Erfahrung lehrt: die Lokalpresse wird die große Zahl der Abonnenten haben und nur hier und da würde auch das Centralorgan gehalten werden. Werner sagte, die Berliner würden über das ihnen anzuthuende Unrecht raisonniren. Ja, das liegt bei uns im Blute. Vor dem Sozialistengesetz war es auch schon so: In Hamburg raisonnirte man auf das Lokalblatt und rühmte die „Berliner Freie Presse"; das sei ein Blatt, das habe Schneid und Courage; kam man aber nach Berlin, so hieß es dort: Ach, die „Freie Presse", die hat zuviel Mängel, aber seht Euch mal das „Hamburg-Altonaer Volksblatt" an, da liegt was drin! (Heiterkeit.) Als dann aber das Sozialistengesetz kam und beide Blätter verboten wurden, hätte man wohl zufrieden sein mögen, das eine oder das andere noch zu haben. Also mit dem Raisonniren auf die Blätter ist es nicht so gefährlich, wir thun das alle gern ein bischen, und es schadet auch nicht, denn es zeugt von Interesse an den Preßorganen. Im Uebrigen werden die Berliner Genossen voll und ganz zu ihrem Rechte kommen, soweit das Blatt für sie Lokalorgan ist und bleiben wird.

Thatsächlich muß ich noch den Genossen Liefländer berichtigen. Er sprach von großen Summen, welche das „Berliner Volksblatt" für den Drucker Profit abwirft, er nannte 100 000 Mark. Das ist nicht wahr. Das Blatt hat schon immer der Partei recht gute Dienste gethan, seitdem es Ueberschüsse hat. Aber bis zur Einführung der Rotationsmaschine hat es nur ca. 10 000 Abonnenten gehabt; von diesen war die Gesammteinnahme ca. 110 000 Mark, dazu 20 000 Mark an Annoncen, macht 130 000 Mark. Daß man dabei nicht 100 000 Mark Profit machen kann, liegt auf der Hand. Uebrigens möge sich Herr Liefländer beruhigen; setzt soll bei uns kein Buchdrucker werden. In Bezug auf seinen Vorschlag auf Gründung einer Genossenschaftsdruckerei will ich bemerken: Die alten Genossen, die bei unseren Genossenschaftsdruckereien ihre Erfahrungen gemacht haben, werden ein wenig Respekt vor der Gründung einer neuen besitzen. Wenn es am Platze ist, gründen wir wieder eine, aber so pressirt's nicht; ich habe auch noch immer Antheilscheine, welche nicht bezahlt sind. (Heiterkeit.)

Bezüglich der Kontrolle der prinzipiellen Haltung der Presse haben mich Vollmar und Keßler mißverstanden, wenn sie ausführen, nach meiner Darlegung solle schon ein einziger Artikel oppositioneller Natur genügen, diese Bestimmung in Kraft zu setzen. Ich habe sagen wollen: Es kann sehr wohl Blätter geben, die sich sogar radikaler aufspielen als unsere übrige Presse, und von denen wir alle trotzdem überzeugt sind, daß die Art und Weise, wie solche Organe wirken, der Partei schadet, und daß dieses radikale Gebahren von einer Seite und aus Gründen betrieben wird, vor denen wir alle Ursache haben, uns zu bewahren. Ich könnte Beispiele davon geben sowohl vor als unter dem Sozialistengesetz. Hier müssen wir vorkehren. Und so schlimm ist es doch mit meinem Despotismus auch nicht; ich verlange nicht im geringsten, der Parteivorstand solle den Censor spielen über die Presse; das ist einfach ausgeschlossen, wir würden dann ein halbes Dutzend Censoren brauchen. Aber erinnern Sie sich z. B. an die „Rothe Fahne" Hasselmann's. Ist sie denn nicht zu dem Zweck ins Leben gerufen worden, um den Mittelpunkt abzugeben für die Bestrebungen, die kaum geeinte Partei wieder zu spalten, auseinanderzureißen? (Zwischenrufe: Volksfreund!) Aehnlich lag es mit dem „Volksfreund", der viel radikaler war als das „Volksblatt", und doch hat man davor gewarnt. Sie wissen, warum; man hat den Stöcker dahinter gewußt. — So war meine Aeußerung zu verstehen: Es muß ein Organ da sein, ob der Vorstand oder eine spezielle Kommission ist Nebensache, das in solchem Fall erklärt, die Partei hat mit dem Blatt nichts zu thun. Zu solchen Preßorganen sind häufig Mittel da, die nicht von den Parteigenossen gegeben werden; wir können das Fortbestehen solcher Blätter nicht hindern, darum müssen wir uns auf andere Weise schützen.

Damit bin ich fertig und will nur wünschen, daß die 25er-Kommission einen Entwurf ausarbeitet, der Allen so gut und praktisch vorkommt, daß er en bloc angenommen wird. (Beifall.)

Liefländer stellt richtig, daß er nicht gesagt habe, der Drucker des „Berliner Volksblatt" verdiene 100 000 Mark, sondern er habe alle Blätter gemeint, die als Parteiorgane in Berlin anzusehen sind, und zwar nach ihrer geschäftlichen Gestaltung in der Zukunft; auch habe er die Broschüren mit darunter verstanden, mit denen in Zukunft ein viel umfangreicheres Geschäft gemacht werden würde.

Der Organisationsentwurf mit sämmtlichen Anträgen geht an die 25er-Kommission, die sich sofort im Gartensaal konstituiren wird.

Vorsitzender Dietz: Es ist eine Anfrage an das Bureau gelangt, folgenden Inhalts: Im Nebensaale sind ein Berliner Regierungsrath und ein Regierungspräsident aus der Provinz Sachsen eingetroffen; ob sich da nicht etwas machen ließe? (Heiterkeit.) — Im Gegentheil, die Herren sind uns sehr willkommen und mögen uns aufmerksam zuhören und recht viel zu ihrem Nutzen von hier mit fortnehmen! (Heiterkeit und Beifall.)

Da Punkt 5 der Tagesordnung: „Vornahme der Wahlen auf Grund der angenommenen Organisation" einstweilen zurückgestellt werden muß, wendet sich der Parteitag zu Punkt 6:

Das Programm der Partei.

Berichterstatter Liebknecht: Genossen! Ich habe hier keine Programmrede zu halten, sondern nur über das Programm der Partei zu reden und darüber, ob und inwieweit Abänderungen an demselben vorgenommen werden müssen. Unser Programm datirt vom Jahre 1875, vom „Einigungskongreß" her und ist ein Kompromißprogramm, wie man es mit Recht genannt hat. Das Wort „Kompromiß" soll hier beiläufig kein Tadel sein. Schon vor fast 20 Jahren schrieb ich: Alle historischen Vorgänge sind Ergebnisse von Kompromissen. Natürlich ist das Wort Kompromiß da in einem anderen Sinne gebraucht, als es jetzt meist geschieht, im Sinne des charakterlosen Aufgebens von Prinzipien. Der Satz hat insofern Geltung, als eine neue Weltanschauung sich niemals sofort fix und fertig verkörpern kann, sondern die alte und die neue eine Zeit lang nebeneinander bestehen, bis die neue die alte vollständig überwunden hat. Unser jetziges Programm war thatsächlich ein Kompromiß zwischen dem Programm der auf dem Boden der internationalen Arbeiterassoziationen stehenden „Eisenacher", und dem des nationalen Allgemeinen deutschen Arbeitervereins. Den Mitgliedern des letzteren zu Liebe wurde bekanntlich z. B. der Lassallesche Vorschlag von den Produktivassoziationen aufgenommen. Dafür erklärten die Lassalleaner ihre Zustimmung zu den demokratischen Forderungen und der internationalen Grundlage unseres Programms. Ich selbst hatte damals die Ehre, die Programmrede zu halten, und damals, wenigstens der Absicht nach, eine wirkliche, da es galt, ein neues Programm zu schaffen, und damals schon betonte ich die Unvollkommenheit des Programms und zeigte, daß es keineswegs ein endgiltiges sein könne, daß es aber ein Produkt der Verhältnisse und eine Nothwendigkeit sei, daß wir überhaupt niemals ein vollkommenes und endgiltiges Programm schaffen können, da die Wissenschaft stets voranschreitet — und daß die Partei sich demnach auch nicht einen papierenen Papst in Gestalt eines unfehlbaren Programms schaffen dürfe.

Kaum war das Einigungs-Programm Gesetz geworden, da wurden schon Abänderungen vorgeschlagen — und schon vor dem Sozialistengesetz wurden auf den Kongressen Anträge auf Revision gestellt, für welche sich allerdings im Fortschreiten unserer Entwickelung das Bedürfniß herausstellte. Man wollte namentlich die Produktivgenossenschaften mit Staatshilfe beseitigt wissen; außerdem wurden noch einige andere Punkte beanstandet, besonders der Satz: „Religion ist Privatsache", der schon in den siebziger Jahren eine ziemlich lebhafte Polemik hervorrief. Es wurden auch Beschlüsse gefaßt zu Gunsten der Revision — da kam das Sozialistengesetz und unsere Partei wurde von dem Boden der Theorie und wissenschaftlichen Entwickelung hinabgedrängt auf den Boden des Handelns, des Kampfes. Sie hat 12 Jahre zu kämpfen gehabt. In dieser langen Zeit ist auch hie und da der Ruf nach Aenderung des Programms erschallt, aber nur sehr vereinzelt, und stets ist er nur von solchen erhoben worden, welche an dem eigentlichen Kampfe, an diesem Kampf auf Leben und Tod, nicht theilzunehmen in der Lage waren. Wer solchen Kampf kämpft, kann sich nicht mit Programmfragen beschäftigen, — das haben sich alle Militenten (Kämpfenden) gesagt, die Masse der Partei wie die „Führer". Unter der Herrschaft des Ausnahmegesetzes haben wir — und wiederholt auch ich — verschiedentlich dazu aufgefordert, die Partei möge in die Diskussion des Programms eintreten; aber der Aufforderung wurde so gut wie nicht entsprochen — nur von wenigen Genossen wurden einige vereinzelte und fast blos untergeordnete Fragen angestreift, zu einer eingehenden Erörterung, zu einer Diskussion des Programms kam es nicht.

Als wir nach langem Ringen so weit waren, daß wir — auch unter der Herrschaft des Sozialistengesetzes — wußten, wir waren die Sieger, — auf dem Kongreß zu St. Gallen — wurde die Programmfrage wieder aufgeworfen und eine Kommission zur Ausarbeitung eines Entwurfes eines revidirten Programms niedergesetzt. Diese Kommission bestand aus Auer, Bebel und mir. Wohlan, wir haben unsere Mission nicht erfüllt — wir müssen uns schuldig bekennen. Unsere Entschuldigung ist: wir haben in den letzten zwei Jahren nicht die Zeit dazu gehabt. Und mit uns schuldig ist die ganze Partei, welche sich — trotz des gefaßten Beschlusses — und trotz eindringlicher Aufrufe im Londoner Parteiorgan, so gut wie gar nicht mit der Diskussion des Programms beschäftigt hat —. Wahrhaftig, aus sehr guten Gründen, denn gerade nach dem St. Gallener Kongreß begann in Deutschland eine politische Krisis, welche mit dem Falle Bismarcks geendigt hat. Unsere Feinde hatten sich überzeugt, daß die Ausnahmegesetzgebung verfehlt, das Sozialistengesetz eine unwirksame Waffe war. Aber es beseitigen, das wollte Bismarck nicht, sonst beseitigte er die Basis seiner Macht: das Gewalt- und Willkürregiment; — er wollte ein verschärftes Gesetz verlangen, da er, in der eigenthümlich-beschränkten Denkweise, in der er befangen war, sich dem Glauben hingab, durch äußerste Steigerung der Polizeiwirthschaft, durch äußerste Steigerung des Druckes, schließlich doch unser Herr zu werden. Der berüchtigte Expatriirungsvorschlag kam; man wollte die „Führer“ der Sozialdemokratie aus dem Lande jagen. Da nahm der Kampf zwischen uns und dem Polizeiregiment verdoppelte Kraft an; wir hatten zu ringen mit Anspannung jedes Nervs. Wir entlarvten die Lockspitzel; wir stellten unsere Feinde vor der Welt an den Pranger; wir erfochten Sieg auf Sieg; doch nach jeder gewonnenen Schlacht wurden wir in neue Kämpfe getrieben, und bis zum 1. Oktober haben wir nicht die Zeit gehabt, auch nur einen Moment auszuruhen, geschweige denn, daß wir Muße gehabt hätten, ein neues Programm berathen zu können. Das neue, das heißt, das revidirte Programm, muß auch der Partei würdig sein. Darum, weil dies Muße erheischt, mußten wir uns auch gegen den Vorschlag erklären, gleich hier und jetzt eine Kommission zur Revision des Programms niederzusetzen. Die Kommission hätte aus den tüchtigsten Kräften des Parteitages bestehen müssen; diese wären dem Kongreß verloren gegangen, und in den 7 oder 8 Tagen, die wir zusammen sein werden, hätte man nur hastig ein Programm improvisiren können, dessen genaue Durchdenkung und Durcharbeitung einfach unmöglich gewesen wäre.

Ich gehe nun auf die einzelnen Punkte unseres Programms ein und werde diejenigen herausgreifen, bei denen die Kritik eingesetzt hat, und diejenigen bezeichnen, welche als besonders revisionsbedürftig erscheinen; ich werde dann eine Resolution vorschlagen, dahin gehend, daß der Parteivorstand beauftragt wird, dem nächsten Parteikongreß einen Revisionsentwurf vorzulegen und diesen drei Monate vor dem Zusammentritt des Parteitags zu veröffentlichen und der allgemeinen Diskussion zu übergeben, damit die Partei Zeit hat, sich schlüssig zu machen. Das Programm der Partei muß die Kollektivarbeit sämmtlicher Parteigenossen sein, und Jeder wird mir beistimmen, daß eine solche Arbeit früher, in der Zeit des Kampfes, nicht gethan werden konnte.

Es ist zunächst Anstand genommen worden an dem Namen unserer Partei: sozialistische Arbeiterpartei Deutschlands. Schon auf dem Einigungskongreß ist darüber viel gesprochen worden, aber damals war man einhellig der Meinung, dieser Name sei der passendste. Es wurde ausgeführt, daß jede sozialistische Partei nothwendig eine demokratische sein muß. Und der Ausdruck „Arbeiterpartei" ward gewählt, weil wir von der Arbeiterklasse als solcher die Durchführung dieses Programms erwarten. Wir wissen ja, daß edeldenkende, erleuchtete Männer aus den sog. „höheren", herrschenden Klassen an dem Emanzipationskampfe der Arbeiterklasse theilnehmen; aber das sind Ausnahmen, die Masse dieser „höheren" Klassen ist aus Klassenbewußtsein und Klasseninteresse uns feindlich —, der Befreiungskampf der Unterdrückten kann also nur von der Arbeiterklasse geführt werden. Darum glaube ich, wir werden es bei dem alten Namen belassen, wie wir auch in dem Entwurf der Fraktion ihn beibehalten haben.

Das Programm selbst besteht nun aus einem allgemeinen und einem besonderen Theil. Es ist wiederholt darauf hingewiesen worden, daß eine solche Trennung manche Bedenken hat, und sie wird in der That von der niederzusetzenden Kommission oder dem künftigen Vorstand, falls dieser mit dem Entwurf betraut wird, nicht aufrecht erhalten werden können.

Dem allgemeinen Theil, die Erklärung der Parteiprinzipien betreffend, ist der Stempel des Kompromisses scharf aufgedrückt; ihm fehlt vielfach die wissenschaftliche Präzision, welche ein Programm unserer Partei unbedingt haben sollte — das Programm einer Partei, die sich mit Recht als die Partei des wissenschaftlichen Sozialismus bezeichnet.

Nehmen wir die einzelnen Punkte:

I. Die Arbeit ist die Quelle alles Reichthums und aller Kultur.

Prinzipiell ist der hier ausgedrückte Gedanke vollkommen richtig. Trotzdem ist die Fassung neuerdings angegriffen worden; es ist gesagt worden: Die Arbeit ist nicht die alleinige Quelle des gesellschaftlichen Reichthums, auch die Natur hilft ihn schaffen, sie ist gewissermaßen — so hieß es wörtlich — die Mutter, und die Arbeit der Vater des Reichthums. Wer das gesagt hat — und diese irrige Ansicht ist wiederholt aufgetaucht — hat — ganz abgesehen von der Sonderbarkeit, die weibliche Arbeit zum Vater zu machen — nur ausgesprochen, was die flache, bürgerliche Nationalökonomie schon lange vorher ausgesprochen hat; französische Nationalökonomen haben, gegenüber der klassischen englischen Nationalökonomie, welche nur die Arbeit als Schöpferin der Werthe kennt, die Natur eingeschmuggelt. Natürlich stehen wir nicht außerhalb der Natur; natürlich giebt es keine Arbeit ohne Natur; der arbeitende Mensch ist selbst ein Stück Natur, wie die Luft, die der Arbeiter athmet, wie die Erde auf der er steht — das alles versteht sich von selbst und braucht nicht gesagt zu werden. Die Natur, als Natur, schafft eben keine Werthe, keine Werthe im nationalökonomischen Sinne. Wie viele Menschen würden sich in der Natur ernähren können ohne menschliche Arbeit? Was wollen die paar Beeren des Waldes besagen? Und nicht ein Mensch wäre im Stande, unseren Winter zu überdauern. Dem, der diesen eigenthümlichen Vorschlag gemacht hat, will ich die Nationalökonomie Roscher's empfehlen; der hat sogar noch einen zweiten Vater oder eine zweite Mutter entdeckt, nämlich das Kapital, sodaß erst die Dreieinigkeit: Arbeit, Natur, Kapital, den Reichthum erzeugen soll. Und das Manchesterthum sagt ja auch: Arbeit ohne Kapital ist nichts; allein, was ist denn das Kapital? Produkt der Arbeit! Also kommen wir immer wieder zur Arbeit, als der Quelle alles Reichthums, zurück.

Ferner hat man gemäkelt an dem Worte „Reichthum". Ob es ganz glücklich gewählt ist, will ich nicht diskutiren; es paßt nicht ganz, weil es ja auch einen andern Sinn giebt und leicht Anlaß zu Mißverständnissen werden kann. Es ist die Uebersetzung des englischen wealth, — gleichen Ursprungs wie das deutsche „Gewalt" — wealth of nations — Nationalreichthum, Reichthum der Nationen, und in diesem wissenschaftlichen Sinn ist das Wort hier durchaus richtig gebraucht. Jedenfalls ist der jüngst vorgeschlagene Ausdruck „Wohlbefinden" gewiß nicht besser; denn er drückt die Sache durchaus nicht aus und bringt uns von dem wissenschaftlichen Gebiet der Nationalökonomie ab. Ein unglücklicherer Ersatz konnte nicht leicht angerathen werden.

Wenn wir sagen: nicht bloß der gesellschaftliche Reichthum ist Produkt der Arbeit, sondern auch alle Kultur, so ist das ebenfalls durchaus richtig. Die Kultur ist nicht vom Himmel heruntergefallen, nicht geschaffen durch irgend ein Wunder, nicht das Werk einiger Leithammel, die nach einer gewissen Theorie von irgendwo hergekommen sind; nicht den sogenannten „großen" Männern, nicht den Propheten verdanken wir die geschichtliche Entwickelung; sie ist die Kollektivarbeit der gesammten Menschheit. Keine Kraft kann nach dem Naturgesetz verloren gehen; gerade die kleinsten Lebewesen haben die größte schöpferische Thätigkeit entfaltet und thun das fortwährend in dem Organismus der Welt, während die großen Lebewesen, die Löwen, Tiger und sonstigen Raubthiere eine höchst überflüssige Thätigkeit ausüben. So trägt auch die Arbeit der Kleinsten bei zur Erhöhung des Kulturniveaus; sie bildet einen Theil der gesammten gesellschaftlichen Arbeit, und ohne diese Collectivarbeit der Millionen und Abermillionen würde der Mensch

11

nichts sein, oder ein Thier — wie denn der Mensch überhaupt nur Mensch ist in der Gesellschaft und durch die Gesellschaft — durch seine und seiner Mitmenschen Arbeit und die Arbeit der tausende von Menschengeschlechtern, die vorausgegangen sind,

„und da allgemein nutzbringende Arbeit nur durch die Gesellschaft möglich ist, so gehört der Gesellschaft, das heißt allen ihren Gliedern, das gesammte Arbeitsprodukt, bei allgemeiner Arbeitspflicht, nach gleichem Recht, Jedem nach seinen vernunftgemäßen Bedürfnissen.

Auch hier stoßen wir auf einige nicht wissenschaftlich präzise Wendungen. Es ist falsch, jedenfalls mißverständlich, daß das gesammte Arbeitsprodukt nach gleichem Recht allen Mitgliedern der Gesellschaft gehört. Der Gesellschaft gehört es, aber „nach gleichem Recht allen Gliedern", das ist wenigstens unklar ausgedrückt. Bei der genossenschaftlichen Produktion wird es nicht möglich zu machen sein, das Arbeitsprodukt jedem Einzelnen individualistisch, in mechanisch gleichen Theilen, zu Gute kommen zu lassen; da würden wir ganz anachronistisch auf dem Boden des Individualismus zurückkehren. Hier müssen wir die sozialistische Organisation der Gesellschaft in Produktion und Konsumtion betonen. Die mechanisch gleiche Vertheilung der Produkte oder des Arbeitsertrags ist eine Unmöglichkeit. — Die „allgemeine Arbeitspflicht" ist dagegen unbedingt ausgesprochen. Die Arbeitspflicht besteht, während das sogenannte „Arbeitsrecht" oder „Recht auf Arbeit" ein sehr problematischer Begriff ist. Die menschliche Arbeit ist eine Pflicht; die Arbeit ist nicht Zweck, sondern Mittel zum Zweck; wir leben nicht um zu arbeiten, sondern wir arbeiten um zu leben. Ohne Arbeit können wir nicht leben; deshalb hat die Gesellschaft das Recht, jedem Mitglied die Arbeit als Pflicht aufzuerlegen. —

Viel ist gespottet worden über die „vernunftgemäßen Bedürfnisse"; hier wird die Kommission eine etwas glücklichere Fassung zu wählen haben.

„In der heutigen Gesellschaft sind die Arbeitsmittel Monopol der Kapitalistenklasse; die hierdurch bedingte Abhängigkeit der Arbeiterklasse ist die Ursache des Elends und der Knechtschaft in allen Formen."

Im Wesentlichen ist auch dieser Gedanke richtig. Ein neuerdings erhobener Einwand richtet sich gegen den Ausdruck „Arbeiterklasse", für den man, angeblich „schärfer", „Proletariat" setzen will. Das wäre aber eine bedeutende Verschlechterung; es wäre nicht nur nicht richtiger, sondern ganz unrichtig und völlig unwissenschaftlich. Der Kampf, welcher gekämpft wird, ist ein Klassenkampf; es ist nothwendig, gerade diesen Klassencharakter des Emanzipationskampfes zu betonen; zu konstatiren, daß die Klasse der Arbeiter gegenübersteht der Klasse Derer, welche das Monopol der Arbeitsmittel besitzen. Und um so nothwendiger ist dies, als gerade in unserer Partei in Bezug hierauf vielfach irrige, unwissenschaftliche Ausdrücke gebraucht werden. Man spricht zum Beispiel vom Arbeiterstand. Den giebt es nicht. Es giebt in der modernen Kulturwelt blos eine Arbeiterklasse. Man hat die Arbeiter den vierten Stand genannt; der Ausdruck konnte gebraucht werden vor Jahrzehnten, heute kann von einem vierten Stand nicht mehr geredet werden — es giebt keinen. Der Ausdruck ist dem französischen tiers état, dem dritten Stand, nachgebildet; der „dritte Stand" in Frankreich aber war das gesammte Volk — 25 Millionen — mit Ausnahme von einigen hunderttausend Geistlichen und Adligen; in diesem dritten Stand, das heißt an 25 Millionen, mit Ausnahme der Geistlichen und des Adels, war das Proletariat, das Handwerkerthum, das Kleinbürgerthum, die Bourgeoisie enthalten. Nachdem der dritte Staud zur Herrschaft gelangt war, hat der Kampf der Stäude sein Ende erreicht, und der Klassenkampf hat begonnen. Der Begriff der Stände ist mittelalterlich; mit dem Untergang der Stäude endete auch das Mittelalter. Von dem Augenblick an, wo die französische Ständeversammlung, die Generalstaaten, sich zur französischen Nationalversammlung erklärten, gab es keine Stäude mehr, keinen dritten, noch weniger einen vierten Stand; da begann die Trennung der Gesellschaft in die Klassen der Besitzenden und Nichtbesitzenden, derer, welche die Arbeitsmittel haben, und derer, welche für die Besitzer der Arbeitsmittel arbeiten müssen. In England, wo die ökonomische Entwicklung rascher vor sich ging, ist der Ausdruck „Klasse" schon weit früher gebraucht worden. Im Interesse der Präzision wird also der Ausdruck „Arbeiterklasse" beizubehalten sein. Für den Ausdruck „Ursache des Elends und der Knechtschaft in allen Formen" ist vielleicht eine genauere und weniger allgemeine Fassung möglich.

„Die Befreiung der Arbeit erfordert die Verwandlung der Arbeitsmittel in Gemeingut der Gesellschaft und die genossenschaftliche Regelung der Gesammtheit mit gemeinnütziger Verwendung und gerechter Vertheilung des Arbeitsertrages."

In diesem dritten Absatz wird es nöthig sein, die Ziele unserer Partei schärfer zu formuliren, schärfer hervortreten zu lassen, wie es nothwendig ist, die kapitalistische Produktion durch die genossenschaftliche zu ersetzen, wie überhaupt eine wissenschaftlichere schärfere Formulirung der Ziele, welche wir verfolgen, nothwendig erscheint.

Es ist neuerdings vielfach daran Anstoß genommen worden, daß unser Parteiprogramm die Grund- und Bodenfrage nicht ausdrücklich erwähnt. Ich kann hierzu nur bemerken, daß wir auf

dem Gothaer Einigungskongreß von der Annahme ausgingen, die
Erde, der Grund und Boden, sei ein Arbeitsmittel, und daß in der
Erklärung, die Arbeitsmittel müßten Gemeingut der Gesellschaft
werden, die Proklamirung des Grund und Bodens zu gesellschaft-
lichem Eigenthum schon eingeschlossen sei. Dem Wunsche, diese
unsere Stellung noch besonders zu betonen, ist eine gewisse agitatorische Berechtigung nicht abzusprechen. Falsch aber ist die Behauptung, daß die Grund- und Bodenfrage für uns erst seit Kurzem
aufgetaucht sei. Schon 1868 stand für uns die Frage auf der
Tagesordnung. Im Leipziger Hochverrathsprozeß finden Sie massenhaft darauf bezügliche Zitate von uns, welche als Glieder in der
Beweiskette des angeblichen Hochverraths gegen uns verwerthet
wurden. Im Jahre 1869 bereits wurde auf dem Baseler internationalen Kongreß unzweideutig von uns Stellung dazu genommen.
Im Auftrage unserer Partei, die mich nach Basel delegirt hatte,
sprach und stimmte ich damals für die bekannte Resolution, welche
die Erklärung des Grund und Bodens zu Gemeingut forderte.
Aufs Heftigste deswegen angegriffen, sand ich mich mit Bebel veranlaßt, in verschiedenen Vorträgen unseren Standpunkt zu rechtfertigen; ich hielt u. A. einen Vortrag, der als Broschüre veröffentlicht und zu der Schrift: „Zur Grund- und Bodenfrage"
erweitert ward. In dieser Schrift führte ich beiläufig u. A. auch
aus, kein größerer Fehler könne von unserer Partei begangen werden,
als die letzten Ziele nicht auszusprechen, — wir müßten stets ganz
und rückhaltlos sagen, was wir wollen, das sei ehrlich und zugleich
die beste Politik. Und das erwies sich in diesem Fall auch als
taktisch richtig. Zuerst entstand ein allgemeines Halloh, man wollte
uns die Bauern und Landarbeiter auf den Hals hetzen; da haben
wir den Stier bei den Hörnern gefaßt und nachgewiesen, daß das,
was wir wollen, schon heute für neun Zehntel aller Grund-
besitzer, sogenannte Bauern, von größtem und unmittelbarem Vortheile wäre. Dies jetzt weiter und eindringlicher der Landbevölkerung
durch Schriften und Agitation klar zu machen, wird von nun ab
eine der wichtigsten Aufgaben für uns sein.

„Die Befreiung der Arbeit muß das Werk der Arbeiterklasse sein, der gegenüber alle anderen Klassen
nur eine reaktionäre Masse sind."

Genossen! An der Richtigkeit des ersten Theils dieses Satzes
ist nicht zu zweifeln — die Arbeiter sind die Unterdrückten und Ausgebeuteten — und die Unterdrücker und Ausbeuter werden ihre
Opfer sicherlich nie freiwillig befreien. Mit Bezug auf den zweiten
Theil hat man uns aber den Vorwurf gemacht, einen „radikalen"
Beschluß gefaßt zu haben, den wir gar nicht ausführen können und
der obendrein nicht ganz richtig sei. Wir seien z. B. genöthigt, mit
der bürgerlichen Demokratie ein großes Stück Weges zusammen,

theilweise Hand in Hand, zu gehen. Ja, in manchen Fragen der
bürgerlichen Freiheit ist allerdings ein Theil des Bürgerthums, bis
zu einem gewissen Grade, mit uns einverstanden; da aber, wo es
gilt, das von allen anderen Parteien scharf abgegrenzte Wesen
unserer Partei zu bethätigen, wo das revolutionäre Ziel unserer
Partei scharf zu Tage tritt, da zeigt sich sofort die Richtigkeit des
Satzes, da sind alle übrigen Klassen uns gegenüber eine reaktionäre
Masse, da sind sie die eine Klasse der Besitzenden, und in den
historischen Momenten, wo das Proletariat handelnd auf der Welt-
bühne erscheint, offenbart sich in grellster Beleuchtung die Wahrheit
des Satzes. Als wir 1871 uns mit der Kommune solidarisch erklärten und sagten, die Kommunarden sind nicht Blutmenschen,
nicht Verbrecher, sondern edle Menschen, die für das Beste der
Menschheit streben und wirken, und als wir nach dem Falle der
Kommune die Sache der Besiegten und mit Koth Beworfenen ver-
theidigten, hatten wir damals auch nur die geringste Unterstützung
durch die fortschrittliche und demokratische Presse? „Frankfurter
Zeitung" und „Kreuzzeitung" griffen uns gleich heftig an; nur ein
Blatt, die allerdings erst etwas später erschienene „Wage" meines
Freundes Guido Weiß hatte die Mannhaftigkeit, für uns und die
Kommune eine Lanze zu brechen.

In Deutschland liegen die Dinge eben so, daß ein Zusammengehen mit den bürgerlichen Parteien bis zu einem gewissen Grade
gar nicht vermieden werden kann. Hätten wir englische Zustände,
das heißt eine ganz scharfe Abgrenzung der Klassen — hätten wir
das Bürgerthum als direkt herrschende Klasse, dann könnte natürlich
von einem Zusammengehen nicht mehr die Rede sein. Aber wir
sind in Deutschland in einer eigenthümlichen Lage. Unser Bürgerthum ist zu seig, zu unentwickelt gewesen, um seine bürgerlich-
demokratischen Forderungen durchzusetzen. Diese Forderungen,
welche in England und Frankreich Gesetz geworden sind, hat unser
Bürgerthum nicht zu verwirklichen vermocht; es hat, mit geringen
Ausnahmen, jetzt auch auf dieselben verzichtet, und so ist es denn
bei uns die Aufgabe der arbeitenden Klassen geworden, das,
was das Bürgerthum in seiner Feigheit versäumt hat, nachzuholen,
auch diese Arbeit zu verrichten und neben unseren sozialistischen
Forderungen auch für die Forderungen der bürgerlichen Demokratie
zu kämpfen — eine Lage, die unsere Arbeit vermehrt, aber unsere
Position günstiger macht. Es wird sich also auch hier möglicherweise eine etwas schärfere Formulirung als nothwendig und zweckmäßig ergeben.

„II. Von diesen Grundsätzen ausgehend, erstrebt die
sozialistische Arbeiterpartei Deutschlands mit allen
Mitteln den freien Staat und die sozialistische Gesellschaft, die Zerbrechung des ehernen Lohngesetzes durch

Abschaffung des Systems der Lohnarbeit, die Aufhebung der Ausbeutung in jeder Gestalt; die Beseitigung aller sozialen und politischen Ungleichheit."

Hier komme ich an einen Punkt, der weniger für Sie, als für
die uns zuhorchenden Gegner erklärt werden muß. Im ursprünglichen Programm stand „mit allen gesetzlichen Mitteln". Dieses
„gesetzlich" haben wir in Wyden gestrichen. In Folge dessen hat
man uns vorgeworfen, wir hätten uns damit einfach auf den Boden
der Gewalt gestellt. Nichts kann falscher sein, als diese Behauptung.
Die Partei hat gethan, was die Pflicht der Selbsterhaltung und
ihre Würde ihr geboten hat. Man hatte uns durch das Sozialistengesetz außerhalb des Gesetzes, außerhalb des gemeinen Rechts gestellt;
da mußten wir entweder uns feig ducken oder richtiger: Selbstmord
begehen, oder wir mußten thun, was wir gethan haben, — erklären:
wir müssen der Gewalt weichen, aber als Recht erkennen wir dies
Gesetz nicht an; auf dem Boden dieses Gesetzes können wir als
Partei nicht existiren, wir existiren aber, und wollen existiren,
und deshalb müssen wir, dem Gebot der Selbsterhaltung folgend,
dieses Gesetz brechen, untergraben, zerbrechen — und das können
wir doch nicht „gesetzlich", d. h. auf dem Boden eben dieses Gesetzes.
Unser Wydener Beschluß war die nothwendige und logische Antwort auf das Sozialistengesetz: es war zugleich unser Aktions-
programm, und die Ausführung ist dem Beschluß gefolgt. (Stürmischer Beifall.)

Ob es sich empfiehlt, das Wort „gesetzlich" wieder aufzunehmen,
ist eine Frage der Erwägung für die Kommission oder die Revisoren.
Ich lege dieser Frage nicht die geringste Bedeutung bei. Der
Charakter des Programms ist klar auch ohne dieses Wort. Aber
wir leben in merkwürdigen Zeiten. Die Welt ist vielleicht niemals
so im Fluß gewesen, wie jetzt. Wir haben in den letzten Monaten
und Jahren wunderbare Ueberraschungen erlebt, und die Zeit der
Ueberraschungen ist noch nicht vorüber; — wer weiß, wie lange
für uns der Sonnenschein dauern wird, wie bald aus der Sammet-
pfote wieder die Kralle hervorbricht! Zum Glück sind wir gewappnet,
wir haben die gute Rüstung aus der Zeit des Sozialisten-Gesetzes
und alle Kampfmittel und Waffen jener Kampfzeit noch heute zur
Verfügung, — und auch manches Kampfmittel, von dem wir noch
keinen Gebrauch gemacht haben. Es hängt von der weiteren Entwicklung der Dinge ab, wie wir uns zu dem Wörtchen „gesetzlich"
zu stellen haben.

Dann kommt hier noch ein Ausdruck, welcher zu mancherlei
Bedenken Anlaß gegeben hat: „der freie Staat." Die bisherige
Fassung „freier Staat" und „sozialistische Gesellschaft" wird sich
schwerlich aufrecht erhalten lassen. Besser wäre vielleicht: „Die
sozialistische Gesellschaft im freien Staat." — Man wird aber sagen,

— und man hat es gesagt — die sozialistisch organisirte Gesellschaft ist gar kein Staat mehr. Der ganze Staatsbegriff ist ein reaktionärer Begriff; es liegt in der ganzen Natur des Staates, daß er zu einer selbstständigen Macht wird, die sich gegen das Volk richtet. Der heutige Staat mit der von ihm eingeschlossenen Gesellschaft läßt sich mit einem Krebse vergleichen. Der Krebs hat eine feste Haut, die sich wie die Schale, zur Kruste verhärtet, und den weichen Körper, die von der Kruste umpanzerte Masse am Wachsthum hindert, und durch eine Revolution gesprengt, beseitigt werden muß, damit der Körper wachsen kann; die Gesellschaft ist der Körper, der Staat die Kruste. — Genug, ich lasse die Frage, ob das Wort „Staat" beseitigt werden muß, offen. Es ist Sache der Theoretiker, welche unsere Forderungen wissenschaftlich zu formuliren haben, dies klarzustellen. Wir kommen hier noch zu einem Ausdruck, der zu Ausstellungen Anlaß gegeben hat: „ehernes Lohngesetz." Ein ehernes Lohngesetz, das mußten wir uns schon in Gotha sagen, existirt thatsächlich nicht. Das sogenannte „Gesetz" ist der Bourgeois-Nationalökonomie entnommen; der Ausdruck ist agitatorisch von Lassalle gebraucht worden und hat seinen Zweck auch herrlich erfüllt. Er hat etwas Greifbares, Anschauliches, allein, wissenschaftlich richtig ist er nicht. Wenn es ein ehernes Lohngesetz gäbe, wenn der Lohn auf das absolute Minimum herabgedrückt werden könnte, dann wäre es ja nicht möglich, daß in einem und demselben Lande in einer und derselben Branche ganz verschiedene Lohnzustände wären. Doch ich kann hier nicht tiefer in die Frage eingehen, die einen besonderen Vortrag erheischen würde. Schon Marx hat das eherne Lohngesetz für eine „ökonomische Fiktion" erklärt. Es muß daher, meines Erachtens, eine präzisere Formel gewählt werden, die die Natur des heutigen Produktionsprozesses, und die systematische Ausplünderung des Arbeiters, welche er bedingt, umfassend und klar zum Ausdruck bringt.

„Die sozialistische Arbeiterpartei Deutschlands, obgleich zunächst im nationalen Rahmen wirkend, ist sich des internationalen Charakters der Arbeiterbewegung bewußt, und entschlossen, alle Pflichten, welche derselbe den Arbeitern auferlegt, zu erfüllen, um die Verbrüderung aller Menschen zur Wahrheit zu machen."

Diese Gedanken sind wohl von unanfechtbarer Richtigkeit. Keiner, der für den internationalen Gedanken noch so sehr begeistert ist, wird sagen, wir haben keine nationalen Pflichten. National und international sind keine Gegensätze. Man muß blos das Wort „national" richtig auffassen. Es handelt sich nur um einen bestimmten, abgegrenzten Theil der internationalen Menschheit. Der Theil gehört zum Ganzen. Und „international" heißt blos, über die Grenzpfähle der Nation, des engeren Vaterlands hinausgehend, den Horizont über das Ganze erweitern, die Menschheit als eine Familie, die Welt als Heimath betrachten. So richtig die Gedanken, so stilistisch ungeschickt ist die Formulirung — was theilweise die Folge des Kompromisses ist, der zwischen der mehr internationalen Auffassung der „Eisenacher" und der mehr nationalen der Lassalleaner abgeschlossen werden mußte. Die Betonung des nationalen und internationalen Standpunktes neben einander wäre sonst kaum für nöthig erachtet worden.

Mit dem allgemeinen Theil des Programms bin ich nun zu Ende, und ich fasse das Gesagte dahin zusammen, daß derselbe unter allen Umständen gründlich umgearbeitet werden, und daß auch für die an sich richtigen Gedanken eine präzisere, den Anforderungen der Wissenschaft mehr entsprechende Form gefunden werden muß.

Nun kommt das engere Programm, welches seinerseits wieder in einen weiteren und engeren Theil zerfällt. Zunächst der weitere:

„Die sozialistische Arbeiterpartei Deutschlands fordert, um die Lösung der sozialen Frage anzubahnen, die Errichtung von sozialistischen Produktivgenossenschaften mit Staatshilfe, unter der demokratischen Kontrolle des arbeitenden Volkes."

Wir zählen heute 1890. Vor fünfzehn Jahren — 1875 — wurde dieser Punkt als Hauptkonzession an die Lassalleaner aufgefaßt. Die Einigung war da, aber noch nicht die Verschmelzung. Diese ist inzwischen erfolgt. Die beiden Ströme, die wie bei Mainz Main und Rhein, noch eine Weile, dem Auge unterscheidbar, verschieden in Diesem und Jenem, nebeneinander herliefen, haben sich nach der Vereinigung der Lassalleaner und Eisenacher so rasch in Eins verschmolzen, und die wissenschaftliche Fortentwicklung unserer Partei hat auch unter den ehemaligen Lassalleanern die volle Klarheit gebracht, daß mit Produktivgenossenschaften und Staatskredit, mögen sie noch so sehr mit demokratischen Garantieen verbrämt werden, die soziale Heilung nicht bewerkstelligt, die Umgestaltung der kapitalistischen Gesellschaft in die sozialistische nicht bewirkt werden kann; daß die dem Lassalle'schen Vorschlage zu Grunde liegende Auffassung vielleicht dem noch etwas primitiven Zustande des deutschen Großkapitalismus aus der damaligen Zeit entsprochen haben mag, aber heute, bei der kolossalen Entwicklung unserer Industrie, absolut unzulänglich erscheint und das Lächeln jedes Großkapitalisten hervorrufen muß. Und auch kein Arbeiter, der vom modernen Industrialismus eine Ahnung hat, kann sich derartigen Illusionen noch hingeben. Hören wir weiter:

„Produktivgenossenschaften sind für Industrie und Ackerbau in solchem Umfange in's Leben zu rufen, daß

aus ihnen die sozialistische Organisation der Gesammtarbeit entsteht."

Sie sehen hier die ganze Naivetät der Auffassung, welcher
damals noch Rechnung getragen werden mußte. Man konnte noch
denken: der Staat stellt sich über die Klassen, er impft der heutigen
Gesellschaft den Sozialismus ein, oder, anders ausgedrückt — er
treibt den Keil des Sozialismus vermittelst solcher Genossenschaften
in die heutige kapitalistische Gesellschaft und sprengt sie dadurch
auseinander. Der heutige Staat ist aber ein Klassenstaat und
muß es sein, so lange er nicht sozialistisch ist. Und die bürgerliche
Gesellschaft geht nicht par ordre du mousti, nicht durch einen Ukas
von oben zu Grunde, sondern durch ihre eignen Widersprüche und
durch ihre Gemeinschädlichkeit, und durch unsere Thätigkeit — sie
wird mehr und mehr zur ökonomischen Unmöglichkeit; sie muß
in klassischer Form schließlich einen Selbstmord be.ehen, indem
sie die Grundlagen ihres Seins zu zerstören genöthigt ist, und sie
hat sich obendrein selber in den Proletariern die eigenen Todten-
gräber herangezogen. Mehr kann man nicht verlangen!

Auf alle Fälle muß dieser Programmpunkt entweder gestrichen
oder vollständig umgestaltet werden.

„Die sozialistische Arbeiterpartei Deutschlands fordert als Grundlagen des Staates:

1. Allgemeines, gleiches, direktes Wahl- und Stimmrecht mit geheimer und obligatorischer Stimmen-
abgabe aller Staatsangehörigen vom zwanzigsten
Lebensjahre an für alle Wahlen und Abstimmungen
in Staat und Gemeinde."

Diese, sozusagen selbstverständliche Forderung hat auch noch
heute ihre volle Bedeutung für uns und bedarf keiner Erörterung.
Ich habe nur auf eins aufmerksam machen wollen. Es ist in der
neueren Zeit wieder die Nothwendigkeit betont worden, in unserem
Programm die Gleichberechtigung der Frauen auszusprechen,
und so hat man vorgeschlagen, hier ausdrücklich zu erklären, daß
auch die Frauen das Stimmrecht haben sollen. Diese Frage wurde
schon auf dem Einigungskongreß behandelt. Damals wurde nun
das Wort „Staatsangehörige" gewählt, im Gegensatz zu dem im
Eisenacher Programm befindlichen Wort „Männer", blos um ein
Wort zu haben, welches sowohl Frauen als Männer umfaßt, also
die Gleichberechtigung in sich schließt. Wohlgemerkt: es heißt
Staatsangehörige, nicht Männer. Ob es sich nun aber nicht
doch empfiehlt, in direkter, positiver Form die Gleichberechtigung
der Frauen auszusprechen, das gebe ich den künftigen Revisoren
anheim. Nothwendig ist es nicht; denn wenn die Sozialdemokratie
die Gleichberechtigung aller Menschen will, so versteht sich die
Gleichberechtigung der Frau mit dem Manne einfach von selbst.

Für die Sozialdemokratie giebt es überhaupt keine Frauenfrage, die Frauenfrage ist in der sozialen Frage einfach inbegriffen; sie ist ein Theil der sozialen Frage, die mit der Umgestaltung der heutigen Gesellschafts- und Produktionsverhältnisse von selbst gelöst wird.

Daß der Wahl- und Abstimmungstag ein Sonn- und Feiertag sein muß, wie es weiter im Programm heißt, ist so selbstverständlich, daß ich darüber kein Wort sagen will.

Im Anschluß an diese Forderung ist nun eine andere vorgeschlagen worden, die unter allen Umständen in das Programm aufzunehmen ist: das proportionale Wahlsystem. Die Sozialdemokratie hat gegenwärtig, im Verhältniß zu ihrer Stimmenzahl, eine viel geringere Vertretung im Reichstage, als die anderen Parteien; etwa nur ein Drittheil so viel als z. B. das Centrum, das, obgleich seine Wählerzahl der unsrigen nachsteht, doch dreimal so viel Abgeordnete hat. Das ist eine flagrante Ungerechtigkeit, der in gründlichster Weise durch das sogenannte Proportionalsystem abgeholfen wird. Dasselbe ist zuerst in Frankreich, dann in England und später in der Schweiz aufgetaucht und von unserer Partei — und von mir seit Jahrzehnten, noch ehe es eine sozialdemokratische Partei gab — empfohlen worden. Das System besteht darin, daß nach Listen im ganzen Lande abgestimmt wird und daß das ganze Land blos einen einzigen Wahlkreis bildet. Jede Partei hat das Recht, auf ihrer Liste so viel Kandidaten aufzustellen, als überhaupt Mandate zu vertheilen sind, und nun geht es ans Abstimmen. Die Stimmzettel der verschiedenen Parteien, welche, zur Vermeidung von Irrthümern, verschiedene Farben haben könnten, werden an den Wahlurnen abgegeben; die im ganzen Lande abgegebenen Stimmen werden zusammengezählt und dann die Gesammtzahl durch die Zahl der Mandate dividirt, und auf die Stimmenzahl, die so herauskommt — sagen wir auf je 9- oder 10 000 Stimmen — entfällt je ein Mandat, und dann vertheilt man einfach. Bei je 10 000 Stimmen auf ein Mandat würde unsere Partei, bei 1½ Millionen Stimmen, 150 Sitze im Reichstage haben. Dieses System hat noch den weiteren Vortheil, daß auch der kleinsten Minorität, die bei dem jetzigen System unvertreten bleibt, die Möglichkeit der Vertretung gewährt wird. Es ist zwar gesagt worden: die Mehrheit ist stets dumm, Verstand ist stets bei Wenigen nur gewesen; was wird da aber aus dem demokratischen Gleichheitsprinzip? Ja wohl, es giebt eitle Gecken, die da glauben, den Verstand mit Löffeln gegessen zu haben, das Monopol des Verstandes zu besitzen. Nun, ein solcher Bursche mag sich doch aufstellen lassen! Jetzt ist er ein verkanntes Genie, und ein solches ist stets unzufrieden; wenn er aber seinen Namen und sein Genie aufpflanzt und sich den Wählern von ganz Deutschland vorstellt, dann ist ganz Deutschland sein Rekrutirungsfeld — da hat er doch bessere Ausfichten, als jetzt. Und wenn eine neue Idee auftaucht, so ist doch, falls sie etwas taugt, wohl zu erwarten, es werden in ganz Deutschland so viel Stimmen für sie abgegeben werden, daß wenigstens ein Vertreter ins Parlament kommt. Und jede Idee, jede Strebung und Strömung soll vertreten sein.

Wir kommen dann zur

„direkten Gesetzgebung durch das Volk."

Ob dieser Satz nicht einer näheren Präzisirung bedürfen wird, ist die Frage. In der Schweiz haben wir die direkte Gesetzgebung durch das Volk, jedoch nur in einigen der kleinsten Kantone uneingeschränkt. Ohne Einschränkung ist sie auch in größeren Staatswesen nicht möglich. Bei uneingeschränkter direkter Gesetzgebung durch das Volk müßte man konsequent das ganze Volk über alle Gesetze berathen und abstimmen lassen, die gesammte wahlfähige oder stimmberechtigte Bevölkerung hätte in Volks- oder Landesversammlungen zusammenzutreten, und über alle Gesetze nicht blos, sondern auch über alle Maßnahmen und politischen Akte zu verhandeln und sich schlüssig zu machen. So ist es bei den altnordischen, den germanischen Völkern gewesen, bei den Angelsachsen, Norwegern u. s. w., wo das gesammte Volk, d. h. die Freien, in Things zusammentrat und die Gesetzgebung, Regierung und Rechtsprechung direkt ausübte — die sogenannte Theilung der Gewalten war unbekannt. Alle Gewalt lag im Volk. In einzelnen Kantonen der Schweiz haben wir die direkte Gesetzgebung und Regierung noch. Im Kanton Glarus z. B. kommt in jedem Jahr die Landesgemeinde, d. h. die ganze Wählerschaft des Kantons, zusammen und giebt sich die Regierung, sitzt zu Gericht über die Regierung und beschließt die Gesetze. Ja, das ist möglich in einem so kleinen Lande, aber in den großen Reichen der modernen Zeit ist dies nicht durchzuführen. Schon in den größeren Kantonen der Schweiz wird die Gesetzgebung so vorgenommen, wie bei uns: durch Vertretung, aber mit der Maßgabe, daß über Gesetze erst eine Volksabstimmung stattfinden muß, ehe sie in Kraft treten können, und daß, wenn eine gewisse Anzahl von Wählern ein bestimmtes Gesetz fordert, ein solches Gesetz dem gesetzgebenden Körper vorgelegt werden muß. Eine Bestimmung in diesem Sinne, überhaupt eine nähere Definition der direkten Gesetzgebung, ist unter allen Umständen in unser zu reformirendes Programm aufzunehmen.

„Entscheidung über Krieg und Frieden durch das Volk".

Das ist für uns, einstweilen freilich, Zukunftsmusik im verwegensten Sinne des Worts. Ein demokratisches Volk, das seine Regierung in der Hand hat, weil es selbst die Gewalt hat, entscheidet natürlich über Krieg und Frieden, und wenn wir einmal eine wirklich demokratische Verfassung haben, wie sie unserem

Programm entspricht, dann kann es keine Regierung mehr geben, die über die Köpfe des Volkes hinaus einen Krieg erklären kann. Zu dieser Forderung gehört die

„allgemeine Wehrhaftigkeit — Volkswehr an Stelle der stehenden Heere".

Während des französischen Krieges, als zuerst die Frage der Annexion in den Vordergrund trat, sagte ich im Reichstage, laßt den Franzosen Elsaß-Lothringen; wenn Ihr das nehmt, dann habt Ihr die Gefahr einer russisch-französischen Allianz, und der Schwerpunkt der europäischen Macht wird, statt von Paris nach Berlin, von Paris nach Petersburg verlegt werden, und Rußland allein hat den Vortheil. Man verlange von den Franzosen, außer einer Kriegsentschädigung, die Abschaffung des stehenden Heeres und die Einführung des Milizsystems, wie es die Schweiz hat; das ist die beste Garantie des Friedens; denn ein wirkliches Volk in Waffen führt keinen Eroberungskrieg, vorausgesetzt, daß es nicht ein Volk von Wilden ist. Wenn jeder deutsche Arbeiter, Bauer, Kleinbürger selbst Soldat ist, dann giebt es nicht zweierlei Staatsbürger im Staat, nicht zwei Völker im Volk — eins ohne und eins mit Waffen, von denen das eine das andere gelegentlich über den Haufen schießen kann; — giebt es nur ein Volk, und das Volk hat alle Macht, dann ist es unmöglich, daß eine Regierung einen Eroberungskrieg oder überhaupt einen Angriffskrieg beginnt, denn die Völker wollen den Frieden. Wenn der schweizer Bundesrath den Schweizern zumuthen wollte, einen Eroberungszug, z. B. gegen irgend ein hübsches Stückchen von Italien zu machen, so würden — auch wenn die Schweiz zwanzig mal so groß wäre — die Schweizer Volkssoldaten antworten: wenn Ihr Lust habt, dummes Zeug zu machen, so machts und laßt Euch selbst todtschießen; wir machen nicht mit. — Eine Miliz, ohne stehendes Heer — denn man hat auch Milizen neben einem stehenden Heere — ist die beste Bürgschaft des Friedens. Daß aber der ersehnte ewige Friede oder Weltfriede erst kommen kann, wenn der soziale Krieg aufgehört hat, das brauche ich Ihnen nicht zu sagen. (Bravo!)

„Abschaffung aller Ausnahmegesetze, namentlich der Preß-, Vereins- und Versammlungsgesetze" — versteht sich von selbst.

Was die

„Rechtsprechung durch das Volk"

betrifft, so hat die Sache doch gegenwärtig auch ihre zwei Seiten. Ich habe, gleich Bebel, einmal das Unglück gehabt, daß ich mich — es war beim Leipziger Hochverrathsprozeß — der Rechtsprechung durch das Volk, d. h. einem Schwurgericht, zu unterwerfen hatte. Wir wurden damals zu je 2 Jahren Festung, wegen Vorbereitung zum Hochverrath, verurtheilt, und wir waren an den uns zur Last gelegten

Vergehen genau so unschuldig, wie jeder der Herren Rechtsprecher aus dem Volk, die uns schuldig befunden hatten. In den modernen Ländern — auch in den politisch freien — wo die Rechtsprechung durch das Volk allgemein ist, erweist sie sich entschieden als eine Klassenjustiz. Die herrschende Klasse sitzt über die arbeitende Klasse zu Gericht. In England, Frankreich und Amerika sind durch die Geschworenen Urtheile von flagrantester Ungerechtigkeit gefällt worden — Urtheile, die von Berufsrichtern, kraft ihrer besseren Schulung im logischen Denken, wenigstens im juristischen Denken, das eine besondere Logik hat, nie und nimmer gefällt worden wären; solche Urtheile kommen jeden Tag vor, und ich sage ganz offen, ich hätte damals in Leipzig viel lieber vor Berufsrichtern gestanden. Es ist mir nach unserem Prozeß von einem Berufsrichter erklärt worden: wenn Sie vor uns gestanden hätten, hätten wir Sie freisprechen müssen, denn es war juristisch unmöglich, Sie zu verurtheilen. Genug, im heutigen Klassenstaat ist die Rechtsprechung durch das Volk ein zweischneidiges Schwert.

Was die

„Unentgeltlichkeit der Rechtspflege"

betrifft, so versteht es sich von selbst, daß wir die Forderung festhalten müssen. Die Unentgeltlichkeit der Rechtspflege hat sich aber auch auf den Rechtsbeistand zu erstrecken. Der Charakter des Klassenstaats unserer Gesellschaft tritt gerade bei der Justiz und nicht blos in der Rechtsprechung, sondern auch — und fast noch schärfer — darin zu Tage, daß das Recht so theuer ist, und daß der arme Mann deshalb sein Recht — und sei es klar wie die Sonne! — in vielen Fällen nicht zur Geltung bringen kann. (Sehr richtig!) Ich bin, namentlich während meines achtjährigen Aufenthalts auf dem Dorfe, hundertmal von Rechtsuchenden um Rath gefragt worden, und ich habe den armen Leuten gar oft sagen müssen: Ihr habt Recht, aber Ihr könnt Euer Recht nicht erlangen, vergleicht Euch lieber, — auf dem Wege des Prozesses seid Ihr verloren; Ihr könnt die Gerichtskosten und den Advokaten nicht bezahlen, und ohne Advokat könnt Ihr nichts machen. — Die Advokaten sind in schlechten Ruf gerathen, ganz ohne ihre Schuld — auch sie sind Opfer des Klassenstaats. Es sind — und da spreche ich aus eigner, sehr reicher Erfahrung — weit mehr Leute dadurch, daß sie, aus Scheu vor den hohen Kosten und vielleicht auch abgeschreckt durch den schlechten Ruf der Advokaten, ihre Sache selbst führen wollten und so verpfuschten, — es sind dadurch weit mehr Leute geschädigt worden, als vielleicht durch die Kniffe und die Unehrlichkeit von Advokaten. In ähnlicher Lage sind, um etwas Anderes, prinzipiell jedoch ganz Gleiches zu berühren, heutzutage auch die Aerzte. Der Bauer geht nicht zum Arzt, wenn er es irgend zu vermeiden im Stande ist, er scheut die Kosten. So kommt es, daß tausende von

Krankheiten, die, von einem Arzt rechtzeitig erkannt und behandelt, mit Sicherheit hätten geheilt werden können, jetzt in unzähligen Fällen, namentlich bei Frauen, einen tödtlichen Ausgang nehmen oder doch zu dauerndem Siechthum führen. Hier ist genau dieselbe Kur nothwendig, wie in der Anwaltsfrage: die ärztliche Behandlung muß unentgeltlich werden, oder mit anderen Worten: der Arzt — wie der Rechtsanwalt — muß Beamter des Staates, der Gesellschaft sein, besoldeter Beamter, der nicht von dem Klienten oder Patienten Honorar zu nehmen hat, sondern den einfach die Gemeinde oder der Staat anstellt, damit er Jedem, der seiner Hilfe bedarf, solche unentgeltlich angedeihen lassen kann.

Die

„allgemeine gleiche Volkserziehung durch den Staat" ist selbstverständlich, ebenso der

„unentgeltliche Unterricht in allen Bildungs- anstalten."

Die

„Erklärung der Religion zur Privatsache,"

zu der ich nun gelange, ist ein kritischer, viel umstrittener Punkt. Man hat den Deutschen vorgeworfen, daß sie sich mit der Erde zu wenig beschäftigen, im Himmel aber eifrig spazieren gehen und dadurch auf der Erde zu kurz gekommen sind. Es ist ein Zeichen geistiger Unfähigkeit und mangelnder Thatkraft, statt auf der Erde seine Energie zu bethätigen, in den unendlichen Himmel hinauszugondeln und Krieg zu führen gegen den bürgerlichen Gott da droben. In Amerika verdarb ich es mit den Freidenkern dadurch, daß ich einmal sagte: der deutsche Arbeiter, der jetzt unter dem Sozialistengesetz den Kampf gegen den schwächsten Gensdarm oder Schutzmann führt, entwickelt in meinen Augen tausendmal mehr Muth, als wie derjenige, der den allmächtigen Jehovah als persönlichen Feind bekämpft und aus dem Himmel wirft. Auf der Erde wirken, das ist's, worauf es ankommt. Wer macht denn — man verzeihe mir den geschäftlichen Ausdruck — in religiöser Freiheit oder Freireligiosität? Ich verfolge das Thun dieser Klasse von Menschen seit vor 1848. Damals war in meiner engeren Heimath, in Offenbach, ein Hauptnest dieser Freireligiosität, der freigemeindlichen Bewegung. Nun, und was sind diese Freidenker geworden? Welche Rolle haben sie in der Revolution von 1848 gespielt? Es waren fast alles jämmerliche Spießbürger. Und jetzt? Ist einer unter diesen „radikalen" Frei- gemeindlern gewesen, der es wagte, den Kampf gegen die Unter- drückung, für gleiches Recht aufzunehmen? Und einer unter ihnen, der den Muth der Konsequenz gehabt hätte, sich Sozialdemokrat zu nennen? Diesen Leutchen, wenn sie unter sich sind, sind wir gar nicht radikal genug, weil wir nicht wenigstens einmal jeden Tag den lieben Herrgott absetzen. Aber vor dem realen politischen Kampf haben sie, mit verschwindenden Ausnahmen, eine heilige Scheu — höchstens, daß sie als Fortschrittler oder Volksparteiler stimmen. Von Konsequenz des Denkens und Handelns keine Spur, — und zum weitaus größten Theil sind sie unsere politischen Gegner. Es giebt Heißsporne unter uns, die sich mit besonderem Eifer auf die Religion werfen, weil noch ein Stückchen vom Jehovah in ihnen ist, den sie nicht ganz los werden können. (Sehr richtig!)

Wir müssen weiter bedenken, daß die Religion an sich und die Kirche an sich nicht fähig sind, uns zu unterdrücken, wenn nicht der Staat sie hält, wenn nicht die Gesellschaft sie hält. Die katholische Kirche so gut wie die protestantische Kirche, sie sind die Bundesgenossen, nein, die Stützen, die Werkzeuge des heutigen Klassenstaats, und zugleich ein Produkt desselben. Sie helfen dem Staat, und sofern sie ihm helfen, müssen wir auch gegen sie Front machen. Wer aber, statt den Klassenstaat selbst, statt die ökonomischen Bedingungen des Klassenstaates und seine politischen Voraussetzungen anzugreifen, sich auf die Kirche verbeißt, der verpulvert seine Kraft gegen falsche Objekte; haben wir erst den Staat erobert, dann ist uns die Religion nicht gefährlich. Glauben Diejenigen unter Ihnen, die vielleicht an dem Kampf gegen Jehovah Gefallen finden, glauben Sie etwa, daß durch radikal-religiöse Phrasen, oder gar durch Schimpfen, der Religion Abbruch gethan wird? Das wäre ein großer Irrthum! Im Gegentheil! Betrachten Sie doch den Kulturkampf! Ich für meine Person bin mit der Religion sehr früh fertig gewesen. Ich stamme aus der Zeit, wo die deutsche Studentenschaft Hegel'sche Philosophie studirte, wo sie durch die Strauß, Bauer, Feuerbach u. s. w. in den Atheismus eingeweiht wurde. Mir war das, da ich sehr frei erzogen war, nicht schwierig. Aber ich habe eines während meines langen politischen Lebens gelernt, das mich praktisch gemacht hat: ich habe gelernt, daß ich nie einen Menschen, der an Religion glaubte, durch Beschimpfung der Religion, durch Angriffe auf die Religion habe belehren können, (Sehr richtig!) Der Religion können wir blos dadurch zu Leibe gehen, daß wir die Religion des Einzelnen ruhig Religion sein lassen, ihm aber Wissen beibringen; die Schule muß gegen die Kirche mobilisirt werden, der Schulmeister gegen den Pfaffen; richtige Erziehung beseitigt die Religion. Angriffe machen sie blos stärker, und Diejenigen unter uns, die gegen die Religion den Hauptkampf führen, verfallen in den Fehler der preußischen Regierung in ihrem Kampf gegen die katholische Kirche: sie machen den Feind nur stärker. (Lebhaftes Bravo!)

Wir haben in unserem Programm gesagt: die Religion ist Privatsache. Ich will nicht sagen, daß dieser Ausdruck ein absolut fehlerloser ist. Ich kann nur bemerken: einen vernünftigeren, praktischeren Satz haben wir nicht unter allen unseren praktischen

Forderungen. Ich bin öfters genöthigt gewesen, in Gegenden zu
agitiren, wo der Katholizismus noch eine Macht ist, aber neben
ihm auch die Sozialdemokratie. Da habe ich durch diesen Punkt
unseres Programms, indem ich ihn richtig erklärte, zahlreiche
Stimmen erlangt von Leuten, die heute noch sozialdemokratisch
stimmen, die aber durch einen Angriff auf die Religion uns ent-
fremdet worden wären. In der Gegend von Mainz gerieth ich
einmal mit einem katholischen Priester in eine Diskussion. Er war
sehr höflich, stimmte sonst im Wesentlichen mit mir überein, aber
daß wir die Religion aus dem Staate verdrängen, sie zur Privatsache machen wollten, das ginge doch nicht. Ich sagte ihm: Sie
irren sich, das ist ja gerade für Sie von großem Vortheil. Sehen
Sie, wenn der preußische Staat die Religion zur Privatsache erklärt hätte, wie wir fordern, dann hätte der Kulturkampf nicht entstehen können. Er bemerkte dann: ja, der Staat
muß christlich sein. Ich erwiderte, welches Christenthum soll denn
der Staat haben? Wir haben ein protestantisches, ein reformirtes,
ein lutherisches, ein katholisches, ein griechischkatholisches Christenthum und noch 20 bis 30 christliche Sekten. Was soll nun der
christliche Staat sein? Soll er protestantisch oder katholisch sein,
oder was sonst? Als protestantischer Staat führt er gerade den
Kulturkampf gegen die katholische Kirche, als katholischer Staat
würde er ihn gegen die protestantische Kirche führen u. s. w. Und
das hat den katholischen Bauern so eingeleuchtet, obwohl der Pfarrer
sich noch sträubte, daß sie einstimmig für mich gestimmt haben.
(Heiterkeit.) Und glauben Sie nicht, ich hätte geheuchelt; ich sagte
den Bauern rückhaltlos: ich bin Atheist, ich glaube nicht an Gott,
aber ich glaube, daß Jeder das Recht hat zu glauben was er will;
wir Sozialdemokraten wollen absolute Gewissensfreiheit, absolute
Meinungsfreiheit; kein Staat, keine Gesellschaft hat das Recht, einem
Menschen mit der Faust an's Gewissen zu greifen, einem Menschen
ein religiöses Bekenntniß oder eine andere Meinung aufzudrängen.
Wenn wir das versuchen, dann schaden wir nur unserer Sache.
(Bravo!) Bei Begründung unseres Antrages auf Aufhebung aller
Ausnahmegesetze, auch der gegen die Jesuiten, habe ich im Reichstage auf das Beispiel der Vendée hingewiesen. Und in der That,
es ist schlagend. Im revolutionären Frankreich war die Herrschaft
der Vernunft eingeführt, die Revolution hatte die Wissenschaft zur
Basis. Die armen, in geistiger Finsterniß lebenden Bauern ergriffen
die Waffen für ihren katholischen Aberglauben und nahmen den
Kampf auf gegen die übermächtige, stürmisch vorandrängende Revolution. Ungleicher konnten die Kräfte nicht vertheilt sein. Und
was war der Erfolg? Kaum war das aufständische Gebiet, von
einem Ende zum andern, mit Feuer und Schwert verwüstet, jeder
Widerstand niedergeworfen, so loderte der Brand wieder in irgend

einer Ecke auf, und die Blutarbeit hatte von Neuem zu beginnen — bis die Sieger erlahmten. Ein Beweis, wie er schlagender nicht gedacht werden kann, daß es absolut unmöglich ist, eine Idee, und wäre sie auch eine falsche, mit Gewalt zu überwinden oder durch irgend einen Machtspruch wegzudekretiren. Unsere Partei ist eine Partei der Wissenschaft. Die Wissenschaft steht der Religion feindlich gegenüber. — aber sie kann und will sie nicht niederschlagen. Die Wissenschaft sorgt für gute Schulen, das ist das beste Mittel gegen die Religion. (Stürmisches Bravo und Händeklatschen.) Und im Uebrigen bekennen wir Farbe. Also ich bin für Beibehaltung des Satzes. In einem Privatschreiben wurde ich neulich ersucht, ich möge doch dahin wirken, daß unserem Programm die alte demokratische Forderung der Trennung der Kirche von der Schule, der Schule von der Kirche und der Kirche vom Staat ausgesprochen werde. Das wäre indeß ein Rückschritt. Indem wir die Religion zur Privatsache erklären, trennen wir eo ipso die Religion vom Staat, und die allgemeine und gleiche Erziehung durch den Staat schließt selbstverständlich die Trennung der Schule von der Kirche mit ein. Die Fassung unseres Programms ist weit besser, umfassender und prinzipiell richtiger, als jene alte, die sich beiläufig noch in unserem Eisenacher Programm befunden hat.

Es kommen nun die Forderungen „innerhalb der heutigen Gesellschaft" — das heißt die dritte Abtheilung des Programms, so daß wir also eine weitere oder allgemeine, eine engere und eine noch engere haben. Hier wird geändert werden müssen. Daß den Forderungen der Partei eine möglichst kurze, klare und scharfe Darlegung der Prinzipien vorausgeht, ist in der Ordnung; aber sie hat gewissermaßen das Fundament zu sein, auf dem die Forderungen sich erheben. Die Forderungen selbst in Forderungen schlechthin, und in solche „innerhalb des heutigen Staates" zu trennen, ist sicherlich nicht zu rechtfertigen. Wo soll die Grenzlinie sein? Stellen wir nicht alle unsere Forderungen „innerhalb des heutigen Staats?" Und wo fängt der heutige Staat an? Wo hört er auf? Ist eine Grenzlinie zu ziehen zwischen dem heutigen Staat und dem sogenannten „Zukunftsstaat" — um einmal das viel mißbrauchte Wort zu gebrauchen. Gehen beide nicht in einander über?

Diese Forderungen im heutigen Staat sind sehr mannigfaltiger Natur, und trotz engeren als engen Charakters zum Theil recht allgemein. Zum Beispiel gleich die erste Forderung:

„Möglichste Ausdehnung der politischen Rechte und Freiheiten."

Wie allgemein! Und zugleich wie selbstverständlich! Gegen den Inhalt ist natürlich nichts einzuwenden — die Form läßt sich vielleicht bessern.

Die Forderungen bezüglich einer einzigen progressiven Einkommensteuer für Staat und Gemeinde, bezüglich des unbeschränkten Koalitionsrechtes, des Normalarbeitstages und des Verbots der Sonntagsarbeit entsprechen noch heute unserem Standpunkte wie von vor 15 Jahren.

Als Ganzes sind die am Schlusse unseres Programms aufgestellten Forderungen des Arbeiterschutzes veraltet, von der Zeit überholt. Seit 15 Jahren sind wir auf diesem Gebiet, wenigstens theoretisch, so weit gekommen. In jedem Wahlprogramm im kleinsten Städtchen Deutschlands sind seitdem weit radikalere und umfassendere Forderungen aufgestellt worden. Damals war das neu, und so unvollkommen es heute erscheint, damals war es eine That, eine bahnbrechende That. Und mit diesen Forderungen haben wir den heutigen Klassenstaat gezwungen, daß er die Arbeiterschutzgesetzgebung als obersten Gegenstand auf die Tagesordnung gesetzt hat. Wie rasch der Fortschritt auf diesem Gebiet ist, das zeigt sich besonders deutlich am Normalarbeitstag. Hätten wir 1875 eine bestimmte Zeit festgesetzt, so wäre es schon kühn gewesen, den zehnstündigen Normal-Arbeitstag zu fordern. Heute würde der zehnstündige Arbeitstag für uns in gewisser Beziehung schon ein überwundener Standpunkt sein, heute würden wir sagen müssen: acht Stunden; und nach zehn Jahren würde vielleicht der Achtstundentag wieder ein überwundener Standpunkt sein. Es war darum sehr vernünftig, daß das Programm nicht einen zeitlich definitiv bestimmten Normal-Arbeitstag, sondern einen „den Gesellschaftsbedürfnissen entsprechenden" fordert. Den Gesellschaftsbedürfnissen und dem Gesellschaftskönnen, auch das muß ausgedrückt werden. Durch die sich immer mehr vervollkommnende Technik, durch die bessere Art des Betriebes, durch die bessere Organisation der Arbeit wird die Arbeit immer produktiver und kann in Folge dessen beständig abgekürzt werden, sodaß man jetzt schon in einigen Kolonien Englands einen sechsstündigen Arbeitstag hat und in Australien einen fünfstündigen erstrebt. Mit Bezug auf unser Streben nach Verkürzung der Arbeitszeit haben allerhand Leute gehöhnt: die Sozialdemokraten wollen nicht arbeiten, sie wollen faulenzen. Dieses alberne, verleumderische Geschwätz kommt regelmäßig aus dem Munde von Leuten, die nicht wissen, was arbeiten heißt, die aber sehr wohl wissen, was faulenzen ist. (Heiterkeit.) Lafargue hat diesem läppischen Geschwätz gegenüber das „Recht auf die Faulheit", das ist auf Muße proklamirt. Der Mensch ist nicht ausschließlich zur Arbeit geboren; wir müssen, um Menschen zu sein, uns harmonisch ausbilden, — das können wir nicht ohne Arbeit; ohne Arbeit können wir überhaupt nicht leben. Die Arbeit ist folglich eine Nothwendigkeit. Aber mehr arbeiten als für den Zweck, Mensch zu sein, nothwendig ist, das heißt den Zweck dem Mittel opfern. Nicht um zu arbeiten leben wir, sondern wir arbeiten, um zu leben. (Sehr richtig!)

Ich muß nun noch nachträglich bemerken, daß neuerdings vorgeschlagen worden ist, es solle im Programm ausgesprochen werden, daß die Sozialdemokratie die Republik erstrebe. Ob es nöthig ist, das auszusprechen, will ich dahingestellt sein lassen. Daß das Staatsideal auf einem demokratischem Boden, einer auf dem Boden der Gleichheit und Freiheit stehenden Partei die Republik ist, versteht sich für jeden denkfähigen Menschen einfach von selbst. Auf der andern Seite wissen wir auch sehr wohl, daß auch in dem republikanischen Klassenstaat, auch in den Bourgeoisrepubliken das Gleichheitsprinzip genau ebenso verletzt wird wie in den Monarchien — und zwar durch jeden Bourgeois. Deshalb steht das Postulat politischer Gleichheit, obgleich wir sie natürlich erstreben, für uns nicht so im Vordergrund, wie f. Z. für die bürgerlichen Parteien. — Mir persönlich ist es gleichgiltig, ob dieser Vorschlag angenommen wird, oder nicht — für uns handelt es sich vor allem um die soziale, die ökonomische Gleichheit, welche die politische von selbst bedingt, während das Umgekehrte nicht der Fall ist.

Ich komme zum Schluß. Ich habe vorher ausgeführt, daß, und warum es bisher unmöglich war, das Programm zu reformiren, und Ihnen schon jetzt einen neuen Entwurf vorzulegen. Wenn da eine Schuld ist, sind Sie Alle mitschuldig, insofern aus dem Schooße der Partei über das Programm Vorschläge in nennenswerthem Maaße nicht gekommen sind, und eine Diskussion im größeren Stil nicht stattgefunden hat. Uebrigens ist dadurch, daß wir das Programm noch nicht reformirt oder revidirt haben, der Partei kein Nachtheil erwachsen. Dies Programm, das Einigungsprogramm, oder Gothaer Programm, ist uns 15 Jahre lang eine Sturmfahne gewesen, die der Partei auf ihrem ununterbrochenen Vormarsch, in all ihren Kämpfen, vorangetragen worden ist. Es war ein Führer und Kompaß, der uns den Weg zeigte, ein Leitstern, der unsere Schritte lenkte. Die Fahne ist zersetzt und zerschossen worden, aber sie hat uns zum Siege geführt; in ihr verkörpert sich ein ruhmvolles Stück Geschichte der sozialdemokratischen Arbeiterpartei; und ich will blos wünschen, daß das neue Programm, die neue Fahne, die wir den Erfordernissen der Zeit entsprechend, uns schaffen werden, der deutschen Sozialdemokratie ebenso glorreich im Kampfe vorangetragen werden möge, wie diese alte, verfolgte Sturmfahne. (Bravo!) Und schlecht ist dies Programm wahrhaftig nicht gewesen und ist es jetzt nicht. — Trotz seiner Mängel spricht es im Großen und Ganzen die Ziele und das Wesen der Partei aus, und — blos als Programm betrachtet, ohne Berücksichtigung der Partei — steht es thurmhoch über den Programmen aller anderer

12*

Parteien, es ist thatsächlich das einzige politische Programm, welches in Deutschland existirt. Keine der bürgerlichen Parteien hat ihre Forderungen zusammengefaßt und formulirt — auch nicht die konservative und nicht die Centrums-Partei. Keine andere Partei hat mit der Rückhaltslosigkeit, die nur dem guten Recht eigen ist, und wie wir sie in unserem Programm bewiesen haben, ihre letzten Ziele hingestellt, keine sich eine solche Richtschnur gegeben, wie wir in diesem unserm Programm. Es hat die Partei nicht falsch geführt, und wir wären Thoren gewesen, wenn wir, ehe wir aus der heißen Schlacht gekommen, es hätten bei Seite werfen und in der Eile durch ein anderes ersetzen wollen. Das Programm ist uns lieb geworden. Seine Mängel hat Jeder von uns gefühlt, in vielen Reden vor den Wahlen ist die Nothwendigkeit der Reform betont worden. Vollkommenes kann niemals geschaffen werden. Das Programm, welches wir in einem Jahr uns geben werden, wird sich gleichfalls überleben. Die Welt geht eben im Sturmschritt voran. Dieses alte Programm aber, welches mit der Geschichte unserer Partei so innig verwachsen, selbst ein Theil der Parteigeschichte ist, leichtsinnig zu vertauschen mit einem rasch über Nacht zusammengestoppeltem neuem Programm, wäre einfach eine Tollheit, eine Impietät gewesen. Das neue Programm soll auch gut werden, und „gut Ding braucht Weile." Die Gegner haben gesagt, das Sozialistengesetz sei für uns ein eiserner Reifen gewesen, der die Partei gewaltsam zusammengehalten habe und die Partei werde zerfallen, wenn das Sozialistengesetz aufhöre. Wohlan, der 1. Oktober und dieser imposante Kongreß haben bewiesen, wie falsch unsere Gegner urtheilen, haben sie Lügen gestraft. Einiger hat die Partei sich nie gezeigt, einiger, ja so einig war sie nie zuvor. Aber ist diese Einigkeit etwa allein herbeigeführt worden durch den gemeinsamen Kampf gegen das Sozialistengesetz und dessen Urheber und Vollstrecker? Nein, wenn das Sozialistengesetz ein eiserner Reif war, dann war unser Programm ein diamantnes Band für uns. (Lebhaftes Bravo!) Mit unserem Programm haben wir das Sozialistengesetz, diesen eisernen Reif, zerbrochen — es hat sich also stärker erwiesen. Diamant ist ein griechisches Wort, Adamas, das heißt: „das nicht zu Bändigende," das „Unbesiegbare," und dieses Band der Unbesiegbarkeit, welches das alte Programm uns gewesen ist, möge und wird uns auch das neue Programm werden. Das neue Programm soll es zu lebendigem Ausdruck bringen, daß die Partei stets fortschreitet, daß es für uns keinen Stillstand giebt auf ewige Zeit, denn Stillstand ist Untergang. Die Wissenschaft ist für uns der Boden, auf dem wir unüberwind[lich] sind, wie es für jenen Riesen des Alterthums die Mutter Erde w[ar]. Die Wissenschaft ist die Mutter des Sozialismus; wenn wir [sie] verlassen, dann sind wir verloren. Auf dem Boden der Wissenscha[ft] und der Wirklichkeit sind wir unbesiegbar und werden alle unsere Feinde überwinden! (Stürmischer, lang andauernder Beifall.)

Vorsitzender Dietz: Nach dieser vortrefflichen Rede Liebknecht's schlage ich vor, die Diskussion bis morgen zu vertagen. Damit ist der Parteitag einverstanden. — Es ist angefragt worden, ob die Rede des Genossen Liebknecht gedruckt werden wird. Ich kann mittheilen, daß die Rede thunlichst ihrem ganzen Wortlaute nach in das Protokoll aufgenommen werden wird. (Bravo!) Damit sind Sie einverstanden.

Es ist eine weitere Reihe von Telegrammen eingegangen.

Liebknecht bringt nunmehr folgende Resolution ein:

In Erwägung:
daß das von dem Einigungskongreß zu Gotha im Jahre 1875 beschlossene Parteiprogramm, so trefflich es sich auch in den Kämpfen der letzten 15 Jahre, namentlich unter dem Sozialistengesetz bewährt hat, dennoch nicht mehr in allen Punkten auf der Höhe der Zeit steht, wie das schon von früheren Parteikongressen ausgesprochen worden ist,

beschließt der Parteitag:
Der Parteivorstand wird beauftragt, dem nächsten Parteitag einen Entwurf eines revidirten Parteiprogramms vorzulegen und den Entwurf mindestens 3 Monate vor Zusammentritt des nächsten Parteitages zu veröffentlichen, damit die Partei hinreichende Zeit zur Prüfung habe.

Schluß der Sitzung 6¼ Uhr.

Vierter Verhandlungstag.

Donnerstag, den 16. Oktober 1890.

Vorsitzender Dietz eröffnet die Sitzung um 9¼ Uhr.

Es ist abermals eine ganze Reihe von Telegrammen und Begrüßungszuschriften eingegangen.

Die Genossen Fr. W. Höppner, Georg Horn, August Frauenlob (Dresden-Land), Ernst Messing, L. Müller (Dresden-Altstadt), Emanuel Wurm (Pirna) und Kaden (Dresden) geben folgende Erklärung zu Protokoll:

Der Genosse Schönfeld erklärte, daß in Bezug auf die Haltung der „Sächsischen Arbeiterzeitung" zum 1. Mai die Arbeiter Dresdens und der Umgegend vollständig auf Seite der Zeitung gestanden, und doch wäre diese Haltung nicht im Einklang mit den Ansichten der Fraktion gewesen. Sollte also dem Parteivorstand die Aufficht über die prinzipielle Haltung der Presse aufgetragen werden, könnten gleiche Vorgänge zur Maaßregelung des Organs führen.

Wir erklären, daß die Arbeiterschaft Dresdens und Umgegend in prinzipieller Beziehung der 1. Mai-Feier vollständig sympathisch gegenüberstand, in Bezug auf die praktische Ausführung jedoch keineswegs der Haltung der „Sächsischen Arbeiterzeitung" zustimmte. Die Genossen hatten jedoch zu keiner Zeit einen genügenden Einfluß auf das Blatt, um ihre Meinung geltend zu machen."

Singer (zur Geschäftsordnung): In der heutigen Nummer des hiesigen „Generalanzeiger" wird eine Notiz verbreitet, wonach die meisten Führer der Partei mit den französischen Gästen in einem hiesigen Hotel eine geheime Berathung gehabt haben sollen. (Gelächter.) Ich würde der Lächerlichkeit dieser Behauptung gegenüber, es nicht für nothwendig erachtet haben, ein Wort zu verlieren. Wir haben, in Rücksicht auf die Nothwendigkeit der freiesten öffentlichen Verhandlung, der Presse einen Raum in diesem Saale eingeräumt, der weit über das hinausgeht, was wir eigentlich in Rücksicht auf unsere Delegirten uns selbst schuldig wären. (Lebhafte Zustimmung.) Wir haben aber gemeint, den vor Zusammentritt des Kongresses schon erhobenen Verdächtigungen dadurch am besten entgegentreten zu können. Wir kümmern uns um das, was die gegnerische Presse von unseren Verhandlungen bringt, garnicht. Wir verlangen weder die Vorlegung der Berichte, die die Herren schreiben, noch wollen wir irgend einen Einfluß auf ihre Berichte ausüben. Wogegen wir aber ein Recht haben zu protestiren, das sind lügnerische, verleumberische Behauptungen. (Sehr richtig!) Die Notiz des „Generalanzeiger" ist von diesem Kaliber. Wir haben keinen Grund, mit unseren ausländischen Genossen in „geheime" Berathung zu treten. Das, was wir gemeinsam wollen, das wollen und können wir so öffentlich sagen und bethätigen, daß die Gegner ihren Schrecken daran haben werden. (Bravo!) Indem ich im Namen des Parteitages jene Behauptung als eine Lüge bezeichne, beantrage ich zugleich das Einverständniß des Parteitages, daß für den Fall dieser Herr Berichterstatter sich im Saale befinden sollte, er sich von diesem Moment an als ausgewiesen zu betrachten hat. (Lebhaftes Bravo!)

Hermann-Dresden erklärt, daß er seine Unterschrift unter die Dresdener Erklärung nicht gesetzt habe, weil in der That die Haltung der „Sächsischen Arbeiterzeitung" zur 1. Mai-Feier im Einklang gestanden hätte zu der Haltung der Genossen in Dresden.

Kaden-Dresden: Unsere Erklärung beruht auf Thatsachen. Wir sind dafür gewesen, daß der 1. Mai soweit wie thunlich gefeiert werde, das heißt, soweit nicht dadurch Maßregelungen entstehen konnten. Ein großer Theil der Arbeiter war mit den Aufforderungen der „Sächsischen Arbeiterzeitung" nicht einverstanden.

Der Parteitag tritt hierauf in die Tagesordnung ein: Generaldiskussion über den Bericht Liebknecht's, betreffend das Parteiprogramm.

Es stehen folgende Anträge zur Diskussion:

1. Die oben mitgetheilte Resolution Liebknecht's.

2. Die Resolution von Fritz Berndt-Berlin V.:

Die Versammlung des sozialdemokratischen Wahlvereins für den V. Berliner Wahlkreis spricht sich entschieden dafür aus, daß die Revision des Parteiprogramms nicht verschoben wird. Sie beantragt folgende Aenderung des Parteiprogramms:

1. Die Forderung: „Erklärung der Religion zur Privatsache" wird statt an die sozialistische Gesellschaft an den heutigen Staat gestellt. — 2. Der die Produktiv-Assoziationen betreffende Satz wird gestrichen. — 3. Jede Beschränkung von Frauenarbeit, im Unterschied von der Männerarbeit, fällt. Die Forderung des gesetzlichen gleichen Lohnes für Mann und Frau fällt, weil ihre Durchführung thatsächlich zur Verdrängung der Frauenarbeit führt. Nur das Verbot der Nachtarbeit verheirateter Frauen ist zu fordern. — 4. Die Forderung des politischen Wahlrechts der Frauen wird in das Programm aufgenommen und zwar unter die Forderungen an den heutigen Staat. — 5. Abschaffung der Gesindeordnung. — 6. Verbot der Naturalienlöhnung an die ländlichen Arbeiter. — 7. In den die Einkommensteuer betreffenden Passus wird die Steuerfreiheit der Einkommen unter dreitausend Mark aufgenommen.

3. Antrag J. Stern:

1. Dem letzten Theil des Programms (Forderungen vom heutigen Staat) die weitere Forderung anzufügen:

„Der Staat hat die Pflicht, allen Erwerbslosen aus Staatsmitteln ausreichenden, den heutigen Kulturverhältnissen entsprechenden Unterhalt zu gewähren, ohne Beeinträchtigung ihrer politischen Rechte."

2. Im allgemeinen Theil des Programms von der Sozialdemokratie, neben dem Charakter der Klassenbewegung, auch den Charakter der Kulturbewegung zu betonen.

4. Antrag von Guben:

Den Absatz im Programm betreffend die Produktivgenossenschaften zu streichen.

5. Antrag Dr. Rübt-Heidelberg:

Der Parteitag wolle den Parteivorstand beauftragen, bei der Ausarbeitung der Programmvorlage in Erwägung zu ziehen, ob das Partei-Interesse es nicht verlange, daß die Forderungen des

Gotha-Wydener Programms: „Erklärung der Religion zur Privatsache" abgeändert werde wie folgt:

Die sozialistische Arbeiterpartei Deutschlands greift zwar
in die religiöse Ueberzeugung der einzelnen Parteigenossen
unmittelbar nicht ein, sie steht, aber als revolutionäre Partei,
auch in religiöser Beziehung auf dem Boden der freien
wissenschaftlichen Forschung. Infolge dessen verwirft sie
prinzipiell jeden Dogmenglauben als eine Quelle geistiger
Knechtschaft und als gewaltiges Hinderniß des Emanzipationskampfes des Proletariats, und bekämpft jede Kirche, die auf
Grund der Glaubensdogmen den sozialen und politischen
Befreiungsbestrebungen der Arbeiterklasse entgegentritt.

6. Antrag der Frauen Ihrer, Gundelach, Blohm und
Steinbach:

Zu Abtheilung 3 des Programms wünschen wir den § 5 so
lautend: Verbot der Kinderarbeit unter 14 Jahren. Beschränkung
aller die Gesundheit besonders schädigenden Arbeit auf höchstens
6 Stunden täglich.

§ 6. Zwischen: gewählte Beamte und — — — ein wirksames: „insonderheit für die gewerbliche Frauenarbeit, weibliche
Beamte."

Der Vorsitzende stellt bezüglich des Antrages Berndt die Unterstützungsfrage; der Antrag wird nicht genügend unterstützt.

Guttenstein-Karlsruhe: Das Parteiprogramm ist das punctum
saliens unserer Verhandlungen. Die Beschlüsse über den Organisationsentwurf können von den Regierungen umgestoßen werden, bei dem
Parteiprogramm haben lediglich und allein die Sozialdemokraten
mitzureden. Der erste Ruf unserer Gegner bei jeder Wahlbewegung
heißt: Heraus mit Eurem Programm! Unser Programm ist der
Niederschlag der sozialistischen Wissenschaft.

Während der 12 Jahre des Sozialistengesetzes war die sozialistische
Literatur unterdrückt, und nur kleine Broschüren konnten auf ver-
botenen Wegen verbreitet werden. Sie werden mir zustimmen, daß
sogar einzelnen Genossen die Bestimmungen des Programms vielfach unbekannt sind. Es war keine Gelegenheit geboten, in den
engeren lokalen Kreisen das Programm zu diskutiren, während es
doch unbedingt erforderlich ist, daß die einzelnen Organisationen
nicht von heute auf morgen, sondern monatelang sich mit jedem
Punkt des Programms in jeder Richtung eingehend befassen. Die
sozialdemokratische Partei ist keineswegs blos eine Arbeiterpartei;
die Arbeiterschaft allein kann die soziale Frage nicht lösen ohne
Mithülfe der Theoretiker, der gebildeten Sozialdemokraten. Was
wir heute bringen, ist nur schätzbares Material für die Feststellung
des künftigen Programms.

Thierbach-Königsberg (Neumark): Was zunächst unsere

Stellung zur Religion betrifft, so werden uns die trefflichen Ausführungen Liebknecht's überzeugt haben, daß dieser Punkt des alten
Programms stehen bleiben muß. In Punkt 4 sollte, anstatt Normalarbeitstag, besser „Maximalarbeitstag" gesagt werden. Es muß
eine feste Norm vorhanden sein. Bei Einführung des Normalarbeitstages wäre den Kapitalisten Gelegenheit geboten, je nach Bedarf auch wieder über diese Grenze hinweg arbeiten zu lassen, der
Normalarbeitstag würde eine Waffe zu Gunsten der besitzenden
Klassen werden. Mit der Wahl einer Kommission bin ich einverstanden.

Blos: Beschränken wir uns auf diejenigen Punkte, bei denen
wir einmüthig sind. Dies sind namentlich die ökonomischen und
theilweise auch die politischen Sätze in unserem Programm. Ich
begreife kaum, wie von so mancher Seite beantragt wird gerade
die Bestimmungen über die Religion abzuändern. Jeder, der einmal
agitatorisch thätig gewesen ist, wird wissen, daß dieser Punkt des
Programms uns sehr gute Dienste geleistet hat (Sehr richtig!),
und wir würden unzweifelhaft eine ungeheure Thorheit begehen,
wenn wir ihn ändern würden. (Sehr richtig!) Gerade jetzt, wo
ein ganz neuer Kampf mit dem Centrum beginnen wird, würden
wir mit einer derartigen Aenderung ohne Zweifel dem Centrum
Waffen in die Hände liefern, die es bisher garnicht besessen. (Sehr
richtig!) Dieser Partei würde es ohne Zweifel gelingen, die Massen
zu einem religiösen Fanatismus zu entflammen, der unserer Agitation
die größten Hindernisse bereiten würde. Wir können auf diesem
Gebiete der freien wissenschaftlichen Forschung und unserer Parteiliteratur ruhig ihren Lauf lassen, wir dürfen unsere Partei nicht
zu einem Laboratorium für freireligiöse und freidenkerische Experi-
mente machen. (Bravo!) Ich begreife, daß diese Strömung, wie
sie namentlich die Berliner Genossen ergriffen, sich in einen Antrag,
wie den von Rüdt, verdichtet hat. Rüdt sagt zwar, man wolle
nicht unmittelbar in die religiösen Anschauungen eingreifen, dieser
Vordersatz ändert aber nichts an der Tendenz des Antrages. Wir
sollen einen Punkt aufnehmen, welcher der freireligiösen und frei-
denkerischen Richtung entspricht. Darauf wollen wir uns aber schon
nun deshalb nicht einlassen, weil nachher ganz ungeahnte Schleusen mit
neuen Wünschen sich eröffnen würden, die uns unangenehm werden
könnten. Es könnten schließlich auch die Vegetarianer kommen, sogar
die „Wollenen". (Heiterkeit und Beifall.)

Die ländliche Agitation hat schon der St. Gallener Parteitag
behandelt. Leider haben wir bisher nicht Gelegenheit gehabt, etwas
Praktisches zu schaffen. Gestehen wir es nur ein: sozialdemokratische
Bauern, im eigentlichen Begriff giebt es bis heute nicht. Unsere
Agitation ist in dieser Beziehung von Erfolg nicht begleitet gewesen,
einerseits der ökonomischen Verhältnisse wegen, andererseits, weil

wir die Bestimmungen in unserem Programm, die wir für eine solche Agitation brauchen, bis jetzt nicht gehabt haben. Wir brauchen, um das ländliche Proletariat zu unserer Bewegung heranzuziehen, vor allen Dingen praktische Forderungen. Wir müssen vor allem unsere Agitation darauf richten, die Lage dieser abhängigen Landbevölkerung einigermaßen zu erleichtern durch eine praktische Thätigkeit der Gesetzgebung u. s. w. Die große Lüge, daß das patriarchalische Verhältniß die Lage des Landvolkes angenehmer machen könnte, hinter der sich die ganze mittelalterliche Brutalität verbirgt, muß gründlich enthüllt werden. Verlangen wir, daß das ländliche Proletariat der Gesindeordnung entzogen wird; das wird uns ein ungeheures Material für die Agitation in die Hände geben. Zunächst müssen wir prinzipiell und sozial-ökonomisch unsere Forderungen gegenüber der Landbevölkerung formuliren. Dazu gehört allerdings ein gewisses Studium; es wird nicht leicht sein und man wird sich gegenwärtig halten müssen, daß die Verhältnisse auf dem Lande ganz andere sind, als in der städtischen Industrie. Mit allgemeinen Redensarten richten wir hier garnichts aus, noch weniger, wenn wir die auf die städtischen, industriellen Arbeiter zugeschnittenen Programmpunkte auf die ländlichen Arbeiter übertragen wollen. (Bravo!)

Liefländer: Wir haben seit Jahren die Produktivassoziationen gefordert. Ich habe bis jetzt noch keinen Vorschlag gehört, der diesen Programmpunkt ersetzen will. Ich meine, um die Lösung der Frage in unserem Sinne anzubahnen, müssen wir sie gründen; es soll ja nur ein Uebergang sein. — Unter den heutigen Verhältnissen werden wir ein proportionales Wahlsystem nicht bekommen, damit würde ja die heutige Gesellschaft sich selbst aufgeben. — Wie das Volk Recht spricht, hat Liebknecht schon richtig geschildert; um das zu sehen und zu würdigen, braucht man nur einer Schöffengerichtssitzung beizuwohnen. Der alte Satz: "Religion ist Privatsache" sollte doch eine Aenderung erfahren; am besten würde er ganz gestrichen, weil sich an ihn fortwährend neue Angriffe und neue Kritiken knüpfen — oder wir können ihn auch behalten, wie er früher war. (Große Heiterkeit und Beifall.) Most hat seiner Zeit für den Austritt aus der Landeskirche agitirt, aber diese Agitation hat nicht die erhofften Früchte getragen.

Auerbach-Berlin V.: Es ist mir gestern in Privatunterhaltungen gesagt worden, daß es gar keinen Werth hätte, sich auf die Diskussion des Programms einzulassen. Ich kann dem nicht beipflichten. Monatelang ist in den Versammlungen und in der gesammten Presse soviel davon die Rede gewesen, daß es mehr als bedenklich sein würde, wenn wir hier nicht in eine ausführliche Erörterung eintreten würden. Die bürgerliche Presse und die Gegner würden immer und immer wieder ihre alte Behauptung wiederholen: das ist eine Partei, die nicht einmal ein festes Programm hat, die es erst auf dem nächsten Parteitage machen will! Darum müssen wir wenigstens die allgemeinen Gesichtspunkte aufstellen.

Was den Namen betrifft, so wissen wir ja, was wir unter der „sozialistischen Arbeiterpartei" zu verstehen haben. Aber die christlich-sozialen Oberwinder und Genossen pflegen auch zu sagen, wir sind Arbeiter und nebenbei Sozialisten. Es wäre deshalb doch vielleicht ganz gut, wenn wir „sozialdemokratische Arbeiterpartei" sagten. — Ueber den Kardinalpunkt unseres Programms, die Umgestaltung der heutigen Gesellschaftsordnung, hat Liebknecht sich gestern so glänzend ausgesprochen, daß da nichts mehr hinzuzusetzen ist. Ich bin dafür, das Wort „gesetzlich" nicht wieder aufzunehmen, ondern es bei „mit allen Mitteln" zu belassen; wir haben nicht nöthig, den herrschenden Klassen gegenüber irgend einen Vorbehalt zu machen, die uns als Unterminirer ihrer Gesellschaft, und mit Recht, betrachten. Die Gleichberechtigung der Frauen auch bei den Wahlen stärker im Programm und auch bei unserer Agitation zu betonen, wäre sehr nützlich; bisher ist letzteres noch sehr vernachlässigt worden, und unter den „Staatsangehörigen" hat man fast überall nur die Männer verstanden. Fordern wir also stets das gleiche aktive und passive Wahlrecht auch für die Frauen. Den „kitzlichen" Punkt: direkte Gesetzgebung durch das Volk, möchte ich so lassen, wie er ist. Das Wählen soll doch nur ein Agitationsmittel sein, und kann es ein glänzenderes Agitationsmittel geben, als wenn wir verlangen: direkte Gesetzgebung durch das Volk, wo jedes Gesetz dem ganzen Volke vorgelegt wird. An der „Rechtsprechung durch das Volk" wollen wir auch nicht rütteln; wenn hier und da ein Schwur- oder Schöffengericht einen falschen oder schlechten Spruch abgiebt, so kann das für eine Aenderung kein durchschlagender Grund sein. Beide Gerichtsformen sind ein Schritt zum besseren, und es ist ganz ersprießlich, wenn Leute aus dem Volk den Richtern beigegeben werden. Das Volk weiß, wo es der Schuh drückt, darum sollen Männer des Volkes die Rechtsprechung haben. Die Eingangsformel „möglichste Ausdehnung dieser Rechte und Freiheiten" möchte ich geändert wissen; ich will keinen Unterschied zwischen der heutigen und der künftigen Gesellschaftsordnung im Programm, nicht „möglichste" Ausdehnung dieser Rechte, nein, alles wollen wir fordern! Ob man es uns giebt, ist gleichgiltig. Die einzelnen Programm-forderungen bezüglich des Arbeiterschutzes werden wir nach den Beschlüssen des Pariser Kongresses umzuändern haben. Den Unterschied zwischen Männer- und Frauenarbeit bitte ich Sie im Partei-programm fallen zu lassen. Für mich giebt es keine verschiedene Sittlichkeit von Mann und Frau, welche geschädigt werden kann; für mich giebt es nur eine allgemeine Sittlichkeit, und reaktionär von uns wäre es, wenn wir die Frau, welche sich wirthschaftlich

selbstständig machen will, irgendwie in ihrer Erwerbsthätigkeit beschränken wollten.

Noch eine Bemerkung zur Geschäftsordnung. Wir sind in einer
Zwangslage; wir haben in St. Gallen beschlossen, daß dem nächsten
Parteitage ein Programmentwurf vorgelegt werden soll. Das Komitee
hat uns keinen Entwurf vorlegen können und kann sich auch nicht
hinsetzen und bis morgen einen solchen ausarbeiten. Da bitte ich
nun, den Entwurf schon 6 Monate vor dem nächsten Parteitag zu
publiziren, damit zur Durcharbeitung allen Interessirten genügende
Zeit bleibt. Endlich eine Berliner Bemerkung. (Heiterkeit.) Ich
gebe die Erklärung ab, daß wir Berliner; trotz aller Unterschiede
in der Taktik; das veränderte, das neue Programm ansehen werden
als einen rocher de bronce und es gemeinsam mit allen Genossen
aus der Provinz hochhalten werden für alle Zeit. (Beifall.)

Ehrhardt-Ludwigshafen: Ich begrüße mit Freuden die
allseitigen Bestrebungen in unserer Partei, das Programm zu
ergänzen, denn das ist, auch im Hinblick auf seine praktische Ausführung ein Bedürfniß. Wohin wir uns wenden, wir treten einem
Reichstagsabgeordneten, oder einem Landtagsabgeordneten, oder
mindestens einem Stadtrath auf die Hühneraugen (Heiterk.it); es
ist also unsere Pflicht, unser Parteiprogramm möglichst deutlich zu
machen, damit unsere Parteigenossen bei der Agitation eine Schablone
haben. Unser Programm ist für uns die Fahne, um die wir uns
unter allen Umständen schaaren. In letzter Zeit ist uns durch
verschiedene Umstände die Agitation sehr erschwert worden, nicht
zum wenigsten durch die Berliner, welche mit ihren langwierigen
Berathungen über die Religion uns in der Provinz beständig den
Prügel zwischen die Beine geworfen haben. (Sehr richtig!) Nichts
ist erbärmlicher, als wenn ich in einer Centrumsversammlung immer
wieder 'Aeußerungen aus jenen Versammlungen vorgehalten be-
komme mit dem Beifügen: „Ihr wollt die Religion beseitigen oder
sie blos vorläufig noch bestehen lassen, um den „dummen Bauern"
nicht vor den Kopf zu stoßen." Wenn ich nun vor diesen Bauern
stehe, muß ich immer erst den Mist wegräumen, den die Berliner auf-
geladen haben. (Zustimmung und Widerspruch.) — Zu den Schluß-
forderungen an den heutigen Staat habe ich einen Vorschlag. Ich
habe die Verstaatlichung der Apotheken im Auge. Keine der
heutigen Einrichtungen eignet sich besser zur Verstaatlichung. Wie
wirksam muß diese Forderung als Agitationsmittel sein, wenn man
erwägt, wie erbärmlich es heute um die Verpflegung der Armen
mit Midikamenten bestellt ist! — Ueber den sogenannten Zukunftsstaat müßte möglichst rasch ein kleines Brochürchen, eine Art
Katechismus herausgegeben werden. Wir wissen nicht, wie lange
die heutige Aera der sogenannten Freiheit dauert; es darf keine
Minute versäumt werden, um das, was wir dem Volke zu sagen

haben, in die Maffen zu werfen. Verwenden wir in ausgedehntestem
Maaße den Riesenfonds, der hinter uns steht, nicht zu Unterstützungs-
sondern zu Agitationszwecken! Im nächsten Jahre wollen wir
soviel arbeiten, wie in den verflossenen zehn Jahren zusammen,
aber praktisch, nicht nur theoretisch; ob das Wort im Programm
so oder so lautet, ist minder wichtig, in der Sache sind wir ja
einig! (Beifall.)

Schwartz-Hamburg: Gegenüber den vielen Ausführungen der
letzten Zeit in der Religionsfrage stehen wir so: Der Staat soll sich
nicht in Religionsangelegenheiten mischen; wer das Bedürfniß hat,
einer Religionsgemeinschaft anzugehören, hat die Kosten dafür zu
tragen, nicht aber soll der Steuersäckel des Volkes herangezogen
werden, um Pfaffen zu besolden. Auch in Hamburg hat sich jüngst
eine Agitation etwas breit gemacht, welche auf den Massenaustritt
aus der Landeskirche hinarbeitet. Das wäre falsch; das Landvolk
würde dann en masse von uns zurückweichen. In der ländlichen
Presse wurde dies besonders gegen uns ausgeschlachtet. Darum
muß dieser Agitation' entgegengewirkt werden. Ich empfehle, den
Passus „Religion ist Privatsache" unverändert bestehen zu lassen.

Molkenbuhr: Ich möchte darauf aufmerksam machen, daß
es eigentlich völlig überflüssig ist, in unserm Programm Bestimmungen über politische Tagesfragen zu haben. Dazu sollte in
Resolutionen Stellung genommen werden, für deren Vereinbarung
die Parteitage, die wir ja jetzt öfter haben werden, der Ort sind.
Das Programm muß die Endziele festlegen, sollte sich aber mit
Tagesfragen nicht befassen. Sonst kommen wir aus dem Dilemma
nicht heraus, daß wir fast jedes Jahr das Programm ändern müssen,
weil uns jedes Jahr neue Fragen aufgedrängt werden. Auch tritt
uns dann unser Programm bei der Agitation gewissermaßen hem-
mend in den Weg; stehen diese oder jene bestimmten Forderungen
im Programm, so können die Leute daraus schließen, wir wollten
nichts anderes, nichts weiter, als was darin steht, und dabei können
doch immer neue berechtigte Forderungen auftauchen, denen Rechnung
getragen werden muß. Zu der Frage „Religion ist Privatsache"
glaube ich, als Bewohner des platten Landes und nach den Erfahrungen meiner Thätigkeit auf den Dörfern, berechtigt zu sein,
mich auch hier zu äußern. Man will den Passus aus dem Programm
beseitigen, weil wir doch den Atheismus als Produkt der wissenschaftlichen Forschung fordern. Nehmen wir alle Produkte wissenschaftlicher
Forschung auf, dann haben wir kein Programm mehr, dann könnten wir
ganze Bände herausgeben. Wir sind doch zunächst eine politische Partei,
und können als solche doch unmöglich die gesammte Wissenschaft in
unser Programm hineinschreiben. Aus dem Verlangen, daß ein
zielbewußter Sozialdemokrat mit der Landeskirche brechen müsse,
folgert man auf dem Lande, daß, wenn die Sozialdemokratie zur

Herrschaft gelangt, Jedem seine Religion verboten, eine große Ketzer-richterei in dem umgekehrten Sinne veranstaltet werden würde, daß man die Gläubigen verbrenne. Und das folgert man mit ziemlicher Nothwendigkeit, wenn wirklich verlangt wird, daß keiner in der Partei geduldet werden soll, der zu einer Kirche gehört. Durch diese Agitation wird auch ein Mißverständniß insofern hervor-gerufen, daß man die freien Gemeinden auf Kosten der sozialistischen Partei zu stärken sucht, denn auf etwas Anderes läuft doch die ganze Sache nicht hinaus. Wir wollen doch keinen Gewissenszwang gegen uns, beanspruchen vielmehr völlige Gedankenfreiheit; also müssen wir sie auch den anders Denkenden lassen. Auf dem Lande kommen wir mit der Religion am besten voran, wenn wir sie ganz aus dem Spiel lassen. Wenn die Leute auf den Dörfern unser Programm, unsere Hauptforderungen kennen gelernt haben, sind sie schon halbe Sozialisten geworden; nun können die Pfaffen es sich nicht versagen, über die Sozialdemokraten herzufallen; sie kommen dann in ihren Predigten auf das Theilen, die Abschaffung der Ehe und alle anderen Lügen. Gerade das ruft dann den Widerspruch der schon halb zu Sozialdemokraten Gewordenen hervor, weil sie sehen, wie leichtfertig da von den Pfaffen Lügen in die Welt ge-setzt werden; das macht sie schwankend, und vielfach haben es auf diese Weise in manchen holsteinischen Orten, wo Sonntags früher ziemlich die ganze Bevölkerung in die Kirche ging, die Herren mit ihren früheren Kirchgängern verdorben. So entsteht von selbst, was jene Heißsporne mit Gewalt herbeiführen wollen. Wir stehen ja doch nicht thurmhoch erhaben über der Bevölkerung; wir wollen sie doch zu unseren Auffassungen herüberziehen; da dürfen wir sie nicht auf diesem Wege zurückstoßen und zwischen ihr und uns eine Scheidewand aufrichten. Das geschähe aber auch dann schon, wenn wir bloß die Nothwendigkeit, Atheist zu sein, betonen würden.

In der Frage der Verstaatlichung von Grund und Boden werden wir, im Interesse der ländlichen Agitation, jedenfalls eine Schrift verfassen müssen, die diesen Punkt festlegt und unseren agitatorisch auf dem Lande wirkenden Genossen eine Richtschnur bietet. Ich bin Zeit meines Lebens im Grunde nichts anderes, als ein Bauernagitator gewesen. Die Landleute sind nicht völlig un-empfindlich für die sozialistischen Lehren, im Gegentheil findet man ein gut Stück praktischen Sozialismus schon oft auf dem Lande (Bravo!), beim Entwässerungswesen, beim Verwenden landwirth-schaftlicher Maschinen, welche den Kleinbetrieb unmöglich machen, im Genossenschaftswesen u. s. w. Dadurch wird dem eigentlichen sozialdemokratischen Grundgedanken Vorschub geleistet; die Leute sind praktisch sozialistischer, als sie selbst glauben, und faßt man die Sache dann am richtigen Ende an, so werden sie auch für unser Programm zugänglich. Es liegt hier kein Fehler im Programm;

es fehlt nur an der nöthigen Litteratur, wonach sich jeder Agitator richten kann. (Beifall.)

Dr. Rüdt: Ich habe das Wort zu einem sehr wichtigen Punkte unseres Programms erbeten und möchte zunächst jedes Vorurtheil gegen mich beseitigen. Ich bin weder ein Freireligiöser, noch ein Freidenker, ich bin ein Feind des Freidenkerthums und bekämpfe es; ich wünsche Ihnen allen· Tretet in die Sozialdemokratie ein, da ist der Platz, wo ihr kämpfen sollt! Ich weide auch nicht auf den Wiesen der grauen Theorie, sondern ich bin wahrscheinlich der praktischste Agitator der Partei. (Heiterkeit.) Das beweisen die Anforderungen, die an mich gestellt werden; ich habe in anderthalb Jahren 140 Reden gehalten. Die Parteigenossen in Bayern, Baden, Württemberg, im Schwarzwald können mir's überall bestätigen.

Ich bin nicht aus Opposition gegen unser Parteiprogramm zu meinem Antrag gekommen, sondern weil ich wünsche, daß unsere herrliche und erhabene Partei bewahrt bleibe vor dem Vorwurf der Heuchelei. Eine solche Partei muß auch wahrhaftig sein. Wir haben gestern selbst von Liebknecht gehört, daß er, wie die meisten andern, auf dem Standpunkt des Atheismus steht. Es soll das nicht ausgesprochen werden im Programm; ich verlange nur, daß wir offen und ehrlich als Partei erklären, daß wir, als Revolutionäre auf dem Standpunkt der Wissenschaft stehend, nichts mit den alten Hirngespinnsten, mit denen die Pfaffen unsere Ziele, unsere Pläne durchkreuzen, gemein haben. Ich habe draußen im Süden Deutschlands unendlich viel mit Pfaffen zu thun, — warum? weil sie uns die Sozialdemokraten vor der Nase wegnehmen wollen! (Heiterkeit.) Deshalb trete ich ihnen entgegen und sage ihnen: Ihr kommt zu spät; auf den Arbeiter macht ihr mit euren Hirngespinnsten keinen Eindruck mehr. Wenn sie vor das Volk hintreten und die Arbeiter warnen vor uns, den Sozialdemokraten, die alles, auch den lieben Herrgott, vernichten wollen, da müssen wir doch einschreiten und den Arbeitern zeigen, daß die Pfaffen sie an der Nase herumführen wollen. Das ist die Aufgabe des Agitators, das beweisen meine Erfolge in den katholischen Ländern. Als die Wahlen kamen, hieß es bei uns: nun wird's gefährlich sein, den Rüdt aufs Land hinauszuschicken, den werden die Pfaffen todtschlagen. (Heiterkeit.) Aber als die Wahlen da waren, hat man den Rüdt doch hinausgeschickt, wo die Pfaffen waren, und da hat er seine größten Erfolge gehabt. Als die Pfaffen vor zwei Jahren gegen Giordano Bruno vorgingen, behaupteten, er sei ein Esel und ein Schwein gewesen, da ging ich nach Köln, und die Kölner können Euch erzählen, was ich da fertig gebracht habe. (Heiterkeit.) Ein freierer Geist war hineingetragen worden; der nützt immer und schadet nie. Dazu meine Erfahrungen im Rheinlande gegen Pastor Thümmel. Die Remscheider Parteigenossen hatten mir geschrieben: wir können nicht fertig werden, wir kommen zu keinem Verein, wir stehen nach Thümmels Erfolgen als gemeine Verbrecher da, Niemand will sich zu uns bekennen. Da bin ich hingekommen und habe gewirkt. Ich bin also thatsächlich kein unpraktischer Parteiphilosoph. Liebknecht sagt selbst, man müsse den Muth haben, nicht vor den letzten Konsequenzen zurückzuschrecken; er hat 1869 in Basel den Kollektivismus auch an Grund und Boden offen verkündet; und wir sollten heute nicht den Muth haben, zu sagen: ja wohl! als Partei brechen wir vollständig mit der Meinung, als gehörten wir noch zu dem alten Zopf, der dem alten Moses nachzieht? Liebknecht meint, die Schule werde schon helfen. Gewiß, aber nur, wenn sie aus den Händen der Pfaffen genommen wird. Bleibt sie so wie heute, oder kommt sie zu ihnen zurück, so haben wir keine Hoffnung, daß diese Schule Sozialdemokraten aus unseren Kindern machen wird. Auf der Pastorenkonferenz in Hannover haben wir ebenfalls dieselben Absichten wieder kennen gelernt: wir brauchen nur wieder einen schönen Himmel, den brauchen wir nur mit unseren schwarzen Kutten zuzudecken, dann wird der Staat mit uns zufrieden, und diese Abwendung wird wieder zurückgedrängt sein. Ich bin der festen Ueberzeugung, diese Abwendung wird nicht zurückgedrängt, aber sie kann gehemmt werden durch das Pfaffenthum. Haben wir nicht in der Geschichte die schlagendsten Beispiele dafür? Nachdem die Revolution niedergeworfen war, sind da nicht diese Ideen von den Pfaffen wieder zur Geltung gebracht worden? Bebel hat das wunderbare Prognostikon gestellt, daß jetzt unsere Thätigkeit stärker gegen die Ultramontanen gerichtet werden müsse; unser Kampf geht aber ebenso gegen die Stöckerei und Muckerei, wie gegen den Ultramontanismus. Denn diese Brüder haben sich untereinander sehr gern und stehen auf demselben Boden. Wir handeln, wie ich praktisch erfahren habe, nicht ganz recht, wenn wir bei jenem alten Satze stehen bleiben. Dreesbach wird mir bezeugen, daß bei der letzten Wahl die Gegner in ihren Flugblättern gerade hier eingesetzt hatten, um die Führer als miserable Heuchler und Lügner hinzustellen; im Programm stände: „Religion ist Privatsache," und die Führer hätten den Atheismus gepredigt. Darum sage ich, die Partei soll sich bekennen, weiter gar nichts, und dann die Pfaffen bekämpfen. Ich brauche nicht auf die enge Verbindung von Thron und Altar hinzuweisen; Sie wissen, wie strikte die beiden immer zusammengehalten haben. — Die große sozialistische Bewegung dreht sich doch nicht blos um den Magen; sie ist eine große Kulturfrage und -Bewegung, und als solche kämpft sie zunächst für die soziale, dann für die politische und dann im Großen und Ganzen für die Geistesfreiheit der Menschen. Sklaven werfen die Kette nicht ab. Ich kann, liebe Freunde, den Vorwurf zurückweisen, daß diejenigen, welche gegen das Pfaffenthum ankämpfen, gegen den lieben Herrgott ankämpfen; ich habe nie mit den Geistlichen um diese oder jene schöne Eigenschaft desselben gestritten, darauf habe ich mich nie eingelassen, sondern stets praktisch den Pfaffen vorgehalten: Ihr wollt das Volk auf dem Boden der blauen Phantasie in der Knechtschaft erhalten. Die Partei selbst fühlt heraus, daß hier etwas geschehen muß. Von allen Gegenden Deutschlands kommen mir seit zwei Jahren Briefe über Briefe, die mich auffordern, in zwei, drei Tagen nach dem Rhein, nach Schlesien Sachsen, Hannover u. f. w. zu kommen. (Rufe: Zur Sache!) Ich bin bei der Sache; ich will damit beweisen, daß ein praktisches Bedürfniß vorhanden ist, daß die Leute selbst verlangen, in Schutz genommen zu werden.

Stolle-Gesau: Der erste Satz unseres Programms: „Die Arbeit ist die Quelle alles Reichthums und aller Kultur" ist von der Manchesterschule angefochten worden, und es verlohnt sich der Mühe, zu untersuchen, ob dieser vor 15 Jahren aufgestellte Satz Stich hält.

Auch an dem Programmpunkt, betreffend die Arbeitsmittel, hat die kapitalistische Presse eingesetzt und eine präzisere Fassung verlangt. Es ist auch bei uns angeregt worden, nicht mehr von Arbeitsmitteln, sondern von Arbeitswerkzeugen zu sprechen. Der Ausdruck „Arbeitsmittel" ist ein Kompromißausdruck; auch die Bodenfrage ist ja in dem Programm nicht buchstäblich erwähnt; früher stand doch an der Stelle das Wort „Kollektiveigenthum". Wenn wir aber heute unser Programm präzisiren, müssen wir das alles hineinnehmen; heute muß ausgesprochen werden, daß der Grund und Boden verstaatlicht werden muß, und daneben muß der Ausdruck „Arbeitsmittel" genauer gefaßt werden. — Die gegen die Rechtsprechung durch das Volk gestern und heute angeführten Thatsachen können mich nicht bestimmen, davon abzugehen; denn wir haben nicht gewählte Volksgerichte, sondern Geschworene, die nach einem Census berufen werden. — In der Religionsfrage besagt unser Programm, daß wir das Bekenntniß zu einer Religionsgemeinschaft Jedem überlassen, wir greifen in die Ueberzeugung nicht ein, wir schreiben nichts vor. Aber damit begegnen wir einem aufgetretenen Uebelstande nicht. Die Kirche, als privilegirte Institution, ist von uns zu bekämpfen, und das muß in dem Programm irgendwie zum Ausdruck kommen. Ich bedaure, daß unsere hierhergehörige frühere Forderung aus dem Eisenacher Programm herausgekommen ist. Die Kirche kann nicht nur Andersdenkende boykottiren, ächten, sie kann sie ganz unschädlich machen und ist so geschützt, daß man gegen die Geistlichen nicht klagbar vorgehen kann. Soll das ewig so fortgehen? Was die Schule betrifft, so schützen selbst unsere Dissidentengesetze uns nicht hinreichend, unsere Kinder freidenkend erzogen zu bekommen. Also Trennung der Schule von der Kirche, der Kirche vom Staat!

13

(Glocke.) Ich komme nur noch kurz auf den Berliner Antrag wegen der Frauenarbeit; dieser Antrag scheint mir gänzlich verfehlt, insofern er die Forderung gleichen Lohnes für Männer und Frauen beseitigen will. Den Frauen müssen in jeder Beziehung die gleichen Rechte zugesprochen werden. Gerade die Konkurrenz der billigeren Frauenarbeit macht jährlich Tausende von Männer arbeitslos. Wer objektiv denkt, wird diesem Antrage nicht zustimmen.

Geyer-Leipzig beantragt den Schluß der Diskuſſion; Klees ist gegen den Schluß; der Schlußantrag wird abgelehnt.

Agster-Stuttgart: Ich will vorweg gegen Dr. Rübt bemerken, daß der größere oder geringere Erfolg der praktischen Agitation nicht in der größeren oder geringeren Zahl der gehaltenen Reden gefunden werden kann. Die längeren Ausführungen bezüglich des Pfaffenthums waren mehr oder minder überflüſſig. So schlimm, wie Dr. Rübt es geschildert hat, ist denn doch die Sache mit dem Pfaffenthum nicht. Wenn wir auch nach dem Fall des Sozialiſtengesetzes das Wort „gesetzlich" weglaſſen, möchte unſerer Agitation, speziell in gewiſſen Kreisen, doch ein unbequemer Hemmschuh angelegt werden, insofern der deutsche Philiſter ja sehr geneigt ist, nunmehr zu glauben, daß wir uns damit auf einen ungesetzlichen Boden stellen wollen. — Daß die Apothekenfrage sehr reformbedürftig ist, unterliegt keinem Zweifel; das Programm würde aber ein Ungeheuer an Umfang werden, wenn wir alle diese Spezialien darin aufnehmen wollten. Die von Auerbach befürwortete Beseitigung der Trennung der Programmforderungen in zwei Gebiete ist eine Frage praktischer Erwägung, die nicht so sehr ins Gewicht fallen kann. Liebknecht hat mit Recht betont, daß wir eine gewiſſe Pietät obwalten laſſen müſſen. — Bei der Forderung der Rechtsprechung durch das Volk muß der Umstand beachtet werden, daß man heutzutage von einer eigentlichen Rechtsprechung durch das Volk noch nicht reden kann; heute hat die besitzende Klaſſe die Rechtsprechung in den Schwur- und Schöffengerichten in der Hand.

Metzner-Berlin I: Ich möchte zunächst auf die Produktivgenoſſenſchaften eingehen. Liebknecht sagte, der Gedanke habe sich überlebt; Andere wollen ihn festhalten. Thatsächlich hat er sich überlebt, denn gerade diese Bestimmung ist in den letzten Jahren vielfach falsch gedeutet worden. Man berief sich auf das Programm, wenn man Produktivgenoſſenſchaften gründen wollte, zum Theil auch, z. B. in Berlin, gegründet hat. Man hat geglaubt, mit solchen Gründungen vorgehen zu ſollen, während doch das Programm nur so aufgefaßt werden kann, daß der Staat, in welchem derartige Aſſociationen begründet werden ſollen, erst herbeizuführen ist, und man hat ganz und gar übersehen, daß, wenn derartige Genoſſenſchaften gegenwärtig begründet werden, sie absolut nicht bestehen können, wenn sie nicht auf dem Boden der heutigen kapitaliftischen Produktion aufgerichtet werden. Sie stellen also nur eine Verlängerung des heutigen Zustandes dar. Solche Mißverständnisse müssen unmöglich gemacht werden, und es hat daher dieser Paffus fortzufallen. Andererseits ist nicht außer Acht zu laffen, daß diese Forderung feiner Zeit aufgestellt wurde, um der Agitation von Schulze-Delitzsch entgegenzuwirken. Von da ist sie in unfer Programm hineingerathen. — Zu dem wunden Punkte der Religionsfrage bemerke ich nur, daß ich, obwohl felbst freireligiös und der Berliner Gemeinde feit Jahren angehörend, mich doch nicht für den Antrag Rüdt erwärmen kann. Gerade weil auch ich unfere Partei vor Heuchelei bewahren will, möchte ich das, was hier in feinem Antrag gefagt ift, nicht in das Programm aufnehmen.

Mit Stolle halte ich es für unfere Aufgabe, dahin zu wirken, daß der konfeffionelle, der dogmatische Unterricht nicht mehr in den Schulen vom Staate protegirt wird; das ift in dem Satze: Religion ift Privatfache, zum guten Theil mit ausgedrückt. Damit ift fchon gefagt, daß der Staat als folcher auch nicht berechtigt fein foll, für irgend welche befondere konfeffionelle Anschauung einzutreten. In der Beziehung wird vielfach den Anhängern der freireligiösen Richtung mit Unrecht ein Vorwurf gemacht. Sie wollen nicht unfere Reihen lichten; im Gegentheil kann ich von Berlin mit Fug behaupten, daß fich auf diefem Gebiete die Anschauungen mehr und mehr klären. Dem Gebahren, welches auf Maffenaustritt aus der Landeskirche gerichtet ift, ftehe ich gleichfalls fehr kühl gegenüber. Nichts hat mir größeren Widerwillen bereitet, als vor einer Reihe von Jahren in Berlin Most direkt in einer großen Volksverfammlung dazu auffordern zu hören; ich habe mir fchon damals fofort gefagt, daß diefe gegen die Stöcker'fche Bewegung gerichtete Demonstration einen nennenswerthen Erfolg nicht haben würde. Es ift leicht, in Volksverfammlungen dazu aufzufordern; aber noch nicht der zehnte Theil führt es nachher aus. Gewiß muß dahin gewirkt werden, unfere Jugend möglichft aus den Feffeln des Dogmenglaubens herauszureißen, aber da haben wir mit uns felbft noch viel zu thun, und auf Kommando läßt fich fo etwas nicht machen. Den Antrag Berndt möchte ich nicht dahin verftehen, daß die Revifion des Programms fofort vorgenommen werden foll, denn fonft würden wir blos ein Programm zufammenftoppeln, das nachher als nicht gehauen und nicht geftochen bezeichnet werden müßte. (Beifall.)

Frau Steinbach-Gera: Daß ich überhaupt hier das Wort ergreife, verdanke ich nicht Ihnen, fondern leider unferen eigenen Kämpfen. Ich habe mich nicht dazu gedrängt, ich bin gedrängt worden noch im letzten Augenblick, wo in einer hämifchen Notiz der „Hamburger Nachrichten", dem Lagerplatz Bismarck'fcher Weisheit, den Sozialdemokraten unterfchoben wurde, daß fie höchftwahr scheinlich beim Kongreß Frauen nicht zulassen würden, trotzdem sie doch im Reichstag beim Gesetz über die gewerblichen Schiedsgerichte die Forderung aufgestellt, daß das Frauenstimmrecht eingeführt werde, und weil dies abgelehnt wurde, das ganze Gesetz abgelehnt haben.

Auch wir Frauen haben uns erlaubt, Ihnen zum Programm einen Antrag zu unterbreiten. Ist die gewerbliche Arbeit nur für einen Theil des Volkes, nur für die Frauen schädigend? Leidet die ganze Familie weniger darunter, wenn der Mann krank, verseucht, elend Familienpflichten übt? Die Fürsorge für die Frauen allein ist eine Beschränkung, die in guter Absicht, scheinbar zu unseren Gunsten, gemacht ist, wir müssen uns aber entschieden dagegen verwahren. Durch ein Verbot der Frauenarbeit in diesen Gewerben würden vielleicht Tausende von Frauen auf das Pflaster geworfen werden, und da sie nicht verhungern können und sollen, — was auch nicht Ihre Absicht sein wird — so sind sie gezwungen, das enorme Angebot von billiger, beinahe schon unbezahlter Arbeitskraft in den übrigen Branchen weiblicher Thätigkeit noch zu vermehren. Gerade die massenhaft durch billige Frauenarbeit hergestellten Artikel vertragen keinen Zuschlag auf den Arbeitslohn. Ich will nur die Spiegelbelege-Industrie erwähnen, die besonders schädlich ist. Ich bitte Sie also im Programm festzulegen, wenn Sie schon auf die Schädlichkeit der Arbeit Rücksicht nehmen, daß beide Geschlechter gleichmäßig berücksichtigt werden.

Ebenso bitte ich Sie unseren zweiten Antrag anzunehmen, worin wir die Einführung weiblicher Fabrikinspektoren fördern. (Beifall.)

Kokosky-Braunschweig: Die „Hamburger Nachrichten" haben einmal eine gute That gethan, denn ohne ihren Artikel wäre unsere Genossin nicht hier erschienen. In unserem Programm ist kein Unterschied gemacht zwischen Mann und Frau. Es sollte aber unverkennbar gesagt werden, daß die Frauen mit uns gleichberechtigt sind.

Man sagte, wir trieben Heuchelei, wenn wir hier nicht ein Rüdt'sches Bekenntniß ablegen. (Heiterkeit.) Ich habe überall den Standpunkt vertreten, daß jede Religion, jedes Bekenntniß zu bekämpfen sei. Nun, es giebt dafür noch eine andere Art der Agitation, als wie die großen Reden des Dr. Rüdt. Ist es nicht auch ein Beispiel von Agitation, wenn man seine Kinder nicht in die Kirche schickt? Wir wollen nicht mehr dem alten Moses folgen, aber auch nicht dem neuen Moses, dem Dr. Rüdt. (Heiterkeit.)

Hoffen wir, daß nach fleißiger Arbeit ein Programm zu Stande kommt, welches auf der Höhe der Wissenschaft steht, gleichgiltig von wem es herrührt. (Beifall.)

Oertel-Nürnberg: Die Sozialdemokratie hat immer die Gleichberechtigung der Frau verlangt, und es ist uns nicht im Mindesten eingefallen, die Genossinnen von hier fernzuhalten. Gleichzeitig möchte ich aber auch betonen, daß mich die Ausführungen der Frau Steinbach nicht überzeugt haben. Die Frauenarbeit ist nur ein Stück der sozialen Frage und kann als einzelne Frage durchaus nicht gelöst werden. So wenig es uns Männern gelingt, innerhalb der heutigen Gesellschaft eine menschlichere Existenz zu erringen, ebensowenig würde es den Frauen gelingen, diejenigen Rechte eingeräumt zu erhalten, die ihnen naturgemäß gehören.

Von allen Rednern, die heute gesprochen, sind nur verschwindend wenig neue Gesichtspunkte bezüglich des Parteiprogramms angeführt worden. Es waren größtentheils nur Wiederholungen dessen, was Liebknecht gestern zusammengefaßt hat. (Sehr richtig!) Ehrhart's Tonart möchte ich nicht folgen. Ich werfe mich hier nicht zum Anwalt der Berliner Genossen auf, aber ich halte es nicht für schön, daß man bei jeder Gelegenheit den Berlinern etwas am Zeuge flicken will. Es ist ein unveräußerliches Menschenrecht der Berliner Genossen, ebenfalls ihre Ansichten geltend zu machen. Wenn einzelne Berliner Genossen zum Austritt aus der Landeskirche auffordern, so wird die Sozialdemokratie daran nicht zu Grunde gehen. Wenn wir uns selbst Furcht einflößen, dann wird es nicht gut: Den Antrag des Dr. Rübt halte ich für vollständig überflüssig. Seine ganzen Erlebnisse sind für mich höchst gleichgiltig, und für die Partei nicht minder. Wir können nicht durch Agitation die Religion von heute beseitigen, sie liegt in der heutigen Gesellschaft begründet, und diese wird die Religion stets aufrecht erhalten, weil sie ein großes Interesse daran hat. Ich glaube mit Liebknecht, daß, wenn wir einmal den sozialistischen Staat haben, wir sehr leicht mit der Religion fertig werden.

Es sind noch ca. 40 Redner gemeldet.

Die Diskussion wird geschlossen.

Persönlich bemerkt Genosse Schmidt-Berlin: Ich bedaure, daß im Laufe der heutigen Debatte wieder einzelne Angriffe gegen die Berliner Genossen gerichtet worden sind, und zwar in einer Weise, die wir entschieden zurückweisen müssen. Es ist da von „Berliner Mist" gesprochen worden. Ich erkläre, daß die Versammlungen in Berlin, welche den Austritt aus der Landeskirche zum Zweck hatten, nicht von der Partei ausgingen, sondern einfach auf die Initiative einzelner Genossen zurückzuführen sind. Denn vorläufig steht im Parteiprogramm nicht, daß jeder Sozialdemokrat Atheist sein muß. Vogtherr sprach also im eignen Namen, nicht für die Partei. Wenn auf dem Lande „Berliner Mist" abgeladen wird, so geht er nicht von Berliner Genossen aus, er wird nicht von ihnen aufgetragen. Ich bitte also den Genossen, der dies gesagt, sich in Zukunft etwas anständigerer und gebildeterer Ausdrücke zu bedienen.

Zubeil: Ich kann mich dem nur anschließen. Wir können hier nicht für die Ausführungen Werner's speziell verantwortlich gemacht werden. Wir unsererseits haben nicht eine einzige, irgendwie beleidigende Aeußerung einem Delegirten gegenüber gebraucht und ich wundere mich, daß derartige beleidigende Ausdrücke gegen die Berliner Delegirten nicht einmal von dem Vorsitzenden unseres Parteitages gerügt werden. Wenn Ehrhart behauptet, daß die Berliner mit solchem „Mist" umgehen, so ersuche ich ihn, eine Zeitlang in Berlin zu leben, vielleicht hat er es dann nicht nöthig, Mist abzuladen.

Lücke-Köln: Rübt hat sich berufen auf seine Erfolge in Köln, und er hat uns, „seine lieben Freunde," angezapft zu einer Aeußerung über seine Erfolge. Ich muß im Namen meiner Genossen in Köln erklären, daß wir die Erfolge, welche die Sozialdemokratie in Köln aufzuweisen hat, nur zum kleinen Theile Herrn Dr. Rübt zuschreiben. Wenn er sich einen großen Theil an den dortigen Erfolgen beimißt, dann möge er es Anderen überlassen, ihm Lorbeerkränze zu flechten.

Gewehr-Elberfeld; Die Partei als solche hat sich niemals an der Angelegenheit Rübt-Thümmel betheiligt, und die Partei als solche hat Rübt auch niemals zu einer Reise nach dem Rhein eingeladen.

Dr. Rübt: Dem Braunschweiger Genossen erwidere ich, daß ich es doch nicht verdient habe, wenn ich in objektiver Weise einen anderen Standpunkt durch meinen Antrag vertrete, so persönlich angegriffen zu werden. Den Vergleich mit Moses habe ich auch nicht verdient, dazu bin ich viel zu blond. Ich will mir nicht ein Verdienst beimessen, daß ich in Köln gesprochen. Aber mein Kampf gegen die Jesuiten in Köln hat wesentlich dazu beigetragen, daß dort ein sehr viel freierer Geist hineingekommen ist. Ich habe mir also nicht zu viel zugetraut. Ich habe allerdings von den Sozialdemokraten eine Einladung bekommen, nach dem Rhein zu kommen. Ich weiß nicht, in welcher Beziehung ich mich irgendwie überhoben hätte. Höchstens war es ein Fehler, daß ich gesagt habe, ich wäre der praktischste Agitator der Partei. Ich habe sagen wollen, daß ich in gewisser Beziehung vielleicht am meisten in dem Kampfe gegen die Pfaffen praktische Erfahrung habe. Ich möchte also bitten, daß man nicht gleich über einen Redner, der unvorbereitet spricht und seine Worte nicht reiflich überlegen und wählen kann, in dieser Weise herfällt.

Lenz-Remscheid: Nach den Rübt'schen Ausführungen mußte es in Remscheid so erbärmlich schlecht mit der Partei bestellt sein, daß Herr Rübt aus Heidelberg kommen mußte, um uns ins Leben zu rufen. Wir haben eine starke Partei gehabt, noch ehe wir Rübt kannten.

Rüdt hat also eine Unwahrheit gesprochen. Es ist eine Uebertreibung, die ich entschieden im Namen meiner Remscheider Genossen zurückweisen muß, wenn er uns gesagt hat, wir hätten ohne ihn nicht fertig werden können. Pfarrer Thümmel ist auch heute noch nicht mundtodt, obwohl allerdings der Vortrag Rüdt's viel zur Aufklärung beigetragen hat.

Jeup-Dortmund verliest, um der Verwirrung, welcher die sozialdemokratische Partei von Seiten der Ultramontanen in Bochum ausgesetzt ist, entgegenzutreten, eine Erklärung, wonach er, Redner, im Gegensatz zu anderen Rednern, der Ansicht ist, daß die Stellung der Partei zur Religion im Programm klar und präzis ausgedrückt ist.

Vorsitzender Dietz: Es ist soeben wieder der Ausdruck „Unwahrheit" gefallen. Der Genosse Rüdt ist der Uebertreibung beschuldigt worden, und vorher hat Genosse Ehrhart gesagt, daß sie „den Berliner Mist ausbaden müßten". Ich habe mich erkundigt, wie Ehrhart das gemeint hat. Er hat sagen wollen, die Berliner Beschlüsse hätten die Leute im Lande nachher auszubaden. Ich muß doch bitten, daß derartige Angriffe unterbleiben, und daß Meinungen, wie die letzteren, in andere Formen gekleidet werden.

Rüdt führt an, daß er vom Vorsitzenden des Lesevereins eingeladen worden sei, worauf Lenz entgegnet, der Leseverein oder ein Genosse seien aber nicht die Remscheider Sozialdemokraten.

Ehrhart-Speyer: Vielleicht geht der Ausdruck „Mist" etwas zu weit. Ich nehme ihn zurück. Ich wollte nicht die Berliner Genossen im Allgemeinen angreifen, sondern ich meinte nur diesen Punkt in Bezug auf die Landeskirche. Rüdt habe ich durchaus nicht für einen Parteiphilosophen gehalten; ich möchte also diesen Ausdruck nicht auf ihn angewandt wissen.

Woldersky-Köln: Ich erkläre, daß von der Parteileitung Kölns Rüdt niemals nach Köln gerufen ist.

Hierauf erhält das Schlußwort

Liebknecht: Man hat mir von gegnerischer Seite den Vorwurf gemacht, daß ich in meinen gestrigen Ausführungen das berühmte Thema des Zukunftsstaates nicht behandelt habe. Als der Sozialismus noch sehr jung war, noch nicht auf der wissenschaftlichen Basis stand, und sich zum modernen Sozialismus verhielt, wie die mittelalterliche Alchymie zur modernen Chemie, da beschäftigten sich die Arbeiter, welche in der sozialistisch-kommunistischen Bewegung standen, auf das Eingehendste mit der Frage, wie der Zukunftsstaat aussehen und wie es im Zukunftsstaat zugehen werde. Ich kam anno 1847, als junges Bürschchen in die Schweiz, gerade als das letzte Nachspiel der Kämpfe zwischen den Kommunisten, geführt durch Weitling, und dem „Jungen Deutschland", dessen Hauptvertreter der jetzt verrückt gewordene Antisemit Marr war, stattfand. Da wurde in jedem deutschen Verein des jungen Deutschland, wie in jedem kommuniſtiſchen Arbeiterverein auf das Eingehendſte die Frage des Zukunftsſtaates erwogen. Und ich erinnere mich, daß damals die Frage ganz beſonders große Schwierigkeiten verurſachte: wer wird in dem kommuniſtiſchen Staate die Stiefel putzen, die Kleider und Kloaken reinigen und die Straßen fegen. Heute lächelt Jeder über dieſe Verſuche, ſich den Zukunftsſtaat auszumalen. Die Schwierigkeiten von damals ſind zum Theil durch die Fortſchritte der Technik, der Wiſſenſchaft, ſchon im Gegenwartsſtaat beſeitigt worden. Die Kloakenreinigung z. B. wird durch's Waſſer weit beſſer beſorgt, als jemals durch Menſchen. Die Eiſenbahnen, die Elektrizität, die Elektrotechnik ſind gekommen und haben die Welt revolutionirt, von Grund aus umgeſtaltet. Die Wirklichkeit iſt der kühnſten Phantaſie vorangeeilt. In Shakeſpeare's „Sommernachtstraum" will Puck, der Zauberer und Genius, einen Gürtel um die Erde legen in 30 Minuten. Heute fährt der elektriſche Funke, der zum Diener des Menſchen gemachte Blitz, in einer Sekunde um die ganze Erde herum. Diejenigen Herren, die Auskunft über den Zukunftsſtaat von uns wollen, mögen bedenken, daß uns jede Vorausſetzung fehlt, auf welche hin vorausgeſagt werden könnte, wie ein Staat, oder eine Geſellſchaftsordnung, ich will ſagen in zehn Jahren — nein in einem Jahr — beſchaffen ſein wird. Was heute als Wahrheit gilt, iſt morgen als Unſinn erkannt. Was heute Ideal, iſt morgen Wirklichkeit, übermorgen Reaktion. Und da will man ſagen, wie künftig der Staat ſich geſtalten ſoll! Nur ein Narr kann das fragen. Wer will ſich unterfangen, zu ſagen, wie es nächſtes Jahr in Deutſchland ausſehen wird? Leute, die ſolche Fragen ſtellen, verſtehen von den ſozialen Fragen nichts, nichts von dem organiſchen Entwickelungsprozeß der Geſellſchaft, und ſie nageln ſich ſelbſt an als vollſtändig unwiſſenſchaftliche, denkunfähige Köpfe. (Sehr richtig!)

Ich komme nun zu der ſoeben beendigten Diskuſſion. Die zu dieſem Punkt der Tagesordnung eingebrachten Anträge ſind, wie ſchon angedeutet worden, einfach Material für die Genoſſen, welche beauftragt werden, der Partei den revidirten Entwurf vorzulegen. Es iſt in dieſer Debatte nicht ein Antrag geſtellt und nicht ein Wort geſprochen worden, welches nicht berückſichtigt werden wird. Unſer Programm kann nicht hervorgehen aus den Köpfen einzelner Weniger, es muß die Kollektivarbeit der ganzen Partei ſein. Alles was noch in der Preſſe, in Verſammlungen Neues an Geſichtspunkten auftauchen wird, wird ſelbſtverſtändlich als Bauſtein verwendet werden für das neue Programm. Nur einen Irrthum habe ich hier zu rektifiziren. Es iſt wiederholt von einer Kommiſſion geſprochen worden, oder von der Kommiſſion, welcher, nach der von mir beantragten Reſolution, dieſe Aufgabe zu übertragen ſei. Ich habe den Antrag geſtellt, den Parteivorſtand zu beauftragen, einen revidirten Entwurf vorzulegen. Wir haben ausdrücklich vorlegen gesagt, und nicht auszuarbeiten. Der Vorstand kann und wird selbst, soweit die Kräfte seiner Mitglieder reichen, an dem Entwurf arbeiten; er hat aber die Pflicht, alle tüchtigen Kräfte in der Partei heranzuziehen und mitarbeiten zu lassen. Kurz: die Partei soll das neue Programm machen, und der Vorstand dieser Kollektivarbeit die würdige Form geben.

Es ist falsch, zu sagen, wir müssen ein definitives Programm schaffen. Es giebt kein definitives Programm für irgend eine Partei, geschweige denn für eine wissenschaftliche Partei, denn es giebt keine definitive Wissenschaft. Lord John Russel, der da glaubte, er habe die politische Weisheit mit seiner Reformbill zum Abschluß gebracht und von der Firality-Endgültigkeit sprach, hat sich durch dieses Wort für ewige Zeiten lächerlich gemacht. Wir behalten auch das neue Programm nur, solange es dem Stande der Wissenschaft entspricht; merken wir, daß die Wissenschaft darüber hinausgegangen ist, dann reformiren wir es abermals. Wir sind niemals zufrieden, wir gehen immer vorwärts! (Sehr richtig!)

Ein Redner hat gewünscht, wir möchten doch das Wort „Normalarbeitstag" durch das deutlichere Wort „Maximalarbeitstag" ersetzen. Dieser Vorschlag liefert einen Beweis für die Richtigkeit der Behauptung, daß unter dem Sozialistengesetz zwar eine kampfesmuthige Generation herangewachsen ist, daß aber die theoretische Ausbildung etwas Noth gelitten hat unter den Erfordernissen des Kampfes. (Heiterkeit.) Sonst würde der Genosse wissen, daß es einen Mann gegeben hat, dessen Name noch nach 1000 Jahren als der des Begründers unseres wissenschaftlichen Sozialismus in hellem Glanze strahlen wird, nämlich einen gewissen Karl Marx, der in seinem monumentalen Werke, dem Kapital, den klassischen Ausdruck „Normalarbeitstag" gewählt hat. Das Wort „Maximalarbeitstag", das absolut nicht mehr sagt als „Normalarbeitstag", ist einfach eine Neuerung, versucht theilweise aus bewußter Opposition gegen Karl Marx von Männern, die wünschten, daß der internationale Charakter, welchen Marx der Bewegung aufgedrückt hat, etwas zurückgedrängt werden möge. Es sind die Anhänger des nationalen und konservativen Rodbertus gewesen, welche den Ausdruck „Normalarbeitstag" durch „Maximalarbeitstag" zu ersetzen versuchten, und es ist der Staatssozialismus, der sich für diesen Ausdruck ins Zeug gelegt hat. Wir halten es mit Marx, und wir bleiben bei unserem „Normalarbeitstag".

Ich komme jetzt zu der Frage der Religion. Ich habe mich mit derselben gestern deshalb so eingehend beschäftigt, weil ich wußte, daß unter uns allerhand Geister das Bedürfniß haben, sich in den luftigen Regionen herumzutummeln. Ich habe gestern schon alle Einwürfe gegen die Fassung unseres betreffenden Programm-

fatzes vorweg widerlegt. Nun hat Herr Rübt gesagt: wir machen
uns einer Heuchelei schuldig, wenn wir nicht Farbe bekennen und
den Atheismus auf unsere Fahne schreiben. Bekennt unser Programm nicht Farbe, stellen wir uns nicht auf den Boden der
Wissenschaft? Und weiß nicht jeder denkfähige Mensch, der weiß,
was Wissenschaft ist, daß Wissenschaft und Religion unvereinbare
Gegensätze sind? Durch den wissenschaftlichen Charakter unserer
Partei ist jede Mißdeutung nach dieser Richtung hin beseitigt. Von
einer Heuchelei ist also keine Rede, wohl aber umgekehrt von einer
mangelnden Kenntniß der Dinge und mangelndem Urtheilsvermögen
auf Seite derjenigen, welche die Auffassung theilen, daß die Religion
in erster Linie zu bekämpfen sei. Die Kirche, die katholische, wie
die protestantische, ist heutzutage nichts anderes, als eine Stütze,
ein Instrument des Klassenstaates, und die Basis des Klassenstaates
ist die kapitalistische Produktionsweise mit ihrer Sklaverei und Ausbeutung in jeder Gestalt. Mit der kapitalistischen Produktion steht
und fällt der moderne Klassenstaat. Jeder General, der den Feind
schlagen will, vergeudet seine Kräfte nicht in einer untergeordneten
Position, die für das Ganze keine ausschlaggebende Bedeutung hat,
sondern er packt den Schlüssel der feindlichen Position, nach dessen
Fall alles Andere fallen muß. Statt mit Nebensachen die Kräfte
zu zersplittern, packen wir die ökonomische Basis an, auf welcher
der heutige Klassenstaat mit sammt den Kirchen oder Konfessionen
und dem Pfaffenthum steht; fällt die Basis, dann fällt alles Andere
mit. (Sehr richtig!) Und dann bedenke man noch, daß die Verpflichtung zur Religionslosigkeit ein Eingriff in die Gewissensfreiheit wäre, in die Freiheit des Denkens, in die persönliche Freiheit, die wir unter allen Umständen achten und schützen müssen.
Kurz, wir, die wir den Satz vertheidigen, daß die Religion Privatsache, sind mehr in Harmonie mit den Grundprinzipien unserer
Partei und obendrein bei weitem radikaler als Diejenigen, denen
in der Bekämpfung der Religion selbst eine gewisse Religiosität
(sehr gut!) oder richtiger, ein Rest von Pfafferei anhängt. Ich liebe
die Pfaffen in keiner Gestalt, und die Antipfaffen genau so wenig
wie die richtigen. (Bravo!)

Und noch eins: Haben wir nicht das, was die Kraft der
Religion bildet, den Glauben an die höchsten Ideale? Ist
im Sozialismus nicht die höchste Sittlichkeit: Selbstlosigkeit,
Aufopferung, Menschenliebe?

Wenn wir unter dem Sozialistengesetz freudig das schwerste
Opfer gebracht haben, uns die Familie und die Existenz zerstören
ließen, uns auf Jahre trennten von Frau und Kind, blos um
der Sache zu dienen, so war das auch Religion, aber nicht
die Religion des Pfaffenthums, sondern die Religion des
Menschenthums. Es war der Glaube an den Sieg des Guten

und der Idee; die unerschütterliche Ueberzeugung, der felsenfeste Glaube, daß das Recht siegen und daß das Unrecht zu Falle kommen muß. Diese Religion wird uns niemals abhanden kommen, denn sie ist Eins mit dem Sozialismus. — Im Reichstage sagte einmal der Abgeordnete Bamberger, als ich über die Gemeinschädlichkeit des Sozialistengesetzes sprach und den Sturz seiner Urheber voraussagte, seufzend zu einem Nebenmann: „Die Sozialdemokraten haben noch den Glauben!" Ja, wir haben noch den Glauben — die Herren Fortschrittler haben ihn nicht —, wir wissen, daß wir die Welt erobern werden. (Lebhaftes Bravo!)

Also mit der Religion wären wir nun fertig.

Es ist ferner von der Frauenarbeit und von dem Frauenstimmrecht die Rede gewesen. Selbstverständlich sind wir alle für das Frauenstimmrecht, für die absolute Gleichberechtigung der Frauen. Diese Gleichberechtigung hat sich auch auf das Gebiet der Arbeit zu erstrecken. Die Genossin, welche vorhin so beredt über dieses Thema gesprochen, ist vollkommen im Recht, zu sagen: Sollen wir die Vergiftung, die Durchseuchung, die Zerstörung des Lebens und der Gesundheit durch die jetzige Produktionsweise beim Manne mehr billigen als bei der Frau? Und sind die vergiftenden, die Gesundheit, das Leben untergrabenden Einflüsse, die wir von dem weiblichen Arbeiter abwenden wollen, nicht auch verderblich für den männlichen Arbeiter? — Prinzipiell ist hiergegen nichts einzuwenden. Und prinzipiell muß auch nach dieser Richtung hin Gleichheit sein. Der Arbeiterschutz-Gesetzentwurf, den wir im Reichstag eingebracht haben, trägt dem Prinzip der Gleichberechtigung, der Gleichheit von Mann und Frau auch Rechnung, soweit es irgend möglich ist, ohne die Interessen der Frau zu schädigen; allein die größere Zartheit des weiblichen Organismus, die Schwäche des Weibes, die zugleich seine Stärke ist, zwingt zu Rücksichten, die das Prinzip der Gleichberechtigung nicht verletzen, von der Humanität aber gefordert werden. Ich will ins Einzelne nicht eingehen — auch diese Frage wird gewiß in vorurtheilslosester, den Interessen der Frauen sicherlich förderlichster Form zur Erledigung gebracht werden.

Die direkte Gesetzgebung durch das Volk, so absolut hingestellt wie in unserem Programm, ist praktisch nicht durchführbar. Aber ich will mich nicht auf Details einlassen. Daß das heutige System der Vertretung, welches man mit dem Namen Parlamentarismus bezeichnet, auch in praktischer, wenn ich so sagen darf: in technischer Beziehung an vielen Mängeln leidet, daß es den Willen des Volkes nicht voll zur Geltung kommen läßt, das unterliegt keinem Zweifel. Vielleicht habe ich im nächsten Jahre die Ehre, als Referent oder Korreferent über das neue Programm zu sprechen, und dann habe ich auch diese Frage ausführlich zu behandeln und auszuführen, wie nach meiner Ansicht die Volksvertretung und Gesetzgebung vernünftig zu gestalten sind.

Die Unentgeltlichkeit der Medizin ergiebt sich von selbst aus der Unentgeltlichkeit der ärztlichen Behandlung.

Es ist gewünscht worden, daß auch die Aufhebung der Gesindeordnung in dem sogenannten praktischen Theil des Programms gefordert werden möge. Das ist eine Frage, die wir hier nicht entscheiden können, aber dem Ermessen der Genossen möchte ich es doch zur Erwägung anheimgeben, daß es sich wohl kaum verlohnen würde, Materien in's Programm aufzunehmen, die schon in einigen Jahren aus der Welt geschafft sein können. Ein Parteiprogramm ist kein Wahlprogramm, kein Gelegenheitsprogramm, welches blos den Bedürfnissen des Tages zu entsprechen hat.

Einen Fehler unseres Programms habe ich gestern nur gestreift, er besteht darin, daß es in verschiedene Abtheilungen zerfällt, bei deren Abgrenzung ziemlich willkürlich und unlogisch verfahren worden ist. Statt organisch aus einem Guß oder Wuchs zu sein, ist es mechanisch in drei Theile zerschnitten, was den organischen Zusammenhang aufhebt und logisch, wissenschaftlich nicht zu rechtfertigen ist. Da heißt es z. B. nachdem die allgemeinen Prinzipien ausgesprochen sind: Die sozialistische Arbeiterpartei Deutschlands fordert, um die Lösung der sozialen Frage anzubahnen, die Errichtung von „sozialistischen Produktivgenossenschaften". Von wem fordert sie das? Doch nicht vom „Zukunftsstaat", sondern vom heutigen Staat. Und wo soll die Lösung „angebahnt" werden? Doch auch nicht im „Zukunftsstaat", wo sie ja bereits erfolgt ist, sondern im heutigen Staat. Nun kommt aber am Schluß dieser Abtheilung des Programms ein zweiter Absatz: „Die sozialistische Arbeiterpartei Deutschlands fordert innerhalb der heutigen Gesellschaft." Sie sehen, diese Trennung ist vollkommen willkürlich, und sie bildet einen der größten Fehler dieses Programms. Wer kann den heutigen Staat von dem künftigen Staat scharf abgrenzen? Der heutige Staat wächst in den Zukunftsstaat hinein, gerade wie der Zukunftsstaat schon in dem heutigen Staat drinsteckt. Es geht nicht wie beim Fall des Sozialistengesetzes, Nachts 12 Uhr hört der alte Staat auf und fängt der neue an. (Heiterkeit.) Dieser kindischen Auffassung, der unsere Gegner huldigen, indem sie fürchten, wir wollten tabula rasa machen — als ob das möglich wäre! — dürfen wir uns nicht schuldig machen; und wir thäten es, wenn wir eine bestimmte Grenze zwischen dem heutigen und dem sogenannten Zukunftsstaat ziehen wollten. Da fällt mir ein: in den Zeitungen war wieder von „Theilerei" die Rede. Kein Anderer als Herr Eugen Richter hat uns wieder das Theilgespenst vorgeführt. Nun, die Herren, die mit solchen Mitteln arbeiten, beweisen dadurch blos, daß sie das ABC des Sozialismus und auch die Nationalökonomie nicht kennen. Ueber derartige Späße geht man hinweg und überläßt die Leute, die solche Dummheiten machen, ihrem Schicksal, der Lächerlichkeit. Aber wenn man sich auch mit solchen Kindereien nicht befassen kann: die Partei hat jetzt in Wahrheit den geistigen Kampf zu kämpfen, von dem jetzt so viel die Rede ist, und für uns ist er Ernst, während er für unsere Feinde blos Spiegelfechterei ist. Indem die Partei in die Diskussion des Programms eintritt, tritt sie zu gleicher Zeit ein in die Diskussion der Parteigrundsätze im weitesten Umfang. Noblesse oblige!*) Mit der Kraft wächst die Pflicht. Die Aufhebung des Sozialistengesetzes, das Wachsthum unserer Partei legt uns Pflichten auf. Unsere erste Pflicht ist, Wissen in die Massen zu bringen. Im Wissen liegt Macht. Hätten die deutschen Arbeiter nicht durch die Sozialdemokratie, d. h. durch die einzige Partei, welche die Erziehung der Massen sich zur Aufgabe gemacht hat, eine große Summe von Wissen und Kenntnissen überkommen, glauben Sie, daß wir den Kampf gegen das Sozialistengesetz ausgehalten und unsere Gegner auch geistig überwunden hätten? Nun wohlan! Zwölf Jahre hat der Kampf unsere ganzen Kräfte in Anspruch genommen. Für die Theorie hatten wir keine Zeit. Jetzt kommt wieder die Zeit des Studiums, der Belehrung, und gerade die Neugestaltung des Programms giebt uns die beste Gelegenheit, und ist ein mächtiger Sporn, diese Mission der Aufklärung in weitester Ausdehnung zu erfüllen.

Und nun bitte ich Sie blos noch, setzen Sie alles daran, daß die Aufgabe, die wir uns gestellt haben, im vollsten Maaße erfüllt wird. Das neue Programm muß stehen auf der Höhe der Wissenschaft, es muß athmen den Geist der Partei, die da weiß, daß sie nicht willkürlich und durch Zufall das geworden ist, was sie ist, und daß wir nicht ein Haufe von verbissenen Unzufriedenen sind, die nicht wissen, was sie wollen — wie unsere Gegner behaupten. Nein, wir sind Sozialdemokraten aus Ueberzeugung und aus Nothwendigkeit. Die Nothwendigkeit zwingt das auf Besserung seiner Lage bedachte, nach seiner Befreiung ringende Volk, sich der Sozialdemokratie anzuschließen. Die ganze gesellschaftliche und staatliche Entwickelung, aus der wir hervorgegangen, ist eine Nothwendigkeit. Diese Nothwendigkeit, die unsere Gegner mit keinen Kanonen, mit keinen Polizeiwaffen aus der Welt schaffen können, besteht, und kraft ihrer bestehen wir. Die Sozialdemokratie ist eine geschichtliche Nothwendigkeit, und unser Sieg ist eine Nothwendigkeit. Nicht die blöde Nothwendigkeit des griechischen Fatums, das mit

---

*) Französisch. Eigentlich: Adel verpflichtet. — Höhere Macht und Leistungsfähigkeit legen höhere Pflichten auf.

dem Menschen spielt, wie die Katze mit der Maus, sondern die
Nothwendigkeit des organischen Entwicklungsprozesses, in welchem
der Mensch als höchst entwickelter Organismus, die entscheidende,
bestimmende Arbeit verrichtet. Irgend ein übel berathener Literat
hat jüngst gesagt, die Marx'sche Lehre schließe die Gefahr in sich,
den Glauben zu erzeugen, wir hätten mit verschränkten Armen da-
zustehen und, während der Entwicklungsprozeß sich von selbst voll-
ziehe, es ruhig abzuwarten, bis die Suppe der Sozialdemokratie ge-
kocht sei. Der Mann, der das geschrieben, hat keine Zeile von
Marx gelesen oder verstanden. Marx gerade hat es scharf ausgesprochen, daß der Mensch selbst mitbestimmender, nein, be-
stimmender Faktor ist, daß er aber nicht willkürlich die Ent-
wicklungsgesetze verändern und deren Wirkungen aufheben kann.
Und wäre diese Lehre nicht richtig, nimmer wäre es uns möglich
gewesen, unsere Gegner zu besiegen. Unsere Gegner verfügen über
alle menschlichen Machtmittel: Geld, Polizei, Soldaten — aber sie
haben uns nichts anhaben können, weil die organischen Entwicklungs-
gesetze, die für uns wirken, sich nicht ändern, nicht fälschen, nicht
in ihr Gegentheil verkehren lassen. Die Machtfülle eines Bismarck
war Ohnmacht im Kampfe mit uns. Gestützt auf unser gutes Recht
und in voller Erkenntniß der Thatsachen, im klaren Bewußtsein
unserer Stärke und der gegenseitigen Machtverhältnisse haben wir
gekämpft und gesiegt — nicht, indem wir die Arme verschränkten,
sondern thatkräftig eingriffen, jeder Einzelne mit äußerster Anspannung seiner Kraft — und so wollen wir fortfahren.

Das alte Programm hat sich überlebt, schaffen wir ein neues.
Dieses wird wiederum alt werden, dann schaffen wir abermals ein
neues. Was wir nicht thun, thun unsere Kinder. Man hat von
„Jungen" und „Alten" gesprochen. Dummes Zeug! Wer das Wort
erfunden, kennt das Wesen der Sozialdemokratie nicht. Unsere
Partei ist eine Partei der Jugend, die Partei des jungen Riesen:
Proletariat, der die Menschheit befreien wird. Die meisten von
uns sind glücklicher Weise jung, andere sind alt an Jahren, aber
als Sozialdemokraten sind wir Alle jung. Gewiß, wie ich am
1. Oktober in Berlin sagte: Wir haben eine junge und eine alte
Garde; die junge Garde ist erzogen worden unter dem Sozialistengesetz und durch das Sozialistengesetz. Neben ihr, nie weit vom
Feind, steht aber auch die alte Garde, und beide müssen mit einander wetteifern, wie die junge und alte Garde der französischen
Armee. Sie müssen einander anspornen und vorantreiben im großen
Emanzipationskampf, damit das Programm der Partei möglichst
gründlich und möglichst bald verwirklicht werde, das Meiste dazu
beitragen, daß unsere Ziele erreicht werden, das sei eines Jeden
Ehrgeiz! Mit diesen Worten komme ich zum Schluß. Nehmen Sie
unsere Resolution womöglich einstimmig an und thun Sie, was

Sie können, daß das Programm zur Verwirklichung, und die Partei zum Siege gelange! (Stürmischer, wiederholter Beifall.)

Nachdem ein Antrag Berndt, die Berathung über das Parteiprogramm sofort vorzunehmen, zurückgezogen ist, wird die Resolution des Genossen Liebknecht einstimmig angenommen. (Bravo!)

Es ist ein Antrag eingegangen, die Liebknecht'sche Rede in 100 000 Exemplaren drucken zu lassen.

Der Vorsitzende theilt mit, daß die Liebknecht'sche Rede thunlichst ausführlich im Protokoll erscheinen wird. Die Presse kann dann diese Rede abdrucken, wodurch eine viel größere Verbreitung gesichert ist, als durch jenen Vorschlag.

Singer beantragt, daß alle in Bezug auf das Parteiprogramm eingegangenen Anträge dem Parteivorstande als Material mitgegeben werden.

Dieser Antrag wird angenommen. In der Tagesordnung wird insofern eine Aenderung beschlossen, daß zunächst über „Streiks und Boykotts" und dann über „die Parteipresse" verhandelt werden soll.

Schluß der Sitzung gegen 1 Uhr.

Nachmittagssitzung.

3¼ Uhr. Den Vorsitz führt Singer.

Auf Wunsch der sämmtlichen im Saale anwesenden Berichterstatter macht der Vorsitzende dem Parteitag die Mittheilung, daß von den Herren, die bisher hier anwesend waren, Niemand die heute Vormittag als Lüge bezeichnete Notiz im „General-Anzeiger" verfaßt hat.

Unter den wiederum an den Parteitag zahlreich eingelaufenen Zuschriften befindet sich, wie der Vorsitzende unter großer Heiterkeit der Versammlung anzeigt, auch eine solche aus London von der Heilsarmee. Dem vielfachen Rufe: Vorlesen! erklärt der Vorsitzende nicht Folge geben zu können, da es sich um ein sehr langes Schriftstück handle, dessen Vorlesung zu sehr aufhalten würde.

Außerdem hat eine gestern in Berlin stattgehabte, von mehreren tausend Personen besuchte Volksversammlung nicht nur dem Parteitag ihre Grüße gesandt, sondern auch das Bureau ersucht, namens dieser Versammlung auch den ausländischen Genossen besonderen Brudergruß zu übermitteln. (Lebhaftes Bravo!)

Einige Genossen wünschen, das Bureau möge für morgen eine Abendsitzung anberaumen, da sie Samstag abreisen müssen. Der Parteitag wird im Laufe des Freitags sich darüber schlüssig machen.

Zur Verhandlung steht, da Punkt 7 der Tagesordnung, die

„Parteipreſſe," wegen Behinderung Auers und Bebels in der 25er Kommiſſion, einſtweilen zurückgeſtellt iſt,

Punkt 8:

Die Stellung der Partei zu Streiks und Boykotts.

Berichterſtatter Kloß-Stuttgart: Obgleich die Stellung der Partei oder wenigſtens der einzelnen Parteigenoſſen, wiederholt in Wort und Schrift zur Kenntniß der Allgemeinheit gebracht worden iſt, dürfte es doch zweckmäßig ſein, einmal auf dem Parteitag dazu Stellung zu nehmen, um nicht immerfort Verdächtigungen ausgeſetzt zu ſein. Es wird ſich wohl zunächſt darum handeln, ob Streiks und Boykotts überhaupt berechtigt ſind, und dazu werden wir einen kurzen Blick auf die gewerblichen Verhältniſſe werfen müſſen, um zu ſehen, ob Streiks und Boykotts durch die Natur unſerer Produktion herausgefordert werden, alſo berechtigt ſind, oder ob unſere Arbeiter ſich blos einbilden, ohne Streiks nicht fertig zu werden, ob die Streiks wirklich häufig blos das Werk von Hetzern ſind.

Unter den heutigen Produktions- und Erwerbsverhältniſſen ſteht der Arbeitsvertrag, der ja das Gleiche ſein ſoll wie ein Kaufvertrag, dieſem garnicht gleich. Bei jedem Kaufvertrag beſtimmt der Eine die Waare, ſei es an Werth oder an Qualität, und der Andere, der dieſe Waare verkauft oder abgeben will, beſtimmt den Preis dafür. Ein Käufer wird nicht ſagen können, ich will die Waare in der und der Qualität und in dem und dem Quantum, werde aber nur dieſen oder jenen Preis zahlen, ſondern der Verkäufer wird den Preis feſtſtellen, und der Käufer wird um dieſen Preis, wenn er mit der Waare einverſtanden iſt, ſie kaufen.

Wie ganz anders beim Arbeitsvertrag! Auch hier iſt der Arbeiter der Verkäufer der Waare Arbeitskraft, der Unternehmer der Käufer derſelben. Da wäre es doch ganz gerechtfertigt, wenn der Arbeiter, der dem Unternehmer die Waare Arbeitskraft nach deſſen Anforderungen ſtellen muß, auch von dieſem den entſprechenden Preis würde verlangen können. Aber ſo iſt es in unſeren Erwerbsverhältniſſen nicht. Die Unternehmer maßen ſich an, nicht nur die Arbeit nach Quantität und Qualität zu beſtimmen, ſondern auch den Preis feſtzuſetzen, unbekümmert darum, ob der Verkäufer damit einverſtanden iſt und bei dieſem einſeitigen Vertrage ſeine Rechnung findet.

In jedem halbwegs geſunden Geſellſchaftsverhältniß beſtreitet die Geſellſchaft den Unterhalt aller ihrer Glieder und muß ihn beſtreiten; andererſeits aber ſtellen alle Glieder ihre Arbeitskraft dieſer Geſellſchaft zur Verfügung, damit ſie alle dieſe Glieder erhalten kann. Das heutige iſt mit dieſem geſunden Geſellſchaftsverhältniß nicht in Einklang zu bringen, weil die heutige Geſellſchaft unter der heutigen kapitalistischen Produktionsweise nicht die Verpflichtung übernimmt, für alle ihre Glieder zu sorgen, sie alle zu erhalten; denn übernähme sie diese, dann würde sie nicht etwa nur die arbeitskräftigen Glieder erhalten, sondern im Interesse der Selbsterhaltung der Gesellschaft liegt es auch, neue heranzubilden, sie wird für ausreichenden Unterhalt auch der Kinder sorgen müssen. Dem ist eben nicht so in der heutigen Gesellschaft. Stellen wir die Arbeit des Einzelnen, als Leistung für die Gesellschaft, dem Lohn oder Unterhalt, als Leistung der Gesellschaft an den Arbeiter, gegenüber, so müßten von diesem Lohne soviel Glieder der Gesellschaft erhalten werden können, als auf jedes einzelne arbeitskräftige Glied entfallen. In unserer heutigen Produktion giebt es aber nur sehr wenig Arbeiter, die sagen können, daß sie mit ihrem Lohn sich, ihre Frau und ihre Kinder ernähren können, und daß weiter der Lohn noch ausreicht, um anderen moralischen Verpflichtungen der Gesellschaft zu entsprechen, nämlich diejenigen, welche im Dienste der Gesellschaft ihre Arbeitskraft eingebüßt haben, Greise und Invaliden, erhalten zu können. Der Lohn reicht in den meisten Fällen nicht entfernt dazu aus.

Sind nun Einrichtungen getroffen, welche den Ausfall an Lohn ersetzen können? Vergeblich blicken wir uns danach um. Keine Einrichtung tritt in Thätigkeit, wenn der Arbeiter mit seinem Lohn nicht die ganze Familie ernähren kann. In letzter Zeit ist allerdings eine Einrichtung getroffen, welche gewissermaßen der moralischen Verpflichtung der Gesellschaft entsprechen sollte, die „große" Sozialreform des Alters- und Invaliditätsversicherungsgesetzes. Hier hatte ja der Staat die Absicht, dafür zu sorgen, daß die Veteranen der Arbeit noch existiren können; aber ein Blick auf die Höhe der Rente, welche diesen Invaliden und Veteranen gezahlt wird, lehrt uns zugleich die völlige Unzulänglichkeit dieser Einrichtung kennen.

Woher kommt es denn, daß die Löhne so gering, so unzureichend sind? Einfach daher, daß der Unternehmer zwar der Repräsentant der Gesellschaft ist, insofern er uns unsere Arbeitskraft abnimmt, aber nicht insofern, daß er die Leistung der Gesellschaft, entsprechend der Verpflichtung derselben, uns gegenüber erfüllt; er ist in dieser Hinsicht nicht der Repräsentant der Gesellschaft, sondern nur seines Geldbeutels; er zahlt einfach den Lohn, den er unter den jeweiligen Verhältnissen zu zahlen gezwungen ist. Jeder Unternehmer weiß ja, wenn er eine Maschine in Dienst stellt, daß er erst Kapital daran zu geben hat, daß er die Maschine kaufen, sie richtig bedienen, den Dampfkessel mit Feuer und Wasser speisen muß; es ist ihm so klar, wie daß $2 \times 2 = 4$ ist, daß, wenn er die Maschine nicht gehörig mit Dampf versorgt, er auch die vorausgesetzte Leistung nicht von ihr erwarten kann. Wie ganz verschieden aber sieht es mit dem Arbeitsmittel Mensch aus! Wenn

14

der Unternehmer ganz genaü weiß, was er der maschinellen Arbeitskraft schuldig ist, der menschlichen Arbeitskraft gegenüber weiß er es allem Anschein nach nicht. Es dürfte uns schwerlich schon ein Unternehmer zu Gesicht gekommen sein, der am Freitag früh seinen Arbeiter fragt: Hast Du noch das nöthige Geld für heute Abend zum Nachtessen für Dich und die Deinen? der da fragt: Hast Du noch genug, um eine gesunde Wohnung miethen zu können, damit Eure Gesundheit erhalten bleibt? Er kümmert sich um alles das garnicht; er baut den Pferden noble Ställe, ob aber der Arbeiter eine gesunde Wohnung hat, danach fragt er nicht. Das Pferd repräsentirt für ihn einen Kapitalwerth, die menschliche Arbeit nicht, weil diese sich jeden Augenblick auf der Straße findet. Und auch mit dem Unterhalt dieser Arbeitskraft geht er nicht vor wie mit dem der thierischen oder maschinellen; er zahlt nicht, was nothwendig ist, um sie zu erhalten und neue heranzubilden, sondern nur, was er nach der jeweiligen Lage des Arbeitsmarktes zahlen muß. Aber damit nicht genug; er geht auch ganz einseitig vor, wenn ihm der Lohn einmal zu hoch erscheint, oder wenn der Reisende, den er ausgesandt hat nach neuen Bestellungen, ihm schreibt: ich kann um den Preis nicht absetzen, der Preis muß zurückgesetzt werden. Da wird denn in allererster Linie am Lohn des Arbeiters abgezwackt, einfach eine Lohnreduktion dekretirt, gleichviel, ob der Arbeiter einverstanden ist oder nicht. Oder wenn gewisse Einrichtungen dem Unternehmer nicht mehr passen, dann fragt er nicht lange, er läßt einfach eine Beschränkung des Arbeitsvertrages eintreten, sei es durch Verlängerung der Arbeitszeit oder dergl. Heute wird der Arbeiter nicht gefragt, er ist nicht der andere Kontrahent beim Abschluß des Arbeitsvertrages.

Wenn nun aber die Verhältnisse sich so verschlimmert haben, daß der Arbeiter mit seinem Lohn absolut nicht mehr auskommen kann, wenn er bei den Einrichtungen der Werkstatt sein Leben gefährdet sieht, wenn der Unternehmer alles das schweigend an sich vorübergehen läßt, was bleibt dem Arbeiter übrig, als dann durch den Zwang des Streiks auf den Unternehmer einzuwirken, um besseren Lohn, bessere Arbeitsbedingungen zu erzielen? Wenn eine Lohnreduktion angekündigt wird, sieht sich der Arbeiter gezwungen, das alte Verhältniß zu erhalten zu suchen, indem er die Arbeit unter dem neuen Verhältniß verweigert. Hier tritt der Abwehrstreik ein, den Jedermann als voll und ganz berechtigt wird anerkennen müssen.

Wenn ferner die Verhältnisse durch irgend welche Vorkommnisse sich verschlechtern, wenn z. B. durch Zollschranken dem Volke die Nahrungsmittel vertheuert werden, wenn durch Viehsperren das Fleisch vertheuert wird, sodaß, entsprechend dieser Vertheuerung, die Lebenshaltung zurückgeschraubt werden müßte, wer wollte es dann dem Arbeiter verargen, daß er durch Erlangung höheren Lohns seine Lage in etwas zu verbessern sucht? Die gegnerische Presse empfiehlt uns ja das Sparen, jederzeit sind Sparapostel aller Art aufgetreten: wir sollen uns nach der Decke strecken. Den Unsinn, der thatsächlich in diesem Rathe liegt, scheinen die Leute gar nicht einzusehen. Sie sagen uns „wir haben vor 20 Jahren viel billiger gearbeitet mit längerer Arbeitszeit," nehmen sich aber nicht die Mühe, zu vergleichen, zwischen der damaligen und der jetzigen Zeit. Sie empfehlen uns das Sparen, denn „wir haben zu große Bedürfnisse und können folglich mit dem uns gewährten Lohne nicht auskommen." Darin liegt eine vollständige Verkennung unserer heutigen Produktionsverhältnisse. Man hat uns nicht nur den Italiener als Muster der Sparsamkeit und Bedürfnißlosigkeit anempfohlen, man hat uns sogar den Kuli als Muster hinstellen wollen. Die Nationalökonomen, die darin die Lösung der sozialen Frage suchen, beweisen dadurch, daß sie thatsächlich von unseren wirthschaftlichen Verhältnissen auch nicht das Mindeste verstehen, sonst würden sie wissen, daß unsere gesammte Produktion auf Massenkonsum und auf Bedürfnißreichthum basirt; wollten wir zu der anempfohlenen Bedürfnißlosigkeit zurückkehren, dann würde die Gesellschaft in kürzester Zeit in sich zusammenbrechen, weil die ganze kapitalistische Produktion nicht mehr gerechtfertigt wäre. Unter solchen Umständen ist jener Rathschlag geradezu ein Hohn auf die heutigen Verhältnisse und die Lebenshaltung des Arbeiters: es ist daran etwa ebensoviel richtig, als wenn man einem 20 jährigen Menschen empfehlen wollte, sich unter der Decke zu strecken, die vielleicht vor 10 Jahren seiner Länge angepaßt war; er wird sich nicht strecken können unter dieser Decke, sondern im höchsten Fall sich darunter zusammenkauern, aber niemals sich darunter behaglich fühlen. Deßhalb ist es richtiger, wenn sie diese ihre Decke der Körperlänge entsprechend machen. Das aber beabsichtigen gerade die Arbeiter, indem sie höheren Lohn verlangen, um ihre Lohndecke entsprechend einrichten zu können.

Wenn nun aber die Vorstellungen der Arbeiter, daß der Lohn nicht ausreicht, daß die Werkstatt ungesund ist, daß die Ventilation gar nicht oder nur mangelhaft vorhanden ist, somit Gesundheit und Leben des Arbeiters untergraben wird, nichts fruchten, wenn der Unternehmer sich entschieden weigert, ihnen Gehör zu geben, was bleibt dem Arbeiter übrig, als wiederum sein Heil darin zu suchen, daß er sich mit seinen Berufsgenossen vereinigt, um bessere Arbeitsverhältnisse herbeizuführen? Nicht nur der Abwehrstreik, auch der Angriffsstreik ist prinzipiell ganz entschieden berechtigt.

Ebenso steht es mit den Boycotts. Wenn die Arbeiter sich in der Ausübung ihrer bürgerlichen Rechte beeinträchtigt fühlen

14*

durch eine Klique von Unternehmern, vielleicht unter Mitwirkung von Behörden, durch Lokalabtreibung u. dergl. daran behindert werden, ihre Interessen zu berathen und darüber zu beschließen, was bleibt ihnen anders übrig, als zur Abhilfe die Ausübung eines Gegendrucks zu versuchen? Wenn ihnen nicht Gelegenheit geboten ist, bei den Wahlen zusammenzukommen, um die Wahlangelegenheiten besprechen zu können, so werden sie dadurch eben in ihren bürgerlichen Rechten beschränkt. Auch da sind die Boycotts prinzipiell berechtigt.

Doch ich will mich dabei nicht aufhalten. Die Genossen aus Berlin, welche ganz speziell damit zu thun hatten, werden in der Diskussion darüber nähere Auskunft geben können.

Wir haben es aber nicht allein mit der prinzipiellen Seite der Frage zu thun, sondern auch mit der taktischen. Diese mit in Betracht zu ziehen, veranlaßt uns ganz besonders das Ueberhandnehmen der Streiks während der letzten Jahre. Da wurden Streiks über Streiks inscenirt, haben aber in der großen Mehrzahl einen unglücklichen Ausgang genommen. Es ist von den Genossen längst darauf hingewiesen, daß der Streik eine zweischneidige Waffe ist, leicht denjenigen verletzen kann, der sich damit vertheidigen wollte. So wird es bei allen Streiks der Fall sein, wo seitens der Arbeiter nicht für die Vorbedingungen gesorgt ist, die einen glücklichen Ausgang in sichere Aussicht stellen. Mit den Streiks wird gar oft Mißbrauch getrieben. Während der letzten Jahre hat die Zahl der Streiks ganz bedeutend zugenommen. Eine zuverlässigere Mittheilung über die Zahl der Streiks kann ich leider nicht geben, dazu ist das mir zugegangene Material zu gering. Aber aus den mir gewordenen Mittheilungen ging nur allzudeutlich hervor, daß die Streiks während der letzten Jahre in weitaus den meisten Fällen ihren Zweck verfehlt haben. Die Gründe dafür waren starker Zuzug, Indifferentismus der Kollegen, die nicht genügend in die Verhältnisse eingeweiht waren, um ihn standhaft aushalten zu können, und vor allem Mangel an Unterstützung. Allein unter den Tischlern Deutschlands haben sich die Arbeiter in ca. 40 Orten Deutschlands geregt, um Lohnbewegungen zu insceniren, und nur durch die Organisation ist es gelungen, zu erreichen, daß die Streiks in den meisten Orten unterblieben, während einige, indem sie sich mit geringen Konzessionen begnügten, auch ohne Streik einigen Vortheil erzielt haben. Aber das in vielen Fällen erzielte Resultat ist später durch ungenügende Organisation, mangelhafte Schulung oder große Indifferenz, Vergessen der Thatsache, daß die Erfolge nur der Solidarität der Gesammtheit zu verdanken waren, wieder in Frage gestellt oder gänzlich verloren worden.

Wie ist nun dem Ueberhandnehmen, dem unvorsichtigen Insceniren von Streiks entgegenzutreten? Die vielen Streiks der letzten Jahre, inscenirt von Arbeitern, die gar nicht oder erst kurze Zeit organisirt waren oder sich erst organisiren wollten, sind gewissermaßen einem Erwachen aus dem Schlafe zu vergleichen, wo der Erwachende sich im Augenblick nicht klar in die wirklichen Verhältnisse hineinversetzen kann; der Arbeiter fühlt das Unbehagen, weiß ihm nicht wirksam entgegenzutreten, und glaubt mit einem Male die Sache durch den Streik bessern zu können. Er weiß nicht, daß ein Schlag nicht genügt, um die Verhältnisse dauernd zu bessern. Die Arbeiter haben so lange in Indifferentismus dahingelebt, sich der Organisation fern gehalten, und erst als sie vielleicht statistisch aufgeklärt wurden oder ein Redner in ihre Kreise drang, der sie durch das lebendige Wort über ihre Lage aufklärte, erwachten sie aus dem Schlummer und glaubten nun, nichts Besseres thun zu können, als zu streiken. Dieses unvorbereitete Vorgehen ist die Hauptursache des mißglückten Verlaufs der meisten Streiks; man befand sich in Unkenntniß der Verhältnisse und war nicht im Stande, die Geschäftslage richtig zu beurtheilen.

Weiter darf ich den Hinweis darauf nicht unterlassen, daß auch das Verhalten der Behörden gegenüber den Streikenden allzu oft ein sehr großer Hemmschuh war, daß dadurch die Organisation verhindert wurde, ihre ganze Kraft zu entfalten, daß aber den Organisationen der Unternehmer Schutz und Hilfe in Aussicht gestellt oder zu Theil wurde. Bei den verschiedenen Streiks, vor zwei Jahren in Magdeburg und an anderen Orten, haben die Unternehmer sofort schwarze Listen angefertigt, um die daran betheiligten Arbeiter zu kennzeichnen. An diesen schwarzen Listen hat sich keine Behörde gestoßen, kein Staatsanwalt hat sich veranlaßt gesehen, dagegen einzuschreiten; als aber die Arbeiter in den Zeitungen vor diesem oder jenem Geschäft warnten, da fanden die Behörden darin sofort einen Verstoß gegen § 153 der Gewerbeordnung. Denken wir ferner an die Vorkommnisse in Hamburg vor drei Jahren und in diesem Jahre. Als 1887 die Tischler in Hamburg streikten, faßte der den Streik leitende Tischlerverein den Beschluß, daß kein Vereinsmitglied bei einem Innungsmeister in Arbeit treten dürfe. Was war die Folge? Die Behörde erblickte in dem Beschluß eine Gefährdung der Innungen, einer staatlich anerkannten Institution. Als aber in diesem Jahre die Unternehmer in Hamburg beschlossen, in ihren Branchen keinen Arbeiter einzustellen, der der fachgewerblichen Organisation angehört, fand sich weder Polizei noch Staatsanwalt, welche hierin einen Verstoß gegen § 153 in dem Sinne erblickten, daß dadurch staatlich anerkannte Institutionen, wie es die Fachvereine auf Grund des § 152 thatsächlich sind, in ihrem Bestehen gehindert wurden. Man ging noch weiter, man hat die Kassirer dieser Organisationen verhaftet, die Kassen beschlagnahmt, diese Leute gleich Verbrechern mit Nummern auf der Brust photographiren laffen. (Rufe: Pfui!) Später stellte sich natürlich heraus, daß man diesen Verhafteten gesetzwidrige Handlungen nicht nachweisen konnte, daß man also Leute, die im vollen Recht waren, einfach mit Gewalt lahm zu legen versucht hatte. Diese Behandlung der Streikenden dürfte zum unglücklichen Ausgang vieler Streiks mit beigetragen haben. Aber noch manches Andere hat mitgewirkt. Vor einigen Monaten fanden wir in jedem Gewerkschaftsblatt regelmäßig wiederholte Warnungen vor Zuzug nach gewissen Orten, oft waren nicht weniger als 20, und darunter ganz bedeutende Orte aufgeführt. Waren nun in drei, vier, sechs Orten gleichzeitig Streiks inszenirt, so suchten natürlich überall die jungen Leute, um die Streikkasse zu entlasten, anderswo unterzukommen; irgendwo mußten sie doch unterkommen, und es war ihnen oft nicht möglich, an all' den Orten vorüberzugehen, wo die Arbeiter ebenfalls im Kampfe lagen: sie traten in Arbeit, und die Klagen lauten denn auch übereinstimmend dahin, daß der Zuzug zu stark war und deswegen die Streiks nicht durchgeführt werden konnten.

Aber wenn auch diese Streiks zum Theil unglücklich verliefen, weil sie unverständiger Weise inscenirt waren, so sind sie deswegen keineswegs absolut verwerflich; im Gegentheil, haben wir sie im Prinzip anerkannt, und der Mißerfolg kann daran nichts ändern. Wesentlich geändert muß aber die Taktik werden. Diese Frage geht auch den Kongreß an.

Seit Jahren ist es in einzelnen Kreisen der Parteigenossen leider gar zu sehr üblich gewesen, über die Fachorganisationen sich weit erhaben zu fühlen. Manche haben die fachgewerbliche Bewegung geradezu als Humbug hingestellt, und gerade durch dieses Ignoriren der Fachvereinsbewegung ist das Wachsthum der Partei sehr aufgehalten worden; die Partei wäre heute ungleich stärker, wenn die Genossen auch für die fachgewerbliche Bewegung durch Erörterung der wirthschaftlichen Fragen und dergleichen vor den Mitgliedern der Fachvereine thätig gewesen wären und sie uns dadurch näher gebracht hätten. Mögen die Genossen zurückdenken; viele von ihnen sind erst durch diese fachgewerbliche Bewegung zu politischen Anschauungen gekommen. (Sehr wahr!) Wäre das geschehen, wir hätten schon 1887 mit einer viel größeren Stimmenzahl rechnen können. Ebenso bestimmt aber glaube ich, daß unsere diesmalige große Stimmenzahl zum guten Theil der fachgewerblichen Agitation zuzuschreiben ist, die ganz bedeutend an Boden gewonnen, in immer weitere Arbeiterkreise das Klassenbewußtsein getragen hat. (Sehr gut!) Deshalb müssen wir uns hier schlüssig machen, ob wir nach wie vor der fachgewerblichen Organisation gegenüber uns passiv verhalten wollen oder ob wir uns nicht vielmehr der Nothwendigkeit klar bewußt werden wollen, daß wir dafür zu sorgen haben, daß die große Masse der Arbeiter sich erst organisirt, um dann nach genügender Vorbereitung mit Streiks und Boycotts auch wirksam und ohne Besorgniß vor Verlusten vorgehen zu können.

Soll nun der lokalen oder der zentralen Organisation der Vorzug gegeben werden? Gegen die letztere ist hervorgehoben worden, daß sie, da sie keine Politik treiben dürfe, der Versumpfung anheimfallen müsse. Es dürfte aber in Wirklichkeit kaum so werden, wenn die Genossen es nur verhindern wollen. So lange letztere sich den Organisationen fernhalten, so lange dort nur Leute sind, die lernen wollen, aber keine Lehrer finden, so lange liegt die Gefahr der Verflachung nahe, wenn aber die Genossen, die das politische Prinzip anerkennen und hochhalten, sich ihnen anschließen, dann wird davon keine Rede sein, dann werden sie ihren Zweck voll und ganz erfüllen, ohne Politik zu treiben. Andererseits sagt man, die Lokalorganisationen dürfen Politik treiben, darum sind sie an sich vorzuziehen. Aber sie werden mit Argusaugen bewacht, wir haben ja den Herfurth'schen Erlaß kennen gelernt, der geringste Fehltritt würde sie zur Auflösung führen. Thatsächlich wurden in Erfurt 3 Lokalorganisationen unter Anklage gestellt, in Verbindung getreten zu sein, weil sie eine gemeinsame Herberge errichtet haben; ein solches Vorgehen ist nicht zu billigen, weil es nicht im Sinne des Gesetzgebers gelegen haben kann. — Also auch diese Organisationen werden keineswegs in der gewünschten Weise vorgehen können, namentlich nicht auf dem Gebiete der politischen Angelegenheiten.

Der Zweck der Organisation ist, Aufklärung in die Reihen der Arbeiter zu bringen, und der Zweck wird im Wesentlichen durch die Agitation erreicht. Als beste Agitationsform empfiehlt sich also die zentrale Organisation. Die lokale Organisation hat kein Interesse daran, daß in der Schwester- oder Nachbarstadt eine ähnliche Organisation besteht, weil sie mit ihr nicht in Verbindung treten kann, bezw. darf; die zentrale aber, die z. B. in Hannover als Zahlstelle existirt, hat ebensoviel Interesse daran, in Königsberg, Kassel oder München eine Zahlstelle entstehen zu sehen. Solche zentrale Organisation kann auch viel leichter Opfer bringen für die Agitation.

Nun haben ja auch diese Organisationen sehr viel mit behördlichen Maßnahmen zu kämpfen gehabt. Zunächst suchte man sie als politisch zu erklären, um sie dann verbieten zu können. Dieser Anschlag ist nur in vereinzelten Fällen gelungen, wo die Organisation am Orte selbst die nöthigen Vorsichtsmaßregeln außer Acht gelassen hatte. Aber auch sonst ist ihnen das Leben recht sauer gemacht worden; es wurde alles aufgeboten, sie als Versicherungsgesellschaften darzustellen, zuerst in Barmen, dann in Frankfurt und Berlin, bis das Oberverwaltungsgericht diesem Versuch einen Riegel vorschob. Aber das wirkte nicht lange; unbekümmert um dieses Urtheil hat man nachher wieder in Magdeburg, Berlin und anderen Orten die Vereinszahlstellen unter Anklage gestellt, Versicherungsgesellschaften zu sein, und erst neuerdings ist noch eine in Erfurt erhobene Anklage vom Kammergericht in Berlin zurückgewiesen worden.

Alles in Allem wiederhole ich, die Genossen sollten die fachgewerblichen Organisationen nach Kräften unterstützen, da sie unbedingt einsehen müssen, daß diese die Sache der Arbeiter nur fördern können. Ein Beispiel aus Stuttgart. Dort bestand 1883 eine lokale Organisation von ca. 500 Mitgliedern; sie erhielt sich trotz der Aussperrung von 1883 auf ziemlich hohem Stand, bis 1885/86 einige Parteigenossen von lokalem Einfluß einfach erklärten, diese Bewegung sei für sie ein überwundener Standpunkt. Die Arbeiter in den großen Werkstätten Stuttgarts, die auf die Sozialdemokraten unter den Vereinskollegen ihr Hauptaugenmerk zu richten gewohnt waren, wollten nun auch nichts mehr davon wissen, und so schmolz der Bestand auf 120 bis 130 zusammen. Erst seit die Genossen eingesehen haben, daß sie im Unrecht waren, ist die Organisation wieder erstarkt und rechnet jetzt nicht mehr mit 120, sondern mit 900 bis 1000; das haben wir lediglich der Unterstützung der Genossen zu danken, die endlich den Bann abgeschüttelt und erkannt haben, daß durch ihr früheres Verhalten auch die Parteiinteressen geschädigt waren. Denn die aus der Gewerkschaftsbewegung Ausgeschiedenen waren auch für die Parteibewegung verloren. Ist Einer ein gutes Fachvereinsmitglied geworden, so müßte es auch kurios zugehen, wenn seine eigene Vernunft ihn nicht in die Reihen der Sozialdemokratie überführte, welche für seine bürgerlichen wie wirthschaftlichen Rechte gleichmäßig eintritt. Dann aber, wenn wir diese Organisationen kräftigen und fördern, wird auch bald dem Uebelstande abgeholfen sein, daß die Streiks als eine so gefährliche Waffe betrachtet werden müssen; denn dann werden die Streiks, wenn sie überhaupt unvermeidlich sind, von ganz anderem Erfolge begleitet sein.

Bis jetzt ist noch auf keinem Parteitage darüber Beschluß gefaßt, noch niemals zur Frage der fachgewerblichen Organisation Stellung genommen worden. Wir hier, auf dem ersten Parteitag nach dem Falle des Sozialistengesetzes, sollten dies nachholen, damit die Genossen allerwärts wissen, wie die höchste Instanz unserer Partei sich zu dieser Frage verhält. Ich erlaube mir daher, Ihnen im Verein mit Grillenberger folgende Resolution vorzuschlagen:

Der Parteitag erklärt:

Unter den heutigen ökonomischen Verhältnissen und bei dem Bestreben der herrschenden Klassen, die politischen Rechte und die wirthschaftliche Lage der Arbeiter immer tiefer herabzudrücken, sind Streiks wie auch Boykotts eine unumgängliche Waffe für die Arbeiterklasse: einmal, um die auf ihre materielle oder politische Schädigung gerichteten Bestrebungen ihrer Gegner zurückzuweisen dann aber auch, um ihre soziale und politische Lage nach Möglichkeit innerhalb der bürgerlichen Gesellschaft zu verbessern.

Da aber Streiks und Boykotts zweischneidige Waffen sind, die, am unrechten Orte oder zur unrechten Zeit angewendet, die Interessen der Arbeiterklasse mehr schädigen als fördern können, empfiehlt der Parteitag den deutschen Arbeitern sorgfältige Erwägung der Umstände, unter welchen sie von diesen Waffen Gebrauch machen wollen; insbesondere betrachtet es der Parteitag als eine zwingende Nothwendigkeit, daß die Arbeiterklasse zur Führung solcher Kämpfe sich gewerkschaftlich organisirt und zwar möglichst in zentralistischen Verbänden, um sowohl durch die Wucht der Zahl, wie die Wucht der materiellen Mittel und nach sorgfältig getroffenen Erwägungen den beabsichtigten Zweck möglichst vollkommen erreichen zu können.

Der Parteitag, von diesen Auffassungen ausgehend, empfiehlt allen Parteigenossen kräftige Unterstützung der gewerkschaftlichen Bestrebungen.

Zugleich protestirt der Parteitag gegen die erneuten Versuche der Regierungen und der Unternehmerklasse, den in Deutschland vorhandenen Rest des Koalitionsrechts durch die reaktionären Bestimmungen in der Novelle zur Gewerbeordnung vollends zu vernichten, und beauftragt die parlamentarischen Vertreter der Partei, diese Versuche mit aller Entschiedenheit zu bekämpfen und dafür einzutreten, daß volle Koalitions- und Vereinigungsfreiheit, diese Grundlage für die Kämpfe der Arbeiterklasse zur Erreichung besserer Existenzbedingungen, erreicht werde.

Ich empfehle Ihnen diese Resolution zur einstimmigen Annahme. (Lebhafter Beifall.)

Ein inzwischen eingegangener Antrag von Horn-Löbtau, Heppner und Frauenlob, wonach für alle aus Streiks und Boykotts hervorgegangenen Prozesse Rechtsschutz durch Bestellung von Rechtsanwälten aus den Mitteln der Parteikasse gewährt werden soll, findet nicht die genügende Unterstützung.

In der Diskussion erhält zuerst das Wort

Bock-Gotha: Das Referat meines Freundes Kloß wird jedenfalls dazu beigetragen haben, jenen Theil der hier vertretenen Genossen, welche bisher dieser Richtung feindlich gesonnen waren, vielleicht etwas umzustimmen. Man macht den Gewerkschaften den Vorwurf, daß sie nicht so voll und ganz für die Partei ausgenutzt werden können, wie man es wünscht. Damit schüttet man aber das Kind mit dem Bade aus. Ich stehe seit 20 Jahren in der Bewegung und muß meiner Ueberzeugung dahin Ausdruck geben, daß unter dem Sozialistengesetz dort, wo der Kampf sich ausschließlich auf das politische Gebiet konzentrirte, diese Auffassung einige Berechtigung hatte; aber nachdem jenes gefallen ist, werden die Genossen,

welche in dieser Bewegung einen Rückschritt sahen oder ihr direkt
feindselig entgegentraten, sich anders stellen.

Mit Recht hat der Referent ausgeführt, daß er sich nicht vor-
stellen kann, daß ein guter Gewerkschafter nicht auch zugleich ein
guter Parteigenosse soll sein können. Unsere älteren Genossen an
der Spitze haben sich sehr oft im günstigsten Sinne über die Bewegung ausgesprochen. Wenn irgend etwas, so muß doch schon
der Umstand die Andern überzeugen, daß die Regierungen zwischen
der gewerkschaftlichen Bewegung und uns in der Bekämpfung gar
keinen Unterschied gemacht haben. (Sehr richtig!) Die Regierung
weiß sehr wohl, inwieweit die gewerkschaftliche Bewegung der
politischen von Vortheil ist. Ich halte es nun überhaupt für verkehrt, daß man den Gewerkschaften einen ausgeprägt bestimmten
politischen Charakter giebt. Wir haben gestern so beredt ausein-
andersetzen hören, daß eine antireligiöse Agitation derart nachtheilig
sein kann, daß wir einem großen Theil der Bevölkerung damit vor
den Kopf stoßen. Ganz genau dasselbe ist auch hier der Fall.
Wenn wir von jedem Arbeiter verlangen, daß er in der gewerkschaftlichen Organisation zugleich der sozialdemokratischen oder
überhaupt einer bestimmten politischen Richtung angehöre, dann
verkennt die gewerkschaftliche Bewegung vollständig ihren Zweck, denn
die Leute kommen nicht als Sozialdemokraten in die Gewerkschaft,
sondern als Arbeiter. Wenn die Gegner der Bewegung meinen,
daß die Gewerkschaften durch Leisetreterei versimpeln, daß sie am
Gange der Arbeiterbewegung nichts bessern würden, so übersehen
Jene, daß, obwohl die Gewerkschaften keine Politik treiben dürfen,
noch keine Generalversammlung, kein Kongreß, keine Zahlstelle gefunden werden konnte, wo nicht zielbewußte Arbeiter an der Leitung
betheiligt gewesen wären. Versumpfen sie, dann ist es nicht Schuld
der Arbeiter, sondern unsere Schuld. Auf dem Gebiet der Fach-
presse ist der Versumpfung vorgebeugt; in diesem Punkt steht unsere
deutsche gewerkschaftliche Bewegung allen anderen Ländern weit
voran. Sie finden in dieser Presse nationalökonomische Aufklärung
in jeder Beziehung, und da sie als selbstständige Unternehmung
neben den Gewerkschaften steht, so kann von Versumpfung wohl
nicht die Rede sein. — Wollen wir die Gewerkschaftsbewegung
pflegen, dann müssen wir nicht nur die zielbewußten Arbeiter an
uns ketten wollen, sondern gerade an die große Masse der Indifferenten herangehen, und die bekommen wir nur dann, wenn wir
den Gewerkschaften nicht einen ausgesprochen politischen Charakter
verleihen. Die Leute politisch aufzuklären, ist Sache der politischen
Partei; in den Gewerkschaften soll man sie widerstandsfähig machen
gegen das Kapital, gegen das Unternehmerthum. Das letzte Jahr
hat den verschiedenen Gewerkschaften in Deutschland großartige
Kämpfe gebracht, und damit ist auch zugleich die gewerkschaftliche

Organisation riesenhaft gewachsen. Meine Gewerkschaft ist von 5000 Mann auf 15000 Mann in einem Jahre gestiegen, und gerade diese Parias mit ihrer längsten Arbeitszeit und dem kümmerlichsten Lohn sind durch die Gewerkschaftsorganisation befähigt worden, eine große Anzahl Kämpfe siegreich durchzuführen. — Der Referent führte aus, es liege im Interesse der Bewegung, nutzlose Streiks möglichst zu verhüten. Dafür giebt es kein besseres Mittel, als eine kräftige, gut organisirte Gewerkschaft. So lange die Arbeiter in einzelnen kleinen Verbändchen zusammen sind, ohne Fühlung mit der Gesammtheit, nicht genügend disziplinirt, so lange werden derartige kleine Streiks jederzeit wiederkehren und die Arbeiter werden ihre Opfer nutzlos vergeuden; eine stramme Organisation aber verbürgt, daß nur da gestreikt wird, wo Aussicht auf Erfolg vorliegt. Wo sind denn die englischen Gewerkschaften hingekommen? Sie selbst werfen jetzt den bisherigen Apparat über Bord und erklären, daß dem Arbeiter nur auf dem politischen Gebiete geholfen werden kann. Bis dahin ist doch noch ein weiter Schritt. (Glocke.) Es thut mir leid, abbrechen zu müssen. Wenn in der Zukunft etwas Praktisches geleistet werden soll, dann muß das Streben der gesammten Arbeiterschaft zielbewußt darauf gerichtet sein, die untersten Schichten und Branchen emporzuheben, da anzufangen, wo die Masse in Elend und Noth versumpft, wo bisher weder politisch, noch gewerkschaftlich etwas gethan wurde. (Beifall.)

Lenz-Remscheid: Betrachten wir die Berliner Streiks. Der Maurerstreik hatte den Zweck, den Stundenlohn von 60 auf 70, womöglich auf 75 Pfennige zu bringen. Die jungen Leute reisen ab, helfen in der Provinz und drücken da den niedrigen Lohn von 20 bis 30 Pfennig noch weiter herunter. Gerade dadurch, daß die Forderungen theilweise in's Unvernünftige hoch hinaufgeschraubt werden, wird unsere Partei ganz entschieden geschädigt. Die Streiks der Baubranchen in Berlin und Hamburg sind zum Schaden der Betreffenden und auch zum Schaden der ganzen Partei ausgeschlagen. Ich bitte Sie daher, alles einzusetzen, um diese theilweise leichtfertig, wenn auch nicht gerade frivol angezettelten Streiks zu verhüten.

Horn-Dresden Land: Was mein Freund aus Remscheid eben angeführt hat, kann keinesfalls die Billigung des größeren Theils der Delegirten finden, weil in Berlin und Hamburg mit ganz anderen Verhältnissen zu rechnen ist, als auf dem platten Lande. Wenn es sich um die Erringung höheren Lohnes handelt, ist doch zunächst zu berücksichtigen, ob der bisher bestandene Lohnsatz auch ausreicht für die Bedürfnisse der am Orte vorhandenen Arbeiter oder Gewerkschaftsmitglieder. Es giebt Gegenden, wo die Leute sich mit einem Stundenlohn von 30 Pf. nur gerade so knapp behelfen müssen, wie in Berlin oder Hamburg mit 60 Pf. — Mit

der Fassung der Resolution bin ich im Großen und Ganzen einverstanden. Wenn ich die bisherigen Kämpfe berücksichtige, muß
ich aber auch dazu kommen, diesen Bestrebungen die möglichste
Unterstützung nach jeder Richtung angedeihen zu lassen. Wo das
Verlangen nach Besserung der Lage der Arbeiter in den Gewerkschaften von uns als berechtigt anerkannt wird, sollte auch aus
Parteifonds Hilfe geleistet werden, und dahin zielte mein Antrag,
der allerdings vorhin leider nicht die genügende Unterstützung fand.
Ein berechtigter Kern liegt aber doch darin.

Molkenbuhr-Altona: Ob wir ein Recht haben, Streiks
und Boykotts anzuwenden, über diese Frage sind wir längst hinweg.
An und für sich sind die Streiks nach meiner Meinung viel weniger
abhängig vom Willen derer, welche daran betheiligt waren, als
von den Verhältnissen, wie sie sich einmal entwickeln. Hier aber
kommt die Frage in Anregung, wie leichtfertige Streiks verhindert
werden können. Darüber zu entscheiden, sind auch wir hier absolut
nicht in der Lage, denn die Höhe der Forderungen, welche gestellt
werden können, läßt sich doch von solchen, welche dem ganzen
Streik fern standen, viel weniger beurtheilen, als von Jenen, die
direkt im Kampfe stehen. Im Ganzen ist doch das Streben der
Arbeitgeber immer darauf gerichtet, die Waare Arbeitskraft so billig
wie möglich zu erhalten; die Arbeiter dagegen streben, sie so theuer
wie möglich zu verkaufen. Daß die Organisation der Arbeiter in
Gewerkschaften absolut nothwendig ist, darüber kann es ebenfalls
keinen Streit mehr geben; in der Zeit der kapitalistischen Produktionsweise sind die Gewerkschaften gerade so nothwendig, wie
die Zünfte im Mittelalter.

Den Boykott will ich als politisches Kampfmittel für durchaus
gerechtfertigt erachten, wenn es die Eroberung von Lokalen für
Versammlungen und dergl. gilt; wenn er aber dazu dienen soll,
irgend Jemand, irgend eine Gesellschaft, die vielleicht von den
Arbeitern materiell abhängig ist, zu zwingen, daß sie Sozialismus
heuchele, das kann ich nicht billigen, das sollte uns völlig fern
bleiben. Ebenso liegt es mit der politischen Gewerkschaft. Die
gewerkschaftlichen Organisationen sollen zentralisirt dem Kapital
gegenüberstehen, damit sie als Macht sich dem Kapital gegenüber
schützen können; da soll man nicht vorher von dem Einzelnen ein
politisches Glaubensbekenntniß verlangen. Das würde nur zur
Zersplitterung führen, wie bei den Hirsch-Dunckerschen. Da sind
Sozialdemokraten ausgeschlossen, sie wollen nur Freisinnige haben.
Würden wir alle Nichtsozialisten ausschließen, dann würden wir
damit mit einem Male den ganzen Arbeiterstand in so und soviel
Gruppen spalten; das Gegentheil des Gewollten wäre erreicht, die
Arbeiter würden zersplittert unter sich im Kampf liegen, und das
würde für den Arbeitgeber, den Ausbeuter von höchstem Nutzen

fein. Diese Zerfplitterung muß auf jeden Fall vermieden werden.

Wilfchke-Berlin II: Es ist hier gefagt worden, es hätten viele Streiks in letzter Zeit stattgefunden, deren unglücklichen Verlauf man hätte vorausfehen können. Es haben in Berlin Streiks stattgefunden wegen Maßregelung einzelner Perfonen, Maßregelungen, welche aus Lohndifferenzen hervorgegangen waren. Da war es allerdings verkehrt, gleich zum Streik zu greifen; man hätte fich begnügen follen, die Gemaßregelten anderswo unterzubringen oder fie, wenn keine Arbeit vorhanden ist, materiell zu unterstützen. Der Kosten- aufwand hierfür ist lange nicht fo groß, als wie bei einem Streik, der dann möglicher Weife einen koloffalen Umfang annimmt und Taufende und Abertaufende kostet. Nun haben wir in Berlin und anderwärts zu einem Mittel gegriffen, welches, wenn auf guter Bafis errichtet, fich bewährt hat und von allen Lokalorganifationen Zustimmung gefunden hat, nämlich eine Streik-Kontrollkommiffion. Es handelt fich nun darum, womöglich hier von den Parteigenoffen eine Erklärung zu erhalten, welche Unterlage einer folchen Kom- miffion zu geben fei, damit diefe Kommiffion nach einem Syftem arbeiten könnte. — Der Referent hat dann auf die Berliner Er- fahrungen in Boykotts hingewiefen. Da hat er wohl blos die Lokalfperre gemeint, in der wir allerdings gefiegt haben. Im vorigen Jahr konnten wir kein größeres Lokal mehr bekommen, da haben wir denn feit April den Boykott über fie verhängt; das hat fich fo bewährt, daß man es überall in den größeren Städten ebenfo gemacht hat. Daß der Boykott gleichwohl nicht allenthalben angebracht ist, ist felbstverständlich. In jüngster Zeit find Boykotts infcenirt worden, die von vornherein als ausfichtslos erfcheinen mußten; zweifellos kann diefe Waffe fich auch einmal gegen uns kehren. Man hat verfucht, wegen Maßregelung einzelner Perfonen einzelne Gefchäftsleute zu boykottiren; das ist unklug und zwecklos. Kommt der Boykottirte dem Drucke nach und stellt den Gemaß- regelten wieder ein, wer will ihn zwingen, wenn er den Arbeiter dann nach 14 Tagen wieder entläßt, diefen trotzdem weiter zu be- fchäftigen? Das ist ein Ding der Unmöglichkeit.

Beim Hamburger Streik und im vorigen Jahre bei den Berliner Maurern ist es vorgekommen, daß alle diejenigen, die fich während des Lohnkampfes in irgend einer Weife bethätigt hatten, namentlich diejenigen, die auf den Bahnhöfen die zureifenden Fremden von der Arbeitsannahme abzuhalten hatten, einfach von der Polizei verhaftet und ins Gefängniß gesteckt wurden, ohne Unterfuchung; in Hamburg ging die Polizei foweit, alle Perfonen, welche fich nur annähernd auf dem Bahnhofe aufhielten und die fie für Maurer, Tifchler, Zimmerleute halten zu dürfen glaubte, einfach beim Kragen zu packen und vom Bahnhof herunter zu transportiren, auch wenn sie ein Billet gelöst hatten. Dieses Vorgehen ist nicht bloß in Berlin und Hamburg, sondern auch anderswo vorgekommen; es scheint systematisch betrieben worden zu sein und auf einer einheitlichen Anordnung der obersten Behörde zu beruhen. In einer Berliner Versammlung wurde ein Protest dagegen beschlossen und die Fraktion aufgefordert, ihn dem Minister zu unterbreiten, diesen zu befragen, ob er die unteren Organe dahin instruirt habe. Es wäre wohl zu verlangen, daß die Fraktion diese Frage an den Minister richtete. Wenn man sich auch nicht viel davon versprechen kann, so wird doch, wenn man die Parlamentstribüne als ein so wichtiges Agitationsmittel anerkennt, auch diese Anregung Beachtung finden müssen; sie wird den unteren Organen, namentlich der Polizei, einen gewissen Stoß geben.

Beyer-Leipzig: Wir können den gewerklichen Kampf nur aufnehmen auf Grund der heute bestehenden gewerkschaftlichen Organisation, deshalb müssen wir die gewerkschaftliche Bewegung in vollem Sinne des Worts unterstützen. Viele Genossen stehen der gewerkschaftlichen Bewegung vollständig fremd gegenüber. Mit ein paar Groschen Beitrag ist es nicht gethan. (Beifall.)

Es ist folgende Resolution eingegangen:

In Erwägung,

daß durch die fortschreitende wirthschaftliche Entwickelung der ökonomische Kampf zwischen Arbeit und Kapital immer schärfere Formen annimmt, und angesichts der ablehnenden Haltung der Regierung gegenüber dem von der sozialdemokratischen Fraktion eingebrachten Arbeiterschutzgesetze, ist es eine Nothwendigkeit, diesen Kampf seitens der Arbeiter zu organisiren. Die geeignete Form dieser Organisation ist die gewerkschaftliche. Der Parteitag ersucht deshalb die Parteigenossen allerorts, den bestehenden gewerkschaftlichen Organisationen sich anzuschließen und wo solche nicht vorhanden sind, sie ins Leben zu rufen.

Glocke-Berlin. Bock-Gotha. Segitz-Nürnberg. Barth-Berlin. Slomke-Bielefeld. Bruhns-Bremen. Fritz-Berlin.

Zubeil-Berlin: Ich kann mich mit den Ausführungen des Genossen Kloß nur einverstanden erklären. Die Gewerkschaftsbewegung muß auf das Lebhafteste unterstützt werden, sie wird unsere Zwecke wesentlich fördern. In Bezug auf ernste Lohnkämpfe wird häufig an einen großen Theil der Arbeiter das Ansuchen gestellt, sofort die Stadt zu verlassen. Diese Arbeiter gehen nun in andere Städte und drücken die Löhne noch tiefer hinab. Man sollte die sogenannte Reiseunterstützung mehr und mehr einschränken. Die Unterstützung sollte vielmehr dazu gebraucht werden, daß die Genossen beim Ausbruch eines Lohnkampfes in der Stadt aushalten können. Niemand darf den Ort verlassen, der es nicht freiwillig thun will. Die Boykotts sind, zur rechten Zeit und mit den rechten Mitteln angewandt, oft bessere Waffen, als die Streiks. Wenn aber gesagt worden ist, daß in Hamburg und Berlin frivole Forderungen gestellt worden sind, so muß ich das entschieden zurückweisen. In großen Städten wie Hamburg und Berlin, sind 60, 70, 75 Pfg. pro Stunde nicht zu viel. Maurer und Zimmerer namentlich haben einen großen Theil des Jahres nichts zu thun und müssen im Winter Noth leiden. Wenn aber auf einem sozial-demokratischen Parteitag derartige Forderungen unvernünftige genannt werden, dann weiß ich nicht, was wir mit dem Lohnkampfe überhaupt anfangen sollen. Selbstverständlich würde diese Aeußerung, wenn sie ins Protokoll kommt, von den Kapitalisten ausgebeutet werden. Unsere Fraktion muß für ein Vereins- und Versammlungs-recht wirken, welches es ermöglicht, in jeder Stadt eine Organisation zu gründen. In Berlin verfahren die Behörden in dieser Be-ziehung sehr willkürlich. Während in der Umgegend Berlins überall Zahlstellen eines Verbandes gestattet sind, ist es bis jetzt in Berlin noch nicht gestattet, eine Zahlstelle zu gründen. Dieses Verfahren kann der Parteitag nicht scharf genug verurtheilen. Die lokale Organisation kann das nicht bieten, was eine zentrale Organisation bietet. Ich bitte Sie, in die Resolution auch die Arbeiterinnenvereine auf-zunehmen.

Haburg-Potsdam: Die Gewerkschaften haben uns bei der letzten Reichstagswahl große Dienste geleistet. Sie haben überall Geld aufgebracht, um uns den Sieg zu ermöglichen. Gegen Boykotts wider solche Lokalbesitzer, welche ihr Lokal zur Wahl u. f. w. nicht hergeben, läßt sich nichts einwenden. Der Boykott darf aber nicht gegen Geschäftsleute verhängt werden, welche eine andere politische Ueberzeugung haben als wir. Wenn man uns wegen unserer politischen Ueberzeugung maßregelt, so dürfen wir dasselbe Ver-fahren nicht anwenden, um einen politischen Gegner in seinem Gewerbe zu schädigen.

Wilke-Braunschweig: Bei der Form der Organisation müssen wir die thatsächlichen politischen Verhältnisse und die Auslegungen der bestehenden Gesetze im Auge behalten. Uebrigens kommt es weniger auf die Form, als auf den Geist an, welcher in der Organisation weht, die wir uns schaffen. Die Ansicht des Genossen Kloß, es könne einer lokalen gewerblichen Vereinigung, z. B. in Braunschweig, gleichgiltig sein, ob sich ein ähnlicher Verein in Magdeburg bilde, kann ich nicht theilen. Es ist uns von außer-ordentlichem Nutzen, wenn rings um uns herum noch recht viele Festungen gegen den Kapitalismus errichtet werden. Der einzelne Verein kann dies zwar nicht veranlassen, es kann aber in einer öffentlichen Versammlung eine Agitationskommission gewählt werden, der es zur Aufgabe gemacht wird, in den umliegenden Ortschaften die Agitation in die Hand zu nehmen. Nach den bisherigen Erfahrungen, besonders der Metallarbeiter, bietet die lokale Organisation eine geringere Angriffsfläche dar, als die zentrale. Die Zentralisation wird ja hergestellt durch die Gewerkschaftskassen. Was Gewerkschaften ohne Statuten leisten können, hat die Organisation der Töpfer gezeigt. Die Zentralisation hat aber ihre besonderen Gefahren. Wenn man in zentralisirten Gewerkschaften einmal über die Gesetze spricht, so gefährdet man den ganzen Verband; wird ein einzelner Verein aufgelöst, so schadet dies nicht so viel. Man sollte es den Einzelnen überlassen, wie sie sich organisiren wollen, es aber Jedem zur moralischen Pflicht machen, sich einer Organisation anzuschließen. Der Hauptzweck dieser Vereine soll zunächst gewerkschaftliche Angelegenheiten sein, und ich habe noch kein Statut gefunden, wo es heißt, es werden nur Sozialdemokraten zugelassen. Ist man dann eine zeitlang zusammen, dann kann ja ein tüchtiger Redner einen lehrreichen Vortrag über ein sozialistisches Thema halten. Was das Abreisen bei Streiks betrifft, so dürfen wir doch auch nicht übersehen, daß durch die ausgewanderten Genossen oft in anderen Ortschaften ein ganz neu pulsirendes Leben hineingekommen ist. Es sind neue Organisationen entstanden, und es ist auf die faulen Zustände aufmerksam gemacht worden.

Die Diskussion wird geschlossen.

Zu persönlicher Bemerkung bestreitet

Stengele-Hamburg die Behauptung von Lenz, daß in Hamburg unvernünftige Forderungen gestellt worden sind.

Das Schlußwort erhält

Grillenberger: Nachdem aus der Versammlung eigentlich Niemand einen gegnerischen Standpunkt gegen die Ausführungen des Referenten eingenommen (Zuruf: wir sind nicht zum Wort gekommen!), kann ich mich kurz fassen. Die gegnerischen Anschauungen würden sich höchstwahrscheinlich nur auf die Form der Organisation bezogen haben; der Parteitag hat Stellung zu nehmen zur Frage der Streiks und Boykotts im Allgemeinen. Wie die Gewerkschaften am zweckmäßigsten zu organisiren sind, wird Sache der demnächst bevorstehenden Gewerkschaftskonferenz und der Gewerkschaftskongresse sein. Wir müssen entscheiden, ob die Partei überhaupt befugt ist, Stellung zur Frage der Streiks und Boykotts zu nehmen. Die Partei hat allerdings ein Recht dazu, weil der ökonomische Kampf heute eine andere Gestalt annehmen muß, als dies noch vor wenigen Jahren der Fall war. Seit dem Fall des Sozialistengesetzes sind die Herren Unternehmer genöthigt, auch auf dem ökonomischen Gebiet eine veränderte Front einzunehmen. Früher hatten die Unternehmer das Sozialistengesetz und dessen Anwendung durch die Behörden zur Verfügung. Man schlug seitens der Behörden einfach alles todt, was einigermaßen danach roch, daß die Massen auf gewerkschaftlichem Gebiete organisirt und das Philister-thum in seiner Ruhe gestört werden konnte. Wo das Sozialistengesetz versagte, stand das Vereinsgesetz zu Gebote, um Körperschaften, sobald sie sich mit sogenannten öffentlichen Angelegenheiten beschäftigten, als politische Vereine zu betrachten, die nicht miteinander in Verbindung treten können. Reichte auch dies nicht aus, so nahm man zu dem Gesetz über das Versicherungswesen seine Zuflucht. Man erklärte einfach solche Vereine, z. B. den Deutschen Buchdrucker-Unterstützungsverein, als Versicherungsgesellschaft (in Bayern) — und verbot sie, weil sie als solche ihre Zulassung in dem betreffenden Bundesstaate nicht nachgesucht hatten.

Jetzt, wo man nach dem Fall des Sozialistengesetzes nicht mehr nach Belieben mit einem polizeilichen Federstrich eine derartige Organisation aus der Welt schaffen kann, fangen neuerdings die Unternehmer an, sich in ähnlicher, aber viel gewichtigerer Weise zu organisiren, wie die Arbeiter seit Jahrzehnten versucht haben. Seit Monaten errichten die Unternehmer allenthalben im Reich, in den verschiedensten Industriebranchen, zentralisirte Verbände, die nicht blos Angehörige irgend eines einzelnen Fachkreises, sondern ganze Branchen umfassen, Ringe, Verbindungen, die jegliche Arbeiterbewegung durch die Gewalt des Kapitalismus lahmlegen und durch Anwendung der Hungerkur gegen die Arbeiter das Sozialistengesetz ersetzen sollen. Demgegenüber fragt es sich eigentlich nur, ob unsere Partei nicht schon längst dazu hätte Stellung nehmen sollen. Es ist allerdings von der weisen Unternehmerpresse und von den Unternehmern selbst vielfach behauptet worden, Streiks und ähnliche Maßregeln der Arbeiter seien nur sozialdemokratische Kampfmittel, um die Unzufriedenheit unter den Massen zu erregen, die Lebenshaltung der Arbeiter zu verschlechtern, und auf diese Weise die rabiat gewordenen Arbeitermassen der sozialdemokratischen Bewegung in die Arme zu treiben. Jeder, der die Entwickelung unserer Gesellschaft einigermaßen kennt und ehrlich ist, muß sich sagen, daß das nichts ist als eine elende Verdächtigung. Der Sozialdemokratie ist es niemals eingefallen, Streiks zu dem Zwecke zu proviziren, um Unzufriedenheit zu erregen. Wir haben stets erklärt, Streiks sind eine zweischneidige Waffe, die nur in dem alleräußersten Falle angewendet werden darf. Wir meinen, daß die Organisirung der Massen an sich schon eine Waffe ist, gewichtig genug, um vielfach die Unternehmer und ihren Uebermuth in Schach zu halten, daß es sogar in verschwindend wenigen Fällen nothwendig sein wird, zu dem Mittel des Streiks zu greifen. Aber wie die Verhältnisse einmal liegen, und da die Gegensätze sich zuzuspitzen begonnen haben, ist es nothwendig, hier zu erklären, daß die Streiks von uns nicht zurückgewiesen, nicht unterdrückt werden können, daß die Streiks für die Arbeiterklasse eben zur Nothwendigkeit geworden sind und daß bei dem Uebermuth des Unternehmerthums die Streiks öfter auf der Bildfläche unserer Bewegung erscheinen werden, als uns selbst lieb ist.

Dasselbe ist auch bei den Boykotts der Fall. Nur dürfte in Bezug auf die Anwendung dieses Mittels, das in Deutschland verhältnißmäßig jung ist, noch größere Sorgfalt am Platze sein, als bei der Gutheißung von Streiks. Boykotts zur Beseitigung von Hindernissen, die den Arbeitern hauptsächlich bei Ausübung ihrer politischen Rechte in den Weg gelegt werden, und meistentheils gerichtet gegen Besitzer großer Lokalitäten, sind von vornherein gut zu heißen, zumal in solchen Fällen, wo in ganz besonders brutaler Weise das Unternehmerthum glaubt, sein Uebergewicht zeigen zu können. Die Boykott aber in allen den Fällen, wo es sich um eine kleine Differenz zwischen Unternehmer und Arbeitern handelt, gleichsam, als ständige Institution in's ganze gesellschaftliche Leben zu übertragen, wäre das Gefährlichste, was seitens der Arbeiterbevölkerung überhaupt geschehen könnte. Man hat der Fraktion in Bezug auf den 1. Mai vorgeworfen, daß ihr Erlaß zu spät oder überhaupt ergangen sei. Man hat also die Fraktion für die Mißerfolge des 1. Mai verantwortlich machen wollen. Ich verweise Sie auf einen Mißerfolg auf dem Gebiet des Boykott, wo die Fraktion keinerlei Einfluß gehabt hat. Ich meine den großen Bierboykott in Berlin, von dem sich die Parteigenossen außerhalb Berlins sofort gesagt haben, daß derselbe nie und nimmer zu einem glücklichen Erfolge führen könnte, weil es ein Unding war, sämmtliche Aktiengesellschaften boykottiren zu wollen, blos um sie zur Schlichtung einer untergeordneten Differenz mit ihren Brauergesellen zu bringen. An dem ist die Fraktion vollständig unschuldig gewesen. Wir können als Partei Streiks und Boykotts umsomehr als berechtigt anerkennen, weil die Maßregeln der Unternehmer von den gesammten politischen Parteien unserer Gegner unterstützt oder doch als berechtigt hingestellt werden. In den Preßorganen dieser Parteien, mögen es Deutsch-Freisinnige, Nationalliberale oder Konservative sein, wird unausgesetzt gegen die Arbeiterverbindungen gehetzt. Dazu kommt noch, daß die nationalliberale Partei auch in Bezug auf die Handhabung der Maßregelungen gegenüber den Arbeitern am gehässigsten vorzugehen pflegt. Gegenüber den buntscheckigen, aber äußerst gefährlichen Mitteln der Unternehmer haben wir nichts, als das Gefühl der Solidarität und die Möglichkeit der Zusammenfassung der großen Massen. Wenn heute ein Streik inscenirt wird und Jemand die indifferenten oder nur mit halber Seele theilnehmenden Genossen auffordert, sich doch dem Streik anzuschließen, und wenn er dabei nur irgend annähernd die Grenzen des „Zulässigen" überschreitet, so wird er sofort wegen sogenannter Verrufserklärung in's Gefängniß gesteckt. Das ist in der letzten Zeit zu einer wahren Kalamität geworden. Sobald ein Arbeiter seinen Kollegen zur Innehaltung des Koalitionsrechts u. s. w. zu veranlassen sucht, wird er in's Gefängniß gesteckt. Wenn aber die Unternehmer sich zusammenthun, um die Arbeiter daran zu hindern, das Koalitionsrecht auszuüben, so ist noch niemals die Polizei oder eine sonstige Behörde gegen das Unternehmerthum aufgetreten. In Sachsen, dem reaktionärsten Lande Deutschlands, hat man dem Boykott gar den „groben Unfugparagraphen" entgegengestellt. Ein sehr beliebtes Mittel der Verrufserklärungen von Seiten der Fabrikanten, sind die schwarzen Listen. Es werden Briefe versandt, in welchen darauf aufmerksam gemacht wird, dieser oder jener Arbeiter war bei mir am Streik betheiligt. Diese Briefe enthalten nicht blos die schwerste Verrufserklärung, sondern zugleich eine Boykottirung, und doch wird gegen diese Fabrikanten nicht vorgegangen. Andererseits hat man neuerdings entdeckt, daß in dem Gebiet des preußischen Landrechts Streiks, wenn sie ohne Einhaltung der Kündigungsfrist inscenirt sind, verfolgt werden können auf Grund des § 110 des Strafgesetzbuches wegen „Ungehorsam!" Wenn dagegen Unternehmer zusammentreten, um bei Arbeitsstockungen, oder lediglich deshalb, um die Preislage der Produkte in die Höhe zu treiben, für längere Zeit ihre Etablissements sperren und deshalb ihre Arbeiter ohne Kündigung auf die Straße setzen, oder wenn in Fabriken, entgegen den getroffenen Vereinbarungen, die Akkordlöhne verkürzt werden, so hat man nicht gehört, daß gegen sie der § 110 angewandt, oder daß gegen letzteres Verfahren auch nur einmal die Untersuchung wegen Unterschlagung des verdienten Arbeitslohnes eingeleitet worden wäre. Das Schönste aber auf diesem Gebiet ist unzweifelhaft das, was das Landgericht der Freien Reichs- und Hansestadt Lübeck fertiggebracht hat. Dort haben Arbeiter am 20. Februar erklärt, sie seien nicht geneigt, an diesem Tage zu arbeiten. Darauf wurde ihnen erklärt, wenn Ihr nicht arbeitet, braucht Ihr auch am Freitag und Samstag nicht zu kommen. Die gemaßregelten Arbeiter wandten sich an ihren Fachverein und dieser setzte sich mit dem Unternehmer in Verbindung und erklärte: Wenn Sie den betreffenden Arbeitern nicht den Lohn für die zwei Tage bezahlen, so werden wir diese Arbeiter als gemaßregelt betrachten und sie aus unserer Vereinskasse unterstützen. Die beim Untersuchungsrichter geäußerte Ansicht des Unternehmers, die Vertreter des Fachvereins hätten mit Streik direkt gedroht, wurde vom Unternehmer selbst nicht mehr aufrecht erhalten, vom Gerichtshof aber als richtige Version angesehen, und darauf wurden die Vertreter des Fachvereins, die den Fabrikanten auf diese Weise gezwungen hatten, seine Arbeiter zu bezahlen, verurtheilt, der eine zu sechs, der andere zu drei Monaten Gefängniß wegen des Vergehens der Erpressung. (Rufe: Hört, Hört!) Was sagen Sie aber dazu, daß vor Kurzem dieses Urtheil, das man allgemein für unmöglich gehalten hat, vom Reichsgericht sanktionirt worden ist! (Erneute Zurufe.) Demgegenüber gilt es nicht mehr einer Gewerkschaftsbewegung anzuhängen, die vielfach nur eine Art Vereinsspielerei gewesen ist, eine Zwergorganisation, sondern es gilt, die Massen zu organisiren, die Arbeiterklasse als solche in den Kampf gegen das Unternehmerthum zu führen. Die Gewerkschaften müssen großartige Dimensionen annehmen, wenn dem Vorgehen des Unternehmerthums mit einigem Erfolg entgegengetreten werden soll. Selbst dann, wenn die Massen in gewaltig großen Organisationen zusammengeballt werden, hat das Unternehmerthum übermächtige Vortheile in Folge des großen Geldbesitzes. Das Einzige, was die Arbeiter gegenüber den Unternehmern noch einigermaßen zu schützen vermag, ist, daß bei gewissen Differenzen die sogenannte Einigkeit derselben regelmäßig nicht lange Stand zu halten pflegt; der Konkurrenzneid ist nicht selten der Bundesgenosse der organisirten Arbeiter. Aber im Großen und Ganzen wird nach dem Fall des Sozialistengesetzes das Unternehmerthum sich hauptsächlich auf das Gebiet des Lohnkampfes werfen, und deshalb haben die Arbeiter alle Ursache, mit allen ihnen zu Gebote stehenden Mitteln die Gewerkschaftsbewegung zu unterstützen. Es handelt sich dabei nicht blos um zentralisirte Verbände im gewöhnlichen Sinne, sondern um große Unionen, ähnlich wie sie in England groß gezogen sind. Die speziellen Organisationen der einzelnen Fächer können ruhig innerhalb der großen Union existiren. Aber es müssen sämmtliche Fächer einer Branche zusammengefaßt werden, so das Baugewerbe 2c.

Der Vorwurf, daß in den großen Städten mitunter unberechtigte oder unvernünftige Forderungen von den Arbeitern erhoben werden, ist bereits zurückgewiesen worden. Es ist aber doch insofern ein Fehler gemacht worden, als man sich mit dem Vorgehen auf gewerkschaftlichem Gebiet allzu sehr in die großen Städte und Industriezentren zurückgezogen hat. Es kann unmöglich eine gedeihliche Entwickelung der Gewerkschaftsbewegung stattfinden, wenn in den großen Städten, in irgend einer beliebigen Branche, bereits für den neunstündigen oder achtstündigen Arbeitstag agitirt wird, während in den Provinzialstädten in derselben Branche noch bis zu 16 Stunden täglich gearbeitet werden muß. Hier muß ein Ausgleich herbeigeführt werden. Jetzt, wo wir in eine Periode des wirthschaftlichen Niederganges eingetreten sind, wo also überhaupt an Angriffsstreiks nicht gedacht werden kann, sondern wo hauptsächlich daran gedacht werden muß, zur Abwehr sich zu vereinigen, müssen wir Organisationen schaffen, um für die Zukunft widerstandsfähig zu sein. Es muß jetzt auf die Agitation in den Provinzen und auf dem flachen Lande das Hauptgewicht gelegt werden, und es müssen diejenigen Genossen draußen, die stets treu zur Sache gehalten haben, aber noch unter dem Druck einer unmenschlich langen Arbeitszeit stehen und allein nicht im Stande sind, etwas zu leisten, besser unterstützt werden. Namentlich muß das Augenmerk darauf gerichtet werden, einen annähernden Ausgleich auf diesem Gebiet herbeizuführen. Das Land und die kleinen Städte müssen auch ihren Theil haben an den bisherigen Errungenschaften des Lohnkampfes und der gewerkschaftlichen Bewegung. Unterstützen Sie diese Arbeiter- und Arbeiterinnenbewegung, so weit dies nur in Ihren Kräften liegt. Deshalb empfehle ich, unsere Resolution nicht nur einstimmig anzunehmen, sondern nach Kräften auch danach zu handeln, wenn Sie wieder nach Hause kommen. (Lebhaftes Bravo!)

Die Resolution Kloß-Grillenberger wird einstimmig angenommen, ebenso auch die Resolution Glocke.

Es würde nunmehr in der Reihenfolge der Berathungsgegenstände der letzte Punkt der Tagesordnung: „Anträge aus der Mitte des Parteitages" zur Verhandlung kommen müssen. Da aber die betreffenden Anträge erst nach Gruppen zusammengestellt, gedruckt und vertheilt werden sollen, so schlägt der Vorsitzende vor, die Sitzung abzubrechen. Der Parteitag ist damit einverstanden.

Schluß nach 6 Uhr.

Fünfter Verhandlungstag.

Freitag, den 17. Oktober 1890.

Vormittagssitzung.

Vorsitzender Singer eröffnet die Sitzung um 9½ Uhr mit folgender Mittheilung:

Es ist dem Parteitag eine Adresse zugegangen von den Mitgliedern des sozialdemokratischen Leseklubs „Lessing" in Berlin. (Bravo!) Ich werde die Adresse ausnahmsweise zur Verlesung bringen. Sie lautet:

„Dem ersten Arbeiterparlament der deutschen Sozialdemokratie auf deutschem Boden, den Vertretern der völkerbefreienden Sozialdemokratie unseren herzlichsten Brudergruß!

„Gleichzeitig geben wir dem Wunsche Ausdruck, daß die Beschlüsse des Kongresses einen bedeutenden Fortschritt bilden mögen in den berechtigten Bestrebungen der Proletarier aller Länder.

„Indem wir den großen kulturgeschichtlichen Moment eines derartigen Kongresses zu würdigen wissen, erkennen wir dessen Einfluß auf die gesammten Emanzipationsbestrebungen des Proletariats, das stolze Bewußtsein sieghaften Vordringens und die Weckung und Verallgemeinerung des internationalen Solidaritätsgefühls.

„Darum vorwärts im zielbewußten Kampf für Freiheit, Gleichheit und Brüderlichkeit!

Die Mitglieder des sozialistischen Leseklubs „Lessing"."

Indem ich Namens des Parteitages den Absendern der Adresse den wärmsten Dank ausspreche, beantrage ich, diese schön ausgestattete Adresse den Halleschen Genossen zum dauernden Andenken an diesen Parteitag zu überweisen. (Lebhafte Zustimmung.) Damit ist der Parteitag einverstanden. Ich ersuche das Lokalkomitee, die Adresse hier in Empfang zu nehmen.

Vor Eintritt in die Tagesordnung erklärt Schönfeld-Dresden, daß seine neuliche Behauptung bezüglich der „Sächsischen Arbeiterzeitung", soweit seine Informationen reichen, richtig sei. Sollte er sich geirrt haben, so nähme er keinen Anstand, seine Behauptung zurückzunehmen.

Höppner glaubt, daß die übrigen Dresdener Genossen durch diese Erklärung befriedigt sein werden.

Der Parteitag tritt in die Tagesordnung ein:

Punkt 7:

Die Parteipresse.

Hierzu hat W. Liefländer-Potsdam-Osthavelland folgenden Antrag gestellt:

„Da die Presse das mächtigste Kampfmittel in Händen der Partei ist und in Erwägung, daß es heiligste Pflicht der Partei sein muß, dieses Kampfmittel bis zur äußersten Grenze anzuwenden und auszunutzen, spricht sich der Parteitag dafür aus, daß zur Herstellung des event. Zentral-Organs und aller von der Parteileitung ausgehenden Schriften eine eigene Druckerei errichtet werde, damit der gesammte, aus Herstellung dieser Preßerzeugnisse resultirende Reinertrag wiederum für Parteizwecke zur Verwendung gelangen kann."

Für den Fall der Ablehnung dieses Antrages beantragt Liefländer:

„Ein etwaiger Kontrakt mit einem Drucker betreffs Herstellung eines von der Parteileitung herausgegebenen Zentralorgans und anderer Druckschriften darf nur bis zum nächsten Parteitag abgeschlossen werden.

Der Antragsteller hat beide Anträge zurückgezogen.

Es liegt nur noch ein Antrag der Gubener Genossen vor.

Es wird beantragt, daß die gesammte sozialdemokratische Presse Eigenthum der Partei sei.

Eine Reihe anderer auf die Presse bezüglicher Anträge wird bei den allgemeinen Anträgen aus der Mitte des Parteitages verhandelt werden.

Berichterstatter Auer: Ueber unsere Parteipresse, insonderheit die Lokalpresse (denn über das Zentralorgan entscheidet ja bis zu

einem gewiſſen Grade bereits unſer Organiſationsſtatut) herrſchen
noch wenig klare Anſchauungen. Das zeigt der Antrag Guben,
der bereits die Expropriation des geſammten Preßeigenthums
beſchließen will. Ein ſolcher Antrag iſt einfach unannehmbar.
Die Lokalpreſſe muß ſich von der Zentralpreſſe vor allem
darin unterſcheiden, daß der Haupteinfluß auf dieſelbe den Parteigenoſſen am Ort, bezw. der Provinz und dem Kreiſe zuſteht,
für den das Blatt ſelber erſcheint, während die Zentralorgane aus-
ſchließlich für die Geſammtpartei vorhanden ſind. Man erhebt nur
gar zu leicht den Anſpruch, daß die Mittel der geſammten Partei
unter Umſtänden für ein einzelnes Lokalorgan zur Verfügung ſtehen
ſollen. Ging doch neulich ein Aufruf durch die Preſſe, behufs
Errichtung einer Druckerei an einem beſtimmten Orte Deutſchlands
die geſammte Partei in Aktion zu ſetzen! Das iſt eine abſolut
falſche Auffaſſung. Die Parteiorgane müſſen getragen werden durch
den Kreis, für den ſie beſtimmt ſind (Sehr richtig!), und das hier
recht präzis auszuſprechen, war mit einer der Gründe, warum wir
den Gegenſtand überhaupt auf die Tagesordnung geſetzt haben.
Daß im Uebrigen die Lokalorgane der Partei zu dienen haben, dem
Geſammtintereſſe, daß ſie in Bezug auf taktiſche und prinzipielle
Fragen ſich der Ordnung und Diſziplin anzuordnen, zu fügen
haben, iſt ſelbſtverſtändlich. Es iſt aber unmöglich, die Lokalpreſſe gewiſſermaßen zu uniformiren. Die Lokalpreſſe muß der
Verſchiedenartigkeit der verſchiedenen Gegenden Rechnung tragen.
Es kann alſo garnicht davon die Rede ſein, daß man der Lokalpreſſe gewiſſermaßen von oben herab eine Direktion giebt in dem
Sinne, daß man ſich in die Einzelheiten hineinmiſcht. Die
Genoſſen der betreffenden Orte und Bezirke ſollen ſowohl in
materieller Beziehung für ihr Lokalblatt aufkommen, als auch die
geiſtige Leitung deſſelben ſoweit wie möglich in der Hand haben.
Selbſtverſtändlich geht es nicht, daß ein einzelnes Organ erklärt,
was kümmern wir uns um die Beſchlüſſe des Parteitages, um
unſer Programm, um unſere Organiſation! Die taktiſche Ausführung und Vertretung der allgemeinen Parteigrundſätze dagegen
kann den lokalen Verhältniſſen angepaßt werden. Alles, was ich
Ihnen zu ſagen hätte, erſchöpft folgende Reſolution, die wir Ihnen
zur Annahme empfehlen:

„Der Parteitag beſchließt:

In Erwägung: daß die Preſſe das beſte und wirkſamſte
Agitations- und Kampfesmittel iſt;

in weiterer Erwägung: daß unſere Parteipreſſe dieſer ihrer
Aufgabe nur entſprechen kann, wenn ihre Exiſtenz genügend ge-
ſichert iſt und jeder maßgebende nicht-parteigenöſſiſche Einfluß
von ihr ferne gehalten wird,

ſpricht der Parteitag die Erwartung aus:

daß die Genossen überall, neben der Agitation für die Verbreitung des Centralorgans und der nichtperiodischen Parteiliteratur, sich vor allem die Unterstützung und Verbreitung unserer bereits existirenden Lokalpresse angelegen sein lassen,

daß sie ferner überall strenge darauf achten, daß unsere Presse nicht Gegenstand von Privatspekulationen werde, die mit dem Parteizweck nichts gemein haben,

daß die erste und oberste Aufgabe unserer Presse: die Arbeiter aufzuklären und zum Klassenbewußtsein zu erziehen, nicht unter Rücksichten auf irgend welche Privatinteressen leide.

Insbesondere empfiehlt der Parteitag den Genossen:

bei Gründung von neuen Parteiblättern möglichst Vorsicht walten zu lassen und solche Unternehmungen unter keinen Umständen zu gründen, bevor sie nicht genau erwogen und sich überzeugt haben, daß die Möglichkeit für die Existenz des Unternehmens aus eigenen Mitteln gegeben, und daß vor allem auch die nothwendigen geistigen, technischen und administrativen Kräfte zur Leitung eines Blattes vorhanden sind."

(Zustimmung.)

Ich mache Sie besonders auf die Rathschläge aufmerksam, die wir in unserem Schlußpassus aussprechen, Genossen! So hochwichtig die Presse für uns ist, so sehr kann sie der Partei geradezu schädlich werden, wenn leichtsinnig mit der Gründung von Preßorganen vorgegangen wird. Dieser Leichtsinn muß unter allen Umständen vermieden werden. Nur eine in ihrer materiellen Existenz gesicherte und geistig wie technisch gut geleitete Presse kann ihre Aufgabe recht erfüllen. So gut wie . nicht Jeder ein geschickter Modelleur, Schneider und Schreiner sein kann, so gut ist auch nicht Jeder von Natur dazu berufen, ein Zeitungsredakteur zu sein. (Heiterkeit.) Die Scheere soll nicht das Zeichen sein, in dem die Redaktion arbeitet und siegt! Solchermaßen hergestellte Blätter gereichen der Partei nicht zum Nutzen. Ebensowenig aber auch solche, die fortgesetzt mit Defizits arbeiten und die Mittel der Partei aufbrauchen, die besser zur Agitation u. s. w., für das Interesse der gesammten Partei, verwendet werden können. Solche Blätter sind wirklich unter Umständen ein Krebsschaden. Außerdem können deswegen unter den Parteigenossen der betreffenden Orte leicht Differenzen entstehen. Wir haben vor allem die Pflicht, unsere bestehende existenzfähige Presse zu unterstützen und zu verbessern. Es ist zweifellos nichts verloren, wenn mit der Gründung neuer Zeitungsunternehmen noch ein bischen gewartet wird. Lassen Sie die alten Organe sich einleben, dann werden sich leichter die Mittel finden, um neu entstandenen helfen zu können. Eine schwache, immer auf dem Aussterbeetat stehende Presse ist ein Uebel. Ich empfehle Ihnen also unsere Resolution. Nehmen Sie dieselbe an und sorgen Sie vor allem dafür, daß sie kein todter Buchstabe bleibt. (Lebhafter Beifall.)

Frau Steinbach-Hamburg: Ich möchte Sie bitten, uns Frauen auch in Bezug auf die Presse Gleichberechtigung zu gewähren. Nicht um blaustrümpflerische Neigungen zu fördern thue ich dies. Der sogenannte Gleichberechtigungsdusel, wie er bisher leider von Frauenrechtlern und Frauenrechtlerinnen auf den Markt geworfen ist, liegt mir am Allerentferntesten. Wie ich für die Frauen nur die nächstliegenden praktischen Forderungen vertrete, nur plaidire für die Gründung von Fachvereinen, um auf dem Arbeitsmarkt den Frauen das gleiche Recht wie den Männern zu erringen, so fordere ich auch von der Presse nur die Unterstützung dieser unserer fachgewerkschaftlichen Bestrebungen. Ich muß mich nun darüber öffentlich beschweren, daß mir in meinem Wohnort, in Hamburg, von dem dortigen Arbeiterorgan nicht in dem gehörigen Maaße der geringe Raum, den ich für meine praktischen Bestrebungen gefordert habe, eingeräumt worden ist. Es wird leider von den Männern noch alles in einen Topf geworfen, was von den Frauen ausgeht. Es ist in der Redaktion gesagt worden, „zu der Tragödie des Männerstreiks dieses traurigen Sommers hat die Frau Steinbach nun auch noch die Komödie eines Hamburger Plätterinnenstreiks hinzugefügt." Dieser Plätterinnenstreik ist leider, gegen meinen Willen, vor sich gegangen. Immerhin ist das Resultat dieser Bestrebung noch ein ganz gewaltiges geworden. Wir haben für einen Theil unserer Arbeitsgenossinnen eine Erhöhung ihres Tagelohnes, eine Verringerung ihrer bisher die Nächte hindurch währenden Arbeitszeit errungen, und wenn wir das auch nur für 40 oder 50 Genossinnen errungen haben, mit einer 5 Monate alten Organisation, so kann ich verlangen, daß meine kurzen, aufklärenden Berichte über diese Bewegung aufgenommen werden, und ich kann einem Redakteur nicht das Recht zugestehen, dies noch zu beschneiden. (Heiterkeit.) Das ist Mehlthau auf unsere Bestrebungen. Persönliche Anzapfungen, Klatsch dürfen die Herren zurückweisen, aber für sachliche Ausführungen verlange ich mein Stückchen weißes Papier. Es giebt ja soviel Lumpen und Papier auf der Welt. Kaufe doch die Redaktion mehr Papier! (Heiterkeit.)

Oertel-Nürnberg: In der letzten Zeit ist eine wahre Zeitungs-Gründungs-Epidemie ausgebrochen. Viele dieser Blätter und Blättchen sind nicht existenzfähig. Sie werden über kurz oder lang von der Parteileitung Unterstützung verlangen oder wieder verschwinden. Man darf solchen Gründern den Vorwurf der Unvorsichtigkeit nicht ersparen. Das Zeitungsgeschäft muß gelernt sein. Vielfach haben Leute die Blätter begründet, sich nicht vorher orientirt, sich nicht von Fachleuten Auskunft geben lassen. Derartigen Dingen kann man am besten dadurch gegenübertreten, daß die Partei beschließt, daß von der Parteileitung irgeno welcher Zuschuß an die Lokalpresse nicht abgegeben werden darf. Der Gründung eines Arbeiterrinnenorgans stehe ich sympathisch gegenüber. Allerdings müßte die Redaktion und Mitarbeiterschaft eines solchen Blattes vorzüglich sein. Bekanntlich müssen unsere Frauen mit der denkbar schlechtesten Zeitungslektüre zur Zeit vorlieb nehmen. Es hat sich in den letzten Jahren eine ganze Anzahl sogenannter parteiloser Blätter breit gemacht, Lokalanzeiger, Generalanzeiger u. s. w. Sie erscheinen unter der Maske der Parteilosigkeit und sind in Wirklichkeit nichts, als reaktionäre Blätter, die mit großem Wohlbehagen die reaktionärsten Ansichten und Bestrebungen verbreiten.. Die Arbeitermassen sind es vor allen, die diese Blätter unterhalten. In Nürnberg hat ein solches Organ in kurzer Zeit 20- bis 25 000 Abonnenten gewonnen. Gegen diese „parteilosen" Blätter muß ein wohlorganisirter Feldzug unternommen werden. Den Antrag Guben bitte ich abzulehnen. Wenn wir die Presse annektiren, dann müssen wir auch für etwaige Defizits aufkommen, dazu haben wir aber gar keine Veranlassung. Unsere Partei ist eine Kampfpartei, die ihre Mittel nicht festlegen darf. Außerdem wäre es auch ungerecht, solche Blätter zu annektiren, die während des Ausnahmegesetzes als private Blätter begründet wurden und nur mit großen Geld- und persönlichen Opfern erhalten werden konnten.

Heinrich-Altona: Ich werde für die Resolution stimmen. Redner führt im Auftrage seines Wahlkreises Beschwerde gegen Baumeister Keßler, wegen dessen Angriffe auf Frohme. Nach längeren, theilweise heftigen Ausführungen bringt er folgenden Antrag ein:

Der Parteitag spricht hiermit seine entschiedene Mißbilligung über das vom Regierungsbaumeister Keßler in seinem Organe „Vereinsblatt" gegenüber den Hamburger Genossen, insbesondere dem Genossen Karl Frohme, beachtete unwürdige Verhalten aus!

Im gleichen Sinne spricht Schwer-Hamburg I.

Kahl-Duisburg beantragt Ueberweisung an die Neuner-Kommission, wogegen Keßler sich ausläßt, weil verschiedene Mitglieder darin mehr oder weniger betheiligt seien. Dagegen erklärt er sich mit einem Schiedsgericht einverstanden, das Bebel zusammenberufen möge. Auf Antrag des Vorsitzenden wird die Bildung und Einberufung dieses Schiedsgerichts dem Vorstande überwiesen.

Von Slomke-Bielefeld ist folgende Resolution eingegangen:

Der Parteitag spricht sich entschieden gegen die Aufnahme von Lotterieannonzen, Geheimmittelempfehlungen und ähnlichen, den guten Charakter der Parteipresse verletzenden Anzeigen aus.

Ein Unterantrag von Slomke, in seinen Prinzipalantrag auch Abzahlungsgeschäfte aufzunehmen, wird nicht genügend unterstützt.

Rüger-Verden ist für die Resolution Auer. Durch Schweigen

könne man am Besten sein Einverständniß mit derselben bethätigen. (Beifall.)

Kittler-Heilbronn: Wollen wir mit der parteilosen Presse konkurriren, so müssen wir unsere Presse möglichst billig abgeben. Sollte auch anfangs mit Defizits gearbeitet werden, das Massenabonnement macht später das Unternehmen doch rentabel.

Ein weiterer Antrag:

Der Parteitag empfiehlt den Genossen allerorts, daß bei Gründungen von sozialdemokratischen Preßunternehmungen der einzelnen Orte und Wahlkreise die Zustimmung der Delegirten eines vorher einzuberufenden Provinzialtages einzuholen ist,

wird bei den allgemeinen Anträgen zur Verhandlung kommen.

Schulze-Magdeburg erklärt Namens seiner Auftraggeber, daß die Magdeburger sich ebenfalls der sogenannten Opposition angeschlossen haben. Er will nun die Gründe für diese Haltung darlegen, wird jedoch vom Vorsitzenden mit dem Hinweis unterbrochen, daß jetzt die Parteipresse zur Berathung stehe. Es bleibe dem Redner ja unbenommen, eine schriftliche Erklärung vom Bureau verlesen zu lassen. Redner wünscht in Bezug auf die Presse, daß so unqualifizirbare Aeußerungen, wie sie in letzter Zeit von einzelnen Parteiorganen gethan seien, in Zukunft vermieden werden.

Gottschalk-Hamburg: Wir stehen unbedingt auf dem Standpunkt, daß die Presse Parteieigenthum sein muß und zwar der Partei am betreffenden Orte. Dieser müßte auch die Kontrole zustehen. Dem Antrag Slomke kann ich nicht zustimmen. Annonzen sind eine sehr ergiebige Einnahmequelle für die Zeitungen. Mache man es doch so, wie in Hamburg, daß man schreibt: für den Annonzentheil übernimmt die Redaktion keine Verantwortung. Was die Blätter für die Frauen betrifft, so glaube ich, daß die Frauen doch nur Kaffeekränzchenblätter haben wollen. . . .

Vorsitzender Singer: Ich kann es nicht für zulässig erachten, daß behauptet wird, die in der Arbeiterinnenbewegung stehenden Frauen wollen nichts wie „Kaffeekränzchenblätter" gründen.

Gottschalk (fortfahrend): Ich sage mir, daß die gleichberechtigte Frau dieselben Blätter lesen kann, die wir schon besitzen. Die Frauen können in politischen Blättern ebenso gut für die Sache wirken, wie in besonderen Blättern, die schon mit Defizits arbeiten. Frau Steinbach hat sich darüber beschwert, daß ein Hamburger Redakteur ihre Berichte beschnitten habe. Wollte der Redakteur allen diesen Vereinsgeschichten Raum geben, dann könnte sein Blatt schließlich nicht 8 Seiten umfassen, sondern müßte zwölfmal so groß sein. Er muß in dieser Beziehung etwas beschneiden. Ich möchte also den Vorwurf zurückweisen, als wolle man die Frauen beschneiden, nein, die Männer werden gerade so gut beschnitten! (Stürmische Heiterkeit.)

Schmalfeld-Stade: Ueber die Gründung eines Lokalblattes sollten nur die Genossen am Ort entscheiden, damit sollte die Partei als solche nicht belästigt werden. Es wird sich bald ein gewisses Gründungsfieber bemerkbar machen. Dem muß mit allen Mitteln entgegengetreten werden. Die Schwindel- und Unsittlichkeits-annoncen müssen unbedingt aus der Presse verschwinden; ich kann es auch nicht billigen, wenn ein Blatt die Verantwortlichkeit für solche Annoncen abzuschütteln sucht. Die Leser sagen sich einfach: die Geschäfte, welche in unserem Blatte annonciren, müssen gut sein; die Redakteure haben eine bessere Uebersicht als die Leser. Anders steht es mit den Annoncen, betreffend die Abzahlungs-geschäfte. Diese sind gewissermaßen ein Produkt unserer heutigen Verhältnisse, sie sind nicht aus der Welt zu schaffen. Es sollte aber von den Blättern darauf hingewiesen werden, daß die Käufer in ganz unverantwortlicher Weise von diesen Geschäften übervortheilt werden. Frau Steinbach steht mit ihrer Klage nicht allein da. Die Einsender solcher Lohnbewegungsberichte sollten sich möglichst kurz fassen. Bei der Gründung neuer Blätter sollte man recht vorsichtig sein, um nicht den bereits bestehenden Abbruch zu thun. Dies gilt besonders von Schleswig-Holstein und Mecklenburg.

Ein Schlußantrag wird abgelehnt.

Köster-Wanzleben: Unsittliche und marktschreierische Annoncen muß unsere Presse zurückweisen. Die Frage der Kontrollkommission hat bei uns in Magdeburg schon praktische Gestalt angenommen. Wir haben selbst eine Kontrolle ausgeübt, welche aus dem leidigen Streit entstand, ob das Recht der freien Meinungsäußerung durch die frühere Redaktion der „Magdeburger Volksstimme" in einer Weise ausgeübt wurde, welche dem Sinn und der Sprache eines Arbeiterorgans angemessen ist, oder in einer Weise, die dem Genossen Bebel das Recht gab, eine Beleidigung für die Parteileitung heraus-zulesen. Die Art der Kontrolle muß sich durchaus nach den lokalen Verhältnissen und Bedürfnissen richten, und deshalb ist man in Magdeburg mit der Kontrolle, wie sie Auer vorgeschlagen, nicht einverstanden. Es könnte darnach leicht vorkommen, daß die Haltung eines Blattes wie der „Volksstimme" als eine Verletzung der Prinzipien der Partei angesehen wird. Um nun zu verhüten, daß Vorkommnisse, wie bei der „Magdeburger Volksstimme", wieder-kehren, möchte ich beantragen: der Parteitag erklärt, daß Streitig-keiten, bei denen es sich nur um eine ungeschickte Kampfesweise handelt, in den Spalten der Zeitung, nicht in Volksversammlungen ausgefochten werden müssen und daß nicht gleich die Kontroll-kommission einschreitet und kurzer Hand einfach tabula rasa mit der ganzen Redaktion macht.

Zappay-Marburg beantragt:

Der Parteitag spricht die Erwartung aus, daß die Partei-

blätter nicht nur Anzeigen von Geheimmitteln u. s. w. zurückweisen, sondern auch von denjenigen Geschäften, welche den am
Ort üblichen Arbeitslohn ihren Arbeitern resp. Arbeiterinnen
nicht bezahlen.

Dieser Antrag findet nicht die genügende Unterstützung.

Gewehr-Elberfeld: Vorkommnisse wie bei der „Magdeburger
Volksstimme" und der „Sächsischen Arbeiterzeitung" sind nicht für
die ganze Partei maßgebend. Ich bin gegen den Antrag Guben
und für den Wunsch von Schulze, daß die Parteipresse Eigenthum
der Partei am einzelnen Orte ist. Ueber die Aufnahme von
Annoncen mögen die Redakteure selbst entscheiden.

Der Schluß der Diskussion wird beantragt und von Ohlig
befürwortet. Es sei ja sicher, daß auch diesmal der Antrag des
Referenten einstimmig angenommen werde. Man solle doch nicht
muthwillig die Arbeit hinauszögern.

Frau Ihrer ist für Fortsetzung der Debatte und protestirt
gegen den Ausdruck „muthwillig".

Der Schlußantrag wird angenommen.

Slomke-Bielefeld verlangt noch das Wort zur Begründung
seines Antrages.

Vorsitzender Singer befragt die Versammlung, ob sie ausnahmsweise und abweichend von der Geschäftsordnung den Genossen
noch hören will.

Die Versammlung entscheidet mit großer Mehrheit dagegen.

Slomke (zur Geschäftsordnung): Es ist doch wohl ganz selbstverständlich, daß man die Einbringer selbstständiger Anträge, die
noch dazu eine Redezeit von 20 Minuten nach der Geschäftsordnung
beanspruchen können, auch zum Worte kommen läßt.

Vorsitzender Singer: Es handelt sich nicht um einen selbstständigen Antrag, sondern um eine Resolution zu einem bereits
vorliegenden Antrag. Der Gegenstand ist erledigt.

In einer dem Bureau überreichten „Erklärung der Delegirten
des ehemaligen nördlichen Belagerungsgebietes" Theiß, Lüttgens,
Hillmer, Schwartz, Hogreve, Schweer, Heinrich und Dubber, wird
dem Parteitage mitgetheilt, daß dieselben mit den Ausführungen
von Gottschalk-Hamburg wegen der Inserate nicht einverstanden sind.

Zur Geschäftsordnung erklärt Bremer-Magdeburg, daß die
Magdeburger Delegirten ohne gebundenes Mandat gewählt seien,
nur mit dem Auftrage, sachgemäß Stellung zu nehmen; auch Schulze-
Magdeburg hätte kein gebundenes Mandat.

Desgleichen erklärt Stengele-Hamburg zur Geschäftsordnung:
Ich erkläre, daß ich der von Frau Steinbach angegriffene Redakteur
des Hamburger „Echo" bin. . . . (Glocke des Vorsitzenden.)

Vorsitzender Singer (unterbrechend): Ich kann Ihnen dazu

das Wort nicht weiter verstatten. Frau Steinbach hat zwar das Blatt, aber nicht mit ihren Namen genannt.

Das Schlußwort erhält

Referent Auer: Ich werde mich auch beim Schlußwort möglichst kurz fassen. Ich fange wieder damit an, Sie zu bitten, möglichst von heute ab sich zu befleißigen, daß Sie die bereits gefaßten Beschlüsse nicht leere Worte sein lassen, sondern sie auch thatkräftig ausführen. Wenn wir bisher schon diesen Rath befolgt hätten, wären heute alle Reden über Annoncenwesen und dergleichen nicht mehr nothwendig gewesen. Ich werde Ihnen die betreffenden Parteibeschlüsse von früher vorlesen, daraus werden Sie ersehen, daß wir zu allen diesen Fragen schon längst Stellung genommen haben. Sind Mißstände vorhanden, so liegt das daran, daß die Parteigenossen die früheren Beschlüsse nicht ausgeführt haben. In St. Gallen wurde am 6. Oktober 1887 folgende Resolution von Bebel eingebracht: „Der Parteitag stellt an die Fraktion das Ersuchen, ihren moralischen Einfluß bei den Herausgebern und Eigenthümern von Arbeiterblättern und sonstigen auf die Arbeiterkreise berechneten Literaturerzeugnissen in Deutschland nachdrücklich dahin geltend zu machen, daß diese Art von Literatur ihrer Aufgabe, die Arbeiter aufzuklären, auch wirklich entspricht, was nicht immer der Fall ist. Insbesondere aber soll die Parteivertretung ihr Augenmerk auch darauf richten, daß der ausbeuterische und korrumpirende Charakter verschiedener dieser auf die Arbeiterkreise berechneten Unternehmungen (marktschreierische Anpreisung von zweifelhaften, literarischen Erzeugnissen, von Geheimmitteln und dergleichen, sowie die Veröffentlichung von Schmutz- und Schwindelannoncen u. s. w.) aufhört. Weigern sich die Herausgeber solcher Preßerzeugnisse, den im Interesse der Arbeiterklasse ausgesprochenen Wünschen der Reichstagsfraktion nachzukommen, so soll letztere öffentlich die Arbeiter vor dem Lesen oder Verbreiten solcher Literatur warnen."

Wenn wir den Beschluß gehalten hätten und darauf achten, ihn in Zukunft zu halten, dann ist alles das auf diesen Punkt bezügliche hier und früher schon Gesagte erledigt. Ich konstatire also nur, daß die Partei in dieser Beziehung bereits eine Marschroute hat.

Es ist nun auch der Vorschlag der „Verstaatlichung" der Parteipresse wieder aufgetaucht, und Einzelne sind mit der von mir vorgeschlagenen Resolution deshalb nicht einverstanden, weil dieser Gedanke darin nicht ausgesprochen ist. In der Diskussion ist aber schon darauf hingewiesen worden, daß es eine reine Unmöglichkeit ist, die gesammte Parteipresse als Parteieigenthum zu erklären. Das geht aus tausenderlei Gründen nicht an, liegt auch garnicht im Interesse der Presse selber. Die Folge davon wäre, daß der eigene Trieb derjenigen Blätter, die noch in etwas unsicherer Stellung sich befinden, sich herauszuhelfen, fortfallen würde, daß wir nur der

Partei als solcher eine Last von Defizits aufbürden würden, welche die Partei nicht tragen kann und soll. Blätter dagegen . . . .

(Hier erfährt die Verhandlung eine Unterbrechung. Ein Delegirter ist plötzlich ohnmächtig von seinem Sitz zu Boden geglitten und wird von den ihm zunächst sitzenden Genossen aus dem Sitzungssaal in einen Nebenraum getragen. In der Versammlung herrscht große Bewegung über den Vorfall. Nachdem die Ruhe wiederhergestellt ist, fährt der Redner fort.)

Die gesammte Parteipresse zum Parteieigenthum in dem Sinne zu machen, daß sie der Gesammtpartei gehöre, wofür wir dann wieder ein eigenes Organ schaffen müßten, welches juristisch dieses Eigenthum übernehmen kann, das ist unmöglich durchzuführen. Es steht ja aber den Genossen an den einzelnen Orten garnichts im Wege, Einrichtungen dahin zu treffen, daß ihr Lokalorgan auch in Bezug auf das Eigenthumsrecht ihr Organ wird und nicht irgend einer Privatperson gehört. Dagegen spricht sich auch die Resolution in keiner Weise aus. Die Genossen können also in dieser Beziehung machen, was sie wollen; was wir nicht annehmen können, ist, daß die Gesammtpartei Eigenthümerin der gesammten Parteipresse sein soll. Was die Genossen wollen, ist wahrscheinlich auch nur das, daß ihnen das Recht eingeräumt werde, sich selbst zu Eigenthümern ihres Lokalorgans zu machen. Das mag gemacht werden, wo es sich irgendwie als zweckentsprechend erweist.

Ferner ist auch hier die Frauenbewegung wieder hereingezogen worden. Es ist eigentlich bedauerlich, daß die Frauen gar so viel zu klagen haben. Das liegt doch wohl nicht blos am mangelnden Entgegenkommen seitens der Parteigenossen, sondern vielleicht sind die Frauen auch in etwas pessimistischer Stimmung. Ihre Bewegung hat ja wirklich noch nicht die Ausbreitung, die wir alle ihr wünschen, und je kleiner die Bewegung ist, — das ist eine alte Erfahrung, die auch wir Männer seiner Zeit gemacht haben — je mehr sie noch in den Kinderschuhen steckt, desto mehr machen sich innere Zwistigkeiten, kleinliche Nörgeleien und ein gewisses Gefühl des Unbefriedigtseins geltend. Es ist das meine persönliche Meinung. Es scheint mir, daß auch die Leiterinnen der Frauenbewegung bei uns nach und nach dahin gekommen sind, daß sie über die Dinge, die sie selbst reformiren und bessern sollen, in Uneinigkeit gerathen und nun uns armen Männern die Schuld dafür geben, daß sie sich untereinander nicht vertragen können. Ich bin ja selbst verheirathet und hoffe, daß mir diese Aeußerung von den Frauen nicht nachgetragen werden wird. (Heiterkeit.) „Komödie des Plätterinnenstreiks," für eine solche in der Aufregung gethane Aeußerung eines einzelnen Blattes müssen Sie nicht die Gesammtheit verantwortlich machen; solchen Ausdruck können Sie ja mit der größten Leichtigkeit zurückgeben, denn für diese einzelne „Komödie" des Plätterinnenstreits mache ich mich sofort anheischig, zwei, drei, vier gleiche „Komödien", die die Männer in Szene gesetzt haben, anzuführen, da sind Sie reichlich entschädigt. Das müssen Sie nicht so genau nehmen. Wir wissen Alle, und das drückt auch unser Organisationsentwurf aus, wie wir voll und ganz bereit sind, die Gleichberechtigung der Frauenbewegung mit der unsrigen anzuerkennen. Liebknecht sagte, die Frauenbewegung ist eben mit die soziale Frage; wir gehören da zusammen und wollen uns nicht scheiden.

Der Genosse Schulze-Magdeburg hat gemeint, es empfehle sich, keine so schroffen Worte bei den Angriffen mehr zu gebrauchen, und Köster-Wanzleben hat gesagt, derartige Streitfragen sollten in den Parteiorganen, nicht in öffentlichen Versammlungen, ausgetragen werden. Ich spreche zunächst meine Genugthuung darüber aus, daß es Magdeburger Genossen sind, welche dem dortigen Organ nahestanden, die solchen Wünschen Ausdruck geben; ich hoffe, daß sie in alle Zukunft diesen ihren eigenen Rath befolgen werden und bedaure nur, daß sie ihn nicht schon vorher befolgt haben. Die Genossen selber waren es übrigens, welche Stellung zu ihrem Partei-blatt nahmen, sowohl in Dresden und in Magdeburg. Es hat wirklich keine Vergewaltigung stattgefunden. Daß in Magdeburg Bebel er-schienen ist, kann doch nicht Wunder nehmen: hat er nicht das Recht der freien Meinungsäußerung, wie wir alle? Und in Dresden wohnte er ja sogar und konnte schon als bloßer Parteigenosse an der Ver-sammlung theilnehmen, wie auch die Genossen am Orte das Recht hatten, seine Meinung, als die des Angegriffenen, zu hören. Gerade die dort erfolgte Beschlußfassung müssen Sie also respektiren. Ich wünsche nur, daß wir in alle Zukunft möglichst mit derartigen Vorkommnissen verschont bleiben. (Beifall.)

In persönlicher Bemerkung zum Schlußwort des Referenten weist Frau Steinbach den Ausdruck „Komödie" nochmals ent-schieden zurück.

Die Resolution Auer wird darauf nochmals verlesen und gelangt sodann einstimmig zur Annahme.

Der Antrag der Gubener Genossen wird gegen eine kleine Minorität abgelehnt, der Antrag Slomke angenommen. Der Antrag der Hamburg-Altonaer Genossen wird, da die Ein-setzung eines Schiedsgerichts beschlossen ist, zurückgezogen.

Vorsitzender Singer: Ich habe dem Parteitage eine tief-traurige Mittheilung zu machen. Der Genosse, der eben, wie wir glaubten, in Folge eines Unwohlseins vom Stuhle fiel, ist, wie leider feststeht, vom Schlage getroffen, gestorben. Wir haben wiederum einen Genossen verloren, der in treuester Pflichterfüllung für die Interessen der Partei gearbeitet hat. Der Delegirte Baumgarten für Hamburg III war einer der ältesten Genossen

Hamburgs; seit langem treu für unsere Sache eintretend, stand er in der Reihe derjenigen, die auch für ihre Person Maßregelungen um ihrer Ueberzeugung willen erlitten haben. Wir empfinden dieses plötzliche Hinscheiden um so schmerzlicher, als der Genosse hier durch seine Thätigkeit mit dazu beigetragen hat, daß die Einheit und Geschlossenheit der Sozialdemokratie glänzender wie je sich manifestirt hat. Wenn es einen Trost für diesen plötzlichen Verlust giebt, so besteht er darin, daß der Genosse die Ueberzeugung in den Tod mitnehmen konnte, daß seine Partei, die Partei des Proletariats, für welche er bis zu seinem letzten Athemzuge gekämpft hat, den vollen, den ganzen Sieg erringen wird. Ich bitte Sie, das Andenken an den von uns geschiedenen Genossen durch Erheben von den Sitzen zu ehren.

(Die Versammelten erheben sich einmüthig von ihren Plätzen.)

Unter der Einwirkung dieses schmerzlichen Ereignisses halte ich es nicht für angemessen, in unseren Arbeiten fortzufahren. Ich bitte Sie, in Würdigung der Stimmung, in der wir uns alle befinden, die Sitzung jetzt abzubrechen und um 2 Uhr wieder aufzunehmen; die Sitzung ist geschlossen.

Schluß 11½ Uhr.

Nachmittagssitzung.

Um 2½ Uhr wird die Sitzung unter dem Vorsitz des Genossen Dietz wieder aufgenommen.

Vor der Tagesordnung verlangt das Wort

Singer: Ich habe bezüglich meiner vor dem Parteitag wegen der Notiz im hiesigen „General-Anzeiger" abgegebenen Erklärung von dem Chefredakteur Herrn Friedrich Baumann an meine Adresse folgende Mittheilung erhalten:

Vor Eintritt in die Tagesordnung der gestrigen Berathungen des sozialdemokratischen Parteitages stellten Sie im Namen des Parteitages die Behauptung des „General-Anzeiger":

Am verflossenen Dienstag Abend, während des Kommerses, hätten Führer der Partei mit den französischen Delegirten in einem hiesigen Hotel eine geheime Berathung gehabt,

als eine verleumderische Lüge hin.

Demgegenüber erkläre ich, daß ich selbst die französischen Delegirten, nachdem ich mit denselben eine halbe Stunde im Saale des Prinz Karl zugebracht hatte, in das bewußte Hotel geführt und dort während mehrerer Stunden in Gesellschaft dieser Herren, des Abgeordneten Liebknecht und anderer Parteimänner verweilt habe. Dieses Zusammensein fand in einem reservirten Zimmer der ersten Etage

16

des erwähnten Hotels statt. Ihre Persönlichkeit habe ich dort-
selbst nicht bemerkt. Angesichts des Charakters der geführten
Unterhaltung, angesichts der Fragen, welche die französischen
Herren an den Abgeordneten Herrn Liebknecht richteten, war ich
vollauf berechtigt, diese Zusammenkunft, fern der Kommersfeier, in
den wenigen Worten, die ich ihr gewidmet habe, mit dem übrigens
unverfänglichen Ausdruck „geheime Berathung" zu bezeichnen.
Die böswillige Absicht, welche Sie mir als Ergebniß Ihrer miß-
verständlichen Auffassung unterschieben, hat mir absolut fern
gelegen. Deshalb erhebe ich energisch Einspruch gegen Ihre
Anschuldigung und erwarte von Ihrem Gerechtigkeitsgefühl, daß
Sie gegenwärtige Erklärung zur Richtigstellung an gleicher Stelle
bekannt geben."

Ich stelle einfach diesem Schreiben den Wortlaut der Notiz
aus dem „General-Anzeiger" gegenüber, wo es heißt: „Ein Genosse
nahte sich ihnen und lud sie im Namen des Abgeordneten Liebknecht
ein, zu ihm ins Centralhotel zu kommen. Hier saßen die meisten
Führer, tranken Bier und pflegten geheime Berathung ꝛc." und
überlasse es dem Urtheil des Parteitages und der Außenstehenden,
ob ich ein Recht hatte, diese Behauptung als eine verleumderische
Lüge hinzustellen, ein Ausspruch, den ich hiermit wiederhole.
(Lebhafter Beifall.)

Darauf tritt der Parteitag in die

Spezialdiskussion über den Organisationsentwurf,

wie er nach den Beschlüssen der 25 er Kommission gedruckt unter
die Mitglieder zur Vertheilung gelangt ist. Dieselbe Kommission
hat dem Parteitage eine Vorschlagsliste für die auf Grund der
neuen Organisation vorzunehmenden Vorstandswahlen überreicht.

Berichterstatter Auer: Die Kommission, welche Sie vorgestern
gewählt haben, hat gestern getagt und zwar den ganzen Tag, und
das Resultat ihrer Arbeiten liegt Ihnen vor in dem Schriftstücke,
überschrieben „Organisation der sozialdemokratischen Partei Deutschlands." Die Kommission hat mich mit der Berichterstattung beauftragt. Sowohl im Interesse unserer Verhandlungen, als auch
angesichts der großen Einmüthigkeit, mit welcher die Kommission
ihre Beschlüsse gefaßt hat, glaube ich, mich möglichst kurz fassen zu
können; ich werde mich auf die allernothwendigsten Erläuterungen
beschränken.

Zunächst haben wir in der Ueberschrift den Parteinamen
geändert in „sozialdemokratische Partei Deutschlands".
Darüber wird es einer weiteren Auseinandersetzung gar nicht bedürfen.

§ 1 lautet jetzt:

Zur Partei gehörig wird jede Person betrachtet, die sich zu den Grundsätzen des Parteiprogramms bekennt und die Partei nach Kräften unterstützt.

Zweierlei ist hier besonders zu beachten.

Mit dem Worte „Person" (wie schon im Entwurf) wird ausgesprochen, daß Männer wie Frauen zur Partei gehören können. Als Kennzeichen ferner für die Zugehörigkeit zur Partei wollen wir das Bekenntniß „zu den Grundsätzen unseres Parteiprogrammes" betrachten, nicht engherzig „zum Parteiprogramm", so daß Jeder jeden Buchstaben anerkennen müßte, sondern in Berücksichtigung dessen, daß der Eine oder der Andere gegen diesen oder jenen speziellen Punkt seine Bedenken habe und eine kleine Abweichung irgend welcher Art gar keine Rolle spiele. Außerdem soll, wer zu uns gehören will, die Partei „nach Kräften unterstützen". Damit ist den Einwürfen gegen „dauernd materiell" Rechnung getragen. Die Unterstützung kann in den verschiedensten Formen geschehen: materiell, durch Agitation, durch theoretische, wissenschaftliche Arbeit; es ist absolut freier Spielraum gelassen. Ich bemerke noch, daß wir auch in Rücksicht auf die vereinsrechtlichen Verhältnisse in Deutschland speziell zu dieser Form gekommen sind, diese Rücksicht war die ausschlaggebende.

§ 2.

Zur Partei kann nicht gehören, wer sich eines groben Verstoßes gegen die Grundsätze des Parteiprogramms, oder wer sich ehrloser Handlungen schuldig gemacht hat.

Ueber die Zugehörigkeit zur Partei entscheiden die Parteigenossen der einzelnen Orte oder Reichstagswahlkreise.

Gegen diese Entscheidung steht dem Betroffenen die Berufung an die Parteileitung und den Parteitag zu.

Auch hier ist nicht mehr von einem groben Verstoß gegen den Buchstabensinn des Programms, sondern gegen die Grundsätze desselben die Rede; die Bestimmung aber, daß, wer sich ehrloser Handlungen schuldig gemacht hat, nicht mehr zu uns gehört, haben wir beibehalten. Auch darüber brauche ich wohl kein Wort zu verlieren. Wir hielten dafür, daß es ehrlose Handlungen giebt, die Jedem gegenüber als ehrlos gelten, und daß da von bürgerlicher und sozialdemokratischer Moral gar nicht die Rede sein kann. In den Augen gewisser bürgerlicher Kreise gilt man ja schon als ehrlos, wenn man einmal das Unglück hatte, einer Majestätsbeleidigung verdächtigt zu werden; daß für uns derlei nicht als ehrlos gilt, ist selbstverständlich. Nach Absatz 2 des § 2 sollen über die Zugehörigkeit zur Partei die Parteigenossen der einzelnen Orte oder Wahlkreise zu entscheiden haben. Der ganze Aufbau der Organisation, wie sie beschlossen ist, läßt gar nichts anderes zu. Nur den

16*

Appell an die Parteileitung und an den Parteitag haben wir offen gehalten.

Bei dem ganzen Kapitel über die Vertrauensmänner will ich mich gar nicht aufhalten; die §§ 3 bis 5 des Entwurfs sind mit kleinen Abänderungen beibehalten worden. Mit Rücksicht auf die verschiedenartige Vereinsgesetzgebung, und weil wir Deutsche uns noch des Vorzugs erfreuen, ein Land innerhalb der Reichsgrenzen zu haben, welches in Bezug auf Konstitutions- und Verfassungslosigkeit mit Rußland und der Türkei konkurriren kann, nämlich Mecklenburg, ohne Vereins- und Versammlungsgesetz, endlich weil in Bayern der Wortlaut des Vereinsgesetzes nach der Interpretation mehrerer Gerichtsbeschlüsse es außerordentlich erschweren dürfte, den Bestimmungen in den §§ 3 bis 5 nachzukommen, haben wir einen neuen § 6 geschaffen, wonach dort den Genossen völlig freie Hand gelassen wird, die Organisation so einzurichten, wie sie ihnen durchführbar und zweckmäßig erscheint.

Die Bestimmungen über den Parteitag sind im Wesentlichen geblieben, wie sie waren. Viele dazu gestellte Anträge haben auf irrthümlichen Voraussetzungen beruht. Im jetzigen § 8 ist aber die Bestimmung, daß die Anträge für den Parteitag spätestens 14 Tage nach der Bekanntmachnng des Termins vorliegen müssen, als eine ganz unnütze Einschränkung gestrichen worden. Jetzt werden die Parteigenossen Anträge stellen können, soviel sie wollen, mit der einzigen Einschränkung, daß sie zehn Tage vor dem Termin bekannt sein müssen. Damit hat sich eine große Anzahl von Anträgen ohne Weiteres erledigt. Zu § 9 (Theilnahme am Parteitage) lagen besonders viele Anträge vor, welche auf eine andere Art der Vertretung und Zulassung zum Parteitage hinausliefen. Sie sind alle abgelehnt worden, weil wir uns über keinen anderen Modus verständigen konnten und es, wie sich herausstellte, ungemein schwer ist, in dieser Beziehung zu reglementiren. Wir haben schließlich beschlossen, zu sagen, daß „in der Regel" kein Wahlkreis durch mehr als 3 Personen vertreten sein darf. Es bleibt danach dem Taktgefühl der Parteigenossen selber überlassen, ob sie glauben, einem späteren Parteitage zumuthen zu können, daß aus ihren Kreisen mehr als 3 Delegirte in maximo erscheinen. Daß es nur loyal und berechtigt sein kann, wenn die großen Wahlkreise mit sehr großer Wählerzahl mehr schicken wollen, dagegen wird auch Niemand etwas haben. Das Recht ist Ihnen jetzt zugesagt; d richtigen Gebrauch davon zu machen, ist Ihrem Taktgefühl u Ermessen überlassen. Auch § 10 (Aufgaben des Parteitages) . geblieben. Desgleichen § 11 (Einberufung eines außerordentliche Parteitages). Hier ist jedoch eine Bestimmung weggefallen, da die Einberufung auch zu erfolgen habe auf Antrag von 10 000 Unter schriften von Parteigenossen. Der Fall, daß ein außerordentliche

Parteitag erst aus der Partei heraus erzwungen werden muß, wird ungemein selten vorkommen; wir werden es wohl nie erleben. Diese Erwägung und die fernere, daß die Kontrolle der 10000 Unterschriften gar nicht möglich ist, und daß damit etwa eine für uns gefährliche Klippe in vereinsgesetzlicher Hinsicht von uns selbst geschaffen werden würde, hat uns veranlaßt, diese Bestimmung des Statuts einstimmig fallen zu lassen. Sie würde doch nur dekoratives Beiwerk gewesen sein und hätte möglicherweise einem findigen Staatsanwalt willkommenen Anlaß geboten, hier eine geheime Verbindung zu konstruiren.

Bei unseren Berathungen über die Parteileitung, dem springenden Punkt des Ganzen, wurde von vornherein von allen Seiten ausgesprochen, daß nicht darauf bestanden werde, irgend eine vorher ausgesprochene, geschriebene oder gedruckte Meinung aufrecht zu erhalten, sondern daß uns Alle in unseren Anträgen, in unserer Kritik, in Presse und Versammlungen nur das Bestreben geleitet habe, das Beste für die Partei herbeiführen zu helfen. So war denn von Anfang an die Möglichkeit einer Verständigung sehr leicht; es frug sich für uns alle nur: Wie wird der mit dem Statut verfolgte Zweck zu erreichen sein, ohne uns der Gefahr auszusetzen, die Organisation sofort wieder aus vereinsrechtlichen Gründen zu gefährden? Nachdem von allen Seiten die Erfahrungen zum Besten gegeben waren, nachdem auch die Vertreter der Fraktion sofort erklärt hatten, daß dieselbe auf der Uebertragung der Kontrolle durchaus nicht bestehe, sondern diesen Vorschlag eigentlich gegen den Willen der Mitglieder, nur dem Zwange folgend, gemacht habe, um damit nach ihrer Meinung eine Schutzwehr gegen die Auflösung der Partei zu errichten, haben wir uns nach längerer Debatte vollständig geeinigt. Der Vorschlag der Hamburger Genossen und theilweise der der Berliner, der nichts anderes ist, als eine gewisse, wenn auch nicht wörtliche Nachahmung der Organisationsbestimmungen, die sich die deutschfreisinnige Partei, auch dem Zwange folgend, gegeben hat, ist die Grundlage unserer Beschlüsse geworden. Der Antrag Theiß unterschied sich von dem Berliner nur in 2 Punkten; einmal setzte er die Zahl der Vorstandsmitglieder geringer an, als der der Berliner, und dann enthielt er die Einschränkung in der Auswahl der Personen nicht, welche sich im Berliner Antrage befand. Der Berliner Antrag wollte 20 Vorstandsmitglieder, von denen 10 der ⸺aktion angehören dürfen, dem Exekutivausschuß von 5 Personen ⸺ten nur 2 Fraktionsmitglieder angehören können. Gegen diese ⸺nschränkungen wurden aber ganz bestimmte Erklärungen abgegeben, ⸺ nach genügender Aussprache schließlich von keiner Seite mehr ⸺ Aufrechterhaltung derselben verlangt, und zwar sind wir alle ⸺s rein praktischen Erwägungen zu der einstimmigen Anschauung ⸺angt, daß eine derartige Einschränkung nicht möglich ist. Bei der ⸺etzung der Vorstandsämter kommt nicht in Frage, ob einer der

Fraktion angehört, sondern ob er die Fähigkeit und die physische und materielle Möglichkeit hat, dem Vorstand anzugehören; die Abgeordnetenqualität ist hierfür vollständig irrelevant. Wir haben festgesetzt einen Vorstand aus 12 Personen, 2 Vorsitzende, 2 Schriftführer, 1 Kassirer, 7 Kontrolleure. Die Wahl erfolgt auf dem Parteitag mittelst Stimmzettel, und zwar so, daß der Parteitag auch gleich ausspricht, welchen Charakter er mit der einzelnen Wahl verbinden will. Die folgenden Bestimmungen dieses Abschnitts sind rein geschäftlicher Natur. Bemerken will ich noch, daß die Meinung dahin ging, daß die 5 Personen, welche die Verwaltung führen sollen, möglichst an einem Platz oder in einem verhältnißmäßig nicht zu großen Umkreis wohnen sollen, daß es dagegen bei den Kontrolleuren, welche die Geschäftsführung zu überwachen haben, weniger darauf ankommt, obwohl auch hier wünschenswerth ist, daß sie nicht allzu entfernt vom Sitze der Parteileitung ihren Wohnort haben.

Diese Parteileitung ist gewissermaßen der Kopf des Ganzen. In der Parteileitung ist der Mittelpunkt für die Verwaltung geschaffen; für die politische Leitung wird ja die Fraktion nachher immer noch ihren sehr bedeutenden und maßgebenden Einfluß haben, gleich wie auch die Parteipresse.

Mit dieser Zusammensetzung des Parteivorstandes aber glauben wir auch zugleich die nothwendige Kontrollinstanz geschaffen zu haben, wodurch eine Extrakontrollbehörde überflüssig wird. Die gewählte Form ist ja wieder auf die vereinsrechtlichen Verhältnisse zurückzuführen; wir waren in der Kommission einstimmig darin, daß, wenn wir uns überhaupt eine Organisation geben können, dies die einzig mögliche Form ist.

Wir haben zuletzt noch den Zusatz beschlossen:

Die Parteileitung verfügt nach eigenem Ermessen über die vorhandenen Gelder.

Dieser Passus klingt etwas selbstherrlich, aber auch diese Vorschrift ist uns durch die Verhältnisse aufgezwungen. Wir haben ja Vermögen, das soll sich vermehren, es ist im Interesse der Partei sehr zu wünschen, daß wir gewisse Fonds haben. Nun können, trotz aller Vorsicht, trotz alles Bestrebens, dem Gesetze möglichst nachzukommen, — man sucht ja immer wieder uns von dem Boden des Gesetzes abzudrängen — wir dennoch nicht wissen, ob wir ni[ ] wieder als Verein erklärt und geschlossen werden; die schließen[ ] Behörde möchte dann vielleicht kommen und verlangen, daß n[ ] mit dem Gelde herausrücken, weil es beschlagnahmt werden müs[ ] Für diesen Fall — denn wir hätten kein Vergnügen daran, b[ ] Polizei das Geld auszuliefern (Heiterkeit) — glaubten wir uns sicher[ ] zu müssen. Ausliefern würden wir das Geld ja nicht, darüb[ ] täuscht sich auch die Polizei nicht; aber wenn wir diese Bestimmu[ ] nicht haben, welche den Vorstand der Partei den Gerichten gegenüber deckt, so könnte nach früheren schlimmen Erfahrungen eine Behörde wieder von uns die Herausgabe verlangen, und im Falle der Weigerung, die Anklage wegen Unterschlagung erheben. Siehe den Prozeß in Mannheim; die Mannheimer sind verurtheilt worden, obwohl eine Unterschlagung im kriminellen Sinne nicht vorlag; aber die Richter sind zu der Ueberzeugung gekommen, weil die Metallarbeiter mit Rücksicht auf ihre Gewerkschaft unter der Aera des Sozialistengesetzes mit der Klarlegung des Thatbestandes nicht offen heraustreten konnten. Wird dies statutarisch so festgelegt, so wird die Leitung einfach bezügliche Beschlüsse fassen. Vielleicht werden wir das Vermögen bei der Bank von England niederlegen — wir sind ja zu allem fähig — und dann werden wir, wie man uns maßgebend juristisch belehrt hat, sagen können, das Geld ist da, aber in der Bank von England; wenn ihr wollt, geht hin und holt's euch! (Heiterkeit.) Ich theile das blos mit, damit nicht nach außen der Eindruck aufkommt, als wenn die Parteileitung, über die Köpfe der Genossen hinweg, mit den Geldern wirthschaften könnte, wie sie wollte. Die Leitung soll vor aller Welt abrechnen über Einnahmen und Ausgaben; aber die Gelder müssen so untergebracht werden, daß nicht irgend Jemand heran kann, für den es nicht gesammelt war. (Heiterkeit.)

Im § 14 wird festgesetzt, daß der Parteitag die Höhe der Besoldung für die Vorstandsmitglieder zu bestimmen hat. Wir folgen damit dem Wunsche zahlreicher Stimmen auf dem Parteitag; die Gründe aber, welche ich in meinem Referat dafür geltend gemacht hatte, daß wir nicht ursprünglich sofort so verfahren sind, wurden in der Kommission als vollkommen zutreffend anerkannt. Einen Ausweg haben wir gefunden in einer Resolution, in der ausgesprochen werden soll, daß bis zum nächsten Parteitag der neuen Parteileitung überlassen wird, die Gehälter festzusetzen, weil man nicht weiß, wie groß der Umfang der Arbeit sein wird, wer ganz und wer nur zeitweise beschäftigt sein wird. Nach dieser Resolution würde die Bestimmung des § 14 für dieses Mal noch nicht zur Ausführung gelangen.

Im § 15 ist die Kontrolle der prinzipiellen Haltung der Parteiorgane durch die Parteileitung beibehalten worden und zwar aus Gründen, die in der Kommission noch näher ausgeführt wurden und so durchschlagend waren, daß ein ganz entschiedener Gegner dieser Bestimmung in der Kommission die Erklärung abgab, daß er keine Ursache mehr habe, gegen diese Vorschrift zu stimmen.

Nach § 16 sollen die Vakanzen dadurch beseitigt werden, daß die Kontrolleure die Neuwahl vornehmen. Wir halten das für die glücklichste Lösung und hoffen außerdem, daß eine Valanz nicht eintreten wird, daß wir fünf so gesunde, kräftige, tüchtige Genossen in den Vorstand bekommen, daß sie alle den nächsten Parteitag noch erleben werden. Daß die Wahl aus dem gesammten Kreise der Parteigenossen erfolgen kann, versteht sich von selbst.

Die so organisirte Parteileitung, die zumal immer nur ein Jahr besteht, garantirt uns vollständig, daß Beschwerden über die Leitung oder die Fraktion schnell und sachgemäß zur Erledigung kommen werden; es ist kein Grund mehr vorhanden, eine besondere Kontroll-behörde einzusetzen, die uns lediglich der Gefahr der Auflösung preisgeben würde.

In Betreff des Parteiorgans sind die ursprünglichen Vor-schläge vollständig beibehalten worden. Da waren sehr viele Wünsche, und wurden auch in der Kommission wieder laut; aber nach nochmaliger gründlicher Erörterung der Für und Wider haben wir uns von der Unmöglichkeit überzeugt, eine andere Lösung, als die vorgeschlagene, zur Zeit zu finden. Auf dem nächsten Parteitag kann auch diese Bestimmung geändert werden; für jetzt wäre dies nur unter Schädigung sehr wesentlicher Parteiinteressen möglich.

Nachdem wir so den ganzen Tag fleißig gearbeitet hatten, nachdem alle Meinungen — und in der Kommission saßen ja die Vertreter der schroffsten Gegensätze, wir waren thatsächlich ein Miniaturbild des Parteitages — nochmals aufs Energischste und mit den sachlichsten Gründen vertheidigt worden waren, nachdem der Abend gekommen war und unsere Arbeit beendet, da war das ebenso für Sie wie für uns in der Kommission erfreuliche Resultat, daß es keine Sieger und keine Besiegten gab, sondern daß wir das ehrliche und offene Geständniß ablegen konnten, daß wir alle nur nach bestem Wollen und Können auf die Wahrung des Partei-interesses bedacht gewesen waren. Einstimmig haben wir alle 25 miteinander nicht blos den Entwurf angenommen, sondern uns auch verpflichtet, einstimmig hier im Plenum für denselben ein-zutreten und Sie im Parteiinteresse zu ersuchen, den Entwurf en bloc anzunehmen. (Stürmischer Beifall.)

Vorsitzender Dietz: Es ist der Antrag eingelaufen, die Kom-missionsbeschlüsse nicht zu diskutiren, sondern sofort en bloc anzu-nehmen. (Allseitige Zustimmung.)

Unter jubelndem Beifall wird, diesem Antrag entsprechend, ohne Diskussion der Entwurf nach den Kommissionsvorschlägen mit allen gegen 1 Stimme angenommen.

Auf Antrag Bebel's wird nunmehr zunächst über die Reso-lution, betreffend die Festsetzung der Gehälter berathen.

Bebel: Es sollen 5 Personen vorhanden sein, welche die eigentlichen Verwaltungsgeschäfte zu leiten haben. Nach unserer praktischen Erfahrung müssen unter diesen 5 mindestens 2 sein, die mit ihrer ganzen Arbeitskraft von früh bis spät sich zur Verfügung stellen; in nicht mehr zu ferner Zeit schon werden 2 vielleicht nicht mehr ausreichen. Neben den beiden Schriftführern wird die meiste Arbeit der Kassirer haben; dann aber werden die 5 Mitglieder sehr häufig, und zwar auch während des Tages, nicht blos in den Abendstunden, zusammenkommen müssen und demnach erhebliche Zeitopfer zu bringen haben. Ohne Rücksicht darauf, wer gewählt wird, und ob ein Gewählter auf materielle Beihilfe verzichten kann, meinen wir doch, daß gewisse materielle Entschädigungen diesen Personen gezahlt werden müssen, unter allen Umständen denjenigen, welche mit ihrer ganzen Arbeitskraft herangezogen werden. Früher erhielten die Schriftführer je 150, der Kassirer 105, die beiden Vorsitzenden je 45 Mark. Diese Beträge werden gegenwärtig nicht mehr auslangen, namentlich wenn Berlin, welches größere Mittel erheischt, zum Sitz der Parteileitung gewählt wird, wie es höchst wahrscheinlich geschehen wird. In Anbetracht der Zeitopfer und der materiellen, in Bezug auf Repräsentation an die Mitglieder zu stellenden Anforderungen glauben wir annehmen zu dürfen, daß in maximo für die beiden Schriftführer monatlich je 250 Mark, für den Kassirer 150 Mark, die beiden Vorsitzenden je 50 Mark auszugeben sein wird. Ist der Eine oder der Andere später in der Lage, auf diese Zuschüsse zu verzichten, um so besser für die Partei; im Prinzip aber halte ich eine derartige Festsetzung für nothwendig. Ich schlage nun vor, von der Detailberathung abzusehen und statt dessen folgende Resolution zu beschließen:

In Erwägung, daß im § 14 des Organisationsstatuts bestimmt ist, daß die Gehälter für die Parteileitung durch den Parteitag festgesetzt werden sollen; in Erwägung, daß noch nicht zu übersehen ist, wie groß die Arbeit der Parteileitung sein wird, also sich die Höhe der nothwendigen Gehälter nicht genau festsetzen läßt, beschließt der Parteitag, daß die Parteileitung ermächtigt ist, das Gehalt bis zum nächsten Parteitag selber festzusetzen mit der Einschränkung, daß das Gehalt der einzelnen Mitglieder, soweit sie überhaupt Gehalt empfangen, den Betrag von 250 Mark pro Monat nicht übersteigen darf.

Für die Kontroleure ist eine bestimmte Entschädigung nicht vorgesehen; doch werden dieselben, wenn sie zusammentreten, sowohl Reisekosten und Auslagen ersetzt erhalten, wie auch entsprechende Diäten bekommen. (Allseitige Zustimmung und Rufe: Abstimmen!)

Ohne Debatte wird die Resolution einstimmig angenommen.

Hierauf wird nach § 10 des Statuts der Sitz der Parteileitung bestimmt.

Dazu liegen 2 Anträge vor: 1. von Elbing-Marienburg, den Sitz nach Danzig (Heiterkeit) zu verlegen, 2. zum Sitze Berlin zu wählen.

Zur Geschäftsordnung bemerkt

Jochem-Danzig: Der Vertreter für Elbing-Marienburg hat mir den Danzig betreffenden Antrag zur Unterschrift vorgelegt. Ich sagte ihm, er solle doch so etwas nicht machen. Er hat ihn mir nochmals vorgelegt, ich habe meine Unterschrift wieder verweigert. Was ich befürchtet habe, ist eingetreten, es wurde über den Vorschlag gespottet, und da habe ich zu erklären, daß die Danziger Genossen und ich mit dem Antrage nichts zu thun haben.

Der Vorschlag, betreffend Danzig wird unter großer Heiterkeit einstimmig abgelehnt, Berlin dagegen einstimmig angenommen.

Auf Grund des § 10, Absatz 3 geht der Parteitag jetzt über zu Punkt 5 der Tagesordnung:

Vornahme der Wahlen auf Grund der angenommenen Organisation.

Von der 25er Kommission ist folgende Vorschlagsliste dem Parteitage unterbreitet worden:

Vorstand

A. Gerisch, Vorsitzender.

P. Singer, „

J. Auer, Schriftführer.

R. Fischer, „

Bebel, Kassirer.

Kontrolleure.

Behrend-Frankfurt a. O.

Dubber-Hamburg.

Ewald-Brandenburg.

Herbert-Stettin.

Jacobey-Berlin.

Kaden-Dresden.

G. Schulz-Berlin.

Hierzu bemerkt Kühn-Langenbielau: Als Mitglied der 25er Kommission bin ich beauftragt, zu motiviren, wie die Kommission dazu gekommen ist, diesen Vorschlag sich zu erlauben. Nach Annahme des § 13 ergab sich ganz von selbst die Frage, ob sich nicht in diesem engeren Kreise eine Verständigung über die geeignetsten Personen finden ließe. Die Kommission war sich völlig bewußt, daß ihr Mandat nicht dahin ging; entschied sich aber einstimmig dafür, es dennoch zu thun. Als Gründe für dieses Vorgehen waren maßgebend zunächst die Rücksicht auf Zeitersparniß in Anbetracht der Geschäftslage; ferner bezüglich der Feststellung der Personenfrage selbst der Umstand, daß es wünschenswerth erschien, wenn die Kontrolleure nicht zu weit vom Sitze der Parteileitung entfernt wohnen, um in dringenden Fällen möglichst an einem Tage zur Erledigung der betreffenden Angelegenheiten zusammenkommen zu können. Von diesem Gesichtspunkte aus sind die vorgeschlagenen Kontrolleure ausgewählt worden; der andere geltend gemachte Wunsch, daß möglichst jeder größere Einzelstaat oder jede Gegend Deutschlands in der Parteileitung berücksichtigt werden möchte, hatte demgegenüber zurückzutreten. Bei der Abwägung der Personenfrage ist natürlich in erster Linie die Qualifikation der einzelnen Vorgeschlagenen erwogen worden. Die Kommission bezweifelt gar nicht, daß es außerhalb ihrer Vorschläge noch andere, für die weitverzweigte, komplizirte Thätigkeit der Geschäftsleitung ebenso geeignete Personen giebt und will dem Recht des Parteitages nicht im Geringsten vorgreifen (Unruhe, Schlußrufe); sie erlaubt sich eben nur, Ihnen nach ihrer Ansicht geeignete Vorschläge zu machen. Der Name Liebknecht fehlt auf der Vorschlagsliste, weil wir der Ansicht waren, daß Liebknecht, als Chefredakteur des Parteiorgans, einmal keine Zeit für die Vorstandsthätigkeit übrig haben, dann aber doch so wie so der geistige Leiter bleiben würde.

Joest-Mainz: Ich habe einen Antrag mit fünf anderen Namen von Kontrolleuren eingereicht, der aber nicht verlesen worden ist. Im Umkreise von Berlin, über Dresden hinaus, befindet sich auf der Kommissionsliste kein einziger Genosse. Der ganze Süden und Westen Deutschlands soll unvertreten bleiben; das begreife ich nicht. (Gelächter.) Ich schlage Grillenberger, Geck-Offenburg und Müller-Darmstadt statt der beiden Berliner und des Frankfurter Genossen vor.

Geyer-Leipzig-Land: Ich finde Joest's Ansicht geradezu partikularistisch. Er spricht von Gerechtigkeitsgefühl; ist es gerecht, Anderen das Gerechtigkeitsgefühl abzusprechen?

Prinz-Frankfurt a. M.: Man sollte doch die Vorschläge der Süddeutschen nicht auslachen; die Süddeutschen haben dieselben Eigenschaften wie die Norddeutschen, mit Ausnahme einiger Berliner. (Oho!) Auch von Darmstadt und Nürnberg kann man in einer Tagereise nach Berlin kommen. Der Vorstand von vor 1878 war über ganz Deutschland verzweigt.

Pittak-Kiel-Rendsburg tritt für den Kommissionsvorschlag ein.

Behrend-Frankfurt a. O. erklärt, im Interesse der Süddeutschen zurücktreten zu wollen.

Frohme kann sich auch mit der Liste nicht ganz befreunden. Der Vorwurf des Partikularismus sei zurückzuweisen; bei dem großen Interesse, welches die Genossen allerorten in Deutschland der Geschäftsleitung entgegenbringen, sei der Hinweis der Süddeutschen auf die Nothwendigkeit, im Vorstand vertreten zu sein, selbstverständlich. Es würde einen höchst üblen Eindruck in Süddeutschland machen, wenn den Wünschen der dortigen Genossen nicht würde nachgegeben werden.

Sittig-Hannover: Meinen Mandatgebern würde es nicht angenehm sein, wenn der gesammte Vorstand aus Personen besteht, deren Wohnorte rings um Berlin liegen. Ich würde noch Meister-Hannover vorschlagen, der als Abgeordneter ohne Unkosten für die Parteikasse dabei sein könnte.

Meister-Hannover: Es ist mir recht peinlich, jetzt das Wort zu erhalten. Ich erkläre vorweg meinen Verzicht auf eine solche Wahl, bin aber ebenfalls mit dem Kommissionsvorschlag nicht einverstanden. Nicht etwa aus Animosität gegen Berlin, sondern weil mir der Gesichtskreis der Kommission sehr enge gewesen zu sein scheint. Für die Kommission hat nur Berlin und Umgegend existirt, das übrige Deutschland nicht. Die Motivirung des Referenten war wohl auch nicht ernst gemeint; die Kontrolleure sollen doch den Vorstand kontrolliren, nicht selbst die Geschäfte des Vorstandes ausführen; die Schlagfertigkeit, die dort im Interesse schleunigen Zusammentretens gewünscht wird, ist also gar nicht so sehr erforderlich. Die Kontrolleure sollten gerade im Interesse ihres Amtes etwas weiter vertheilt sein. Ich vermisse in der Liste auch ganz Rheinland und Westfalen.

Lüttgens-Hamburg: Die Kommission ist von der Erwägung ausgegangen, daß eine Eisenbahnfahrt von höchstens vier bis fünf Stunden ausreichen müsse, um an den Sitz der Parteileitung zu gelangen. In diesem Sinne ist der Kommissionsvorschlag durchaus der richtige. Wir dachten damit besonders praktisch zu verfahren. Hintergedanken haben wir absolut nicht gehabt. Zwei Genossen aus Berlin hielten wir der Schnelligkeit der Kontrolle halber für mindestens nöthig im Vorstande.

Theiß-Hamburg: Es müssen wenigstens zwei Beisitzer in Berlin sein, um Gegenstände von geringerer Bedeutung sofort erledigen zu können. Welche Personen das sein sollen, darüber werden wir bis morgen Nachmittag nicht einig werden. Die zwei Genossen sind vorgeschlagen, weil sie in persönlichen Angelegenheiten in Berlin die unparteiischste Anschauung haben. (Sehr richtig!) Die Wahl süddeutscher Genossen haben die Süddeutschen selbst als partikularistisch zurückgewiesen.

Kokosky-Braunschweig: Die beiden wichtigsten Aemter ruhen doch in süddeutschen Händen. Die beiden Schriftführer Auer und Fischer sind Bayern.

Vollmar-München: Ich bin so zu sagen auch ein Süddeutscher und habe als solcher in der Kommission den Gedanken bekämpft, einen Theil der Kontrolleure nach Süddeutschland zu setzen. Es ist viel praktischer, wenn die Leute nahe zusammen wohnen, welche diese Sachen machen. (Beifall.)

Lutz-Baden: Man will eine Mainlinie gewissermaßen zwischen

uns wieder aufrichten. (Oho!) Ich bitte also, auch Süddeutschland zu berücksichtigen.

Schmidt-Burgstädt schlägt vor, an Stelle von G. Schulz-Berlin Schulz-Magdeburg zu wählen.

Fritz Berndt-Berlin will statt G. Schulz Zubeil gewählt wissen, den die Berliner Delegirten mit 16 gegen 5 Stimmen zum Kontroleur vorzuschlagen beschlossen hätten.

Behrend-Frankfurt a. O. will an seine Stelle Pfannkuch-Cassel treten lassen.

Es wird beschlossen, daß Vorschlagslisten vertheilt werden, welche nach Wunsch geändert werden können und als Stimmzettel gelten sollen. Diese Stimmzettel sollen von drei Genossen nach einer halben Stunde gesammelt werden.

Von einer Seite wird Auskunft gewünscht über die Person der Genossen Gerisch und Fischer.

G. Schulz-Berlin fragt die Berliner Genossen, ob er sich während seiner 22jährigen Thätigkeit in der Partei etwas habe zu schulden kommen lassen, was seine Nichtwahl rechtfertige.

Hiernach wird zur Beschlußfassung über den Ort des nächsten Parteitages geschritten. Maßgebend ist § 7 des Statuts:

Alljährlich findet ein Parteitag statt, der von der Parteileitung einzuberufen ist.

Hat der vorhergehende Parteitag über den Ort, an welchem der nächste Parteitag stattfinden soll, keine Bestimmung getroffen, so muß die Parteileitung mit der Reichstags-Vertretung hierüber sich verständigen.

Auf Antrag Gottschalk-Hamburg wird es dem Parteivorstande überlassen, den Ort des nächsten Parteitages zu bestimmen.

Damit sind, bis auf die Feststellung der Wahlen, die Punkte 4 und 5 der Tagesordnung erledigt.

Es folgt der letzte Gegenstand der Tagesordnung:

Punkt 9:

Anträge aus der Mitte des Parteitages.

Das Bureau hat diese Anträge, in 4 Gruppen vertheilt, drucken lassen. Außerdem sind gestern einige 20 Anträge eingegangen, die nicht mehr gedruckt werden konnten, weil ihre Vertheilung erst kurz vor Schluß des Parteitages möglich ist. Sie sind übrigens, ihrem Inhalte nach, großentheils schon in den gedruckten Anträgen mit enthalten.

Der Vorsitzende schlägt vor, diese Anträge, sowie die Anträge in Gruppe III und IV (s. Anhang) dem Parteivorstande zur Erledigung resp. Berücksichtigung zu überweisen.

Der Parteitag beschließt demgemäß.

Es gelangen zunächst die Anträge der Gruppe III zur Verhandlung.

Der erste Antrag lautet:

Folgende Thatsachen setzen wir als bekannt voraus:

Die Arbeiter, Arbeiterinnen, jugendliche Arbeiter und Kinder, welche in der Landwirthschaft, Forstwirthschaft, Gärtnerei, beim Fuhrwesen, Binnenschifffahrt, Fischerei und zu persönlichen Dienstleistungen beschäftigt werden, stehen nicht unter der Reichsgewerbeordnung, sondern unter den Gesindeordnungen der Einzelstaaten.

Diese Gesindeordnungen sind ausnahmslos auf dem Grundsatz errichtet, daß Arbeiter Staatsbürger zweiter Klasse sind. So enthält die sächsische Gesindeordnung in ihren Motiven den Satz: „Dienstloses Gesinde bildet jedenfalls eine der besonderen polizeilichen Aufsicht bedürfende Menschenklasse." Diese polizeiliche Aufsicht schreibt besagte Gesindeordnung auch vor.

Die preußische Gesindeordnung vom Jahre 1810, die sächsische und die meisten anderen gestatten der Herrschaft und deren Stellvertretern, das Gesinde, also alle oben genannten Arbeiter, Arbeiterinnen u. s. w. körperlich zu züchtigen. Widerstand gegen derartige körperliche Züchtigung wird beim Arbeiterstand eventuell mit Gefängniß bestraft. Ebenso Ungehorsam gegen die Herrschaft u. s. w.

Wir beantragen daher:

Der Parteitag wolle beschließen:

Es ist Pflicht jedes Parteigenossen, insbesondere der Reichstagsfraktion, dahin zu wirken, daß obengenannter Theil des Arbeiterstandes der deutschen Gewerbeordnung unterstellt und die Gesindeordnungen der Einzelstaaten aufgehoben werden.

Otto Jochem. Robert Greiner-Aschersleben. Gottfr. Baitz-Kalbe a. S. August Trautmann-Quedlinburg a. H. Robert Dahlen-Halberstadt. Albert Bartels-Wernigerode. August Noack-Eilenburg. Ernst Titze-Minden. Christian Schrader-Osnabrück. Wilh. Fehl-Burgsteinfurt i. W. Alois Kretschmar-Lüneburg. C. Weichelt-Pirna. Herm. Herzog-Leutersdorf b. Zittau. Carl Neu-Reichenbach i. V. W. Hänsler-Mannheim. Th. Lutz-Baden-Baden. J. Zarbock-Bromberg. C. Bertram. Otto Böttcher. Emil Hähle. Carl Schultz-Königsberg. F. Geserick-Egeln. C. Beneke-Celle.

In derselben Richtung bewegt sich der zweite Antrag dieser Gruppe:

Der Pateitag fordert die Fraktion auf, in der nächsten Session des Reichstages einen Antrag einzubringen, der vom sozialreformatorischen Standpunkt aus die Arbeitsverhältnisse

a. der Land- und Forstarbeiter,

b. der heute unter die Bestimmungen der Gesindeordnung fallenden Personen,

regelt.

Halle a. S., den 14. Oktober 1890.

Auerbach-Berlin. Fr. Zubeil-Kalau-Luckau.
F. Trosiener-Grevesmühlen-Hagenow.

Greiner-Aschersleben als Mitantragsteller: Die ländlichen Arbeiter haben sich bei den Wahlen mit Recht darüber beschwert, daß wir nichts für die Beseitigung der drückenden Gesindeordnung gethan haben. In der Gesindeordnung steht, daß das Züchtigungsrecht nicht überschritten werden darf, und doch ist ein Brotherr freigesprochen worden vom Gericht, „weil er sich der Strafbarkeit seiner Handlung nicht bewußt" war. Die ländlichen Arbeiter und Arbeiterinnen müssen unter die Gewerbeordnung gestellt werden schon in Rücksicht auf Lohndifferenzen und auf die Kündigungsfrage.

Dahlen-Halberstadt: Bei den letzten Wahlen sind Knechte, die für uns gestimmt haben, sofort auf die Straße gesetzt worden. Das darf nicht so weiter gehen.

Riemann-Chemnitz beantragt, beide Anträge der sozialistischen Reichstags- resp. sächsischen Landtagsfraktion zu überweisen.

Geyer: Die Reichstagsfraktion kann keinen direkten Antrag auf Aufhebung der Gesindeordnung einbringen, weil diese Frage nicht vor den Reichstag gehört. Sie ist Sache der Landesgesetzgebung. Im sächsischen Landtage haben unsere Abgeordneten einen solchen Antrag gestellt, natürlich ohne Erfolg. Die Agitation darf deswegen nicht ruhen.

Trautmann-Quedlinburg: Der Protest gegen die Gesindeordnung wäre ein wirksames Agitationsmittel. Redner führt, unter lebhaften Entrüstungsrufen der Versammlung, einige drastische Fälle an, wo das Züchtigungsrecht überschritten worden, und trotzdem eine Freisprechung erfolgt ist.

Der Antrag Riemann wird angenommen.

Es werden nunmehr die Anträge Gruppe I zur Debatte gestellt.

Antrag 1 lautet:

In Erwägung, daß unter den Genossen vielfach die Ansicht vorherrscht, es seien manche der früheren Genossen im „Sozialdemokrat" ganz ungerechtfertigterweise in den Verdacht gebracht worden, der Polizei Dienste zu leisten, beschließt der Parteitag, eine aus 7 Genossen (Delegirten) bestehende Kommission zu wählen, welcher die Parteileitung das gegen die betreffende Person vorliegende Material zur Prüfung zu übergeben und die dann nach erfolgter Kenntnißnahme dem Parteitag kurz Bericht zu erstatten hätte.

Gustav Keßler. Werner. Wernicke. Jacobey. Berndt. Auerbach-Berlin. Zubeil. Trosiener. Schwarz. Jochem. J. Zwiener. Slomke. E. Jhrer. Wilh. Liefländer. Adolph Schultze. Friedr. Katurbe. Ed. Gutmann. H. Altermann. Fr. Schwabe. E. Ernst. W. Gießhoit. J. Wernau. H. Heine. Fr. Blohm. Fr. Gundelach. Louis Fichtmann. Heinrich. R. Bräuer.

Riemann beantragt, diesen Antrag der Neuner-Kommission zu überweisen.

Zubeil will den Antrag einfach der Parteileitung überwiesen wissen. Die übrigen Antragsteller würden hoffentlich damit einverstanden sein.

Singer: Parteigenossen! Ich bitte für die Behandlung dieses Antrages um Ihre ernste Aufmerksamkeit. Das Bureau hat mich beauftragt, über diesen Antrag, in Verbindung mit einigen, dem Parteitag zugegangenen Beschwerden, zu referiren. Das gesammte Bureau hat einstimmig beschlossen, dem Parteitag zu empfehlen, und ich beantrage es hiermit, den Antrag Keßler und Genossen abzulehnen. Es liegt dem Parteitage eine Zuschrift von Oskar Krohm, Medailleur in Berlin, vor, in der er den Parteitag anruft, seine durch eine Beschuldigung im „Sozialdemokrat" verloren gegangene politische Ehre wiederherzustellen. Herr Krohm ist im „Sozialdemokrat" als im Dienste der Polizei stehend angezeigt worden, und er hat das bestritten. Er hat den Redakteur der „Volkstribüne", den Genossen Schippel, welcher diese Mittheilung in sein Blatt aus dem „Sozialdemokrat" übernommen hatte, verklagt. Schippel ist verurtheilt worden, weil es ihm nicht möglich war, den Beweis der Wahrheit zu führen; das Berliner Polizeipräsidium hat die Erlaubniß zur Vernehmung derjenigen Beamten, auf deren Zeugniß Schippel sich berufen hatte, verweigert. Herr Krohm verlangt nun vom Parteitag unter der Mittheilung, daß die Beschuldigung eine falsche sei, Remedur und wünscht, daß die Sache untersucht werde. Aehnlich liegt der Fall mit dem Herrn Conrad von Breslau. Auch er wendet sich an den Parteitag als oberste Instanz, mit der Bitte, die Mittheilung, welche der „Sozialdemokrat" über ihn gebracht, deren Wahrheit er bestreitet, zu annulliren, resp. die Sache zu untersuchen. Dann liegt hier, veranlaßt durch den Antrag Keßler, der durch die Presse gegangen ist, ein Schreiben des Buchdruckereibesitzers Römer aus Berlin vor, der in längerer Auseinandersetzung die auf ihn bezüglichen Mittheilungen des

„Sozialdemokrat" bestreitet. Und zum Schluß ist ein Schreiben eingelaufen, gerichtet an unseren Genossen Liebknecht, von Herrn Maximilian Schlesinger in Breslau, der den Partei- tag ersucht, falls der Antrag Keßler wegen Einsetzung einer Untersuchungskommission betreffend unbegründeter Verdächtigungen u. s. w. angenommen würde, auch seine Sache zu verhandeln. Nach meiner Auffassung — ich spreche in diesem Falle nur persönlich, weil dem Bureau diese Sache nicht vorgelegen, — hat der Parteitag mit Herrn Maximilian Schlesinger überhaupt nichts zu thun (hört, hört!) weil derselbe kein Parteigenosse ist. Was sodann den Antrag Keßler betrifft, so wird in der Partei gewiß nicht ein Mitglied existiren, welches es nicht auf das Allerlebhafteste bedauern würde, wenn mit der Bezeichnung „Polizeispitzel" irgend Jemand Un- recht geschehen wäre. Das muß ausgesprochen werden gegenüber den Verdächtigungen, die gegen einzelne unserer Parteigenossen ver- breitet sind, als ob es sich für sie darum gehandelt habe, aus Gründen privater Rache, aus Gründen persönlicher Natur zu einem Mittel zu greifen, welches allerdings die Ehre eines Mannes schwer schädigen und vernichten muß. Ich weise Namens der ganzen Partei, insbesondere aber auch Namens der bisherigen Parteileitung und Namens der Fraktion diese Verdächtigung auf das Entschiedenste zurück. Niemand in der Partei kann und darf solchen Vergehens beschuldigt werden. Denn wäre es wahr und könnte es bewiesen werden, daß Jemand aus Gründen persönlicher Natur mit der Ehre eines Parteigenossen so verfahren ist und denselben bewußt fälschlich als „Polizeiagent" bezeichnet hat, so würde in der ganzen Partei Nie- mand sein, der nicht ein solches Verfahren als ehrlos und ver- werflich erklären würde. Der Antrag Keßler und Genossen weist aber dem Parteitage eine Aufgabe zu, die zu erfüllen er nicht im Stande ist. (Sehr richtig!) Der Antrag verlangt vom Parteitage, er solle Mittel und Wege finden, Aufklärung zu schaffen über Dinge, die aufzuklären er nicht die Macht in Händen hat. Dieser Antrag muthet dem Parteitage zu, zu erforschen, wer die „eiserne Maske" ist. Ich frage, ob hier in der Versammlung ein Mensch in der Lage ist, darüber Auskunft zu geben? Und nun, was soll mit diesem Antrag geschehen? Keßler und Genossen verlangen: die Parteileitung solle das gegen die betreffenden Personen vorliegende Material einer Kommission zur Prüfung übergeben. Ja dazu müßte die Parteileitung doch erst „Material" haben. Haben die Antrag- steller den geringsten Grund zu der Annahme, die Parteileitung sei im Besitze solchen „Materials?" Sollen wir, die bisherige Parteileitung oder der frühere Vorstand, durch diesen Antrag veranlaßt werden, eine Anfrage an unsere Freunde in Zürich und London zu richten, von denen die betreffenden Mittheilungen gekommen sind? Und wie dann, wenn dieselben sagen — was sie als Ehrenmänner müssen —

17

bei aller Freundschaft zu Euch, wir sind nicht in der Lage, Euch Material zur Prüfung zu liefern, wir sind nicht gewillt, diejenigen, von denen wir die Mittheilungen haben, zu nennen. Dann steht die Parteileitung vor der Unmöglichkeit, den Beschluß des Parteitages auszuführen. Aber nicht nur dieser formelle Grund veranlaßt mich, Sie zu bitten, den Antrag abzulehnen. Wohl kann ich mit den Antragstellern auf das lebhafteste bedauern, wenn wirklich ungerechtfertigte Beschuldigungen in dieser Beziehung erhoben worden sein sollten, jedoch weit über dem Interesse des Einzelnen, steht das Interesse der Partei, und diese hat weder die Möglichkeit, noch Ursache sich in diese Angelegenheit hineinzumischen. Die Partei hat allen Grund, dem unter dem Namen „eiserne Maske" existirenden Unbekannten dankbar zu sein dafür, daß es möglich gewesen ist, die Enthüllungen über Schröder-Haupt, Ehrenberg u. s. w. zu machen. Wir müssen uns doch sagen, daß, nachdem die Wahrheit dieser schwerwiegenden Behauptungen auf das glänzendste nachgewiesen ist, gewiß kein Grund vorliegt, Mißtrauen gegen weitere Mittheilungen aus derselben Quelle zu hegen. Immer zugegeben, daß für den Fall wirklich Jemand Unrecht geschehen ist, dies sehr bedauerlich wäre, glaube ich doch, daß die sozialdemokratische Partei keine Ursache hat, Fragen zu stellen, an deren Beantwortung ein Interesse einzig und allein die Polizei hat. (Sehr richtig!) Vergegenwärtigen Sie sich einen Augenblick die Situation; Machtmittel, Aufklärung zu erzwingen, haben wir nicht; die wichtigsten und weittragendsten von den Mittheilungen, welche durch den „Sozialdemokrat" gekommen, sind auf ihre Richtigkeit geprüft und für zutreffend befunden worden; daß unter dem Sozialistengesetz das Spitzelthum gezüchtet worden, ist weltbekannt. In Berücksichtigung aller dieser Umstände werden Sie mit mir zu der Ueberzeugung kommen, daß es das Interesse der Partei gebieterisch verlangt, den Antrag abzulehnen, und unter der zwingenden Wucht der Verhältnisse über die „eiserne Maske" nicht weiter verhandeln. — Ich habe mich bemüht, diese Angelegenheit durchaus in den Grenzen sachlicher Diskussion zu halten, und ich bin überzeugt, daß der Parteitag die Frage mit dem Ernste, welchen sie gewiß verdient, diskutiren, sich aber auch bewußt bleiben wird, daß hierbei ein höheres Interesse, das der Gesammt-Partei, zur Geltung gebracht werden muß. Namens des Bureaus, welches diesen Beschluß einstimmig gefaßt hat, beantrage ich, der Parteitag wolle den Antrag Keßler und Genossen ablehnen und durch die Ablehnung dieses Antrages die eingegangenen Beschwerden von Krohm, Konrad und Röwer für erledigt erachten, sowie erklären, daß er mit Schlesinger in Breslau überhaupt nichts zu thun hat. (Lebhafte, allseitige Zustimmung.)

Heisig-Breslau: Ich erkläre auf Ehrenwort, daß Conrad

im Geheimbundsprozeß einen Genossen bloßgestellt hat. Er hat —

Vorsitzender Dietz: Ich kann Angriffe auf Conrad und andere in die Sache Verwickelte nicht gestatten. Es ist keiner von den Betreffenden da, sich zu vertheidigen.

Wernau-Berlin erklärt, daß sein Name ohne sein Zuthun unter den Antrag Keßler gekommen ist. Er empfiehlt ev. Uebergang zur Tagesordnung.

Keßler (zur Geschäftsordnung): Der Antrag ist mir zur Unterschrift vorgelegt worden und ich habe ihn unterstützt, weil ich es für zulässig hielt, daß man über diesen Antrag spreche. Ich bin der Antragsteller nicht.

Der Antrag Singer wird mit allen gegen zwei Stimmen angenommen. Damit sind die übrigen Anträge beseitigt.

Antrag 2 lautet:

„Der Parteitag wolle beschließen: Die verbündeten Regierungen aufzufordern, um die durch das verurtheilte Ausnahmegesetz angerichteten Schäden einigermaßen gut zu machen, das auf Grund der willkürlichen Bestimmungen dieses Gesetzes weggenommene Eigenthum von Körperschaften und Personen wieder herauszugeben.

Vollmar. Schmid. Göschl. Götzenberger. Birk.

Wird ohne Debatte angenommen.

Es folgt die Resolution unter 3:

„In Erwägung, daß durch die Aufhebung des Ausnahmegesetzes gegen die sogenannten gemeingefährlichen Bestrebungen der Sozialdemokratie vom 21. Oktober 78 eine Reihe von staatsbürgerlichen Rechte ausgeübt werden kann, ohne von Strafe bedroht zu sein;

in fernerer Erwägung, daß auf Grund desselben Gesetzes eine große Zahl von Bestrafungen von Rechtswegen erfolgt sind, welche von den Betroffenen zur Zeit verbüßt werden; daß weiter die Bestimmungen des zitirten Gesetzes die grundlegende Tendenz vieler Bestrafungen auf Grund der §§ 128 und 129 des R.-St.-Gesetzbuches bilden, deren Verbüßung zum Theil zur Zeit noch nicht erfolgt, erklärt der Kongreß der deutschen Sozialdemokratie zu Halle, indem er den Opfern des Sozialisten-Gesetzes seine Sympathie und seinen Dank für ihr mannhaftes Eintreten für ihre Ueberzeugung und die Emanzipation der Proletarier aus politischer und ökonomischer Knechtschaft ausspricht — daß es mit den Aufgaben eines Rechtsstaates nicht vereinbar und daher Pflicht desselben ist, die Aufhebung bezüglicher Strafvollstreckungen auszusprechen, und beauftragt der

17*

Kongreß das Bureau, diese Resolution der Staatsregierung zu übermitteln.

M. Lücke-Köln.   Ernst Moritz-Köln.   Franz Werner-Köln. Jos. Kenfenheuer-Mühlheim a. R.   H. Hager-Mühlheim a. R Heinr. Altermann-Nossen.   Otto Klein-Berlin Ernst Wilschke-Berlin.   Janiszewski-Berlin R. Salomon-Oberbarnim.   H. Schibolsky. Adolf Hofmeister-Köln Landkr.   Hugo Woldersky-Köln Landkr. Lorenz Kurth.   Carl Riemann 9. sächs. Kreis. Carl Porges 21. sächs. Kreis.   Adolph Albrecht-Halle a. S. Otto Schmidt-Querfurt.   Ad. Hoffmann-Merseburg. H. Hirt-Niederbarnim.   A. Plaffe-Niederbarnim. Ernst Hahn-Gera.   H. Müller.

Lücke-Köln: Unsere Resolution verlangt nicht gerade Amnestie von der Staatsregierung, sondern sie verurtheilt die Bestrafungen und die fernere Inhafthaltung der Genossen, welche unter dem Sozialistengesetz verurtheilt wurden.

Bebel: Ich bitte diesem Antrage nicht zuzustimmen. Bei aller Vorsicht der Fassung, um den Schein zu vermeiden, als wenn wir unsererseits für unsere Genossen eine Amnestie beantragen wollten, kann die Sache doch auf keinem anderen Wege, als auf dem der Amnestie erledigt werden. Die Erledigung dieses Antrages ist auf gesetzlichem Wege überhaupt nicht möglich. Wir sollen z. B. hier in Bezug auf die §§ 128 und 129 einen Vorschlag an-nehmen, der schon deshalb unannehmbar ist, weil beide Paragraphen dem gemeinen Recht angehören, das durch den Fall des Sozialisten-gesetzes garnicht berührt wird. Die Geheimbundsprozesse sind mit dem Fall des Sozialistengesetzes nicht unmöglich geworden. Polizei und Staatsanwälte können jeden Augenblick neue Geheimbunds-prozesse insceniren, sobald ihnen „Thaten" bekannt würden, die unter dem Sozialistengesetz als Geheimbündelei sich qualifiziren ließen. Er warne nachdrücklich sich irgend welcher Täuschung hin-zugeben und zu glauben, mit den Geheimbundsprozessen sei es vorbei. Vergehen gegen die §§ 128 und 129 verjähren erst nach 5 Jahren nach begangener That, wenn nicht mittlerweile diese Frist durch eine gerichtliche Untersuchungshandlung unterbrochen worden ist. Die Staatsanwaltschaft kann also auf Grund von Thatsachen, welche sich als Geheimbündler qualifiziren, innerhalb dieser Frist jeden Augenblick einen Geheimbundsprozeß anstrengen (hört! hört!). Außerdem wäre es eine Inkonsequenz, nur die Vergehen auf Grund der §§ 128 und 129 herauszugreifen, dagegen die Verurtheilungen wegen Majestätsbeleidigung, Hochverrath, Widerstand gegen die Staatsgewalt, Aufruhr rc. zu übergehen. Ferner: Sie schlagen vor, sich an die Staatsregierung zu wenden, an welche? Wir haben in Deutschland 23 Staatsregierungen. Stände die Reichsregierung, dann könnte die preußische Regierung als Reichsbehörde in Frage kommen; aber nach der bestehenden Gesetzgebung kann eine gerichtlich erfolgte Verurtheilung nur auf dem Wege der Amnestie aufgehoben werden, und die Amnestie kann nur im Einzelstaat erlassen werden. Eine Amnestie wollen wir aber nicht, und auch Diejenigen nicht, die heute im Gefängniß sitzen. Haben Hunderte und Tausende unter dem Sozialistengesetz ihre Strafen bis zum Ende abgebüßt, so mögen es auch Diejenigen thun, die heute noch im Kerker sitzen. (Bravo!)

Die Resolution wird abgelehnt.

Antrag 4 lautet:

Unterzeichnete stellen den Antrag, die Fraktion möge im Reichstag den Antrag stellen auf Aufhebung aller französischen Gesetze in Elsaß-Lothringen.

B. Böhle-Straßburg i. Elf. Jacob Haug-Mülhausen i. Elf.

Böhle weist auf die Nothwendigkeit hin, die Rechtsungleichheit in Elsaß-Lothringen zu beseitigen.

Bebel: So sehr ich die Tendenz des Antrages als berechtigt anerkenne, so muß ich mich doch gegen denselben erklären, weil die Antragsteller so zu sagen das Kind mit dem Bade ausschütten. Es wird verlangt die Aufhebung aller französischen Gesetze. Bekanntlich ist aber die Civilgesetzgebung in Elsaß-Lothringen, die auf die Gesetze der großen Revolution aufgebaut ist, der deutschen weit vorzuziehen. Hätten die Antragsteller ganz bestimmte Gesetze bezeichnet, dann ließe sich über den Antrag reden. So müssen selbstverständlich der Diktaturparagraph für Elsaß-Lothringen und die Preßgesetze und die Gesetze über das Vereins- und Versammlungswesen aufgehoben werden.

Der Antrag wird abgelehnt.

Antrag 5 lautet:

Der Parteitag wolle beschließen, die Fraktion zu beauftragen, ein Vereins- und Versammlungsgesetz auszuarbeiten und im Reichstage einzubringen, welches unter vollständiger Wahrung der Vereins- und Versammlungsfreiheit dem unhaltbaren Zustande der betreffenden Landesgesetze ein Ende macht. G. Fell-Leipzig.

Der Antragsteller betont die Nothwendigkeit eines Vereins- und Versammlungsgesetzes, nach welchem alle Einschränkungen, außer der Anmeldung der Vereine und Versammlungen, wegfallen. So habe z. B. in den Versammlungen kein überwachender Polizeibeamter zu erscheinen u. s. w. In Sachsen sei schon die Agitation zu Gunsten eines besseren Gesetzes im Gange.

Vorsitzender Dietz: Ich habe Ihnen mitzutheilen, daß unser verstorbener Kollege, der Delegirte Baumgarten aus Hamburg, jetzt in den Sarg gebettet ist und von hier nach dem Bahnhof geleitet werden soll. Das Bureau drückt den Wunsch aus, daß die Mitglieder des Parteitages dem Verstorbenen das Geleit bis zum Bahnhof geben. Ferner stellt das Bureau den Antrag, daß die

Parteikasse die Kosten der Beerdigung zu übernehmen hat. Dagegen erfolgt kein Widerspruch. Ich schließe die Sitzung.

Schluß 5¼ Uhr.

Sechster Verhandlungstag.

Sonnabend, den 18. Oktober 1890.

Schlußsitzung.

Vorsitzender Singer eröffnet die Sitzung um 9¼ Uhr.

Vor Eintritt in die Tagesordnung erhält das Wort

Stengele-Hamburg: Parteigenossen! Im Namen der Delegirten aus dem ehemaligen Hamburger Belagerungsgebiet spreche ich Ihnen unseren wärmsten Dank aus für die erhebende Art und Weise, wie Sie unserem theuren, unvergeßlichen Todten die letzte Ehre erwiesen haben. Ich danke insbesondere den Genossen von Halle dafür, daß sie uns bei dem Trauerfall mit Rath und That zur Seite gestanden haben. Wenn etwas den Schmerz der Familie lindern kann, so ist es das Bewußtsein, daß dem Heimgegangenen noch im Tode der Dank abgestattet wurde für sein treues, unverdrossenes Wirken. Wir wollen den Todten dadurch ehren, daß wir, seine Kampfesgenossen, fortarbeiten, wie er es bis zum letzten Athemzuge gethan hat, und daß wir die Fahne der Sozialdemokratie hoch halten! (Lebhafte Zustimmung.)

Vorsitzender Singer: Es sind folgende Zuschriften eingegangen:

Eine Anzahl Berliner Genossen erhebt Protest gegen das Auftreten des Genossen Berndt auf dem Parteitag.

Berliner Genossen protestiren dagegen, daß Werner sich hier als Vertreter der Berliner Genossen bezeichnen konnte. Herr Dolinski von Berlin bittet den Parteitag, eine Beschwerde, die er gegen das „Volksblatt" hat, zu untersuchen, und beantragt die Einsetzung eines Schiedsgerichts.

Ein Schreiben aus Hamburg, in welchem Beschwerde gegen die Redaktion des „Echo" erhoben wird, kommt zu demselben Resultat.

Ich beantrage Namens des Bureaus, diese Schriftstücke dem Parteivorstande zur Erledigung zu überweisen. Der Parteitag ist damit einverstanden.

In einer Zuschrift aus Berlin wird energisch Protest erhoben gegen die Bezeichnung, welche Ehrhart in Bezug auf die Berliner Genossen gebraucht; der damalige Vorsitzende hat den Ausdruck gerügt und Ehrhart hat ihn zurückgenommen. Damit ist die Sache erledigt.

Ein Herr Eduard Isfert-Berlin wünscht dagegen Schutz, daß er, wie es nach seiner Ansicht mehrere Genossen thun, als Agent der Polizei betrachtet werde. Dieser Brief an den Parteitag ist nach den gestrigen Beschlüssen als erledigt zu betrachten. Damit ist der Parteitag einverstanden.

Seitens der sämmtlichen **Berliner Delegirten** auf unserem Parteitag ist folgende **Erklärung** eingegangen mit der Bitte, sie zu verlesen und dem Protokoll einzuverleiben:

In Erwägung, daß durch die auswärtige und hiesige gegnerische Presse die Behauptung ging, daß die Berliner Parteigenossen im prinzipiellen Gegensatz zur Partei und Parteileitung stehen und einer Spaltung der Partei zustreben, erklären die Vertreter von Berlin, Teltow-Beeskow-Storkow und Nieder-Barnim:

Es liegt uns nichts ferner, noch haben wir jemals auch nur im entferntesten die Absicht gehabt, derartiges zu unternehmen. Wir werden alle dahingehenden Versuche mit Entschiedenheit zurückweisen. Wir stehen nach wie vor auf dem Boden unserer Parteigrundsätze.

Alle diese Verdächtigungen beruhen vielmehr nur auf falschen, die Partei schädigenden Unterstellungen, benutzt von der gegnerischen Presse, um ihre schon oft bemerkten, unehrlichen Absichten gegenüber unserer Partei zu bethätigen.

Wir wahren uns aber auch das Recht der freien Kritik, und wünschen im Interesse unserer Partei, daß alle persönliche Gereiztheit in der Presse und in Versammlungen wie bei jedem Einzelnen verschwinden möge.

Wir werden mit allen Kräften weiterarbeiten an der Einheit, Entwickelung und dem Aufbau der Partei. (Bravo!)

Berlin I.: Täterow, Th. Metzner. Berlin II.: Otto Klein, Janiszewski, Wilschke. Berlin III.: Fritz, Gründel, Barth. Berlin IV.: Robert Schmidt, Johann Petersen, Franz Berndt, Adolph Scholz. Berlin V.: Berndt, Auerbach, Jacobick. Berlin VI.: Jul. Wernau, W. Gieshoit, Franz Schwabe, E. Ernst. Niederbarnim: A. Plasse, H. Hirsch, H. Schibolsky. Teltow-Beeskow-Storkow-Charlottenburg: H. Wernicke-Charlottenburg, W. Schütze, Werner.

Die gestern vorgenommene **Wahl der Parteileitung** hat folgendes Resultat gehabt: Es wurden 368 Stimmen abgegeben, die sämmtlich als giltig zu erachten sind. Es wurden gewählt zu Vorsitzenden: Singer mit 368, Gerisch mit 357 Stimmen; zu Schriftführern: Auer mit 368 Stimmen, Fischer mit 364 Stimmen; zum Kassirer: Bebel mit 367 Stimmen; zu Kontrolleuren: Dubber-Hamburg mit 359, Herbert-Stettin mit 339, Ewald-Brandenburg mit 336, Kaden-Dresden mit 326, Jacobey-Berlin mit 294, G. Schulz-Berlin mit 168, Behrend-Frankfurt a. O. mit 159 Stimmen. Auf Pfannkuch-Kassel fielen 121, auf Zubeil-Berlin 126, auf Grillenberger 52, auf Müller-Darmstadt 44, auf Geck-Offenburg 38 Stimmen. Die übrigen Stimmen waren zersplittert.

Demnach ist die **Parteileitung gewählt** und die Partei dadurch definitiv konstituirt. (Bravo!)

Ich glaube Namens aller Gewählten mit dem Dank für die Wahl die Versicherung verbinden zu können, daß wir uns der Wahl würdig zeigen werden, durch treue, aufrichtige Pflichterfüllung. (Bravo!)

Grillenberger: Die an Einstimmigkeit grenzende Wahl des eigentlichen Parteivorstandes beweist in glänzender Weise die Disziplin und Einigkeit der Partei. Daß eine andere Zusammensetzung des Parteivorstandes stattfinden mußte, als es bisher unter dem Ausnahmegesetz der Fall war, ist selbstverständlich. Es konnte beispielsweise unser Freund Meister nicht mehr in den Parteivorstand gewählt werden, und es war selbstverständlich, daß auch die Uebrigen darauf verzichten mußten, da eben die Gewählten ihren Sitz in Berlin haben müssen. Es ist aber von einigen Parteigenossen darauf hingewiesen worden, daß man es nicht für richtig halte, ein Mitglied des früheren Parteivorstandes, das seinen Sitz in Berlin hat, nicht in den Parteivorstand mit hineinzuwählen, nämlich unseren altbewährten Genossen und Freund Liebknecht. Darauf ist zu erwidern: Es ist von jeher Gebrauch gewesen, daß der Redakteur des offiziellen Parteiorgans nicht zu gleicher Zeit Mitglied des Parteivorstandes sein kann; dies war unter der alten Organisation sogar statutarisch verboten. Von diesem Grundsatz ausgehend, ist davon abgesehen worden, Liebknecht mit in Vorschlag zu bringen. Es ist aber doch ein kleiner Lapsus insofern untergelaufen, als man es unterlassen hat, die Wahl des Chefredakteurs des offiziellen Parteiorgans dem Parteitage zu übertragen. Liebknecht gehört zwar seit dem 1. Oktober der Redaktion des nunmehr zum leitenden Parteiorgan in Deutschland ernannten Blattes an, aber ich meine, es ist Pflicht des Parteitages, diese Wahl zum Chefredakteur des offiziellen Organs auch offiziell zu sanktioniren. Es gehört sich, daß dieser Chefredakteur dem Parteivorstande in allen Dingen koordinirt ist. Der Parteivorstand hat eine gewisse Aufsicht über das Blatt zu üben, aber der Chefredakteur des Centralblattes muß in allen Dingen Aufschluß haben über das, was in der Partei vorgeht. Er muß in ununterbrochenem Kontakt mit dem Parteivorstande sein, und deshalb ist es selbstverständlich, daß dieser Redakteur ebenso als Parteibeamter betrachtet wird, wie die Mitglieder des Vorstandes, daß er an allen Sitzungen derselben theilzunehmen und berathende Stimme hat. Er kann nicht als Bediensteter des Parteivorstandes betrachtet werden. Auch aus einem Akt des Vertrauens und der Dankbarkeit für unseren altbewährten Parteigenossen Liebknecht, der seit mehr als 40 Jahren für unsere Prinzipien kämpft und auch auf diesem Parteitage bewiesen hat, wie nahezu unersetzlich er für uns ist, beantrage ich, der Parteitag wolle beschließen: Liebknecht wird als Chefredakteur des offiziellen Parteiorgans bestätigt und ist als solcher gleichberechtigt mit dem Parteivorstande. (Bravo!)

Dieser Antrag wird einstimmig angenommen.

Vorsitzender Singer: Der Parteitag hat mit diesem Beschluß eine offizielle Stellung mehr geschaffen, und ich kann der Partei zu diesem Beschluß nur Glück wünschen.

Es ist abermals eine Reihe von Begrüßungstelegrammen eingegangen.

Von Frau Ihrer-Berlin liegt folgendes Schreiben vor:

Um Mißverständnissen vorzubeugen, erkläre ich, daß ich die Antragstellerin des sogenannten Antrages Keßler (Eiserne Maske betreffend) bin, und zwar in Rücksicht darauf, daß mir der Fall Rohmann nicht aufgeklärt erscheint.

Ferner wird folgende „Erklärung" zur Kenntniß des Parteitages gebracht:

Als Delegirte des Wahlkreises Lennep-Remscheid-Mettmann geben Unterzeichnete die Erklärung ab, daß die vom Delegirten Lenz gethane Aeußerung bezüglich der Berliner und Hamburger Streiks von unseren Mandatgebern nicht getheilt wird.

Carl Meist. Max König.

Hierauf wird in der Tagesordnung fortgefahren und die gestern abgebrochene Diskussion über Antrag 5 sub I fortgesetzt.

Aßmann-Braunschweig und Kerrl-Bremen weisen auf die Verschiedenartigkeit der Vereinsgesetzgebung in den einzelnen Staaten und auf die agitatorische Wirkung hin, welche eine Behandlung dieser Materie haben würde, die reichsgesetzlich geregelt werden müsse.

Blos: Wir schneiden hier eine sehr gefährliche Materie an. Ich glaube, daß die von anderer Seite gewünschte reichsgesetzliche Regelung sich bald in Wirklichkeit übersetzen wird. Unsere Fraktion wird dann gerade genug zu thun haben, um die Angriffe auf die Vereins- und Versammlungsfreiheit abzuwehren. (Sehr richtig!) Wir wollen dann froh sein, wenn wir mit einem blauen Auge davonkommen. Es ist nicht blos von konservativer, sondern auch von freisinniger Seite bereits die Ansicht ausgesprochen worden, daß man bei einer Neuregelung dieser Gesetzgebung einfach die Grundsätze des preußischen Vereinrechts auf das ganze Reich zu übertragen gedenke. Sogar Munckel hat dieser Anschauung zugestimmt. Wir werden dagegen auf's schärfste opponiren. Wenn wir aber diese Frage selbst anregen, so könnte uns von der öffentlichen Meinung die Verantwortung für die neue Beschneidung des Koalitionsrechtes aufgebürdet werden, und davor sollten wir uns in Acht nehmen. (Sehr wahr!)

Die Diskussion wird geschlossen und der Antrag abgelehnt.

Es wird beantragt, die übrigen noch unerledigten Anträge der Parteileitung zur Erledigung resp. Berücksichtigung zu überweisen. (Zustimmung.)

Der Vorsitzende bittet, in der Diskussion der Anträge so lange fortzufahren, bis die Neunerkommission, welche ihre Berathungen noch nicht beendet hat, fertig ist.

Der Antrag wird zurückgezogen.

Inzwischen ist folgender Antrag eingegangen:

Der Parteitag wolle beschließen, der Einladung des Generalraths der belgischen Arbeiterpartei, den nächstjährigen internationalen Arbeiterkongreß in Brüssel abzuhalten, Folge zu leisten.

Bebel.

Zur Diskussion steht weiter Antrag 6:

Der Parteitag wolle beschließen, die Fraktion der sozialdemokratischen Arbeiterpartei im Reichstage zu ersuchen, nach Kräften dahin zu wirken, daß die Mißstände beim Auswanderungswesen möglichst beseitigt werden; so insbesondere die Regierungen zu ersuchen, den Transport der Auswanderer, wie auch die Unterbringung derselben in den Hafenstädten so scharf wie möglich zu überwachen und zu kontrolliren, da die bisherigen Einrichtungen, sowohl was Transport wie Unterbringung der Reisenden anbelangt, den einfachsten Forderungen der Hygieine Hohn spricht.

Watermann-Bremerhaven. F. Kerrl-Bremen. L. Funke.

Kerrl-Bremen schildert die Mißstände in den Häfen und auf den Auswandererschiffen. Dietz habe bei der Dampfersubventionsvorlage das ganze Material im Reichstage vorgebracht, auch auf die große Zahl der Selbstmorde und darauf hingewiesen, daß, wenn diese Thatsache wahr, die Staatsanwaltschaft schon längst hätte dagegen einschreiten müssen. Der Vertreter des Norddeutschen Lloyd, Meier, habe damals nicht geantwortet, und seither sei garnichts geschehen. Die Fraktion müsse die Sache in die Hand nehmen.

Bebel: Mit der Annahme des Antrags stoßen wir offene Thüren ein. Wir haben bereits thatsächlich Reichskommissare, welche das Auswanderungswesen zu überwachen haben, insbesondere auch die Unterbringung der Auswanderer in den Seehäfen, Logirhäusern und auf den Schiffen kontrolliren, und alljährlich wird dem Reichstage darüber Bericht erstattet. Jedesmal ist auch ausführlich darüber gesprochen worden; das Centrum hat sich der Sache in sehr anerkennenswerther Weise angenommen. Ich werde aber dem Antrage dennoch zustimmen, in der Erwartung, daß die Genossen, welche solche Anträge stellen, den Vertretern im Reichstage das Material zusammenstellen, um für Bremen, Hamburg u. s. w. auch im Reichstage der Diskussion eine beglaubigte Unterlage zu liefern. Wenn die Genossen sich an Ort und Stelle unterrichten, den Zustand der Logirhäuser untersuchen und über ihre Erfahrungen an die Fraktion regelmäßig Bericht erstatten wollen, dann wird auch die Erörterung im Parlament fruchtbarer sein. Die Mittheilungen über die Behandlung der Kohlenzieher in den Schiffen haben ja seiner

Zeit das größte Aufsehen erregt. Ich wiederhole also meine Bitte an die Parteigenossen, in dieser Richtung eine besondere Thätigkeit zur Feststellung der Thatsachen zu entfalten.

Millarg-Friedeberg: Es kommen hier nicht blos die Seestädte, sondern auch Berlin in Betracht als Centralpunkt für die Auswanderer der östlichen Provinzen. Die Berliner Agenten in der Invalidenstraße lassen den Auswanderern eine geradezu unwürdige Behandlung angedeihen; durch das feine Vordergebäude die Leute in die elenden Schuppen der Hinterhäuser zu führen, geniren sie sich, deshalb haben sie von der Hinterseite, von der Charitee her, ein Loch als Zugang ausbrechen lassen, durch welches die Auswanderer ihren Eintritt in diese elende Herberge nehmen müssen. Und solcher Mißstände giebt es noch mehr, die diese Berliner Kommissionäre verschulden. Da muß irgendwie eingeschritten werden.

Die Diskussion wird geschlossen und der Antrag angenommen.

Es folgt die Berathung des Antrags 7:

In Anbetracht der elenden Lage, in der sich die große Mehrzahl der seefahrenden Bevölkerung Deutschlands befindet, beauftragt der Parteitag die sozialdemokratische Fraktion im Reichstage, die Forderung auf Revision der deutschen Seemannsordnung zu stellen.

J. Schwarz-Hamburg III und Genossen.

Schwarz-Lübeck: Ich darf mir wohl gestatten, zu diesem Antrag Stellung zu nehmen. Als Seemann lange Jahre auf Segel- und Dampfschiffen thätig gewesen, kann ich über die Lage der Seeleute erschöpfende Auskunft geben. Hier will ich nur in einigen Punkten die Revisionsbedürftigkeit der Seemannsordnung darthun. Am 1. April 1891 treten die Verordnungen in Kraft, welche darauf hinzielen, daß die Zahl der Unfälle im Seefahrtsbetriebe möglichst eingeschränkt wird. Nach dem Buchstaben ausgeführt, würden diese Verordnungen allerdings geeignet sein, die Unfälle möglichst zu verhüten und die Menschenleben mehr als bisher zu schützen. Aber bleibt man bei den heutigen Gewohnheiten, so fällt die gute Absicht dieser Erlasse einfach ins Wasser, wenn nicht der Seemann bei der Ausführung mitzuwirken befugt ist. Bis heute ist das nicht der Fall. Wenn auch ein Paragraph der Seemannsordnung besagt, daß ein Schiffsoffizier und zwei Mann der Besatzung beim Seeamt oder Konsulat die Untersuchung eines Fahrzeuges auf seine Seetüchtigkeit, die genügende Ausrüstung mit Lebensmitteln u. f. w. beantragen können, so steht dem ein anderer Paragraph gegenüber, wonach, falls die Untersuchung den guten Zustand des Schiffes und seiner Ausrüstung ergiebt, die Antragsteller mit schweren Strafen belegt werden können. Dadurch wird die Möglichkeit der Beschwerde so beengt, daß der Seemann sich schwerlich entschließen wird, einen solchen Antrag zu stellen. Und daß der Schiffsoffizier ihn stellen wird, ist noch weniger schwerlich anzunehmen, da er, wenn er es thäte, eigentlich nicht mehr in der Lage wäre, noch ferner als Schiffsoffizier zu fungiren. So haben wir es mit der geltenden Seemannsordnung noch zu keinem nennenswerthen Fortschritt in dieser Beziehung bringen können. Aber auch in anderen Richtungen ist eine Reform dringend nothwendig. Manche Schiffsführer sind notorische Trinker, dem Seemann aber ist es auf keine Weise möglich, sich gegen solche unzurechnungsfähigen Führer zu helfen; er muß den verworrensten Befehlen sich fügen, wenn er nicht schwere Strafe erleiden will. Es ist ferner in der Seemannsordnung eine einheitliche Speiserolle für das ganze Deutsche Reich herzustellen; es muß auch festgestellt werden, was für Speisen zu liefern sind. Heute übergeben die großen Rhedereien die Menage einfach dem Führer, welcher dabei noch einen Verdienst für sich herausschlägt. Butter wird auf den wenigsten Schiffen gegeben; wird sie aber wirklich gegeben, dann ist es eine gewisse Schmiere, welche auf dem Lande Niemand essen würde, oder gar Margarine, welche nie und nimmer als Butter zu betrachten ist. Die Seemannsordnung stammt aus den 70er Jahren, sie war, den damals vorhandenen Zuständen gegenüber, immerhin ein Fortschritt, aber jetzt ist sie in zahlreichen Punkten ungenügend geworden. Ich bitte Sie also, dem Antrage zuzustimmen. (Beifall.)

Da sich Niemand zum Worte meldet, wird die Diskussion geschlossen und zur Abstimmung geschritten. Der Antrag wird angenommen. Ein Antrag der Bautzener Genossen: die Fraktion solle selbstständige Gesetzentwürfe, vor Einbringung im Reichstage, erst der Gesammtpartei zur Begutachtung vorlegen; ferner, daß jeder Genosse das Recht haben solle, dem Vorstande, zur Begutachtung durch die Gesammtpartei, selbstständige Gesetzentwürfe oder Vorschläge einzureichen, und daß endlich die Fraktion die Pflicht habe, solche Gesetzentwürfe, für welche zwei Drittel der Abstimmenden sich entschieden, dem Reichstage vorzulegen, wird durch Uebergang zur Tagesordnung erledigt.

Ein Antrag Zubeil und Genossen, aus der Parteikasse den einzelnen Kreisen, die noch Wahlschulden haben und sie zu zahlen nicht im Stande sind, die nöthigen Mittel anzuweisen, wird zurückgezogen.

Es folgt die Berathung des Antrags 10:

Der Parteitag empfiehlt den Parteigenossen, überall da, wo Erfolge in Aussicht stehen, in die Wahlagitation einzutreten, sei es für den Reichstag, die Landtage oder Gemeindevertretung.

Dreesbach. Zubeil. Metzner. Heine. Tutzauer. Gottfr. Schulz. Bamberger. Berndt. Klein. Gründel. Brietz. Barth. Millarg. Täterow.

Dreesbach: Wir haben selbstverständlich die Pflicht, überall in die Wahlagitation einzutreten, nicht nur da, „wo Erfolge in Aussicht stehen." Wir sagten uns aber, daß es bei den Landtags- und Gemeindewahlen in einzelnen Distrikten des deutschen Reiches kaum möglich ist, durchzudringen, ohne Kompromisse einzugehen. So betrachte ich die Betheiligung an diesen Wahlen in Preußen als einfach unmöglich für unsere Genossen, weil sie dort im günstigsten Falle nur die Wahlmänner der dritten Klasse ohne Kompromiß mit den bürgerlichen Parteien durchbringen können, also ein wirklicher Erfolg nicht denkbar ist. Wir haben den Antrag eingebracht, weil man in sehr vielen Gegenden noch zweifelhaft ist, ob man sich bei diesen Wahlen betheiligen soll oder nicht. Ich halte es für eine Pflicht der Partei in ihrer jetzigen Entfaltung, sich überall am politischen Leben zu betheiligen; ich weiß speziell, daß in den Gemeindevertretungen wir kaum in der Lage sein werden, unsere Endziele zum Durchbruch zu bringen, aber wir haben zu zeigen, daß wir eine lebensfähige Partei sind und von dem Wahlrecht den möglichst weitgehenden Gebrauch machen wollen.

In der Diskussion bemerkt

Schmidt-Berlin: Wir werden für den Antrag stimmen, wie er hier vorliegt. Man hat uns in jüngster Zeit vorgeworfen, wir wollten den Parlamentarismus negiren und würden damit aus Sozialdemokraten zu Anarchisten. Es sind aber lediglich aus falschen Anschauungen heraus Fehler gemacht worden. Wir haben einfach erklärt, der Parlamentarismus ist der Mantel, mit welchem sich der Absolutismus unserer heutigen Gesellschaftsordnung zudeckt, und von dieser Auffassung werden wir nicht abgehen. Nicht ein Sozialdemokrat, nein hunderte von Sozialdemokraten haben in Wort und Schrift bewiesen, daß der Parlamentarismus in unserer heutigen Gesellschaft unendlich faul ist. Aber deshalb lehnen wir doch nicht die Betheiligung an den Wahlen ab, sondern nehmen das Kampfmittel, welches uns die Bourgeoisie bietet, auf und betheiligen uns überall, wo es möglich ist, am Wahlkampfe. Wir haben auch bisher damit sehr gute Erfolge errungen. Betreffs unserer besonderen Stellung zu den Stadtverordnetenwahlen kann ich mich auf Liebknecht berufen; Liebknecht führte aus, er habe 1869 noch nicht gewußt, daß 1871 das geeinigte Deutsche Reich bestehen würde; wir sagen, wir wußten 1887 nicht, daß 1890 das Ausnahmegesetz fallen würde; wir ändern jetzt ebenfalls unsere Taktik, wir werden jetzt wieder energisch an den Gemeindewahlen uns betheiligen, das erklären wir hiermit. (Sehr gut!) Niemand wird verkennen, daß wir unter dem Gesetz sehr schwere Arbeit, unendlichen Kampf mit der Polizei hatten, daß das alles die Agitation sehr zurückgehalten hat. In der Auswahl der Vertreter haben wir auch Fehler begangen, wir waren darin nicht vorsichtig genug, aber auch das lag an den bösen Verhältnissen; unsere besten Genossen waren ausgewiesen, ein großer Theil hatte sich vom öffentlichen Leben zurückgezogen, thatsächlich war Mangel an geeigneten Kandidaten vorhanden. Diese Umstände veranlaßten uns und verschiedene Andere damals dazu, den Wahlen zur Gemeindevertretung nicht die frühere Sympathie entgegenzubringen. Wir haben uns aber der Majorität gefügt; und wenn auch jetzt die Meinungsverschiedenheiten über den Nutzen des Parlamentarismus wieder stärker hervortreten, wir werden immer gemeinsam weiter arbeiten. Wie die Zukunft sich gestaltet, kann Niemand voraussehen. (Beifall.) Unsere Stadtverordneten sind keine Geschäftssozialisten; sie haben Geschäfte eingerichtet, weil sie auf andere Weise keine Existenz mehr fanden.

Franzen-München-Gladbach bittet, daß in Zukunft den Schwarzen etwas energischer auf den Leib gegangen werde.

Glocke-Nordhausen: Es könnte zweifelhaft sein, ob eine längere Diskussion über den Antrag am Platze ist; aber da thatsächlich nach der Erörterung dieser Frage in St. Gallen dieselbe immer wieder, und besonders stark in Berlin, diskutirt worden ist, scheint es angebracht, daß der heutige Parteitag endlich einmal eine bestimmte Stellung vorschreibt und die Streitigkeiten damit abschneidet. Vielfach haben persönliche Momente die Berliner Genossen veranlaßt, eine gewisse Antipathie gegenüber den Stadtverordnetenwahlen an den Tag zu legen. Aber auch prinzipielle Momente haben, wenn auch nicht in Berlin, zu der theilweisen Enthaltsamkeit mitgewirkt; es muß ferner an die Arbeiter im Staats- oder Gemeindedienst gedacht werden, die ungeheuren Maßregelungen ausgesetzt sind. Wir stehen nicht mehr auf dem Protest-Standpunkt der alten Demokraten, sondern wir betheiligen uns an den Wahlen, um sozialistische Elemente in die Stadtvertretung zu bringen. Art, Charakter und Handhabung der Agitation zu den Kommunalwahlen muß prinzipiell korrekt festgelegt werden. Natürlich können Stadtverordnete, die schwere Fehler sich zu Schulden kommen ließen, nicht mehr aufgestellt werden; wir blamiren uns und die Partei zu sehr damit.

Horn und Genossen beantragen, hinter „Erfolge" im Antrag Dreesbach einzuschalten:

„und seien dieselben auch nur propagandistischer Art."

Die Diskussion wird geschlossen und zunächst der Eventualantrag Horn und sodann mit diesem der ganze Antrag angenommen.

Die Berathung wendet sich zu Antrag 11:

Die Genossen von Marburg beantragen, daß in Anbetracht des Vordringens der antisemitischen Bewegung auf immer weitere Kreise und der verwerflichen Kampfesweise, welcher sich die Antisemiten speziell gegen die Sozialdemokraten bedienen, die Partei die Parteigenossen Marburgs in irgend einer Weise unterstützt, damit am Heerde der antisemitischen Agitation eine kräftige Gegenagitation entwickelt werden kann.

Zappan-Marburg.

Von vier verschiedenen Seiten wird beantragt, diesen Antrag der Parteileitung zu überweisen.

Ohne Debatte wird demgemäß beschlossen.

Zwei Anträge von Hamburg II. unter Nr. 12, auf Einsetzung eines ständigen Schiedsgerichtes und eventuelle Einsetzung eines Partei-Ausschusses werden als erledigt zurückgezogen.

Vorsitzender Singer: Bevor wir in der Erledigung der Tagesordnung fortfahren, theile ich auf Wunsch mit, daß im Ganzen 251 Telegramme und 55 Zuschriften und Adressen an den Parteitag eingegangen sind.

Ferner bringe ich eine dem Genossen Kühn-Langenbielau zugegangene Mittheilung zur Verlesung:

Soeben erhalte ich aus Langenbielau in Schlesien von dem mir als durchaus zuverlässig bekannten Genossen Lux folgende Nachricht: Am 14. Oktober hat sich dort in meiner Wohnung eine Person als Kaiserdeputirter Schröder aus Westfalen vorgestellt und erklärt, er sei vom Agitationskomitee der westfälischen Bergarbeiter beauftragt, im Schlesischen Kohlenrevier Versammlungen abzuhalten, um den Zuzug nach Westfalen zu verhindern, da dort gestreikt werden solle; es ständen zu diesem Zweck 1 800 000 Mark zur Verfügung, und davon könne er bis zu 5000 Mark für Schlesien zur Verfügung stellen. Legitimation hat der Mann verweigert mit dem Bemerken, er habe sich bereits auf der Polizei legitimirt. Da nun Bergarbeiter Schröder mir soeben mündlich erklärt, daß er diese Woche hier gewesen, überhaupt noch nie nach Schlesien gekommen sei, so muß angenommen werden, daß ein Schwindler seinen Namen mißbraucht, wahrscheinlich zu dem Zwecke, die im Werden begriffene Organisation der schlesischen Bergleute durch einen vorzeitigen Koup zu hintertreiben.

Zur Abgabe einer Erklärung nimmt das Wort

Liebknecht: Genossen! Aus Italien ist uns ein Brief zugegangen, in welchem man uns ankündigt, daß aus Ravenna ein telegraphischer Gruß an den hiesigen Parteikongreß ergangen sei, und nun zeigt man uns brieflich an, daß der Kongreß der italienischen Arbeiterpartei, die auf unserem Boden steht, morgen, Sonntag, in Ravenna zusammentritt. Nach dem ganzen Wortlaut dieses Briefes nun, der die größten Hoffnungen für die sozialistische Bewegung in der ganzen Welt durch die Entwicklung der Partei in Deutschland ausspricht, hielt ich uns für verpflichtet, dem Wunsch, der hier vielfach ausgesprochen wurde, nachzukommen und den italienischen Arbeiterkongreß von Seiten des hiesigen telegraphisch zu begrüßen und ihn zu ermuntern, auf dem eingeschlagenen Wege fortzufahren. Ich habe deshalb im Einklang mit den Freunden hier, gemeinsam mit unserem Freund Anseele, ein französisches Antworttelegramm aufgesetzt, welches deutsch folgendermaßen lautet:

„Der Kongreß der deutschen Sozialdemokraten in Halle begrüßt im Namen der Verbrüderung der Völker und der Solidarität der Arbeiter aller Länder die Sozialisten Italiens, die zum Kongreß versammelt sind: Unser Kongreß hofft, daß der Kongreß von Ravenna fruchtbar sein möge für den italienischen und den internationalen Sozialismus, und er ladet die dort versammelten Deputirten der Arbeit ein, den allgemeinen Weltkongreß von 1891 in Brüssel zu beschicken, um dort das Werk der Befreiung der Arbeiterklasse und der Befreiung der Menschheit vollenden zu helfen.

Ich bitte, den Wortlaut des Telegramms einstimmig anzunehmen und das Bureau zur Absendung desselben an die angegebene Adresse zu ermächtigen.

Unter lebhafter Zustimmung genehmigt der Parteitag diesen Vorschlag.

Darauf wird in der Berathung der selbstständigen Anträge fortgefahren.

Der Antrag 13:

„Die Parteigenossen Danzigs nehmen den vor Erlaß des Ausnahmegesetzes gemachten Vorschlag, Gründung einer Parteibibliothek, wieder auf und beantragen demgemäß beschließen zu wollen.

Unter Parteibibliothek ist zu verstehen: In Berlin soll eine Bibliothek errichtet werden, welche nur werthvolle wissenschaftliche Werke führt, die den agitatorisch wirkenden Genossen im ganzen Reiche zur Benutzung stehen sollen, da es den meisten Genossen nicht möglich ist, größere Summen für Anschaffung solcher Bücher zu verwenden,

wird ohne Debatte auf Antrag Bebels der Parteileitung überwiesen.

Dasselbe geschieht hinsichtlich des Antrags 14:

„Unterzeichneter beantragt hiermit, daß die Parlamentsberichte des Reichstags in Zukunft in Form eines Nachschlageheftes in größeren Auflagen gedruckt und zum möglichst billigen Preis an die verschiedenen Parteiblätter als Beilage abgegeben werden.

Die Ausführungen werden der Parteileitung übertragen.

Georg Johannes-Zittau i. S.

Antrag 15 lautet:

Der Kongreß beschließt:

„Der 1. Mai ist dauernd ein Feiertag der Arbeiter, der, entsprechend dem Beschluß des internationalen Pariser Arbeiterkongresses den Einrichtungen und Verhältnissen des Landes gemäß zu begehen ist. Wenn sich der Arbeitsruhe an diesem Tage Hindernisse in den Weg stellen, so haben die Umzüge, Feste im Freien u. s. w. am 1. Sonntag im Mai stattzufinden."

W. Liebknecht. Jensen-Stade. Arnold-Konstanz.

Ein Gegenantrag von 4 Berliner Genossen will die Feier des 1. Mai stets auf den ersten Sonntag im Mai verlegen, wenn nicht der 1. Mai ein Sonntag ist.

Liebknecht: Genossen! Eine Rede werde ich nicht halten, dazu ist die Zeit schon zu weit vorgerückt und sachlich sind wir in dieser Frage ja auch vollkommen einig. Den Antrag, die Feier des 1. Mai allgemein auf den ersten Sonntag im Mai zu verlegen, wie das in England, theils weil dort die großen Arbeitermeetings seit Jahrzehnten am Sonntag stattfinden, theils zur Vermeidung von Konflikten geschehen ist, kann ich nicht empfehlen. Ich glaube nicht, daß wir in Deutschland diese Konzession machen können. Der 1. Mai ist nicht blos durch Beschluß des internationalen Pariser Kongresses ein historischer Tag, sondern er ist schon seit Jahrtausenden ein Volksfeiertag der germanischen, gallischen, zum Theil auch der lateinischen Völker. Im größten Theil Deutschlands, in ganz England, Italien, Frankreich und der Schweiz wird der 1. Mai noch heute mehr oder weniger festlich begangen als Tag der Wiederauferstehung der Natur. Die Amerikaner, welche den 1. Mai als Feiertag der Arbeit proklamirten, haben dabei allerdings im Auge gehabt, daß es der Partei, welche die Wiedererweckung der Menschheit aus tausendjährigem Elend, aus dem geistigen Tode und aus der Knechtschaft bewerkstelligen wird, vor Allem zukommt, das Frühlingsfest feierlich zu begehen und in einem Fest die Auferstehung der Natur und der Menschheit zu feiern. Am 1. Mai müssen wir also unter allen Umständen festhalten. Andererseits wollen wir aber auch nicht unnütze Konflikte herbeiführen; darum geht mein Antrag weiter dahin, den 1. Mai in jedem Falle zu feiern, und zwar in würdigster Weise, durch Versammlungen, Vorträge, Feste und, wo es möglich ist ohne Konflikte oder sonstige Unannehmlichkeiten oder Nachtheile für die Bewegung selbst, auch durch Ruhenlassen der Arbeit, Umzüge u. s. w. Wo dieser letzteren Art der Feier sich aber Hindernisse entgegenstellen, da soll am 1. Mai von solchen Kundgebungen abgesehen werden, sollen nach der 1. Mai-Feier, nicht mit Ausschließung derselben, am ersten Sonntag im Mai die großen Kundgebungen, Umzüge und der-

18

gleichen stattfinden. Ich will nur wünschen, daß der Antrag möglichst ohne Debatte angenommen werde. (Beifall.)

Der Berliner Antrag wird zurückgezogen.

Eine Debatte erhebt sich nicht.

Im Schlußwort bemerkt Genosse Liebknecht: Ich bin darauf aufmerksam gemacht worden, daß der Gegenantrag Konflikte eben vermeiden will, während der meinige vielleicht zu Konflikten, ähnlich wie sie in diesem Jahre gewesen sind, führen möchte. Diese Ansicht ist vollkommen hinfällig. In diesem Jahre waren wir durch die Wahlen derart in Anspruch genommen, daß rechtzeitig ein anderer Rathschlag nicht möglich war. Das aber wird künftig nicht geschehen. Wir haben nicht jedes Jahr Wahl, und dann haben wir doch diesmal praktische Erfahrungen gemacht; diese Befürchtung ist also grundlos.

Mit allen gegen drei Stimmen wird der Antrag angenommen.

Der Antrag 16, der letzte Antrag der ersten Gruppe, lautet:

Beantragen, daß bei Stichwahlen zwischen den bürgerlichen Parteien sich die Genossen der Abstimmung zu enthalten haben.

Herbert-Stettin.   F. Kandt-Rostock.
Bortmann - Randow-Greifenhagen.

Antragsteller Kandt-Rostock: Es könnte scheinen, als ob nach Ertheilung der nachträglichen Zustimmung zum Verhalten der Fraktion in der Stichwahlfrage sich die Erledigung dieses Antrages erübrige. Ich bin jedoch anderer Meinung. Der Wortlaut meines Antrages ist im Wesentlichen in St. Gallen zum Beschuß erhoben worden. Durch das Ausgeben der bekannten Parole zu den 1890er Stichwahlen ist vielfach Verwirrung erzeugt worden. Solche Inkonsequenz ist nicht korrekt. Ich bitte um Annahme meines Antrages, damit ein korrekter Zustand hergestellt wird.

Kalnbach-Karlsruhe: Der Antragsteller schüttet das Kind mit dem Bade aus. Es ist oft von äußerster Wichtigkeit, die reaktionärsten, volksfeindlichsten Abgeordneten aus dem Reichstag zu verdrängen. Das kann aber nicht erreicht werden, wenn wir nach dem Antrage beschließen. Ein klassischer Beweis für das Gegentheil ist unsere letzte Wahl in Karlsruhe, wo es galt, den erzreaktionären Staatsanwalt Fieser zu schlagen. Es wurde der freisinnige Pflüger vorgeschlagen, zwar keine bedeutende Persönlichkeit, aber durchaus freiheitlich gesinnt und überall für die Arbeiter einzutreten bereit. Durch unsere Betheiligung an der Stichwahl haben wir ihm zum Siege verholfen und einen großen Feind der Arbeiter verdrängt. Wir sollten uns also nicht generell binden, sondern von Fall zu Fall, nach der Persönlichkeit und den Verhältnissen entscheiden. Ich bitte den Antrag abzulehnen.

Joeft-Mainz: Auch ich möchte vor solchem Beschluß warnen; wir sind alle überzeugt, daß er doch nicht wird gehalten werden können. (Sehr richtig!) Auf dem St. Gallener Kongreß ist allerdings so beschlossen worden, aber die Genossen haben ihn kaum zur Hälfte respektirt. Auch die thatsächlichen Verhältnisse sprechen dagegen. Der Oberstaatsanwalt Hartmann soll einmal im Reichstage gesagt haben: Ihr Sozialdemokraten gehört gesellschaftlich hier gar nicht hinein! Wenn man an einem solchen Herrn ein Exempel statuiren und dabei erreichen könnte, daß ein minder rücksichtsloser Gegner in den Reichstag kommt, dann sollte man doch diese Gelegenheit nicht unbenutzt lassen, weil man durch einen Beschluß in der Richtung des Antrags gebunden wäre. Ich bin es müde, immer wieder Beschlüsse zu fassen, von denen wir alle im Voraus wissen, daß man sie nicht respektirt; wir verlieren höchstens dadurch nach außen an Ansehen. (Beifall.)

Es wird der Schluß der Diskussion beantragt.

Auerbach-Berlin hält die Debatte für so wichtig, daß er dringend bittet, sie fortzusetzen.

Der Schlußantrag wird angenommen und der Antrag Herbert-Kandt-Borkmann, gegen eine geringe Minderheit, abgelehnt.

Damit ist die Berathung der gedruckt vorliegenden Anträge erledigt.

Der vorher mitgetheilte Antrag Bebel, betreffend den Brüsseler Kongreß, wird einstimmig angenommen.

Folgender Antrag:

In Erwägung, daß diejenigen Parteigenossen, welche im Besitz eines Reichstagsmandats sich befinden, die Pflicht haben, den Parteitag zu besuchen, erscheint es erforderlich, daß denselben die ihnen entstehenden Unkosten zurückerstattet werden. Daher wolle der Parteitag beschließen, die Höhe der täglichen Spesen für den genannten Zweck festzusetzen.

Franz Berndt-Berlin, 4. Wahlkreis. Fr. Riesop-Konitz, W.-Pr. Fritz Berndt - Berlin, 4. Wahlkreis. Fr. Zubeil-Kalau-Luckau. R. Jakobey-Berlin V. v. Wietersheim-Hamm-Soest. Kahl-Duisburg. Ad. Schultze-Magdeburg. Karl Grünberg-Hartha. Anton Guhmann-Döbeln. Emil Busch-Güstrow. H. Schwerdtfeger-Neubrandenburg. Wendt-Malchin-Waren.

dessen prinzipieller Theil bereits entschieden ist, wird, soweit es sich um die finanzielle Regelung handelt, dem Parteivorstande überwiesen.

Hiermit sind die Geschäfte des Parteitages beendet, bis auf den Bericht der Neunerkommission, der noch nicht fertiggestellt ist.

Es tritt eine Pause von 25 Minuten ein.

———

18*

Um 11 Uhr 15 Minuten wird die Sitzung wieder eröffnet.

Vorsitzender Singer: Wir würden nunmehr den Bericht der Neunerkommission entgegennehmen können. Zunächst möchte ich aber den prinzipiellen Standpunkt des Parteitages in der Behandlung dieser Angelegenheit feststellen. Wir haben die Neunerkommission als einen Gerichtshof zur Untersuchung und Beurtheilung der ihr überwiesenen Angelegenheit gewählt. Wir haben mit der denkbar größten Objektivität diese Kommission zusammengesetzt und dadurch vermieden, daß irgendwie an der Sache interessirte Personen einen Einfluß auf die Fassung des Urtheils ausüben konnten. Da nun der Parteitag nicht in der Lage sein würde, in irgend einer Weise in eine Nachprüfung des Aktenmaterials einzutreten, so halte ich es für nothwendig, daß der Parteitag schon jetzt, ehe Jemand das Urtheil kennt, erklärt, daß die Mittheilungen der Kommission, mögen sie ausfallen wie sie wollen, für ihn als verbindlich erachtet werden und daß der Parteitag es von vornherein ablehnt, in eine Erörterung des Kommissionsberichts einzutreten.

Gießhoit-Berlin: Damit sind wir Berliner nicht einverstanden. Man hat in der Kommission nur 3 Zeugen aus Berlin vorgeschlagen. Die Kommission hätte andere Berliner auch als Zeugen vernehmen sollen (Rufe: Abschlachtungstheorie, weiter nichts!).

Slomke-Bielefeld: Ich bin mit vielen Anordnungen des Präsidiums zufrieden gewesen, wenn unnöthige Angelegenheiten vom Parteitage ferngehalten wurden. Wir wollen aber in dieser Sache den Vorwurf der Abschlachtung dem Parteitage zuguterletzt ersparen.

Schippel: Wir können ja nicht einmal wissen, ob der Beschluß der Kommission nicht dem Organisationsentwurf der Partei überhaupt widerspricht. Ueber die Zugehörigkeit zur Partei entscheiden die Parteigenossen der einzelnen Orte und Reichstagswahlkreise. Es ist also formell absolut unzulässig, daß, ehe alle Instanzen durchgegangen sind, der Parteitag hier irgend etwas entscheidet. Ich kann mir recht wohl denken, daß wir vielem zustimmen, was die Kommission vorschlagen wird, wir können aber nicht debattelos dem, was die Kommission vorbringt, beistimmen.

Vorsitzender Singer: Um jeden Schein zu vermeiden, als ob von hier aus irgend welche Besorgniß, in die Diskussion dieser Angelegenheit einzutreten, herrscht, ziehe ich meinen, übrigens auf Wunsch einer größeren Anzahl Genossen gemachten Vorschlag zurück und überlasse das Weitere dem Verlauf der Verhandlungen. (Bravo!)

Berichterstatter Geck-Offenburg: Parteigenossen! Die Neunerkommission hat folgendes Urtheil gefällt. Dieselbe wurde vom Parteitage beauftragt, die in dem beigefügten Antrage verlangte Untersuchung vorzunehmen. Sie ist nach einer dreitägigen Verhandlung des in thatsächlicher und rechtlicher Beziehung geprüften

Materials dazu gekommen, die 5 vorgelegten Hauptfragen also zu beantworten:

Bericht der Neuner-Kommission.

Frage A. Ist Grillenberger Geschäftssozialismus vorzuwerfen? **Nein!**

Frage B. Haben die Verhandlungen in der Kommission ergeben, daß sich eine Mittelsperson verhetzend zwischen Fraktion und die Berliner Genossen gestellt hat? **Nein!**

Frage C. Ist die Behauptung Werner's über die Art seiner Nichtanstellung beim Volksblatt wahr? **Nein!**

Frage D. Ist das Vorgehen der Fraktion gegen Schippel als ein zu schroffes und ungerechtfertigtes zu bezeichnen? **Nein!**

Frage E. Ist in der Anwendung des Wortes „Spitzel" bei Charakterisirung der Berliner Parteizustände eine bewußte oder unbewußte Beleidigung der Berliner Genossen zu erblicken? **Nein!**

Die Beantwortung sämmtlicher Fragen ist nach eingehender Prüfung **einstimmig** erfolgt.

Es handelt sich zunächst um den Vorwurf des Geschäftssozialismus, welcher von Berlin aus durch Wille gegen den Reichstagsabgeordneten Grillenberger, als Angestelltem der Buchdruckerei Wörlein & Co. in Nürnberg, erhoben wurde. Grillenberger entgegnete: „Wille habe jedenfalls den Geschäftssozialismus von seinem Freunde Werner kennen gelernt."

Hierauf antwortete Buchdrucker Werner im Sprechsaal des „Berl. Volksbl." vom 23. August d. J.: „Grillenberger habe eine Menge allgemeiner Verleumdungen zu Tage gefördert. — Hoffentlich kommen wir beide nach Halle. Ich werde dort Material gegen Grillenberger bringen."

Werner ist nun seinem Vorgeben nicht nachgekommen; sein der Kommission vorgelegtes Material beschränkt sich auf zwei in Nürnberg erschienene Flugblätter aus dem Jahre 1884, worin unwahre Behauptungen enthalten sind, wegen denen der Verfasser der verleumderischen Beleidigung schuldig befunden wurde. Ein weiterer Beweis wurde nicht versucht; der Hinweis auf die Aeußerung einer untergeordneten Person kann nicht als solcher betrachtet werden. Dagegen konnte im Verlauf der Verhandlung festgestellt werden, daß die Wörlein'sche Druckerei in Nürnberg in ihrem geschäftlichen Verhältniß zur Partei eine Praxis befolgte, über welche man nur die größte Befriedigung haben kann. Diese Thatsache war unter den Berliner Parteigenossen seit Jahren so bekannt, daß man sich nur wundern muß, wie heute Genossen, welche öffentlich auftreten, eine gegentheilige Auffassung kolportiren dürfen. Es steht durch die Verhandlung fest, daß Genossen sich von der Unhaltbarkeit derartiger Anschuldigungen jederzeit bei solchen, die seit längerer Zeit mit den Parteiverhältnissen bekannt sind, hätten Auskunft verschaffen können.

Grillenberger bringt seinerseits eine Anzahl von Thatsachen vor, welche als Kriterien für eine Geschäftspraxis des Buchdruckers Werner dienen sollen, die den Vorwurf „Geschäftssozialismus" verdiene. Es ist nicht zu leugnen, daß die Summe der einzelnen Bilder den Eindruck erzeugt, daß Buchdrucker Werner, nachdem er vom Arbeiter zum Geschäftsmitinhaber avancirte, eine geschäftliche Usance entwickelt, welche an der Grenze des Zulässigen sich bewegt.

Mag es auffallen, daß die „Tribüne" aus den Händen des bisherigen Druckers ohne äußeren Anlaß genommen und der Werner'schen Druckerei zugetheilt wurde, so kann es doch nicht als erwiesen angesehen werden, daß Werner direkt diese Veränderung anregen bezw. herbeiführen half; ebensowenig liegen Anhaltspunkte dafür vor, daß Werner Vorbereitungen traf, auch den Druck des „Volksblatt" an sich zu reißen; es ist allerdings auffallend, warum Werner gerade gegen das Volksblatt und Leute, die bei dem Volksblatt angestellt sind, öffentliche Angriffe macht. Es sei gleich hier betont, daß durch die Verhandlung festgestellt wurde, daß Werner nicht durch Maßregelung oder Arbeitslosigkeit gezwungen war, sich zu etabliren.

Werner macht kein Geheimniß daraus, daß er in letzter Zeit Schritte that, um auch den Druck des Vereinsblattes zu erhalten.

In diesen und ähnlichen Fällen gehen die Bemühungen Werner's um Druckaufträge Hand in Hand mit der von der allgemein üblichen Geschäftskonkurrenz befolgten Praxis.

Dagegen wurde die Ueberzeugung gewonnen, daß das Geschäftsgebahren Werner's, wie solches bei der Schaffung verschiedener Druckarbeiten, insbesondere des Berliner Verkehrs-Almanach, zur Geltung kam, als sehr zweifelhaft und verdächtig zu bezeichnen ist. Die geschäftliche Manipulation, durch welche der Verkehrs-Almanach geschaffen wurde, gilt als noch nicht genügend aufgeklärt; Werner, als Vorsitzender der betreffenden Kommission und zugleich als Unternehmer des Werkes, hätte im eigenen, wie im Interesse der Berliner Genossen bemüht sein müssen, in diesem Geschäfte nach jeder Hinsicht volle Klarheit walten zu lassen. Andererseits entlasten ihn die betreffenden Berliner Genossen insofern, als diese sich dem Vorwurfe nicht entziehen können, in diesem Falle die in der Partei übliche Gründlichkeit außer Acht gelassen zu haben.

Zur Beurtheilung der Frage, ob Werner der geeignete Mann sei, über den Charakter anderer Leute öffentliche Kritik zu üben, wurden einige Angaben zur Prüfung vorgelegt, welche sich auf das private Leben W.'s beziehen. Dieselben liegen in der Zeit zu weit zurück, als daß man zu ihrer Prüfung hätte die nothwendigen Erhebungen machen können. Herr Werner, der von diesen gegen ihn im Umlaufe gewesenen Gerüchten früher wiederholt Kenntniß erhielt, unterließ es, sie durch ein gerichtliches Vorgehen gegen die Verbreiter derselben zu beseitigen.

Die Behauptung Werner's von einer Zwischenperson, die sich zwischen die Fraktion und die Berliner Genossen verhetzend drängte, richtet sich gegen einen Parteigenossen, dem nicht nachgewiesen werden kann, daß er in seinem freundschaftlichen Verkehr mit den Fraktionsmitgliedern der Berliner Parteigenossenschaft irgend welche Verlegenheiten bereitete. Die Freundschaft zu Fraktionsmitgliedern ist kein Anlaß, jemandem Mißtrauen entgegenzubringen. Dies sollte Buchdrucker Werner um so mehr bedenken, als er in seinem Geschäfte Personen anstellte, deren Vergangenheit einen Verkehr mit Sozialdemokraten ausschließt. Ohne jeden Rückhalt ist auch der Versuch Werner's, zwei Artikel des „Berliner Lokalanzeiger" auf Inspiration eines Mitgliedes der Bading'schen Druckerei zurückzuführen. Es hat sich die große Wahrscheinlichkeit ergeben, daß dieselben von Dr. Hamburger herrühren.

Die Meinungsverschiedenheit über die Feier des 1. Mai sollte im Volksblatt ungehindert zum Ausdruck kommen; daß eine von den Freunden Werner's eingesandte Erklärung nicht erschien, daran trifft, nach dem Ergebniß der Untersuchung, die genannte Redaktion keine Schuld; die Aufnahme unterblieb auf Wunsch der Einsender selbst. Von der Beseitigung irgend eines Schriftstückes kann durchaus keine Rede sein.

Bezüglich seines öffentlichen Auftretens macht Werner nicht den Eindruck, daß er seine Angriffe immer auf Thatsachen stützt, sondern mehr die subjektive Ansicht dritter Personen unterlegt. Seine Art, sich auszudrücken, trägt dazu bei, ihn in der Entwickelung seiner Themata immer mehr vom sachlichen Boden zu entfernen. Er gesteht dies selbst zu, indem er einräumt: „In der Hitze des Gefechtes kommen mir oft Worte, die ich nicht gebrauchen wollte." — „Hätte ich gewußt, daß es mir so ausgelegt würde, so hätte ich nicht gewagt, es zu sagen."

Zeugen, die von ihm selbst vorgeschlagen und mit ihm befreundet sind, sagten aus: „Werner ist thatsächlich ein Mann, dem die Zunge durchgeht ꝛc." „Er ist ein guter Kerl, aber er kann sich nicht beherrschen."

Werner sagte, er habe wegen einer Mehrforderung von 3 Mark Lohn die Maschinenmeisterstelle in der Bading'schen Druckerei nicht erhalten, und knüpft daran die Behauptung, er (W.) hätte sich niemals etablirt, wenn er damals diese Stellung bekommen hätte.

Die Verhandlung ergab, daß die Behauptung Werner's nach dieser Richtung der Wahrheit vollständig entbehrt. Nach der anderen Seite besteht für Werner — selbst für den Fall, daß es sich um eine Preisdifferenz von 3 Mark handelte, kein Anlaß sich zu beschweren. Es ist bewiesen, daß Werner bei Vergebung von Einbinden von Parteidruckschriften Nichtparteigenossen deshalb bevorzugte, weil sie billiger arbeiteten, als Parteigenossen.

Die Vernehmung Schippels und der Mitglieder der Kommission zur Herausgabe des Verkehrs-Almanachs haben dies ergeben.

Die Behauptung Werner's, daß er wegen seines öffentlichen Auftretens eine Maßregelung im Geschäfte seines damaligen Prinzipals zu befürchten hatte, ist durch Zeugen ebenfalls als unrichtig erwiesen.

Es ist unwahr, daß Grillenberger die Berliner Parteigenossen als solche mit Polizeispitzel titulierte. Nach Feststellung der betreffenden Aeußerung Grillenberger's ergiebt sich, daß er sagte, es gab eine Zeit, wo man nicht sicher war, daß unter 3 Personen in Berlin ein Spitzel sich befand. Die Vernehmung Berliner Genossen als Zeugen ergab die Berechtigung dieser Behauptung.

In Anbetracht aller gegen Werner vorgebrachten Thatsachen mußte der äußere Anschein nothwendig zur Annahme führen, daß Werner nicht würdig sei, unserer Partei als Genosse anzugehören; jedoch konnte sich die Kommission, nach eingehender Prüfung des vorliegenden Materials, nicht entschließen, einen Antrag auf Ausschluß zu stellen. Die Kommission gewann vielmehr, unter Zusammenfassung aller Punkte, die Ueberzeugung, daß Werner weder das Taktgefühl noch die Fähigkeit besitzt, die Tragweite seiner Handlungsweise in Bezug auf die Wahrung der Interessen der Partei abzuwägen.

Halle, 18. Oktober 1890.

Die Kommission:

W. Geck-Offenburg. Aug. Kaden-Dresden. Kloß-Stuttgart. Hermann Grimpe-Elberfeld. Ewald-Brandenburg. Meist-Köln. Reißhaus-Erfurt. Pfannkuch-Cassel. Müller-Darmstadt.

Werner: Ich möchte den Referenten bitten, die ganze von mir im „Volksblatt" veröffentlichte Sprechsaalnotiz vorzulesen.

Berichterstatter Geck: Es ist im Urtheil nicht behauptet, daß Werner den Grillenberger des Geschäftssozialismus bezichtigte. (Der Berichterstatter verliest den betreffenden Passus der Urtheilsgründe.)

Werner: Ich bestehe darauf, daß meine ganze Sprechsaalnotiz verlesen wird.

Berichterstatter Geck kommt diesem Wunsche nach.

Die Erklärung im „Sprechsaal" lautet:

In einer Rede, die Grillenberger am vergangenen Montag in Nürnberg hielt, und die nun durch die Presse läuft, hat derselbe eine Menge allgemeiner Verleumdungen zu Tage gefördert. Meine Person beehrt er ganz besonders damit.

Herr Wille habe — das läßt er so mit unterfließen —

den „Geschäftssozialismus", von dem Herr Wille in Berlin sprach, wohl von seinem Freunde Wilhelm Werner kennen gelernt. Herr Wille, den ich höchstens vier Mal gesehen und mit dem ich in meinem Leben höchstens zwanzig Worte gewechselt habe, sogar nicht einmal über Parteiverhältnisse, wird von Grillenberger im Handumdrehen zu meinem Freunde gemacht — jedenfalls durch falsche Einflüsterungen von einer bestimmten Seite, welche ein Interesse daran zu haben scheint, den Zwist zwischen Fraktion und Berliner Genossen zu schüren, um für allein würdig gehalten zu werden, mit ersterer verkehre zu dürfen. Warum auch nicht? So kompromittirt man beide gleich auf einmal: mich als Geschäftssozialist und ihn als meinen Freund. Ich weise die Verdächtigung Grillenbergers mit aller Entschiedenheit zurück.

Ich habe ja noch nicht Gelegenheit gehabt, durch langjährige Thätigkeit im Reichstage den parlamentarischen Anstand zu studiren und meine Kampfesweise danach einzurichten. Aber ich halte es augenblicklich für besser, meine Ausführungen, Grillenberger gegenüber, bis auf den Parteitag aufzusparen, es könnte sonst der gegnerischen Presse etwas neuer Stoff gegeben werden. Hoffentlich kommen wir beide nach Halle. Ich werde dort Material gegen G. bringen.

Er soll mir auf dem Parteitag Rede und Antwort in dieser Frage stehen. Ich bin bereit. Kann er dort seine Behauptungen nicht aufrecht erhalten, kann er mir den Geschäftssozialismus nicht beweisen, so wird er sich gefallen lassen müssen, wenn ich ihn einen ehrlosen Verleumder nenne.

Berlin, den 22. August 1890.

W. Werner, Buchdrucker.

Es ist der Antrag eingegangen, den Bericht der Neunerkommission sobald als möglich drucken zu lassen und den Delegirten zuzusenden.

Werner: Sie werden Alle in meiner Sprechsaalnotiz im „Berliner Volksblatt" nicht gefunden haben, daß ich darin Herrn Grillenberger des Geschäftssozialismus geziehen habe. Wie kommt aber Herr Grillenberger dazu, in jener Nürnberger Versammlung einfach zu erklären: „Den Geschäftssozialismus, von dem Herr Wille sprach, hat derselbe wohl durch seinen Freund Werner kennen gelernt. Gewisse Leute in Berlin hatten das Bestreben, das dortige „Volksblatt" an sich zu reißen; das ist nicht gelungen, da das „Berliner Volksblatt" zum Centralorgan der Partei bestimmt wurde." Ich habe zur Genüge den Beweis geliefert, daß dies nicht wahr ist, und einen Theil meiner Berliner Genossen, die alle über die internen Vorgänge in Berlin ganz genau unterrichtet sind, als Zeugen vorgeschlagen, sie sind aber nicht verhört worden. (Hört! Hört!)

Grillenberger hat selbst in der Kommission erklärt, daß er nicht aus eigener Erfahrung mich beschuldigt habe, sondern daß er es von dem Prokuristen des „Berliner Volksblatt", Herrn Jacob Bamberger, habe. Zu derselben Zeit, als der Abgeordnete Grillenberger vom Geschäftssozialismus sprach, erschienen in der „Berliner Volkszeitung" mehrere Notizen und Artikel, in denen ich als Schildknappe Schippel's hingestellt wurde und als Mann mit den geschäftspolitischen Machenschaften. Ich wußte gar nicht, wie nur diese „geschäftspolitischen Machenschaften" in die „Berliner Volkszeitung" gekommen waren. Ich ging in Folge dessen in Versammlungen gegen die „Volkszeitung" vor, und eine große Parteiversammlung auf Tivoli beschloß, die „Berliner Volkszeitung" habe sich in die Parteiverhältnisse der Sozialdemokraten nicht hineinzumischen. Das „Volksblatt" druckte diese Resolution ab und erklärte, wir haben mit der „Volkszeitung" nichts mehr zu thun. Darauf erschien eine ziemlich gehässige Erklärung in der „Volkszeitung" im Briefkasten: Endlich haben wir einmal das „Berliner Volksblatt" auf einer Doppelzüngigkeit ertappt. Damals, als wir die geschäftspolitischen Machenschaften gegen das „Volksblatt" aufdeckten, war man mit denjenigen Theil, welcher die Angelegenheit provozirte, einverstanden, jetzt aber, wo die Angriffe nur gegen die „Berliner Volkszeitung" gehen, zieht man sich einfach von dieser Sache zurück." Das ist doch ein Beweis von einer ziemlichen Dreistigkeit. Wir haben uns nun die größte Mühe gegeben, danach zu forschen, was es denn eigentlich mit dieser Notiz für eine Bewandtniß hat, und wir haben selber nachher klargestellt bekommen, daß eben Herr Jacob Bamberger, der Prokurist des Volksblatts, thatsächlich auf der Redaktion des Berliner Volksblatt verkehrte und daß, wenn er zu der Zeit zu Hause gewesen wäre, als der Streit mit der Volkszeitung und dem Volksblatt entstand, nie und nimmer diese Polemik hätte entstehen können. Ledebour, der jetzt weg ist von der Volkszeitung, erklärte später seinem Freunde Wille in Gegenwart des Redakteurs Scherbel aus Berlin, daß die Anzapfungen dem Genossen Schippel gegenüber auf Veranlassung der Redaktion des Berliner Volksblatts geschehen seien. Damit halten sie zusammen, daß Herr Jacob Bamberger, der als Prokurist gar nichts weiter zu thun hat, als die Druckaufträge des Blattes entgegenzunehmen, sich permanent in der Redaktion befindet. Herr Bamberger sollte eben Thatsachen gegen meine Person aufbringen, und darum sage ich, daß er als Zwischenperson viel mehr Schuld hatte als Grillenberger. Man hat mich nun deswegen des Geschäftssozialismus geziehen, weil ich angeblich Druckarbeiten, die ich in unserer Druckerei nicht schaffen konnte, an eine andere Druckerei die nicht tarifmäßig bezahlte, weggegeben habe. Felgentreff und Mohrbach haben dieses Material zusammengebracht. Sie sind, um

Erkundigungen einzuziehen, bei den verschiedensten Druckereien wegen des Auftrages des „Almanach" gewesen. Mohrbach ist hier garnicht erschienen, weil Unregelmäßigkeiten gegen ihn vorliegen. Das sind die Elemente, die man gebraucht, um Material zusammenzusuchen gegen andere Parteigenossen, die es einmal gewagt haben, Herrn Jacob Bamberger oder irgend Jemand Anderem entgegenzutreten. Wegen Abgabe eines Druckauftrages kann man mich des Geschäftssozialismus nicht beschuldigen. Die erwähnte Druckerei zahlt zur Zeit tarifmäßig. Dagegen kann ich beweisen, daß Bamberger, seit 20 Jahren ein Freund verschiedener Fraktionsleute, nachdem er mit Herrn Bading die Druckerei in Händen hat, seine Druckerei drei Jahre lang gesperrt gesehen hat, weil er nicht tarifmäßig zahlte. Man hat nun, um der Sache eine persönliche Spitze zu geben, Dolinski mit in die Debatte gezogen. Dolinski ist seit 3 Wochen in unserem Geschäft thätig. Er ist gewerkschaftlich so engagirt, daß er in Berlin keine Arbeit mehr bekommt und da haben wir gemeint, ihn anstellen zu müssen, gleichviel ob er gewerkschaftlich ruinirt ist oder nicht. Bamberger erklärte, daß die Kaution, weswegen man den Dolinski immer verdächtigte, nicht verloren gegangen sei, sie sei gerettet worden, aber man kann es nur nicht dem Dolinski sagen, sonst könnte er schließlich sich nicht alles so gefallen lassen, was über ihn geredet werde. Eigenthümlich ist das Verfahren Bambergers resp. des Volksblatt in Bezug auf den von Wille geschriebenen Artikel in der „Sächsischen Arbeiterzeitung". Es wurde gesagt, es ist hier ein Artikel geschrieben worden, aber das wahre Streitobjekt brachte man nicht zur Kenntniß der Leser, sondern schrieb unten in einer Note, wir halten es nicht für werth, diesen Artikel zu veröffentlichen, weil wir nicht die Ansichten theilen, die darin enthalten sind. Ja, wenn man ein Streitobjekt aufwirft, so erfordert es die Gerechtigkeit, daß man dieses Streitobjekt auch abdruckt. Nun erschien dies Streitobjekt in der „Berliner Volkstribüne", infolgedessen sich die Polemik zwischen Liebknecht und Schippel entwickelt hat. Der Abgeordnete Liebknecht hat hier vom Podium herab erklärt, daß der Artikel in die Volkstribüne gekommen sei, weil man dem Redakteur, der selbst nicht daran Schuld sei, die Pistole auf die Brust gedrückt habe (Liebknecht: Ist auch wahr!) Redakteur Schmidt hat hier eine Erklärung niedergelegt, in der er behauptet, daß daran kein Wort wahr sei, daß aus seinem eigenen Ermessen dieser Artikel hineingekommen sei. Dr. Konrad Schmidt hat Bebel ersucht, er möge es hier konstatiren, daß ohne jegliches Zuthun irgend welcher Berliner Genossen der Artikel aus der Sächsischen Arbeiterzeitung in die Tribüne gekommen sei. Bebel. hat ihm nun, wie mir Schmidt mitgetheilt hat, gesagt, daß er diese Mittheilung telephonisch aus dem Bureau erhalten habe. Als Schmidt etwas darauf entgegnete, erklärte Bebel, ja der Mann hat etwas gehört, das sind seine Vermuthungen, er hat sich ein Urtheil darüber gebildet und dieses Urtheil hat man mir mitgetheilt, das kann ich den Leuten gar nicht verdenken (Bebel: das habe ich nicht gesagt; bekannte Verdrehung!) Nun, da ist wohl zur Evidenz bewiesen, daß eine Zwischenperson (Unruhe) vorhanden ist. Und noch eins. Herr Bamberger hat sich unter dem Sozialistengesetz öffentlich in Berlin gar nicht bemerkbar gemacht. Wie konnte er da mit einem Mal auf dem Parteitag mit einem Mandat erscheinen? (Fortgesetzte Unruhe.) Meine Behauptung in Bezug auf meine Anstellung beim „Berliner Volksblatt" halte ich voll und ganz aufrecht. Wäre ich beim „Volksblatt" angestellt worden, ich hätte mich nie und nimmer selbstständig gemacht. Ich konnte mich nirgends halten, weil ich überall von der Polizei umlagert war. Ich bin deshalb mit Einem, der schon eine Druckerei hatte, in Verbindung getreten, ohne einen Pfennig Geld. Herr Bading hat mir allerdings 500 Mk. auf zwei Wechsel gegeben. Aber die Dankbarkeit dafür kann mich doch nicht abhalten, Sachen, die mir in der Partei nicht gefallen, zu mißbilligen und ihnen entgegenzutreten. Man hat mir weiter vorgeworfen, der Direktor des „Münchener Brauhaus," Arndt, hätte mir 20 000 Mk. geboten, um ein Konkurrenzblatt gegen das Volksblatt zu gründen. Ich habe das schon einmal in der Lipsversammlung widerlegt und gesagt, ich hätte Jeden, der mir derartiges angesonnen, ganz energisch zurückgewiesen. Ich weise diese Unterstellung noch einmal ganz entschieden zurück und berufe mich auf meine Berliner Parteigenossen, die nicht meine persönlichen Feinde sind. Wenn ich Geschäftssozialist bin, dann sind es alle, die vielleicht nur ein Geschäft machen, und die ganz andere Sachen gemacht, die den Bierstreik in Berlin ausnutzten, um das Fürther Bier aus Nürnberg durch Bamberger in Berlin einzuführen, wo er von Nürnberg Prozente in Anspruch nimmt (Bebel: wieder unwahr! große Unruhe.) Ich werde Beweise bringen. Es ist mir dann eine unanständige Handlung in der Kommission vorgehalten worden. Ich könnte nun sagen, ich war zu der Zeit, als die Sache geschehen ist, 20 Jahre alt, und habe es vielleicht in meiner Dummheit gemacht. Aber ich erkläre auf Ehrenwort, daß ich es niemals gethan habe. In Berlin ist eine Kommission darüber eingesetzt worden, wozu der Betreffende geladen war, er ist aber nicht erschienen, um seine Beschuldigung gegen mich aufrecht zu erhalten. Ich habe in der Kommission auf Ehrenwort, ich weiß ja nicht, ob ich noch eins habe, erklärt, daß ich diese That nicht begangen habe. Ich meine, was sich ein Parteigenosse nicht erlauben darf, dürfen sich die Fraktionsmitglieder auch nicht erlauben; die Fraktionsmitglieder sind nicht mehr, als die anderen Parteigenossen. (Bebel: selbstverständlich!) Die Volkstribüne ist ein Organ, welches vollständig mit der Polizei nichts zu thun hat, und doch geht ein Theil

der Fraktionsleute nach Hannover, Köln, Solingen u. s. w. und erklärt, das Organ sei ein Polizeiorgan und sein Redakteur ein zwei-
deutiger Mensch. Da habe ich ein Recht, zu sagen, diese Sachen
gehören sich nicht, und ich werde mich nicht scheuen, auch wenn ich
die Herren Abgeordneten gegen mich habe, derartige Unregelmäßigkeiten zu rügen. Sie können mit mir machen, was sie wollen. Ich
gebrauche nicht erst Hinterthüren, sondern was ich zu sagen habe,
— das ist meine Ungeschicklichkeit und Plumpheit — das sage ich
den Leuten ins Gesicht. Davon soll man mir erst einmal das Gegentheil beweisen. Ferner ist mir ein schwerer Vorwurf daraus gemacht
worden, daß ich in Magdeburg eine Versammlung abgehalten habe,
wo ich mich kolossal mißbilligend über den Organisationsentwurf
ausgesprochen haben soll. Nach den Berichten habe ich aber im
Eingang der Rede gesagt: Wir erkennen ja die Ueberlegenheit jener
Genossen Bebel, Liebknecht, Singer gern an, haben sie auch nie angegriffen, aber wir haben das volle Recht, den Maßstab der Kritik
an sie zu legen und zu sagen, das und das gefällt uns nicht von
euch — und das Recht der freien Kritik darf ich mir doch wohl
noch erlauben. Wenn ich dann über die theuren Wohnungen der
Abgeordneten gesprochen habe . . . . (Glocke des Vorsitzenden.)

Vorsitzender Singer (unterbrechend): Der Parteitag ist gewiß
gewillt, dem Redner möglichst Zeit für seine Ausführungen zu gestatten, dann sollte er sich aber doch dazu entschließen, nur zu dem
im Berichte Vorgetragenen zu sprechen. Von der Magdeburger
Versammlung z. B. steht im Bericht kein Wort, von vielen anderen
Dingen, die der Redner bespricht, auch nichts.

Werner (fortfahrend): Es sind Dinge verbreitet worden, die
jeder Basis vollständig entbehren. (Unruhe.) Ich soll mich um das
Vereinsblatt beworben haben. Ist denn das nicht eine ganz geschäftliche Handlung? Wenn dann später in Berlin, und zwar
wieder vom Volksblatt, verbreitet wurde, ich sei bei Wernigerode
auf dem Brocken gewesen und hätte dorthin die ganze Opposition
zu einer geheimen Sitzung bestellt. (Heiterkeit.) Wenn solche Gerüchte verbreitet werden, so sind das ganz unanständige Unterstellungen. Wenn man mir den Geschäftssozialismus nicht nach-
weist, so werden mir alle Parteigenossen nachsagen müssen, daß
bei mir davon nicht die Rede sein kann. Verurtheilen Sie mich
oder nicht, es ist mir ganz egal; ich gebe hiermit die Erklärung ab:
ich bleibe nach wie vor Sozialdemokrat und sage mit Wille: „Es
giebt noch einen Ort, wo man sich zurückziehen kann!"

Pfannkuch: Ich mache darauf aufmerksam, daß durch Beschluß
des Parteitages, auf Grund des Antrags Stadthagen, der Neuner-
kommission ihr Arbeitspensum und Arbeitsgebiet vorgeschrieben war
und wir durchaus kein Interesse daran hatten, es aus eigener
Initiative zu erweitern. Daß wir nicht alle von Werner vor-

geschlagenen Zeugen gehört haben, beruht darin, daß schon zwei zu seinen Gunsten dasselbe bekundet hatten, wir also einen dritten und vierten nicht brauchten.

Schmidt-Burgstädt: Ich bitte um möglichst einstimmige Annahme des Kommissionsberichts. Ich kenne Werner sehr lange, kenne auch die Berliner Opposition und bin geradezu erstaunt über die Objektivität des Urtheils. Die Berliner Genossen müssen mir bestätigen, daß das Urtheil ihnen aus der Seele gesprochen ist; es stellt den Sachverhalt so naturgetreu hin, daß gar nicht mehr daran zu rütteln ist. Sprechen wir der Kommission unser volles Vertrauen dadurch aus, daß wir einstimmig bestätigen, daß sie ein durchaus objektives Urtheil gefällt hat.

Meister-Hannover: Es soll Jemand die Niedertracht begangen haben, die „Volkstribüne" als Polizeiorgan zu bezeichnen, und dabei wurde auch Hannover genannt. Da mir nun selbst in Berlin eine derartige Niederträchtigkeit vorgeworfen wurde, so richte ich an Werner die Frage, wer das gethan hat. (Werner ruft: Der Abgeordnete Frohme!) Wir in Hannover wissen von einer solchen Aeußerung Frohme's nichts.

Pfannkuch: Wir haben die Form dieser so viel umstrittenen Aeußerung genau festzustellen gesucht und es ergab sich folgendes: Frohme erklärt, und das ist auch anderweitig bekannt durch andere Fraktionsmitglieder, er habe ausgeführt, die Schreibweise Schippel's sei eine derartige, daß, wenn er bewußter Weise im Dienste der Polizei stände, er nicht geschickter diese Schreibweise ausüben könnte. (Vereinzelte Pfuirufe.)

Zu einer Erklärung bezüglich des „Berliner Volksblatt" erhält das Wort der als Berichterstatter auf dem Parteitag anwesende

Redakteur des „Berliner Volksblatt" Baake: Genossen! Das Bureau hat mir gestattet, obgleich ich nicht als Delegirter hier anwesend bin, eine kurze Erklärung im Namen der Redaktion abzugeben. Herr Werner sagt, Wille hätte ihm mitgetheilt, der Redakteur Ledebour von der „Volks-Zeitung" habe in Gegenwart eines anderen Redakteurs Namens Scherbel erklärt, die Angriffe gegen Schippel in der „Volks-Zeitung" seien auf Veranlassung der Redaktion des „Berliner Volksblatt" erfolgt. Wenn eine solche Aeußerung in der That gefallen ist, so ist damit eine unwahre Behauptung ausgesprochen worden. Ich als Mitglied der Redaktion weiß nicht das Geringste darüber, daß unsererseits ein Eingreifen der Volks-Zeitung veranlaßt sein soll. Die Schilderung des Verhältnisses, in welchem Bamberger zur Redaktion steht, ist in den meisten Punkten übertrieben. Wir stehen wohl im Verkehr mit Bamberger, der auch häufig auf die Redaktion kommt, aber daß er bestimmenden Einfluß auf unsere Entschlüsse und Handlungen hätte, bestreite ich entschieden im Namen der Redaktion des „Berliner Volksblatt". (Bravo!)

Bebel: Herr Werner hat auch heute wieder genau dieselbe Taktik in seinen Ausführungen verfolgt, welche wir bereits während der früheren Verhandlungen an ihm beobachtet haben, obgleich er sich hätte angelegen sein lassen sollen, hier angesichts seiner bisherigen Erfahrungen nicht wieder in diese Taktik zurückzufallen. Da es ausgeschlossen ist, daß der Parteitag unzurechnungsfähig ist, so muß es sich wohl bei Werner um eine Art von Geistesverfassung handeln, die sehr zu seiner Entschuldigung spricht. Eine andere Frage ist freilich, ob ein Mann, der absolut außer Stande ist, Wahres von Unwahrem zu unterscheiden, immer und immer wieder schon erlebigte Dinge in der früheren unwahren Weise hier vorbringen soll; ich überlasse das ganz der Beurtheilung des Parteitages.

Die ganze Taktik Werner's ist auch jetzt wieder darauf ausgegangen, die Ausführungen der Kommission möglichst zu umgehen und eine Menge von Dingen vorzuführen, auf welche die Kommission kein Gewicht gelegt oder welche sie als durch die Zeugenaussagen erledigt angesehen hat. Auf diese Art zwingt Werner uns wieder in eine lange Debatte hinein, die in seinem eigenen Interesse möglichst hätte vermieden werden sollen. Er zerrt die Magdeburger Vorgänge hier herein, die in der Kommission, unter meiner Zuziehung erörtert worden sind und auf die die Kommission nicht mehr zurückgekommen ist. Dann erwähnt er auch die Harzzusammenkunft, über welche alle, die davon hörten, gelacht haben. Wenn Werner und seine Freunde wirklich zusammengekommen sind, warum soll man ihnen das Recht dazu bestreiten? Haben die einzelnen Männer der Opposition gemeinsame Zielpunkte, dann haben sie gewiß nur ihr Recht wahrgenommen, wenn sie zusammenkamen.

Nun schreitet er aber zu neuen Verdächtigungen fort. In der Bading'schen Druckerei soll vor Jahren nicht tarifmäßig bezahlt worden sein. Bamberger erklärt, es ist allerdings wahr, daß in dem Organ der Buchdrucker dem „Correspondent" unsere Druckerei vor einigen Jahren unter den nicht tarifmäßig zahlenden aufgeführt worden ist; darauf haben wir die Kommission der Buchdrucker herangezogen, ihr die Bücher vorgelegt, und die Kommission hat sich von der Einhaltung des Tarifs überzeugt.

Wer aber war der Mann, der diese niederträchtige Verleumdung veröffentlicht hat? Das war derselbe Herr Dolinski, der jetzt bei Werner beschäftigt ist. (Hört! Hört!) Mit Dolinski haben wir ja noch näher zu thun, ich kenne ihn sehr genau, zu genau, seit 13, 14 Jahren; es ist da allerlei vorgekommen, was wir untersuchen werden und was wesentlich anders ausfallen dürfte, als es ihm lieb sein wird. Ferner soll Bamberger wegen der Kaution irgend etwas zugegeben haben. Dolinski war Redakteur der „Freien Presse"; er wurde gegen 1500 Mark Kaution aus der Untersuchungshaft entlassen und ging ins Ausland, nach der Schweiz, wo ich ihn gesehen habe und wo er eine solche Haltung eingenommen hat, welche ganz besonders die untersuchende Thätigkeit der Parteileitung herausfordern wird. Dann stellte er sich den Gerichten und nun war selbstverständlich diese Kaution fällig. Ich halte es für ganz undenkbar, daß Bamberger gesagt haben sollte: „Die Kaution ist zurückgezahlt worden, aber Dolinski darf das nicht erfahren." Dolinski mußte doch vom Gericht selbst unterrichtet werden, daß die Kaution durch seine Gestellung hinfällig geworden sei und an wen sie gezahlt werden solle. Da Rackow die Kaution gestellt hatte, ist sie nach London gesandt worden und Rackow hat sie mir überwiesen für die Parteikasse. Ich habe sie erhalten, Dolinski aber mußte davon, als der erste, unterrichtet sein.

Weiter behauptet Werner, Bamberger habe den Bierboykott in Berlin — einen der verhängnißvollsten Schritte, die je unternommen worden sind und wobei Werner der Hauptattentäter war — benutzt, um Nürnberger Bier nach Berlin zu schaffen, und für diese Organisation des Bierabsatzes von dem betreffenden Brauer Prozente erhalten. Redner weist nun des Längeren aus persönlicher Kenntniß nach, wie diese Werner'sche Behauptung unwahr und völlig grundlos sei, und fährt fort:

Es wird auch hierbei wieder nur zu klar, was für Mittel und Wege angewandt werden, jemand zu verdächtigen. Bamberger gehört zu den verhaßtesten Personen bei Werner und einigen seiner Freunde (Ruf: In ganz Berlin!) — ja, das sind die alten Redensarten, man spricht von ganz Berlin, ohne ein Recht dazu zu haben. Bamberger ist seit mehr als 20 Jahren in der Partei; eine Anzahl Personen, welche zufällig auch Reichstagsabgeordnete sind, kennen ihn, haben mit ihm verkehrt, einige häufiger, wozu ich nicht gehöre. Daß dabei auch die Berliner Vorgänge erörtert werden, liegt auf der Hand. Der weitere Umstand, daß Bamberger Prokurist beim Volksblatt ist und als solcher mit der Redaktion in Verbindung steht, macht es erklärlich, daß bei diesem Verkehr die verschiedensten Dinge besprochen werden, Gutes und Schlechtes, wie Sie wollen. Aber da man Bamberger geradezu als die Mittelsperson bezeichnet hat, die sich zwischengedrängt und systematisch auf die Verhetzung der Berliner Genossen hingearbeitet habe, so erkläre ich, daß von allem diesem kein Wort wahr ist! Ist es nicht zugleich die stärkste Beleidigung, die man uns einzeln und insgesammt anthun kann, daß ein Einzelner die Macht haben soll, uns gegen die Genossen zu verhetzen? Ich verwahre mich dagegen aufs entschiedenste (Lebhafter Beifall), ich verwahre dagegen auch alle meine Freunde; ich würde mich dessen in der Seele schämen. Als Kassirer muß ich doch am besten wissen, wie groß die Opferwilligkeit der Parteigenossen in Berlin ist; wer da bestrebt sein wollte, dieselben bei uns zu verdächtigen, der würde schön von uns heimgeschickt werden.

Eins aber muß ich erklären. Allerdings sind nicht blos erst

in der letzten Zeit, sondern vom ersten Augenblick der Wirksamkeit des Ausnahmegesetzes an, immer von einem mehr oder weniger großen Theil, mitunter blos von einzelnen, bei der Fraktion, die verschiedensten Versuche gemacht worden, die Fraktion unter das Aufsichtsrecht der Berliner Genossen zu stellen. Man hat mir sogar Deputationen geschickt, durch die man von mir Abrechnung verlangte, und Derjenige, der einmal in diesem Auftrage kam, ist hintennach unzweifelhaft als Polizeispitzel entlarvt worden. (Hört, hört! Große Bewegung.) Sie drangen auf Abhaltung von Konferenzen, welche nothwendigerweise das Material zu einem Geheimbundprozeß geliefert hätten! Weil wir dies alles wußten, haben wir solchen Zumuthungen den entschiedensten Widerspruch entgegengesetzt. (Lebhafte Zustimmung; Ruf: Mit Recht!) Wir sind dadurch in viele persönliche Unannehmlichkeiten gekommen, welche ganz wesentlich dazu beigetragen haben, allmählich eine gewisse Entfremdung zwischen einem Theil der Berliner Genossen und der Fraktion herbeizuführen. Es ist das die Schuld eines mehr oder weniger großen Theils der Berliner Genossen, welche innerhalb der Ausnahmegesetzperiode unausgesetzt diese Bestrebungen zur Geltung bringen wollten.

Ueber diese Verhältnisse und Vorgänge ist in der Fraktion ungemein oft gesprochen worden; es ist daselbst häufig zu heftigen Auseinandersetzungen gekommen, schließlich haben wir uns aber stets verständigt, wir müßten jeden solchen Versuch der Berliner, sich als kontrollirende Behörde aufzuspielen, zurückweisen. Ich will nicht weiter auf diese Dinge eingehen, ich müßte da zu Vorgängen kommen, die hier öffentlich zu erörtern für beide Theile bedenklich und unangenehm wäre. Ich glaube, ich habe genug gesagt.

Herr Werner hat weiter erklärt, er würde sich nicht nehmen lassen, Vorgänge, die zwischen einzelnen Abgeordneten und dem Redakteur der „Volkstribüne" sich abgespielt hätten, zu rügen und öffentlich zu besprechen. Es liegt hier immer wieder der fortgesetzte Versuch vor, den Verdacht zu erwecken, als gäbe es einen Menschen in der Partei oder in der Fraktion, der ihm und seinen Freunden das Recht der Kritik nehmen wollte. Aber die Kritik soll anständig, mit Wahrheit und Wahrhaftigkeit, geübt werden. Im Genter Manifest steht der schöne Satz: „Wir sind verpflichtet, gegen uns selbst und allen Menschen gegenüber Wahrheit und Wahrhaftigkeit im Umgange zu pflegen." Es möchte vielleicht nothwendig sein, diesen Satz in das Parteiprogramm aufzunehmen für die, die das nicht begreifen, und dazu gehört in erster Linie Werner. (Heiterkeit.) Schippel hat sich durch meine Mittheilungen über die Verhandlungen in der Fraktion über die Vorgänge, auf die Werner anspielt, für zufriedengestellt erklärt. Das weiß Werner, und doch tritt er immer

19

wieder mit diesen Verdächtigungen vor uns. Werner hat gesagt, Konrad Schmidt, der Redakteur der „Volkstribüne", habe ihm erklärt, daß mir aus der Redaktion des „Berliner Volksblatt" verdächtigende Aeußerungen über Berliner Genossen zugegangen seien. Ich habe zu erklären, daß Bamberger, den er hierbei im Auge hatte, bei dieser ganzen Sache nicht in Frage kommen konnte, weil er sich zu jener Zeit auf einer Erholungsreise auf Rügen befand, und daß Konrad Schmidt, mit dem ich die Sache in der freundschaftlichsten Weise besprach, wie es sich unter Genossen versteht, in Plauen, wohin er auf meine Einladung kam, mir gesagt hat, es sei ihm nun unendlich viel klar, was ihm früher nicht klar gewesen, er sei in verschiedenen Richtungen getäuscht worden. Wenn viele Genossen über die Parteiverhältnisse sich mehr zu informiren suchten, so würde unendlich viel Streit, Zank und Unannehmlichkeiten vermieden werden. (Sehr richtig!) Werner aber hat es stets verschmäht, sich an der Quelle Aufschluß zu verschaffen. Was die telephonische Mittheilung betrifft, so habe ich Schmidt gesagt, daß Baake mir die betreffende Mittheilung gemacht habe. Schmidt hat sich mit Baake ins Einvernehmen gesetzt und mir gesagt, daß meinerseits ein Irrthum vorliege; ich habe meinen Irrthum unbedingt zugegeben; ich war zu jener Zeit mit Arbeiten überhäuft, sodaß der Irrthum sehr verzeihlich war. Ich kann also nicht konstatiren, wer mir jene Mittheilung aus dem Volksblatt telephonisch zurief; Bamberger aber war es nicht, sonst hätte ich ihn an der Stimme erkannt.

Werner hat dann, entgegen den klaren und bestimmten Ausführungen des Urtheils, auch jetzt wieder erklärt, er wäre nie Unternehmer geworden, wenn er noch fernerweit in Berlin hätte Beschäftigung finden können. Ich will zugeben, daß er im Laufe seiner Thätigkeit in Berlin ein oder mehrere Male gemaßregelt worden ist. Aber ich konstatire, daß seine letzte Stellung eine solche war, daß der betreffende Buchdruckereibesitzer garnicht an seine Maßregelung gedacht hat. Der Mann hat bezeugt, daß Werner ihm freiwillig gekündigt hat mit der Motivirung, daß er sich selbstständig machen wolle. (Hört! Hört!) Ich habe nichts hinzuzufügen.

Ueber eins will ich noch in der Partei volle Klarheit schaffen. Ich wiederhole hier, daß ich selbst es auf das Allerentschiedenste verurtheilt habe, daß die Berliner „Volkszeitung" damals, als die Konflikte zwischen uns und der Opposition ausbrachen, sich in einer Art und Weise gegen die Opposition benommen und dieselbe kritisirt hat, wozu ihr nach meiner Auffassung kein Recht zustand, da sie kein Parteiblatt ist. Aber ich muß weiter erklären, daß, soviel ich unterrichtet bin, zum Mindesten kein Fraktionsmitglied hinter diesen Dingen stand. Was die Volkszeitung gethan, haben die Redakteure

auf eigene Fauſt gethan, und wenn ſie von manchen inneren Vorgängen in der Partei, die wir ſehr viel lieber begraben ſein laſſen
wollten, eine Kenntniß, die uns ſelbſt ſehr unangenehm iſt, hatten,
ſo ſind nicht wir es, durch die ſie dieſe Kenntniß erlangt haben.
(Lebhaftes Bravo!)

Von den Chemnitzer Delegirten wird folgende Reſolution
mitgetheilt:

> Die heute im Gaſthaus Wieſenthal verſammelten Partei-
> genoſſen von Chemnitz Stadt und Land erklären ſich mit der
> Haltung ihres Abgeordneten, Herrn Max Schippel, voll und ganz
> einverſtanden und beauftragen die heute zum Parteitage gewählten
> Delegirten, dieſe Reſolution dem Parteitage zu unterbreiten.

Chemnitz, 8. Oktober 1890.

Wagler. Winneberg. Heiner. Hendel. Krauß.

Schippel: Ich bin in der merkwürdigen Lage, daß ich für
einen Parteigenoſſen ſprechen muß — ich betrachte ihn als ſolchen —
mit dem ich in den letzten Monaten in ziemlich hartem Kampfe
gelegen habe. Sehe ich mir unſer Parteileben an, ſo geſtehe ich
offen, daß Werner, allerdings etwas rückſichtsloſer und weniger
anſtändig, als es ſonſt der Fall, aber doch ſo ziemlich daſſelbe
thut, was Tag für Tag in unſerer Partei maſſenhaft geſchieht.
Das Benehmen Werner's auf dieſem Kongreß war weder gut noch
beſonders anſtändig. Aber wenn ihm Geſchäftsſozialismus vorgeworfen wird: nun, wie viele ſind unter uns, über welche in
ſolchen Fällen, wo etwas nicht ſicher zu beweiſen war, doch in der
Oeffentlichkeit derartige Gerüchte kolportirt wurden? Wir haben
es ſelber hier auf dem Parteitage erlebt von einem angeſehenen
Parteigenoſſen, daß er ruhig Gerüchte als Thatſachen ausgeſprochen
hat. Unſer alter Parteigenoſſe Liebknecht, ich will nicht ſagen, daß
er die Unwahrheit wiſſentlich hat ſagen wollen, hat geſagt, er wiſſe
ganz beſtimmt, daß dem Redakteur der „Volkstribüne“ die Piſtole
auf die Bruſt geſetzt worden wäre, damit er eine Erklärung gegen ihn,
Liebknecht, aufnähme. Am nächſten Tage bekamen wir einen Brief
von Schmidt ſelber, worin er das ganz entſchieden zurückweiſt.
Nun, das iſt eben eine Art zu reden und zu kämpfen in unſerer
Partei, die ſich unter dem Sozialiſtengeſetz bei uns eingelebt hat.
Und wenn der Eine dies thut, dann wollen wir deswegen auf den
Anderen keinen Stein werfen. Herr Liebknecht hat ſogar die Erklärung
von Schmidt gehört und doch ſeine Behauptung aufrecht erhalten. Alſo,
wenn wir das alles ſoweit kontrolliren wollten, daß wir es gleichſam
gerichtlich erhärteten, dann dürfte man ſich wohl über Weniges in
der Partei ausſprechen. Ungerechtfertigte Vorwürfe wegen des
Geſchäftsſozialismus kommen in unſerer Partei alle Tage vor.
Auch Grillenberger, wie wir aus der Volksblattnotiz geſehen, hat
Werner vorgeworfen, ſeine ganze Oppoſition rühre daher, daß er

19*

das Volksblatt nicht zum Druck bekommen habe. Ich will mit Grillenberger nicht darüber rechten, daß er dies gesagt; aber er hätte vorsichtiger und sich mehr erkundigen sollen. Das sind Vermuthungen, für die der Beweis fehlt. So hat es auch Werner gemacht. Wir sollten die ganze Gelegenheit viel weniger benutzen, um Werner eine Lektion zu ertheilen, sondern wir alle sollten für uns selber eine Lehre daraus ziehen. Was Werner dutzendfach gethan, hat jeder Einzelne von uns ein oder zwei Mal gethan.

Es hat in der letzten Zeit den Anschein gewinnen können, als ob die Fraktion als Körperschaft irgendwie gegen mich vorgegangen wäre. Das hat sie niemals gethan, auch früher nicht. Die ganze Fraktion kann nicht verantwortlich gemacht werden für das, was vielleicht Zwei oder Drei einmal gethan haben. Ich konstatire weiter, daß die Fraktion sogar, wo Uebergriffe vorgekommen, diese korrigirt hat und daß die Sache für mich erledigt ist und für die Partei. Wenn Werner mal ein Wort fallen läßt, was uns nicht gefällt, so wollen wir ihm das nicht so verübeln. Entnehmen wir für uns die Lehre daraus, daß wir Alle zusammen nicht so viel unnützes Zeug schwätzen sollen.

Grillenberger: Werner hat den Thatbestand, der durch die eingehenden Zeugenvernehmungen in der Kommission festgestellt ist, verwirren wollen. Er hat behauptet, ich hätte in der Kommission erklärt, daß das, was ich in Bezug auf seinen Geschäftssozialismus wisse, mir durch Bamberger mitgetheilt sei. Dies ist unwahr. Ich habe ausdrücklich erklärt, daß das, was Anderen bekannt geworden ist über jene Geschichte, über die Vergangenheit Werner's, daß das nicht auf meine eigene Wissenschaft zurückzuführen sei, sondern daß mir die Mittheilungen darüber von Bamberger geworden sind. In Bezug auf den Geschäftssozialismus habe ich ausdrücklich angegeben, daß andere Berliner Parteigenossen Mittheilungen gemacht haben, und in der Kommission ist auch eine Reihe von Briefen verlesen worden, die mir ungefordert zugegangen sind. Also nicht die Angaben über den Geschäftssozialismus habe ich von Bamberger erhalten, sondern über die andere Affaire, auf welche die Kommission nicht eingegangen ist, weil sie zu weit in der Zeit zurückgelegen hat, als daß wir uns darüber vergewissern könnten. In Bezug auf diesen Punkt wird Werner nichts anderes übrig bleiben, als die Personen, die ihm das vorgeworfen, gerichtlich zu belangen und so den Thatbestand festzustellen.

Im Kommissionsbericht heißt es unter A: Wille habe mir persönlich den Vorwurf des Geschäftssozialismus gemacht Das ist nicht ganz richtig. Wille hat den Vorwurf erhoben gegen die gesammte Parteileitung und gegen die Partei im Allgemeinen, und als Angehöriger der Parteileitung habe ich selbstverständlich diesen Vorwurf zurückgewiesen und gesagt, Wille könne sich über den Begriff des Geschäftssozialismus durch seinen Freund Werner belehren lassen. Ich bitte, diese Aenderung im Protokoll wiederzugeben, damit mir nachher kein Vorwurf gemacht werden kann.

Herr Schippel hat gemeint, ich hätte ja auch eine Unrichtigkeit verübt, indem ich Werner vorgeworfen hätte, derselbe habe das „Berliner Volksblatt" an sich reißen wollen. Es geht aber aus meiner Erklärung klar hervor, daß die eigene Person von Werner dabei garnicht in Betracht gekommen ist. Ich habe in der Nürnberger Versammlung erklärt, daß in Berlin gewisse Leute vorhanden sind oder waren, die das „Berliner Volksblatt" gern an sich gerissen hätten. Damit meinte ich den Theil der Genossen, die zur sogenannten inneren Bewegung gehören, welche das Blatt für diese Bewegung reklamiren wollten, während die Fraktion die Absicht hatte, dasselbe zum Centralorgan der Partei zu erklären. Es war gar keine Rede davon, daß ich in jener Versammlung Werner vorgeworfen, er hätte das Volksblatt zum Druck an sich reißen wollen.

Ob Schippel ein- oder zweimal gethan, was Werner dutzendmal gethan hat, kann ich nicht untersuchen, aber ich für meine Person, und ich kann das wohl auch für meine übrigen Kollegen in der Fraktion aussprechen, wir verwahren uns dagegen, daß wir mit Werner auch nur in einem Punkt in Vergleich gestellt werden. (Sehr gut!)

Schmidt-Berlin (große Unruhe): Ich kenne keine „innere" Berliner Bewegung, sondern nur eine Berliner Bewegung. Ich bedaure, daß Werner in etwas leichtfertiger Weise Verdächtigungen gegen einzelne Personen erhoben, nur möchte ich ihn gegen den Vorwurf des Geschäftssozialismus in Schutz nehmen. Der Druck der „Volks-Tribüne" wurde ursprünglich einem Drucker übergeben, der bis dahin kein Parteigenosse war und vielleicht auch bis heute noch nicht Parteigenosse ist. Wir hatten eben in Berlin keinen Parteigenossen, der die Tribüne hätte drucken können. Mittlerweile gründete Werner eine Druckerei mit einem Genossen zusammen und wir übergaben ihm den Druck, weil er unser Gesinnungsgenosse ist. Wäre Grillenberger in Berlin gewesen, so wäre er vielleicht in Frage gekommen. Werner hat also nicht die Tribüne zu sich herübergezogen, um Geschäfte zu machen, sondern die Genossen haben in ihrer Mehrheit beschlossen, diesem Parteigenossen die „Volks-Tribüne" zum Druck zu geben. In derselben Weise verhält es sich auch mit dem Almanach. Auf Wunsch Schippel's wurde beschlossen, die „Arbeiterbibliothek" vorläufig bei dem anderen Drucker, Posekel, zu lassen, um ihm nicht sofort den ganzen Erwerb zu nehmen. Ich glaube, Grillenberger hat etwas gesündigt, wenn er sagte: unter drei Berliner Parteigenossen ist immer ein Spitzel. —

Vorsitzender Singer: Grillenberger hat nur gesagt, man sei zu gewissen Zeiten in Berlin nicht sicher gewesen, ob nicht, wenn drei Parteigenossen beieinander waren, ein Polizeispitzel dazwischen war.

Schmidt (fortfahrend): Ich nehme das Wort zurück. (Große Unruhe.) Grillenberger wird nicht bestreiten, daß die Bemerkung der „Fränkische Tagespost" von wegen der „silbernen Löffel" direkt gegen Werner gerichtet war. Nun ist ja diese Angelegenheit noch nicht ganz aufgeklärt. Aber selbst wenn es Wahrheit gewesen wäre, was Grillenberger andeutete, so ist es doch nicht nöthig, unseren Feinden das Schauspiel zu geben, in solch gehässiger Weise gegen einen Genossen vorzugehen. Wäre es wahr, dann wäre der betreffende Parteigenosse hinausgeworfen worden. Es war aber nicht gut, zum Gaudium unserer gegnerischen Presse so etwas vorzubringen. (Fortdauernde Unruhe.)

Es werden Schlußanträge gestellt.

Thierbach erklärt sich gegen den Schluß, damit nicht von den Berliner Genossen der Vorwurf erhoben werden könne, sie seien vergewaltigt worden. (Gelächter.)

Der Schluß der Debatte wird gegen eine verschwindende Minderheit angenommen.

Persönlich bemerkt:

Liebknecht: Genosse Schmidt hat mir bestritten, daß er zur Aufnahme der bekannten denunziatorischen Notiz gegen mich in die „Volks-Tribüne" genöthigt worden wäre. Ich erkläre hierauf: meine Quelle ist Herr Felgentreff gewesen, der mir noch gestern hier wiederholt hat, Schmidt habe zugegeben, er, der Redakteur, habe sich nicht erwehren können der Aufforderungen, die von gewisser Seite ihm zugegangen sind. Hier ist mein Gewährsmann, ich kolportire nichts gegen meine bessere Ueberzeugung, wie das Andere thun. Ich erkundige mich genau. Wollen Sie es untersuchen, so untersuchen Sie es.

Schippel: Ich habe vorhin ausdrücklich betont, daß ich es für selbstverständlich halte, daß Liebknecht in bester Ueberzeugung seine Aeußerung gethan hat. Aber die Quelle Felgentreff ist für mich eine trübere, als die Quelle Konrad Schmidt.

Werner: Die sog. Brockenverschwörung war nichts weiter als eine ganz gewöhnliche Landpartie, wo Männlein und Weiblein zusammen waren. (Heiterkeit.)

Warnecke beklagt sich darüber, daß ihm das Wort abgeschnitten ist; er wird sich darüber bei der Parteileitung beschweren.

Werner: Schmidt hat dem Zeugen Felgentreff in meiner Gegenwart, in Gegenwart von Zeugen erklärt, daß Niemand ihn gedrängt habe, diesen Artikel aufzunehmen. Wenn Herr Felgentreff etwas anderes zu Liebknecht gesagt hat, dann hat er gelogen. (Rufe oho! pfui!)

Schwabe-Berlin: Felgentreff ist nach dem Eingesandt auf der Volkstribüne erschienen und hat Schmidt Vorhaltungen gemacht. Eine Kommission hat über diesen Fall entschieden, und in dieser Kommission, der ich angehört habe, hat Schmidt entschieden erklärt, daß ihm von Berliner Parteigenossen kein Auftrag geworden ist, dies in die „Tribüne" hineinzusetzen. Es ist eine ganz gewöhnliche Verdächtigung gewesen, die Felgentreff hier ausgesprochen hat.

Vorsitzender Singer: Ich bin der Meinung, daß wir uns in der letzten Stunde unseres Beisammenseins nicht mit so umfangreichen Geschäftsordnungsdebatten aufhalten sollten; ich kann es überhaupt nicht genug bedauern, daß der enorme Eindruck, den unser Parteitag unstreitig auf die ganze zivilisirte Welt gemacht haben wird, beeinträchtigt wird durch Erörterung solch' kleinlicher, rein persönlicher Streitigkeiten. (Zustimmung.)

Der Vorsitzende verliest hierauf nochmals das Urtheil der Neuner-Kommission und verkündet sodann den Eingang folgender, von 10 Genossen unterzeichneten Resolution:

„Der Parteitag erklärt, daß die Anführungen Werner's über den Bericht der Neuner-Kommission keinen Gegenbeweis enthalten haben, und stimmt den Erklärungen der Kommission in jedem Punkte bei."

Die Resolution wird genügend unterstützt. Mit allen gegen etwa 24 Stimmen entscheidet der Parteitag im Sinne der eben eingegangenen Resolution:

Ein weiterer Antrag ist eingelaufen:

„Der Parteitag erklärt, nachdem er von dem Bericht der Neuner-Kommission, den der Parteitag als objektiv gehalten anerkannt hat, Kenntniß genommen, den zur Verhandlung stehenden Fall Werner gegen die Fraktion für erledigt und macht es jedem Parteigenossen zur Pflicht, im privaten wie im Parteileben stets die größte Wahrhaftigkeit zu bewähren."

Vorsitzender Singer: Dieser Antrag enthält eigentlich eine Beleidigung der Partei; ich bringe ihn nicht zur Abstimmung. Die Pflicht, im privaten wie im öffentlichen Leben sich stets wahrhaftig zu erweisen, wird wohl von jedem Parteigenossen als selbstverständlich anerkannt werden. Ich habe nur den dringenden Wunsch, daß der eben erledigte, nicht angenehme Theil der Verhandlungen des Parteitages seine Früchte dahin tragen möge, daß die künftigen Parteitage von ähnlichen Verhandlungen verschont bleiben. (Lebhafte Zustimmung.)

Namens des Parteivorstandes ersucht der Vorsitzende die Mitglieder der Parteileitung, sich Nachmittags 3 Uhr im Restaurationssaale zur Erledigung geschäftlicher Angelegenheiten zusammenzufinden.

Gottschalk-Hamburg: Das Mitglied der Parteileitung, Dubber, ist bereits abgereist.

Das Wort ergreift nunmehr

Tölcke-Dortmund (mit lebhaftem Beifall empfangen): Parteigenossen! Ich bin wohl einer der ältesten Parteigenossen in ganz Deutschland. Ich habe das Bedürfniß gefühlt, an diesem Parteitage theilzunehmen selbst dann, wenn ich mir hier den Tod geholt hätte. Ich habe die Beweggründe dazu geschöpft aus meiner langjährigen Thätigkeit in der Partei; ich bin deren Angehöriger seit dem Beginn der Arbeiterbewegung in Deutschland; ich habe fast allen Generalversammlungen des Allgemeinen Deutschen Arbeitervereins angehört, und nach der Vereinigung der beiden Fraktionen, allen Kongressen beigewohnt, bis dann meine Theilnahme an den inneren Angelegenheiten der Partei theils durch das Sozialistengesetz gehindert wurde, theils aber auch in Folge einer Verhaftung, die ich auf Grund des Preßgesetzes erduldet habe als Redakteur einer Parteizeitung in Westfalen. Während der Haft habe ich mir schwere Krankheiten zugezogen, so daß ich aus dem Gefängniß zu meiner Familie entlassen werden mußte. Ein Rest von dieser Strafe und zwei Preßstrafen blieben noch rückständig, elf Monate weniger einen Tag. Es war das 1879. Seitdem habe ich von Jahr zu Jahr von der Staatsanwaltschaft Aufschub erhalten, und zwar zehn Jahre hindurch, auf Grund eines Zeugnisses des Kreisphysikats und anderer ärztlicher Atteste, die mir bescheinigten, daß ich unmöglich den Rest meiner Strafe aushalten könnte, weil mein Leben ganz bestimmt in Gefahr kommen würde. Schließlich habe ich die Strafe nicht zu verbüßen brauchen, weil Kaiser Friedrich eine Amnestie erließ, worin auch die Preßvergehen inbegriffen waren. Ich habe mich gefragt, ob ich mich der sogenannten Amnestie fügen sollte; ich habe deshalb nicht dagegen protestirt, weil ich auch nicht im Stande gewesen wäre, die Strafe zu verbüßen, ich hätte keine acht Tage im Gefängniß zubringen können, dann wäre ich auf dem Gefängnißhofe beerdigt worden. Zu diesem Entschluß haben mich die ärztlichen Atteste gebracht, sodaß ich die Amnestie habe Amnestie sein lassen; die Staatsanwaltschaft hat unter diesen Umständen am Ende mehr Vortheil davon gehabt wie ich. Ich war früher einer der stärksten Männer Deutschlands, und nach dem Gutachten meiner Aerzte hätte ich vielleicht 100 Jahre alt werden können, wenn nicht, eine Folge der Haft, mein Körper vollständig ruinirt wäre.

Ich mußte unbedingt diesen Parteitag besuchen. Ich wollte mich überzeugen, inwieweit die sozialdemokratischen Grundsätze in Deutschland sich verbreitet und ihre Anhänger zugenommen. Ich habe die Verhandlungen dieses Parteitages mit großem Interesse und mit möglichster Aufmerksamkeit verfolgt und gefunden, daß die Partei in diesem Augenblick, nach 12jähriger Pause, eine

Sicherheit für die Weiterentwickelung ihrer Grundsätze und Bestrebungen in Deutschland bietet, wie ich sie kaum erwartet
hätte. Die wichtigsten Beschlüsse hat der Parteitag gefaßt mit
Einstimmigkeit, andere untergeordnete Punkte sind erledigt worden
mit fast eben derselben Einstimmigkeit. Die Anträge wegen vor-
gekommener Streitigkeiten sind mit möglichster Gründlichkeit erledigt worden, und ich bin überzeugt, daß von jetzt ab in der
Partei derartige Sachen kaum mehr vorkommen werden. Der
Parteitag hat endgültig auch in dieser Frage entschieden und die
Partei wird sich den gefaßten Beschlüssen, auch in anderer Beziehung, unbedingt fügen. Das ist keine absolute Disziplin, wie
man sie uns von gewisser Seite vorhalten könnte, daß man sagt,
es müsse den bekannten Vorstehern Folge geleistet werden. Aber
es muß von jedem Parteigenossen unbedingt vorausgesetzt werden,
daß er die gefaßten Beschlüsse respektirt und ihnen folgt bis sie
abgeändert werden.

Ich weiß nicht, ob es mir noch möglich sein wird an einem
künftigen Parteitag theilzunehmen. Ich habe mich auch diesmal
an der Diskussion nicht betheiligt. Ich habe mich zwar zweimal
zum Wort gemeldet bei prinzipiellen Fragen, wurde aber daran
durch die Annahme des Schlusses verhindert. Ich habe das aber
durchaus nicht bedauert, weil ich meine Theilnahme an der Diskussion
für vollständig überflüssig gehalten habe. Ich hätte Ihnen nichts
anderes sagen können, als was Sie selbst zur Sache gebracht haben.
Ich habe die Versicherung abzugeben, daß die ganzen Verhandlungen,
der Verlauf des Parteitages für mich ein durchaus erhebender
gewesen ist. Wenn ich über kurz oder lang sterbe, dann sterbe ich
getrost in der Ueberzeugung, daß die Prinzipien der Sozialdemokratie
allein die zukünftigen Geschicke der Menschheit gestalten werden.

Nun habe ich auch noch, als wohl ältester Parteigenosse unter
den anwesenden Delegirten, von vielen Seiten den Auftrag erhalten,
der Leitung des Parteitages den Dank der Delegirten auszusprechen
für die Unparteilichkeit, für die rastlose Thätigkeit und Umsicht der
Vorstandsmitglieder des Parteitages und ich bitte Sie, Ihre volle
Ueberzeugung darüber mit mir auszudrücken, daß eine bessere Leitung
gar nicht hätte stattfinden können. (Stürmisches Bravo!)

Vorsitzender Singer: Parteigenossen! Wir sind am Schluß
unserer Arbeiten angelangt. Ich will zunächst dem Gefühl herzlichen
Dankes für die soeben gehörten Worte des Seniors unserer Versammlung Ausdruck geben. Wir alle sind erfreut darüber, daß er
an diesem Parteitag hat theilnehmen können. Wir wünschen und
hoffen, daß es unserem verehrten Freund Tölcke möglich sein werde,
noch recht viele unserer Parteitage zu besuchen, und bei der geistigen
Regsamkeit und Frische, von der er eben ein glänzendes Zeugniß
abgelegt hat, bin ich überzeugt, daß wir ihn dann auch in der

Diskussion hören werden. Für die freundlichen Worte, mit welchen
Tölcke der Thätigkeit des Bureaus gedacht hat, und für Ihre Zustimmung hierzu, danke ich im Namen des gesammten Bureaus
herzlich. Ich bitte Sie, diesen Dank auch übertragen zu dürfen
auf die Genossen, welche in den Kommissionen thätig waren, und
die in gewissenhafter Erfüllung der ihnen vom Parteitage über-
tragenen Aufgaben sich nicht so lebhaft an den Verhandlungen des
Plenums betheiligen konnten, wie sie es wohl gewünscht und
beabsichtigt haben. Ich bin überzeugt, daß der Parteitag mit der
Uebertragung des Dankes an die Kommissionen einverstanden ist.
(Lebhafte Zustimmung.) Und nun werthe Genossen, lassen Sie mich
in Ihrem Namen den Halleschen Genossen unseren wärmsten Dank
aussprechen für die mühevolle, opferfreudige Thätigkeit, welche sie
nicht allein bei den Vorbereitungen für den Parteitag, sondern auch
während der Verhandlungen desselben bewiesen haben. Alle, die
mit solchen Arbeiten schon einmal beschäftigt gewesen sind, wissen,
wie schwierig gerade die befriedigende Lösung solcher Aufgaben ist;
wir alle wissen, was dazu gehört, eine Versammlung von über
vierhundert Personen häuslich so unterzubringen, daß sie sich in
den ihr zugewiesenen Räumen wohl und behaglich fühlt. Was nach
Lage der Verhältnisse möglich war, haben die Halleschen Genossen
redlich gethan. Während der Verhandlungen waren sie bemüht,
die Gastfreundschaft in ausgiebigstem Maaße zu gewähren, sie haben
unsere Thätigkeit in nie ermüdender, stets bereiter Weise unterstützt,
aber auch dafür gesorgt, daß die Geselligkeit zu ihrem Recht gekommen ist. Sie haben einen Kommers veranstaltet, der alle Theilnehmer desselben auf das Höchste befriedigt hat und den Jeder im
allerbesten Andenken behalten wird. Sie sind gewiß alle damit
einverstanden, daß ich den Halleschen Genossen für ihre thatkräftige
Unterstützung und die brüderliche Gastfreundschaft unsern wärmsten
Dank ausspreche. (Lebhafte Zustimmung.)

Gestatten Sie mir nun noch einen kurzen Rückblick auf unsere
Verhandlungen. Genossen! Wir sind zusammengekommen in dem
Bewußtsein und der Ueberzeugung, daß auf diesem Parteitage die
Einigkeit und Geschlossenheit der Partei sich glänzend manifestiren
werden. Aber die gegnerischen Parteien sowohl wie die gegnerische
Presse, welche mit wahrer Wollust in nimmersatter Gier eine
Spaltung in der sozialdemokratischen Partei herbeisehnen, hatten
dem Parteitage das Prognostikon gestellt, daß in Halle, als er[s]
Wirkung der Aufhebung des Sozialistengesetzes, die Partei si[ch]
spalten und auseinanderfallen werde.

Genossen! Unsere Verhandlungen haben gezeigt, daß dies[e]
Hoffnungen, diese Vermuthungen zwar den Wünschen der Gegne[r]
aber nicht den thatsächlichen Verhältnissen entsprochen haben. Ic[h]
darf dreist behaupten: der Beweis, daß es sich nicht um wirkli[ch]

ernsthafte, prinzipielle und taktische Gegensätze in der Partei handelt, ist in so eklatanter Weise durch unsere Verhandlungen erbracht worden, wie fast auf keinem früheren Parteitage.

Wenn man bedenkt, daß in der gegnerischen Presse systematisch seit Wochen und Monaten gehetzt worden ist, daß versucht wurde, rein persönliche Differenzen zu wirklich prinzipiellen Streitigkeiten aufzubauschen, wenn man die rastlose Minirarbeit der Gegner beobachtet hat, so muß man sagen: der Parteitag hat durch seine Verhandlungen und Beschlüsse über diese Bestrebungen ein vernichtendes Urtheil gesprochen. (Lebhafte Zustimmung.) Die Verhandlungen dieses Parteitages beweisen den Gegnern, was den Parteigenossen längst zur felsenfesten, unerschütterlichen Ueberzeugung geworden, daß derjenige, der da glaubt, auf eine Spaltung in der Sozialdemokratie rechnen zu können, sich gründlichst irrt; sie beweisen, daß die Sozialdemokratie fest und treu auf dem Boden ihrer Prinzipien und ihres Programms steht, daß in ihren Reihen zwar Meinungsverschiedenheiten möglich sind, daß aber auch diejenigen Genossen, welche in einzelnen Punkten abweichender Meinung sein mögen, sich stets dem Willen und Ausspruch der Partei unterordnen und niemals an der Einheit und Geschlossenheit der Partei rütteln werden. (Bravo!) Ich darf es aussprechen, gerade die Delegirten, welche unter dem Namen der sogenannten Opposition nach Halle gekommen sind, sie haben in ihrer erdrückenden Mehrheit durch ihr Verhalten auf dem Parteitage, namentlich durch ihr Verhalten unseren Beschlüssen gegenüber, bewiesen, daß, obgleich sie in einzelnen Punkten verschiedener Ansicht waren, das Solidaritätsgefühl in ihnen so mächtig ist, daß sie unseren Beschlüssen fast einstimmig beigetreten sind; gerade diejenigen Delegirten, auf welche unsere Feinde die größten Hoffnungen gesetzt hatten, die Berliner, haben sich durch ihre zu Protokoll gegebene Erklärung ein Denkmal für ihre Parteitüchtigkeit gesetzt, sie haben damit gezeigt, daß die Berliner Genossen nach wie vor die Alten sind und auch bleiben wollen. (Bravo!)

Genossen! Wir dürfen sicher sein, daß unsere Verhandlungen einen Ansporn bilden für weite Kreise im Volke. Wir haben uns eine Organisation geschaffen, wir haben Einrichtungen getroffen, um die Verbreitung unserer Parteiliteratur in regeren Fluß zu bringen; wir haben Stellung genommen zu dem Parlamentarismus und zu einer Reihe augenblicklich die ganze Kulturwelt bewegender Fragen, namentlich in Bezug auf die Arbeiterschutzgesetzgebung; aber auch unsere Prinzipien, das Ziel, welchem wir zustreben, haben wir vor aller Welt klargelegt. Wir sind was wir waren, und bleiben was wir sind: die Partei der Armen und Ausgebeuteten, welche erst mit der Beseitigung der Klassenherrschaft ihre Aufgabe erfüllt sieht. Der Zusammentritt und der Verlauf dieses

Parteitages hat bewiesen, daß es keine Macht der Erde giebt, welche mit der Sozialdemokratie fertig wird! Es ist durch unsere Verhandlungen sichergestellt, daß wir nach wie vor unentwegt und unbeirrt unsere Bahnen ziehen, daß wir nicht ruhen und rasten werden, bis das große Ziel erreicht ist, dem wir uns zugeschworen haben, das Ziel der Befreiung der Proletarier aller Länder! (Stürmischer Beifall.)

Beim Schluß unserer Verhandlungen wollen wir uns geloben, daß Jeder, nach seinem besten Wissen und Können, dem Banner, welches jetzt wieder frei entfaltet in Deutschland weht, in alter Treue dient. Unsere Fahne, das Wahrzeichen der Menschenliebe, der Freiheit, Gleichheit und Brüderlichkeit ruft uns! Wohlan, lassen Sie uns unsere Standarten der Arbeiterklasse zu immer neuen Kämpfen, zu immer neuen Siegen vorantragen. Hoch die deutsche, dreimal hoch die internationale, völkerbefreiende Sozialdemokratie! hoch! und abermals hoch! und zum dritten Mal hoch! (Die Versammlung hat sich erhoben und fällt in stürmischer Begeisterung in die Hochrufe ein. Stehend singen die Delegirten darauf die erste Strophe der Arbeitermarseillaise.)

Vorsitzender Singer: Hiermit erkläre ich die Verhandlungen des Parteitages der deutschen Sozialdemokratie, der nach dem Fall des Sozialistengesetzes zum ersten Mal seit 13 Jahren wieder auf deutschem Boden getagt hat, für geschlossen.

Schluß 2 Uhr.

Vor Schluß des Parteitages sind abgereist die Delegirten: Altermann, Eims, Goldstein, Grünberg, Knuth, Nelleßen, Pelz, Riemann, Schiel, Schuhmacher, Schäfer-Metz, Sperka, Stern, Stolle-Meerane, Wehner, Wendt.

Nichtverhandelte Anträge;

laut Beschluß des Parteitages — cfr. Protokoll Seite 253 — dem Parteivorstand zur Erledigung event. zur Berücksichtigung überwiesen.

Gruppe III.

1. Unterzeichneter beantragt die Gründung eines Blattes in Elsaß-Lothringen. Böhle-Straßburg i. E.

2. Unterzeichnete stellen den Antrag, daß der künftige Partei-Vorstand beauftragt wird, mit aller Energie dahin zu wirken, in Elsaß-Lothringen ein Partei-Organ ins Leben zu rufen und die dazu erforderlichen Mittel aus der Parteikasse zu bewilligen.

Böhle. Hickel-Straßburg i. E. J. Haug-Mühlhausen i. E.

3. Der Kongreß möge beschließen, auf Kosten der Partei eine speziell für Elsaß-Lothringen passende Agitationsbroschüre in deutscher und französischer Sprache zu schaffen.

Thies-Mannheim.

4. Die durch den Schuhmacher Julius Zarbock auf dem sozial-demokratischen Parteitage zu Halle a. S. vertretenen Genossen des Bromberger Wahlkreises beantragen:

Der Parteitag wolle beschließen, daß eine in polnischer Sprache einmal wöchentlich erscheinende Zeitung zu dem viertel-jährlichen Preise von 75 Pfennige herausgegeben werde. Der Zweck des Blattes soll sein: der großen Masse der Land-bevölkerung die sozialdemokratischen Anschauungen in gemeinver-ständlicher Weise zugänglich zu machen.

5. Die Unterzeichneten beantragen hierdurch zu Punkt 7 der Tagesordnung „die Presse" die Unterstützung der Gründung einer wöchentlich einmal erscheinenden Zeitung in polnischer Sprache für Posen, Schlesien und das russische und österreichische Polen. Die Herausgabe hat in Breslau zu erfolgen.

Fritz Kunert und Genossen.

6. Unterzeichneter beantragt, in Erwägung, daß als Kampf- und Agitationsmittel die Presse absolut nothwendig ist, der Partei-tag wolle beschließen, daß aus Parteifonds in denjenigen Wahl-kreisen, wo die sozialdemokratische Parteibewegung eine fruchtbare Zukunft zu erwarten hat, die Gründung von sozialdemokratischen Blättern zu erleichtern sei. H. Krewinkel-Aachen und Genossen.

7. Die durch den Kaufmann Robert Rüger auf dem sozial-demokratischen Parteitage zu Halle a. S. vertretenen Genossen des 6. hannoverschen Wahlkreises beantragen:

Der Parteitag wolle beschließen, daß neben dem Centralorgan eine täglich erscheinende Zeitung zum vierteljahrespreise von 1 Mark herausgegeben werde. Der Zweck des Blattes soll sein, der großen Masse der Landbevölkerung die sozialdemokratischen Anschauungen in gemeinverständlicher Weise zugänglich zu machen.

8. Es ist ein Unterhaltungsblatt herauszugeben, welches, in unserem Sinne geschrieben, sämmtlichen sozialdemokratischen Zeitungen als Wochenbeilage dient.

Volderauer-Karlsruhe. Hans Arnold.

9. Der Parteitag beschließt:

Der Parteivorstand ist gehalten, allmonatlich, unter Hinzu-ziehung ihm geeignet erscheinender Kräfte, eine Agitations-nummer, gerichtet an die indifferenten Arbeiter und Arbeiterinnen, besonders an die ländliche Bevölkerung, herauszugeben. Diese Flug-schrift ist unentgeltlich an die Genossen größerer, an die Landbistrikte angrenzender Städte zu senden, und von diesen besonders auf dem Lande zu verbreiten.

Halle a. S., den 13. Oktober 1890.

Auerbach-Berlin. Berndt-Berlin, 5. Wahlkreis. Jacobick-Berlin, 5. Wahlkreis. Werner-Teltow-Beeskow. Wernicke-Teltow-Beeskow. Schütze-Teltow-Beeskow. Schäfer-Metz. Frantzen-M.-Gladbach. Ebert-Düsseldorf. Wilh. Busch-Neuß-Grevenbroich. H. Heine-Düsseldorf. Wilke-Braunschweig, Kreis Holzminden, Ruppin-Templiner Kreis. Fr. Riengs-Konitz. Zubeil. J. Jensen-Stade. J. Schmalfeldt-Stade. Troßlener-Grevesmühlen. Peters-Schwerin i. Mecklbg. v. Wietersheim-Hamm-Soest. Klüß-Elmshorn. Florin-Halle a. S. Pittack-Rendsburg. Heinr. Mahlke. Steph. Heinzel. H. Lienem. W. Kellermann. W. Benthien. H. Schwertfeger. H. Paegelow. Emil Busch-Güstrow.

10. Die Genossen des Wahlkreises Friedberg-Büdingen be-antragen, der Parteitag wolle beschließen, in den ländlichen Wahl-kreisen von Zeit zu Zeit, auf Kosten der Partei, ein Flugblatt er-scheinen zu lassen, welches geeignet ist, die Agitation, den anti-semitischen wie den anderen reaktionären Bestrebungen gegenüber, zu fördern. H. Westphal. H. Prinz-Friedberg-Büdingen.

11. Der Parteitag wolle beschließen, der künftigen Partei-leitung aufzugeben, für die Broschürenliteratur größere Summen zu verwenden, besonders Schriften für die ländliche Arbeiter-bevölkerung herauszugeben. Auch möge ein Preis ausgesetzt werden

für die Abfassung einer Schrift, gerichtet an die ländlichen Arbeiter, in welcher in populärer Weise unsere Forderungen klargelegt werden. Dieser Vorschlag ist übrigens nicht neu, sondern er wurde kurz vor Erlaß des Sozialistengesetzes gemacht.

Die Gründung von Zeitungen für ländliche Arbeiter, welche uns in Aussicht gestellt wird, ist mit Freuden zu begrüßen. Es ist aber nothwendig, daß Leute, welche doch nur eine geringere Kenntniß unserer politischen und sozialen Verhältnisse haben, zuerst im allgemeinen aufgeklärt werden müssen. Otto Jochem-Danzig.

12. Die Unterzeichneten beantragen:

Den Parteivorstand aufzufordern, eine umfassende Geschichte der deutschen Arbeiterbewegung, die unmittelbar aus den Quellen, mit gründlicher Verwerthung des gesammten Materials, gearbeitet ist, abfassen zu lassen.

Begründung.

Es handelt sich bei dem Gegenstand des Antrages gleichmäßig um eine Ehrenpflicht, wie um ein praktisches Interesse unserer Partei.

Bei dem ausnahmslos tendenziösen, die Thatsachen verfälschenden Charakter der Literatur über die deutsche Arbeiterbewegung ist es Ehrenpflicht, eine Darstellung zu veranlassen, die der Entwickelung unserer Partei und ihren Bestrebungen gerecht wird.

Bei dem Umstand aber, daß die genaue Kenntniß unserer eigenen Geschichte eine der Bürgschaften für das sichere und in glücklichen Bahnen sich bewegende Fortschreiten der Partei bildet, ist das an jene Untersuchung sich knüpfende Interesse auch von hoher, praktischer Bedeutung.

Dieses Interesse wird vollkommen nur dann gewahrt werden, wenn die geforderte Untersuchung nicht auf eine Glorifizirung unserer Partei hinausläuft, sondern mit der Strenge und Unparteilichkeit wissenschaftlicher Methode Licht und Schatten gleichmäßig gerecht vertheilt. Wir verlangen darum eine wissenschaftliche Arbeit, die dabei in einer schönen, allgemein verständlichen Sprache geschrieben sein soll.

Wir fordern die Untersuchung im jetzigen Moment, weil der 30. September 1890 den Abschluß einer geschichtlichen Epoche bedeutet, und weil gegenwärtig, besser als in einem späteren Zeitpunkt, das für die Arbeit nöthige Quellenmaterial vollständig beschafft werden kann. Kaden-Dresden u. Genossen.

Gruppe IV.

1. In Erwägung, daß die ländlichen Wahlkreise in Deutschland seither nicht in der Weise bearbeitet werden konnten, wie dies mit Rücksicht auf die proletarische Bevölkerung dieser Gegenden geboten erscheint;

in fernerer Erwägung, daß die Unterstützung solcher Wahlkreise aus Parteimitteln für die Ausbreitung unserer Prinzipien nur
von Vortheil sein kann, beschließt der Parteitag:

Der Parteivorstand wird ermächtigt, mehr als dies seither
geschehen, die ländlichen Wahlkreise Deutschlands finanziell und
agitatorisch zu unterstützen.

Müller-Darmstadt u. Genossen.

2. Der Parteitag wolle beschließen, daß dafür Sorge getragen
wird, daß bei der ländlichen Bevölkerung mehr für Aufklärung
gethan wird, und zwar sowohl durch Auswahl einer geeigneten
Literatur, als auch durch Anstellung von Agitatoren.

Chr. Schrader-Osnabrück.

3. Der Parteitag ermächtigt den Parteivorstand, größere Geld-
mittel der Parteipresse in denjenigen Landestheilen, wie z. B.
Posen, Elsaß-Lothringen, Ost- und Westpreußen und Thüringen
zuzuwenden, wo unsere Genossen nicht in der Lage sind, aus
eigenen Mitteln die Parteipresse in der nöthigen Weise zu fördern.

Carl Schultze-Königsberg und Genossen.

4. Die Genossen des Kreises Waldenburg beantragen hiermit,
fernerhin die Agitation in der Provinz viel mehr zu fördern und die
tüchtigsten Agitatoren zu senden, damit die Provinz ebenfalls in
gleicher Linie marschiren kann mit der Großstadt, und nicht, wie
es bisher geschehen, wo bloß die Großstädte die beste Agitation genossen haben. Jüttner.

5. Der Parteitag beschließt:

In den ländlichen Bezirken Distriktsorganisatoren oder Ver-
trauensleute zu ernennen, welche, wenn es die Umstände erheischen,
in einer von der Parteileitung zu bestimmenden Höhe entschädigt
werden.

Die Ernannten haben die Verpflichtung, der Parteileitung
mindestens allmonatlich einen Bericht über ihre Thätigkeit einzu-
senden. A. Kerrl-Bremen.

6. Der Parteitag wolle beschließen:

Den Agitatoren und Rednern der Partei, die nicht Abgeordnete
sind, in Anbetracht, daß den ersteren das zur Agitation jeweilig
wichtigste Material selten zu Gebote steht, von Partei- bezw. Vor-
standswegen, die etwaigen statistischen, stenographischen oder sonst
wichtigen Unterlagen parlamentarischer Körperschaften, wenn möglich, zugänglich zu machen. Des Weiteren, vor jeder Reichstagswahl einen „Leitfaden für die Agitation" nach Art der „Parlamentarischen Thätigkeit der Reichs- und Landtage" auf Kosten
der Partei erscheinen zu lassen. Goldstein-Dresden.

Präsenz-Liste.

Name	Wohnort	Vertreter des Wahlkreises
Abel	Siegen	Wittgenstein-Siegen
Agster	Stuttgart	Göppingen-Gemünd
Albrecht	Halle a. S.	Delitzsch-Bitterfeld
Altermann	Nossen	Nossen-Roßwein
Anderhub	Hechtsheim	Mainz
Apel	Frankenhausen	Schwarzburg-Rudolstadt
Arnold	Konstanz	Ueberlingen
Aßmann	Braunschweig	Holzminden
Auer	Berlin	
Auerbach	Berlin	Berlin V
Baerer	Harburg	Harburg-Buxtehude
Bamberger	Berlin	Rinteln-Hofgeismar
Bartels	Halberstadt	Oschersleben-Halberstadt
Barth	Berlin	Berlin III.
Bartling	Limmer	Münden-Hameln.
Bauer	Plauen	Plauen i. V.
Bauer	Nieder-Zwönitz	Stollberg-Schneeberg
Baumgarten*)	Hamburg	Hamburg III.
Bebel	Berlin	
Becker	Hannover	Hannover
Beetz	Marktzeulen	Kronach
Behrend	Plötzin	Jüterbogt-Luckenwalde
Behrend	Frankfurt a. O.	Frankfurt-Lebus
Beneke	Celle	Fallersleben-Gifhorn
Bennewitz	Oberlungwitz	Glauchau-Meerane
Benthien	Kleinen	Schwerin-Wismar
Bentrup	Flensburg	{ Apenrade-Flensburg / Tondern-Husum
Berndt, Franz	Berlin	Berlin IV.
Berndt, Fritz	Berlin	Berlin V.
Berndt	Guben	Guben-Lübben
Berthold	Darmstadt	Worms-Heppenheim
Bertram	Hannover	Hildesheim
Beyer	Schönefeld-Leipz.	Leipzig, Land
Bieber	Spremberg	Cottbus-Spremberg
Birk	München	{ München I / Kaufbeuren
Blohm, Frau	Hamburg	Harburg-Buxtehude

*) Berschied während der Verhandlung des Parteitages am 17. Oktober.

Name	Wohnort	Vertreter des Wahlkreises
Blos	Stuttgart	Pforzheim
Bock	Gotha	Gotha
Böhle	Straßburg i. E.	Straßburg, Stadt*)
Böttcher	Chemnitz	Chemnitz
Borkmann	Grabow a. O.	Randow-Greifenhagen
Bräuer	Velten	Potsdam-Osthavelland
Breder	Nürnberg	Nürnberg
Breil	Hagen i. W.	Hagen
Bremer	Magdeburg	Magdeburg
Brey	Hannover	Lüchow-Uelzen
Brühne	Frankfurt a. M.	Usingen-Höchst-Homburg
Bruhns	Bremen	Bremen
Buchwald	Altenburg	Sachsen-Altenburg
Burkhardt	Glauchau	Glauchau-Merane
Busch	Güstrow	Güstrow-Ribnitz
Busch	Neuß	Neuß-Grevenbroich
Colbitz	Crimmitschau	Zwickau-Crimmitschau
Dahlen	Halberstadt	Halberstadt-Oschersleben
Daßbach	Hanau	Hanau-Gelnhausen-Orb
Demmler	Geyer	Stollberg-Schneeberg
Dick	Heidenheim	Ulm-Heidenheim
Dietz	Stuttgart	
Dittus	Pforzheim	Pforzheim
Doerr	Mainz	Bingen-Alzey
Dreesbach	Mannheim	Mannheim
Dubber	Hamburg	Hamburg I
Eckert	Cölln b. Meißen	Meißen
Ehrhardt	Ludwigshafen	Speyer
Eims	Mittweida	Mittweida-Limbach
Eitzinger	Nürnberg	Nürnberg
Emmel	Frankfurt a. M.	Aschaffenburg
Epple	Stuttgart	Stuttgart
Erbert	Düsseldorf	Düsseldorf
Erfurth	Herzberg	Goslar
Ernst	Berlin	Berlin VI
Ernst	München	Schweinfurt
Ewald	Brandenbrg. a. H.	Westhavelland
Faber	Frankfurt a. O.	Frankfurt-Lebus
Feer	Schweinfurt	Schweinfurt
Feiler	Neustadt a. O.	Weida-Auma
Felber	Augsburg	Augsburg
Fell	Plagwitz	Leipzig, Land
Fichtmann	Elbing	Elbing-Marienburg
Fischer	London	Aichach-Lechhausen

---

*) Die Wahl, welche in Straßburg durch die Polizei verhindert wurde, fand in Kehl i. Baden statt.

Name	Wohnort	Vertreter des Wahlkreises
Fischer	Mühlhausen i. Th.	Mühlhausen-Langensalza
Flaßig	Finsterwalde	Kalau-Luckau
Fleischmann	Wiesbaden	Caffel
Foerster	Hamburg	Greiz (Reuß ä. L.)
Franßen	M.-Gladbach	M.-Gladbach
Frauenlob	Potschappel	Ger.-Bez. Dresden
Friedrich	Eisenach	Eisenach
Friesecke	Rathenow	Westhavelland
Fritz	Berlin	Berlin III
Fröhlich	Katscher O.-Schl.	Leobschütz
Frohme	Hamburg	Altona
Funke	Hastedt	Bremen
Galm	Seligenstadt	Dieburg-Offenbach
Geck	Offenburg	Offenburg
Gentzel	Nordhausen	Nordhausen
Germer	Großprießligk	Borna-Pegau
Geserick	Egeln	Wanzleben
Gewehr	Elberfeld	Barmen-Elberfeld
Geyer	Leipzig	Leipzig, Land
Giertz	Weimar	Weimar-Apolda
Gießhoit	Berlin	Berlin VI
Glocke	Berlin	{ Jerichow I und II Nordhausen
Göschl	München	München I
Gößenberger	München	München II
Goldbach	Anger-Crottendf.	Leipzig, Stadt
Goldstein	Dresden	Meißen
Gottschalk	Hamburg	Hamburg II
Greiner	Sonneberg	Sonneberg
Grenz	Chemnitz	Annaberg-Eibenstock
Grillenberger	Nürnberg	{ Nürnberg Regensburg
Grimpe	Elberfeld	Barmen-Elberfeld
Grothe	Halle a. S.	Saalkreis Halle
Grothe	Sprottau	Sagan-Sprottau
Grünberg	Hartha	Nossen-Roßwein
Gründel	Berlin	Berlin III
Grundstein	Ebingen	{ Reutlingen-Tübingen Bahingen-Rottweil
Guhmann	Döbeln [beiterin.	Nossen-Roßwein
Gundelach, Frau	Magdeburg Ar-	Magdeburg
Guttenstein	Karlsruhe i. B.	Karlsruhe
Haburg	Potsdam	Potsdam-Osthavelland
Haeckel	Berlin	Schönau-Hirschberg
Hähle	Gablenz b. Chmn.	Chemnitz
Hänsler	Mannheim	Mannheim
Häuschen	Jahnsbach	Zschopau-Gelenau

20*

Name	Wohnort	Vertreter des Wahlkreises
Hager	Gladbach	Mühlheim-Wipperfürth
Hahn	Gera	Reuß j. L.
Hahnfeld	Essen a. R.	Essen a. R.
Haug, F.	Freiburg i. B.	Freiburg i. B.
Haug, I.	Mülhausen	Mühlhausen i. E.
Heilmann	Zierndorf	Erlangen-Fürth
Heine	Düsseldorf	Düsseldorf
Heine	Halberstadt	
Heinrich	Altona	Altona
Heinzel	Kiel	Kiel-Rendsburg
Heisig	Breslau	Breslau-West
Herbert	Stettin	Stettin
Herrling	Sangerhausen	Sangerhausen-Eckartsberga
Herrmann	Gronau	Tecklenburg-Ahaus
Herrmann	Dresden	Dresden r. d. Elbe
Herzog	Leutersdorf	Zittau
Hickel	Mülhausen i. E.	Mühlhausen i. E.
Hildebrandt	Gotha	Gotha
Hillmer	Hamburg	Hamburg II
Hirsch	Weißensee	Niederbarnim
Hirschmeier	Neustadt O.-S.	Neustadt O.-S.
Hochbaum	Olvenstedt	Neuhaldensleben-Wolmirstedt
Höhle	Büdelsdorf	Schleswig
Höppner	Cotta	Ger.-Bez. Dresden.
Hoffmann	Merseburg	Merseburg-Querfurt
Hoffmann	Zeitz	Naumburg-Zeitz
Hofmann	Saalfeld	{ Schwarzburg-Rudolstadt Sonneberg-Saalfeld
Hofrichter	Kalk	Köln a. R. Landkreis
Hogreve	Wandsbeck	Altona
Hoppe	Lüdenscheid	Altona-Iserlohn
Horn	Löbtau	Ger.-Bez. Dresden
Hosang	Dessau	Dessau-Zerbst
Hüttig	Gößnitz	Sachsen-Altenburg
Hug	Bant	{ Weener-Leer-Emden Aurich-Wilhelmshafen Oldenburg Varel Delmenhorst
Hugo	Eschwege	Eschwege-Schmalkalden
Jacobick	Berlin	Berlin V
Jahn	Greiz	Reuß ä. L.
Janiszewski	Berlin	{ Berlin II Posen
Jensen	Stade	Otterndorf-Neuhaus
Jeup	Gelsenkirchen	Bochum
Ihrer, Frau	Velten Arbeiterin.	Berlin
Jochem	Danzig	Danzig-Stadt

Name	Wohnort	Vertreter des Wahlkreises
Joest	Mainz	Mainz
Johannes	Zittau	Zittau
Johannsen	Einbeck	Einbeck-Northeim
Jüttner	Waldenburg i.Schl.	Waldenburg i. Schl.
Kaben	Dresden	Dresden r. d. Elbe
Kaempfe	Bamberg	Bamberg
Kahl	Duisburg a. Rh.	Duisburg
Kalnbach	Karlsruhe	Bretten-Sinsheim
Kambach	Kunersdorf	Schönau-Hirschberg
Kandt	Rostock	Rostock-Doberan
Kater	Barleben	Neuhaldensleben-Wolmirstedt
Katurbe	Burg	Jerichow I u. II
Kaulich	Halle a. S.	Saalkreis Halle
Keck	Fürth	Erlangen-Fürth
Kegel	München	Bamberg
Keinitz	Wurzen	Oschatz
Keller	Görlitz	Lauban-Görlitz
Kellermann	Itzehoe	Nord- und Süd-Dithmarschen
Kenfenheuer	M.-Gladbach	Mühlheim-Wipperfurth
Kerrl	Bremen	{ Bremen / Lippe-Detmold
Keßler	Berlin	Bernburg
Kettel	Oberweimar	Weimar-Apolda
Kießling	Braunschweig	Braunschweig
Kittler	Heilbronn	Heilbronn-Besigheim
Klees	Magdeburg	Magdeburg
Klein	Berlin	Berlin II
Kloß	Stuttgart	{ Stuttgart / Böblingen-Vaihingen
Klüß	Elmshorn	Nord- und Süd-Dithmarschen
Knuth	Uetersen	Ottensen-Pinneberg
König	Remscheid	Lennep-Mettmann
Körner	Cöthen	Bernburg
Köster	Gr. Ottersleben	Wanzleben
Kokosky	Braunschweig	Braunschweig
Konrad	Mainz	Mainz
Kramer	Kirchberg	Kirchberg-Auerbach
Kretschmann	Hamburg	Rostock-Doberan
Kretschmer	Harburg	{ Harburg-Buxtehude / Lüneburg-Winsen
Krewinkel	Aachen	Aachen
Kricke	Naumburg a. S.	Naumburg-Zeitz
Kühn	Langenbielau	Reichenbach-Neurode
Kunert	Breslau	
Kurth	Kalk	Köln a. Rh. Landkreis
Lampe	Quittelsdorf	Schwarzburg-Rudolstadt
Langenstein	Plauen i. B.	Plauen i. B.

Name	Wohnort	Vertreter des Wahlkreises
Langer	Chemnitz	Chemnitz
Langner	Breslau	Breslau-West
Lauke	Dessau	Dessau-Zerbst
Lechte	Bovenden	Göttingen-Münden
Lenz	Remscheid	Lennep-Mettmann
Leutert	Apolda	Weimar-Apolda
Leven	Wald	Solingen
Liebknecht	Berlin	{ Gießen / Cassel
Liefländer	Berlin	Potsdam-Osthavelland
Lienau	Neumünster	Kiel-Rendsburg
Löwenstein	Nürnberg	Hof
Lorenz	Königsberg i. Pr.	Königsberg (Stadt)
Lücke	Köln a. Rh.	Cöln a. Rh. Stadtkreis
Lütjens	Hamburg	Hamburg I
Lutz	Baden-Baden	{ Pforzheim / Baden-Rastadt
Maier	Frankfurt a. M.	Frankfurt a. M.
Malke	Flensburg	{ Hadersleben-Sonderburg / Apenrade-Flensburg
Mathies	Elbingerode	Goslar
Meist	Köln a. Rh.	Lennep-Mettmann
Meister	Hannover	{ Grönenberg-Melle / Einbeck-Northeim / Fallersleben-Gifhorn
Messing	Dresden	Dresden links der Elbe
Metzger	Hamburg	
Metzner	Berlin	Berlin I.
Meyer	Hamburg	Hamburg III
Meyer	Pirmasens	Zweibrücken
Millarg	Berlin	Friedeberg-Arnswalde
Mösler	Gotha	Gotha
Molkenbuhr	Ottensen	Ottensen-Pinneberg
Moritz	Köln a. Rh.	Köln a. Rh., Stadtkr.
Müller	Bamberg	Bamberg
Müller	Berlin	Glatz-Habelschwerdt
Müller	Darmstadt	{ Darmstadt / Erbach-Bensheim
Müller	Dresden	Dresden, links der Elbe
Müller	Schkeuditz	Merseburg-Querfurth
Nelleffen	Süchteln	Kempen a. Rh.
Neu	Reichenbach	Kirchberg-Auerbach
Neubeck	Brandenbrg. a. H.	Westhavelland
Niemann	Rheydt	M.-Gladbach
Noak	Eilenburg	Delitzsch-Bitterfeld

Name	Wohnort	Vertreter des Wahlkreises
Oertel	Nürnberg	{ Bayreuth Forchheim
Ohlig	Heusenstamm	Dieburg-Offenbach
Orb	Offenbach a. M.	Dieburg-Offenbach
Orbig	Gießen	{ Gießen Wetzlar-Altenkirchen
Pägelow	Parchim	Parchim
Palmer	Eutritzsch	Leipzig, Stadt
Pape	Lübeck	Lübeck
Pelz	Nürnberg	Ansbach-Schwabach
Peters	Schwerin	Schwerin-Wismar
Petersen	Berlin	Berlin IV
Pfannkuch	Cassel	Cassel
Pinkau	Thonberg	Leipzig, Stadt
Pittack	Rendsburg	Kiel-Rendsburg
Plasse	Friedrichsberg	Niederbarnim
Plorin	Halle a. S.	Halle-Giebichenstein
Poitzmann	Goslar	Goslar
Porges	Buchholz	Annaberg-Eibenstock
Postelt	Dresden	Löbau-Ebersbach
Potthast	Hannover	Hannover
Prinz	Frankfurt a. M.	Friedberg
Proß	Eßlingen	Eßlingen-Nürtingen
Raecker	Burgsteinfurt	Tecklenburg-Ahaus
Rebner	Wurzen	Oschatz
Reinemer	Erbenheim	Cassel
Reißhaus	Erfurt	{ Erfurt-Schleusingen Sonneberg-Saalfeld
Rempe	Essen	Essen a. R.
Richter	Striegau	Jauer-Bolkenhain
Riemann	Chemnitz	Freiberg-Dederau
Riepold	Rheine	Tecklenburg-Ahaus
Riesop		Konitz
Röder	Schneeberg	Stollberg-Schneeberg
Rohleder	Elsterberg	Kirchberg-Auerbach
Rüdt, Dr.	Heidelberg	{ Müllheim Lahr Heidelberg Kaiserslautern
Rüger	Verden	Verden-Hoya
Salomon	Wriezen	Oberbarnim
Schaefer, A.	Augsburg	Augsburg
Schaefer, Fr.	Metz	Metz
Schalling	Olbernhau	Zschopau-Gelenau
Schenck	Greiz	Reuß ä. L.
Scherm	Nürnberg	Kronach

Name	Wohnort	Vertreter des Wahlkreises
Schibolsky	Bernau	Niederbarnim
Schiel	Coblenz	Coblenz-St. Goar
Schippel	Friedrichshagen	
Schlichtholz	Coswig	Dessau-Zerbst
Schlossared	Brieg	Brieg-Namslau
Schmalfeldt	Stabe	Stade-Bremervörde
Schmid	München	München II
Schmidt	Berlin	Berlin IV
Schmidt	Blankenburg	Braunschweig
Schmidt	Bernburg	Bernburg
Schmidt	Burgstädt	Mittweida-Limbach
Schmidt	Querfurt	Merseburg-Querfurt
Schmidt	Zwickau	Zwickau-Crimmitschau
Schnabel	Dresden	Pirna
Schneidenbach	Brunndöbra	Plauen i. B.
Schönfeld	Dresden	{ Dresden links der Elbe { Bautzen
Scholz	Berlin	Berlin IV
Schrader	Osnabrück	Osnabrück-Jburg
Schröder	Dortmund	Dortmund
Schütz	Breslau	Breslau-Ost
Schütz	Rixdorf	Telt.-Beesk.-Stork.Charlottenb.
Schulenburg	Osterode	Einbeck-Northeim
Schultze	Königsberg i. Pr.	Königsberg-Stadt
Schultze	Magdeburg	Magdeburg
Schulz, G.	Berlin	Coburg
Schulz	Jena	Weida-Auma
Schulze	Erfurt	{ Weimar-Apolda { Erfurt-Schleusingen
Schumacher	Solingen	Solingen
Schwabe	Berlin	Berlin VI
Schwartz	Zeitz	Naumburg-Zeitz
Schwartz	Lübeck	Lübeck
Schwarz	Hamburg	Hamburg III
Schweer	Hamburg	Hamburg I
Schwerdtfeger	Neubrandenburg	Meklenburg-Strelitz
Segitz	Fürth	Würzburg
Seifert	Zwickau	
Seige	Poeßneck	Sonneberg-Saalfeld
Semmler	Limbach	Limbach-Mittweida
Sievers	Limmer	Münden-Hameln
Singer	Berlin	Fallersleben-Gifhorn
Sittig	Hannover	Hannover
Slomke	Bielefeld	Bielefeld
Sperka	Stuttgart	Stuttgart
Spindler	Zschopau	Zschopau-Gelenau
Stadthagen	Berlin	
Stamm	Bautzen	Bautzen

Name	Wohnort	Vertreter des Wahlkreises
Stamm	Cannstadt	Cannstadt-Ludwigsburg / Backnang-Hall
Starke	Bunzlau	Bunzlau-Lüben
Steinbach, Frau	Gera Arbeiterin.	Gera
Steinfatt	Hamb.-Eimsbüttel	Oldenburg-Plön
Steiten	Meerane	Glauchau-Meerane
Stengele	Hamburg	Hamburg II
Stephan	Hildesheim	Hildesheim
Stephan	Oschatz	Oschatz
Stern	Stuttgart	Cannstadt-Ludwigsburg / Backnang-Hall
Stölzer	Tangermünde	Stendal-Osterburg
Stolle, W.	Gesau	
Stolle, H.	Meerane	Borna-Pegau
Stolz	Liegnitz	Haynau-Liegnitz
Strobel	Ravensburg	Ravensburg-Tettnang
Stürmer	Barmen	Barmen-Elberfeld
Sturm	Speier	Speier
Tabert	Luckenwalde	Jüterbogk-Luckenwalde
Taeterow	Berlin	Berlin I
Tewes	Schwelm	Hagen
Theiß	Langenfelde	Ottensen-Pinneberg
Thierbach	Berlin	Königsberg N.-M.
Thies	Mannheim	Mannheim
Titze	Breslau	Breslau, Ost
Titze	Minden i. W.	Minden-Lübbecke
Tölcke	Dortmund	Dortmund
Trautmann	Quedlinburg	Quedlinburg
Trosiener	Schwerin	Hagenau-Grevesmühlen
Tutzauer	Berlin	
Ullrich	Offenbach	
Ulrich	Heidingsfeld	Würzburg
Urban	Forst i. L.	Sorau
Urban	München	München I
Vetterlein	Gera	Reuß j. L.
Vogel	Marienthal	Zwickau-Crimmitschau
Vogenitz	Altenburg	Sachsen-Altenburg
Volderauer	Karlsruhe	Villingen / Karlsruhe
v. Vollmar	München	München II / Rosenheim / Passau / Straubing / Weilheim / Ingolstadt / Landshut / Illertissen

Name	Wohnort	Vertreter des Wahlkreises
Wassermann	Braunschweig	Kreis Helmstedt
Watermann	Geestemünde	Otterndorf-Neuhaus
Wehner	Salzungen	Meiningen-Hildburghausen.
Weichelt	Pirna	Pirna
Weisel	Arnstadt	Schwarzburg-Sondershausen.
Wenbler	Erlangen	Erlangen-Fürth
Wendt	Penzlin	Malchin-Waren
Weniger	Harburg	Harburg-Buxtehude
Wentzel	Halberstadt	Halberstadt
Wernau	Berlin	Berlin VI / Landsberg a. W.-Soldin
Werner	Berlin	Telt.-Beesk.-Stork.Charlottenb.
Werner	Köln a. R.	Köln a. R. Stadtkr.
Wernicke	Charlottenburg	Telt.-Beesk.-Stork.Charlottenb.
Wesch	Crefeld	Crefeld
Westphal	Frankfurt a. M.	Friedberg
v. Wietersheim	Soest	Hamm-Soest
Wilke	Braunschweig	Kreis Holzminden / Ruppin-Templin
Wilschke	Berlin	Berlin II
Wittmann	Suhl	Erfurt-Schleusingen
Woldersky	Köln	Köln a. Rh. Landkreis
Wunderlich	Bochum	Bochum
Wurm	Hannover	Pirna / Reuß j. L.
Zappay	Marburg	Marburg-Frankenberg
Zarbock	Bromberg	Bromberg
Zerm	Wolffenbüttel	Kreis Helmstedt
Zubeil	Berlin	Kalau-Luckau
Zwiener	Bielefeld	Herford-Halle

Zuschriften und Telegramme.

a. Deutschland.

Altenburg. Die Buchwald'schen Hausbewohner.
Altona. Der Frauen- und Mädchen-Verein zu Altona.
Altona. Die Genossen.
Altona. Ein Kreis von Genossen bei Haberfeld.
Apolda. Wirkergehilfen Apolda's.
Aschersleben. Mehrere Eisenarbeiter.
Baden-Baden. Der Arbeiter-Wahlverein f. Baden-Baden u. Umgegend.
Barleben. Die Genossen.
Barmen. Die Genossen.
Bergedorf. Die ausgesperrten Glasarbeiter.
Berlin. Einige Genossen.
Berlin. Genossen aus dem Lokal „International".
Berlin. Fachverein der Feilenhauer.
Berlin. Fachverein der Former.
Berlin. Fachverein der Klempner.
Berlin. Fachverein d. Schlächtergesellen.
Berlin. Freie Vereinigung der Posamentirer und Berufsgenossen.
Berlin. Freie Vereinigung d. Maurer Berlins (Versamml. v. 16. Oktober).
Berlin. Geselliger Klub „Proletariat".
Berlin. Lese- u. Diskutirklub „Internationale".
Berlin. Mehrere Genossen des IV. Berliner Wahlkreises.
Berlin. Metallarbeiter-Verein (Versammlung Norddeutsche Brauerei).
Berlin. Personal d. „Berl. Volksbl."
Berlin. Rauchklub „Ohne Zwang".
Berlin. Die sozialdemokrat. Fraktion der Stadtverordneten Berlins.
Berlin. Die sozialdemokrat. Kaufleute und Handlungsgehilfen Berlins.
Berlin. Sozialdem. Leseklub „Lessing".
Berlin. Vereinigung deutscher Maler, Filiale 5.
Berlin. Versammlung für Frauen und Männer vom 12. Oktober.
Berlin. Versammlung für Männer und Frauen in Moabit.
Berlin. Versammlung vom 15. Oktbr. in Joel's Saal.
Berlin. Die Zimmerer Berlins.
Bernburg. Arb.-Gesangverein Bernburg.
Bernburg. Tabakarbeiter Bernburgs.
Biebrich. Die Arbeiter von Biebrich.
Bielefeld. Festversamml. von 2000 Pers.
Bochum. Die Genossen.
Bockenheim. Frankfurter Festgenossen.
Braunsberg. Die Genossen.
Braunschweig. Die Genossen.
Bremen. Die Bremer Schneider.
Bremen. Tischlerversammlung.
Bremerhaven. Die Genossen v. Bremerhaven und des 19. Wahlkreises.
Breslau. Die Genossen.
Breslau. Der Klub „Lassalle".
Bruchsal. Die Genossen.
Buchholz i. S. Der Wahlverein von Annaberg i. S.
Calbe a. S. Arbeiter-Bildungsverein.
Cassel. Die Genossen.
Celle. Die Cigarrenmacher von Celle.
Charlottenburg b. Berlin. Die Genossen.
Chemnitz. Die Arbeiter in der Werkzeugfabrik.
Coburg. Wahlverein Coburg.
Cöthen. Die Genossen.
Colmar i. Els. Die Genossen.
Danzig. Die Genossen.
Darmstadt. Festversammlung.
Dessau. Die Genossen.
Dortmund. Druckerei d. „Westf. Presse".
Dresden. Genossen des 6. sächsischen Wahlkreises.
Dresden. Genossen des 8. sächsischen Wahlkreises.
Dresden. Freie Vereinigung d. Barbiere.
Dresden. Die Tischler Dresdens.
Dresden. Tischler und Schuhmacher Dresdens.
Dresden. Die Dresdener Töpfer.
Düsseldorf. Mehrere Wehrleute.
Ebersbach i. S. 2. sächs. Wahlkreis.
Eilenburg i. S. Die Schuhmacher.
Einbeck. Die Genossen.
Elberfeld. Von den Verurtheilten des Elberfelder Prozesses a.d. Gefängniß.
Elbing. Die Genossen.
Elmshorn. Die Genossen.
Erfurt. Personal d. „Thüring. Tribüne".
Essen a. Ruhr. Die Genossen.
Eßlingen i. Württ. Die Genossen.
Flensburg. Die Parteigenossen.
Forst. Die Genossen v. Forst u. Umgeg.
Frankenhausen a. Kyffh. Die Genossen.
Frankenthal. Genossen von Frankenthal und Oggersheim.
Frankfurt a. M. Der Fachverein der Steinmetzer und Marmorarbeiter.

Frankfurt a. M. Die Schreiner bei Holzmann u. Co.

Frankfurt a. M. Versammlung der Metallarbeiter aller Branchen.

Freiburg i. S. Die Genossen.

Freiburg i. Baden. Genossen.

Freiburg i. B. Die Zähringer Genossen.

Freienwalde a. O. Die Genossen.

Fürth i. Bayern. Restaurant Zirl.

Gaarden. Centralverband der Werftarbeiter, Filiale Kiel.

Geestemünde. Das Personal d. „Norddeutschen Volksstimme".

Gelsenkirchen. Die Genossen.

Gera. Die Schneider.

Gernsheim. Der Arbeiter-Wahlverein.

Gießen. Die Genossen.

Glauchau. Wahlverein Gesau.

Gößnitz. Die Genossen.

Göttingen. Der 12. Hann. Wahlkreis Göttingen.

Gotha. Die Genossen.

Greiz. Die Genossen v. Dölau-Rothenthal-Sachswitz, Kreis Greiz.

Greiz. Häkers Lokal, Greiz.

Großenhain i. S. Genossen.

Hagen i. W. Die Genossen.

Hamm i. W. Die Genossen.

Hamburg. Die Arbeiter der Krahnschen Schuhwerwerkstätte.

Hamburg. Der 59. Bezirk des zweiten Hamburger Wahlkreises.

Hamburg. Druckereipersonal v. F. Meyer.

Hamburg. Die Genossen Georgsplatz 11.

Hamburg-Eimsbüttel. Genossen des 2. Hamburger Wahlkreises.

Hamburg. Die Liedertafel von 1872, Hamburg-Hohenfelde.

Hamburg. Markenfabrik v. Jean Holze.

Hamburg. Die organisirten Schneider.

Hamburg. Verband der Werftarbeiter.

Hamburg. Versammlung von Frauen und Mädchen von Hamburg u. Umg.

Hannover. Die Genossen v. Hannover-Linden.

Hannover. Lese- u. Diskutirklub „Vorwärts".

Hannover. Parteigenossen.

Hannover. Die Damen-Schneider und -Schneiderinnen von d. Georgstraße.

Hannover. Die Schneider.

Hannover. Stiftungsfest d. vereinigten Arbeiterinnen Hannover-Lindens.

Harburg. Die Arbeiter bei Aug. Plath.

Hartha i. S. Die Hutmacher.

Heidingsfeld. Die Genossen.

Hildesheim. Die Maler u. Genossen.

Hildesheim. Tischlerverbb. Hildesheim.

Höchst a. Main. Die Genossen.

Hof i. B. Textilarbeiter-Versammlung.

Jena. Die Genossen.

Kaiserslautern. Genossen.

Kall. Genossen des Landkreises Köln.

Karlsruhe. Gesangverein „Vorwärts".

Karlsruhe. Die Ortsverwaltung der allgem. Metallarbeiter-Kranken- und Sterbekasse Karlsruhe.

Kiel. Die Genossen.

Kiel. Gesangverein der Tischler Kiels.

Kiel. Die Parteigenossen.

Kiel. Die Tischler Kiels.

Kirchheimbolanden. Die Genossen.

Köln. Die Former Kölns und Umgeg.

Köln a. Rh. Sozialdem. Verein Köln.

Königsberg i. Pr. Die Genossen.

Königsberg i. Pr. Die Tischler Königsbergs.

Lambrecht i. Pf. Die Genossen.

Landeshut i. Schl. Die Genossen.

Langenbielau i. Schles. Arbeiter von Langenbielau.

Langenbielau. Herbergsvater Stolzenberg.

Lauenburg a. Elbe. Die Arbeiter Lauenburgs.

Leipzig. Die Malergehilfen.

Leipzig. Die Schuhmacher.

Leipzig. Die Vergolder Leipzigs.

Luckenwalde. Die Genossen.

Ludwigshafen. Wahlverein Ludwigshafen.

Ludwigshafen a. Rh. Wahlverein Friesenheim (Pfalz).

Lübeck. Buchdrucker Lübecks.

Lübeck. Die Former Lübecks.

Lübeck. Die Schneider Lübecks.

Lübeck. Die Schuhmacher Lübecks.

Lübeck. Die Tischler.

Magdeburg-Buckau. Die Genossen.

Mainz. Die Genossen.

Mannheim. Die Genossen der Neckarvorstadt Mannheim.

Mannheim. Gewerkschaftskartell Mannheim.

Martendorf b. Berlin. Die Genossen.

Markenkirchen i. Voigtl. Die Genossen.

Meißen. Stiftungsfest des Metallarbeiter-Vereins zu Meißen.

Memmingen. Wahlkreis Memmingen-Illertissen.

Metz. Die Parteigenossen.

Minden. Die Genossen.

Mühlhausen i. Els. Die Genossen.

München. Die Genossen.

München. Die Genossen von Thalkirchen bei München.

M.-Gladbach. Die Gladbacher Sozialdem.

Münster i. Westf. Die Genossen.

Netzschkau i. S. Formerverein Reichenbach-Netzschkau.

Neumünster. Die Parteigenossen.

Neurode. Die Genoss. d. Kreises Neurode.

Niefern b. Pforzheim. Wahlversammlg.

Nortorf. Die Genossen.

Offenbach a. M. Oeff. Metallarb.-Vers.

Offenbach a. M. Sozialdemokraten Heusenstamms.

Ohlau i. Schl. Der soz. Arbeiterverein.

Osterode a. Harz. Gesangverein Männer-Quartett Osterode a. H.

Osterwieck. Die Genossen.

Ottensen. Die Parteigenossen.

Passau. Die Genossen.

Penig i. S. Genossen.

Pforzheim. Die Genossen.
Pirna i. S. Die Genossen des 8. sächs. Wahlkreises.
Plauen i. Voigtl. Die Genossen.
Plauen.Plauen'scheGenoss.(Jägersruh).
Potschappel i. S. Genossen im Plauenschen Grunde.
Potsdam. Die Genossen.
Pyrmont. Die Pyrmont = Waldecker Genossen.
Quackenbrück. Die Bürstenmacher.
Rastenburg i. Ostpr. Die Genossen.
Rathenow. Ein Gedicht.
Rathenow. Die Genossen.
Reinickendorf b. Berlin. Die Genossen.
Remscheid. Die Genossen.
Rendsburg. Die Genossen.
Rixdorf b. Berlin. Weberverein.
Ronneburg i. S. Die Genossen.
Ronsdorf. Selbeck's Wirthschaft.
Roßwein i. S. Die Roßwetner Arbeiter.
Rostock. Mehrere Maurer.
Ruhla i. Th. Allgem. Arbeiterverein.
Schleusenau. Genossen.
Schneeberg i. S. Die Genossen.
Schönebeck a. Elbe. Die Genossen.
Schwabach. Versammlung des Wahlkreises Ansbach=Schwabach.
Schwedt a. O. Die Genossen des Prenzlau-Angermünder Wahlkreises.
Schwerin i. Meckl. Die Genossen.
Sebnitz i. S. Die Genossen.
Siegmar. Der Verein zur Förderung volksthümlicher Wahlen in Siegmar.

Solingen. „Bergische Arbeiterstimme."
Solingen. Die Parteigenossen.
Sonneberg i. Th. Die Arbeiter.
Spandau. Die sozialb. BäckerSpandaus.
Speyer. Die Genossen.
Stettin. Die Lohn = Kommission der Schneider und Näherinnen Stettins.
Stettin. Sozialdemokrat. Wahlverein.
Stockelsdorf. Die Fackenburger Genoff.
Stuttgart. Der Arbeiterverein Heslach.
Tannenberg i. S. Die Genossen von Geyer und Tannenberg.
Tettnang. Die Genossen.
Velten. Die Genossen.
Viersen. Die Sozialdemokraten des Kreises Gladbach.
Wandsbeck. Die Genossen.
Wandsbeck. Das Harmonia = Quartett Wandsbeck.
Weimar. Zahlstelle des Deutschen Tischlerverbandes.
Weißensee b. Berlin. Der Arbeiterbildungsverein.
Wermelskirchen. Die Genossen.
Wiesbaden. Die Drechsler Wiesbadens.
Wiesbaden. Genossen.
Wilhelmsbad. Gold= u. Silberarbeiter Hanaus.
Winsen a. d. L. Die Genossen.
Wolmirstedt. Die Genossen.
Würzburg. Wahlversammlung.
Zwickau i. S. Die Genossen v. Planitz·
Zwickau. Die Genossen v. Schedewitz.
Zwickau. Mehrere Genossen.

b. Ausland.

Amerika.
Boston. Deutsche Sektion Boston der sozialistischen Arbeiterpartei v. Nordamerika.
Buenos-Aires. Verein „Vorwärts."
Chicago. Exekutiv = Komitee der soz. Arbeiterpartei d. Vereinigten Staaten von Nordamerika.
Milwaukee. Die Sozialisten Milwaukee's.
New=York. National-Exekutiv-Komitee der amerikanischen Sozialdemokratie.

Dänemark.
Kopenhagen. Dän. Sozialdemokraten.

England.
London. Komm. Arb.=Bildungsverein.
London. Eight Hours and International Labour League.
London. General Council of the Social Democratic Federation.
London. National Union of Gasworkers and General Labourers of Great Britain and Ireland.
London. The Political Council of the North Camberwell Radical Club and Institute.

Frankreich.
Paris. Le cercle des socialistes roumains.
Paris. Le Congrès regional de la Federation des travailleurs socialistes de France.
Paris. Polnische Delegirte zum soz. Kongreß zu Paris.
Paris. Redaktion b. „L'Idee Nouvelle", Revue Sociale et Litteraire.
Paris. Une groupe des Proscrits de la Commune de Paris 1871.

Holland.
Amsterdam. Sozialdemokratischer Bund in Amsterdam.

Italien.
Mailand. Lega Socialista Milanese.
Mailand. Il Consolato Operaio Milanese.
Mailand. Radikaler Verein.
Ravenna. Congrès nationale du Parti socialiste d'Italie.

Oesterreich.
Bielitz. Die Genossen v. Bielitz-Biela, Oesterr. Schlesien.
Budapest. Ungarländische allgemeine Arbeiterpartei.

Floridsdorf. Genossen von Florids=
dorf und Donaufeld.
Jägerndorf. Die Genossen.
Klagenfurt. Die Genossen.
Kronstadt. Kronstädter Arbeiterklub.
Meidling. Die Genossen.
Reichenberg i. Böhm. Redaktion des
„Freigeist".
Salzburg. Die Arbeiterschaft Salzburgs.
Triest. Die Genossen.
Villach. Die Genoss. v. Villach=Kärnthen.
Warnsdorf. Die Genossen v. Warns=
dorf (Böhmen).
Wien. Zehn junge Theoretiker.
Wien. Vereinigte Perlmutter=Drechsler
in Wien.
Wien. Vereinigte Steinnußknopf=Ar=
beiter in Wien.

Polen.

Aus Genf. Redaktionen der polnischen
sozialist. Blätter „Walka Klas" und
„Przedswit".
Lemberg. Polnische Sozialisten.

Schweden.

Stockholm. Distrikt steyrelsen.

Schweiz.

Basel. Arbeiterbund Basel.
Basel. Deutsche sozialdemokr. Mitglied=
schaft. Deutscher Arbeiterverein.
Basel. Genossen v. Basel und Lörrach.
Bern. Die Parteigenossen.
Bern. Soz.=dem. Partei der Schweiz.
Cheaux=de=fonds. Genossen v. Cheaux=
de=fonds und Locle.
Frauenfeld. Deutscher Verein.
Genf. Ligue internationale de la Paix
et de la Liberté.
Glarus. Deutscher Verein Glarus.
Payerne. Internat. Arbeiterverein.
St. Gallen. Mitgliedschaft St. Gallen.
Winterthur. Deutsche Sozialisten.
Zürich. Redaktion des russ. „Sozial=
demokrat".

Spanien.

Madrid. Partido Socialista Obrero
Espanniol. Comite National.